Look Your Best with Word® for Windows™

Designs and Text by Sue Plumley

Look Your Best with Word for Windows

Copyright © 1992 by Que Corporation

All rights reserved. Printed in the United States of America. No part of this book may be used or reproduced in any form or by any means, or stored in a database or retrieval system, without prior written permission of the publisher except in the case of brief quotations embodied in critical articles and reviews. Making copies of any part of this book for any purpose other than your own personal use is a violation of United States copyright laws. For information, address Que Corporation, 11711 N. College Ave., Carmel, IN 46032

Library of Congress Catalog No.: 92-70881

ISBN:0-88022-927-6

This book is sold *as is*, without warranty of any kind, either express or implied, respecting the contents of this book, including but not limited to implied warranties for the book's quality, performance, merchantability, or fitness for any particular purpose. Neither Que Corporation nor its dealers or distributors shall be liable to the purchaser or any other person or entity with respect to any liability, loss, or damage caused or alleged to be caused directly or indirectly by this book.

95 94 93   4 3 2

Interpretation of the printing code: the rightmost double-digit number is the year of the book's printing; the rightmost single-digit number, the number of the book's printing. For example, a printing code of 92-1 shows that the first printing of the book occurred in 1992.

Publisher: Lloyd J. Short

Acquisitions Manager: Rick Ranucci

Managing Editor: Paul Boger

Product Development Manager: Thomas H. Bennett

Book Designers: Scott Cook and Michele Laseau

Production Team: Claudia Bell, Michelle Cleary, Christine Cook, Terri Edwards, Mark Enochs, Kate Godfrey, Dennis Clay Hager, Audra Hershman, Carrie Keesling, Phil Kitchel, Bob LaRoche, Loren Malloy, Linda Quigley, Linda Seifert, Sandra Shay, Kevin Spear, Kelli Widdifield, Allan Wimmer

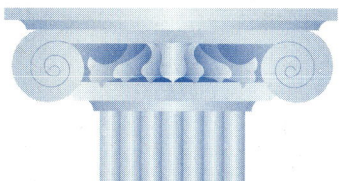

DEDICATION

With all my love and thanks to my husband, Carlos.

CREDITS

Product Director
Charles O. Stewart III

Acquisitions Editor
Tim Ryan

Production Editor
Mike La Bonne

Editors
Jo Anna Arnott
Don Eamon
Micci Swick-Volk

Technical Editor
Smita Desai

Composed in Garamond and MCPdigital by Que Corporation.

ABOUT THE AUTHOR

Susan Plumley owns and operates Humble Opinions, an independent consulting firm that offers training and seminars in most popular software programs. Her BA is in Art and English from Marshall University. She worked as a teacher, a typesetter, a graphic artist, and as a purchaser and supervisor in a commercial print shop before starting her own business in southern West Virginia.

TRADEMARK ACKNOWLEDGMENTS

Que Corporation has made every effort to supply trademark information about company names, products, and services mentioned in this book. Trademarks indicated below were derived from various sources. Que Corporation cannot attest to the accuracy of this information.

CorelDRAW! is a registered trademark of Corel Systems, Inc.

Hewlett-Packard, and HP Graphics Gallery are registered trademarks of Hewlett-Packard Company.

ITC Bookman, ITC Zapf Dingbats, and ITC Zapf Chancery are registered trademarks of International Typeface Corporation.

Linotronic is a trademark and Helvetica, Times, and Palatino are registered trademarks of Allied Corporation.

Microsoft, Microsoft Excel, and Microsoft Windows are registered trademarks of Microsoft Corporation.

PC Paintbrush is a registered trademark of Z-Soft Corporation.

PostScript is a registered trademark of Adobe Systems Incorporated.

WordPerfect is a registered trademark of WordPerfect Corporation.

Trademarks of other products mentioned in this book are held by the companies producing them.

ACKNOWLEDGMENTS

I thank the many people who contributed to the completion of this project. Foremost, I am grateful to the Que team for their dedication and assistance during the writing of this book. Thanks to Rick Ranucci and Tim Ryan in Acquisitions for their encouragement and support. Thanks also to Chuck Stewart for his guidance and insight in developing and organizing this book. Thanks, too, Chuck, for the entertaining talks about Irish music! And a special thanks to Mike La Bonne, who shared his patience, his time, and his knowledge in editing this book.

I also express my appreciation to Hugh Manning and Carlos Plumley for their encouragement and technical assistance as well as the loan of some supplementary hardware. Last, I am grateful to Microsoft's excellent customer service technicians for their advice and support in both Word and Windows.

CONTENTS at a GLANCE

Introduction 1

I Understanding Design and Typography

1 Explaining Design Strategies 13
2 Using the Elements of Design 27
3 Defining and Explaining Typography 69
4 Planning and Purchasing Printing 101

II Creating Business Documents

5 Producing a Letterhead 121
6 Producing a Letter 151
7 Producing Envelopes 173
8 Producing a Resume 189
9 Producing a Program 207
10 Producing a Memo 233

III Creating Business Forms

11 Producing a Fax Cover Sheet 255
12 Producing a Purchase Order 279
13 Producing a Travel or Expense Report 307
14 Producing an Order Form 329

IV Creating Sales Documents

15 Producing an Advertisement 359
16 Producing a Flier 381
17 Producing a Brochure 407

V Creating Newsletters

18 Producing a Basic Newsletter 441
19 Producing a Complex Newsletter 477

VI Creating Long Documents

20 Producing a Business Report 517
21 Producing a Book 547

A Getting to Know Word 581
B Using Other Programs with Word 611
C Using Printers and Output 623
D Glossary of Desktop Publishing Terms 633

Index 651

CONTENTS

Introduction 1

    The Advantages of Using Word for Windows 1
    Who Should Read This Book? 3
    What Is in This Book Overall? 4
    What Is in This Book in Detail? 4
    How To Use This Book 7
    Conventions Used in This Book 8

I Understanding Design and Typography

1 Explaining Design Strategies 13

    Deciding the Purpose of Your Document 14
        Understanding Your Audience 14
        Knowing What You Want to Communicate 15
        Determining the Life of Your Document 15
    Planning Your Document 16
        Organizing the Text 16
        Selecting the Format 17
        Determining the Size 18
        Choosing the Finish 18
    Maintaining Consistency 19
    Adding Emphasis 21
    Recapping 25

2 Using the Elements of Design 27

    Planning with Thumbnail Sketches 28
    Creating a Rough Draft 29

Choosing Page Orientation	31
Portrait	32
Landscape	33
Planning the Size of the Document	34
Balancing Design Elements	35
Using Symmetrical Balance	35
Using Asymmetrical Balance	36
Using Modular Balance	37
Using White Space for Contrast	38
Establishing Margins	39
Using Margins with Headers and Footers	42
Using Margins with Bleed	43
Using Binding Margins	44
Planning Columns	44
Establishing Line Length	45
Including Gutters	47
Producing Columns in Word	47
Using Format and Section	47
Using the Table Feature	48
Creating Facing Pages	48
Enhancing the Page With Graphics	50
Using Rules	51
Using Borders	53
Adding Screens	55
Using Graphic Images	55
Describing Types of Documents	56
Using Fliers	56
Using Brochures	57
Using Newsletters	59
Using Forms	61
Using Books	62
Recognizing Design Flaws	63
Recapping	66

3 Defining and Explaining Typography 69

- Understanding Typography Terms 70
  - Defining Typeface 70
  - Examining Type Families 72
  - Discussing Fonts 74
  - Working with Styles 74
- Measuring Type 75
  - Working with Body Text 76
  - Using Headings 76
  - Using Subheads 76
  - Using Display Type 76
  - Measuring Guidelines 77
- Using Attributes to Improve Your Document 78
- Using Spacing 79
  - Spacing Between Letters 80
  - Spacing Between Words 81
  - Spacing Between Lines 82
  - Spacing Between Paragraphs 84
- Using Text Alignment 85
  - Using Left Alignment 85
  - Using Right Alignment 86
  - Using Center Alignment 86
  - Using Full Justification 87
- Using Indentation 87
- Using Tabs 88
- Placing Text on a Page 89
  - Using Display Heads 89
  - Using Heads 90
  - Using Subheads 90
  - Using Captions 90
  - Using Body Text 91
  - Using Text for Emphasis 92
- Producing Style Sheets 96
- Understanding Design Flaws 96
- Recapping 100

4 Planning and Purchasing Printing 101

- Reviewing Design for Printing 101
  - Working with Paste-Up 101
  - Working with Output 105
- Printing Services 105
  - Examining Types of Print Shops 105
- Getting Price Quotations 107
- Choosing Paper and Ink 108
  - Size 108
  - Weight 108
  - Finish 108
  - Opacity 109
  - Brightness 109
  - Grain 109
  - Color 109
  - Types 110
- Working with Ink 111
  - Using Standard Inks 112
  - Using PMS and Special Inks 112
- Finishing Techniques 113
  - Folding 113
  - Fastening the Final Product 116
- Recapping 117

II Creating Business Documents

5 Producing a Letterhead 121

- Creating a Simple Letterhead 122
- Creating a Letterhead That Uses a Logo 127
- Creating a Traditional Letterhead 134
- Creating an Innovative Letterhead 141
- Storing the Letterhead in a Glossary 148
- Recapping 149

6 Producing a Letter 151

Creating a Traditional Business Letter 151
Using Summary Information 155
Creating a Letter by Using Type and Graphics 156
Creating an Innovative Styled Letter 163
Using Other Letter Designs 169
Recapping 169

7 Producing Envelopes 173

Planning Your Envelope Design 174
Understanding Postal Regulations and Guidelines 175
    Size 175
    Boundaries 175
    Additional Copy 176
    Postal Permits 177
    Print Quality 177
Producing a Basic Envelope 177
    Using a Horizontal-Feed Printer 178
    Using a Vertical-Feed Printer 179
    Using a Vertical-Feed Laser Printer 180
Opening a Template 182
Designing a Graphic and Type Envelope 182
Creating an Innovative Envelope 184
Looking at Return Address Designs 186
Recapping 188

8 Producing a Resume 189

Designing a Traditional Resume 191
Creating a Graphic and Type Design 194
Creating an Innovative Resume 198
Looking at Design 203
Recapping 205

XV

9 Producing a Program 207
Creating a Basic Program 208
Producing a Type and Graphic Design 214
Working with a Printer 220
Producing an Innovative Program 221
Looking at Design 228
Recapping 231

10 Producing a Memo 233
Customizing Word's Memo Template 234
Practicing with the Template 237
Creating a Memo with a Numbered List 240
Using the Template 243
Creating an Innovative Memo 244
Looking at Design 248
Recapping 250

III Creating Business Forms

11 Producing a Fax Cover Sheet 255
Producing a Basic Fax Cover Sheet 257
Producing a Fax Cover with Rules 260
Producing a Cover Sheet with a Graphic Box 262
Creating an Innovative Fax Cover Sheet 265
Looking at Design 268
Recapping 277

12 Producing a Purchase Order 279
Producing a Purchase Order for Use
  With a Typewriter 281
Producing a Purchase Order for Reproduction 286
Producing a Purchase Order for Use with Fields 292

Contents

 Adding Field Codes and a Macro to a Form 299
  Brief Summary of Field Codes 299
  Brief Summary of Macros 301
  Creating Fields and a Macro for Your Form 301
 Looking at Design 304
 Recapping 306

13 Producing a Travel or Expense Report 307

 Producing a Travel Log 307
 Producing a Travel Report 312
 Producing a Daily Expense Report 316
 Producing a Small Expense/Reimbursement Form 322
 Recapping 327

14 Producing an Order Form 329

 Producing a Basic Order Form 330
 Producing a Business-to-Business Order Form 336
 Producing an Order Form with Tabs 343
 Looking at Design 349
 Recapping 354

IV Creating Sales Documents

15 Producing an Advertisement 359

 Examining Sources for Advertisements 359
 Planning and Designing Ads 360
  Using Type in Ads 361
  Using Art Work in Ads 361
  Using Color and Logos in Ads 361
  Using Borders in Ads 362
  Placing the Ad 362
 Producing a Display Newspaper Ad 362
 Producing a One-Column Newspaper Ad 365

xvii

Producing a Five-Column Ad	369
Creating and Designing a Circular	373
Using Direct Mail	374
Looking at Design	374
Creating Multipurpose Ads	376
Recapping	380

16 Producing a Flier 381

Producing a Price List Flier	382
Producing a Coupon Flier	389
Producing a Flier with Hanging Indents	395
Looking at Design	399
Recapping	405

17 Producing a Brochure 407

Learning About Brochures	407
Using Typesetting and White Space	408
Selecting the Paper and Ink	408
Determining the Size	409
Producing a Basic Brochure	409
Producing a Traditional Brochure	416
Producing an Innovative Brochure	425
Looking at Design	434
Recapping	435

V Creating Newletters

18 Producing a Basic Newsletter 441

Determining the Size	441
Working with Paper Stocks	442
Learning the Basics	442
Developing Consistency	442
Creating a Nameplate	443
Producing a Type Solution Newsletter	449

Producing a Type and Graphic Newsletter 455
Producing an Innovative Newsletter 463
Looking at Design 472
Recapping 476

19 Producing a Complex Newsletter 477

Creating an Innovative Newsletter 478
    Creating Page One 481
    Creating Page Two 486
    Finishing Page Two 487
    Save and Print 488
Creating a Newsletter with a Page Border 488
Creating an Innovative Newsletter with Tables 497
    Creating the Nameplate 501
    Inserting Text into Tables 502
    Creating a Text Box 504
    Creating the Headers 505
    Creating Page Two 506
    Save and Print the Newsletter 509
Looking at Design 509
Recapping 513

VI Creating Long Documents

20 Producing a Business Report 517

Planning the Design Elements 517
    Choosing the Layout 518
    Determining the Size 518
    Selecting the Paper and Binding 518
Creating a Traditional Business Report 519
Looking at an Innovative Business Report 536
Looking at Design 538
Recapping 543

xix

Look Your Best with Word for Windows

21 Producing a Book 547

Planning Your Book 547
    Setting Up Files and Directories 547
    Considering Front and End Material 548
Planning the Design Elements 549
    Determining the Size 549
    Selecting the Paper 550
    Planning the Page Elements 550
Producing a Traditional Book Design 551
Producing Another Traditional-Styled Book 561
Creating a Master Document 570
    Creating an Index 571
    Creating a Table of Contents 572
Looking at Design 573
Recapping 579

A Getting to Know Word 581

Understanding Word Version 1.1 581
    Working with the Titlebar 582
    Working with the Menu 582
    Understanding the Ribbon 587
    Understanding the Ruler 588
    Understanding the Status Bar 590
    Understanding the Scroll Bar 590
    Understanding the Text Area 591
    Using the Mouse 591
    Using the Keyboard 592
    Microsoft Word For Windows Version 1.1
        Shortcut Keys 592
    Using Direction Keys 593
    Using Alphanumeric Keys 594
Word Version 2.0 595
    Understanding the Screen 595
    Understanding the Titlebar 596
    Understanding the Menu 597

Contents

    Understanding the Toolbar 601
    Understanding the Ribbon 602
    Understanding the Ruler 604
    Understanding the Status Bar 604
    Understanding the Scroll Bars 605
    Understanding the Text Area 605
    Using the Mouse 605
    Using the Keyboard 606
    Microsoft Word For Windows Version 2.0
      Shortcut Keys 606
    Using Direction Keys 608
    Using Alphanumeric Keys 609

B Using Other Programs with Word 611

    Converting Text Files 611
      Word Version 1.1 612
      Word Version 2.0 613
    Importing Graphics 614
      Word Version 1.1 617
      Word Version 2.0 618
    Using Data Exchange 620
      Linking 620
      Embedding 621
      Include 621
      DDE 621

C Using Printers and Output 623

    Understanding Resolution 623
    Using Page Description Languages 624
      Working with HP Printer Control Language 624
      Working with PostScript Page
        Description Language 624
    Using Screen and Printer Fonts 625
    Choosing a Printer 625
      Dot Matrix Printers 625

xxi

Inkjet Printers	626
Basic Laser Printers	626
PostScript Laser Printers	627
Image Setters	627
Understanding Printer Installation Terminology	628
Selecting Your Printer Driver	628
Choosing a Printer Port	629
Configuring Your Printer	629
Setting Up Your Printer	630

D Glossary of Desktop Publishing Terms 633

Index 651

Introduction

If you're one of the many Word for Windows users in the country today, you probably purchased this book to learn more about working with design, using type, formatting documents, improving the look of your word processing documents, and enhancing your proficiency with Microsoft Word for Windows. Chances are you know that Word for Windows is a remarkable program that can produce distinguished documents, and you're ready to learn how to produce such documents. The first step on your journey is to learn about the following benefits of using this superb program.

The Advantages of Using Word for Windows

Word offers you many advantages when you design your own documents. Whether you use Version 1.1 or 2.0, Word will make your task easier. If you like Version 1.1, you'll be even happier with Version 2.0, because it works better with page formatting.

As a powerful page-formatting program, Word indexes, footnotes, sets headers and footers, draws rules and borders, imports graphics, and makes designing documents easy. Also, as an equally powerful word processing program, Word for Windows checks spelling; performs mail merge; and formats tabs, indents, margins, columns, and type. As you work with Word for Windows, you'll discover that the following four features are the major benefits of using the program:

Look Your Best with Word for Windows

Feature	Benefit
Time Saver	When you typeset your own documents, you save time writing copy, making corrections and alterations, and gain quick turnaround. Word's special features make spell-checking, revisions, replacing, and copy and layout changes quick and easy. Word Version 2.0 even has a grammar-checker.
Document Control	By typesetting your own work, you have complete control over the final document. If you don't like the way it looks, you can change the design. Also, you can make last-minute copy changes easily.
Software Integration	One of Word's most important benefits is its compatibility with other software, both Windows and non-Windows applications. You can convert other word processing programs to Word, and import spreadsheets, graphics, and databases. Version 2.0 offers even more selections when importing graphics, and when working with draw and paint programs, clip art, and scanned images.
Money Saver	Formatting your own documents in Word saves you money. Doing it yourself reduces errors, thus reducing typesetting costs. Reduced turnaround and publication time also saves you money.

Introduction

Who Should Read This Book?

Look Your Best with Word for Windows is a book for blue-collar workers, business people, graphic artists, or even the casual user. Word for Windows is for anyone who wants to learn step-by-step how to design professional-looking documents.

If you need to produce a creative letterhead design, forms, brochures, a company newsletter, an elaborate business report, or even a book, *Look Your Best with Word for Windows* is for you. This book explains not only how to create the design, but also how to implement it in specific documents.

If you've worked with Microsoft Word for Windows but lack practical experience in design and page layout, *Look Your Best with Word for Windows* teaches you the rules, terms, and proper application of the design elements. The document chapters offer itemized instructions for both Versions 1.1 and 2.0.

If you're new to Microsoft Word for Windows and to page formatting, the design and typography chapters in this book teach you how to plan and produce an attractive, well-designed document. *Look Your Best with Word for Windows* also gives you detailed, step-by-step instructions for producing actual letterheads, forms, brochures, and newsletters.

If you're a graphic artist experienced in design but unfamiliar with desktop publishing, you'll benefit from the design and typography chapters. Also, the document chapters demonstrate creative arrangements of text and graphics on which you can build your own designs.

Finally, for anyone who has ever worked with a print shop, Chapter 4 provides detailed information about planning and purchasing printing. From special design considerations, to ink and paper choices, this chapter will help you plan your next project with confidence and a new understanding of how print shops work.

What Is in This Book Overall?

Look Your Best with Word for Windows offers not only ideas and techniques to improve the look of your documents, but also a basic understanding of why some printed documents (or pieces) look good and others don't. You'll learn about what design elements attract the reader and what elements maintain that interest.

Today's market generates an abundance of brochures, fliers, pamphlets, newsletters, notices, and advertisements, all in competition with your material. The materials you notice, read, and keep are well-designed and creative. *Look Your Best with Word for Windows* shows you how to produce these kinds of high-quality materials.

Study the beginning of this book well—learn all you can about purpose, planning, design, typography, and dealing with a print shop. With these basics under your belt, follow the directions in the document chapters to apply your knowledge to actual business, sales, and promotion pieces. You'll be creating and producing your own quality material quickly.

What Is in This Book in Detail?

Part I: Understanding Design and Typography, explains in detail the design and typographical elements of documents produced by desktop publishing. From planning your document to having it printed, this section covers every aspect of page design.

Chapter 1, "Explaining Design Strategies," shows you how to prioritize and organize your copy and how to choose a format. Included are tips on how to target your audience, how to develop design consistency, and how to add emphasis to your document.

Chapter 2, "Using the Elements of Design," shows you how to plan the size, shape, and type of your document. It tells you how to balance text and graphics on the page, create margins and columns, add graphics for emphasis, and produce templates.

Also included are tips on readability, adding white space and contrast, steps to successful planning, and what not to do in a design.

Chapter 3, "Defining and Explaining Typography," expands on the design chapter by defining and explaining the use of type, fonts, spacing, alignment, text arrangement on the page, and producing style sheets in desktop publishing. The terms that Word users and typesetters use are also defined and illustrated. Tips show you how to size heads and body text, emphasize type such as bullets and callouts, and produce logos.

Chapter 4, "Planning and Purchasing Printing," is an overview of printing terms and services. This chapter suggests what print shops to use for certain jobs, describes the different kinds of paper and ink available, and identifies finishing options such as various folds and fastening techniques.

Part II: Creating Business Documents, gives you step-by-step instructions in producing specific documents. Each chapter discusses designs ranging from fundamental typeface solutions to more intricate typeface and graphic designs. Also, each chapter gives instructions and keystrokes for several designs, and offers extra design alternatives with critiques of each.

Chapter 5, "Producing a Letterhead," offers designs you can produce in Word. Also described are bullets, line spacing, and storing your letterhead in a glossary for later use.

Chapter 6, "Producing a Letter," shows you how to produce different letter layouts. Also included are tips on using spell- and grammar-checkers and adding boxes and borders. From the formal business letter to a creative advertising letter, this chapter presents several design options.

Chapter 7, "Producing Envelopes," explains how to create separate envelope designs, set up your printer, match your letterhead design, and work with mailing regulations.

Chapter 8, "Producing a Resume," offers resume design strategies that include the traditional, type only, type and graphic blend, and innovative styles.

Chapter 9, "Producing a Program," gives printer tips, layout suggestions, and design completion instructions.

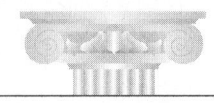

Chapter 10, "Producing a Memo," discusses Word's template and how to change it for your specific purposes. The Summary Info box helps you track your memos. Also offered are keystrokes for several designs.

Part III: Creating Business Forms

Chapter 11, "Producing a Fax Cover Sheet," teaches you how to produce distinctive fax layouts. Also included are tips on what material will and won't fax well and how to attract attention with your fax.

Chapter 12, "Producing a Purchase Order," discusses form strategies, including setting a form to typewriter spacing, saving in a glossary, and Word's table feature.

Chapter 13, "Producing a Travel or Expense Report," shows you how to set up the basic form and several design alternatives.

Chapter 14, "Producing an Order Form," also shows you how to make the form and shows you design alternatives.

Part IV: Creating Sales Documents, delves into the printed matter you give to customers. With several design strategies included in each chapter, this part of the book could be the one you use the most.

Chapter 15, "Producing an Advertisement," covers designs for use in a newspaper ad, an insert, or a mailing. Tips include ways to grab the customer's attention, and overwhelm your competition.

Chapter 16, "Producing a Flier," presents individual designs that you can use in any business.

Chapter 17, "Producing a Brochure," details distinct ideas for creating and typesetting a brochure for your business. Included in this chapter are directions on incorporating tables and charts, as well as using graphics such as rules and borders.

Part V: Creating Newsletters, explains the basic techniques of producing complex newsletters for customers or employees.

Chapter 18, "Producing a Basic Newsletter," includes tips on style sheets, consistency between issues, headers and footers, mailings, and mastheads. Several design choices are also offered.

Chapter 19, "Producing a Complex Newsletter," takes the design and layout a step further. Among the valuable points incorporated

Introduction

in this chapter are creating a masthead, using logos, and adding tables and charts.

Part VI: Creating Long Documents, introduces you to Word's special features and how to apply them. This section includes instructions on cross-references, footnotes, page numbering, first-page design features, and how Word makes it easy to produce long documents.

Chapter 20, "Producing a Business Report," offers ideas and solutions for designing business reports. Tips include updating with Word's data exchange features.

Chapter 21, "Producing a Book," explains specific formulas. Included are tips on how to use or create Word's revision marking, first-page design features, chapter and master documents, and page numbering.

Look Your Best with Word for Windows also provides four appendixes.

Appendix A, "Getting to Know Word," explains the basics of Word to the new user. Covering both Versions 1.1 and 2.0, Appendix A includes information on and illustrations of the screen, the keyboard, and the mouse. Several shortcut keys are also listed.

Appendix B, "Using Other Programs with Word," encompasses the use of both Windows and non-Windows applications. Tips include using the Clipboard, converting text, importing graphics, and applying data exchange methods.

Appendix C, "Using Printers and Output," tells you about the different printers used with Word and output samples. Included are definitions, applications, and advantages and disadvantages of dot-matrix, inkjet, laser printers, and image setters. You also learn how to configure your printer.

Appendix D, "Glossary of Desktop Publishing Terms," provides you with the most recent language associated with desktop publishing.

How To Use This Book

Look Your Best with Word for Windows is divided into sections for easier use. Part I teaches design and typography, and Parts II through VI teach how to format actual documents.

Part I is a tutorial in design. Beginning with Chapter 1, you progress to a better understanding of what it takes to produce a professional document. Part I is also a reference book that provides guidance in the use of type and other design elements.

The rest of the book concentrates on specific projects you can produce with Word. Each lesson and each document chapter becomes progressively more difficult. However, if you do each lesson in order, by the time you complete this book you'll be quite proficient with Microsoft Word for Windows.

On the other hand, if you just want to use particular designs or documents, *Look Your Best with Word for Windows* suits that purpose, too. Each lesson is self-contained—it explains all the steps required to produce a particular document.

Although this book assumes some previous knowledge and use of Word for Windows, the directions are clear and easy to follow. After reading *Look Your Best with Word for Windows*, and a little practice, anyone can produce a professional-looking document. As an extra bonus for new users, Appendix A offers the basic screen, keyboard, and mouse uses with Word.

Conventions Used in This Book

The document chapters (5 through 21) give specific instructions that contain mouse movement, combination keys, and typing on your part. Icons also are used in the margins to distinguish between Word Versions 1.1 and 2.0.

If you're not familiar with mouse terms, such as click, double-click, and drag, refer to Appendix A.

Word uses many combination keys to carry out commands. When you see a plus sign between two keys—as in Ctrl+B—you press and hold down the first key, press the second key, let up on the second key, then let up on the first key.

Word underlines one particular letter in each menu and dialog box command. The underlined letter signifies a keyboard option. By pressing the Alt key plus the underlined letter key, you can

Introduction

access that particular menu or function by using the keyboard. In this book, the underlined letter is **boldfaced**.

Any typing you do, whether it be text or in a dialog box, will appear in **boldface**. Screen messages appear in a `special typeface`. And *Italic* type is used to emphasize the author's points or to introduce new terms.

Icons will be used in the margins to distinguish between Version 1.1 and Version 2.0.

SAVE ON
OFFICE SUPPLIES

- Chairs
- File Cabinets

- Calculators
- Electric Typewriters

- Computer Paper
- Legal Pads

2 DAYS ONLY-JUNE 12 & 13
9:00 a.m. to 5:00 p.m.

Davis Office Supplies
112 East Street

Part I

Understanding Design and Typography

Includes

1. Explaining Design Strategies
2. Using the Elements of Design
3. Defining and Explaining Typography
4. Planning and Purchasing Printing

Explaining Design Strategies 1

Creating a successful design involves many steps. Because each step builds on the last, the first step is the most important: planning and preparing your design for a specific purpose. For example, the main purpose of all printed material is to convey a message to the reader. Likewise, the main purpose of design is to convey its own message, a message that attracts the reader's attention, that persuades the reader to pick up the printed material and read it. The main purpose of design is to convert a browser into a reader.

With so many printed documents competing for readers' attention these days, a design must be exceptional to win out. Creating a good design takes skill. It is an art. Typesetters in print shops work for years to develop proficiency in layout and design. This proficiency doesn't develop overnight and doesn't grow without knowledge of the elements of design. Practice also is an important part of learning good design elements. This book gives you the tools and hands-on practice you need to produce attractive, professional-looking designs and develop design proficiency quickly.

Desktop publishing has changed the way the public perceives the typeset page. Before the appearance of the personal computer and desktop publishing programs, professional typesetters produced high-quality pages that attracted the attention and respect of the public. However, the popularity and affordability of the PC with desktop publishing capabilities has made it easy for anyone to create documents. A great many of these people are not trained in design and typography, thus they produce unattractive and

PART I

Understanding Design and Typography

unprofessional material. The declining quality of printed documents has desensitized the public to where only masterful designs grab their attention. Consequently, to get your message noticed in this kind of environment, you must create professional, high-quality designs that convert browsers into readers.

As mentioned earlier, the elements of design are the building blocks you use to convey a message. In this chapter, you learn how to determine the purpose of your document, your intended audience, the message you want to convey, and the steps you take to plan the successful design of your project. After you accomplish these tasks, you begin organizing the elements of type and graphics to create your design. Such preparation and planning are essential to the success of any document.

Deciding the Purpose of Your Document

When you begin planning a document for publication, you need to know the specific purpose of that document. What do you want to achieve? To sell a product? To inform employees of new benefits? To tell fellow workers about an improved service? Answers to questions like these will help you define the purpose of your document.

Understanding Your Audience

Before you begin planning the specific design of your document, you need to know your intended audience. Who are your readers? Who are you trying to reach with your document? Customers or prospective customers? Fellow employees? Your boss? Are you trying to reach a group of professionals or the general public? Are your intended readers men or women? Young or old? Rich or poor? You cannot successfully communicate with readers unless you know who they are. Each audience has its own communication needs. The more you know about your readers, the easier it is to plan and prepare the appropriate design for your document.

After you identify your readers, you can better plan and prepare your document to meet their needs. Remember to address the

CHAPTER 1

Explaining Design Strategies

reader directly and focus on the points that interest them. Consider, too, the design and typeface choices for this particular audience. The more you can custom-design each document to meet the needs of the readers, the more successful you'll be in getting your message across.

Knowing What You Want to Communicate

After you determine the specific purpose of your document and identify the audience, the next step is to determine what you want to communicate, so that you can design your document accordingly. For example, say that the purpose of your document, or piece, is to sell a product. You must determine the price of the product, describe the product's features, and list the specific benefits the product offers customers. You then design your piece to present these facts to the reader in the best possible way. To enhance the piece, you can choose the price, or one feature, or one benefit to emphasize by using boldface or italic type, rules, screens, and so on.

Determining the Life of Your Document

The intended shelf life of your document depends on the content of the piece (which directly affects design) and the kind of media you use to get your message to the reader. To demonstrate this point, consider the differences between a newspaper ad selling a product, and a brochure describing forthcoming semester classes.

The purpose of a newspaper ad is to pique readers' interest sufficiently enough to get them into the store that sponsors the ad. The ad usually runs from one day to one week. This short duration of exposure alone makes for an extremely limited shelf life. Also contributing to the short shelf life is the competitive nature of newspaper ads. Because newspaper ads are usually surrounded by other ads battling for the reader's eye, some ads

PART I

Understanding Design and Typography

may be scanned too quickly and others may not be scanned at all. Finally, newspapers are almost always tossed after being read one time.

On the other hand, a brochure that describes a list of forthcoming semester classes has a longer shelf life. The content is such that the customer may refer to it this week, next month, or three months from now. The brochure is a stand-alone publication whose main competition is other similar brochures. The design of this type of brochure encourages relaxed and comfortable reading.

When you begin your initial design, you need to consider the shelf life you want your document to maintain and then plan your document accordingly.

Planning Your Document

Now that the preliminary work is done, you can begin organizing the text, selecting the format, determining the trim size, and choosing the finish for your document. Again, the purpose of the document helps determine the size, shape, format, and appearance of the final product.

Organizing the Text

Write your copy, keeping in mind the purpose of the document. Outline your main topics and subtopics first, then form them into well-written and interesting copy. The outline helps you organize your material and write concise but descriptive sentences.

Don't be afraid to change, revise, and rewrite your copy to get it exactly the way you want. As most successful writers will attest, often the best writing comes from rewriting. Anything less than superbly written copy will not hold the readers' interest. Even the heads and subheads should pique the readers' interest and persuade them to read the copy. Finally, make sure that your message is clearly stated and easy to understand, and your terminology, spelling, and grammar are impeccable.

CHAPTER 1

Explaining Design Strategies

Keep any elements you cut from the page, along with other information you may wish to add, just in case page formatting opens up unexpected holes in the copy.

Gather tables, charts, art work, photos, or any other graphic images that reinforce the message. Graphics are elements that take up space just like the text. Be sure that any graphic you use directly supports the message. Anything less is wasted space and may cost you readers. Graphic images get a message across many times faster and more efficiently than the text. Whether a photo, illustration, or diagram, the first thing readers see on a document is the image. If the image is trivial or doesn't contribute directly to the message, readers may skip the entire document. Remember that everything—graphic images, type, white space—must directly support the message.

Selecting the Format

Part of your design strategy includes the format of your document: flier, brochure, letter, newsletter, book, and so on. The format you choose depends on the purpose of the document, the size, the amount of copy, and the method of distribution. If the method of distribution is the mail, for instance, the piece has to conform to postal regulations in size and shape.

For example, a flier is a good format for hard-sell, dated material. Usually printed on one side of an 8 1/2-inch-by-11-inch sheet of low-grade paper, it may contain short lists, brief descriptions, and just the facts. Hard-sell employs high-pressure techniques that command the readers' attention. Display type, bold or bulleted lists, and words such as "Save," "One Week Only," and "Red-Hot Specials," are some examples of these techniques.

A brochure, on the other hand, is appropriate for soft-sell, reference material. Brochures usually print both sides in two or more colors on high-quality paper, and fold into two, three, or four panels. Soft-sell assumes the reader's initial interest in the product or service. In this example, you use detailed descriptions in small but readable type, restrict the use of very large type, and may refer to the benefits and advantages to the customer in a bulleted list or a screened box.

PART I

Understanding Design and Typography

Determining the Size

The size of the document depends on the amount of copy, the format, the quantity printed, and the method of distribution.

Depending on the amount of copy and the format, you can use any size document from flier to newsletter (or even smaller or larger) if you need it. A newsletter, for example, is usually 11-by-17 inches folded to an 8 1/2-by-11-inch format. Chapter 2 lists more of these common sizes and the reasoning behind each size.

Quantity refers to the number of copies you want printed of the final document. Do you want 50 on a laser printer, or 500 on a photocopier, or 10,000 done at a print shop? The size has a direct effect on the cost and time involved in reproducing a document. You'll find more information about quantity in Chapter 4.

The size of a document also depends on the method of distribution. Some documents designed for distribution through the U.S. postal system are limited in size. For example, a document formatted as a postcard must conform to specific postal regulations. However, a newsletter can be mailed in any size, although the cost will be significantly higher than that of a postcard.

When determining the size, you should also consider what happens when readers get the document. Can they easily store the document? Can they slide it into a pocket or insert it in a standard three-ring binder?

Finally, does the size of the document help it stand out among competitors' documents? An unusual size can bring special attention to a document surrounded by a sea of advertisements. Carefully consider all these factors before deciding size.

Choosing the Finish

Certain formats require specific finishing techniques. For example, some documents must be folded, some must be stapled, and some must be folded and stapled. Other documents require padding and numbering. A brochure, for example, usually folds; a booklet staples; and invoices pad and number. Chapter 4 explains these techniques and more.

CHAPTER 1

Explaining Design Strategies

Maintaining Consistency

As in life itself, first impressions are critical in a printed document. If the document doesn't impress a reader at first glance, the document is ignored. Consistency can help you create a positive first impression. A consistent page is clear, organized, and simple. Consistency in design and typography is vital to the success of any document.

Design elements such as balance, margins, columns, rules, and screens promote consistency. Balancing, or distributing, the type and design elements on the page creates a pleasing typeset piece. For example, keeping individual pages balanced throughout the document by using the same number of columns and the same margin widths enhances consistency. Chapter 2 explains these design elements in detail.

Typography, typeface, type size, spacing, and alignment can also contribute to consistency. For example, if the type on the page is consistently easy to read throughout the document, the reader is more likely to read the entire message. Chapter 3, further defines typography and its related components.

Organization is another key. By arranging your text and graphics on the page in a pleasing and logical manner, you add a sense of consistency. You can design this arrangement by putting the most important part of your text first, then the second most important part and so on, to give the reader a sense of order and structure.

Repetition also lends itself to consistency. You can repeat important words or facts in your copy, such as "save" in a sales ad, or "Now Due" on an invoice, to help achieve consistency.

Consistency can also be achieved by repeating design and type elements. For example, you can use 2-point rules above all heads, or end each section with the company logo, or use the same size and style of heads throughout the document, or use equal spacing in all body text, or use the same size bullets on all pages. Figure 1.1 shows consistency within an advertisement. Notice the typeface, type size, margins, and graphics. Figure 1.2 shows the same ad with much less consistency.

PART I

Understanding Design and Typography

FIG. 1.1.
Consistency in a newspaper advertisement.

> **GRAND OPENING**
> # humble opinions
> **OFFERING INSTRUCTION**
> - Desktop Publishing
> - Word Processing
>
> June 3
> 9:00 a.m. - 5:00 p.m.
> 117 E. Main Street • (304) 555-2323

FIG. 1.2.
Inconsistency in the same advertisement.

> *Grand Opening*
> # humble opinions
> **OFFERING INSTRUCTION**
> - Desktop Publishing
> - Word Processing
>
> *June 3*
> **9:00 A.M. - 5:00 P.M.**
> **117 E. MAIN STREET**
> (304) 555-2323

Consistency is just as important in company documents as it is in stand-alone special fliers, brochures, and so forth. Company letterheads, newsletters, and business reports can use similar

CHAPTER 1

Explaining Design Strategies

elements to bind them together. You don't have to format all of these documents in the same way. But, use one logo, or a particular typeface, or a color to tie the documents together. Customers respond well to such consistency. Seeing a familiar logo over and over or recognizing the same typeface or graphic elements makes readers feel more comfortable and more willing to read a document. Figure 1.3 demonstrates consistency among a letterhead, an envelope, and a brochure for the same company. Subsequent chapters will refer to figure 1.3 frequently.

Adding Emphasis

As mentioned earlier, first impressions influence a reader, and you can help generate a favorable first impression by using design elements consistently. Another tool you can use to garner a good first impression is *emphasis*.

You can emphasize a subject in a variety of ways. For example, you can use a graphic element to frame a photograph, or white space to offset a story, or a pie chart to track profits, or column rules to lead the reader's eye to an important item.

Typography is another way you can add emphasis. For instance, you can use 72-point type to emphasize the word "Sale," and headline type to make the names of products stand out. You also can use bullets, callouts, jumplines, boldface, italics, and so on.

Another method of adding emphasis is by using color. A splash of color around an important topic, a four-color chart or photograph, or a contrasting color for a large headline are possible uses of color. Of course, to apply this option, you need either a color printer or a print shop.

Besides knowing when to use emphasis, knowing when not to use it is equally as important. Too much emphasis in a document creates disorder and clutter. With too much emphasis, the reader will not understand the truly important information because everything stands out. Chapters 2 and 3 cover additional ideas you can use. For example, figure 1.4 shows a flier with the proper amount of emphasis added. Figure 1.5 demonstrates the abuse of emphasis in the same flier. Remember to add emphasis to only one idea or topic per document.

FIG. 1.3. *Three documents from one company, tied together for consistency.*

CHAPTER 1

Explaining Design Strategies

OPENING NIGHT!

Manhattan Players Present

BEYOND ENMITY

A PLAY BY S. J. BENDER

featuring

Erin Linkous
Brandon McIntyre

Hattan Theatre
111 W. 24th Street

FIG. 1.4. *Emphasis applied properly.*

No one design solution can fit all documents. The design elements you choose for your documents should depend on the specific purpose of the document, the audience, the copy, and your personal preferences. The following chapters of this book offer guidelines to help you make these decisions, with suggestions that allow your creativity to shine through.

PART I

Understanding Design and Typography

> # OPENING NIGHT
>
> MANHATTAN PLAYERS
> PRESENT
>
> # BEYOND ENMITY
>
> A PLAY BY S.J. BENDER
>
> FEATURING
> # ERIN LINKOUS
> # BRANDON
> # MCINTYRE
>
> HATTAN THEATRE
> 111 W. 24TH STREET

FIG. 1.5. *Overuse of emphasis.*

CHAPTER 1

Explaining Design Strategies

Recapping

You've covered a lot of important information in this chapter that you'll need to remember as you work your way through this book. The following steps are provided as a recap to help refresh your memory, and to give you a quick reference guide whenever you need it:

1. Decide the purpose of your document, understand your audience, and know what you want to say.

2. Write the copy and gather supporting graphic images.

3. Organize the copy by logically ranking the important items.

4. Decide format, size, quantity, distribution method, and finishing techniques. Also remember the intended shelf life.

5. Create consistency throughout the document.

6. Select one important topic or point to emphasize.

Using the Elements of Design

After you've determined the specific purpose of a document, your next step is to choose the document design, which will include elements such as size, shape, format, and layout. These and other elements help make a document attractive, practical, and effective. Also, because the primary purpose of any document is to communicate a message to readers, effective use of basic design elements can help you accomplish this task. In this chapter, you learn more about using the elements of design to produce professional-looking documents.

One way to learn about design is to look at all the documents you can. Keeping in mind that the mission of good design is to entice readers to pick up a document, try to determine what persuades you to pick up a document. Is it graphics, headlines, color, white space, or a combination of these elements?

After you study these documents and identify the design elements that interest you, you'll have a basis on which to build your own designs. Build on this base with the rules about the elements of design presented in this chapter to produce documents that first attract readers, then communicate your message to them. The elements of design not only organize your message, but also complement it. By following the time-tested rules of typesetting, you can produce attractive, professional-looking documents.

Modern typesetters still use the language and rules from the early newspaper days of hand-set type: leading (LED-ing), galleys, parallel columns, picas, uppercase and lowercase, and so on. This chapter and Chapter 3 will cover these rules, most of which are still in use today.

PART I

Understanding Design and Typography

The typewriter also had an effect on design, particularly in page formatting. For years the typewriter was an everyday necessity in business. Some of the language and rules from the typewriter days include double-spacing, narrow margins, caps to emphasize, 5-space indenting at the beginning of a paragraph, and two spaces between sentences. Most of these leftovers are no longer proper or suitable for today's documents.

With so much competition in today's market, only the most attractive and professional-looking documents succeed. This chapter presents design alternatives to the typewriter "leftovers" that have a positive influence on the reader. In addition, you learn, step by step, the most effective way to design your document to communicate your message. The first of these steps is planning. You should read Chapters 2 and 3 completely before doing any planning, sketching, or designing in Word for Windows so you understand how the elements interrelate.

Planning with Thumbnail Sketches

As discussed in Chapter 1, the first step in creating a successful design is to plan your design for a specific purpose. For example, if the purpose of the document is to sell a product, then you should plan your design to support that purpose. Knowing the purpose is the easy part, however. The hard part is to get your design from initial concept to finished product. A helpful tool many designers use to go from rough idea to finished design is a thumbnail sketch. A *thumbnail* is a rough sketch or layout of the document page, although usually smaller than the actual page. In these rough sketches, draw in all heads, columns, rules, and boxes for graphics. Use no detail, no actual type, but concentrate on design elements such as balance, white space, and facing pages. Combine these elements until the result you see is pleasing to the eye. These elements are explained and shown in detail later in this chapter. After you complete these sketches, (see fig. 2.1), create a rough draft of one or two pages.

CHAPTER 2

Using the Elements of Design

FIG. 2.1.
Thumbnail sketches for a flier design.

Creating a Rough Draft

A *rough* draft is a detailed expansion of the thumbnail sketch, in the same size as the final document, that specifies the design elements you'll use. Plan the number of columns and their placement, for example, and consider the width of the page before choosing how many columns the page will use. Determine how much copy you have and how you plan to format it. For instance, do you have copy that can form narrow columns, such as lists or short sentences, or do you have copy and graphics that need wider columns? Also, be sure that you plan for sufficient *gutter* or *alley* space (the space between columns).

Choose where to locate text and images; place related articles or captions near art or photos. Consider clustering similar photos or art works instead of spreading them out. For example, clustering five photographs of new products on one page instead of spreading them over three pages attracts readers and persuades them to look more carefully at all of the photos. Also, be sure that all related items within the document are kept close together. Items that relate, such as an article about the rising cost of housing, a line graph comparing housing costs from 1985 to 1990, and photographs of a $45,000 home and a $100,000 home have more impact on the reader when placed close together.

PART I

Understanding Design and Typography

Plan the type sizes to use. After you write the body of your message, prioritize it. Choose important words and phrases as heads and subheads. These heads should stand out so the reader immediately recognizes them. Chapter 3 explains in detail ways to emphasize these heads and subheads.

You can make a grid of horizontal and vertical lines that cross periodically on the page to form guidelines for text and graphic placement (see fig. 2.2). In the figure, the grid on the left plans for two columns with gutter space. The horizontal rules divide areas for heads, subheads, graphics and body type, as shown on the right. Using a grid is especially helpful when planning the document in this stage.

FIG. 2.2.
A sample grid and a layout designed by using the grid.

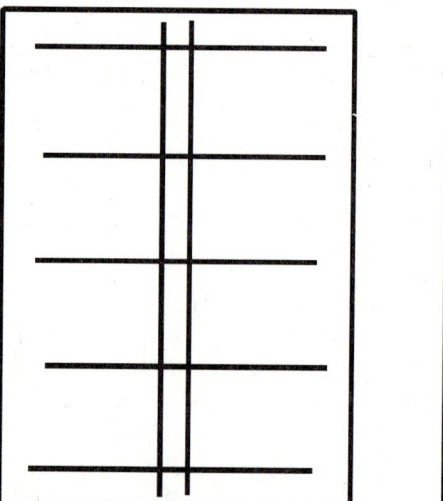

If you haven't already done so, you need to decide whether the document will be folded, mailed, perforated, fastened, and so on. Each of these processes effects the layout of your piece. As examples, a photograph placed on a fold will crease, which makes it less attractive and less effective; a mailing piece must have sufficient space for address labels and postage; and any ticket or card that perforates must leave room for the perforation, and should be placed on at least two edges of the document for easier removal. For more information about these procedures, refer to Chapter 4. As figure 2.3 shows, a rough draft isn't necessarily the final design. Before you're finished, you may have to change the layout because of copy length, additional graphics, design constraints, or unforeseen circumstances.

CHAPTER 2

Using the Elements of Design

FIG. 2.3.
A sample rough draft for a flier.

As you prepare the thumbnails and rough draft, apply the design elements outlined in this book. Remember that you can use emphasis to set off the more important ideas but no one design element should overwhelm the others. Rather, the elements should work together to create a whole effect, a oneness. This unity allows the reader to concentrate on the message, not the design. A design should do nothing but invite the reader to read.

Choosing Page Orientation

A basic element of design is the page orientation of the document: portrait (vertical), or landscape (horizontal). Each has specific uses and each employs the design elements in particular ways that will be covered in the following sections. Which orientation you choose depends on four conditions that affect your document: purpose, copy, dimensions, and quantity.

Purpose: Traditionally, the purpose of a piece dictates its shape. Documents must be easy to read, use, and store to attract the attention of the reader. Therefore, the printing trade assigns orientations to particular documents. If, for example, a document is designed for a standard three-ring binder, or to be slipped easily into a pocket (both vertical formats), the orientation will be portrait. On the other hand, a travel log or newsletter (traditionally horizontal formats) is more efficient as landscape. Similarly,

PART I

Understanding Design and Typography

any document designed for mailing must conform to landscape orientation because of postal regulations.

Copy: Determine how much copy you have and how the information flows on the pages. Is the copy in short lists that you can include in narrow columns, or in long paragraphs of text that need wide columns? Do you have many headlines or subheads, or both? Can you separate these heads with rules or boxes? Is the art horizontal or vertical? Can the text also fit the same orientation as the artwork? If so, mirror this orientation with the page.

Dimensions: The finished size of the document is determined mainly by the amount or type of copy. If you list text by priority—the most important fact first, then the second, and so on—you can include only the text necessary to get the message across. However, tables, charts, and graphics take up much more room than text and frequently require larger-sized documents. The method of distribution may also affect document size. For instance, documents you hand out on the street will be considerably smaller than those designed for display in a store window.

Quantity: Reproduction costs weigh heavily in determining the ultimate size of your document. For example, the cost to print 1,000 small fliers is considerably less than that to print 1,000 store-window displays. Additional factors under this heading include paper and postage. The lighter the paper stock the less expensive it is to mail.

Portrait

Although portrait orientation is vertical, or tall, it is measured by width first then height (8 1/2 inches by 11 inches). Lists of words or short sentences, graphics or photos more tall than wide, shorter headlines, and many subheads fit portrait orientation. You can use large amounts of text in this mode if you use two or three columns per page.

Usually, you produce letters, newsletters, resumes, and business reports in portrait orientation (see fig. 2.4). Some types of fliers and books, however, also can be in portrait mode.

CHAPTER 2

Using the Elements of Design

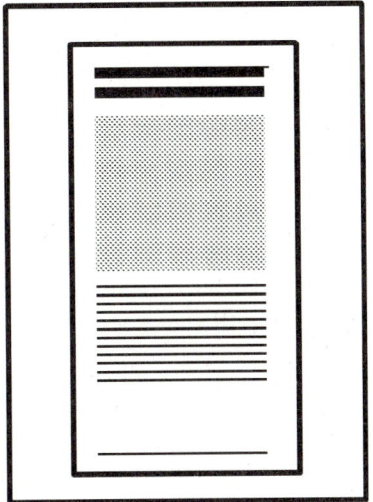

FIG. 2.4.
Sample of flier in portrait orientation. All design elements fit the vertical arrangement.

Landscape

Landscape, or wide, orientation (see fig. 2.5) is measured by height first then width (11 inches by 8 1/2 inches). Long headlines, wide graphics or photos, and more pictures than text use this orientation. This mode is also well-suited for spreadsheets, tables, charts, fliers, brochures, envelopes, programs, some forms, and many books.

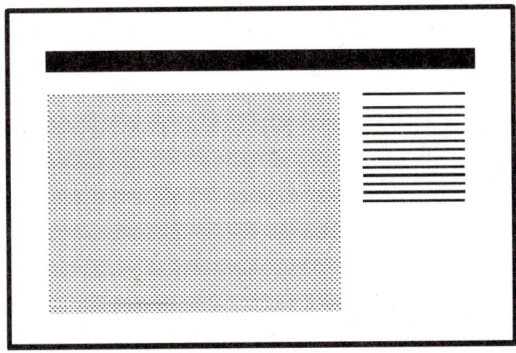

FIG. 2.5.
A sample layout of a flier in landscape orientation.

If you use both orientations in one document, make sure that landscape pages are placed with the heads at the spine of the book (the inside margin). This orientation makes turning the book to view the charts or tables an easier task for the reader.

33

PART I

Understanding Design and Typography

Planning the Size of the Document

The size of your document depends on many factors. Consider the purpose and the traditional sizes that fit this purpose. For instance, a book that has many pages should be a small trim size so it can easily be held; a form with little fill-in can be small; and a newsletter for people with sight disorders may use large type and a large format to accommodate the information. Before you can communicate your message successfully, the reader must be comfortable with the document (easy to read, use, and store). Choosing the proper size for your purpose helps you accomplish this task.

The following factors govern the size of the document:

- The amount of copy
- The number of images (photos, art, spreadsheets, tables, or charts)
- The kind of document: brochure, newsletter, flier, program, book, or magazine
- Distribution
- The paper size limit of your laser printer
- Budget constraints
- The kind and size of paper

As you consider the preceding information, remember that over the years some document sizes have proved efficient and advantageous. Print shops use these sizes over and over again mostly because of the paper sizes, which reflect press run sizes and other automated shop equipment. Print shops purchase paper in large sheets and cut them to standard sizes, which keeps waste to a minimum. Even if you aren't taking the finished document to a print shop for printing, you still can take advantage of the following common cut sizes:

CHAPTER 2

Using the Elements of Design

Paper Size (inches)	Kinds of Use
8 1/2 by 11	Folded to 5 1/2 by 8 1/2 inches or to 3 2/3 by 8 1/2 inches, as in a brochure
11 by 17	Folded to 8 1/2 by 11 inches for a 4-page newsletter or presentation folder
3 5/8 by 8 1/2	For a rack card
6 by 9	For a book or magazine
6 by 10	For a book cover or presentation document

Depending on the laser printer, you may be able to use only 8 1/2-inch-by-11-inch paper or smaller. Some laser printers allow for 8 1/2-inch-by-14-inch paper. This problem is not insurmountable. If, for example, you want to do an 11-inch-by-17-inch newsletter that folds down to 8 1/2 inches by 11 inches, you can format the four 8 1/2-inch-by-11-inch pages on the computer that a copy shop or print shop can use to produce an 11-inch-by-17-inch finished document.

Balancing Design Elements

Text and graphics must balance on the page. One cannot dominate the other. Balance is nothing more than a page of text and graphics designed so well that it attracts readers to the document then leads them through the document in logical steps. A balanced document also helps readers mentally organize the information after one reading, which in turn makes the information stick in their minds longer. Page layout uses three major kinds of balance: symmetrical, asymmetrical, and modular. To keep from confusing the reader, stick with only one kind of balance throughout each document.

Using Symmetrical Balance

Symmetrical balance is the distribution of the text, graphics, and white space so that in terms of size, form, and arrangement all correspond on opposite sides of a point (usually the center). Thus, what you see on one side of the center guide is produced exactly on the opposite side. Figure 2.6 shows two examples of symmetrical balance; the center guide on both samples is the gutter space between columns.

The text and graphics, however, aren't exactly the same; you must measure the visual weight of each page, by the elements. Consider text as the gray of the page (a page of nothing but type gives the impression of being gray). Graphics, art, photos, and illustrations are gray if they are light, but are black if very dark or heavy. Measure the white of the page in margins, gutter space, the area around headlines and graphics, and even within the text (left-aligned or right-aligned text has more white space than justified text). Therefore, by balancing the grays, blacks, and whites on a page, you end up balancing the actual text, graphics, and white space.

Symmetrical balance is a formal, sophisticated, even balance that usually guarantees consistency within the document.

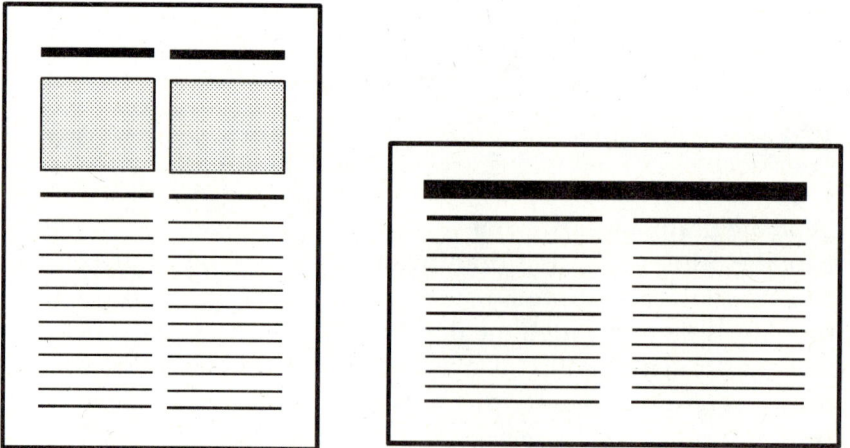

FIG. 2.6. Symmetrical balance in portrait and landscape orientations.

Using Asymmetrical Balance

With *asymmetrical balance*, the elements on either side of the center guide don't exactly correspond but the overall *weight* of the elements remains about the same. In this mode, you balance large areas of gray with large areas of white, or small black areas

CHAPTER 2

Using the Elements of Design

with larger gray areas. Asymmetrical balance results in a more free-form, informal, and interesting document to look at than symmetrical and also is a harder balance to use properly and consistently (see fig. 2.7).

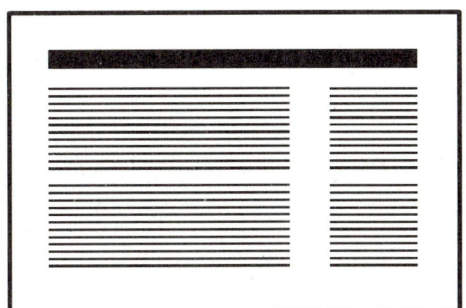

*FIG. 2.7.
Asymmetrical balance in portrait and landscape orientations.*

Using Modular Balance

Modular balance uses intersecting guidelines to form boxes across the page and places text and graphics in the boxes to form an ordered, systematic layout. You can begin forming the grid, or modules, by dividing the page into two or three sections. Then divide these sections into two or three more sections (see fig. 2.8).

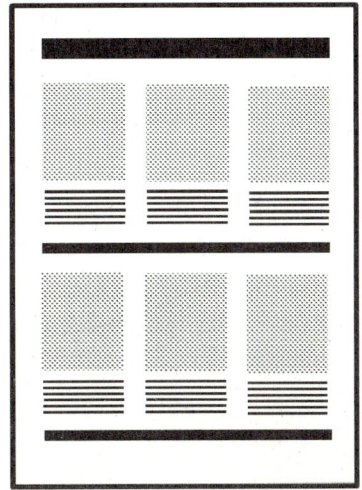

*FIG. 2.8.
The grid modules on the left, converted to a page using symmetrical balance.*

PART I

Understanding Design and Typography

The modular layout can be either symmetrical or asymmetrical. You achieve symmetrical balance by dividing the page in half, either vertically or horizontally, and then placing the text and graphics within the guidelines. You accomplish asymmetrical balance with the grid by combining several boxes to construct various size areas for text, or by varying placement. Figure 2.9 shows the preceding sample grid with asymmetrical balancing of text and graphics.

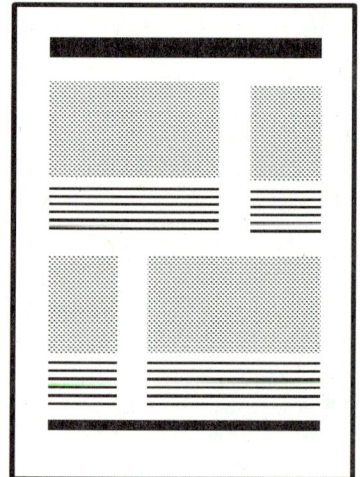

FIG. 2.9.
The grid, converted to an asymmetrically balanced layout.

The balance you choose should be consistent throughout the document. Slight variations, such as adding white space within asymmetrically balanced pages, can add emphasis and interest.

Using White Space for Contrast

To provide contrast, emphasis, and a rest for the reader's eyes, use white space within a document. A headline, text, or a graphic has far more effect when surrounded by white space. As a rule, balance white space throughout the page with text and graphics (gray space) on a 50-50 ratio. This amount of white space may seem like a lot, but many ways are available to apply white space.

Margins are perhaps the most effective way of implementing white space. If you have a small amount of copy, you can make the

CHAPTER 2

Using the Elements of Design

margins one inch, two inches, or even wider. The margins don't have to be even on top, bottom, left, and right. Often, a design is more effective with a large margin on one side and smaller, equal margins on the other three sides (see fig. 2.10).

When designing your page, squeeze white space to the outside of the page. Sometimes this practice can result in odd-shaped margins, but that's better than trapping large pockets of white space inside the page. Such pockets prevent you from achieving balance, waste a lot of valuable space, and are obstacles to the eye.

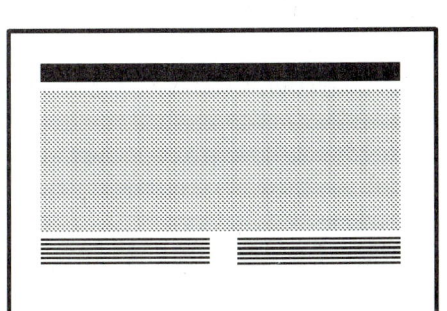

FIG. 2.10.
Some examples of white space.

Establishing Margins

Margins are important to any document. Margins are the areas surrounding the text blocks and the graphics. This space serves both as white space and as breathing room in contrast to the gray areas of text and graphics. Although gray space is often referred to as the active or live part of the page, don't consider the white space as a dead area. White space serves an important function, especially when used as margins; white space provides ease of reading, higher impact, and emphasis on the message.

Margins also help provide consistency from page to page throughout a document. After you choose a formula for the margins of a particular document, stay with that formula throughout the document. Don't change margins just for design sake (unless you mirror the margins for facing pages); don't change the margins to squeeze in an extra bit of text (see alternative methods in Chapter 3).

PART I

Understanding Design and Typography

The size of the margins depends on the amount of copy you're working with. The more copy and fewer pages you have, the smaller you should make the margins. Always leave at least 3/8 inches of margin on all four sides of a document (unless the document bleeds, which is covered in a following section of this chapter). Maintaining this minimum margin is necessary for the following reasons:

- For your laser printer. All printers set an invisible margin around the edge of the paper that will not print. Yours may be 3/8 inch or 1/2 inch. (You can easily test the printer by creating a 1-inch-thick ruled box around the edges of an 8 1/2-inch-by-11-inch page and then print the page. Measure the portion of the rule the printer did not print and use it as a guideline for the smallest possible margin.)

- For the gripper, if you have the document printed at a print shop. *Gripper* is a term used by the press operator that refers to the point where the press grabs the paper to pass it through the press. No ink or printing can be present on this part of the design. Depending on the type of press used, the gripper may be at the top of the page, at the bottom, or on the side. Therefore, to be safe, always leave at least a 3/8-inch margin all the way around the document.

A far better alternative, however, is to leave more margin. (Recall the 50-50 white space rule). If you want contrast, emphasis, and a fighting chance to get the reader's attention, use more margin. Readers who are looking at a gray page of text and crowded graphics may take their attention elsewhere. Margins of 1/2 inch, one inch, or larger are not merely acceptable, but preferable.

Keep the top margin fixed throughout the document; text and graphics should line up evenly along the top. If the top margins are kept intact, the document will have a sense of unity and continuity.

The bottom margin is more flexible. Years ago, printers thought that even, flush bottom lines of text were the only way to set type. Now, however, the only flush lines of text necessary are the lines at the top. Columns that you deliberately leave uneven at the bottom can create valuable white space. Leave out everything that isn't important to the overall message and let the white space speak for itself.

CHAPTER 2

Using the Elements of Design

As a rule, use less margin on top and more on the bottom. The side margins (unless you're producing a book) should measure the same as the top margin. You can set up a flier, for example, with a bottom margin of 1 1/2 inches, and top, left, and right margins of 3/4 inches, or a bottom margin of 2 inches and top and sides of 1 inch each. These rules are traditional in typesetting. If the document demands order and evenly balanced pages—such as a legal brief, a company report, or a formal letter—use these guidelines. If you can apply wider margins with a wealth of white space, don't hesitate to do so. Consider the copy, the kind of document you're doing, and the design elements you apply to it. Unequal margins are unusual in today's market; most typeset pieces employ the traditional rules of measurement because they are easy and safe. Because uneven margins are so distinct and demand attention in any document, using this technique assures you that your message is communicated. Figure 2.11 shows common margins for a newsletter and a brochure. Figure 2.12 shows a more creative use of margins and white space.

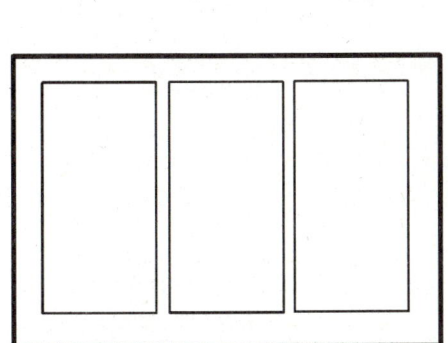
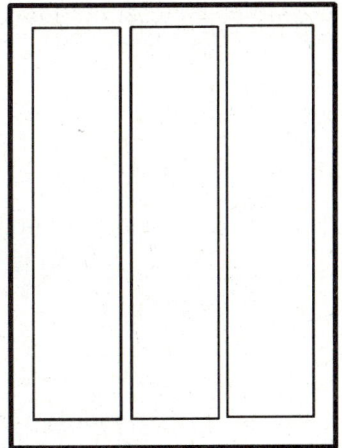

FIG. 2.11.
Landscape and portrait orientations showing layouts that have three columns surrounded by margins and separated with gutters.

There are minor exceptions to these guidelines on margin rules. The following sections describe a couple of exceptions you may encounter.

PART I

Understanding Design and Typography

***FIG. 2.12.**
Columns surrounded by unequal margins create a different perspective than even ones.*

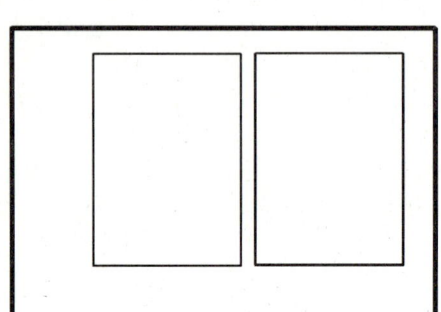
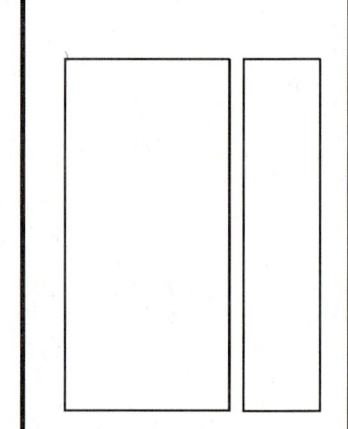

Using Margins with Headers and Footers

Another important function of margins is to provide room in the document for headers and footers. To incorporate those elements, margins must be wide enough for the added type when you produce a newsletter, book, paper, or any document with page numbers.

When planning a document of this nature, you need to plan for a wider margin at the top if you use a header or a wider margin at the bottom if you use a footer. Allow at least an extra 1/4 inch to 3/8 inch.

A header or footer consists of text or graphics that describe the body of the document in some way—for example, company name, logo, page number, author's name, chapter or document title, date, or subject matter contained on the particular page. You can place headers or footers on odd numbered pages only, on even numbered pages only, or on facing pages. Never place a header or footer on the first page of a document or the first page of a chapter.

You can format a header or footer in a variety of ways. Usually the type is bold or italic and the point size is smaller than the body text. Also, headers and footers frequently incorporate a horizontal rule—from margin edge to margin edge—to separate them from the body of the document. Notice, for example, the headers and footers in this book.

Using Margins with Bleed

A *bleed* is when any element on the page except white space goes through the margin and *runs* off the edge of the paper. Although bleeds offer a nice effect, they can be difficult to design. When you use this element, never bleed only off the bottom of the page. When the element bleeds only off the bottom, the reader's eye is lead off the page and away from the document. An element that bleeds top and bottom, or side and bottom, works well. The better way is to bleed off the top or sides, or off both at the same time. That way, the photo drops into the page and so does the reader's eye. Side bleeds can give a nice effect with graphic lines, screens, or boxes. Another option is a three- or four-sided bleed. Figure 2.13 shows a bleed on three sides in landscape orientation and a bleed off one side in portrait orientation.

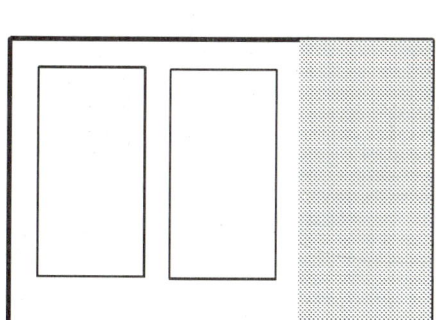

FIG. 2.13.
Two examples of bleed.

Laser printers cannot execute a bleed. All printers have a margin around the edge that doesn't print. Therefore, if you want to bleed something in a document, you have to take it to a print shop. Printers charge extra for bleeds because bleeds take over-sized sheets of paper that must be trimmed to the final size (remember the gripper needed for the press). Also, a bleed on four sides is more expensive than a bleed on one, or two, or three sides.

PART I

Understanding Design and Typography

Using Binding Margins

When you format a book, the margin rules differ from most other publications. A book, paper, or report that is side-stitched (stapled on the left) or punched with holes for a binder of some kind, must have a wider margin on the binding side. Without the extra margin space, the text near the middle of the book becomes unreadable because the binding covers this inner information.

A binding margin is never less than 1/2 inch. The margin usually is 3/4 inch to 1 inch, even larger if the book is extremely thick. If you're printing on both sides of a page, the binding margins shift for left and right pages. The right-hand pages have a larger margin on the left; the left-hand pages have the binding margin on the right (see fig. 2.14).

FIG. 2.14. The binding margin of a book. The figure on the left is a left-hand page; the figure on the right is a right-hand page.

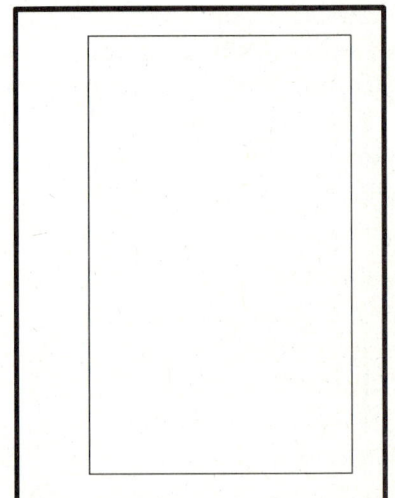

Planning Columns

Some documents may require a division of copy by columns. *Columns* help you organize the placement of text and graphics. Nonprinting vertical guides create boundaries by which you lay out the columns on the page. The first point to remember when designing columns is that Americans read from left to right. Therefore, text should flow from the left-hand column to the

CHAPTER 2

Using the Elements of Design

right. Because the main purpose of the document is to present information to the reader in an easy-to-understand, easy-to-follow format, don't be so creative with the columns that you confuse the reader. The flow of text must be logical.

On portrait-oriented pages, use no more than four columns per page; on landscape-oriented pages, use no more than six columns per page. Too many columns can become cluttered and hard to follow. Also, lines of text have to be short to fit in narrow columns, and graphics may be too small to be effective. Figure 2.15 shows a landscape-oriented page that holds six-columns.

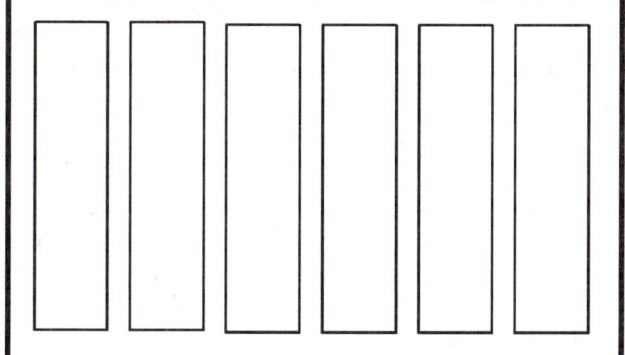

FIG. 2.15.
Six even columns for a brochure design.

For design purposes, columns need not be equal widths (see fig. 2.16). You can combine wide and narrow columns on the page to create interest. Beginning with a grid, experiment with various column widths as you sketch the rough draft. Lay out one wide column and three narrow ones, or two wide and one narrow. When you're satisfied with the layout, fit your copy into the columns according to content. For example, include a brief, bulleted list or a tall, thin graphic in the narrow columns; and place a wide photograph or a lengthy story in the wide columns. Remember the following points when experimenting in this manner: be sure that your copy fits the column layout throughout the entire document, and be consistent with the width and placement of the columns.

Establishing Line Length

When you plan the width of your columns, you need to consider the line length of the type. The width of the column determines

PART I

Understanding Design and Typography

line length, which influences readability. Using lines too long or too short can be hard to read. Newspapers follow a general rule that the optimum line length is 1 1/2 times the lowercase alphabet. Another rule to consider is the type size: the smaller the size of type, the shorter the line will be; the larger the size of type, the longer the line will be. Figure 2.17 shows two examples of line length.

*FIG. 2.16.
A brochure using landscape orientation and uneven columns.*

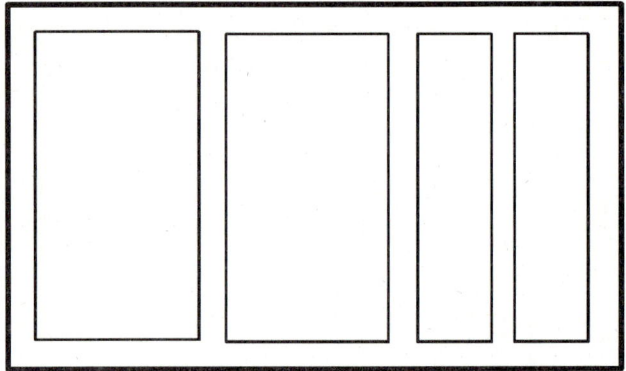

*FIG. 2.17.
The difference in line length between 8-point and 12-point type.*

8-point type works best in a 1-1/2- to 2-inch column. This is 8-point type in a 2-inch column. A longer line length would make it difficult to read.

12-point type is more readable in a 3- to 3-1/2-inch column. This is 12-point type in a 3-1/2-inch column. Anything more or less would make it more difficult to read.

Another way to measure line length is by characters per line (cpl). The optimum number is 35 to 40 characters per line (1 1/2 lowercase alphabets at 10-point type is 39 characters). If you follow this system, make sure that you count letters, spaces, and punctuation marks. The minimum would be 20 cpl and the maximum would be 60 cpl. If you must use wide columns, such as 60 characters per line, choose a typeface with a wide font. You could use 60 cpl, for example, in a letter to the elderly. Use 12-point type in one column to make it easier for failing eyes to read. However, because the majority of readers find 35 to 40 characters per line the most comfortable to read, try to limit your line length to these confines. New Century Schoolbook and Goudy are examples of wide typefaces.

Including Gutters

A *gutter* (sometimes referred to as an alley) is the white space between two columns. Look at a gutter as a margin or breathing room. Leaving enough space between columns is important (refer to fig. 2.15). Narrow gutters can make the text in columns hard to read or force a reader's eye to jump to the column to the left or to the right when following a sentence. Very wide gutters, however, tend to separate ideas or a continued story. Limiting gutters to between 1/4 inch and 1/2 inch is a good compromise. Remember to keep the gutters consistent throughout the document.

Producing Columns in Word

Microsoft Word for Windows offers two ways of producing columns in a document: by using Format, Section, which enables you to set up the columns with gutter space and optional vertical rules; or by creating a table.

Using Format and Section

By choosing the Format menu and selecting Section (with the mouse, click Format, then Section; with the keyboard, press Alt-T,S) you can snake or flow text from one column to the next quickly and easily. *Snake* means that the text continues to fill columns without prompting. So, as you continue typing at the end of the first column, Word automatically moves the cursor to the top of the second column. Word also enables you to balance these columns as equal lengths or, if you choose, to break the columns. Broken column bottoms usually are uneven, so be sure that the tops are flush.

Unlike other word processing programs, Word permits you to edit the text in page view, while in column format. Chapter 18, "Producing a Basic Newsletter," describes this procedure in detail.

PART I

Understanding Design and Typography

Using the Table Feature

Another way to create columns in Word is by using the Table feature. A table consists of columns and rows of cells that contain text, graphics, or both. By choosing **Insert Table** (with the mouse, click **Insert** then **Table**; with the keyboard, press Alt-I,A) and typing the number of rows and columns you want to appear, you can format text in either tabular columns or side-by-side columns. Again, Word enables you to edit within the table columns. You can also add vertical or horizontal rules. Chapter 14, "Producing an Order Form," covers this procedure.

Creating Facing Pages

Documents are often only one or two pages long. You can arrange pages as singles or all the copy on the front and back of one sheet. However, if the document has four or more pages, you must arrange pages as *facing* (or double-sided) pages.

In a four-page newsletter, for example, page one is a right-hand page; page two is a left-hand page, which faces page three; and page four is a left-hand page. Right-hand pages are always odd numbered (1, 3, 5, and so on); left-hand pages are always even numbered (2, 4, 6 and so on). Odd pages always face even pages (see fig. 2.18).

FIG. 2.18.
Facing pages of a four-page newsletter.

BACK (left)	FRONT (right)		INSIDE (left)	INSIDE (right)
Pg. 4	Pg. 1		Pg. 2	Pg. 3

This page-numbering system works the same whether you're producing a four-page, eight-page, or 64-page publication (magazine, newspaper, book, and so forth). You can apply facing pages to either portrait or landscape orientation.

CHAPTER 2

Using the Elements of Design

Designing facing pages so that they look good together is important. Be consistent with columns, margins, gutters, graphics, rules, headlines, and body text. The design of each page may work separately, but when viewed as facing pages, the elements may fight each other. Be sure that all elements and design choices complement each other. If the design elements are distracting, inconsistent, or too cluttered, the result distracts and therefore prevents the reader from concentrating on the message. Figure 2.19 shows a common layout for a four-page newsletter that demonstrates consistency between the facing pages.

FIG. 2.19.
The top illustration represents pages 4 and 1 of a newsletter; the bottom represents pages 2 and 3.

You can add contrast to facing pages by mirroring the design—the columns, balance, and white space on one page are reflected on the facing page. This method of organization looks good, is consistent throughout, and adds just a touch of variation (see fig. 2.20).

49

PART I

Understanding Design and Typography

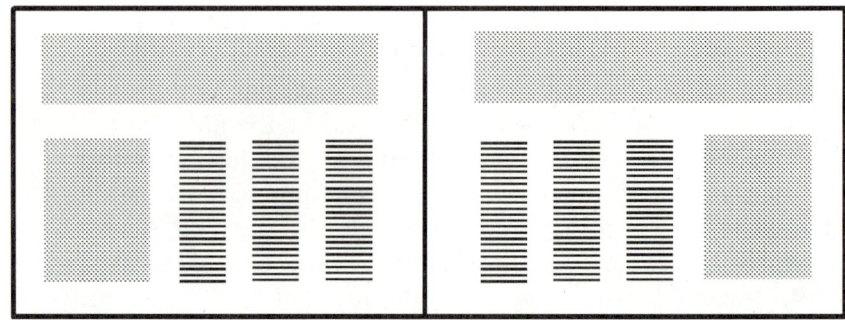

FIG. 2.20.
Landscape orientation using a mirrored balance.

Because consistency is important in typeset documents, use the tools that help achieve this goal whenever possible. A template is a perfect example of a tool that helps the design remain consistent.

A *template* is a list of descriptions frequently used in a document. These descriptions can include margins and columns; type size, style, and face; line and paragraph spacing; tabs and indents; text alignment; and so on.

After you create a template, use it repeatedly to create consistency between documents. When producing a monthly newsletter, for example, build the document on the same template each time. In this way, regular readers immediately recognize the style and format, and feel comfortable before even opening the newsletter.

In Word for Windows, a template contains extra features—boilerplate text, style sheets, glossary items, and macros—to help you with the design. Word also supplies many document templates, or you can create custom templates. The following table explains the contents of a template. For more information, consult the Word for Windows Reference Manual.

Enhancing the Page With Graphics

Besides the design elements previously mentioned, graphics—including rules, borders, boxes, screens, vertical rules (bars), and images—are essential components to good design. Using graphic elements on the page adds interest and diversity. Too many elements, however, can create chaos. The purpose of using graphics

CHAPTER 2

Using the Elements of Design

is to enhance, not ornament or decorate, the text. Decorating the text can distract the reader from the message. This section covers the guidelines that govern the judicious use of graphics.

Table 2.1 Contents of a Template

Contents	Definition and Function
Boilerplate Text	Any text that may be the same in every document, such as the return address in a letter or "To," "From," and "Comments" in a memo.
Style sheet	Determines the character and paragraph formatting, such as font, type size, spacing, alignment, tabs, and indents. Chapter 3 covers style sheets in detail.
Glossary items	All text or graphics, or both, used in several documents: letterhead, logo design, and masthead are glossary items.
Macros	Mini-programs you use to perform specific functions in Word for Windows, such as searching and replacing, finding bookmarks, and so on.

Using Rules

Rules are any lines included on the page. A rule can extend from margin to margin, gutter to gutter (to border a column), or add emphasis to a word, phrase, or headline by extending the width of the type. Rules are usually measured in points, and can be of varying widths.

In Word for Windows Version 1.1, the terms for the widths of rules are single (a 1-point line), double (2 parallel 1-point lines), or thick (a 2-point line).

Word's Version 2.0 added more rule widths. You can apply rules of .75, 1.5, 2.25, 3, 4.5, and 6 points, vertically or horizontally.

Rules can be vertical (bars in Word Version 1.1) or horizontal (above or below the paragraph).

Use a rule to direct the eye. For example, a wide rule above a major head and smaller rules above the subheads. This design

PART I

Understanding Design and Typography

strategy helps tie together the main points of the document, as shown in figure 2.21. Notice that the rules are above the heads. This practice evolved from the typewriter days—typewriters underlined text because neither bold nor italics was available. Because underlining is no longer necessary for emphasis, and bold or italics look better, typesetters steer as far away from underlining as they can, even when using a rule.

FIG. 2.21.
A brochure design that incorporates rules to tie together main topics and the subheads.

Use rules to tie together certain elements, such as columns, or pages within a document. Adding a margin-to-margin rule to a header or footer establishes continuity between pages. Rules placed above or below columns also tie these elements with each other and with columns on other pages. A rule also can establish a stopping point for the eye. A thick rule at the bottom of the page can signal the reader to stop. Be careful with these, however; use a stopping rule only if you want the reader to stop.

Vertical rules (bars in Word Version 1.1) are useful in designing the document. Vertical rules come in the same widths as horizontal rules. Use vertical rules to separate columns of left-aligned text. A thin rule between the columns keeps the reader's eye from jumping to the adjacent column.

CHAPTER 2

Using the Elements of Design

> **NOTE**
>
> Don't use vertical rules in place of gutter space. Add the rule to the gutter space. Also, don't place a vertical rule in a fold. The gutters of a brochure, for example, are for the folds. If you place a rule in the gutter, you not only defeat the purpose of the fold (to divide the columns) but also make it difficult for the person who has to fold the brochures exactly on the rule. A rule in the fold doesn't look good and may cost you more money.
>
> Don't use vertical rules with justified text; the page is already gray enough. The white gutter space is more important than a rule. With left-aligned text, however, the line endings naturally create white space and a rule becomes a desirable element to add.

You can use rules to divide lists, graphics, and numbers. To divide such items in a table, for example, use the single rules. Use the thick or double rules to divide the heads from the items. A *callout* is another example. Often separated from body text with a rule above and below, a callout is a phrase taken from the text and set in 14- to 18-point type that pulls the reader's interest to the story. You have many opportunities to use rules in almost every document. As always, be consistent when using rules. Don't vary thicknesses, length, and direction too much, and especially without a plan to promote the message of the type. Every element you use on the page should in some way promote the message.

Using Borders

A border, or box, is another graphic element meant to direct attention to specific items. Rules make up a box or border, so the measurements of the widths are similar—with one great addition, the shadow box. A shadow box creates a three-dimensional look—a pleasing effect.

Including white space with any box you use is important. Never draw a box into the gutters; instead, draw no further than the column guides. The outside of a box shouldn't butt against other

PART I

Understanding Design and Typography

type; leave room around the box. Elements within the box, whether type or text, must also have space around them. Otherwise, the box just clutters the document.

Use a box to isolate certain messages from the rest of the copy. Use related information in the box. For example, assume that in a newsletter on design, an article about margins and columns takes two of the three columns on a page. In the third column, you could add a box with a short article about the importance of white space on the page.

Place an announcement in a box to isolate the text from other text and to make the information stand out. A double rule or thick rule around an announcement can help reinforce importance. Also, to further enhance the box, you can add a screened background as shown in figure 2.22. The figure combines a box, a screen, and type to draw attention to the message. Notice, too, that the box has sufficient margin space between the text and the borders of the box.

*FIG. 2.22.
Example of an announcement box with a 20 percent screen (Word Version 2.0).*

> **Announcing**
> **GRAND OPENING**
>
> **humble opinions**
> JANUARY 9-12
> 9:00 a.m. - 5:00 p.m.

A box can encompass the entire page, one column, or part of a column; can divide cells and rows in a table; and contain text or graphic images. Only your imagination limits the uses. Just recall the guidelines suggested when you use graphic elements in documents.

Adding Screens

A screen (shaded background) is an added element to Word for Windows 2.0. Use screens as you use boxes. Add a screen to an announcement or to a story. You also can add a border around the screen. Screens are transparent, so type shows through; but be careful that you keep the screen light enough to read the type. Printing type over a 10 percent to 40 percent screen makes reading easier. Anything darker than 40 percent, however, makes the type blend in with the background. Observe the same margin rules when using screens. When using a screen without a border, don't run the type to the very edge of the screen. Allow the screen to exceed the line of type by one or two characters. Your document will look better.

Using Graphic Images

A graphic image can originate from any number of sources. Word for Windows Version 1.1 accepts paint or draw programs, scanners, or any graphic program that can save images in a TIFF format (see Appendix B).

Word for Windows 2.0 accepts many more file types: EPS, TIF, DRW, WPG, PCX to name a few (see Appendix B for more information). Word enables you to scale, crop, add a border around, or frame images. The borders available for the frame of a picture are the same as rules and boxes.

As with a box that contains text, be sure that a graphic image is surrounded by enough white space to let the image *breathe*. Scaling or cropping gives you control over white space within a framed graphic.

The space on the outside of the graphic also is important. Place a margin on all sides of the frame between the graphic and the text (see fig. 2.23).

Consider clustering images, such as photos, illustrations, clip art, and scanned art rather than spreading these elements out. A grouping of images is more appealing to the eye. Also, consider resizing images to allow a dominant picture to take precedence over the others. The largest photo (or image) attracts the reader's eye. The smaller images in the cluster then guide the reader's eye through the remainder of the page.

PART I

Understanding Design and Typography

FIG. 2.23.
A scanned graphic in a framed box. Notice the white space.

Graphic Images

A logo design for Humble Opinions, this graphic image was scanned as a TIFF and then brought into Word for Windows to demonstrate a frame around a graphic, including white space inside and outside the frame.

If a graphic that fills the frame is used, then more white space should be added around the outside of the frame. Graphic images must be allowed to breathe. They are much more effective and provide more emphasis when offset with white space.

Remember that the purpose of any graphic image in the document is to help the reader comprehend the message. Effective use of graphics will enhance, rather than minimize, the message.

Describing Types of Documents

As many kinds of documents exist as there are people to read them. Brochures, newsletters, books, forms, magazines, programs—the variety is endless. The following list describes some of the more common kinds of documents and popular sizes. Included are some sample layouts.

Using Fliers

A flier is a quick-sell advertisement designed to announce, introduce, or remind. A flier can quickly describe sales, grand openings, new items, or products.

Use a flier to attract immediate attention and get the point across quickly. When you design the flier, use a short, hard-sell technique that includes a list of the products, items, or services, or a short list of dates, times, and places with no unnecessary explanations. Use descriptive adjectives and a minimum of type.

CHAPTER 2

Using the Elements of Design

You can print a flier on one side of a sheet of paper, one column or two, with large type and bullets. Common flier sizes, in portrait or landscape orientation, include 5 1/2 by 8 1/2 inches, 8 1/2 by 11 inches, or 8 1/2 by 14 inches. The orientation and placement of text and graphics depend on the copy.

Fliers have no shelf life. Consider them throw-a-ways because of dated information or because of the distribution method. Figure 2.24 shows a sample rough of a flier. In Chapter 16, you produce a flier.

FIG. 2.24.
Sample layout of a flier in portrait mode.

Using Brochures

Because a brochure explains, instructs, details, or informs, design this document for a longer shelf life, to be kept by the customer for future reference. A brochure may include a list and description of products, a detailed explanation of services, or a price list.

Design the cover (or page 1, or front panel—whatever is appropriate for the document) for soft-sell, to gently invite the reader to open and read the contents. Inside, describe the details of the

PART I

Understanding Design and Typography

service or product, perhaps with art, logos, or pictures. Titles, headlines, subheads, and captions accompany body text in a brochure. The back panel contains summary points in a bulleted or numbered list, return address, logo, and often a mailing panel. A logical development of ideas should lead the eye through the brochure starting with the front panel or cover, continuing through the inside, and finishing with the back panel.

Figure 2.25 shows a sample rough draft for the outside three panels of a six-panel brochure. A graphic image is used on panel 1 (the right panel) with several large headlines. The middle panel (panel six) is for mailing, and panel 5 (to the far left) contains a summary of points and the address of the company.

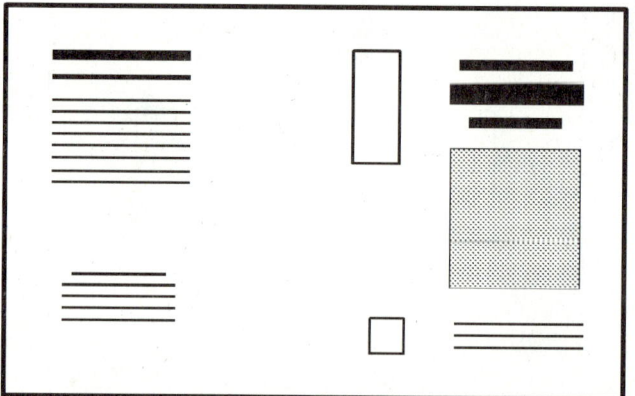

FIG. 2.25.
The outside three panels of a six-panel brochure.

On the inside of the brochure (from left, panels 2, 3, and 4, respectively), figure 2.26 shows a rule (to tie the three columns together) above the text. In this example, one graphic image along with the type are set up in a simple three-column format.

FIG. 2.26.
The inside three panels of a six-panel brochure.

CHAPTER 2

Using the Elements of Design

Brochures usually are printed in the landscape mode (11 inches by 8 1/2 inches for three columns or 14 inches by 8 1/2 inches for four columns). A brochure can also be in the portrait mode (11-by-17 inches, folded to 8 1/2 by 11 inches; or 8 1/2 by 11 inches, folded to 5 1/2 inches by 8 1/2 inches; or 8 1/2-inch-by-11-inch single sheets, fastened together). Chapter 17 describes the details of producing a brochure.

When you design a brochure as a permanent reference, make sure that the information is up to date (prices that may change, for example) throughout the intended shelf life of the document.

> **TIP**
>
> If you're marketing a product, make sure that the information in the brochure interests the customer. Customers want to know what you can do for them, not what you're doing for yourself.

Using Newsletters

Newsletters come in many sizes, shapes, and designs. A newsletter generally has one to 16 pages with one to four columns per page, in either portrait or landscape mode (although portrait is the most common). Depending on the purpose, a newsletter can be a throw-away or a keeper.

Newsletters can explain, instruct, detail, inform, announce, introduce, repeat—just about anything. Some companies use newsletters to inform clients, or employees; many companies use newsletters to sell products and services. Some companies even make a business of selling informational newsletters.

Newsletters usually have a logo on the front cover (page 1). A logo is an easily recognized symbol—decorative type, catchy word, short phrase—that appears on every issue (remember that consistency is important). A dateline, or folio, also should appear under the logo. Sometimes centered, sometimes on left and right tabs, the dateline can include the date and perhaps the volume and number of the document.

PART I

Understanding Design and Typography

Headers or footers also provide consistency. Although some printers say that these elements are unnecessary in a four-page document, a header or footer always adds a professional touch. However, never place a header or footer on the first page. A header should include the page number and may also give the publication's name, the date, the volume, or issue number.

Although not absolutely necessary, a table of contents is a good idea if the newsletter is more than four pages long. By placing a small box on the first page that showcases four or five items of interest in the publication, you can help draw the reader into the newsletter.

Always include a masthead, usually on page two. A masthead contains the editor's name and address, circulation, contact people, reporters, deadlines for copy, volume number, date, fees, credits, and so on.

If a newsletter is sent by mail, you need to provide each copy with a return address, postage permit, and a place for the mailing labels. Be sure that the postage permit is agreeable with the Post Office. The U.S. Mail has many regulations that govern the exact placement, wording, and even punctuation in a postage permit box.

The most important design point of a newsletter is consistency between issues. Although individual page layouts will differ from issue to issue, the masthead, dateline, publication information, and design elements such as column number and width, balance, gutter space, white space, and so on, should remain nearly the same each time. Type styles, spacing, and graphic elements should also be the same. A newsletter also should reflect the design of other publications produced by the same company to tie all the publications together and make them quickly recognizable. You can accomplish this consistency by adding the company's logo in a particular spot each time, or by using the same colors of ink or paper.

Popular sizes for newsletters are: 8 1/2 by 11 inches and printed on both sides; 11 by 17 inches, folded to 8 1/2 by 11 inches or smaller, for mailing (see fig. 2.19 for example); or 22 by 17 inches, both sides, folded to 11 by 17 inches and then to 8 1/2 by 11 inches (see fig. 2.27).

CHAPTER 2

Using the Elements of Design

FIG. 2.27.
One side of a 22-inch x 17-inch newsletter. Notice the mirrored balance of columns.

Using Forms

So many different forms are used every day in business that identifying all of them is impossible. A form usually contains text, lines, boxes, and whatever else you want to add.

Most forms leave spaces for information such as name, address, phone number, perhaps descriptions of items, quantities, total costs, sales tax, and so on. As many kinds of fill-in formats exist as there are forms.

If a typewriter is required to fill in a form, placing the rules on typewriter spacing is important. When setting paragraph spacing (leading) for the body text, 12-point leading equals single line typewriter spacing, 18-point leading equals one-and-a-half typewriter spacing, and 24-point leading equals double spacing. Word

PART I

Understanding Design and Typography

for Windows makes this part easy by describing leading in terms of line spacing or points. Be sure that you measure from the top in the same spacing when placing heads, subheads, and so on. For instance, place the company name, address, logo, and name of form on single-, one and one-half-, or double-spacing so you don't throw the first typewritten line off. If you change the type size in the middle of the form, also re-check the spacing. With Word for Windows you can produce forms easily with the Table format features (described in Chapter 12).

Using Books

With books of 8 to 12 pages or more (excluding newsletters), use headers and footers, page numbers, a table of contents, and an index. Chapter 21 discusses more detailed information.

When publishing a book with many chapters and miscellaneous elements, organizing the directories or floppy disks properly is important. Organize all information—such as text files, graphics, spreadsheets, and formatting—according to individual chapters. Save all related data in the same directory or on the same disk.

> **NOTE**
>
> The computer works faster and more efficiently if you work off the hard drive (instead of a floppy disk) and then save to a floppy disk or tape back-up after you complete each chapter. With large projects, back-ups are especially important.

Creating or loading a template from Word for Windows to apply to each chapter is a good idea. A template defines page orientation, margins and columns, headlines, body text, headers, footers, page numbers, macros, glossaries, and so on. Such a template can also help you achieve consistency throughout the book.

Traditionally, book margins are designed for easy reading. The bottom margins are usually the largest, inside margins the next largest (to accommodate a binding), and the top and outside margins are the same. Remember that books have facing pages, so create your design accordingly.

CHAPTER 2

Using the Elements of Design

Finally, plan the length of the book in sets of four pages or eight pages because of the way a commercial print shop prints a book. All documents with four or more pages print in a signature, or imposition, which is folded to form the proper page order. Depending on the trim size of the book, signatures can run on a press in 4-page, 8-page, or 16-page sets. Figure 2.28 shows a sample 4-page signature (meaning four pages up). Don't be concerned with setting up the signature on the computer, but try to plan the document in groups of four. After all, you don't want to pay for three blank pages at the end of the book.

> **TIP**
>
> To see where page numbers fall in a four-page signature, take a sheet of typing paper and hold it in the portrait mode. Fold the top edge down to align with the bottom edge. Then fold the left edge to align with the right edge. Now number each page (front and back) consecutively from 1 to 8. Unfold the sheet and your page numbers should match the numbers shown in figure 2.28.

FIG. 2.28.
The front of the sheet has pages 5, 4, 8, and 1; the back has pages 3, 6, 2, and 7.

Recognizing Design Flaws

When designing page formats, certain rules apply that you should never break. The reasons for these rules vary, but most important is readability. A summary of things *not* to do is shown in the following list:

PART I

Understanding Design and Typography

- Don't overwork the design by including too many graphics, rules, boxes, screens, heads, subheads, bolds, or italics. Be consistent, and add some contrast. Figure 2.29 shows an example of an overworked design.

- Don't start working at the computer without first forming a plan. Gather all text and graphics and prepare a rough draft before you format.

- Don't change the balance in the middle of a document (see fig. 2.30). Be consistent.

- Don't forget the 50-50 white-space rule. Figure 2.31 shows a page with too much gray; the reader may give up even before beginning to read this kind of design flaw.

- Don't work with margins under 3/8 inch. Remember: with margins, more is better.

- Don't stray from the margin or column guides.

- Don't change column sizes from page to page to fit copy. Plan ahead.

- Don't use a line length either too-long or too-short. Both can distract the reader.

- Don't take space away from gutters to fit in more text. See Chapter 3 for alternative ways to add type effectively.

- Don't design facing pages that fight each other (see fig. 2.32). Consistent balance and graphic elements can help hold a design together.

- Don't use too many graphic rules, borders, or boxes (see fig. 2.29). The general rule is no more than one boxed element per page.

- Don't forget the white space (*breathing room*) on the outside of a box or frame and on the inside.

CHAPTER 2

Using the Elements of Design

FIG. 2.29.
This design uses too many boxes and rules.

FIG. 2.30.
An example of balance changing from page to page in a document. Although individually either balance may work well, this combined design is distracting and unsettling.

PART I

Understanding Design and Typography

FIG. 2.31.
The page is crowded and too gray. Edit or move text to another page and add more white space.

FIG. 2.32.
These facing pages fight each other. Cluster the graphic images, make rules more consistent, and even out top margins.

Recapping

The following steps are provided as a recap to help refresh your memory and to give you a quick reference guide whenever you need it:

1. Prepare a disk or directory on which to save the document and all the components.

CHAPTER 2

Using the Elements of Design

2. Prepare the copy. Convert and transfer handwritten and typewritten material into a word processor.
3. Prepare the graphics.
4. Make thumbnail sketches of the proposed layout.
5. Make a rough draft of two or three pages.
6. Start Word for Windows.
7. Create a template or use one of Word for Windows'.
8. Set page size, orientation, margins, and columns.
9. Set up the style sheet.
10. Begin to format in Word for Windows.

Defining and Explaining Typography

One of the most important elements of design is typography. Typography is the style, arrangement, or appearance of typeset matter; it also refers to the general appearance of the printed page. The subject of typography is so comprehensive that it merits an entire book by itself. In fact, there are many books on the market about typography. This chapter presents information about typography as it applies to desktop publishing and to Microsoft Word For Windows.

This chapter is not just about the font, the style, or the size of the type you choose. It's also about your message, the design of your document, aesthetics, readability, and your reader. A reader judges the type you choose for your document and the way you present it. When looking at a printed page, the reader decides whether to pick up the document and read it, and whether to keep the document or immediately throw it away—all determined by one critical factor: the strength of your design.

Remember, the purpose of any printed document is to convert a browser into a reader, to attract and maintain a reader's attention. With careful planning and consideration, you can produce documents that attract and keep a reader's attention.

PART I

Understanding Design and Typography

Understanding Typography Terms

Terms and uses of type date back to the days of hand-set type. *Roman*, *kerning*, *serif*, *x-height*, *leading*, and *fonts* are just a few familiar terms. Many of these definitions are in use today by typesetters (they compose the typeset page), printers, and users of word processing and desktop publishing programs.

The word *type* essentially means printed characters. In the days of hand-set type, type referred to the actual blocks the typesetter used to print. The term *type* has many derivatives: typeface, type style, font, and type family. The traditional terms have changed in definition because of the development of desktop publishing. The following sections provide a brief description of the terms, their traditional meaning, and their significance today.

Defining Typeface

A *typeface* is a specific style or design of the actual letters of type. Helvetica, for example, is a typeface as is Times Roman. All typefaces have the following characteristics in common: x-height, ascenders, descenders, and they all rest on a common baseline.

The *x-height* is the height of a font's lowercase letters (such as *a*, *c*, and *x*) that do not have ascenders or descenders.

An *ascender* is the portion of the lowercase letters *b*, *d*, *f*, *h*, *k*, *l*, and *t* that rises above the x-height of the typeface.

A *descender* is the portion of the lowercase letters *g*, *j*, *p*, *q*, and *y* that hangs below the baseline.

> **NOTE**
>
> Because many fonts have unusually long or short ascenders and descenders, the x-height is a better measurement of the actual size of a font than the type size measured in points.

CHAPTER 3

Defining and Explaining Typography

The *baseline* is the invisible line on which all characters sit, as shown in figure 3.1.

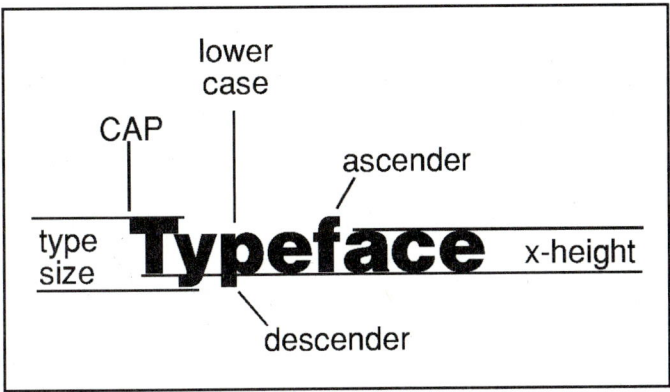

FIG. 3.1.
The common elements of all typefaces.

In a typeface, each character has components similar to the other characters in the typeface (see fig. 3.2). All Helvetica letters, for example, are sans serif with a uniform stroke and vertical emphasis. Vertical emphasis refers to the upright stress of the stroke. All Times Roman letters have serifs and are of varied stroke. The serifs of Times Roman soften its vertical emphasis. Helvetica and Times Roman are the two most popular typefaces used today.

Helvetica

Times Roman

FIG. 3.2.
Helvetica and Times Roman typefaces.

Stroke describes the thickness or weight of the lines that form the letter. *Serifs* are the fine cross strokes across the ends of the main strokes of a character (curved or adorned shapes). A serif can be rounded, curved, or stressed. *Stress* is another factor sometimes used to refer to typefaces. Stress refers to the distribution of weight in an individual letter. Helvetica has an even stress; Times Roman is "weighted" to the left. Stress also can refer to slant—as in italic or script types.

It is very important to limit the number of typefaces you use in a document. Use no more than two different typefaces. Use one

PART I

Understanding Design and Typography

typeface consistently throughout the document for headlines, bylines, and captions; use the other for body text. Helvetica and Avant Garde, for example, are good headline typefaces. For contrast, use Times Roman or Bookman as body text. You can think of this as the two-font rule. Too many typefaces can be distracting to the reader.

Examining Type Families

A *type family* encompasses many typefaces. The common elements of stroke, stress, and serifs identify a particular typeface and the type family to which it belongs. Five major families, or categories, of type are used in most desktop publishing programs and font packages. They are Roman, Sans Serif, Miscellaneous, Text, and Script. Each is very distinctive in look and mood. Figure 3.3 illustrates each type family described here.

FIG. 3.3.
The five major type families.

Roman

Sans Serif

Script

Text

MISCELLANEOUS

Roman

Roman type, as illustrated by Times Roman, is a serif type with a varied stroke. It is a dignified, classical, legible type. Times Roman, the most popular Roman type, is extremely common. Newspapers, books, and magazines use it almost exclusively because it is so easy to read. The serif adds a horizontal flow to the type, making the letters easily recognizable to the reader, which makes Times Roman perfect for body text. Bookman is another example of

CHAPTER 3

Defining and Explaining Typography

Roman type, as are Garamond and New Century Schoolbook. Any Roman type is excellent for body text. Another traditional category of Serif type is the Square Serif. However, the onset of desktop publishing has combined Roman and Square into one type family.

A Square Serif type has a blunt, blocked serif. It projects a forceful, somewhat disjointed appearance. Although excellent for display type or headlines, Square Serif type is not appropriate for body text. The shape of the serifs makes the type hard to read. The Square Serif family includes Palatino and Bodoni.

Sans Serif

Sans serif type has no serifs (characters are straight with little or no curved shapes or adornment). Usually, a sans serif type has a uniform stroke and vertical stress. Sans serif type gives a modern, contemporary, and efficient appearance to the text. The most popular sans serif type is Helvetica. Although hard to read in very large amounts, you can use sans serif type successfully in captions, headlines, forms, and contracts. Other sans serif typefaces include Futura and Avant Garde. You shouldn't use Avant Garde for body text, however. Its rounded letters are exceptionally hard to read.

Sans serif type families usually include a condensed version of the typeface and a black or heavy version. Either of these versions is excellent for display type.

Script

Script is a decorative, cursive type family that simulates handwriting. Script is graceful and fluent. You should reserve the script family for use in invitations, diplomas, or announcements. Chancery is a popular script, as are Brush and Linoscript. Never use script as body text and never use script in all capital letters. Script is hard enough to read without adding the extra burden of all capital letters.

PART I

Understanding Design and Typography

Text

Text is another decorative type family. It's stately and noble and should be used only for small amounts of text in formal pieces, invitations, and diplomas. Text also is very difficult to read and is illegible in all uppercase. Old English is the most popular Text font in use today.

Miscellaneous

The Miscellaneous category has become especially popular with the advent of desktop publishing and drawing programs. Miscellaneous includes any type that is shadowed, outlined, mirrored, or extremely ornate. Use this type for very short display heads (preferably only one per document) and never as body text.

The Miscellaneous category also can include symbol and dingbat fonts. These are fonts in which the letters are symbols, such as pi and accent grave, or arrows, pointing hands, scissors, bullets, numbers with circles around them, and so forth. These fonts are useful in many documents, but don't overuse them.

Discussing Fonts

The original meaning of the word *font* was a collection of all characters of one size and typeface. Times, 10 point, italic is an example. With the advent of desktop publishing, however, font has become a catch-all term that encompasses all sizes and styles of a particular typeface. Now, for example, Times, bold, italic, 6-point to 96-point is considered a font.

Working with Styles

Styles, or attributes, denote the characteristics of a typeface, such as bold, italic, light, condensed, extra bold, or any combination of these attributes. Most typefaces include at least bold and italic; many typefaces also include condensed and extra bold. Never use any of these styles as body text.

Defining and Explaining Typography

Measuring Type

Type *size* is the size of a font, measured in *points* from the top of the tallest ascender to the bottom of the lowest descender. One point equals 1/72 inch; 12 points make a *pica*; 6 picas make an inch (thus, 72 points to the inch). Picas are the printer's and typesetter's alternative to measuring in inches. With 6 picas per inch, close measurements of gutter, spaces, type, and the like make for easier measurements than 1/16-, 1/8-, 1/4-inch, and so on. Most desktop publishing programs offer the user the choice of measuring in picas or inches. The measurement you use is simply a personal preference. Figure 3.4 shows the common sizes and uses of type.

Body Text
9-point type
10-point type
11-point type
12-point type

Subheads
12-POINT BOLD
14-Point Italics

Heads or Headlines
18-Point Bold Italics
24-POINT BOLD
36-Point Bold Italics
48-POINT BOLD

Display Type
60-Pt. Narrow
72-Pt. Bold

FIG. 3.4.
Common type sizes.

PART I

Understanding Design and Typography

Working with Body Text

The main portion of any document is the body text. The common sizes for body text are 9, 10, 11, and 12 points. Type smaller than 9 points is too small to read comfortably, although a great deal of advertising text today is written in sizes smaller than 9-point. Also, body text larger than 12-point type is difficult to read, unless geared to visually impaired readers.

Using Headings

For major headings, type in 18-, 24-, 36-, or 48-point serves best. Heads can be bold, bold italic, or, if short (two to four words), all uppercase. Notice that the common sizes do not include sizes such as 19, 23, 37, or 44. Although most programs offer you the choice of these odd sizes, you should not use them. The common sizes have been time-tested as the most effective sizes in most situations. An 18-point head, for example, fits 10-point body type well and is comfortable to read. A 19-point head may not be that different in size, but it will look different on the typeset page. Also, your screen may not show the proper size if you choose an odd point size, and your printer may not be capable of printing it. For more information about screen and printer fonts, see Appendix C.

Using Subheads

Use a subhead to categorize main topics. The subhead is more significant than the body text, yet less important than the heads. Usually bold, italic, or all uppercase if short, a subhead can be 12- or 14-point type, depending on the size of the document. The larger the page, the larger the point size.

Using Display Type

Display type is large, sometimes ornamental type, used sparingly in documents to grab attention. The size of display type depends on the size of the document, the length of the word or words, and the space the rest of the copy takes. Display type sizes can be

CHAPTER 3

Defining and Explaining Typography

48-, 60-, 72-point or even larger. At this time, the largest available type in a desktop publishing program is 256-points. However, some programs allow you to create a 125-point font, then scale it from 100 percent to 400 percent when printing. The size of the type you use depends on the program, and the fonts installed in your printer. Bit-mapped fonts are seldom larger than 72-point; whereas, PostScript fonts allow for the largest sizes.

Measuring Guidelines

Different typefaces of the same size may not measure the same. Furthermore, each manufacturer of type has its own version of each face. Script and text fonts, for example, are almost always smaller than serif or sans serif fonts. Text in 18-point Chancery looks more like 14 point when printed. Similarly, 28-point Old English text looks more like 18 point when printed. Any font made by ITC is larger than other manufacturers' type of the same size. Helvetica and Avant Garde are generally larger than Times Roman or Palatino (see fig. 3.5).

Chancery
Helvetica
Times Roman

FIG. 3.5.
The size differences are obvious in these examples of 18-point Chancery, 18-point Helvetica, and 18-point Times.

Although desktop publishing programs offer more type sizes for use in documents, you need to limit the number of sizes you use in one document. Use no more than four different sizes in a one-page document, and no more than eight in a longer document. Too many type sizes can be distracting to the reader. Figure 3.6 shows proper sizing for types in an 8 1/2 inch -by-11-inch sales flier. Notice the use of display type, heads, and subheads.

When choosing type sizes, determine the most important ideas in your copy. Set up your copy from the most important ideas to the least important. Decide what information will most attract the reader and make the headline the largest type on the page. Keep

PART I

Understanding Design and Typography

proportion in mind, as well. A flier with 60-point display type and 10-point body text is not proportional. You should strive for balance in your visual presentation.

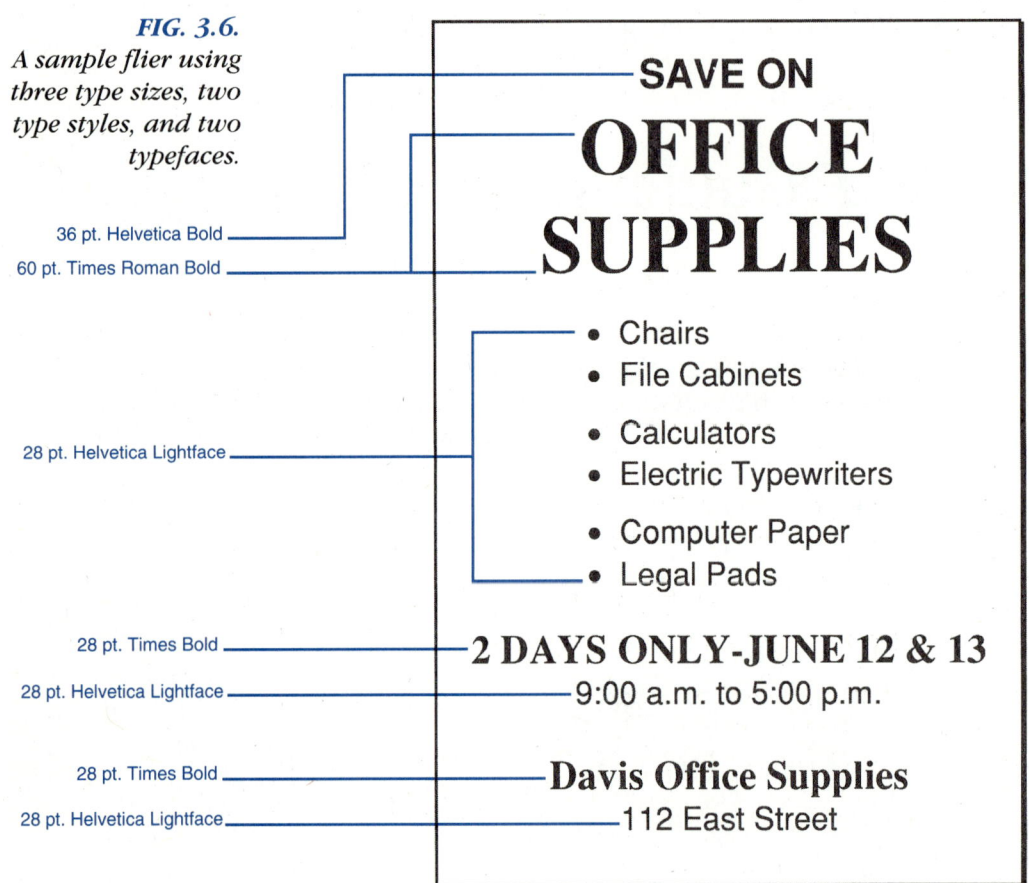

FIG. 3.6.
A sample flier using three type sizes, two type styles, and two typefaces.

Using Attributes to Improve Your Document

As discussed earlier, *styles*, or *attributes*, are used to emphasize a word or group of words. Examples of attributes are bold, italic, bold italic, all capital letters in short headings or subheads, and condensed or expanded type. Applying an attribute to a small amount of text is more emphatic than applying it to large blocks

CHAPTER 3

Defining and Explaining Typography

of text. You shouldn't use too many different attributes in a document. A little bold and italic is fine; but using bold, italic, all uppercase, and condensed type in one document is too much. In figure 3.7, you can see the appropriate use of attributes in a document.

FIG. 3.7.
Appropriate use of attributes for emphasis in a document.

It is easy to misuse attributes. For example, don't underline anything except a column of numbers. Underlining not only makes reading the document more difficult, but also looks unprofessional. Double underlining should be reserved for under the total of a column of numbers.

Using bold, italic, and all uppercase letters in the same document, particularly on the same page, works against readability. If the reader must strain to read your document, chances are it will not be read (see fig. 3.8)

Capital letters often are used at the beginning of each word in a headline or subhead, or for just the first word. Sometimes all uppercase letters are used for the entire head, if it is short. Never use all uppercase letters for body text—just as you would never use all lowercase letters for a heading.

Using Spacing

You need to include white space in your document. This space is important to your document not only for the sake of design, but also for readability. Crowded text—words too close together—and too much "gray" on the page, fatigues a reader's eyes. To include

PART I

Understanding Design and Typography

white space in a document, you can use wider margins (as discussed in Chapter 2). You also can increase the white space by controlling the spacing within the text.

FIG. 3.8.
Too many attributes in a document.

HUMBLE OPINIONS

Software Packages
Do you want to learn more about your **software programs,** *spreadsheets, databases, word processing,* and *desktop publishing programs?* **Humble Opinions** offers *training and instruction* in many of the popular **software packages** for the Personal Computer.

Purchasing Printing
How well do you communicate with your *print shop?* Is your job always *printed right?* If not, you may need help with your projects. Learn *terms* your printer uses, and how they apply to you and your print job. **Humble Opinions** can help you get that job done, *precisely and on time.*

Planning Your Future
What are your **software needs?** Which program can help you organize your daily chores? A growing business needs *proper tools* to expand. **Humble Opinions** can help you evaluate and choose *effective* **software programs** that help you plan your future.

When reading, the eye does not look closely at each word. Instead, the reader uses the shape of words—the shape of the ascenders and descenders in relation to the body of the word—to recognize what the word is. This condition is one reason all uppercase is so hard to read. You can use the spacing of letters, words, lines, and paragraphs to help your reader get through your material quickly and easily.

Four main categories of spacing are used in typesetting documents: letter spacing, word spacing, line spacing, and paragraph spacing. When applying any kind of spacing, be consistent. Consistency in spacing keeps the reader on track, offering no diversions to interrupt the train of thought.

Spacing Between Letters

The spacing between the letters of a word can make it easier or harder to read. Certain letters fit together to form instantly recognizable pairs. For example, *th*, *er*, *sp*, and *ly* are just a few of many familiar pairs of letters. When you have too much space between letters, recognizing letters as pairs is more difficult. This problem is the main reason typesetters rarely use monospaced fonts, such as Courier, for documents. In a *monospaced* font, such as Courier, each letter takes up exactly the same amount of space, no matter whether the letter is an *i* or an *m*. Figure 3.9 shows both

CHAPTER 3

Defining and Explaining Typography

Courier and Helvetica type. Notice the difference in the letter spacing. Helvetica is easier to read.

```
Courier is a monospaced font. Each letter and
punctuation mark occupies exactly the same
amount of space. For this reason, Courier is
difficult to read.

Helvetica is a proportionally spaced font. Each letter is only
as wide as it needs to be. Helvetica is much easier to read
than Courier.
```

FIG. 3.9.
Different letter spacing in Courier and Helvetica typefaces.

Kerning is a part of letter spacing. To kern letters is to bring them closer together so that their spacing looks right. Most desktop or word processing programs space letters properly without adjustment by you. Some letter pairs, however, may need manual adjustment—for example, A and V, or W and A (see fig. 3.10).

AVANT   AVANT

FIG. 3.10.
Letter pairs before (left) and after (right) kerning.

In most cases, Word For Windows automatically spaces letters. If you need to kern letter pairs, Word enables you to do so by expanding or condensing type (by clicking **Format**, then **Chara**c**ter**; or by pressing Alt-T,C).

Spacing Between Words

The correct spacing between words is critical to ease of reading. Words too close together create a dense gray page, uninviting to a reader. On the other hand, words spaced too far apart create "holes" on the page. Large areas of white space between words are apparent in the overall gray of the page. Too much or too little spacing makes the reader work hard to get through the message (see fig. 3.11).

PART I

Understanding Design and Typography

FIG. 3.11.
Words too close together (top), and too far apart (bottom), make documents difficult to read.

> Words can be spaced too close together. If word spacing is too tight, the gray of the page is too dense, causing the reader to search for each word. Justified text can be the root of the problem, combined with a column that is too narrow.
>
> Word spacing is important to readability. Too much space between words can create "rivers" of white space that flow through the page. Text that is justified tends to create wide word spacing if hyphenation is turned off.

Fully justified text often causes problems with spacing. *Fully justified* text—aligned both flush left and flush right—often creates large gaps between words or letters. To avoid this problem when fully justifying text, you can use *discretionary hyphens*, created by pressing Ctrl+- (hyphen). Word uses the discretionary hyphen only when necessary to better space the line of type. Be aware that a discretionary hyphen is different than a plain hyphen. A discretionary hyphen appears only when needed; a plain hyphen is a permanent part of the word. If you insert a plain hyphen by pressing just the hyphen key, and then you later insert or delete text, causing the text to move, the hyphen will still appear in the middle of the word, which is not what you intended.

One final note about word spacing: never use two spaces after a period. This method is a leftover from the typewriter days and monospaced fonts. When typesetting, two spaces at the end of a sentence will create holes in the text. If you have a hard time remembering not to press the space bar twice, you can type the way you usually do, and then perform a search and replace to get rid of the double spaces.

Spacing Between Lines

Line spacing, interline spacing, and leading (*LED-ing*) all refer to the amount of space between two lines of text. You're probably familiar with single-, one-and-a-half-, and double-line spacing from your typewriter; Word uses the same terms to describe line spacing. In Word, you also can measure line spacing in points (by clicking Forma**t**, **P**aragraph; or by pressing Alt-T,P). If you prefer,

CHAPTER 3

Defining and Explaining Typography

Word automatically spaces lines for you, increasing the space in proportion to the size of the type. Most of the time, you probably will not need to adjust the spacing.

The tallest character in a particular typeface and size is the guideline for measuring line spacing. Capital letters, ascenders, and descenders all must have enough space to prevent them from overlapping letters above or below them. Space equal to 20 percent of the size of the font is the normal line spacing, although many word processors and desktop publishing programs use 30 percent.

Because type sizes are measured in points, you may want to learn the measurements for leading in points as well. For example, 10-point type uses 12-point leading (called 10 on 12 and written as 10/12). 14-point type uses 16-point leading, and 18 point-type uses 20- or 22-point leading.

What happens if you need to adjust the leading? Some layouts will require more or less line spacing. The larger the x-height of a typeface, for instance, the more leading you need. The smaller the type, the less line spacing needed. Sans serif type, because of its vertical emphasis, also needs extra leading to improve readability. Headlines may need less leading for effortless reading; body text may require more for the same purpose. You can enlarge the spacing as much as you need to meet the needs of your document; however, you can reduce the leading only to the size of the body type. (For example, 10-point type on 10-point leading, 14-point type on 14-point leading, and so on.) This spacing is close and not the best, but it will work. Figure 3.12 shows three examples of leading with the same size body type.

> This is 10-point Times Roman on 12-point spacing. This spacing works well for body text. It is comfortable to read because there is enough space between the lines.
>
> This is 10-point Times Roman on 14-point spacing (auto). This spacing is still comfortable for the reader, and it allows you to spread out your copy to fill extra space.
>
> This is 10-point Times Roman on 16-point spacing. You may want to use this spacing if your line length is longer than usual for 10-point type or to fit copy.

FIG. 3.12.
Three examples of leading with the same size body type.

Line spacing is also a good way to achieve extra white space. A headline or subhead always needs space above and below it to set it apart from the page. Typesetters handle that problem by creating a *space*. A space is a template (usually 4-point or 6-point type on 6-point leading) that provides a set amount of extra space. When needed, the space is applied above or below the head or subhead to give it more breathing room. Nothing is on the line but a paragraph return. You can accomplish the same thing by adding extra line spacing.

Spacing Between Paragraphs

After the letters, words, and lines of your document have the proper amount of space, you may want to add extra space between paragraphs. You should remember this simple rule: if you indent the first line of the paragraph, don't add an extra line of space between paragraphs; if you don't indent the first sentence, add at least one line of space between each paragraph. Figure 3.13 shows examples of paragraph spacing and indentation. The reason for this rule is ease of reading. If the reader can find the first sentence of a paragraph, it is easier to understand the division of topics in the document. Your task is to help the reader understand.

FIG. 3.13.
In the first example, the sentences are indented, so no added paragraph space is required. In the second example, the sentences are not indented, so added paragraph space is needed.

> Indent the first line when you are not adding extra space between paragraphs. Formatting your body text in this manner allows you to fit more copy on the page.
> The indent of the first line indicates the beginning of the paragraph and adds valuable white space to a gray page. Indenting the first line looks better when your type is justified.
>
> If you left-align your text, consider using extra spacing between the paragraphs instead of indenting the first line. The ragged right adds white space and an indented first line on the left would serve to confuse the reader.
>
> Of course, applying left-aligned text with extra paragraph spacing means you will not fit as much copy on the page. Perhaps you can add more pages.

CHAPTER 3

Defining and Explaining Typography

Using Text Alignment

Alignment is a method of organizing text. Body text, headlines, tabs, and all text must have an alignment (left aligned, or right aligned, or centered, or fully justified). However you align your type, make sure that the alignment remains consistent throughout the entire document. Changes in alignment from page to page can be confusing and disconcerting to the reader. Figure 3.14 illustrates each of the four alignments discussed.

Left-Aligned Subhead
Left-aligned heads, subheads and body text provide consistency of design. The reader always knows where the next line begins. In addition, the ragged right line endings create white space.

Right-Aligned Subhead
Text that is right-aligned should be short and interesting.

Center-Aligned Subhead
Any centered text should be short and well-arranged. Also make sure that line length is pleasing to the eye.

Justified Text
Never justify a subhead or head. Because the type is larger, it will space unequally to fit. It would not look good. Therefore, this justified text has a left-aligned head. Again, justified text allows you to fit more copy on the page.

FIG. 3.14. Examples of left-aligned, right-aligned, centered, and fully justified type.

Using Left Alignment

Left-aligned text has a flush left margin and a ragged right margin. Using left-aligned text for body text has many advantages, which are covered in the next section. The ragged right margin adds valuable white space to break up the page. Of course, if your right margin is too ragged, the white space can be distracting. Usually, left-aligned text has very little or no hyphenation. You can use discretionary hyphens, however, to keep the ragged right line

PART I

Understanding Design and Typography

endings more even. Never use more than two hyphens in succession. If the right margin is too ragged and has many hyphens, you should adjust your column width.

Another advantage of left-aligned text is that equal word spacing occurs naturally, providing an even texture to the gray of the page. Left-aligned text also works well in narrow columns because the reader can find the beginning of a line easier and faster with left-aligned text. The flush left directs the eye easily. When you use left-aligned headlines and subheads, readers are able to find the next topic easily and it adds additional white space. When left-aligning text, place a vertical rule in the gutters to help divide the columns. The vertical rules add a professional touch to the page.

One disadvantage to left-aligned text is that you cannot fit in as much copy as you can with fully justified text. If you have much copy and few pages on which to set it, left-aligned text may take up too much space.

Using Right Alignment

Right-aligned text has a flush right margin and a ragged left margin. Right-alignment rarely is used for body text. Usually right alignment is reserved for a headline or subhead to attract attention. If you use right-aligned heads, be sure to use uppercase and lowercase (never all uppercase) and make sure that the heads are very short and that the overall design of the piece somehow reflects and reinforces the use of right-aligned text.

Never use right-aligned text for any head or subhead more than three or four short lines long. Never use right alignment in a caption or callout. Never use right-aligned text for body text—it is very difficult to read.

Using Center Alignment

Centered text has ragged left and right margins. Center alignment most often is used for headlines, subheads, and datelines. Center alignment provides even word spacing, visual interest, and an air of dignity to the document. Center-aligned heads work well with fully justified body text.

CHAPTER 3

Defining and Explaining Typography

Although rarely used for body text, you can center-align certain items: lists of names or dates, invitations or announcements, and very short lines of text in a flier. Center-aligned body text is hard to read; the reader's eyes must search for the beginning and end of each line.

Using Full Justification

Fully justified text has both a flush-left and flush-right margin. Fully justified text is perfect for long materials, such as books, articles, or reports. The page appears organized, quiet, and comfortable for the reader.

Fully justified alignment enables you to fit more copy on the page. Avoid any temptation to reduce gutters with justified text; because of the even gray appearance of the page, you need the white space in the gutters. Add extra space to the gutter if possible.

Watch out for uneven word spacing with fully justified text. Justification sometimes forces long words to the next line or squeezes short words to the current line. When using fully justified text, always make sure that automatic hyphenation is turned on. Manual manipulation of the line sometimes is necessary. Manual manipulation includes editing the text or adjusting the letter spacing of just one line of text or both. Discretionary hyphens often are handy, too.

Never use fully justified text for headlines. A headline, or subhead, is larger type than the text. Large type is hard to justify without unequal and unsightly word spacing.

Using Indentation

An *indentation* (indent) is the distance from the left margin to the beginning of the text, or from the right margin to the end of the text. In this way, indents control the width of the paragraph. You can apply an indent to the first sentence of a paragraph, or to the left or right of a paragraph so that it stands out from the rest of the text.

A positive measurement, such as two inches, indents the text toward the center of a page or column. A two-inch indent from the left would indent the paragraph two inches. A negative number

PART I

Understanding Design and Typography

used as an indent, such as -1 inch, produces an *outdent*, or *hanging indent*. Used for bullets, numbered lists, or subtitles, a hanging indent is a useful tool for text formatting (see fig. 3.15).

FIG. 3.15.
A hanging indent used for a subtitle.

> OUTDENT   An outdent is where a subtitle, a bullet, a number, and so on, hangs to the left while the rest of the paragraph indents.

Using Tabs

A *tab* is a tool of organization that enables you to line up lists of items across a line. You can align names, numbers, prices, or any list with tabs. A tab stop enables you to move to a specific point quickly and efficiently; all you need to do is press the Tab key.

A tab can align to the left, right, center, or by decimal. These alignments are similar to text alignments. Left tabs are flush left and ragged right.

Right tabs are flush right, and excellent for use with a left tab and leaders as shown in figure 3.16. *Leaders*, pronounced *leeders*, are periods, hyphens, or solid lines between the items on the left and the items on the right that lead the eye to the end of the line. If you use a leader with a right tab, be sure to press Tab and the space bar before typing the item to be aligned on the right tab. This space separates the leader from the item so that it is easier to read.

FIG. 3.16.
The text in the first column is aligned on a left tab. The text in the second column is aligned on a right tab. The leaders help guide the eye to the text in the second column.

> Humble Opinions --------------------------- C. O. Plumley
> Computer Supplies --------------------------- S. U. Blackwell
> Software Unlimited--------------------------- T. O. Angle
> Modems R Us --------------------------------- R. I. Barlow

Defining and Explaining Typography

Use the center tab for names, places, or other special items. When you use a center tab, be sure to allow enough space from the margin for the longest line; otherwise, the tab will not work.

A decimal tab is especially useful when typing lists of numbers, percentages, or currency. The tab stop is on the decimal point; any numbers containing a decimal point, automatically align on the decimal point. Figure 3.17 shows examples of center tabs and decimal tabs.

```
Dell Industries---------------------------- $12,702.00
HO Consultants----------------------------    1250.00
Bender Products, Inc. --------------------      34.99
```

FIG. 3.17.
Center tabs (left) and decimal tabs.

Placing Text on a Page

Now that you understand the basic terms of typesetting and the characteristics of type, you can begin organizing your text on the page. Chapter 2 discusses using design elements as ways of organizing the page. Producing thumbnails and roughs is an excellent way to organize the page; columns and grids also help you place your text.

After composing the body of your document, create heads and subheads that describe the text in an interesting and stimulating way. Use active verbs in the heads if at all possible, so you attract the reader to the text. The heads can then be set in a type that separates them from the body of the document and attracts the reader even more. The definitions presented in the following sections will help you choose type sizes for heads, subheads, and body text.

Using Display Heads

A *display head* is a heading in a very large size and, sometimes, in an ornate font. A display head attracts attention, both by its size and by its content—*Sale*, *Announcement*, and *Grand Opening* are all candidates for a display head. Don't make a head a display

head if it contains more than three or four words, and be sure to use only one display head per document. Of course, you don't have to use any display heads at all; many documents look better with regular headlines instead.

Using Heads

Heads, or *headlines*, attract attention and organize the page. Heads should be short, concise phrases that attract and maintain the reader's interest. You can use a different type style from the body text, or use the same style but make the head larger and bold. Heads can be left-aligned, right-aligned, or centered; they can be bold, bold italic, or all uppercase if short. Sample headlines might be *Refrigerators Half Price*, or *Designer Scarves Are Here*, or *Newsletter Wins Award*.

Using Subheads

To further divide a topic under a heading, use *subheads*. Smaller than the head but larger than the body text, a subhead should be bold or italic to make it noticeable. Subheads help to break up the copy for easier reading. They also supply visual contrast to a gray page and identify the contents of specific paragraphs.

Subheads can be in a contrasting typeface, bold, italic, or indented. They can be left-, right-, or center-aligned.

Be consistent throughout the document and don't use too many different typefaces (remember the two-font rule). Suppose that your body text, for example, is Times Roman and your heads are bold Helvetica. The subheads can be bold Times, or bold italic Helvetica. Some sample subheads might be *All Brands of Refrigerators are in Stock*, or *Choosing Your Scarf to Match Your Shoes*, or *Company Newsletter Editor is Proud*.

Using Captions

A *caption* is text used to briefly explain illustrations, artwork, photos, or figures. A reader often will look at a caption before deciding to read the body text of a document. Therefore, captions are important tools in getting the message to the reader.

CHAPTER 3

Defining and Explaining Typography

Place captions next to, above, or below the illustration or photo. Traditionally, captions are places beneath the photo or illustration. Changing the tradition by offsetting the photo and placing the caption to its left or right creates an exciting change in design, thus attracting more attention. Placing a caption above a photo or illustration produces a mini-head effect, which can also pull the reader into the document.

Align the caption with the body text and make it the width of the illustration if possible. You can center-align short captions to match your headlines. Remember: be consistent. Because captions usually are 8- or 9-point italic type with close leading, a typeface such as Helvetica or another sans serif font is easy to read.

Using Body Text

Body text makes up the bulk of your copy. Set body text in paragraph form, make it left-aligned or fully justified, and choose a typeface easy to read, such as Times Roman. Most people who browse through printed material read the heads first, then the subheads, and then the captions. Body text is the last thing read. Keep this in mind when designing and writing your heads and subheads.

> **NOTE**
>
> When a document contains photos—especially striking, interesting photos—the reader's eye will go there first in almost all instances, then to the caption. If those two keep the reader's interest, and an accompanying story or article is also provided, that's where the eyes will go next. These are important design considerations you should be aware of. They point out that you can indeed direct the reader's eye wherever you want on the page.

PART I

Understanding Design and Typography

Using Text for Emphasis

Besides the methods already described, you can also attract attention to topics in a document by using several techniques, such as jumplines, callouts, large first characters, bullets, and logos.

Working with Jumplines

A *jumpline* continues a story or article on another page. Sometimes a jumpline also can be a method of leading the reader into the document. By placing the beginning of an interesting story or article on the first page of a newsletter, for example, you can use a jumpline to direct the reader to page 3 to continue. The reader must open the newsletter to complete the story, and, you hope, will find something else of interest. Newspapers use jumplines in this way—they begin several important articles on the front page and continue them elsewhere in the paper.

> **NOTE**
>
> Be aware that whenever jumplines are used, some readers will not make the jump. Instead, they will read other articles, which means that the remainder of the jumped article probably will not be read. A good use of jumplines, providing that the main head is strong enough to attract the reader's interest in the first place, is to direct the reader to the following page.

A jumpline usually is written in all lowercase italics and placed in parentheses at the end of the column. The type can be a point or two smaller than the body text. The alignment can be centered, left, or right. All that is necessary is a statement such as the following:

(continued on page 3)

Try to break the story at the end of a paragraph, or at the end of a sentence. To continue the story, place a small, abbreviated head at the break, telling readers where they can find the rest of the story. On the jump page, repeat the abbreviated jump head, and tell readers the page number from which the story was jumped.

CHAPTER 3

Defining and Explaining Typography

Working with Callouts

A *callout* is a short, pithy statement or phrase taken from the body text to entice the reader into reading the entire piece. A callout is usually set in 12- or 14-point bold or italic text, centered or left-aligned, high up on the page (ideally, in the center column of a three-column page). The callout is always the same width as the column, and be sure to leave plenty of white space around it. A nice touch is a box or rules above and below the callout text. Figure 3.18 shows a callout in a column of text from a newsletter.

FIG. 3.18.
A good callout can draw the reader's attention to the rest of the story.

Working with Large First Characters

When designing longer documents, such as newsletters, magazines, or books, you may use a large first character, or *drop cap*, for emphasis at the beginning of each section. A large first character is usually just the first letter of the first sentence in a section or chapter. You can break up large amounts of text in this manner, instead of using subheads. A good rule of thumb is to use no more than one drop cap per page. However, for gray pages, one drop cap at the top of the page and one at the bottom also is acceptable.

93

Any more than that makes your document look cluttered. A similar, but infrequently used, technique is to raise the capital letter so that it extends well above the first line of type.

When using 12-point body text, a large first character can be 28 to 36 points and bold. It also can be a different typeface, or enclosed in a shadow box for more emphasis. Be consistent with large first characters: if you choose 36-point bold to use with 12-point body text, stick to it throughout the document. Figure 3.19 shows a paragraph with a large first character.

FIG. 3.19.
In this example, the drop cap is 36-point Times bold and the body text is 12-point Times.

> Large first characters, sometimes called drop caps, are decorative effects with no other real value. Although they are nice, use them sparingly. For example, use them at the beginning of a chapter, or a section. Under no circumstances should you use them at the beginning of every paragraph.

Working with Bullets

A bullet is a dot, or asterisk, or other symbol used to organize and attract attention to a list of items. Beginning each item on a new line and placing a bullet in front of it makes the list easier to read (see fig. 3.20). Bullets should be consistent in size, indention, and space between the bullet and the beginning of the text throughout the document. Bullets assume that no one thing on a list is more important than the others. If a bulleted item has more than one line, make sure that the bullet is on a hanging indent so that it doesn't get lost in the text.

FIG. 3.20.
Using bullets makes a list easier to read.

> Use bullets to emphasize a list:
> - Always indent the bullet and text
> - If a line wraps, be sure it is at the same indent of the previous line
> - Never use different bullet symbols within one document

CHAPTER 3

Defining and Explaining Typography

Working with Numbered Lists

In contrast to bulleted lists, numbered lists signify an order of importance to the items they contain. Numbers also let the reader know how many items the list contains. Use a hanging indent for numbered lists to make lists more organized and easier for the reader to find the next number.

Working with Logos

A logo is another emphasis tool. A logo, generally a symbol of identity, can project an image for a company or product. You can design a logo out of text by stretching, condensing, reversing, or rotating the type. You can place the logo type on a curve, in an envelope to stretch it, or in perspective. You also can reduce the leading so that two words touch, place text in a box, or position a rule above or below the text.

Word for Windows offers many possibilities for designing logos. Figure 3.21 shows four logos designed in Word. When designing logos, you can ignore most type rules. As long as the logo is easily recognizable, fairly small, and used consistently, it is open to all your creativity.

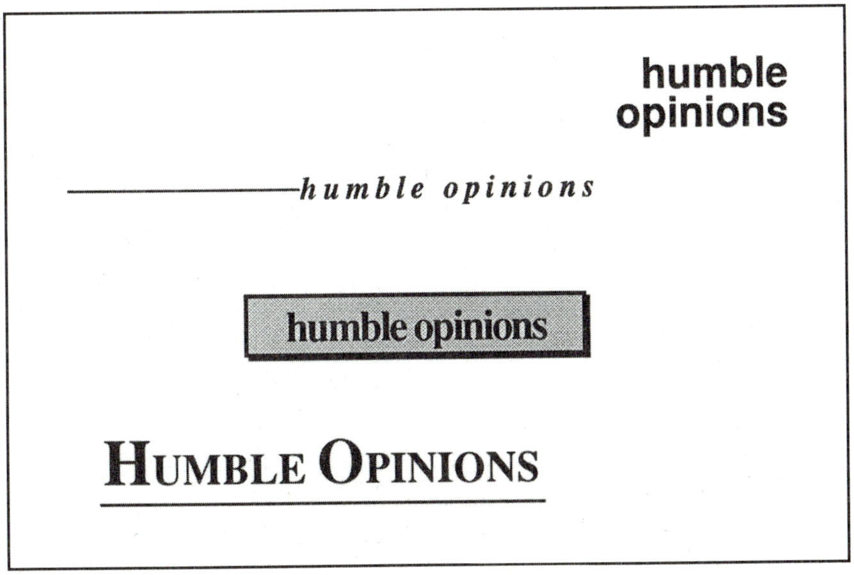

FIG. 3.21.
Sample logos designed in Word for Windows.

95

PART I

Understanding Design and Typography

Producing Style Sheets

A style sheet refers to the text in a template. The template is the overall design: columns, margins, boilerplate text, and so forth. The style sheet is a list of assignments that describes typeface, type size and style, spacing, alignment, and tabs and indents. You use a particular style sheet for a particular type of document. A newsletter style sheet, for example, would be different from a form style sheet. You can, of course, format each individual paragraph of body text, each head, each tab, and so on. But it is so much easier to format the item once, save it as a style, and then use it over and over again throughout the document, and then later in similar documents.

A style sheet is an excellent way of ensuring consistency in a document and between documents. Suppose, for example, that in the first issue of a newsletter, all major headings were set 18-point, bold, and centered. Every head in the document conforms to that same description. Next month, when you produce the second issue of the newsletter, you can use the style sheet created for the first newsletter. The style sheet ensures that the two issues look alike and saves you much time setting up the styles.

As mentioned in Chapter 2, Word has built-in style sheets. You can also create your own style sheets. For consistency and efficiency, use a style sheet with any document you frequently produce.

Understanding Design Flaws

Readability is among the primary reasons for making good design and type choices. If your work is not easy to read or the design is distracting, then you're wasting your time producing it. The most important thing to remember is the comfort and interest of the reader. Following is a list of items you should not do when setting type:

- Don't use too many typefaces in one document. Remember the two-font rule.

- Don't use all uppercase with Script and Text fonts (see fig. 3.22).

- Don't use bold or italic as body text (see fig. 3.23).

CHAPTER 3

Defining and Explaining Typography

- Don't use all uppercase for more than three or four words (see fig. 3.24).
- Don't place two spaces after a period (see fig. 3.25).
- Don't use too many type styles or sizes in a document. Too much variation confuses and distracts the reader.
- Don't use type larger than 12 points or smaller than 9 points for body text.
- Don't use more than two hyphens in a row. Watch your letter and word spacing. If you have a problem, try adjusting the column width.
- Don't use hyphens. Use discretionary hyphens.
- Don't use inconsistent line and paragraph spacing (see fig. 3.26). The reader should be able to scan effortlessly across the page.
- Don't apply more than one alignment to body text in a document. Match the alignments of body, heads, and subheads.
- Don't make captions as large as body text, but don't make them too small to read. As a general rule, make the caption one or two points smaller than the body, in either bold or italic.
- Don't indent a paragraph too much. Use the line length as a guide. For example, a 2 1/2-inch line length needs no more than a 1/4-inch indent. However, a 4-inch line length could stand up to a 1/2-inch indent. Indents of less than 1/4-inch and more than 1/2-inch should not be used.
- Don't indent the first sentence more than 1/4 inch. Always use a tab to indent, never spaces (see fig. 3.27).
- Don't use too many callouts, jumplines, bullets, bold, or italic.
- Don't use different styles of bullets in the same document.
- Don't work without a style sheet.
- Don't forget consistency.

PART I

Understanding Design and Typography

***FIG. 3.22.**
The Script type family. The Chancery typeface in all uppercase is very hard to read.*

> *THIS IS CHANCERY, 18-POINT. IT IS HARD ENOUGH TO READ BECAUSE IT'S SCRIPT; IT IS ALSO ALL CAPS, WHICH MAKES IT ABSOLUTELY IMPOSSIBLE.*

***FIG. 3.23.**
Body text in all bold or all italic is a strain on the reader's eyes.*

> **Body text that is all bold is difficult to read. The eyes tire easily, and so does the reader. The smaller the type, the harder it is to read. Use bold only for emphasis in body text.**
>
> *Likewise, body text that is all italic strains the eyes of the reader. You can use italic for one- or two-word emphasis within body text. Italic is also an excellent substitute for normally underlined text, such as book titles.*

***FIG. 3.24.**
When you use all uppercase as body text, the eye has a difficult time recognizing the shapes of the words.*

> A PARAGRAPH OF ALL CAPS IS HARD TO READ BECAUSE THEY LACK THE ASCENDERS AND DESCENDERS THAT HELP US RECOGNIZE THE SHAPES OF THE WORDS. USE ALL CAPS ONLY ON SHORT HEADS OR SUBHEADS.

CHAPTER 3

Defining and Explaining Typography

When typesetting pages, never place two spaces after a period. Typeset material is much more sensitive to two spaces than one. Two spaces after a period is a leftover from the typewriter days. The two spaces create a pothole effect, or large gaps, such as you see in this paragraph.

FIG. 3.25.
Placing two spaces after periods creates wide gaps in the typeset page.

IRREGULAR SPACING - HEADS
The space between heads and the body text should always be the same. If you start with 1.5 line spacing, stick with it throughout the document.

IRREGULAR SPACING - BODY

Never vary your line or paragraph spacing. Keep all spacing throughout the document consistent. If you begin with 2 lines between paragraphs, finish with 2 lines between paragraphs.

You can handle copyfitting in many different ways. If you must squeeze a little more text in, then reduce spacing of all heads first. Then you can reduce leading within the body — but do it with all of the body.

Inconsistency of spacing is distracting. In addition, it is harder to do.

FIG. 3.26.
Inconsistent line spacing between heads and body text and inconsistent spacing between paragraphs, makes your document look unprofessional.

FIG. 3.27.
The first lines of the sentences indented (unevenly) with spaces.

> Never use spaces to indent the first sentence of a paragraph, or to indent for bullets, numbers, and so on. If you miscount your spaces even once, it will be noticeable on the page.
>
> Uneven indents change the white space. It is no longer a rest for the eyes of the reader, but a point of diversion.
>
> Don't forget to set tabs or indents for the first line of a sentence in a paragraph if you want it to be indented.

Recapping

The following steps are provided as a recap to help refresh your memory and to give you a quick reference guide whenever you need it:

1. Gather and organize all materials before beginning your project.

2. Put your copy in an order of priority. For example, put your most important facts at the top of the page with large headlines to match, then your next most important items with smaller heads, and so on.

3. Set up a style sheet for your document. Plan the typefaces (no more than two), type sizes, type styles, alignment, and spacing.

4. Plan any emphasis type, such as callouts, bullets, and logos.

5. Refer to the Recapping steps in Chapter 2.

Planning and Purchasing Printing

Now that your document is complete, you need to get it reproduced. If you need only a small number of copies, you can print it on your laser printer. However, if you need a large number of copies, using your laser printer is not a cost effective way of getting them. Rather, you need the services of a commercial printer.

This chapter covers printing services, price quotations, paper and ink choices, and a few finishing procedures, such as folding and fastening techniques. The information is presented as an overview only. If you have more detailed questions, you should consult your print shop.

Reviewing Design for Printing

Designing a document for offset or photocopy printing is different from designing a document for laser printing. Certain tasks you perform during layout make it easier and cheaper to have your document printed. Printing is expensive; the more you prepare for a commercial printer's procedures, the less you pay.

Working with Paste-Up

Paste-up means to bring together in final form on the page all the pieces of your completed document to be photographically reproduced. With Word for Windows, you can create pages that need little paste-up. When you format a page that needs no changes, modifications, additions, or deletions, it is *camera ready*. Camera-ready copy goes to the camera department where a negative is made of the final document. The negative is then used to make a plate, which goes to the final step—the press. However, if your document requires crop marks, photographs, artwork, illustrations, and so forth, it is not camera ready. Instead, it needs paste-up work.

Crop Marks

In Word, you cannot add crop marks as you can in many desktop publishing programs. Crop marks are lines (drawn outside the actual document) that define the trim area (see fig. 4.1). If the trim area, or actual size of your document, is 8 1/2 inches by 11 inches, you draw crop marks to define that size. In Word, a formatted page would not be camera ready unless you put the crop marks on yourself. You can, of course, let the print shop do it (at an extra charge).

*FIG. 4.1.
The crop marks on the page tell the printer what size to make the final, or trim, size of the document.*

CHAPTER 4

Planning and Purchasing Printing

PMTs and Halftones

Art work and illustrations can be pasted up in their original form if they are clear, clean (no smudges), and black or red. Other colors, such as blue and green, do not reproduce well. If your art is not satisfactory, the print shop makes a PMT. A *PMT* is a black-on-white reproduction of the art, printed on photographic paper, just like a photograph but without gray tones.

A photograph cannot be printed without reproduction in the camera department. Any photograph that you want to use in your printed document must first be made into a *halftone*. Halftones can either be PMT halftones (on photographic paper) or negative halftones (on negative film). Negative halftones are primarily for very large, detailed photographs or in books that feature photographs. The quality is very high and so is the price. PMT halftones are much less expensive and look fine in most cases.

A halftone breaks up the image of a photograph into a series of dots. These dots vary in size, and they combine to trick the eye into seeing the grays of a photograph.

Layout

As mentioned in Chapter 2, pay special attention to the margins of a document. Gripper, the area that the press uses to pass the sheet of paper through, is important. Always leave at least 3/8 inch on all sides of your document for gripper. If you don't, the print shop either will reduce the overall size of your document or cut the paper larger to allow the room the press needs. Either option costs more money.

You may decide to bleed one, two, three, or all four sides of your design, in which case you'll not need the gripper. As you might recall, a bleed is when the graphics run off the edge of the printed document. To accomplish a rule or border bleed, you either must paste up the bleed or let the print shop do it. Remember, a laser printer cannot print to the edges of a sheet of paper.

When a print shop cuts paper for a document that bleeds, the paper is cut larger than the trim size so that the ink doesn't run off the edge of the paper and ruin the blanket of the press. After printing, the document is trimmed to size. To bleed one side of your document is expensive; to bleed more sides is even more expensive.

PART I

Understanding Design and Typography

Mailing

If you want to mail your document, you may have to contend with additional design considerations. First, leave room for the mailing labels. If you squeeze the mailing panel information into a small area, the labels could cover the permit or the return address. You, or the print shop, must add a mailing permit, unless you use stamps. You also need a return address. Consider, too, the weight of your document when printed and the cost to mail it.

Another important suggestion from the post office is that no type other than the address be placed below the address line (see fig. 4.2). The OCR scanners used to read addresses read the address from the bottom up. Text printed along the bottom of an envelope or other mailed materials is rejected by the OCR and must be hand sorted. That rejection means it takes more time for your document to reach its destination.

If you have questions concerning mailing regulations, contact your postmaster.

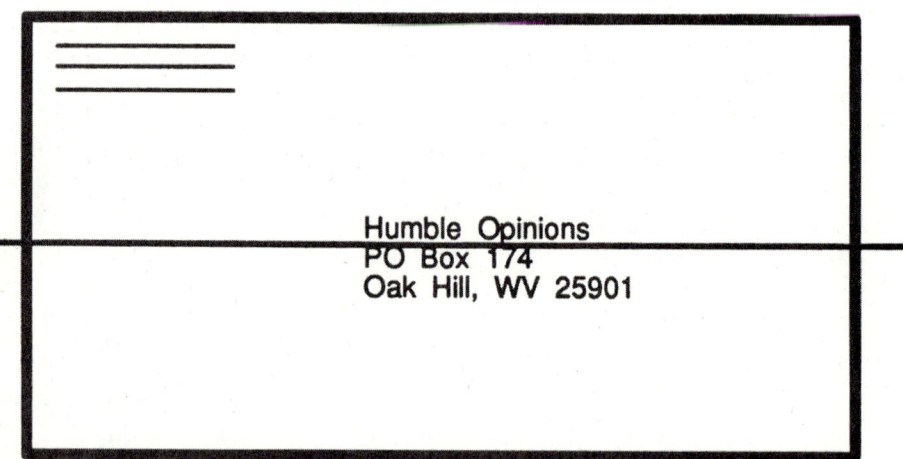

FIG. 4.2.
No text should appear below the address line.

One last point about mailing, if you have a bar code, you can print it directly onto the document. The post office supplies a slick (camera-ready PMT) of your bar code and FIM for you to use. An FIM (Facing Identification Mark) is a type of bar code located along the top edge of the envelope. An FIM assists the OCR scanner to identify and separate certain business and courtesy reply mail. If you place the bar code yourself, be extremely careful. The regulations state that both the bar code and FIM must be in exact positions. If in doubt, let your print shop place it for you.

Working with Output

Output is the page as it comes from your laser printer. Depending on your printer, the resolution could be good enough for use at a print shop. Some printers (dot matrix and pin printers) produce output that works best for proofing purposes only. Most laser printers produce 300 dpi (dots per inch) output. This resolution is satisfactory for photocopying and most offset printing. Appendix C discusses various printers to use with Word.

An option that may be available to you is an output service. Your print shop may have the facilities to output your type to a 1,265 dpi, 2,530 dpi, or higher resolution system. *Resolution* refers to the concentration of dots per inch (dpi). The higher the resolution of your output, the sharper and clearer your type and graphics.

When searching for a print shop, be sure to ask about high resolution output. Also make sure that the shop has a compatible computer, disk size, printer fonts, and version of Word. Appendix C explains more about printers, output, and screen and printer fonts.

Printing Services

Before you choose a print shop, visit several in your area. Ask questions and ask to tour the shop. After you choose a couple of shops as possibilities, request quotes on the work from each of them. Comparing quotes gives you the best value for your money.

Examining Types of Print Shops

If your priorities are quick turnaround, inexpensive price, and fair quality, a quick copy shop may suffice. If, however, you want high-quality work and you're willing to pay for it, you may want to take

PART I

Understanding Design and Typography

your job to a commercial print shop. Each has its advantages and disadvantages. In addition, several other types of shops may be available. This section concentrates on the two most common print shops: quick copy printers and commercial printers.

Quick Copy Shop

A quick copy shop (quick print) is one that does mostly photocopying by using the xerographic process. The shop can copy short to medium-length jobs quickly. Standard page sizes for photocopying are 8 1/2 by 11 inches and 11 by 17 inches, although these shops usually can copy almost anything smaller.

Quick copy shops sometimes have a small press and can do some offset printing, usually using only black ink (and charging quite a bit more for color). These shops usually farm out work such as large offset jobs, typesetting, bindery work, or camera work. Be careful when considering a quick copy shop for a large job (calendars, booklets, or a document with many photographs). If the shop farms out the work, the price may be higher.

The quality of quick copy shop work can range from poor to excellent. When requesting a quote, ask for some samples of the shop's work. Remember to ask if they do your work in-house.

Commercial Printer

A commercial print shop can print almost anything in almost any size. Commercial print shops also run any number of ink colors from one color to four-color process. The selection of colors is wider and the color-printing process can be less expensive than at a quick copy shop. A commercial shop generally has one or more people in the typesetting, paste-up, and camera departments, as well as pressmen and bindery workers. Most commercial printers do their work in-house, although they may use a special-purpose printer from time to time.

The quality from a commercial shop is usually high, although these shops can make mistakes. Offset printing always looks better than copy work. The turnaround time can be from a week to a month, depending on the job. The price is almost always higher than at a quick copy shop. When you're considering a commercial printer, remember to ask for samples and a quote.

CHAPTER 4

Planning and Purchasing Printing

The print shop you choose should suit the particular job. It's wise to find two or three shops of each type and spread out your work.

Getting Price Quotations

It's important to get price quotations for all your jobs before they are printed. Consider getting price quotations from several printers; prices vary greatly from shop to shop. Make sure that the quote is in writing, and keep your copy in case of any questions later (from you and from the printer). Most quotes are good for 30 days (as long as you don't make alterations after the document is in process).

The printer's quote includes the cost of materials and labor for your job: paste-up, camera, stripping, plate-making, paper, ink, and press and bindery time. The more information you give the printer, the more accurate the quote. Describe your document in detail and, if possible, add a mock-up of the job.

Following are items you should include when requesting a price quotation from a printer:

- Today's date, your name, and phone number.
- The date your document is needed.
- The type of document (brochure, flier, or newsletter, for example).
- Quantity (usually three quantities are quoted, such as 1,000, 2,500, and 5,000).
- The trim size and the finished size. For example, a four-page newsletter measuring 11 by 17 inches (the trim size) and folding to 8 1/2 by 11 inches (the finished size).
- The number of ink colors (black is a color) and whether the ink is specially mixed or standard.
- Whether the document is printed on one side or two.
- The type of paper (such as 70#, white linen offset).
- Whether the document is camera ready (includes crops, PMTs, and so forth) or is typeset, but needs minimum paste-up.
- Number of halftones.

PART I

Understanding Design and Typography

- Number and type of folds.
- Finishing techniques (padding or stapling, for example).
- Any special instructions (such as bleeds, negative halftones, numbering, mailing, and so forth).

Choosing Paper and Ink

Papers come in many sizes, finishes, colors, and weights. Certain papers suit certain jobs. Your printer can suggest the proper paper for your job. Request samples of paper from the shop before you get a price quote. Because the cost of the paper can account for 30 percent to 50 percent of the cost of the entire job, it's important to choose the right paper. This section briefly discusses the characteristics of paper.

Size

Papers at a print shop usually come in large sizes and are cut down for each job. Although many more sizes are available, two common sizes are 23 inches by 35 inches and 25 inches by 38 inches. Eight 8 1/2 inch-by-11-inch pieces of paper can be cut from a 23-inch by-35-inch sheet with little waste. If you keep the trim size of your document within a common size range, the paper for your job can be cut more efficiently, making your job less expensive.

Weight

The weight of the paper is important when choosing the right paper for the job. Weight is calculated by the ream (500 sheets). The weight of 500 sheets of 23-by-35-inch paper may be 50#, 60#, 70#, or 80#. The heavier the weight of the ream, the heavier each individual sheet.

Finish

The finish affects the way the printed text and images look. Some standard finishes are smooth, vellum, linen, and enamel. Enamel, smooth, or vellum are the best finishes for the rich, dark tones of photographs (halftones). Text looks good on just about any finish. The finish of the paper you choose for your document is primarily a personal preference; choose the finish according to price and the look. The look of linen, for example, is classy and sophisticated. A smooth-finish paper is basic and simple. Ask for samples of different finishes from the print shop.

Opacity

Opacity is important if you want to use both sides of a sheet of paper, as you would when printing a newsletter or brochure. The greater the opacity of a sheet of paper, the less you can see through it. If your document has large, heavy images to print, avoid a low-opacity paper. Weight also affects the opacity of paper; the heavier the paper, the more opaque it is.

Brightness

Brightness describes the capability of the paper to reflect light. A very bright paper improves halftone reproduction.

Grain

Grain is the direction in which the majority of the paper fibers run. The grain affects the way the paper runs on the press and the way it folds. The grain should always run parallel to the spine fold of a newsletter, book, or magazine. Your printer should know how to use the grain of your paper with your particular document.

Color

Papers come in many colors. The more common colors usually are stocked at a print shop. White is always available, as is ivory. Pastel colors—pink, green, blue, canary—are common in most paper types. Accent colors such as Apache red, prime yellow, or cobalt blue, are also usually stocked. These colors are a bit more expensive. Florescent and metallic colors are generally special-order

PART I

Understanding Design and Typography

items and are expensive. Paper samples from the print shop can help you choose the color you want.

Types

There are as many paper types as there are colors. Common types of paper include book, bond, and letterhead. Each paper type has specific uses. You wouldn't, for example, use the same paper to print a flier and a post card.

Book Paper

Book paper is the most common paper used. Book paper comes in three types: offset, coated, and text. These types are interchangeable, but each has its own special properties.

Offset is used for newsletters, booklets, programs, and so forth. Common finishes are smooth, vellum, linen, and laurentine. Many colors are available and weights range from 50# to 80#. Offset book paper is fairly inexpensive.

Coated is perfect for photographs. Coated book paper comes in glossy or matte finishes. Usually white or ivory, the weights range from 50# to 100#. Don't, however, use 50# enamel. This weight is not opaque, it is a nightmare to print and fold, and it looks cheap. Prices of coated papers vary, although this type should cost no more than an offset paper of the same weight.

Text book paper is a heavier, more deeply finished paper. Reserve this paper for special projects, such as invitations, booklets, or programs. The weights available are from 60# to 80#. Many colors are available. The finish is rough and toothy, which makes text book paper unsuitable for photographs. Text paper has a classy look and is usually expensive.

Bond and Sulphite Paper

Very inexpensive papers, bond and sulphite come in 16# and 20# weights. These papers are available in many colors and either smooth or vellum finishes. These papers are very inexpensive and are ideal for fliers, scratch pads, and one-sided printing.

CHAPTER 4

Planning and Purchasing Printing

Letterhead Paper

Letterhead paper (with matching envelopes) is available in 20# or 24# weights and has a watermark. A good-quality paper in the letterhead family is rag paper (*rag* refers to the cotton content, such as 25 percent or 100 percent). A variety of colors is available. Finishes include smooth, laid, and linen. Considering the quality of the paper and the impression nice letterhead paper makes, this paper is not too expensive.

Cover Paper

Cover paper is a heavier "board" grade used for business cards, rack cards, booklet covers, tickets, and so forth. Cover paper is available in coated and uncoated finishes. Uncoated cover paper matches letterhead and offset papers in finish and color so you can use them in combination (for example, a letter and business card). Uncoated cover paper comes in 65# and 80# weights; many colors; and smooth (called antique), linen, or laurentine finishes. Uncoated cover paper is the least expensive of the cover papers.

Coated cover paper matches other coated papers. Coated cover paper is measured differently. The weights are 8-, 10-, and 12-point cover (8-point cover is equal to 100#). Coated cover paper is available in white or ivory, and can be coated on one side or both. Coated cover paper can range from inexpensive to very costly.

Many other paper types exist: carbonless for forms, label paper for bumper stickers, index and tag for inexpensive posters or post cards, and the list goes on. The best advice is to check with a printer for suggestions on the paper type, finish, and color to suit your job.

Working with Ink

When choosing your paper, consider the color(s) of ink you want to use. Any one color of ink, in combination with a colored paper, can create a two-color effect without the added expense. Outlined letters, graphic rules, boxes, and especially screens, produce the

PART I

Understanding Design and Typography

effect of a two-color job. Remember, however, that black is a color to a printer. If you use black and red ink on a document, that is a two-color job.

Black ink runs on presses every day; it's the most common color. Black is used extensively because it's very effective and the least expensive ink. Black ink on any color of paper looks good, and black ink used with any other color of ink looks good, as well.

Generally, if you're using two colors of ink, you should choose two contrasting colors, such as black and any color, red and blue, or red and green. Using two colors is more expensive, but can be quite dramatic in your document design.

Avoid using white ink. It doesn't print very heavy and you must use a dark paper, which can be hard to read. Don't use yellow for text—it is very difficult to read. Save yellow for screens, lines, or graphic elements.

Using Standard Inks

Standard colors of ink are those that come premixed. Many standard colors are attractive and inexpensive. Common standard inks are black, dutch fireball red, warm red, wedgewood blue, process blue, forest green, pantone purple, and process yellow. Ask a printer to show you a standard ink chart or some samples.

Using PMS and Special Inks

PMS stands for Pantone Matching System. The PMS Swatch Book contains 500 ink colors in various shades and tints. These ink colors are more expensive than standard inks. The pressman mixes the color when the job is ready to run. For that reason, if you later have your document printed a second time, the PMS color you chose may not exactly match that of the first print run.

You might ask a printer whether any already-mixed PMS colors are available. If so, you shouldn't be charged extra, and you might find a color you really like.

Special inks include thermographed, metallic, and florescent. These inks are expensive and difficult to run.

CHAPTER 4

Planning and Purchasing Printing

Thermographed ink is raised ink, and the process is difficult. A document is run through the press, printing the text in ink. Powder is then sprinkled on it while the ink is wet, and the document is run through an oven to set the powder. Thermographed ink is an expensive process, especially if the print shop does the work in-house.

Metallic and florescent inks usually are thin and difficult to run on the press. For this reason, these inks cost more and may not look good. Always ask a printer for samples if you plan to use one of these inks.

Finishing Techniques

The finishing processes take place in the bindery of a print shop. Some printed pieces require more time in the bindery than others. Finishing includes trimming, folding, inserting, gathering, padding, perforating, die-cutting, punching, scoring, laminating, numbering, and fastening. This section offers an overview of the common procedures you might encounter.

Folding

Many of the jobs discussed so far need folding. A mechanical folder does the majority of folding in a print shop. Some folds are easier, taking less time and costing less than other types of folds. The most common folds are parallel, barrel, French, and accordion.

Parallel Fold

Brochures, letters, and fliers usually are folded twice, with a parallel fold. The most common fold, the parallel fold also is the easiest and least expensive. Figure 4.3 shows a brochure marked for two parallel folds.

PART I

Understanding Design and Typography

*FIG. 4.3.
The dashed lines
indicate the folds of
the brochure.*

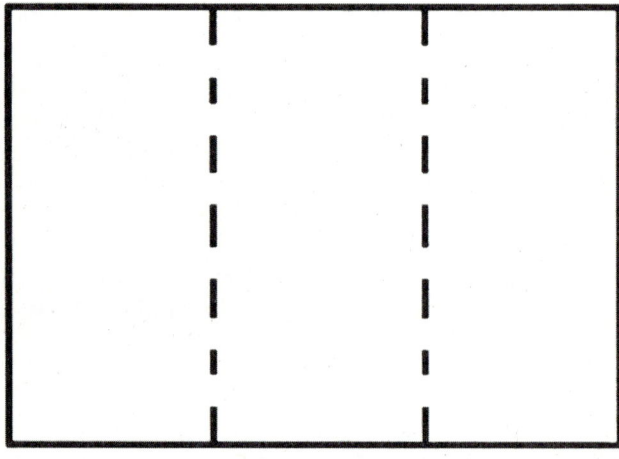

Barrel Fold

A barrel fold is used, for example, with a six-page newsletter printed on 25 1/2-by-11-inch paper. After folding, the finished size is 8 1/2 by 11 inches (see fig. 4.4). A barrel fold is a bit more complicated than a parallel fold.

*FIG. 4.4.
The barrel fold.*

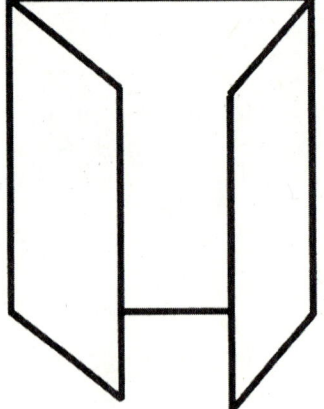

French Fold

A French fold is commonly used for note cards and invitations, and it's difficult to do well. The first fold is lengthwise and the second is at a right angle to the first fold (see fig. 4.5). The problem with a French fold is that one fold must go against the grain of the paper, causing it to crack and fold unevenly. Many times, a mechanical folder executes the first fold, and the second fold is made by hand, which, of course, makes the French fold more expensive.

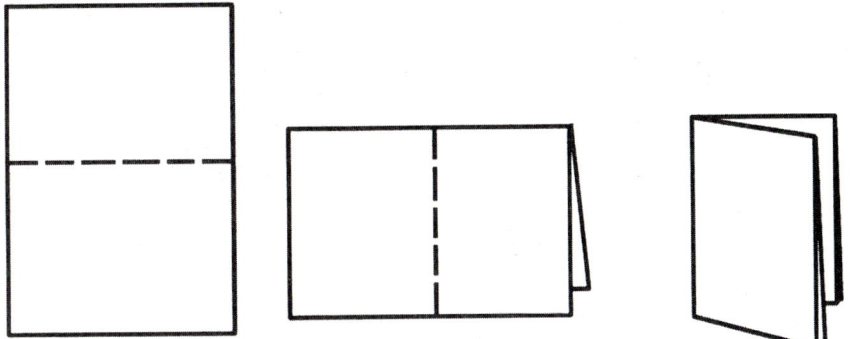

FIG. 4.5.
The French fold.

Accordion Fold

Accordion folds are like those in a road map. They are the most difficult type of fold. The setup of the folding machine changes many times during the process; therefore, the accordion fold is expensive. Figure 4.6 shows a common accordion fold.

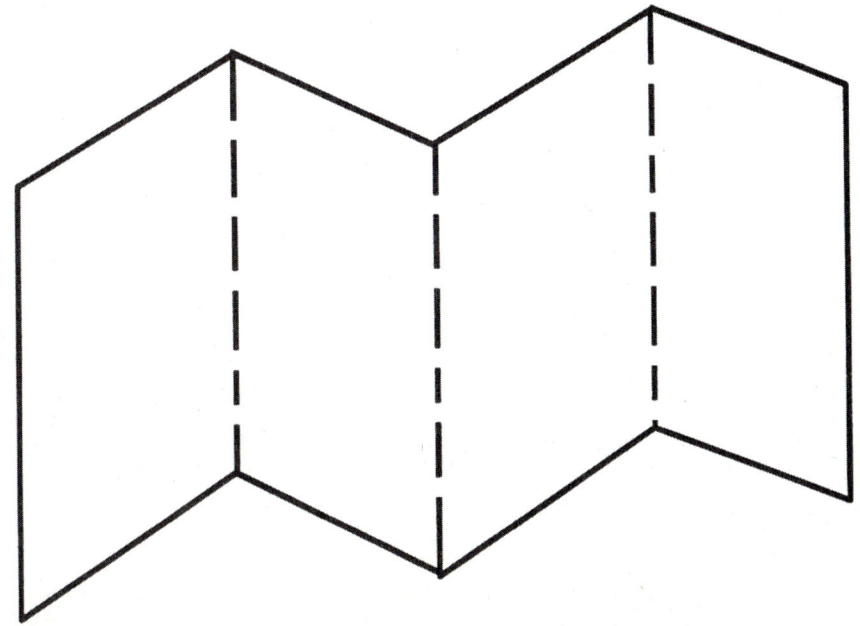

FIG. 4.6.
An accordion fold.

PART I

Understanding Design and Typography

More than five folds to one document is very difficult to do. You'll pay more for this service, and you probably will not be happy with the results. Folding sometimes cracks the spine of a book cover or heavy paper, because the paper is being folded against the grain without first being scored. (Scoring is a process that uses a strip of hardened steel to crush the grain of the paper, thereby creating a straight line for folding.) If this happens, it's the print shop's fault and should be corrected at no charge. Enamel and cover papers are difficult to fold. Always check your final printed piece to be sure it has been folded evenly and looks good.

Fastening the Final Product

The most common type of finishing is some sort of fastening. Stapling is the customary method; padding and drilling also are possibilities. The binding of the document depends completely on its purpose and size.

Looseleaf

A very common method of fastening is to drill or punch holes on the left margin of single pages. These pages are gathered and inserted into a ring binder or plastic binding. Plastic binding is a most efficient way of fastening. It looks somewhat like spiral binding but pages can be removed and replaced easily. Plastic binding is suitable for many types of documents, such as reports, programs, and catalogs.

Side Stitch

Side stitch, or side binding, is a method of fastening single sheets on the left side with staples. Side-stitched documents must have at least a 3/4-inch margin on the fastened side; pages in the middle of the document will not be readable if you don't allow a sufficient margin. Side stitching is a good method of fastening for jobs with 100 to 300 pages, and is inexpensive.

Planning and Purchasing Printing

Saddle Back

Saddle back, or saddle stitch, uses staples on the fold. A common and efficient method of fastening, saddle stitching often is used for newsletters and magazines. This method is inexpensive and works well with booklets up to 64 pages long.

Padding

Padding can be used for any document that requires temporary fastening, such as scratch pads, calendars, and forms.

Fastening and folding are the two most common finishing techniques you probably will need to use for your documents. If, however, your document requires a different treatment, ask a printer for advice.

Recapping

The following steps are provided as a recap to help refresh your memory and to give you a quick reference guide whenever you need it:

1. Plan and lay out your document keeping in mind gripper, bleed, and mailing requirements.

2. As you design your document, consider finishing techniques such as fastening and folding.

3. Prepare your document for the print shop by adding crop marks, PMTs, halftones and so on, or by transferring your files to a disk for high-resolution output.

4. Choose the quantity on reproduction process for your document.

5. Visit several print shops; request paper and ink samples.

6. Prepare a quotation request including all information and a mock-up of your document.

7. Get quotes from several printers before choosing the shop to do your job.

HUMBLE OPINIONS CORPORATION
P. O. Box 174, Suite 114
Oak Hill, West Virginia 25901
(304) 555-2234

OFFICERS
D. A. Halsey, President
D. S. Campbell, V. President
P. A. Houck, Secretary
W. M. Bender, Treasurer

BOARD
K. A. Smith
J. O. Blackwell
W. A. Acord
L. E. McKinney
B. I. Halsey
L. U. Taylor
J. O. Fink
T. A. Janney
C. L. Hatcher
D. A. Friley
J. I. Holiday

Part II

Creating Business Documents

Includes

5. Producing a Letterhead
6. Producing a Letter
7. Producing Envelopes
8. Producing a Resume
9. Producing a Program
10. Producing a Memo

5

Producing a Letterhead

The letterhead is one of the most important tools of a successful business. Every day, businesses dispatch letters that contain general correspondence, inquiries, quotes, or requests. An impressive letterhead sells a business as well as its products and services. A company logo, along with its name, address, and phone number, serves as a reminder of that business each time a customer receives a letter.

Letterheads contain the company name (and perhaps a person's name), an address, and a phone number. Many businesses include more information—president's name, CEO's or vice president's name, board members, office and home phone numbers, alternate addresses, a catchy phrase, and a logo or graphic (clip art, drawn images, rules). Don't add so many elements that your letterhead looks crowded. Keep your design simple.

Pay close attention to the margins when creating a letterhead. The top margin is usually 3/4 inch to 1 inch, and side margins are at least 1/2 inch. If you produce a letterhead with type near the bottom, be sure to specify at least a 3/8-inch margin (1/2 inch if possible).

The space a letterhead takes depends on the information, placement, and art. At the top of the page, the letterhead should take a minimum of 1/2 inch of vertical space and no more than 1 1/2 inches. Any more would defeat the purpose of a letterhead—to identify the writer without overwhelming the contents of the letter.

PART II

Creating Business Documents

This chapter presents four letterhead designs and the steps to produce them in Word Versions 1.1 and 2.0. Each design builds on the previous one. Although you can use any one separately, you'll find it beneficial to try all the letterheads described. Each design highlights different features in Word.

At the end of this chapter, you save a letterhead in Word's glossary so that you can use it in later documents. A glossary entry consists of any amount of text or graphics. You save the glossary, and then you can insert it into other documents as you'll do in Chapter 6, "Producing a Letter."

> **NOTE**
>
> Because directions for both Versions 1.1 and 2.0 are described in this book, different icons represent each version. Choose the icon that corresponds with the version of Word you use.

If you use Version 2.0 of Word, some instructions refer to the graphic rules and borders by size (.75 rule, 2.25 rule, and so on). The Border dialog box does not give you the size of the rule in numbers; however, you should learn the size of each rule represented in this dialog box. If you're not familiar with the measurements, see Appendix A.

Creating a Simple Letterhead

The first letterhead uses the style of type to create an air of distinction (see fig. 5.1). This design consists of the company name, address, and phone number center-aligned. The company name is in Times Roman font (24- and 18-point), which contrasts with the Helvetica font (12- and 8-point) used for the address. Using both large and small capital letters lends a dignified presence to the otherwise simple design. If you're familiar with Word and already know the procedures described here, you may want to skip to the second design.

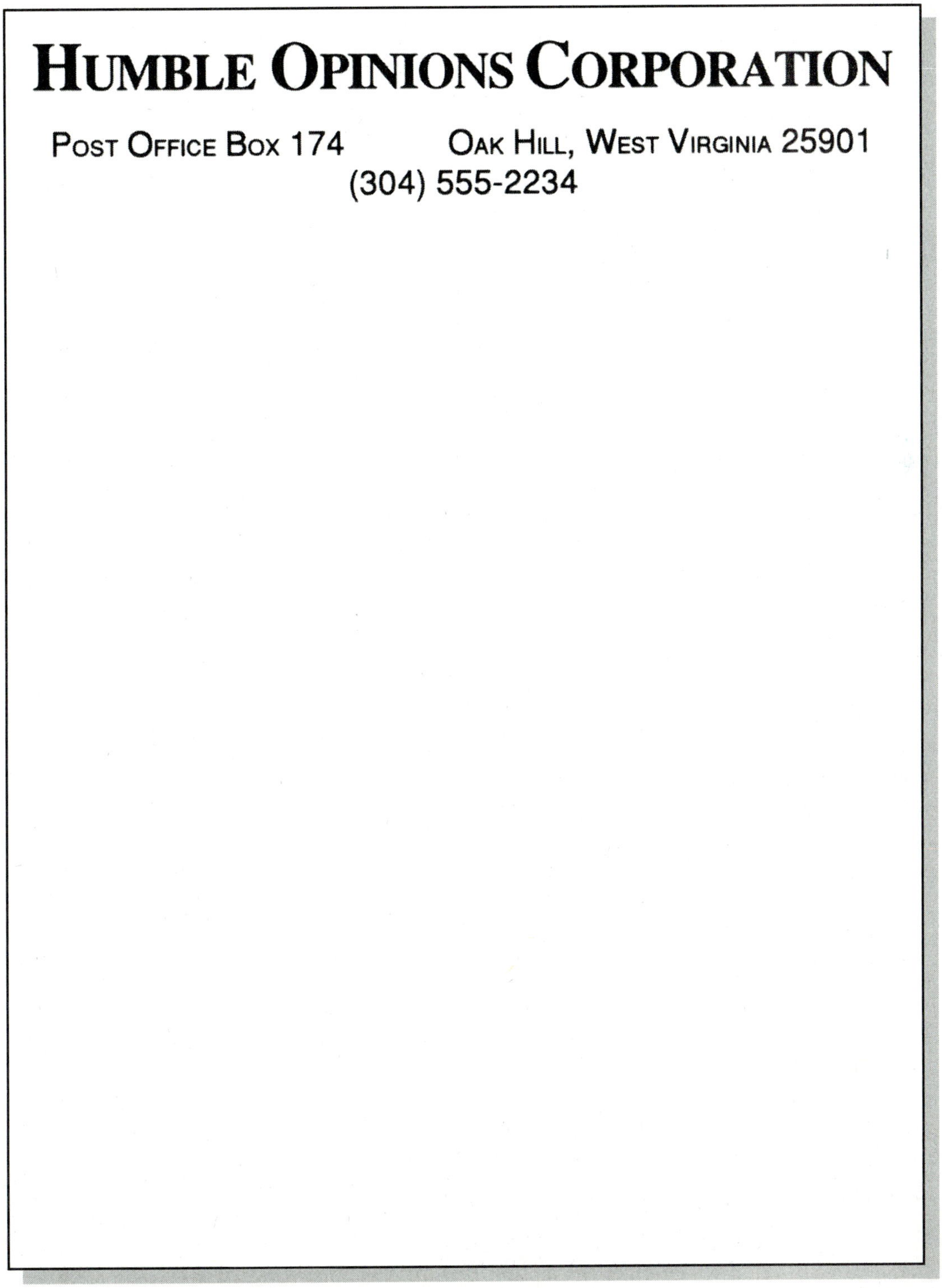

HUMBLE OPINIONS CORPORATION

Post Office Box 174   Oak Hill, West Virginia 25901
(304) 555-2234

FIG. 5.1. *A simple letterhead design.*

PART II

Creating Business Documents

To create the letterhead, you first must set up a new document as follows:

1. From the File menu, select New to begin and a dialog box appears. Choose New Document. Or, press Alt+F,N, and in the dialog box, press N,D. Use the Normal template.

2. Select OK or press Enter.

3. In the View menu, be sure Page, Ribbon, and Ruler are turned on. When you click the command (or press the boldfaced letter) a checkmark appears to the left of the command indicating that it is turned on.

4. If you're using Word 1.1, you set the margins by selecting Document from the Format menu. A dialog box appears, displaying information about the page of your new document. In Word 1.1, the default page width is 8 1/2 inches; the default page height is 11 inches. Both of these values are right for this example letterhead.

3. In Version 2.0, go to View and turn on the Toolbar.

4. If you're using Word 2.0, set the page margins by selecting Page Setup from the Format menu. In Word 2.0, the defaults for size and orientation are Width 8 1/2 inches and Height 11 inches. These values are fine for the letterhead.

5. Click the Top margin box to the left of the number, or press Alt-T. Press Del to delete the 1" and type **.75** (you don't have to include the 0 or the inch mark).

6. Press the tab key twice to move to the Left margin box. Or click the mouse cursor in the Left margin box. Delete the number and type **.5**. Do the same with the Right margin.

7. Click OK or press Enter to close the dialog box and accept the changes you've made.

   You see the cursor blinking at the top left of the page, inside the margins.

Now you're ready to enter and format the text of your letterhead. To do so, follow these steps:

1. Type the following text as your letterhead, pressing Enter and leaving space as indicated:

CHAPTER 5

Producing a Letterhead

HUMBLE OPINIONS CORPORATION (Enter)

POST OFFICE BOX 174 (10 spaces) **OAK HILL, WEST VIRGINIA 25901** (Enter)

(304) 555-2234

The **N**ormal template you chose specifies that the type is left aligned, Times Roman, 10-point.

2. To format the name of the company, position the cursor in front of the H in HUMBLE. Press and hold the mouse button and drag the cursor across the entire first line to highlight it. Release the mouse button. HUMBLE OPINIONS should appear as white type in a black block. Or, position the cursor in front of the H. Press and hold the Shift key and, using the right arrow on the keyboard, move the cursor to the end of the line so that HUMBLE OPINIONS is selected.

3. On the Ribbon, change the size of the font to 24-point by typing **24** in the Points box or scrolling through the sizes and choosing 24. On the keyboard, press Ctrl+D to go to the Points Box, then type **24**.

4. With HUMBLE OPINIONS still highlighted, use the icons at the top of the screen to select **C**enter justification and **B**old. Or, press Ctrl+B, then press Ctrl+E to center in Version 2.0, and Ctrl+C to center in Version 1.1

5. To condense the name of the company, access the Forma**t** menu and select the **C**haracter command. When Word displays the Character Spacing box, click the circle beside **C**ondensed, or press Alt+T, then C.

5. To condense the name of the company, access the Forma**t** menu and select the **C**haracter command. When Word displays the Spacing box, click the arrow and scroll to select **C**ondensed, or press Alt+T,C and then C.

6. The default setting 1.75pt appears in the By: box. Click the box and change the spacing to **.75pt**. Click OK or press Enter to confirm your change.

    On the keyboard, press Alt+: (colon), then type **.75pt**.

    On the keyboard, press Alt+Y, then type **.75pt**.

125

PART II

Creating Business Documents

7. For both versions of the program, click anywhere on the page to deselect the first line of the letterhead, or press the right arrow on the keyboard.

8. Next, you want to change all but the first capital letter to small capitals in HUMBLE OPINIONS. To do so, highlight the letters UMBLE. On the Ribbon, change the size to 18 points.

9. Repeat the procedure for PINIONS, highlighting the letters you want smaller and changing the size to 18 points.

10. Click anywhere on the page to deselect the highlighted text, or press the right arrow on the keyboard.

11. Next, highlight the address and phone number.

12. In the Font box on the Ribbon, scroll to Helv and click to select it; or press Ctrl+F, then use the down arrow key to select Helv.

13. In the Ribbon, change the point size of the address and phone number text to 12.

14. Select **C**enter alignment by clicking the icon on the Ribbon. Or by pressing Ctrl+C in version 1.1, or Ctrl+E in Version 2.0.

15. Click anywhere on the page to deselect the address and phone number text.

16. To add space between the company name and the address, highlight the address and click the 1 1/2 spacing button in the Ribbon. Click anywhere on the page to deselect the address. Or press Ctrl+5. Press the right arrow to deselect the text.

16. To add space between the company name and the address, highlight the address and select **P**aragraph from the Forma**t** menu. Word displays the Spacing box.

17. In the **B**efore box, type **.5li** or scroll to .5li.

18. Click anywhere on the page to deselect the address, or press the right arrow.

19. To create the small caps in the address line, highlight OST and use the Ribbon to change the point size to 8.

20. Repeat this procedure to create small capital letters for the rest of the address line (FFICE, OX, AK, ILL, EST, and IRGINIA).

126

CHAPTER 5

Producing a Letterhead

Now that your letterhead is formatted, you want to see how it looks, and then print it. To do so, follow these steps:

1. From the **File** menu, select Print **P**review to see how the letterhead will look when you print it.

2. Press Esc to return to your working view.

3. To save the document with your letterhead, access the **File** Menu and select Save **A**s.

4. Specify where you want the file saved by selecting [a] or [b] for floppy disk or [c] for your hard disk.

5. If there is text in the File **N**ame box, press Del to remove it and type **Letter1**.

6. Click OK or press Enter.

7. To print your letterhead, open the **F**ile menu, select **P**rint and click OK or press Enter.

A letterhead of this type is perfect for use in a glossary. After you insert the glossary, you begin typing the letter or other text beneath it. You still save a glossary at the end of this chapter; then insert it into a letter in the next chapter.

Creating a Letterhead That Uses a Logo

This letterhead design is somewhat more sophisticated. It employs a logo, a bullet, and center tabs to create a different look. Use this letterhead design when using two or more names, addresses, or phone numbers in your letterhead that need to be spaced with tabs (see fig. 5.2). The logo shown in figure 5.2 was created in CorelDRAW!

If you have access to a drawing program, scanner, clip art program, or so forth, you may want to create a logo for this letterhead. See Appendix B for information about compatible programs. If you don't have a TIFF file of your own and you want to practice inserting a picture, Word has a TIFF file you can borrow. Your finished letterhead will not look exactly like figure 5.2. The only difference will be in the TIFF you use.

127

humble opinions

P. O. Box 174 • Oak Hill, West Virginia 25901

D. J. Halsey, President
(304) 555-1211

D. S. Campbell, Vice President
(304) 555-2234

FIG. 5.2. Using a logo in a letterhead.

CHAPTER 5

Producing a Letterhead

To create the letterhead with a logo, you must start a new document and enter the necessary text for your letterhead. You can do so by following these steps:

1. From the **File** menu, select **New** to begin. A dialog box appears. Use the **Normal** template. Select New **Document**.

2. Select OK or press Enter.

3. In the **View** menu, be sure **Page**, Ri**b**bon, and **R**uler are turned on. By selecting each command, a checkmark appears that indicates it is turned on.

3. Select the **T**oolbar in Version 2.0 to turn it on.

4. If you're using Word 1.1, set the margins by accessing the Forma**t** menu and selecting **D**ocument. A dialog box appears.

4. If you're using Word 2.0, set the margins for the page by opening the Forma**t** menu and selecting Page Set**u**p. A dialog box appears.

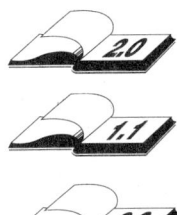

5. In the Margins box, click the **T**op margin box to the left of the number. Or press Alt+T to access the Top margin box. Press Del to delete the 1" and type **.75** (you don't have to include the 0 or the inch mark).

6. Press the tab key twice to move to the **L**eft margin box. Or click in the box. Delete the number and type **.5**. Do the same with the **R**ight margin.

7. Click OK or press Enter to close the dialog box and accept the changes you've made.

   You see the cursor blinking at the top left of the page, inside the margins.

Type the following text as your letterhead, entering spaces and pressing Tab and Enter as indicated:

(Enter)

P. O. Box 174 (four spaces) **Oak Hill, West Virginia 25901** (Enter)

(tab) **D. J. Halsey, President** (tab) **D. S. Campbell, Vice President** (Enter)

(tab) **(304) 555-1211** (tab) **(304) 555-2234**

PART II

Creating Business Documents

Notice that you did not type the name of the company. Instead of using text for the name of the company, you'll import a logo, scanned art, or art from a drawing program. To import the artwork, follow these steps:

1. Position the cursor on the top line of the document (at the first Enter or hard return you entered at the beginning of this document). If you don't have a TIFF file readily available, Word has one that you can use for practice.

2. From the Insert menu, choose **Picture**. A dialog box appears listing files and directories.

3. Press Del to clear the **Picture File Name** box.

3. Press Del to clear the **File Name** box.

4. If the picture file is on a floppy disk, select [a:] or [b:] for the disk drive and select OK. A list of files appears. Select the TIFF file you want and choose OK or press Enter.

5. If the file is on your hard drive, select [c:] and enter the name of the directory and file.

6. If you want to use Word's TIFF file for practice, type **c:\winword\library** and select OK. Scroll through the list of files until you find MONIQUE.TIF, and then select it; or you can type **monique.tif** in the **Picture File Name** box. Choose OK or press Enter. (See fig. 5.3.)

The artwork is inserted into your document at the cursor position.

Next, you want to make the artwork the correct size and center it. To do so, follow these steps:

1. To crop or change the size of the artwork, click inside it. Handles (small black boxes) appear on the four corners and in the middle of each side. Or, place the cursor in front of the picture, hold down the Shift key while pressing the right arrow.

2. To crop the artwork, click a handle and drag the handle in or out. Or, choose Format, Pictu**r**e (Alt+T,R). In the Crop box, type in your measurements.

3. To change the size of the artwork, press and hold the Shift key while you drag any handle in or out. Using the corner handles scales the picture in proportion. Or, choose Format,

CHAPTER 5

Producing a Letterhead

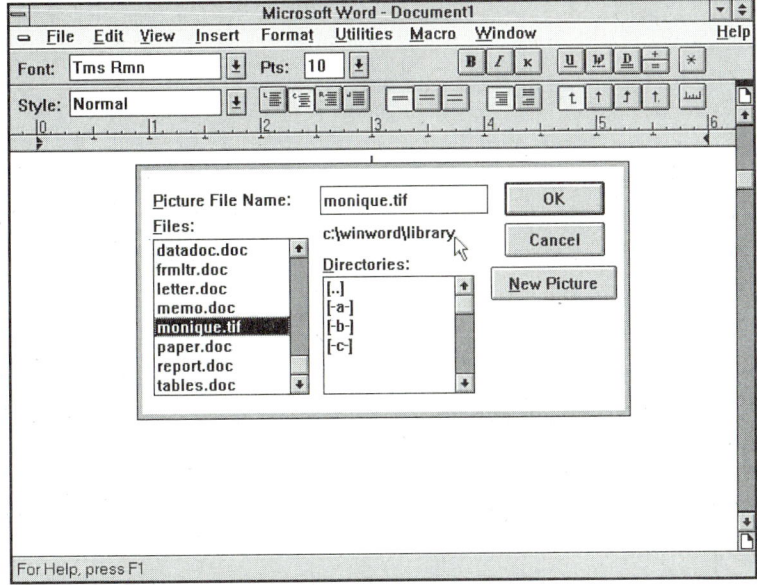

FIG. 5.3.
The Insert Picture dialog box showing the correct path for using the MONIQUE.TIF file.

Picture (Alt+T,R). In the Scaling box, type the percentage for **H**eight and **W**idth.

For this example, make the graphic 7 1/2 inches long and 3/4 inches tall. The ruler along the top will help you measure the 7 1/2 inches. You can also go to Forma**t**, Picture (Alt+T,R) to set the size.

4. After the graphic is sized, center it between the margins. Position the cursor in front of the graphic (so a cursor shows instead of handles) and choose **C**enter alignment in the Ribbon. Or, press Ctrl+E for Version 2.0 or Ctrl+C for Version 1.1.

Your next step is to format the address, as follows:

1. Highlight the address.
2. On the Ribbon, confirm that the font is Times Roman.
3. Change the size of the address to 12 points.
4. Change the address to **C**enter aligned.

As the next step, you're going to add a bullet between the P. O. Box 174 and Oak Hill. A bullet is a symbol (sometimes an asterisk, a dot, hollow box, or filled box) used to add emphasis or importance to a list, or as a decorative element.

PART II

Creating Business Documents

In Word Version 1.1, you must create a macro for a bullet key. After you've created the macro, you only have to press a combination key to insert a bullet. Follow these steps:

1. From the **M**acro menu, select Re**c**ord.

2. Type **Bullet** in the Record Macro **N**ame box and select OK or press Enter. This procedure turns on the Re**c**ord feature so that the following steps will be recorded in memory.

3. From the Forma**t** menu, select **C**haracter.

4. Select Symbol in the **F**ont box and select OK or press Enter. If you use a PostScript printer, choose Dingbat instead of the Symbol font.

5. Be sure Num Lock is on (located on your keypad). Press and hold down Alt while typing **0149** on the numeric keypad. 0149 is the ANSI character for the bullet in the Symbol font. Alt+108 is the Dingbat character for a bullet.

6. Release the Alt key.

7. Press Ctrl+space bar. This step returns you to the original font when you use the bullet in text (you don't want text following the bullet to be in the Symbol font.)

8. From the **M**acro menu, select Stop Re**c**order.

9. From the **M**acro menu, select Assign to **K**ey. Select Bullet in the list box.

10. To assign the Bullet to a key, press any key combination to represent it. (Using Ctrl as the first key is a good idea because most Alt keys in Word are already assigned. Try Ctrl+8—it's not assigned by Word).

11. Select **G**lobal so that you can use the bullet key anytime, in any document.

12. Select **A**ssign, and then Close.

13. From the **F**ile menu, select Sav**e** All. When Word prompts you to confirm making global macro changes, select yes or type **Y**.

To place the bullet into your letterhead, position the cursor between 174 and Oak Hill (in the middle of the four spaces) and press Ctrl+8 (or the key combination you assigned to the bullet).

CHAPTER 5

Producing a Letterhead

In Word Version 2.0, creating a bullet is very simple. Follow these steps:

1. Position the cursor in the middle of the spaces between Box 174 and Oak Hill.

2. From the **Insert** menu, choose **S**ymbol. The Symbol dialog box appears.

3. Be sure the Symbols From box shows `Symbol`. Symbol is a font.

4. Choose the bullet character (fifth row down, ninth character from the right) by clicking it with the mouse, or by using the arrow keys. Or select a different symbol, if desired.

5. Select OK or press Enter. Word inserts the bullet at the insertion point you chose, in the point size of the surrounding text.

To finish formatting your letterhead, follow these steps:

1. First, you need to add space between the logo and the address in Version 1.1. Highlight the address and click the 1 1/2 spacing button in the Ribbon. Or press Ctrl+5 to access the spacing

1. Add space between the head and the address by dragging the cursor to select the entire address in Version 2.0. From the Format menu, select **P**aragraph. In the Spacing, **B**efore box, select 1.5li. and click OK.

2. Highlight the names and telephone numbers. Check the Ribbon to make sure that the text is 10-point, Tms Rmn, and left aligned.

3. From the Format menu, select **T**abs, and then Clear **A**ll.

4. Place the cursor in the **T**ab Position box and press Del.

5. Type **.7**, select Center Alignment, and click **S**et.

6. Place the cursor in the **T**ab Position box and press Del again.

7. Type **6.5**, select Center Alignment, and click **S**et.

8. Select OK or press Enter.

9. Next, position the cursor somewhere in the name of `Halsey`. From the Format menu, select **P**aragraph. In the dialog box,

133

PART II

Creating Business Documents

use the arrow to choose Above in the **B**order box. Single should appear as the default **P**attern; if it does not, select it. Choose OK or press Enter.

9. Position the cursor somewhere in the name of Halsey. From the Forma**t** menu, select **B**order. In the Bo**r**der box, click the top margin to apply a rule above your text. Or press the down arrow until the top margin is highlighted. In **L**ine, choose 1.5, and then select OK press Enter.

10. With your cursor still positioned on the word Halsey, click the inter-paragraph spacing box in the Ruler to add some extra space between the lines. On the keyboard, press Ctrl+5.

10. With the cursor still positioned on the word Halsey, open the Forma**t** menu and select **P**aragraph. In the Spacing, **B**efore, box, choose 1.5li to add some extra space above the line of type.

Now that your letterhead is formatted, you want to see how it looks, and then print it. To do so, take these steps:

1. From the **F**ile menu, select Print Preview to see what your letterhead will look like when printed. Press the Esc key to return to your working view.

2. From the **F**ile menu, select Save **A**s. Be sure that when you save, either on a floppy disk ([a] or [b]), or on your hard drive, that you keep track of your directory; it would be wise to save all your practice documents in one directory or on a single disk.

3. Press Del to clear the box, and then type **Letter2**.

4. Select OK or press Enter.

5. From the **F**ile menu, select **P**rint and OK or press Enter.

Creating a Traditional Letterhead

Sometimes a letterhead may need to be more formal. The kind of business dictates the style. In this format, you can add more type, such as a listing of officers or board members, alternate names or addresses, or lists of services or products.

CHAPTER 5

Producing a Letterhead

Unlike the previous designs, this letterhead with all its entries is not practical for use in a glossary. Because Word inserts the text as is, you would have too many paragraph returns in the original to use as a letter. This design is ideally suited for a commercial or quick-copy print shop as camera-ready copy after you print it on your laser printer.

Figure 5.4 shows one alternative to the traditional letterhead format. The vertical rule as a border adds a sense of order to the conventional design. In addition, it's possible to use a horizontal rule above the company name to focus attention on the name (see fig. 5.5). Or, you could use a horizontal rule under the address and phone instead of a vertical for separation.

When you produce a formal letterhead, don't use overwhelming type or graphic elements, or type that is too decorative (avoid scripts and texts). Also remember the two-font rule—too many type styles on one page is distracting and unprofessional-looking. Times Roman for the company name reinforces its importance; Helvetica for the rest of the letterhead adds contrast and makes the smaller names easy to read.

If you have a lot of type, as in this example, refrain from using large type sizes. Notice that the officers and board members are in 8-point type. The fact that they are listed on the letterhead shows their importance; they don't have to stand out any more than that.

1. In the **File** menu, select **New** to begin. In the dialog box, choose New **Document**. Use the **Normal** template.

2. Select OK or press Enter.

3. In the **View** menu, be sure **Page**, **Ribbon**, and **Ruler** are turned on. Selecting each of these commands displays a check mark to indicate that it is activated.

3. Turn on the **Toolbar**, from the **View** menu.

4. If you're using Word 1.1, set the margins by opening the Forma**t** menu and selecting **D**ocument. The Document dialog box appears.

4. If you're using Word 2.0, set the margins for the page by accessing the Forma**t** menu and selecting Page Set**u**p. The Page Setup dialog box appears.

5. Position the cursor in the **T**op margin box to the left of the number. Press Del to clear the box, and then type **.75**.

135

HUMBLE OPINIONS CORPORATION
P. O. Box 174, Suite 114
Oak Hill, West Virginia 25901
(304) 555-2234

OFFICERS
D. A. Halsey, President
D. S. Campbell, V. President
P. A. Houck, Secretary
W. M. Bender, Treasurer

BOARD
K. A. Smith
J. O. Blackwell
W. A. Acord
L. E. McKinney
B. I. Halsey
L. U. Taylor
J. O. Fink
T. A. Janney
C. L. Hatcher
D. A. Friley
J. I. Holiday

FIG. 5.4. *An alternative to the traditional letterhead format.*

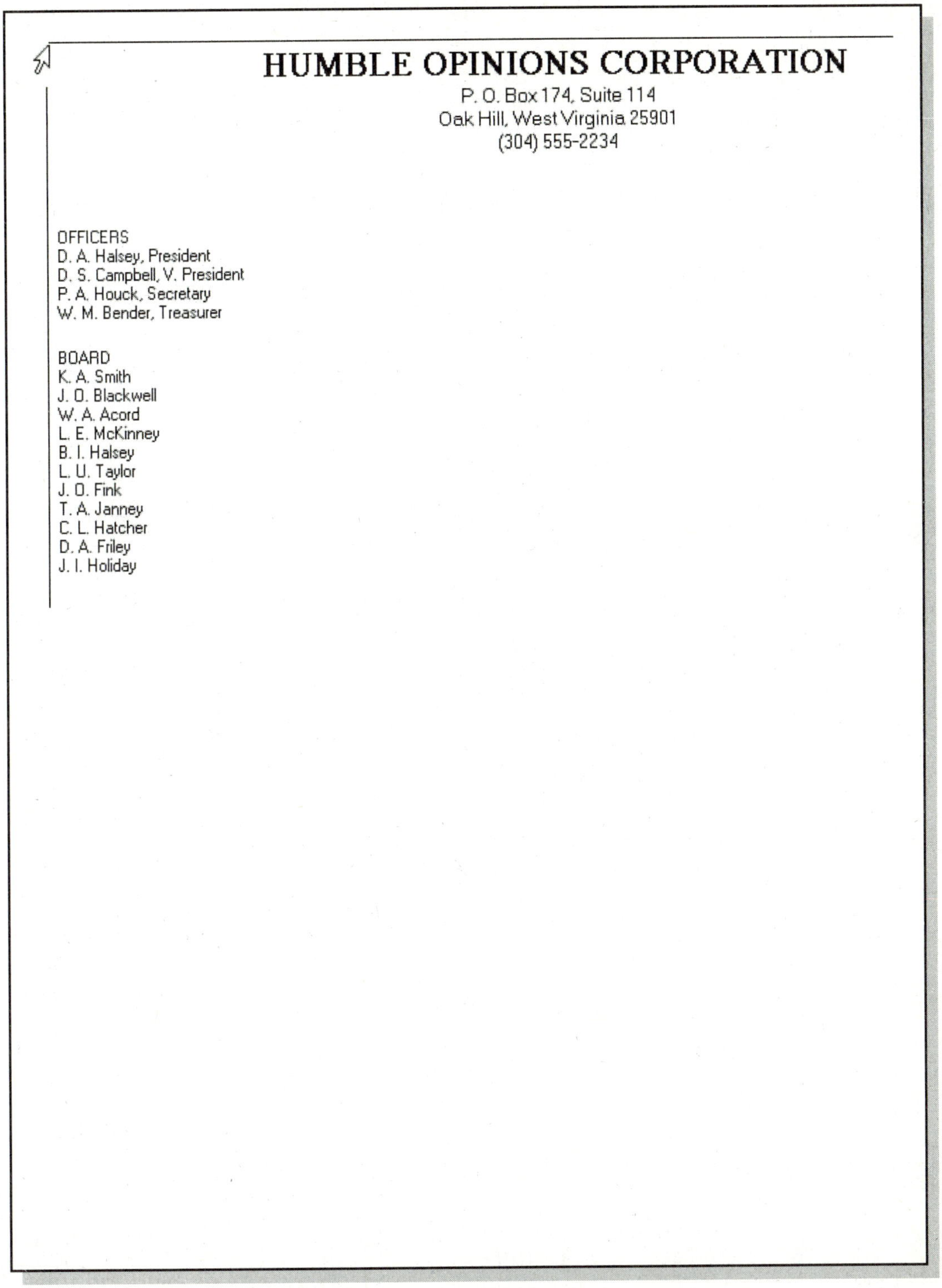

HUMBLE OPINIONS CORPORATION

P. O. Box 174, Suite 114
Oak Hill, West Virginia 25901
(304) 555-2234

OFFICERS
D. A. Halsey, President
D. S. Campbell, V. President
P. A. Houck, Secretary
W. M. Bender, Treasurer

BOARD
K. A. Smith
J. O. Blackwell
W. A. Acord
L. E. McKinney
B. I. Halsey
L. U. Taylor
J. O. Fink
T. A. Janney
C. L. Hatcher
D. A. Friley
J. I. Holiday

FIG. 5.5. *Adding a horizontal rule focuses attention on the name.*

PART II

Creating Business Documents

6. Move to the **Bottom** margin box. Delete the number and type **.5**.

7. Change the **L**eft and **R**ight margins to **.5** in the same way.

8. Click OK or press Enter to close the dialog box and accept the changes you've made.

Type the following text as your letterhead, entering spaces and pressing Enter as indicated:

HUMBLE OPINIONS CORPORATION (Enter)

P. O. Box 174, Suite 114 (Enter)

Oak Hill, West Virginia 25901 (Enter)

(304) 555-2234 (Enter, Enter)

(space) **OFFICERS** (Enter)

(space) **D. A. Halsey, President** (Enter)

(space) **D. S. Campbell, V. President** (Enter)

(space) **P. A. Houck, Secretary** (Enter)

(space) **W. M. Bender, Treasurer** (Enter, Enter)

(space) **BOARD** (Enter)

(space) **K. A. Smith** (Enter)

(space) **J. O. Blackwell** (Enter)

(space) **W. A. Acord** (Enter)

(space) **L. E. McKinney** (Enter)

(space) **B. I. Halsey** (Enter)

(space) **L. U. Taylor** (Enter)

(space) **J. O. Fink** (Enter)

(space) **T. A. Janney** (Enter)

(space) **C. L. Hatcher** (Enter)

(space) **D. A. Friley** (Enter)

(space) **J. I. Holiday** (Enter)

Next, you want to format your letterhead text. To do so, take these steps:

CHAPTER 5

Producing a Letterhead

1. Position the cursor in front of the H in HUMBLE, and then highlight the first line.

2. In the Ribbon, change the size to 18. Check the font, if it is not Tms Rmn, click the arrow and change it. Select the **Center** justification box, and select **B**old.

3. Click anywhere on the page to deselect the first line of the letterhead. Or, press the right arrow on the keyboard.

4. Next, highlight the company address and phone number.

5. In the Ribbon, change the font to Helv, 12 point, **C**enter aligned.

6. Click anywhere on the page to deselect the highlighted text. Or, press the right arrow.

7. To format the officer and board names, first you must highlight them.

8. In the Ribbon, change the font to Helv, 8 point, **L**eft aligned.

Next, you want to insert the vertical rule that runs down the left side of the paper (see fig. 5.4). Because the Border command is paragraph-oriented, you must select any paragraph that is to contain the rule; pressing Enter inserts paragraph markers (empty lines) that you can select.

To select the entire page, press and hold down Ctrl while clicking the mouse button in the left margin. Notice the cursor—when it's in the left margin, it turns into a white arrow. With the keyboard, place the cursor at the top of the page, press F8 repeatedly until the entire page is selected. You'll know you selected the entire page if the text is white on a black block (see fig. 5.6).

> **Caution:** If you have more than one page in a document and select an entire page with the mouse in this manner, you'll highlight all pages in the document. Under this condition, Word adds any changes, such as a vertical rule, to all pages. This situation is also true when you use the combination keys Ctrl+Shift+End to select to the end of the document.

PART II

Creating Business Documents

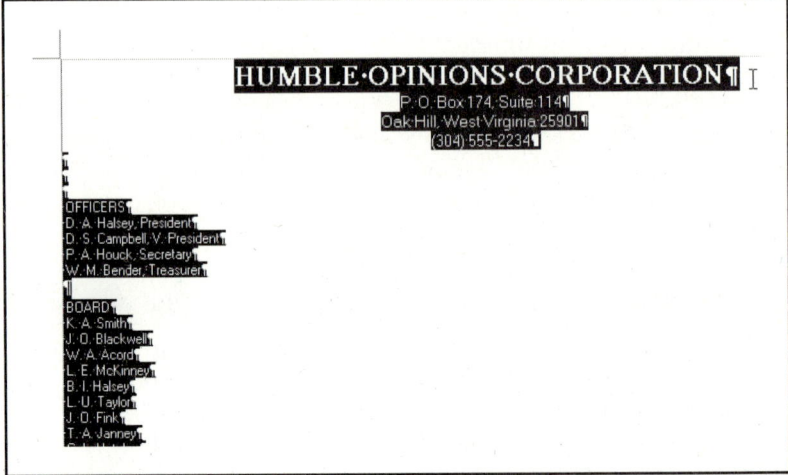

FIG. 5.6.
The entire page is selected and nonprinting characters show.

If you don't want this change to occur throughout the document, select everything on the single page by scrolling to the top of the page. Place the cursor at the very top and left of the page. Press Ctrl+Shift+down arrow (to select a line at a time). Continue to select the entire page. This method selects the entire page without affecting other pages in the document. You also can change views to full screen in Version 2.0, and easily select the entire page by dragging the cursor.

To add the vertical rule to the example letterhead, follow these steps:

1. To add the vertical rule to the left side of the page, place the paragraph returns (Enter) from after Holiday's name to the end of the page.

2. Select all the text.

3. If you're using Word 1.1, from the Format menu select **Paragraph**. Word displays a dialog box.

3. If you're using Word 2.0, from the Format menu, select **B**order. Word displays a dialog box.

4. For Word 1.1, in the **B**order box, click the arrow or press the down arrow, and choose Bar and Single Pattern.

4. For Word 2.0, click the left margin in the B**o**rder box, and then choose the 1.5 rule in the **L**ine box. On the keyboard, press Alt+T,B. Press Alt+R then press the down arrow key to select the left border. Move to the Line box (Alt+L) and use the down arrow key to select the line.

CHAPTER 5

Producing a Letterhead

5. Select OK or press Enter. The vertical bar (rule) should now extend the length of your page.

   Word places a small margin after the vertical bar. The extra space you placed before each left-aligned name, however, will open it up even more.

Now that your letterhead is formatted, you want to save it, see how it looks, and then print it. Follow these steps:

1. From the **File** menu, select Save **As**. Choose the correct disk drive and directory.

2. Press Del to clear the box and enter the file name **Letter3**.

3. From the **File** menu, select Print Preview to view the Document (see fig. 5.7). Press Esc to return to the normal working view.

4. From the **File** menu, select **P**rint and choose OK or press Enter.

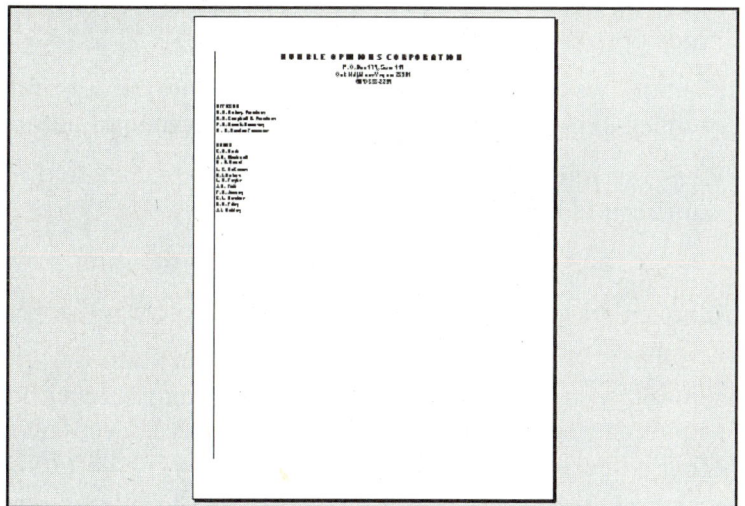

FIG. 5.7.
The finished letterhead shown in Print Preview.

Creating an Innovative Letterhead

Word allows many options when working with text, including line spacing, character spacing, and condensing and expanding text. This section uses several of these options to create a letterhead and show you some of the many alternatives available to you.

141

PART II

Creating Business Documents

This design, less formal than the previous ones, is simple, yet unique (see fig. 5.8). Even if this particular design doesn't appeal to you, the techniques used (centering vertical words, line spacing, and indentations) may help you with other documents.

This design would not work as a glossary in Word Version 1.1, but would be excellent to have printed as camera-ready copy. In Word Version 2.0, this letterhead could be a glossary. You would insert the letterhead in a frame at the bottom of the page, and then type normally. To create this style of letterhead, take these steps:

1. In the **F**ile menu, select **N**ew to begin. A dialog box appears. Use **N**ormal Template and choose New **D**ocument.

2. Select OK or press Enter.

3. If you're using Word 1.1, set the margins by selecting **D**ocument from the Forma**t** menu. The Document dialog box appears.

3. If you're using Word 2.0, set the margins for the page by accessing the Forma**t** menu and choosing Page Se**t**up. The Page Setup dialog box appears.

4. Position the cursor in the **T**op margin box to the left of the number. Press Del to clear the box, and then type **7.25**.

5. Press Tab to move to the **B**ottom margin box. Delete the number and type **.5**

6. Change the **L**eft and **R**ight margins to **.5** in the same way.

7. Click OK or press Enter to close the dialog box and accept the changes you've made.

    You set the top margin to 7.25 inches because it enables you to start on the bottom of the page. If, however, you have other pages in this document, all margins will be set to 7.25 inches, which may not be appropriate for the other pages.

8. In the Ribbon, display non-printing characters so that you can see margins on the page and the symbols for tabs and returns.

Type the following text as your letterhead, entering spaces and pressing Tab and Enter as indicated:

(Tab) **H** (Enter)

(Tab) **U** (Enter)

FIG. 5.8. *A less formal letterhead design.*

PART II

Creating Business Documents

    (Tab) **M** (Enter)

    (Tab) **B** (Enter)

    (Tab) **L** (Enter)

    (Tab) **E** (Enter)

OPINIONS (five spaces) **PO BOX 174** (five spaces) **OAK HILL** (two spaces) **WEST VIRGINIA 25901**

Next, you want to format your letterhead text. You can do so by following these steps:

1. Highlight the word HUMBLE (be sure to get the first tab).
2. From the **F**ormat menu, select **C**haracter. A dialog box appears.
3. Change the type to Helvetica, 30-point, and **B**old.
4. Select OK or press Enter.
5. On the Ruler, check to be sure that the text is left-aligned.
6. From the Forma**t** menu, select **T**abs and Clear **A**ll.
7. In the **T**ab Position box, type **.3**.
8. Select **C**enter align and **S**et.
9. Select OK or press Enter. Word centers each letter so that the widest letter (M) does not hang over the edge as it would if it were left-aligned.
10. With HUMBLE still highlighted, from the Forma**t** menu, select **P**aragraph.

11. For Word 1.1, in the Spacing box, select **L**ine and type **-0.4**.

For Word 2.0, in the Line Spacing box, choose Exactly. In the At: box type **28pt** (be sure to type the **pt**).

Line spacing is the same as *leading*.

Word Version 1.1 enables you to designate spacing in either lines or points. Specify 2li for double-spacing, 3li for triple-spacing. Use a positive number for minimum line spacing (each line has a minimum height; if a character exceeds it, the line height adjusts so that characters don't overlap). Negative line spacing is the same as fixed line spacing (meaning if characters exceed the line height, they overlap each

CHAPTER 5

Producing a Letterhead

other when printed). Auto spacing adjusts the leading to the height of the tallest letter. Set auto by typing **Auto** or **0**, in Forma**t**, **P**aragraph, Spacing, **L**ine.

Word Version 2.0 enables you to designate spacing in points or lines; specify 2li for double-spacing, 1li for single-spacing, 1.5 lines for one-and-a-half. The At Least option enables you to set the minimum line spacing that Word can increase. Exactly sets a fixed line spacing that is not adjustable.

12. In Word 1.1, from the Forma**t** menu, select **P**aragraph. In the B**o**rder box, choose Bar; in the Pat**t**ern box, choose Single, and then select OK or press Enter.

12. In Word 2.0, from the Forma**t** menu, select **B**order. Click the left margin in the B**o**rder box, and select the .75 rule. Or, on the keyboard, press Alt+T,B. Press Alt+R then use the down arrow to select the left margin. Move to the Line box (Alt+L) and use the down arrow to select the .75 rule. Select OK or press Enter.

13. Next, highlight OPINIONS.

14. From the Forma**t** menu, select **C**haracter.

15. Change the **F**ont to Helvetica, 30-point, and **B**old. Select OK or press Enter.

16. In the Ribbon, make the text **L**eft aligned.

    The next step is to expand the word OPINIONS.

    The value limits for expanded type are 3 (maximum) and 0 (minimum). Figure 5.9 shows normal and expanded type. In the Spacing box, you also can select condensed type. The value limits for condensed type are 1.75 (maximum) and 0 (minimum). Figure 5.10 shows normal and condensed type. You may want to experiment with these limits now to discover the possibilities for use in later documents.

17. From the forma**t** menu, select **C**haracter. In the dialog box, select **E**xpanded in the Character Spacing box (or Spacing box in Word 1.1).

18. In the By: box, type **1.5**.

145

PART II

Creating Business Documents

FIG. 5.9.
An example of normal and expanded (by 1.5-pt and 3-pt) type.

> Normal Type - 14 pt. Helv
> Expanded Type By: 1.5pt
> E X P A N D E D   T Y P E   By :   3 p t

FIG. 5.10.
An example of normal and condensed (by .5-pt and 1.25-pt) type.

> Normal Type - 14 pt. Helv
> Condensed Type By: .50
> CONDENSED TYPE By:1.25

19. Click the page to deselect the type. Or press the right arrow key.
20. Highlight the address.
21. In the Ribbon, change the font to Helvetica, 12-points in Version 1.1 and 13-points in Version 2.0, **B**old, and **L**eft aligned.
22. Deselect the text.
23. Highlight the text on the bottom line.

24. In Word 1.1, from the Format menu, select **P**aragraph. In the B**o**rder box, choose Below. In the Pa**t**tern box, select Single.

24. In Word 2.0, from the Format menu, select **B**order. In the B**o**rder box, click the bottom margin for a line below. Choose the .75 rule from the **L**ine box, and select OK or press Enter.

To add the logo to the bottom left of your letterhead, follow these steps:

1. Position the cursor in front of the O in OPINIONS.
2. From the **I**nsert menu, select **P**icture. Choose a TIFF file to insert. Use MONIQUE.TIF if you don't have one of your own; the path is C:\WINWORD\LIBRARY.

You need to size the graphic to make it small enough to fit in the area provided. After you insert the graphic, Word may move it to the next page because of its size. After you resize the graphic, it returns to the original page.

CHAPTER 5

Producing a Letterhead

To size the graphic, follow these steps:

1. Click inside the graphic to activate the handles. Or, on the keyboard, position the cursor before the graphic. Hold down the Shift key while pressing the right arrow to select.

2. Press and hold the Shift key. Click the handle in the lower right corner and drag it toward the center of the graphic. Or, on the keyboard, go to Forma**t**, **P**icture and size graphic to 1/2 inch. Press Enter.

3. When the graphic is the proper size, release the mouse button and the Shift key. Figure 5.11 shows the letterhead on-screen with the MONIQUE.TIF file inserted.

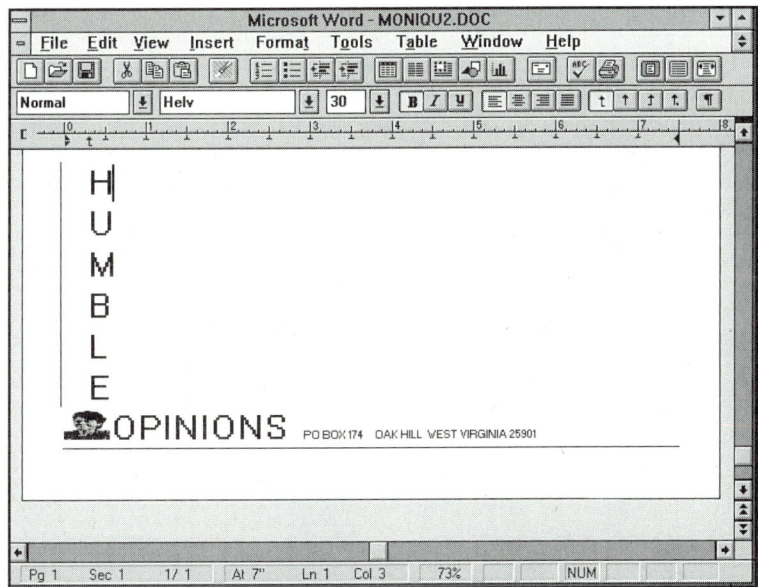

FIG. 5.11.
An example of normal and condensed (by .5-pt and 1.25-pt) type.

Now that your letterhead is formatted, you want to save it, see how it looks, and then print it. Follow these steps:

1. From the **F**ile menu, select Save **A**s.

2. Type **Letter4** in the proper directory and drive.

3. From the **F**ile menu, select Print **P**review to view the finished letterhead.

4. Press Esc to return to the normal working view.

5. From the **F**ile menu, select **P**rint and choose OK or press Enter.

147

PART II

Creating Business Documents

Storing the Letterhead in a Glossary

The final step in this section is to save one of the letterhead designs in a Glossary, which is a file consisting of any amount of text or graphics that you use regularly. You store a letterhead in a glossary, and then retrieve it anytime you want to produce a letter.

To store the letterhead in a glossary, follow these steps:

1. Open the file LETTER1.DOC or LETTER2.DOC by accessing the **F**ile menu and selecting **O**pen.

2. Select OK or press Enter.

3. Highlight the entire letterhead. You can position your cursor at the very top of the page, press the mouse button, and drag to the end of your text. Or, on the keyboard, position the cursor at the top of the page and press F8 to extend the selection.

4. From the **E**dit menu, select Gl**o**ssary.

5. In the Glossary **N**ame box, type **letterhead**.

6. Select **G**lobal-all documents, so that the letterhead can be used anytime in Word.

7. Select Define. Word returns you to the page view.

8. From the **F**ile menu, select **S**ave.

9. When you exit Word, you're asked whether you want to save global glossary and command changes. Tell it yes by clicking on Yes or typing **Y**.

10. When you close your document or this template, Word may also ask you whether you want to save changes to the Normal template (because you created a glossary entry). Tell it yes by clicking on Yes or typing **Y**.

CHAPTER 5

Producing a Letterhead

Recapping

In this chapter, you learned how to produce a simple letterhead, a letterhead that uses a logo, traditional and innovative letterheads, and how to store the letterhead in a glossary.

In the next chapter, you learn how to produce a letter.

Producing a Letter

Letters are the foundation of today's business world. On a daily basis, nearly every transaction in business is preceded or followed by (usually both) some kind of letter. Businesses are frequently judged by the letters they send. In today's competitive economic climate, it's safe to say that in some cases, letters can make or break a business.

This chapter shows you how to create three letter designs. The first is a traditional business letter that uses the glossary saved in the last chapter. The second is less formal and uses a table in the body of the letter. The final design is more appropriate for commercial possibilities such as a mass mailing. At the end of the chapter are two additional designs that give you ideas for your own letters.

When you create your letter designs, remember that your primary goal is to convey your message as clearly and efficiently as possible. Remember to use language appropriate to the reader and to the message, and be extra careful with punctuation, grammar, and spelling.

Creating a Traditional Business Letter

The letter style in this section is the style typically used in business. Formal, symmetrical, and proper, this style often is useful in daily correspondence. Left alignment and Times Roman type

PART II

Creating Business Documents

reflect the formality, and the addition of the letterhead sets it off from other letters. With this first letter, you'll insert the glossary letterhead you saved in Chapter 5. Figure 6.1 shows the finished letter. If you saved your letterheads on a floppy disk, you'll need that disk to do this first letter.

To begin a new document and set up the margins, take the following steps:

1. From the File menu, select New. The New dialog box appears.

2. Choose Document and, for Use Template, select Normal.

3. Select Format, Document and choose OK.

3. From the Format menu, select Page Setup.

    The Page Setup dialog box appears.

4. Select Margins and set the margins as follows: Top 1", Bottom 1", Left and Right 1".

5. Select OK or press Enter. Word returns you to the blank document.

6. The cursor is at the top of the page.

To import the Glossary from the Letterhead chapter, do the following:

1. From the Edit menu, select Glossary. A dialog box appears.

2. Select "letterhead" from the list and choose Insert.

    The letterhead is imported at the cursor.

3. Place the cursor on the next line.

4. On the Ribbon, set the font size to TmsRmn, 12 points, left aligned.

Next, you need to enter the text of your letter. Type the following, pressing Tab and Enter as indicated:

    (Enter, Enter)

    (Tab) **April 15, 1992** (Enter, four times)

    Mr. J. C. Gillenwater (Enter)

    Oak Hill Post (Enter)

HUMBLE OPINIONS CORPORATION

Post Office Box 174   Oak Hill, West Virginia 25901
(304) 555-2234

April 15, 1992

Mr. J. C. Gillenwater
Oak Hill *Post*
Drawer PO
Oak Hill, West Virginia 25901

Dear Sir:

Thank you for your recent purchase of software and training. I believe this package offers enormous advantages for your company. After we install the software, someone will schedule your employees for training at your convenience.

Please do not hesitate to call us if you have any problems, questions, or comments. We look forward to working with you and your staff.

Sincerely,

D. J. Halsey

FIG. 6.1.   *A letter using an inserted Glossary.*

PART II

Creating Business Documents

> **Drawer PO** (Enter)
>
> **Oak Hill, West Virginia 25901** (Enter, twice)
>
> **Dear Sir:** (Enter, twice)
>
> **Thank you for your recent purchase of software and training. I believe this package offers enormous advantages for your company. After we install the software, someone will schedule your employees for training at your convenience.** (Enter, Enter)
>
> **Please do not hesitate to call us if you have any problems, questions, or comments. We look forward to working with you and your staff.** (Enter, twice)
>
> (Tab) **Sincerely,** (Enter, four times)
>
> (Tab) **D. J. Halsey**

Next, you need to check the spelling of your letter. To do so, follow these steps:

1. At the top of the letter, position your cursor in front of April.
2. From the **U**tilities menu, select **S**pelling. The Spelling dialog box appears.
3. Select **S**tart. Word begins scanning your document for spelling errors.

   In Word 1.1, you can select the following options during the spell check: **I**gnore, **C**ancel, **A**dd, **S**uggest, or **C**hange.

1. At the top of the letter position your cursor in front of April.
2. From the **T**ools menu, select **S**pelling. Word begins scanning your document for spelling errors.

   In Word 2.0, you can select the following options: **I**gnore, **I**gnore All, **A**dd, **C**hange, **C**hange All, **U**ndo Last, **S**uggest, **O**ptions, and **C**ancel.

After you've checked the document for spelling errors, format it the way you want it by taking these steps:

1. Highlight the word Post and choose the italic icon on the Ribbon.

CHAPTER 6

Producing a Letter

2. Select April 15, 1992; on the Ruler set the tab to 4.75".

3. Repeat with Sincerely, and D.J. Halsey.

4. From the **File** menu, select Print Preview to see how the letter will look when it is printed.

5. To print the letter, select **P**rint. The Print dialog box appears.

6. Select OK or press Enter.

7. To save your letter, from the **F**ile menu select Save **A**s. The Save As dialog box appears.

8. Make sure that the drive and directory are correct. In the File Name text box, type **Letter1** and choose OK or press Enter.

   When you save your file, Word automatically prompts you to fill in a Summary Info box, which is discussed in the next section.

Using Summary Information

You can use summary information about your document to help you organize and easily find any letter in your files:

1. From the Utilities menu, select **C**ustomize. When the additional Customize choices appear, choose P**ro**mpt for **S**ummary Info.

2. Select OK or press Enter.

3. From the Edit menu, select Summary **I**nfo. The Summary Info box appears.

3. In Word Version 2.0, when you save your file, Word automatically prompts you to fill in a Summary Info box.

4. For **T**itle, enter **Gillenwater**, for **S**ubject, enter **Recent Purchases**, and for Comments, enter **Third Correspondence**.

5. Select Stat**i**stics to view information about the document.

6. Select **S**ave and **C**lose. Word returns you to your document.

You can print the statistics of a Summary Info Box from within the document by selecting File **P**rint. In the Print dialog box, specify Summary Info in the **P**rint text box, and then print as normal.

155

PART II

Creating Business Documents

You also can print the summary information along with the document by selecting **F**ile **P**rint. In the Print dialog box, select **O**ptions and choose Include Summary Info.

To view summary information for a particular letter or document, select **F**ile F**i**nd. Select the file from the list and click Su**m**mary to view the information about that particular document.

Creating a Letter by Using Type and Graphics

The letter presented in this section is informal—from one friend to another—but it still concerns business. In this situation, a company letterhead may be too formal. The design is simple and includes graphic rules. The table makes the information easy to read and refer to (see fig. 6.2).

Word's table feature enables you to organize information in columns and rows, with or without rules. Each row and column intersects at a cell. In the following instructions, those cells are referred to with letters and numbers. The columns are labeled A, B, C and D; the rows are labeled 1, 2, 3, and so forth. You also have a figure to help you identify each cell.

1. Select **F**ile, **N**ew, **D**ocument, **U**se Template: Normal, and choose OK or press Enter.

2. To set the margins, select **D**ocument from the Forma**t** menu.

2. To set the margins, select Page Set**u**p from the Forma**t** menu.

3. In the Margins box, set the **T**op and **B**ottom margins at **1.25"** and the **L**eft and **R**ight margins at **1.30"**.

4. On the Ribbon, set the font as TmsRmn, 12 points, left aligned. (Ctrl+F to choose font; Ctrl+P to choose points; Ctrl+L for left aligned.)

5. From the Format menu, select **T**abs. Set the **T**ab Position at **4.25"**, **L**eft aligned. Choose **S**et and select OK or press Enter. Or, you can set tabs on the ruler by clicking the left tab stop and clicking 4.25". To set the tab on the Ruler with the keyboard, activate the Ruler by pressing Ctrl+Shift+F10. Use the right arrow to move along the ruler. Delete tab stops you don't want, position the cursor at 4.25", press 1 for left tab stop.

D. J. Halsey
Humble Opinions • P. O. Box 174 • Oak Hill, WV 25901

May 1, 1992

Ms. D. E. Campbell
212 Forest Dr.
Fayetteville, WV 25840

Dear Della:

Thanks for requesting information about our new courses. I have gathered some figures I am sure will interest you. Following is a table describing the facts you need to fill out the order form:

Number	Course Title	Course Description	Cost
12345	Desktop Publishing	Microsoft Word Version 1.1 or 2.0	$240
23456	Word Processing	Microsoft Word Version 1.1 or 2.0	$240
34567	Spreadsheet	Microsoft Excel	$225
45678	Planning Printing	Design, Paper, Ink, Finishing	$290

I would be happy to answer any further questions you may have. Feel free to call me at 252-9922. I hope to see you and your staff for training soon.

Sincerely,

Dan Halsey

FIG. 6.2. *A letter using graphic rules and a table for organization of the material.*

PART II

Creating Business Documents

6. Type the following information:

    D. J. Halsey (Enter)

    Humble Opinions (six spaces) **P. O. Box 174** (six spaces) **Oak Hill, WV 25901** (Enter, twice)

    (Tab) **May 1, 1992** (Enter, twice)

    Ms. D. E. Campbell (Enter)

    212 Forest Dr. (Enter)

    Fayetteville, WV 25840 (Enter, twice)

    Dear Della: (Enter, twice)

    Thanks for requesting information about our new courses. I have gathered some figures I am sure will interest you. Following is a table describing the facts you need to fill out the order form: (Enter, four times)

    I would be happy to answer any further questions you may have. Feel free to call me at 252-9922. I hope to see you and your staff for training soon. (Enter, Enter)

    (Tab) **Sincerely,** (Enter, Enter)

    (Tab) **D.J. Halsey** (Enter, four times)

7. At the top of the page, select D. J. Halsey and the entire address line. Center align both lines on the Ribbon (Ctrl+C in Version 1.1; Ctrl+E in Version 2.0). Click anywhere on the page to deselect or press the right arrow.

8. Select D. J. Halsey. In the Ribbon, change the point size to 18, **B**old.

9. With the text still selected, access the Forma**t** menu and choose **P**aragraph. A dialog box appears.

10. In the **B**order box, select Above; in the Pa**t**tern box, select Thick and press Enter. Deselect the type.

9. With the text still selected, access the Forma**t** menu and choose **B**order. A dialog box appears.

10. In the **B**order box, click the margin above. Change the Line to 2.25 points. Select OK or press Enter, and deselect the text.

CHAPTER 6

Producing a Letter

11. Select the address line. On the Ribbon, change the font to Helv, 10 points.

12. With the text selected, access the Format menu and choose **P**aragraph. A dialog box appears.

13. In the B**o**rder box, select Below. In the Pat**t**ern box, select Thick and select OK or press Enter. Deselect the text.

14. Position the cursor in the middle of the six spaces between `Opinions` and `P. O. Box`. Insert a bullet by using the Macro key you created in Chapter 5. Do the same between `Box 174` and `Oak Hill`.

12. With the text selected, open the Format menu and choose **B**order. The Border dialog box appears.

13. In the Bo**r**der box, click the margin below. Change the Line to 2.25 points. Choose OK or press Enter and deselect the text.

14. Position the cursor between `Opinions` and `P. O. Box`, select Insert, **S**ymbol. Double-click the bullet character. Or, on the keyboard, use the right and down arrows to select the bullet. Choose OK or press Enter. Select the bullet symbol on your page. From the Ribbon, change the point size to 10. Choose **C**opy (Ctrl+C) and then **P**aste (Shift+Ins) the bullet between `Box 174` and `Oak Hill`.

15. From the Ribbon, turn on nonprinting characters. Place the cursor on the second paragraph return after the paragraph ending with `...the order form`.

16. Choose Insert, **T**able. A dialog box appears.

16. Choose Table, **I**nsert. A dialog box appears.

17. In the Number of **C**olumns, type **4**, in the Number of **R**ows, type **5**. The Column **W**idth default is Auto. Select OK or press Enter.

18. Using the right mouse button, select cells A-1 through A-5 (see fig. 6.3).

19. From the Forma**t** menu, select **T**able. Figure 6.4 illustrates the dialog box for Version 1.1.

19. Select Ta**b**le, Column **W**idth.

159

PART II

Creating Business Documents

***FIG. 6.3.**
Letters represent each column; numbers represent each row. These designations should help you locate the proper cells in the instructions. The screen shown is Version 1.1.*

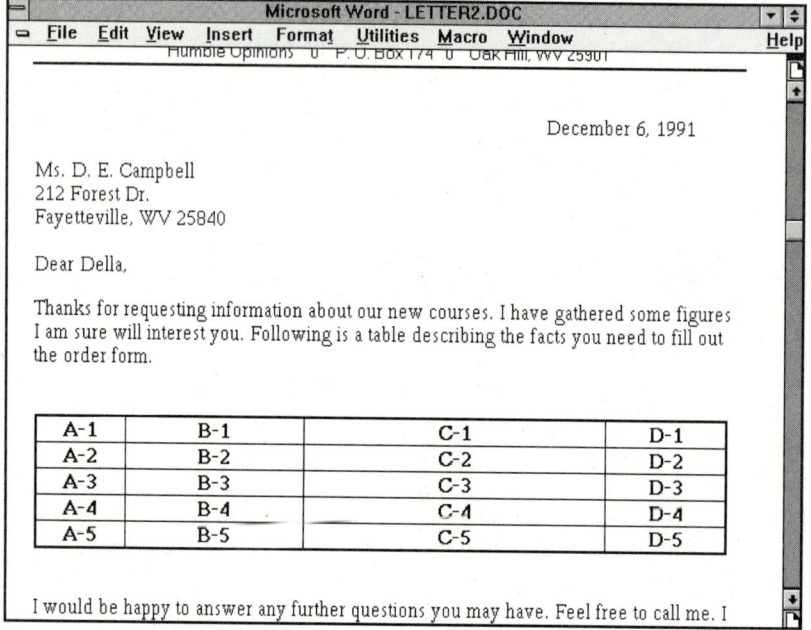

20. In the **W**idth of Column 1:, type **.75"**. Select **N**ext Column. In the box now labeled **W**idth of Column 2:, type **1.5"**. Select **N**ext Column. For the **W**idth of Column 3, type **2.5"**. Select **N**ext Column again and enter **1"** in the column width box. Choose OK or press Enter.

21. Select the entire table. From the Forma**t** menu, select **T**able. A dialog box appears. In the box labeled In**d**ent Rows, type **0.1"**. Select OK. Deselect the text or press Enter.

21. Select the table. Choose **T**able, Row **H**eight. A dialog box appears. Indent from Left **0.1"**. Select OK or press Enter.

22. To move from cell to cell, use the Tab key. Position the cursor in cell A-1. Type the following:

   Number (Tab) **Course Title** (Tab) **Course Description** (Tab) **Cost** (Tab)

   12345 (Tab) **Desktop Publishing** (Tab) **Microsoft Word Version 1.1 or 2.0** (Tab) **$240** (Tab)

   23456 (Tab) **Word Processing** (Tab) **Microsoft Word Version 1.1 or 2.0** (Tab) **$240** (Tab)

CHAPTER 6

Producing a Letter

34567 (Tab) **Spreadsheet** (Tab) **Microsoft Excel** (Tab) **$225** (Tab)

45678 (Tab) **Planning Printing** (Tab) **Design, Paper, Ink, Finishing** (Tab) **$290**

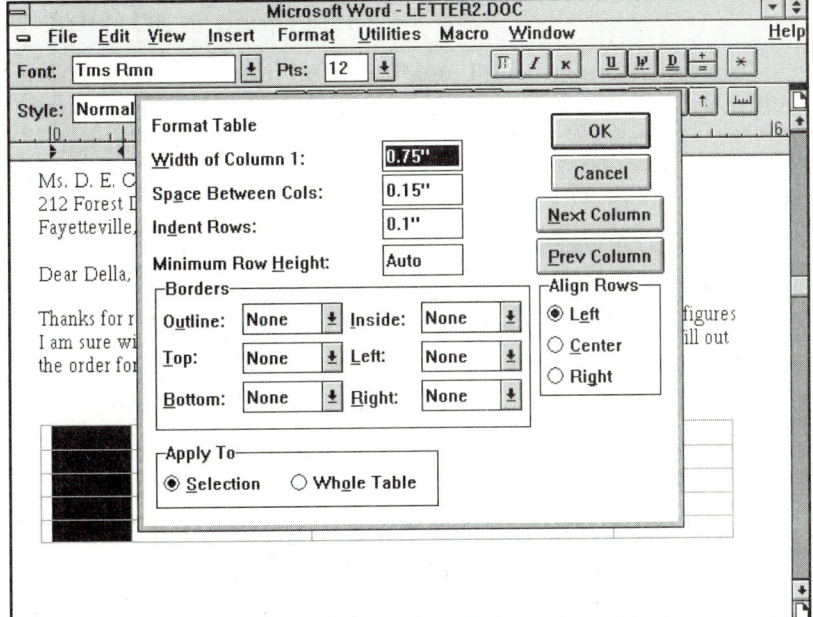

FIG. 6.4.
The Format Table dialog box (Version 1.1).

23. To set the "Cost Column" numbers on a decimal tab, select the column (column D) with the right mouse button or by holding down the Shift key and using the right and down arrows.

24. From the Forma**t** menu, select **T**abs, Clear **A**ll. Type **.63"**, select **D**ecimal tab, choose **S**et, and select OK or press Enter.

25. Position cursor in front of the dollar sign in cell D-2. Press Ctrl+Tab. Repeat this step in cells D-3 through D-5.

    In the Table mode, a Tab moves you from cell to cell. Ctrl+Tab inserts the Tab character.

26. Select the text in row 1 (cells A-1 through D-1) of the table. In the Ribbon, **C**enter align and bold the selected text. Deselect the text.

161

PART II

Creating Business Documents

27. Select the text from cell A-2 to D-5. From the Forma**t** menu, select **P**aragraph. In the Spacing box, **B**efore, add **0.5**li. In the **A**fter box, add **0.5**". Select OK or press Enter. Deselect the text.

28. To add the rules, select the entire table (A-1 through D-5). From the Forma**t** menu, select **T**able. In the **B**orders box, change **Ou**tline to Thick (the **T**op, **B**ottom, **L**eft, and **R**ight should change automatically). Change the **I**nside to Single. Select OK or press Enter. Deselect the text.

29. At the top of the page, position the cursor to the left of the date. Choose **U**tilities, **S**pelling, and **S**tart. Answer with the appropriate responses to the spell checker.

30. Press Ctrl+End to move to the bottom of the page. From the Forma**t** menu, choose **P**aragraph. In the **B**order box, choose Below; Pat**t**ern Thick. Select OK or press Enter.

31. Add a Summary Box by selecting **E**dit, Summary **I**nfo.

28. To add the rules, select the entire table (A-1 through D-5). From the Forma**t** menu, select **B**order. Under **P**reset, choose **G**rid. A 1.25 **L**ine automatically is set on the outside borders; .75 automatically is set on inside lines. Select OK or press Enter. Deselect the text.

29. At the top of the page, position the cursor to the left of the date. Choose **T**ools, **S**pelling. Answer with the appropriate responses to the spell checker.

30. Press Ctrl+End to move to the bottom of the page. From the Forma**t** menu, choose **B**order. Click the margin below, Change the **L**ine to 2.25. Select OK or press Enter. Or, press the down arrow key until the bottom margin is selected.

31. When you Save **A**s, Word prompts you with the Summary Info box.

32. Choose **F**ile, Save **A**s. The Print dialog box appears. Type **Letter3**.

33. Choose **F**ile, Print Preview, and select **P**rint.

CHAPTER 6

Producing a Letter

Creating an Innovative Styled Letter

Businesses send various styles of letters every day. Instead of correspondence, your letter may be an advertisement. With the availability of mailing lists and computer programs to sort and label, more and more advertisements are sent as letters. The design of the letter in this section is an advertisement. The boxes repeat for unity. The justified text mirrors the vertical lines of the box, and the bullets add emphasis. Figure 6.5 shows the finished letter.

To create the advertising letter, take the following steps:

1. Choose **F**ile, **N**ew, **D**ocument, **U**se Template: Normal. Select OK or press Enter.

2. To set the margins, select Forma**t**, **D**ocument. The Document dialog box appears.

3. Set all margins to **1.25"** in the Margin box.

4. From the Forma**t** menu, select De**f**ine Styles, and choose **O**ptions to add a new style. In the **D**efine Style Name box, type **Body Text**. Click **D**efine to add it to the list.

2. To set the margins, select Forma**t**, Page Set**u**p.

3. Set the **T**op and **B**ottom margins to **1.25"**; the **L**eft and **R**ight to **1.00"**.

4. From the Forma**t** menu, select S**t**yle. In the **S**tyle Name dialog box, press the backspace key and type **Body Text**. Click **D**efine or press Alt+D.

5. In the **S**tyle Name dialog box, go to **C**haracter. The font should be TmsRmn, and the point size 12.

6. In the same dialog box, go to **P**aragraph and choose **J**ustified; in the Spacing box, **A**fter, type **1li**. Select OK.

6. Still in the dialog box, go to **P**aragraph and choose Align-ment, Justified; in the Spacing box, Aft**e**r, type **1li**. Click **A**dd or press Alt+A and Enter, Apply.

7. In the Style box, choose Body Text, if it is not already showing.

163

Congratulations!

You have been selected for a special promotion! We are offering this deal to only 300 homes in your state – and you live in one of those homes! Let me begin by telling you there is absolutely no obligation to buy. All we ask is that you allow us a few minutes of your time, and for doing that, you win a **FREE**, all-expense-paid vacation to Florida!

Five days and four nights at a luxurious hotel, three meals a day, **FREE** limousine service, and **FREE** tickets to the sights and attractions in and around Alligator Bend, Florida. Just hours away from tourist hot spots, your vacation awaits you! And there is no obligation to you whatsoever!!

> **Tickets for FREE admission for two:**
> - Visit the spacious, sensational Alligator farms
> - Fish in the famous Insectivorous Swamp
> - Spend a fun day at Rickety Rick's Amusement Park

Once again, you are under no obligation to buy. A few minutes of your time is all we ask. We will be calling you in a few days to discuss this exciting vacation with you. We hope you will consider traveling to our palatial resort and touring our complex (we're located just 7 hours from you!). After you visit us, you're ready to begin your once-in-a-lifetime, all-expense-paid vacation!!!

We are looking forward to meeting you.

Sincerely,
Rookem Resorts, Inc.

P.S.   Rookem Resorts, Inc., is in no way affiliated with Cheatem Resorts, Swindle Homes, or any of their subsidiaries.

FIG. 6.5.   *An advertisement letter.*

CHAPTER 6

Producing a Letter

8. To add the graphic box to the page, select Forma**t**, **D**ocument. The Document dialog box appears.

8. To add the graphic box to the page, select Forma**t**, Page Set**u**p. A dialog box appears.

9. In the margins box, change the **T**op margin to a negative number, –1.25". Select OK or press Enter.

10. Choose **E**dit, **H**eader/Footer. Select Header. Select OK or press Enter.

11. From the Forma**t** menu, select **P**aragraph. In the B**o**rder box, choose Box; Patt**e**rn, Thick.

12. Set the **L**ine to **53li**. This line is the height of the box. Select OK or press Enter.

10. Choose **V**iew, **H**eader/Footer. Select Header. Select OK or press Enter.

11. From the Forma**t** menu, select **B**order. In Preset, choose **B**ox and choose **L**ine 1.25.

12. From the Format menu, select **P**aragraph. In the Spacing box, **A**t: type **53li**. In the same box, change the Indentation From **L**eft to .3" and change From **R**ight to .3". Select OK or press Enter.

13. In the following letter, the code Alt+0150 represents an em-dash. Be sure that Num Lock is on. Place one space before and one space after the em-dash. Type the following:

> **Congratulations!** (Enter)
>
> **You have been selected for a special promotion! We are offering this deal to only 300 homes in your state (Alt+0150) and you live in one of those homes! Let me begin by telling you there is absolutely no obligation to buy. All we ask is that you allow us a few minutes of your time, and for doing that, you win a free, all-expense-paid vacation to Florida!** (Enter, Enter)
>
> **Five days and four nights at a luxurious hotel, three meals a day, free limousine service, and free tickets to the sights and attractions in and around Alligator Bend, Florida. Just hours away from tourist hot**

PART II

Creating Business Documents

spots, your vacation awaits you! And there is no obligation to you whatsoever!! (Enter, twice)

(Tab) **Tickets for free admission for two:** (Enter)

(Tab) **Visit the spacious, sensational Alligator farms** (Enter)

(Tab) **Fish in the famous Insectivorous Swamp** (Enter)

(Tab) **Spend a fun day at Rickety Rick's Amusement Park** (Enter)

Once again, you are under no obligation to buy. A few minutes of your time is all we ask. We will be calling you in a few days to discuss this exciting vacation with you. We hope you will consider traveling to our palatial resort and touring our complex (we're located just 7 hours from you!). After you visit us, you're ready to begin your once-in-a-lifetime, all-expense-paid vacation!!! (Enter, Enter)

We are looking forward to meeting you. (Enter, Enter)

(Tab) **Sincerely,** (Enter)

(Tab) **Rookem Resorts, Inc.** (Enter, three times)

P.S. (Tab) **Rookem Resorts, Inc., is in no way affiliated with Cheatem Resorts, Swindle Homes, or any of their subsidiaries.**

14. Press Ctrl+Home to move to the top of the page. Choose **U**tilities, **H**yphenate, turn Confirm off. Select OK or press Enter. Choose **U**tilities, **S**pelling, and **S**tart.

14. Press Ctrl+Home to move to the top of the page. Choose **T**ools, **H**yphenation, turn Confirm off. Select OK or press Enter. Choose **T**ools, **S**pelling.

15. Select the word Congratulations!. On the Ribbon, change it to Helv, 18-point, **Bold**.

16. With the text still selected, choose Forma**t**, **P**aragraph. Set Spacing After to **1.5li**. Deselect the type.

CHAPTER 6

Producing a Letter

17. Choose **E**dit, **R**eplace. **S**earch for the word `free`, **R**eplace with `FREE`. Select the word `FREE` and press Ctrl+B to make it **B**old. Turn Confirm off. Select OK or press Enter.

17. Choose **E**dit, **R**eplace. In the Fi**n**d What: box, type the word **free**. In the **R**eplace With: box, type **FREE**. Choose Replacement Formatting, **C**haracter. Click **B**old or press Ctrl+B. Select OK or press Enter. Choose Match **W**hole Word Only and Replace **A**ll. Choose Close.

18. Turn on nonprinting codes. Select the paragraph return above `Tickets for FREE admission for two`. On the Ribbon, make the font size 6 points. From the Forma**t** menu, select **P**aragraph. In the Spacing box, change Aft**e**r to **0**, and **L**ine to **0**. Select OK or press Enter. You've created a space between lines that is smaller than .5 inches.

18. Turn on nonprinting codes. Select the paragraph return above `Tickets for FREE admission for two`. On the Ribbon, make the font size 6 points. From the Forma**t** menu, select **P**aragraph. In the Spacing box, change Aft**e**r to **0** and **L**ine to Exactly, A**t:** to **0**.

19. Select the next three lines of type (from `Tickets for FREE...` to `Insectivorous Swamp`). From the Forma**t** menu, select **P**aragraph. In the Spacing box, change Aft**e**r to **.5li**. Select OK or press Enter. Deselect the text.

20. Select the last line, `Spend a fun day...`. From the Forma**t** menu, select **P**aragraph, change Aft**e**r spacing to **1li**. Select OK or press Enter. Deselect the text.

20. Press Enter after the last line, `Spend a fun day...`. On the Ribbon, change the font of this paragraph return to 6 points. From the Forma**t** menu, select **P**aragraph. Change Spacing, Aft**e**r to **1.5li**; **B**efore should be 0. Select OK or press Enter. Click the line `Spend a Fun Day...`. Select Format, **P**aragraph, and change Spacing, Aft**e**r to **.5li**.

21. Select `Tickets for FREE...`. On the Ribbon, select **B**old. Choose Format, **T**abs. Set the tab Position to **1"**, left aligned, and select **S**et. Select OK or press Enter. Deselect the text.

22. Select the three lines beginning with `Visit the spacious...` and ending with `Rick's Amusement Park`. From the Forma**t** menu, select **T**abs. Set the tab Position to **1.5"**, left aligned, and select **S**et. Select OK or press Enter.

167

PART II

Creating Business Documents

23. Position the cursor in front of the paragraph return (the 6-point space), select it and the next four lines to the end of `Rickety Rick's Amusement Park`.

24. From the Format menu, select **P**aragraph. In the **B**order box, select Box. In Patt**e**rn, select Single. Select OK or press Enter. Deselect the text.

25. Position the cursor in front of `Visit the spacious, sensational....` Add a bullet and two spaces. If you don't have a bullet macro key, refer to Chapter 5 for instructions.

23. Position the cursor in front of the paragraph return (the 6-point space), select it and the next five lines, including the 6-point space at the end of `Rickety Rick's Amusement Park`.

24. From the For**ma**t menu, select **B**order. In Preset, choose **B**ox. In **L**ine, choose the .75 rule. Sclect OK or press Enter.

25. Click in front `Visit the spacious, sensational....` Add a bullet and two spaces. Choose Insert, **S**ymbol to add the bullet.

26. Repeat step 25 with the next two lines.

27. Select the lines `Sincerely` and `Rookem`. From the For**ma**t menu, select **T**abs. In the **T**ab Position box, type **4.20"**. Choose Left align and **S**et. Select OK or press Enter. With the text still selected, choose For**ma**t, **P**aragraph. Change Spacing, After to **0**. Select OK or press Enter.

28. To format the hanging indent in the `P.S.`, select the type. Choose Format, Paragraph. Indent from the Left **.40"**. Indent the First Line **–.45"**. Select OK or press Enter. Deselect the text. Select the `P.S.` and use the Ribbon to make it bold.

28. To format the hanging indent in the P.S., select the type. Choose Format, **P**aragraph. Indent from the Left **.78"**, indent the First Line **–.45"**. Select OK. Deselect the text. Select the `P.S.` and use the Ribbon to make it bold.

29. Create a Summary box by selecting **E**dit, Summary **I**nfo.

29. Choosing Save **A**s creates a Summary Info box automatically.

30. Choose File, Save **A**s. The File dialog box appears. Type **Letter3**.

31. Choose File, Print Preview, and **P**rint.

Using Other Letter Designs

This section presents two additional designs you can use for letters. Both were produced on Word Version 2.0; therefore, it may not be possible to reproduce them exactly by using Version 1.1. If you have Version 2.0, consider using Microsoft Draw and WordArt for interesting logo and letterhead designs.

The first letter, shown in figure 6.6, is particularly suitable for a short letter. The vertical rule defines the length of the letter, making it more interesting than a letter without a graphic. The rule also emphasizes the left alignment of the text.

Figure 6.7 shows a letter with a shaded border defining the margins of the letter. The white space created by the wide right and bottom margins makes the letter design interesting. Justified type also defines the margins.

Recapping

In this chapter, you learned about the importance of business letters and how to create well-designed letters ranging from the traditional to the innovative.

In the next chapter, you learn how to produce envelopes.

S. Plumley
P. O. Box 174
Oak Hill, WV 25901
May 13, 1992

Mrs. P. A. Houck
211 Reservoir Drive
Beckley, WV 25801

Dear Patsy:

In response to your request, I have enclosed several paper samples. I believe the white offset linen, 70#, may be the best one for your job. It matches other materials your company has printed, it fits the proposal, and the price is right.

Imagine the white linen with your shade of blue and the warm red of your logo. The logo, in particular, would be very prominent on white. The texture of the linen would make the graphic rules stand out.

If I can be of further help, don't hesitate to call me at 252-6166. I look forward to working with your newest project.

Sincerely,

Sue Plumley

FIG. 6.6. A design for a short letter.

humble opinions P. O. Box 174 • Oak Hill, West Virginia 25901

March 30, 1992

L. W. McKenzie
1455 West 48th Street
Huntington, WV 25705

Dear Mr. McKenzie:

We wish to express our gratitude for your business throughout the past year. Your company has been a pleasure to serve; your staff is always courteous, patient, and friendly.

We are pleased to take this opportunity to offer you, our special customer, a chance to enter our free giveaway! There is no purchase necessary. All you have to do is fill out the enclosed card and return it to us within 14 days.

At the end of this month, our company is giving away a personal computer worth over $2,000. It is our way of saying thank you to special customers like you.

Please return the postage-paid card to us as soon as possible. We will contact you by April 30 to let you know if you won this valuable computer.

Again, thank you for your patronage. We hope to continue doing business with you for many years.

Sincerely,
D. J. Halsey, President
Humble Opinions

FIG. 6.7. *A letter design with interesting white space.*

Producing Envelopes

Producing envelopes is easy in Word for Windows; both Versions 1.1 and 2.0 have special features that support you and your printer. This chapter explains the many aspects of planning, creating, and printing envelopes.

When planning your envelope design, think about matching your letterheads. The designs created in Chapters 5 and 6 can be reproduced on envelopes. Remember that envelopes contain just the name (and logo) of a company, the street address, city, state, and ZIP code. Information such as phone numbers and board members' names never go on an envelope. However, you may want to add the name of the person sending the letter, such as the president, secretary, or a specific board member.

Postal regulations require that the return address be in the upper left corner; the delivery address has a specific position, as well. Regulations and guidelines further specify the size of the mailed piece, placement of extraneous type, bar code, and FIM placement. This chapter summarizes the guidelines that may effect you.

You can print your envelopes on your own printer, or at a print shop. If you print your envelopes yourself, make sure that your printer can handle the job. Printers vary widely in their capability to print envelopes.

PART II

Creating Business Documents

Planning Your Envelope Design

Planning your envelope is an important first step. You should know about your printer and its proficiency with envelopes, observe any postal regulations, and then plan your design elements.

The designs in this chapter are for No. 10 envelopes (9 1/2-inch x 4 1/8-inch business size), but can be adapted to monarch-sized (7 1/2 inches x 3 7/8 inches) envelopes (or even smaller if your printer can print it). Be sure to consult the Post Office's minimum size for mailing, which is discussed later in this section.

Each printer handles envelopes in a different way; some cannot print them at all. Before you spend time designing and creating an envelope, make sure that your printer is capable of printing it. Check your printer manual, which gives valuable information about size, orientation, and feed.

Your printer may have a platen feed; if so, you feed envelopes one at a time. Your printer might have a built-in envelope feeder; if so, you can print many envelopes before refilling. Most laser printers have a vertical feed so that you feed the narrow edge. Inkjet or dot-matrix printers may have a horizontal feed.

If you use a laser printer without a built-in feed, be sure to set the printer for "manual feed" on the printer menu.

If you have a dot-matrix printer, you may have to remove the tractor-fed paper to insert an envelope. Try aligning the left edge of the envelope with the zero mark on the paper holder. You might have to roll the envelope into the printer a little to get it to feed.

The following sections show you how to create envelopes by using both feed types. You may have to adjust measurements, depending on the printer. After printing your first envelope, you'll know more about adjusting measurements and envelope placement.

CHAPTER 7

Producing Envelopes

Understanding Postal Regulations and Guidelines

The U.S. Postal Service has guidelines and regulations concerning mailed materials. The guidelines help ensure that your mail is processed quickly, efficiently, and accurately. Pay special attention to the guidelines if you mail large quantities of materials, such as advertising letters. You can learn more about postal requirements by reading, *Postal Addressing Standards* and *A Guide to Business Mail Preparation,* which are available from the Post Office.

The Postal Service recommends the following guidelines so that your mail is compatible with its OCR scanners. All major post offices use *OCR* (Optical Character Recognition) scanners to read addresses and sort 36,000 envelopes per hour. If your envelope qualifies for the OCR, delivery will be much faster. If your mail does not qualify for the OCR, it will be rejected by the scanner. After rejection, your mail is hand-sorted. This task can take many hours or even days longer; thus, your mail delivery is slower.

Size

Postal Service regulations require that a piece of mail be no smaller than 3.5 inches high by 5 inches wide. Anything smaller will not be processed. Make sure that postcards or return reply cards you want printed conform to this size.

For the maximum size, Postal rules allow 6.125 inches high by 10.5 inches wide. This size is the largest that the OCR equipment can accommodate. Mail can be larger, but it won't move as quickly.

Boundaries

The envelope in figure 7.1 shows where the Postal Service wants the address and bar code placed.

The delivery address should be indented at least 1 inch from the left and right edges of the envelope. The first line of the address should be no more than 2 3/4 inches from the bottom of the envelope. The last line (usually the city, state, and ZIP) should be at least 5/8 inch from the bottom.

The placement of bar codes and FIMs are by regulation; consult your postmaster if you have questions. At one time, the bar code had to go at the bottom of the envelope. Now, you can put it at the end of the address box, following the city, state, and ZIP line. As you can see in the figure, the bar code also can be placed in an area 5/8 inches by 4 1/2 inches in the lower right corner of the envelope. If you place the bar code in the corner, you must measure carefully to conform to official specifications. The location of the FIM is the top, right-hand corner of the envelope. Measuring from the right edge of the envelope, place the right edge of the FIM at 2.125 inches. It may extend no further than 3 inches. The top of the FIM must be lined up with the top edge of the envelope. There are no specific regulations concerning the return address, as long as it does not fall below the delivery address.

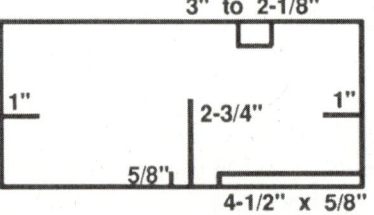

FIG. 7.1. Recommended placement for the mailing address, bar code, and FIM (left) and sample addressed envelope (right).

If you plan to include a bar code on your envelopes, your postmaster will assign you the bar code and FIM along with instructions for exact placement.

Additional Copy

Printing additional logos or copy below the delivery address causes the OCR to reject the envelope. The envelope then must be hand-sorted, which makes delivery slower. Part of your overall envelope design strategy should include the value of additional copy versus the delivery time you want.

Notice, also, that an OCR scanner cannot read anything printed in red. Consequently, if you have your envelopes printed at a print shop, you can include advertising copy in red ink below the address line and avoid problems with the scanner.

CHAPTER 7

Producing Envelopes

Postal Permits

The Postal Service is very particular about postal permits. A postal permit, used in place of a stamp, allows you to mail large quantities at a less expensive rate than stamps. There are bulk rate permits, nonprofit permits, business reply permits, and so on. An individual, a corporation, anyone can purchase a permit from the Post Office to use in large mail bags. There are many rules governing the use of the permit. You must place words such as *bulk rate* and *non-profit* correctly. General rules are that the type must be readable (9-point Helvetica, all caps, centered, for example); you must confine the permit in a graphic box; and you cannot use punctuation in the permit. You must use the specific wording the postmaster assigns to you. For more information, prices, and viability of using your own permit, consult your local post office. Once you receive your permit, you can typeset it directly onto your mailing pieces.

Print Quality

Laser-quality type works fine for envelopes or mailed materials. If you use a dot-matrix or inkjet printer, however, make sure that the type is not broken or fuzzy. Also, make sure that you design sufficient contrast between the address and the background. For example, blue type on a blue envelope may be hard to read.

Use readable lettering and word spacing. The OCR has difficulty reading letters that are too close, lines that are too close, and slanted or script type. The Post Office recommends sans serif type, such as Futura, Helvetica, or Univers. Serifed types that also work are Century Schoolbook and Friz Quadrata. Be sure to left-align the type; use no more than 20 percent screens; and avoid bold, italic, expanded, or condensed type.

Producing a Basic Envelope

The envelope design presented in this section is simple. You can format the page and type for your return address, and then save it as a template for later use. Any time you open the template, your return address and the position for the delivery address automatically appear. Figure 7.2 shows the return address for the basic envelope.

PART II

Creating Business Documents

FIG. 7.2.
The return address.

> **HUMBLE OPINIONS**
> POST OFFICE BOX 174
> OAK HILL, WEST VIRGINIA 25901

This first envelope design instructs you in basic set-up procedures for horizontal- and vertical-feed printers. The envelope designs discussed later in this chapter refer to these set-up instructions.

Using a Horizontal-Feed Printer

The following instructions are for printers that feed horizontally, such as a dot matrix or inkjet printer, or even some laser printers.

1. Select **File**, **New**. Select New **Template**, **Use** Template: Normal. Select OK or press Enter.

2. From the Forma**t** menu, select **Document**. The Document dialog box appears.

3. In Page **W**idth, type **9.5"**. In Page **H**eight, type **4.12"**.

2. From the Forma**t** menu, select Page Set**u**p. The Page Setup dialog box appears.

3. Choose **S**ize and Orientation. In the Paper Size box, choose Custom. Change the **W**idth to **9.5"** and the **H**eight to **4.12"**.

4. Set the Top margin to .4" and the Left margin to .4". Select OK or press Enter.

5. Type the following, pressing Enter and Tab as indicated:

    HUMBLE OPINIONS (Enter)

    POST OFFICE BOX 174 (Enter)

    OAK HILL, WEST VIRGINIA 25901 (Enter eight times)

    (Tab)

6. Select the H in HUMBLE. On the Ribbon, change the size to 18 points; the typeface should be TmsRmn. Do the same to the O in OPINIONS.

7. Select UMBLE. On the Ribbon, change the size to 14 points; the typeface should be TmsRmn. Do the same for PINIONS.

CHAPTER 7

Producing Envelopes

8. Select the two address lines and make sure that they are 10-point TmsRmn.

9. Position the cursor on the last line. On the Ruler, set the tab as left aligned at 4.5".

10. Select **F**ile, Save **A**s. On your hard drive in directory C:\WINWORD, save the template as Envelop1. Word adds the extension DOT, which indicates that the file is a document template.

11. Select **F**ile, Print Preview.

    A message appears whenever you go to print preview or to print, stating that `Document Page size is different from printer page size....` Select OK or press Enter. Word Version 1.1 tells you that you are using a page size other than 8 1/2 inches x 11 inches; this feature will come in handy later when you go back to the normal document size but you forget to change paper size in Forma**t**, **D**ocument.

12. Be sure that your printer is set up for the envelope. Select **P**rint and OK or press Enter.

Using a Vertical-Feed Printer

Vertical feed works on the following types of printers. If your laser printer feeds envelopes from the left of the paper source, or if your printer vertical feeds to the left (align the left edge of the envelope with the zero mark on the printer's paper holder, use these instructions:

1. Select **F**ile, **N**ew. Select New **T**emplate, **U**se Template: Normal. Select OK or press Enter.

2. Select **F**ile, **P**rinter Setup. In **S**etup, change the Orientation to **L**andscape.

3. From the Forma**t** menu, select **D**ocument. A dialog box appears.

2. From the Forma**t** menu, select Page Set**u**p. Choose **S**ize and Orientation. Select **L**andscape.

3. Select **M**argins.

179

4. In the Margins box, set the **T**op margin to .40" and the **L**eft to .40". Select OK or press Enter.

5. Type the following:

    HUMBLE OPINIONS (Enter)

    POST OFFICE BOX 174 (Enter)

    OAK HILL, WEST VIRGINIA 25901 (Enter eight times)

    (Tab)

6. Select the H in HUMBLE. On the Ribbon, change the size to 18 points and typeface to TmsRmn. Do the same to the O in OPINIONS.

7. Select UMBLE. On the Ribbon, change the size to 14 points; and typeface to TmsRmn. Do the same for PINIONS.

8. Select the two address lines and make sure that they are 10-point TmsRmn.

9. Position the cursor on the very last line, the Tab. On the Ruler, set the tab as left aligned at 4".

10. Select **F**ile, Save **A**s. On your hard drive directory C:\WINWORD, save the template as Envelop1. Word adds the extension DOT, which indicates that the file is a document template.

11. Select **F**ile, Print Preview.

    Whenever you go to print preview or to print, a message tells you Document Page size is different from printer page size.... (Word is checking to be sure that you know the page orientation and size are different than normal). Select OK or press Enter.

12. Be sure that your printer is set up for the envelope. Choose **P**rint and OK.

Using a Vertical-Feed Laser Printer

If you have a laser printer with an envelope feed in the center of the paper source, you position the envelope differently. You print

CHAPTER 7

Producing Envelopes

toward the center of an 11-inch-by-8.5-inch landscape-oriented page, using an envelope instead of paper.

1. Select **File**, **New**. Select New **Template**, **U**se Template: Normal. Select OK or press Enter.

2. Select **File**, **Pr**inter Setup. In **S**etup, change the Orientation to **L**andscape.

3. From the Forma**t** menu, select **D**ocument. A dialog box appears.

2. In the Forma**t** menu, select Page Set**u**p, choose **S**ize and Orientation. Change the orientation to **L**andscape.

3. In the same dialog box, choose **M**argins.

4. In the Margins box, set the **T**op margin to **2.5**" and the **L**eft to **.5**". Select OK or press Enter.

5. Type the following text:

   HUMBLE OPINIONS (Enter)

   POST OFFICE BOX 174 (Enter)

   OAK HILL, WEST VIRGINIA 25901 (Enter eight times)

   (Tab)

6. Select the H in HUMBLE. On the Ribbon, change the size to 18 points and TmsRmn. Do the same to the O in OPINIONS.

7. Select UMBLE. On the Ribbon, change the size to 14 points and TmsRmn. Do the same for PINIONS.

8. Select the two address lines and make sure that they are 10-point TmsRmn.

9. Position the cursor on the last line, the Tab. On the Ruler, set the tab as left aligned at 4".

10. Select **F**ile, Save **A**s. On your hard drive directory C:\WINWORD, save the template as Envelop1. Word adds the extension DOT, which indicates that the file is a document template.

11. Select **F**ile, Print Preview. Whenever you go to print preview or to print in Version 1.1, a message appears telling you Document Page size is different from printer page

181

size... (Word is checking to be sure that you know the page orientation and size are not the norm). Select OK or press Enter.

12. Be sure that your printer is set up for the envelope. Choose **Print**. Select OK or press Enter.

Opening a Template

To open and use the template you created, select **File**, **New**. In the **Use Template** box, type **Envelop1**. (You can scroll through the template list.) Select OK or press Enter. After you type the delivery address, select **File**, **Save As**. A dialog box appears for you to save your document. Type the name of your document in the **File Name** box. Word will save it as a document, with a copy of your template attached. Your original template is still available for use with other documents.

Designing a Graphic and Type Envelope

Graphically speaking, you have many ways to add rules and boxes to an envelope. Word Version 2.0 offers even more options. You should keep your design simple. If you don't have a logo, you may want to add a rule above, below, or to the side of your return address. Figure 7.3 shows a simple design with a single vertical rule beside the return address. The type in the company name is expanded and uses large and small capitals. The entire address is in Helvetica, yet it's interesting. Figure 7.4 shows the same design with a rule above and below the return address.

FIG. 7.3.
A Vertical rule used to enhance the return address.

```
| HUMBLE OPINIONS
| P. O. Box 174  •  Oak Hill, WV 25901
```

CHAPTER 7

Producing Envelopes

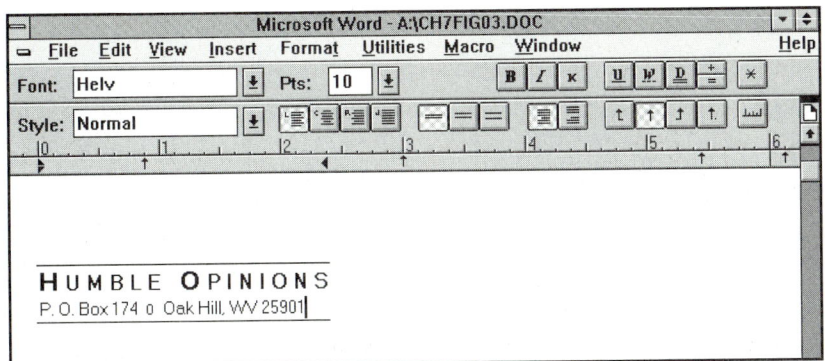

FIG. 7.4.
Rules above and below the return address (Word Version 1.1.)

1. Select **F**ile, **N**ew. Choose New **D**ocument and Use Template: Normal. Select OK or press Enter.

2. Set up the page, orientation, and margins for your printer as explained earlier in the chapter.

3. Type the following:

    HUMBLE OPINIONS (Enter)

    P. O. Box 174 (four spaces) Oak Hill, WV 25901

4. Select HUMBLE OPINIONS. On the Ribbon, change the font to Helv, 18-point, **B**old. It should be left aligned.

5. With the text still selected, select Forma**t**, **C**haracter. In the Character Spacing box, choose **E**xpanded, By: and type **3pt**. Deselect the type.

6. Select UMBLE and on the Ribbon, select the K button for Small **K**aps (Ctrl+K). Repeat with PINIONS.

6. Select UMBLE and choose Forma**t**, **C**haracter. Turn on **S**mall Caps, In the **P**oints box, change the size to 14. Select OK or press Enter. Repeat with PINIONS.

7. Select the address line. On the Ribbon, change the type to Helv. It should be left aligned. Deselect the text.

8. Position the cursor in the middle of the spaces between Box 174 and Oak Hill. Insert a bullet.

    Use the Macro assigned bullet key (Ctrl+8) you created in Chapter 5.

    Select **I**nsert, **S**ymbol. Select the bullet and OK or press Enter.

183

9. Select both lines of type. Choose For**mat**, **P**aragraph. The dialog box appears.

10. In the **B**order box, select Bar. In the Pat**t**ern box, select Double. Select OK or press Enter.

9. Select both lines of type and choose For**mat**, **B**order.

10. In the Bo**r**der box, click the left margin. Or, for the keyboard, press Alt+R, then press the down arrow until the left margin is highlighted. In the **L**ine box, choose a double rule.

11. Select **F**ile, Save **A**s. Type **envelop2** in the File **N**ame box.

12. Select Print Preview, **P**rint.

Creating an Innovative Envelope

Word enables you to make many changes to type. You can condense or expand the character spacing, increase and decrease the line and word spacing, and use attributes, such as bold, italics, and small capitals. You also can apply superscript (part of the type raised above the x-height) and subscript (part of the type hanging below the x-height) attributes to characters. The envelope design presented in this section uses the subscript effect. Although not suitable for many businesses, subscript provides an interesting effect. Figure 7.5 shows a return address design using a rule and subscript characters.

FIG. 7.5.
A return address design using subscript letters.

h$_{}$umble $_o$pinions
P. O. Box 174
Oak Hill, WV 25901

To create a return address that uses subscript characters, take the following steps:

1. Select **F**ile, **N**ew, New **D**ocument, Use Template: Normal. Select OK or press Enter.

CHAPTER 7

Producing Envelopes

2. Set up the page, orientation, and margins for your particular printer as explained earlier in the chapter.

3. Type the following:

   humble opinions (Enter)

   (Tab) P. O. Box 174 (Enter)

   (Tab) Oak Hill, WV 25901

4. Select humble opinions and choose Forma**t** menu, **C**haracter. The Character dialog box appears.

5. Change the type to 18-point bold Helv. In the Spacing box, choose **C**ondensed, **B**y: and type **1pt**. Select OK or press Enter. Check the Ribbon to make sure that the text is left aligned.

6. With the text still selected, choose Forma**t**, **P**aragraph. The Paragraph dialog box appears.

7. In the B**o**rder box, choose Above, Pat**t**ern, Thick, select OK or Enter. Deselect the text.

5. Change the type to 18-point bold Helv. In the Spacing box, choose **C**ondensed, **B**y: and type **1pt**. Select OK or press Enter. Check the Ribbon to make sure that the text is left aligned.

6. Select Forma**t**, **B**order. The Border dialog box appears.

7. In the B**o**rder box, select the margin above. In Line, choose the 1.25 rule. Select OK or press Enter. Deselect the text.

8. On the Ruler, set the right indent to 2".

9. Select the h. On the Ribbon, click the button with an equal sign to subscript the character. On the keyboard, press Ctrl+equal sign. Repeat this procedure with the o. Deselect the text.

9. Select the h and select Forma**t**, **C**haracter. In the Super/subscript box, choose Subscript. In the **B**y: box, type **3pt**. Select OK or press Enter. Repeat the procedure with the o. Deselect the text.

10. Position the cursor in the line P. O. Box 174. On the Ribbon, click the 1.5 space button.

185

10. Click the line P. O. Box 174. Select Forma**t**, **P**aragraph. In the Spacing box, choose **B**efore and scroll to .5. Select OK or press Enter.

11. Select the two address lines. Choose Forma**t**, **T**abs. In the dialog box, set the Tab Position to **.80**, **C**enter and select **S**et. Select OK or press Enter. You can set the tab position on the Ruler, too.

12. Select **F**ile, Save **A**s. Save this envelope design as envelop3.

13. Select **F**ile, Print Preview, and **P**rint.

Looking at Return Address Designs

In this section are some designs for the return address. Although you can produce some of these addresses with Word 1.1, these examples were created with Word 2.0. Some of the design effects may not be available in Version 1.1.

Figure 7.6 shows a graphic presentation of the text. *Humble opinions* was first created in CorelDRAW!, saved as a TIFF file, and then inserted into Word, Version 2.0. The address lines were typed into a frame (not available in Version 1.1). The frame was placed in the logo design. This design is an interesting variation of the normal return address.

FIG. 7.6.
An unconventional look to the return address.

Created in Word Version 1.1, figure 7.7 shows an attractive envelope design. The rules on both sides of the company name are centered in the line. To accomplish this effect, place a tab and a space before the company name, and a space and tab after it. Then, select the tabs and use Forma**t**, **C**haracter, **S**trikethrough to add the rules.

—— humble opinions ——
P. O. Box 174
Oak Hill, WV 25901

FIG. 7.7.
Use a strikethrough to create rules on both sides of the company's name.

Figure 7.8 shows a simple boxed design with centered type. The graphic box can be thick, double, or even shadowed. You also can box just the company name or the address. You can produce this design and many variations in either version of Word.

humble opinions
P. O. Box 174
Oak Hill, WV 25901

FIG. 7.8.
A simple boxed text.

Created in Word Version 2.0, figure 7.9 shows how you can use rules to follow the corner of the envelope for a distinguished effect. Version 2.0 enables you to choose a ruling line above text and a vertical rule for the same selected paragraph. Version 1.1 does not.

h u m b l e   o p i n i o n s
P. O. Box 174 • Oak Hill, WV 25901

FIG. 7.9.
Horizontal and vertical rules follow the lines of the envelope corner.

Figure 7.10 shows a return address with a background screen of 20 percent. Created in Version 2.0, this effect cannot be reproduced in Version 1.1. The screen could encompass the company name and the address lines, or just the two address lines.

HUMBLE OPINIONS
P. O. Box 174
Oak Hill, West Virginia 25901

FIG. 7.10.
A 20 percent screen applied to the company name.

PART II

Creating Business Documents

Recapping

In this chapter, you learned the importance of postal regulations and guidelines and how they can affect your designs. You also learned how to produce several different types of envelope designs and return address designs.

In the next chapter, you learn how to produce a resume.

Producing a Resume

The better your resume looks, the more likely your prospective employer will consider you for the job. Although it's important to show education, experience, and references on your resume, it's equally important to present the information in an attractive manner. A clear and concise summary of the relevant information presented in a professional-looking document will help impress your prospective employer.

You should print your resume on letterhead paper, and use paper with a watermark. For example, use a rag paper (Strathmore, for one), or a linen finish (Swan Linen), or a laid finish (Classic Laid). Also, because so many people use white and ivory paper, you might try blue or green paper to make your resume stand out in the stack. No matter what color paper you use, however, make sure that you also use black ink, which is the easiest to read. It isn't necessary to have your resume printed at a print shop. If you have a laser printer, you can run off your own resumes and save money in the process.

Restrict the length of your resume to one page. More than one page can be extra information that no one will read. You can limit your text by using bulleted lists of information instead of explaining in paragraph form. Just present the facts, and be precise in citing dates, places, and duties. Remember that white space is especially important in a resume. Prospective employers who read 40 to 100 resumes for one job opening, appreciate the short, to-the-point summary. You can always add a one-page cover letter explaining any information about you that is pertinent to a particular job.

PART II

Creating Business Documents

The information usually included on resumes has changed over the years. You no longer must put your age, sex, marital status, or even your health on a resume, although you can. You should, however, put education, experience, and references along with your name, address, and phone number. Career objectives or a brief statement about the job you seek are also important, although you may do this in your cover letter.

Under education, start with your most recent experience. List the name of the college or university, the town, and state. Then cite degrees, majors, and (if appropriate) a few pertinent classes. Be sure to include high school information, but leave out junior high or elementary school (unless this information is pertinent).

When accounting for job experience, be careful with dates, names, and places. Usually the dates are first in each listing. Then, list the name of the company, city, and state. You also can list duties performed.

Although you can include references on the resume, you also can state: "References submitted on request." If you do list names, include full names, company names, addresses, and phone numbers. Three references are usually sufficient.

This chapter presents designs for traditional, graphic, and innovative resumes. If you're a lawyer, or accountant, or engineer, you might want to stick with the traditional designs. However, if you're an artist, or a writer, or a salesman, you might try the innovative design as a more interesting approach. For example, an artist might design a resume with graphics or pen and ink drawings included. A writer might make his resume into a short story. And a salesman could do a sales pitch for himself. Creativity in today's job market, especially in the design of the resume itself, is a distinct advantage.

To save you from retyping each of the example resumes in this chapter, the steps for the first resume include directions for saving your unformatted type for use in the second and third designs. You also may want to type your own resume instead of using the example text.

CHAPTER 8

Producing a Resume

Designing a Traditional Resume

Resumes today enjoy many popular designs, all of which are variations of placing the type. The important point of the resume is that it is readable; if its design stands out in the crowd, then that's a bonus. Use lots of white space and a few bold heads for the best results. Figure 8.1 shows the first resume.

The following instructions guide you to create a traditional resume. Note that the text for this resume is the same as the next two.

1. Select **File**, **New**. Choose New **D**ocument, **U**se Template: Normal, and Select OK or press Enter.

2. To set the margins, select Forma**t**, **D**ocument. The Document dialog box appears.

2. To set the margins, select Forma**t**, Page Set**u**p. A dialog box appears.

3. In the margins box, type **1"** for **T**op, **B**ottom, **L**eft, and **R**ight.

4. On the Ribbon, set the point size to 12. The typeface should be Tms Rmn, left aligned.

5. Type the following text, pressing Enter as indicated:

   Bessie E. Berry (Enter)

   128 Smith Street (Enter)

   Beckley, West Virginia 25801 (Enter)

   (304) 252-1111 (Enter, three times)

   CAREER OBJECTIVE (Enter)

   Position typesetting with desktop publishing, graphic art design on the computer. (Enter, three times)

   EDUCATION (Enter)

   WV College of Graduate Studies, Beckley, WV (Enter)

   Graduate courses in education. (Enter, twice)

   Marshall University, Huntington, WV (Enter)

Bessie E. Berry
128 Smith Street
Beckley, West Virginia 25801
(304) 252-1111

CAREER OBJECTIVE

Position typesetting with desktop publishing, graphic art design on the computer.

EDUCATION

WV College of Graduate Studies, Beckley, WV
Graduate courses in education.

Marshall University, Huntington, WV
Graduate courses in pottery, art history.

Marshall University, Huntington, WV
BA in Art, English, graduated 1976

Huntington East High School, Huntington, WV
Graduated 1971

EXPERIENCE

5/91 - Present - Self-employed
Contract typesetting to various individuals and print shops in the area.

4/90 - 5/91 - BJJ Printing Company, Beckley, WV
Purchaser, proofreader, typesetter, graphic artist.

3/87 - 4/90 - BJJ Printing Company, Beckley, WV
Typesetter and graphic artist.

2/77 - 6/88 - Alcove Printing Company, Huntington, WV
Typesetter and graphic artist.

8/76 - 2/77 - Alcove Printing Company, Huntington, WV
Paste-up artist.

REFERENCES

Submitted upon request.

FIG. 8.1. A finished resume.

CHAPTER 8

Producing a Resume

Graduate courses in pottery, art history. (Enter, twice)

Marshall University, Huntington, WV (Enter)

BA Art, English, graduated 1976 (Enter, twice)

Huntington East High School, Huntington, WV (Enter)

Graduated 1971 (Enter, twice)

EXPERIENCE (Enter)

5/91 - Present - Self-employed (Enter)

Contract typesetting to various individuals and print shops in area. (Enter, twice)

4/90 - 5/91 - BJJ Printing Company, Beckley, WV (Enter)

Purchaser, proofreader, typesetter, graphic artist.(Enter, twice)

3/87 - 4/90 - BJJ Printing Company, Beckley, WV (Enter)

Typesetter and graphic artist. (Enter, twice)

2/77 - 6/88 - Alcove Printing Company, Huntington, WV (Enter)

Typesetter and graphic artist (Enter, twice)

8/76 - 2/77 - Alcove Printing Company, Huntington, WV (Enter)

Paste-up artist (Enter, twice).

REFERENCES (Enter)

Submitted on request (Enter)

6. You should spell-check your text.

7. Before formatting the type, select **File, Save As**. A dialog box appears. Type **resume** in the File **N**ame box. You use RESUME.DOC in later designs so that you don't have to type the information again.

8. Select **File, Save As** again and type **resume1**. RESUME1.DOC is the file you use in this example.

9. Select the first four lines of text (from *Bessie* to the phone number). On the Ruler, choose center alignment or press Ctrl+E in Version 2.0. Deselect the text.

9. Select the first four lines of text (from *Bessie* to the phone number). On the Ribbon, choose center alignment. Deselect the text.

10. Select the first line. On the Ribbon, change the point size to 14 and change the type to bold. Deselect the type.

11. Select CAREER OBJECTIVE and, on the Ribbon, click the **B**old button or press Ctrl+B. Do the same for EDUCATION, EXPERIENCE, and REFERENCES.

12. Position the cursor in the line beginning with Position typesetting....

13. Select Forma**t**, Define **S**tyles. Press Del. In the Define **S**tyle Name: box, type **Indent**.

14. Choose the **P**aragraph button. In the Indents box, From Le**f**t: type **1.5"**. Select OK and OK again or press Enter twice.

15. With the text still selected, on the Ruler, in the Style: box, choose Indent.

13. Select Forma**t**, **S**tyles. Press the Del key. In the **S**tyle Name: box, type **Indent**.

14. Select the **D**efine button, and then the **P**aragraph button. In the Indentations box, From **L**eft: type **1.5"**. Choose OK or press Enter. Select **A**dd, **A**pply, and Close.

15. On the Ribbon, in the style box, select Indent.

16. Select the text from WV College of Graduate Studies... to Graduated 1971. In the Style box, change the type to Indent. Repeat with the text under EXPERIENCE and under REFERENCES.

17. Select **F**ile, **S**ave.

18. Select **F**ile, Print Pre**v**iew. Choose **P**rint and Select OK or press Enter.

Creating a Graphic and Type Design

The second resume, shown in figure 8.2, is a more informal design, which works well when you need a less conventional

CHAPTER 8

Producing a Resume

resume. The rules and centered heads grab attention. The name is larger and more noticeable. The resume also uses plenty of white space. If you have a great deal of material to present in your resume, this design would not work well.

To create a graphic and type resume, take these steps:

1. Select **F**ile, **O**pen. In the File **N**ame box, type or click **RESUME.DOC**. Select OK or press Enter.

2. Select **F**ile, Save **A**s. Type **Resume2** and Select OK or press Enter.

3. Place a paragraph return (Enter) in front of *Bessie*. Select Bessie E. Berry. Press Shift+F3, F3 to change the name to all capital letters.

4. On the Ribbon, change the name to Helvetica, bold, 18-point and center.

5. Select Forma**t**, **P**aragraph. A dialog box appears.

6. In the Border box, choose B**o**rder, Above. In the Pa**t**tern box, choose Thick. Select OK or press Enter.

5. Select Forma**t**, **B**order.

6. In the Bo**r**der box, click the margin above. In the **L**ine box, choose the 2.25 rule. Select OK or press Enter.

7. Position the cursor at the end of the second line (after *Street*). Insert four spaces, and then press Del to move the city and state up onto the same line.

8. Insert a bullet in the middle of the four spaces.

   Use the Macro key created in Chapter 5 (Ctrl+8).

8. Select **I**nsert, **S**ymbol. A dialog box appears. Select the bullet and OK or press Enter.

9. Select the address line and the phone number, and use the Ruler to center them.

9. Select the address line and the phone number, and use the Ribbon to center them.

10. Add a paragraph return (Enter) after the phone number.

BESSIE E. BERRY

128 Smith Street • Beckley, West Virginia 25801
(304) 252-1111

CAREER OBJECTIVE

Position typesetting with desktop publishing, graphic art design on the computer.

EDUCATION

WV College of Graduate Studies, Beckley, WV
Graduate courses in education.

Marshall University, Huntington, WV
Graduate courses in pottery, art history.

Marshall University, Huntington, WV
BA in Art, English, graduated 1976

Huntington East High School, Huntington, WV
Graduated 1971

EXPERIENCE

5/91 - Present - **Self-employed**
Contract typesetting to various print shops in area.

4/90 - 5/91 - **BJJ Printing Company**, Beckley, WV
Purchaser, proofreader
Duties: purchased paper, bindery supplies; scheduled jobs; checked plates and proofread; typesetting and graphic arts.

3/87 - 4/90 - **BJJ Printing Company**, Beckley, WV
Typesetter and graphic artist.

2/77 - 6/88 - **Alcove Printing Company**, Huntington, WV
Typesetter and graphic artist.

8/76 - 2/77 - **Alcove Printing Company**, Huntington, WV
Paste-up artist.

REFERENCES

Submitted upon request.

FIG. 8.2. *The second resume design incorporates centered type and graphic rules.*

CHAPTER 8

Producing a Resume

11. With cursor positioned on the paragraph return, select Form**at**, **P**aragraph. A dialog box appears.

12. In the **B**o**r**der box, choose Below; and in the Patt**er**n box, select Thick. Select OK or press Enter.

11. With cursor positioned on the paragraph return, select Form**at**, **B**order. A dialog box appears.

12. In the Bo**r**der box, click the bottom margin. Choose the 2.25 rule in **L**ine.

13. Select CAREER OBJECTIVE. On the Ribbon, change the font to Helvetica, 14-point, bold, and centered. Repeat this procedure for EDUCATION, EXPERIENCE, and REFERENCES.

14. Select WV College of Graduate Studies and use the Ribbon to make it bold. Repeat this process with each college and high school name. Use the same procedure for Self-employed and each company name in the EXPERIENCE section.

15. Position cursor in the line Graduate courses in education.

16. Select Form**at**, **S**tyles. Press Del. In the **S**tyle Name box, type **Indent**. Select the **D**efine button.

17. Indent should appear in the Define **S**tyle Name: box. Choose the **P**aragraph button or press Alt+P. In the Indents box, From Le**f**t: type **1"**. Select OK twice or press Enter twice.

18. In the Style box on the Ruler, choose Indent. Apply this style to the rest of the text that is indented (the second, third, and fourth lines).

16. Select Form**at**, **S**tyle. A dialog box appears with the cursor in the **S**tyle Name box. Press Del. In the **S**tyle Name box, type **Indent**. Select the **D**efine button.

17. Select the **P**aragraph button. In the Indentation box, From Left: type **1"**. Select OK and click Apply, or press Enter and Alt+A.

18. In the Style box on the Ribbon, choose Indent. Apply this style to the rest of the text that is indented (see fig. 8.2 for the lines that indent).

19. Select the last line, Submitted on request. Center-align it. Place two paragraph returns (Enter) after the text.

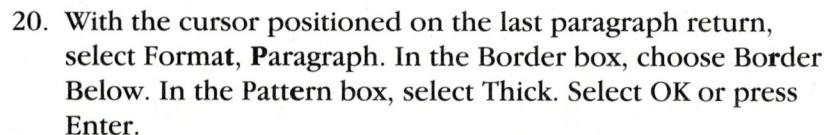

Creating Business Documents

20. With the cursor positioned on the last paragraph return, select Forma**t**, **P**aragraph. In the Border box, choose Bo**r**der: Below. In the Pat**t**ern box, select Thick. Select OK or press Enter.

20. With the cursor positioned on the last paragraph return, select Forma**t**, **B**order. In the Bo**r**der box, click the bottom margin. In the **L**ine box, choose the 2.25 rule. Select OK or press Enter.

21. Select **F**ile, **S**ave.

22. Select **F**ile, Print Preview. Select **P**rint and choose OK.

Creating an Innovative Resume

You have available many creative alternatives to the conventional resume. The resume presented in this section may give you some ideas for your own design. Changing the page orientation and adding boxes makes this design eye-catching. The size and double-sided printing also make it unique (see figs. 8.3 and 8.4).

The artwork (logo) was created by using Microsoft Draw in Word Version 2.0. If you use Word Version 1.1, you can create a resume like the one show in figure 8.5 by applying superscript to one letter, subscript to one letter, and condensing the type. You can also insert a graphic in place of the drawing.

To get you started on creating your own innovative design, take the following steps:

1. Select **F**ile, **O**pen. You can open and use the original RESUME.DOC because this is the last design in this chapter.

2. Select Forma**t**, **D**ocument. Set all margins at 1". Select OK or press Enter.

3. Select **F**ile, **P**rinter Setup. Choose the **S**etup button. In the Orientation box, change to Landscape. Select OK twice or press Enter twice. Word may display the message, `Change current document size to`.... Select **Y**es by clicking on Yes or typing **Y**.

CHAPTER 8

Producing a Resume

FIG. 8.3.
The cover of the resume. The folded size is 5 1/2 inches by 8 1/2 inches.

2. Select **F**ormat, Page Set**u**p. Set all **M**argins to **1**".
3. Select **S**ize and Orientation. Set Orientation to **L**andscape. Select OK or press Enter.

PART II

Creating Business Documents

B. E. Berry 128 Smith Street • Beckley, West Virginia 25801 • (304) 252-1111

Career Objective

Position typesetting with desktop publishing, graphic art design on the computer.

Education

WV College of Graduate Studies
Beckley, WV
Graduate courses in education.

Marshall University
Huntington, WV
Graduate courses in pottery, art history.

Marshall University
Huntington, WV
BA in Art, English, graduated 1976.

Huntington East High School
Huntington, WV
Graduated 1971

References

Submitted upon request.

Employment Experience

5/91 - Present - **Self-Employed**
Contract typesetting to various individuals and print shops in area.

4/90 - 5/91 - **BJJ Printing Company**
Beckley, WV
Purchaser, proofreader, typesetter, graphic artist.

3/87 - 4/90 - **BJJ Printing Company**
Beckley, WV
Typesetter and graphic artist.

2/77 - 6/88 - **Alcove Printing Company**
Huntington , WV
Typesetter and graphic artist.

8/76 - 2/77 - **Alcove Printing Company**
Huntington, WV
Paste-up artist.

FIG. 8.4. *The inside of the resume, using landscape orientation.*

BB   **B. E. BERRY**   128 Smith Street   Beckley, West Virginia 25801   (304) 252-1111

FIG. 8.5. *The BB logo created in Word Version 1.1.*

4. Position the cursor at top left corner of page. Place one paragraph return (Enter) in front of B. E. Berry. Move to the end of the phone number and enter three paragraph returns.

5. Select the first six lines (from the first extra return to the return below the phone number).

CHAPTER 8

Producing a Resume

6. Select Forma**t**, **P**aragraph. In the **B**order box, choose **B**ox. In Patt**e**rn box, choose Thick. Select OK or press Enter.

6. Select Forma**t**, **B**order. In the Preset box, choose Box. In the **L**ine box, choose the 2.25 rule.

7. Select B. E. Berry and use the Ribbon to change it to Helvetica, 24-point, bold. Deselect the text.

8. Position the cursor at the end of Berry. Add five spaces and press Del. At the end of Street, add three spaces. Insert a bullet, add three more spaces, and press Del. Repeat this procedure for the phone number.

   Insert the bullet by pressing Ctrl+8 (the bullet key you created in Chapter 5).

   Insert the bullet by pressing Alt+I,S, then by using the down and right arrows to select the bullet. Press Enter.

9. To add the graphic, you can insert a picture or format the type. To format the *BB*, position the cursor at the beginning of the name and address line. Type **BB** and insert five spaces. Select the BB, change the point size to 48 (or as large as your printer can accommodate) and make it bold. Select Forma**t**, **C**haracter, Character Spacing. Set **C**ondensed, By: to **1.5pt**. Select OK or press Enter. Deselect the type. Select the first B only. On the Ribbon, select superscript (the plus button). Select the second B and change it to subscript (the equal sign button). Deselect the type.

9. Double-click the Microsoft Draw button. When the screen appears, draw the BB or any object you want. When finished drawing, select the objects and select **E**dit, **C**ut. Choose **F**ile and return to the document. Position the cursor in front of *B. E. Berry*, and press Shift+Ins to paste. You may have to size the graphic.

10. Position the cursor in front of the C in Career.

11. Select **I**nsert, **B**reak. In the Section Break box, choose **C**ontinuous and Select OK or press Enter.

12. Select Forma**t**, **S**ection. In Column **N**umber, type **2**. In **S**pacing, type **2"**. Select OK or press Enter.

12. Select Forma**t**, **C**olumns. In **N**umber of Columns, type **2**. In **S**pace Between, type **2"**. Select OK or press Enter.

201

PART II

Creating Business Documents

13. Select Career Objectives. In the Ribbon, change the type to Helv, 14-point, bold.

14. With Career Objectives still selected, Select Forma**t**, **S**tyle(s). Press Delete. In the **S**tyle Name: box, type **Head**.

15. Click the **D**efine button, and choose **P**aragraph. In the Spacing box, **A**fter, type **.5li**. Select OK or press Enter and select Apply. The message Define Style *Head* based on selection? may appear. Select **Y**es or type **Y**.

16. Select Education, Employment Experience, and References. Change each to Head in the Style box.

17. Position the cursor in the first paragraph (Position typesetting with desktop...). Select Forma**t**, **S**tyle(s). Delete the contents of the **S**tyle Name: box and type **Body text**.

18. Select the **D**efine button. In **C**haracter, change the type to 10 points. Select OK or press Enter. In **P**aragraph, Indent From Left **.35"**. Select OK twice or press Enter, and Apply.

19. Select the rest of the text and change to Body text by selecting Body in the Style box.

20. Make each college, university, and high school name bold. Make Self-employed and the name of each printing company bold.

21. Select References and Submitted on request. Press Shift+Del to cut the text. Position the cursor at end of the Education list. Press Shift+Ins to paste the text. This procedure should move Employment Experience to the top of the next column. Be sure that the column tops are even (you may have to delete a paragraph return).

22. Place the cursor at the bottom of the second column and insert a page break by pressing Ctrl+Enter.

23. On the next page, the section formatting for two columns is still in effect. To format the page, you need to be in the column on the right. To move the cursor, press Enter twice.

24. Select Insert, **B**reak. Choose **C**olumn Break. Select OK or press Enter.

25. With the cursor in the right column, use the Ruler to center-align the column.

CHAPTER 8

Producing a Resume

25. With the cursor in the right column, use the Ribbon to center-align the column.

26. Select Forma**t**, **P**aragraph. In the B**o**rder box, choose Box; in the Pa**t**tern box, choose Thick. Select OK or press Enter.

27. For Indents, set the **L**eft indent to **0**.

26. Select Forma**t**, **B**order. In Preset, choose **B**ox. In **L**ine, choose the 2.25 point rule.

27. Select Forma**t**, **P**aragraph. In the Indentations box, change the **L**eft indent to **0**.

28. Type the following, pressing Enter as indicated:

    (Enter, three times) **RESUME** (Enter)

    OF (Enter)

    BESSIE (Enter)

    BERRY (Enter)

29. Select the four lines of text. In the font box, select Helv. Deselect the text.

30. Select RESUME and make it 18-point, bold. Select OF and make it 14-point, bold. Select BESSIE BERRY and make it 48-point bold.

31. Place the cursor at end of BERRY. Press Enter twice. Select the logo on page 2. Select **E**dit, **C**opy. go to page 1 and **P**aste the logo.

32. Press Enter enough times to make the box even with the bottom margin.

33. Select **F**ile, **S**ave.

34. Select **F**ile, Print Pre**v**iew, and **P**rint.

Looking at Design

Resumes should be one page in length, but no more than two. However, some can be very long or very short. If yours is short, use that brevity to your advantage. The white space can make your resume stand out in the crowd. Figure 8.6 shows a short resume. The vertical rule and left-aligned heads balance the large right margin. Indentations help to fill out the space as well.

203

B. E. Berry
128 Smith Street
Beckley, West Virginia 25801
(304) 252-1111

Career Objective
    Position typesetting with desktop publishing, graphic arts.

Education
    WV College of Graduate Studies, Beckley, WV
        Graduate courses in education.

    Marshall University, Huntington, WV
        Graduate courses in pottery, art history.

    Marshall University, Huntington, WV
        BA Art, English, graduated 1976

    Huntington East High School, Huntington, WV
        Graduated 1971

Employment Experience
    5/91 - Present - Self-Employed
        Contract typesetting to print shops in area.

    4/90 - 5/91 - CPP Printing Company, Beckley, WV
        Purchaser, proofreader
        Duties: purchased paper, bindery supplies;
        checked plates and proofread;
        typesetting and graphic arts.

    3/87 - 4/90 - CPP Printing Company, Beckley, WV
        Typesetter and graphic artist.

    2/77 - 6/88 - Alcove Printing Company, Huntington , WV
        Typesetter and graphic artist.

    8/76 - 2/77 - Alcove Printing Company, Huntington, WV
        Paste-up artist.

References
    Submitted upon request.

FIG. 8.6.   A design for a short resume.

If your resume is long, try to pare it down to one page. You can do so in many ways: using justified type with hyphenation, using one address line instead of three, using a smaller point size for the text, and using less space between paragraphs. Figure 8.7 shows a long resume. All the text makes the page more gray than the short resume; however, enough white space is included to enable the reader's eyes to rest.

Recapping

In this chapter, you learned that the ideal resume is one page long and that it can include a cover page. You also learned how to design various resumes, from the traditional to the innovative.

In the next chapter, you learn how to produce a program.

B. E. BERRY

128 Smith Street • Beckley, West Virginia 25801 • (304) 252-1111

CAREER OBJECTIVE
Supervisory position of typesetting, paste-up, and camera departments; production scheduling, purchasing, proofreading; typesetting and graphic arts.

EDUCATION
West Virginia University, Morgantown, WV. MA English, 1980
WV Institute of Technology, Montgomery, WV. BA Printing, 1982
WV College of Graduate Studies, Beckley, WV. Graduate courses in education.
Marshall University, Huntington, WV. Graduate courses in pottery, art history.
Marshall University, Huntington, WV. BA. Art, English, graduated 1976
Huntington East High School, Huntington, WV. Graduated 1971

EMPLOYMENT EXPERIENCE
5/91 - Present - **Self-employed**
Contract typesetting to various individuals and print shops in area. Contract software instruction including word processing, desktop publishing, databases, and spreadsheets. Presenting seminars on Planning and Purchasing Printing; Software Needs; Desktop Publishing.

4/84 - 5/91 - **CPP Printing Company**, Beckley, WV
Purchaser, production manager, scheduler, supervisor typesetting and paste-up, proofreader. Duties included paper and stockroom ordering, bindery supplies, scheduling jobs throughout entire shop, customer needs, sales, plate-checking, proofreading, designing books and magazines for customers.

3/82 - 4/84 - **CPP Printing Company**, Beckley, WV
Typesetter, paste-up, graphic artist, proofreader, purchaser. Duties included typesetting; page layout; designing logos, art work for customers; design and layout of company materials; proofreading; purchasing toner, paper, film, plates, etc., for camera, typesetting, and paste-up departments.

2/78- 3/82 - **Davis Printing**, Morgantown, WV
Typesetter and graphic artist; purchaser. Duties included typesetting, page layout and design, logo design, and purchasing paper, ink and bindery supplies.

8/76 - 2/77 - **Alcove Printing Company**, Huntington, WV
Typesetter, paste-up artist. Duties included page make-up and design, paste-up, and purchasing typesetting and paste-up supplies.

REFERENCES
Submitted upon request.

FIG. 8.7. *A sample of a long resume.*

Producing a Program

Businesses use printed programs for many purposes: conventions, seminars, classes, entertainment, and even golf tournaments. Programs come in all shapes and sizes, printed on one side or two, and with and without graphics or art work. There are no rules for producing a program.

Common program sizes are 8 1/2 inches by 11 inches and 5 1/2 inches by 8 1/2 inches. An 8 1/2-inch by-11-inch program, printed on one side of the paper or both, affords you more page width if you have much text. A 5 1/2-inch by-8-1/2-inch program is usually created by printing on an 8 1/2-inch by-11-inch piece of paper, and then folding it in half. This format provides four pages per sheet of paper. If you have many times, activities, and names to list, this design may be the one you choose. This chapter shows you samples of both common sizes, with instructions on how to reproduce them.

The purpose of a program is to inform. Times, dates, speakers, and activities are all listed in a program. When designing a program, remember that the spectators are already in attendance. Don't waste valuable space persuading them to attend. Instead, concentrate on the information they need once they arrive. The events, times, and places are important. You might include some descriptions of activities as well.

All the program designs in this chapter are appropriate for conventions, seminars, classes, any business event, or personal presentations. You get the necessary keystrokes for three of the designs; the three additional concepts at the end of the chapter are provided to give you ideas for your own programs.

PART II

Creating Business Documents

The designs include many details of typesetting, such as right-aligned tabs, extra line spacing beneath heads, using single quotation marks, and slight indentations. The designs use only one or two typefaces, three to five type sizes, and few styles. Details such as these make a piece look professional.

Creating a Basic Program

The first program design is a basic, two-column, 8 1/2-by-11-inch program (see fig. 9.1). Notice that the times are right-aligned. Traditionally, typesetters align numbers (whether times, outline numbers, or figures) by using a right tab for ease in reading. Because the text following the times is left-aligned, the information is easy to read. Word makes dividing your page into columns easy with Section formatting.

To create a basic, one-page program, perform these steps:

1. Select **F**ile, **N**ew, New **D**ocument. Choose **U**se Template: Normal. Select OK or press Enter.

2. Select Forma**t**, **P**aragraph. The Paragraph dialog box appears.

2. Select Forma**t**, Page Set**u**p. The Page dialog box appears.

3. Set all margins to **.75"**. Select OK or press Enter.

4. Type the following, entering spaces and pressing Enter and Tab as indicated:

   Desktop Publishers Convention (Enter)

   and Trade Show (Enter, three times)

   PROGRAM (Enter, Enter)

   THURSDAY, JUNE 11 (Enter)

   10:00 a.m. - 4:00 p.m. (Enter)

   Trade Show in Progress (three spaces) **Room 117** (Enter, Enter)

   (Tab) 9:00 a.m. (Tab) **Continental Breakfast** (Tab) **Room 212** (Enter, Enter)

   (Tab) 9:30 a.m. (Tab) **Welcoming Address** (Tab) **Room 214** (Enter)

208

Desktop Publishers' Convention and Trade Show

PROGRAM

THURSDAY, JUNE 11
10:00 a.m. - 4:00 p.m.
Trade Show in Progress   Room 117

9:00 a.m.	Continental Breakfast	Room 212
9:30 a.m.	Welcoming Address Speaker: Jeff Barrett, DT Pub	Room 214
10:00 a.m.	Personal Computers Speaker: Jane Wilson, T & L	Room 215
11:00 a.m.	Round Table Discussion The PC in Business Speakers: David Conners, T & L Sara Franks, Litcom Publishing Tom Patten, Satern Inc.	Room 216
12:00 noon	Lunch Break	
1:00 p.m.	Software Packages Speaker: Jeff Barrett, DT Pub	Room 223
2:00 p.m.	Round Table Discussion Today's Market - Software Speakers: Wyatt Franklin, L & M Cheryl Thomas, Level Best, Inc. Debra Dickerson, Ware Experts	Room 216
3:00 p.m.	Demonstrations PC's and Software Packages	Room 223

FRIDAY, JUNE 12
10:00 a.m. - 4:00 p.m.
Trade Show in progress   Room 117

9:00 a.m.	Continental Breakfast	Room 211
10:00 a.m.	Dot Matrix Printers Speaker: Jim Sanders, LTOP	Room 212
11:00 a.m.	Ink Jet Printers Speaker: Geneva L. Johnson, J Assoc.	Room 213
12:00 noon	Lunch Break	
1:00 p.m.	Laser Printers Speaker: C. P. Odell, Plum Corp.	Room 244
2:00 p.m.	High Resolution Output Speaker: C. P. Odell, Plum Corp.	Room 233
3:00 p.m.	Demonstrations	Room 333

SATURDAY, JUNE 13
10:00 a.m. - 12:00 noon
Trade Show in progress   Room 117

10:00 a.m.	Service Bureaus Speaker: Jeff Barrett, DT Pub	Room 212
11:00 a.m.	Planning Printing Speaker: Sue Plumley, HO	Room 212

WHITE HAVEN INN AND RESORTS
JUNE 11 - 13, 1992

FIG. 9.1.   A simple program design.

PART II

Creating Business Documents

(Tab, Tab) **Speaker: Jeff Barrett, DT Pub** (Enter, Enter)

(Tab) **10:00 a.m.** (Tab) **Personal Computers** (Tab) **Room 215** (Enter)

(Tab, Tab) **Speaker: Jane Wilson, T & L** (Enter, Enter)

(Tab) **11:00 a.m.** (Tab) **Round Table Discussion** (Tab) **Room 216** (Enter)

(Tab, Tab) **The PC in Business** (Enter)

(Tab, Tab) **Speakers: David Conners, T & L** (Enter)

(Tab, Tab) **Sara Franks, Litcom Publishing** (Enter)

(Tab, Tab) **Tom Patten, Satern, Inc.** (Enter, Enter)

(Tab) **12:00 noon** (Tab) **Lunch Break** (Enter, twice)

(Tab) **1:00 p.m.** (Tab) **Software Packages** (Tab) **Room 216** (Enter)

(Tab, Tab) **Speaker: Jeff Barrett, DT Pub** (Enter, Enter)

(Tab) **2:00 p.m.** (Tab) **Round Table Discussion** (Tab) **Room 216** (Enter)

(Tab, Tab) **Today's Market - Software** (Enter)

(Tab, Tab) **Speakers: Wyatt Franklin, L & M** (Enter)

(Tab, Tab) **Cheryl Thomas, Level Best, Inc.** (Enter)

(Tab, Tab) **Debra Dickerson, Ware Experts** (Enter, Enter)

(Tab) **3:00 p.m.** (Tab) **Demonstrations** (Tab) **Room 223** (Enter)

(Tab, Tab) **PC's and Software Packages** (Enter, Enter)

CHAPTER 9

Producing a Program

FRIDAY, JUNE 12 (Enter)

10:00 a.m. - 4:00 p.m. (Enter)

Trade Show in progress (three spaces) **Room 117** (Enter, Enter)

(Tab) **9:00 a.m.** (Tab) **Continental Breakfast** (Tab) **Room 211** (Enter, Enter)

(Tab) **10:00 a.m.** (Tab) **Dot-matrix Printers** (Tab) **Room 212** (Enter)

(Tab, Tab) **Speaker: Jim Sanders, LTOP** (Enter, Enter)

(Tab) **11:00 a.m.** (Tab) **Inkjet Printers** (Tab) **Room 213** (Enter)

(Tab, Tab) **Speaker: Geneva L. Johnson, J Assoc.** (Enter, Enter)

(Tab) **12:00 noon** (Tab) **Lunch Break** (Enter, Enter)

(Tab) **1:00 p.m.** (Tab) **Laser Printers** (Tab) **Room 244** (Enter)

(Tab, Tab) **Speaker: C. P. Odell, Plum Corp.** (Enter, Enter)

(Tab) **2:00 p.m.** (Tab) **High Resolution Output** (Tab) **Room 233** (Enter)

(Tab, Tab) **Speaker: C. P. Odell, Plum Corp.** (Enter, Enter)

(Tab) **3:00 p.m.** (Tab) **Demonstrations** (Tab) **Room 333** (Enter, Enter)

SATURDAY, JUNE 13 (Enter)

10:00 a.m. - 12:00 noon (Enter)

Trade Show in progress (three spaces) **Room 117** (Enter, Enter)

(Tab) **10:00 a.m.** (Tab) **Service Bureaus** (Tab) **Room 212** (Enter)

(Tab, Tab) **Speaker: Jeff Barrett, DT Pub** (Enter, Enter)

PART II

Creating Business Documents

(Tab) **11:00 a.m.** (Tab) **Planning Printing** (Tab) **Room 212** (Enter)

(Tab, Tab) **Speaker: Sue Plumley, HO** (Enter, four times)

WHITE HAVEN INN AND RESORTS (Enter, Enter)

JUNE 11 - 13, 1992

5. Position the cursor at the beginning of the page. Select **U**tilities, **S**pelling. Select OK or press Enter.

5. Position the cursor at the beginning of the page. Select **T**ools, **S**pelling. Select OK or press Enter.

6. Select **F**ile, Save **A**s and save this document as PROGRAM. Select **F**ile, Save **A**s. Save the document again, this time as PROGRAM1.

7. Select the first two lines of text (Desktop Publishers' Convention and Trade Show). Use the Ribbon to make the text 24 points, bold, and center-aligned.

8. Place the cursor to the right of the s in Publishers. To add the single quotation mark, select **F**ile, **O**pen. Select C:\WINWORD. In the list of files, select KEYCAPS.DOC. Choose the single closed quotation mark. With the keyboard, press Alt+F,O; select the KEYCAPS.DOC and use the arrows to select the quotation mark.

KEYCAPS.DOC is a collection of symbols that you can copy to the clipboard. The first screen that appears shows two keyboard templates with symbols that you can select. To find the quotation mark, scroll down to the next screen. To select an item, double-click it or use the arrows and press Enter.

9. Select **F**ile, **C**lose KEYCAPS.DOC. With the cursor positioned at the end of Publishers, press Shift+Ins to place the quotation mark.

10. Select the quotation mark. On the Ribbon, change the font to 24 points, bold.

11. Select PROGRAM. On the Ribbon, change the size to 18 points, bold, and center-aligned.

12. Position the cursor on the next line (the line with only a paragraph return). Select **I**nsert, **B**reak. In Section Break,

CHAPTER 9

Producing a Program

choose Continuous. Select OK or press Enter. Make sure that you're in Page View.

13. Select Forma**t**, **S**ection. The Section dialog box appears. In the Columns box, **N**umber, type **2**. In **S**pacing, type **.5**". In **S**ection Start: choose No Break. Select OK or press Enter.

13. Select Forma**t**, **C**olumns. The Columns dialog box appears. In **N**umber of Columns, type **2**. In Space Between, type **.5**". In **A**pply To, choose This Point Forward. Select OK or press Enter.

14. Position the cursor on the paragraph return above the line FRIDAY, JUNE 12. Select **I**nsert, **B**reak. A dialog box appears. Insert a **C**olumn Break. Select OK or press Enter.

15. Select the heading in the first column (from THURSDAY to Room 117). On the Ruler, center-align these three lines. Repeat for the FRIDAY and SATURDAY headings.

15. Select the heading in the first column (from THURSDAY to Room 117). On the Ribbon, center-align these three lines. Repeat for the FRIDAY and SATURDAY headings.

16. Select THURSDAY, JUNE 11. On the Ribbon, change the size to 14 points, bold. Repeat with FRIDAY, JUNE 12 and SATURDAY, JUNE 13.

17. Position the cursor in the line, 9:00 a.m. Continental Breakfast. Select Forma**t**, **S**tyle(s). Delete the contents of the **S**tyle Name box and type **Program**.

18. Click **D**efine, **T**abs. In the **T**ab Position box, type **.60**. Choose **R**ight align and **S**et. Press the Del key and type **.75**. Select **L**eft aligned and **S**et. Press Del and type **2.20**. Select **L**eft aligned and **S**et.

19. Select OK twice or press Enter twice.

19. Select OK and Apply or press Enter and Apply.

20. Select all the text in the first column. In the Style box, change the text to Program. In the second column, select all the text except the centered heads. Change the text to Program in the Style box.

21. At the end of the second column, place the cursor at the end of the text. Select **I**nsert, **B**reak. A dialog box appears. In Section Break, choose Con**t**inuous. Select OK or press Enter.

213

PART II

Creating Business Documents

22. Select Forma**t**, **S**ection. The Section dialog box appears. In the Column **N**umber box, type **1**. Select OK or press Enter.

22. Select Forma**t**, **C**olumns. The Columns box appears. In the **N**umber of columns, type **1**. Select OK or press Enter.

23. Select the last two lines of text, WHITE HAVEN INN AND RESORTS JUNE 11 - 13, 1992. Make the text bold and center-aligned. Deselect the text.

24. Select WHITE HAVEN INN AND RESORTS and change the size to 18 points. Deselect.

25. Select JUNE 11 - 13, 1992 and change the size to 14 points.

26. Select **F**ile, **S**ave.

27. Select **F**ile, **P**rint Preview, and **P**rint.

28. If you plan to continue with the next design, select the single quotation mark (which you copied from KEYCAPS.DOC) and copy it. When you open and save the next document, you can use the Paste command to insert the quotation mark instead of opening KEYCAPS.DOC again.

Producing a Type and Graphic Design

The next program is in a traditional format, using an 11-inch by-8 1/2-inch page (landscape orientation), printed on both sides and folded in half. The horizontal rules reinforce the page design. You should make sure that the rules line up when you print the program (see the next section on printer tips).

The tabs make the columns of times, activities, and room numbers neat and easy to read. One advantage of this format is more room for text in a list form. The front cover contains a clip art graphic, and the back cover lists exhibitors. Figure 9.2 shows the outside front and back covers of the program; figure 9.3 shows the two inside pages.

To create a four-page, folded program, take the following steps:

1. Select **F**ile, **O**pen. Open PROGRAM.DOC. Select Save **A**s and type **program2**.

CHAPTER 9

Producing a Program

TRADE SHOW EXHIBITS AND DEMONSTRATIONS
10:00 a.m. to 4:00 p.m.

TRADE SHOW EXHIBITORS

DT Publishers

T & L, Ltd.

Satern, Inc.

Litcom Publishing

Humble Opinions

L & M

Ware Experts

J Associates

Plum Corporation

White Haven Inn and Resorts
June 11 - 13, 1992

Desktop Publishers' Convention and Trade Show

PROGRAM

White Haven Inn, Washington, DC
June 11 - 13, 1992

FIG. 9.2. *Front and back covers of a program set up in landscape orientation.*

2. Select **F**ile, **P**rinter Setup, **S**etup. A dialog box appears. Change the orientation to Landscape. Select OK twice or press Enter twice. Word may ask, `Change current doc size`. Select **Y**es by clicking **Y**es or pressing **Y**.

3. Select Forma**t**, **D**ocument. Check all margins to make sure that they are .75". Select OK or press Enter.

2. Select Forma**t**, Page Set**u**p. The Page Setup dialog box appears. In **S**ize and Orientation, change the Orientation to **L**andscape.

3. In the same dialog box, **M**argins, check to make sure that all margins are **.75"**.

215

PART II

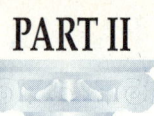

Creating Business Documents

Thursday, June 11			Friday, June 12		
10:00 a.m. - 4:00 p.m.	Trade Show in progress	Room 117	10:00 a.m. - 4:00 p.m.	Trade Show in progress	Room 117
9:00 a.m.	Continental Breakfast	Room 212	9:00 a.m.	Continental Breakfast	Room 211
9:30 a.m.	Welcoming Address Speaker: Jeff Barrett, DT Pub	Room 214	10:00 a.m.	Dot Matrix Printers Speaker: Jim Sanders, LTOP	Room 212
10:00 a.m.	Personal Computers Speaker: Jane Wilson, T & L	Room 215	11:00 a.m.	Inkjet Printers Speaker: Geneva L. Johnson, J Assoc.	Room 213
11:00 a.m.	Round-Table Discussion The PC in Business Speakers: David Conners, T & L Sara Franks, Litcom Publishing Tim Patten, Satern Inc.	Room 216	12:00 noon	Lunch Break	
			1:00 p.m.	Laser Printers Speaker: C. P. Odell, Plum Corp.	Room 244
12:00 noon	Lunch Break		2:00 p.m.	High-Resolution Output Speaker: C. P. Odell, Plum Corp.	Room 233
1:00 p.m.	Software Packages Speaker: Jeff Barrett, DT Pub	Room 223	3:00 p.m.	Demonstrations	Room 333
			Saturday, June 13		
2:00 p.m.	Round-Table Discussion Today's Market - Software Speakers: Wyatt Franklin, L & M Cheryl Thomas, Level Best, Inc. Debra Dickerson, Ware Experts	Room 216	10:00 a.m. - 4:00 p.m.	Trade Show in progress	Room 117
			10:00 a.m.	Service Bureaus Speaker: Jeff Barrett, DT Pub	Room 212
3:00 p.m.	Demonstrations PCs and Software Packages	Room 223	11:00 a.m.	Planning and Purchasing Printing Speaker: Sue Plumley, HO	Room 244

FIG. 9.3. The inside two pages of the program.

4. Position the cursor in front of the words `Desktop Publishers` and press Enter. Move up one line and press Enter five times. Type the following, pressing Enter as indicated:

> **TRADE SHOW EXHIBITS AND** (Enter)
>
> **DEMONSTRATIONS** (Enter)
>
> **10:00 a.m. to 4:00 p.m.** (Enter, four times)
>
> **TRADE SHOW EXHIBITORS** (Enter, Enter)
>
> **DT Publishers** (Enter, Enter)
>
> **T & L, Ltd.** (Enter, Enter)
>
> **Satern, Inc.** (Enter, Enter)

216

CHAPTER 9

Producing a Program

      Litcom Publishing (Enter, Enter)

      Humble Opinions (Enter, Enter)

      L & M (Enter, Enter)

      Ware Experts (Enter, Enter)

      J Associates (Enter, Enter)

      Plum Corporation (Enter, four times)

      White Haven Inn and Resorts (Enter)

      June 11 - 13, 1992 (Enter, three times)

5. Select Forma**t**, **S**ection. The Section dialog box appears. In the Columns box, **N**umber, type **2**. In the **S**pacing box, type **1.5"**. Select OK or press Enter.

5. Select Forma**t**, **C**olumns. The columns dialog box appears. In the **N**umber of Columns, type **2**. In **S**pace Between, type **1.5"**. Select OK or press Enter.

6. Select the third paragraph return after June 11 - 13, 1992. Select Insert, **B**reak. Choose **C**olumn and Select OK or press Enter.

7. Select all the text in the left column (from TRADE SHOW EXHIBITS to June 11 - 13, 1992) and center align it. Deselect the text.

8. Position the cursor at the top of the page. Select Forma**t**, **P**aragraph. In the **B**order box, choose Above; in the Patt**e**rn box, choose Thick. Select OK or press Enter. Repeat this procedure at the bottom of the column.

8. Position the cursor at the top of the page. Select Forma**t**, **B**order. In the Bo**r**der box, click the top margin. In **L**ine, choose the 2.25 rule. Select OK or press Enter. Repeat this procedure at the bottom of the column.

9. Select TRADE SHOW EXHIBITS AND DEMONSTRATIONS. On the Ribbon, make the text 14 points, bold.

10. Select TRADE SHOW EXHIBITORS and make it bold. Repeat with White Haven Inn and Resorts.

11. At the top of the right column, press Enter three times. Position the cursor on the top line (the paragraph return).

217

PART II

Creating Business Documents

12. Select Forma**t**, **P**aragraph. The Paragraph dialog box appears. In the **B**order box, select Above; in the **P**attern box, select Thick. Select OK or press Enter.

12. Select Forma**t**, **B**order. In the B**o**rder box, click the top margin; in the **L**ine box, click the 2.25 rule. Select OK or press Enter.

13. Select `Desktop Publishers Convention and Trade Show`. On the Ribbon, change the text to 32 points, bold, center-aligned. Place a paragraph return after `Publishers`, after `and`, and after `Show`.

14. Place a single closed quotation mark after the `s` in `Publishers`.

    If you copied the quotation mark before you closed the document in the previous example, you can paste the single quotation mark. Or, you can select **F**ile, **O**pen, and choose C:\WINWORD. Open KEYCAPS.DOC and copy the single closed quotation mark. Select **C**lose, and then use the **P**aste command to place the quotation mark.

15. Select Insert, **P**icture. If you have clip art or a graphic you can use, insert it. If you need to borrow Word's art, switch directories to C:\LIBRARY. Change the File **N**ame extension to *.TIF and press Enter. Choose the MONIQUE.TIF file to insert. Add an extra paragraph return after the graphic.

16. Select `PROGRAM`. On the Ribbon, change the type to 18 points, bold, center-aligned. Press Enter after `PROGRAM`.

17. Type the following, pressing Enter as indicated:

    White Haven Inn, Washington, DC (Enter)

    June 11 - 13, 1992

    Select both lines and use the Ribbon to make them 14 points, bold, center-aligned.

18. Select the last return in the column and select Forma**t**, **P**aragraph. In the **B**order box, choose Below; in the **P**attern box, choose Thick. Select OK or press Enter.

18. Select the next to last paragraph return in the column and select Format, **B**order. In the B**o**rder box, click the bottom margin or use the down arrow to select the bottom border;

CHAPTER 9

Producing a Program

in the **L**ine box, choose the 2.25 rule. Select OK or press Enter.

19. Make sure that the borders of the left and right columns are even. You may have to add or delete a paragraph return, depending on the size of your graphic.

20. Place the cursor at the end of the column on the right (on the last paragraph return, below the border). Select Insert, **B**reak. The Break dialog box appears. Insert: **P**age Break. Select OK or press Enter.

21. At the top of the second page, press Enter three times. Place the cursor at the top on the first paragraph return. Repeat step 8 to format a border.

22. Select THURSDAY, JUNE 11. Press Shift+F3 to change the type to uppercase and lowercase. On the Ribbon, change the size to 12 points and bold. Repeat with FRIDAY, JUNE 12 and SATURDAY, JUNE 13.

23. Select Forma**t**, **P**aragraph. In the Spacing box, Aft**e**r: type **.5li**. Select OK or press Enter. Repeat for Friday and Saturday.

23. Select Forma**t**, **P**aragraph. In the Spacing box, Aft**e**r: type **.5li**. Select OK or press Enter. Repeat for Friday and Saturday.

24. Position the cursor at the end of the next line (10:00 a.m....Room 117), add two spaces and press Del. After the tabs are set in the next step, you must adjust the Room tab on this line. You do this on the Ruler by dragging the tab symbol to make it even with the lines below it. On the keyboard, press Ctrl+Shift+F10 to activate the ruler. Use the right arrow key to adjust the tab. Repeat this with the same time line under the Friday and Saturday headings.

25. Position the cursor in the line beginning 9:00 a.m.... Select Forma**t**, St**y**le(s). Delete the contents of the **S**tyle Name box and type **Program**. Select **D**efine, **T**abs. In the **T**ab Position box, type **.6**, choose **R**ight align, **S**et. Press Del, type **.75**, and select **L**eft align, **S**et. Press Del, type **3.15**, and select **L**eft align, **S**et.

26. Select OK twice or press Enter twice.

26. Select OK and Apply or press Enter and Alt+1A.

219

PART II

Creating Business Documents

27. Select all the text in the left column. In the Style box, select Program.

28. In the first column, at the end of the line PC's and Software Packages, press Enter four times. On the next to the last Enter, repeat step 18 to insert a border.

29. Position the cursor on the last paragraph return in the first column and select **Insert**, **B**reak. The Break dialog box appears. Select **C**olumn Break.

30. In the right column, repeat step 8 to position the borders. Make sure that the left and right column borders are even.

31. Check to make sure that Friday is even with Thursday; you may have to insert a paragraph return. Select the text under the Friday and Saturday headings. In the Style box, change the text to Program.

32. Delete the text WHITE HAVEN INN AND RESORTS JUNE 11 - 13, 1992. Repeat step 8 to add a border to the last return in the column.

33. Select **F**ile, **S**ave.

34. Select **F**ile, Print Preview, and **P**rint. You may want to refer to the next section before printing.

35. Copy the single closed quotation mark if you plan to create the next design.

NOTE

Don't forget to change the page orientation in **P**rinter Setup before creating a portrait-oriented piece. Word reminds you the next time you print, but the orientation is still landscape.

Working with a Printer

If you don't plan to have your program professionally printed, you may need to experiment with your printer. When printing on two sides of a sheet of paper, you should line up the vertical rules and the margins. For a proper fold (one that has even margins), make

CHAPTER 9
Producing a Program

sure that the front and back margins are aligned. If your printer has a left-hand feed, align the top of the program along that feed. If your laser printer has a centered feed, make sure that the paper is straight in the tray. You can wedge a piece of heavy cardboard between the paper and the side of the paper tray to help guide the paper.

Producing an Innovative Program

A program may contain more information than just times, activities, and places. You may want to add descriptions of workshops or speaker biographies, for example. The program design presented in this section lends itself to this type of information. The addition of boxed text directs attention to the special discussions and demonstrations. The rest of the information is centered horizontally on the page to add white space. Figure 9.4 shows the first page of the program. Figure 9.5 shows the second page.

The rules for the boxes are thick to "restrain" the type; the rules also contrast with the white space. A shadowed box also would work well. If you're using Word 2.0, you might want to add a 10 percent screen to the boxes. Using graphics is another idea; a logo would look good in the top right corner of both pages.

To produce this innovative program, take the following steps:

1. Select **F**ile, **O**pen. Because this is the last program you create in this chapter, open and use PROGRAM.DOC.

2. Select Forma**t**, **D**ocument. The Document dialog box appears. Change the **T**op and **B**ottom margins to **.5**". The **L**eft and **R**ight margins remain .75". Select OK or press Enter.

2. Select Forma**t**, Page Set**u**p. The Page Setup dialog box appears. Change the **T**op and **B**ottom margins to **.5**". The **L**eft and **R**ight margins remain .75". Select OK or press Enter.

3. Select `Desktop Publishers Convention and Trade Show`. On the Ribbon, make the text 24 points, bold, left-aligned. Insert a single closed quotation mark by pasting from the last document, or by opening C:\WINWORD\KEYCAPS.DOC, copying the quotation mark to the clipboard, and then pasting it into place.

Desktop Publishers' Convention and Trade Show

THURSDAY, JUNE 11

9:00 a.m.	Continental Breakfast	Room 212
9:30 a.m.	Welcoming Address Speaker: Jeff Barrett, DT Pub	Room 214
10:00 a.m.	Personal Computers Speaker: Jane Wilson, T & L	Room 215
11:00 a.m.	Round-Table Discussion The PC in Business	Room 216

ROUND-TABLE DISCUSSION - THE PC IN BUSINESS

Speakers: David Conners, T & L; Sara Franks, Litcom Publishing; Tim Patten, Satern Inc. What are the advantages of the Personal Computer in business today? These experts discuss programs such as word processing and desktop publishing, their applications to the business world, the system requirements and costs, and the future of the Personal Computer.

12:00 noon	Lunch Break	
1:00 p.m.	Software Packages Speaker: Jeff Barrett, DT Publishers	Room 223
2:00 p.m.	Round-Table Discussion Today's Market - Software Speakers: Wyatt Franklin, L & M Chery Thomas, Level Best, Inc. Debra Dickerson, Ware Experts	Room 216
3:00 p.m.	Demonstrations PCs and Software Packages	Room 223

DEMONSTRATIONS - PCS AND SOFTWARE PACKAGES

Fifty-Four Personal Computers, each set up with a different software package. Demonstrations will last as long as there's someone to watch. Hands-on demonstrations available. Visit all 54! Refreshments will be served.

FIG. 9.4. A program in portrait orientation, with additional white space for contrast.

FRIDAY, JUNE 12

9:00 a.m.	Continental Breakfast	Room 211
10:00 a.m.	Dot Matrix Printers Speaker: Jim Sanders, LTOP	Room 212
11:00 a.m.	Ink Jet Printers Speaker: Geneva L. Johnson, J Assoc.	Room 213

INK JET PRINTERS

J Associates brought 27 inkjet printers, 10 of which are color, to demonstrate output. These printers are new and hot. If you've ever thought about buying an inkjet, don't miss this demonstration!!

12:00 noon	Lunch Break	
1:00 p.m.	Laser Printers Speaker: C. P. Odell, Plum Corp.	Room 244
2:00 p.m.	High Resolution Output Speaker: C. P. Odell, Plum Corp.	Room 233
3:00 p.m.	Demonstrations	Room 333

SATURDAY, JUNE 13

10:00 a.m.	Service Bureaus Speaker: Jeff Barrett, DT Pub	Room 212

SERVICE BUREAUS

Speaker Jeff Barrett is from DT Pub, one of the largest Service Bureaus in the DC area. He has brought samples of output and valuable costing information.

11:00 a.m.	Planning and Purchasing Printing Speaker: Sue Plumley, HO	Room 244

TRADE SHOW IN PROGRESS
10:00 a.m. - 4:00 p.m.   Room 117

WHITE HAVEN INN AND RESORTS

FIG. 9.5. *The second page of the program.*

PART II

Creating Business Documents

4. Position the cursor in the first line (Desktop Publishers). Select Format, Paragraph. In the Border box, choose Above. In the Pattern box, choose Thick. Select OK or press Enter.

4. Position the cursor in the first line. Select Format, Border. In the Border box, click the top margin. In the Line box, choose the 2.25 rule. Select OK or press Enter.

5. Delete the word PROGRAM. Press Del twice to remove two paragraph returns.

6. Select THURSDAY. On the Ribbon, make the text 14 points, Helv, bold, left-aligned. Select Format, Paragraph. In the Spacing box, After, type **.5li**.

6. Select THURSDAY. On the Ribbon, make the text 14 points, Helv, bold, left-aligned. Select Format, Paragraph. In the Spacing box, After, type **.5li**.

7. Delete 10:00 a.m. - 4:00 p.m. Trade Show in Progress Room 117. Press Del again to remove its paragraph return. Repeat steps 6 and 7 for Friday and Saturday.

8. Position the cursor in the next line, 9:00 a.m.... Select Format, Style(s). Delete the contents of the Style Name box. Type **Program**. Click Define, Character. The Character dialog box appears.

9. Change the size of the font to 12 points. Select OK or press Enter.

10. In the Styles box, click Tabs. In the Tab Position box, type **2**, and select Right align, Set. Press Del, type **2.4**. Select Left align, Set. Press Del, type **4.5**. Select Left align, Set.

11. Select OK twice or press Enter twice.

11. Select OK and Apply or press Enter and Alt+A.

12. Select all of Thursday's activities, from 9:00 a.m. to 3:00 p.m. Demonstrations Room 223, PC's and Software Packages. In the Style box, make the text Program. Repeat for Friday and Saturday.

13. Turn on Non-Printing Symbols. Position the cursor at the end of the line under 11:00 a.m., The PC in Business. Press Enter twice. The cursor is positioned one paragraph return above the Speakers line. Select this return, the speakers, and one return after the list of speakers.

CHAPTER 9

Producing a Program

14. Select Forma**t**, **P**aragraph. In the **B**order box, select Box; in the Pa**t**tern box, select Thick. Select OK or press Enter.

15. Select Forma**t**, **P**aragraph. In the Indents box, From Left and From Right, type **.35**. Select OK or press Enter.

14. Select Forma**t**, **B**order. In Preset, choose **B**ox; in the Line box choose the 2.25 rule. Select OK or press Enter.

15. Select Forma**t**, **P**aragraph. In the Indentation box, From **L**eft and From **R**ight, type **.35**. Select OK or press Enter.

16. Position the cursor in the box, in front of the two tabs and the word Speakers. Press Enter. Move the cursor up one line. Type the following:

    ROUND-TABLE DISCUSSION - THE PC IN BUSINESS

17. Select the line you just typed. On the Ribbon, make the text Helv, 12 points, bold, center-aligned. Deselect the text.

18. Position the cursor at the beginning of the next line, Speakers. Delete all the tabs. Position the cursor at the end of the line T & L. Enter a semicolon and a space, and then press Del. Press Del twice more to remove the tabs. Repeat this procedure at the end of the line (Litcom Publishing). Center-align this line.

19. At the end of the Speakers, type the following, pressing Enter and Shift+Enter as indicated:

    (Enter) **What are the advantages of the personal computer in business today? These experts** (Shift+Enter) **discuss programs such as word processing and desktop publishing, their applications to** (Shift+Enter) **the business world, the system requirements and costs, and the future of the personal** (Shift+Enter) **computer.**

20. Select the text in the paragraph and Left align it. Select Format, **T**abs. The Tabs dialog box appears. Clear **A**ll. In the **T**ab Position box, type **.75**, and select **L**eft align, **S**et. Select OK or press Enter.

21. Deselect the type. Position the cursor in front of What are the advantages and press Tab. Repeat for the next three lines.

225

PART II

Creating Business Documents

22. Place the cursor in front of the tab before `12:00 noon`. Press Enter.

23. Place the cursor at the end of `3:00 p.m. Demonstrations Room 223, PC's and Software Packages`. Press Enter twice.

24. Type the following, pressing Enter and Shift+Enter as indicated:

    DEMONSTRATIONS - PC'S AND SOFTWARE PACKAGES (Enter)

    See 54 personal computers, each set up with a different software package. (Shift+Enter) **Demonstrations will last as long as there's someone to watch. Hands-on demon-**(hyphen,Shift+Enter) **strations available. Visit all 54! Refreshments will be served.**

25. Select the text in the paragraph, including the paragraph returns above `DEMONSTRATIONS` and after `will be served`.

26. Select Forma**t**, **P**aragraph. In the **B**orders box, choose Box; in the **P**attern box, choose Thick. Select OK or press Enter.

26. Select Forma**t**, **B**order. In the Preset box, select **B**ox; in the **L**ine box, choose the 2.25 rule. Select OK or press Enter.

27. Select Forma**t**, **P**aragraph. The Paragraph dialog box appears. Indent **L**eft and **R**ight **.35**. Select OK or press Enter.

28. Select the first line, `DEMONSTRATIONS`. On the Ribbon, make the text 12 points, Helv, bold, center-aligned.

29. Select the paragraph beginning with `See 54` to `will be served`. Select Forma**t**, **T**abs. The Tabs dialog box appears. Clear **A**ll. In the **T**ab Position box, type **.75**, and select **L**eft aligned, **S**et. Select OK or press Enter.

30. Place a tab in front of each of the three lines in the graphic box.

31. Select page 2. Place a paragraph return in front of `FRIDAY, JUNE 12`.

32. Place the cursor on that paragraph return and select Forma**t**, **P**aragraph. In the **B**order box, choose Above; in the **Pa**ttern box, choose Thick. Select OK or press Enter.

CHAPTER 9

Producing a Program

32. Place the cursor on that paragraph return and select Forma**t**, **B**order. In the Border box, click the margin above; in the Line box, choose the 2.25 rule. Select OK or press Enter.

33. Position the cursor after the 11:00 a.m. speaker, `Geneva L. Johnson, J Assoc`. Press Enter twice and type the following:

    INKJET PRINTERS (Enter)

    J Associates brought 27 inkjet printers, 10 of which are color, to demonstrate output. These printers are new and hot. If you've ever thought about buying an inkjet, don't miss this demonstration!!

34. Select the text in the paragraph. Follow steps 26 through 30 to format this paragraph.

35. At the end of the line containing Saturday's 10:00 a.m. speaker, `Jeff Barrett, DT Pub`, press Enter twice. Type the following, pressing Enter and Shift+Enter as indicated:

    SERVICE BUREAUS (Enter)

    Speaker Jeff Barrett is from DT Pub, one of the largest Service Bureaus in the DC (Shift+Enter) **area. He has brought samples of output and valuable costing information.**

36. Select the text in the paragraph. Follow steps 26 through 30 to format this text box.

37. At the end of the last line, `Speaker: Sue Plumley, HO`, press Enter and type the following, inserting spaces and pressing Enter as indicated:

    TRADE SHOW IN PROGRESS (Enter)

    10:00 a.m. - 4:00 p.m. (three spaces) **Room 117**

38. Select the text from `TRADE SHOW IN PROGRESS` to `WHITE HAVEN INN AND RESORTS`. Make the text bold and center-aligned. Select `WHITE` and make it 12 points. Delete the last line, `JUNE 11 - 13, 1992`.

39. Select **F**ile, **S**ave.

40. Select **F**ile, Print Preview, and **P**rint.

227

PART II
Creating Business Documents

Looking at Design

Many innovative ways are available to format a program. The size doesn't have to be standard or common. You can have a 6-inch-by-9-inch program, or you can use an 11-inch-by-17-inch sheet of paper folded to 8 1/2 inches by 11 inches. An 8 1/2-inch-by-14-inch program also can work; divide it into four columns on either side. You can format your program with either landscape or portrait orientation. Different page orientation enables you to use interesting column arrangements. If you have a variety of fonts available to you, you might try using two different ones. Graphics, photos, and clip art all add an exciting change. Biographies, definitions, or any type of material also can be added.

Figure 9.6 shows another design for a program. The 8 1/2-inch-by-11-inch, portrait-oriented program contains ample white space in the wide margins and spacing between lines. The leaders from the activities to the speakers' names guide the eye across the page. Times of activities are aligned on a right tab and are easy to read.

The wider page design and open space gives a different feel to the program.

The clip art added to the left helps by widening the margins. The graphics also were distorted, which contributes an interesting effect. This format takes up only two pages for the entire program (just one page is shown here). You can produce this design by using either version of Word.

Figure 9.7 shows another example program. This design works well in either portrait or landscape orientation.

The shadow boxes with 10 percent screens clearly define each day's activities. In each box is a list of times, an abbreviated list of activities, and the locations. You could add more logos or line art in the white space. But the white space around the boxes helps to balance the gray of the page.

This design was created by using Word Version 2.0. Word Version 1.1 can create everything but the screens in this design.

Figure 9.8 combines right-aligned heads with plenty of white space. This design requires three pages, but it's an exciting change from the everyday program. The heavy rule along the top defines the margin, as does the right-aligned text and the vertical rule of the box.

Desktop Publishers' CONVENTION AND TRADE SHOW

White Haven Inn, Washington, DC
June 11 - 13, 1992

PROGRAM

THURSDAY, JUNE 11

9:00 a.m.	Continental Breakfast Room 212	
9:30 a.m.	Welcoming Address Room 214	Jeff Barrett, DT Publishers
10:00 a.m.	Personal Computers Room 215	Jane Wilson, L & M
11:00 a.m.	Round-Table Discussion - The PC in Business Room 216	David Conners, T & L Software, Inc. Sara Franks, Litcom Publishing Tim Patten, Satern Inc.
12:00 noon	Lunch Break	
1:00 p.m.	Software Packages Room 223	Jeff Barrett, DT Publishers
2:00 p.m.	Round-Table Discussion - Today's Market - Software Room 216	Wyatt Franklin, L & M Products Cheryl Thomas, T & M Inc. Debra Dickerson, Ware Experts
3:00 p.m.	Demonstrations - PCs and Software Packages Room 223	

FRIDAY, JUNE 12

9:00 a.m.	Continental Breakfast Room 211	
10:00 a.m.	Dot Matrix Printers Room 212	Jim Sanders, LTOP
11:00 a.m.	Inkjet Printers Room 213	Geneva L. Johnson, J Assoc.
12:00 noon	Lunch Break	

FIG. 9.6. This program design shows how to use white space effectively.

DESKTOP PUBLISHERS' CONVENTION AND TRADE SHOW

THURSDAY, JUNE 11

9:00 a.m.	Continental Breakfast	Room 212
9:30 a.m.	Welcoming Address - Jeff Barrett	Room 214
10:00 a.m.	Personal Computers - Jane Wilson	Room 215
11:00 a.m.	Round-Table - David Conners The PC in Business	Room 216
12:00 noon	Lunch	
1:00 p.m.	Software Packages - Jeff Barrett	Room 223
2:00 p.m.	Round-Table - Wyatt Franklin Today's Market - Software	Room 216
3:00 p.m.	Demonstrations - PCs and Software	Room 223

FRIDAY, JUNE 12

9:00 a.m.	Continental Breakfast	Room 211
10:00 a.m.	Dot Matrix Printers - Jim Sanders	Room 212
11:00 a.m.	Inkjet Printers - Geneva L. Johnson	Room 213
12:00 noon	Lunch	
1:00 p.m.	Laser Printers - C. P. Odell	Room 244
2:00 p.m.	High-Resolution Output - C. P. Odell	Room 233
3:00 p.m.	Demonstrations	Room 233

SATURDAY, JUNE 13

9:00 a.m.	Continental Breakfast	Room 212
10:00 a.m.	Service Bureaus - Jeff Barrett	Room 212
11:00 a.m.	Planning Printing - Sue Plumley	Room 212

TRADE SHOW THURSDAY, FRIDAY, AND SATURDAY
10:00 a.m. - 12:00 noon   Room 117

WHITE HAVEN INN
JUNE 11 - 13, 1992

FIG. 9.7. Somewhat unconventional, this design presents screened boxes in an asymmetrical balance.

CHAPTER 9

Producing a Program

> **DESKTOP PUBLISHERS' CONVENTION AND TRADE SHOW**
>
> PROGRAM
>
> THURSDAY, JUNE 11
>
> | | | |
> |---|---|---|
> | 10:00 a.m. | Trade Show in Progress | Room 117 |
> | 9:00 a.m. | Continental Breakfast | Room 212 |
> | 9:30 a.m. | Welcoming Address
Speaker: Jeff Barrett, DT Pub | Room 214 |
> | 10:00 a.m. | Personal Computers
Speaker: Jane Wilson, T & L | Room 215 |
> | 11:00 a.m. | Round-Table Discussion
The PC in Business
Speakers: David Conners, T & L
Sara Franks, Litcom Publishing
Tom Patten, Satern Inc. | Room 216 |

FIG. 9.8. Right-aligned text plus wide left and bottom margins create a new look for the program.

In contrast to the other programs presented in this chapter, the design shown in figure 9.8 uses Times Roman for the headings and Helvetica for the body text. The headings are composed of large and small capitals, which adds a distinguished and sophisticated feel. Helvetica type is easy to read and adds a light, open appearance.

In Version 2.0, you can use very thick rules, but not in Version 1.1. Other than the rule, you can produce this design on either version of Word.

Recapping

In this chapter, you learned how to produce program designs that concentrate on the information people need when they attend such events as seminars, conventions, classes, and business meetings, or when they make personal presentations.

In the next chapter, you learn how to produce a memo.

10

Producing a Memo

Everyone in business sends memos. Among many other things, memos inform, remind, list, question, and confirm. Memos are dispatched in-house to presidents, board members, supervisors, secretaries, staff, and to all employees of a company. They also can be sent to lawyers, accountants, bankers, or branch offices. Memos can contain times, dates, names, regulations, steps, instructions, appointment reminders, or just a friendly hello.

Generally, business memos include the company name, address, phone number, and logo. Memos can also incorporate banner lines such as To, From, Date, and Subject. Sometimes, you can also add a space for a reply. The last component of a memo is the text, which can include anything from one sentence to several pages. The text always refers to the Subject, explaining it in some detail. This chapter gives instructions for creating several memo designs, from a basic, business-oriented layout, to some creative alternatives.

Word for Windows comprises many features to create and track your memos easily. You can create templates, fields, and macros to fill out the memos. A glossary also can help you with memo production.

You should use the Summary Info box with each memo. The box enables you to assign various titles, key words, and comments to each memo. After you save the Info box, you can view or print the statistics about that document. You also can use Word's Find feature to search for statistics in the Info boxes and identify any

PART II

Creating Business Documents

document by its contents. The first memo design presented in this chapter includes a Summary Info box.

Templates are especially convenient for use with a memo. After you format and save a basic template, you can recall it and fill in the required information quickly and easily. In this chapter, you create memos in template form for later ease of use. You may want to substitute your own header information for those in the designs so that you can produce your own memos immediately.

Fields and macros are parts of automatic memo completion. Although they are not necessary, fields and macros can make your task swift and simple. Word includes a memo template, which you change in the first design. Contained in the memo template are fields and macros that you can apply to your own memos and other documents.

In Chapter 5, you saved a letterhead design as a glossary to incorporate into other documents. Although the following designs don't use a glossary, you can easily use the one you created for a memo. Refer to Chapter 5 for information on creating and saving a glossary and Chapter 6 for implementing it.

Customizing Word's Memo Template

Word supplies many templates with which to work; your Reference Manual describes all of them. The memo template (MEMO.DOT) is a useful one for people not accustomed to creating documents in Word. You can set up this template with your company's information, and then have others in your office use it.

Word includes an *autonew* macro that prompts the user with questions to fill in the memo. A *macro* is a set of instructions, programmed by Word or you, that tells the program to perform specific tasks. Autonew is a macro that automatically runs when you begin a new document. The macro tells Word to prompt the user for certain information.

The information prompts are dialog boxes with questions, such as `Type the names of the people you want to send the memo to`. When filled in by the typist, the information is entered into the

CHAPTER 10

Producing a Memo

proper area of the memo. This proper placement of information is accomplished with fields. FILLIN is a commonly used field in Word. By creating a document with this field, you can prompt Word to ask any question; Word then positions the information in the proper area in the document. For more information about macros and fields, consult your Reference Manual.

This first design uses the MEMO.DOT file, which contains built-in macros and fields. You can customize the memo to fit your company, and then use it over and over as a template. You don't have to create any macros or fields; Word creates them for you. If you're interested in learning more about using fields and macros, Chapter 12, "Producing a Purchase Order," explains how to write and implement them.

Figure 10.1 shows the finished memo template.

Humble Opinions Corporation
P. O. Box 174
Oak Hill, WV 25901
(304) 255-5555

To:

From:

Date:

Subject:

FIG. 10.1.   *Word's MEMO.DOT template with revisions.*

To change Word's MEMO.DOT to one your company can use, follow these steps:

1. Select **File**, **Open**. From the Open Dialog box, select the C:\WINWORD directory.

2. In the File **Name** box, delete the contents, type *****.dot**, and press Enter.

PART II

Creating Business Documents

2. In the List of File **T**ypes: box, select Document Templates [*.DOT] and press Enter.

3. Choose the MEMO.DOT template. Select OK or press Enter.

4. Select **U**tilities, **C**ustomize and Typing **R**eplaces Selection. Select OK or press Enter.

4. Select T**o**ols, **O**ptions. In the **C**ategory box, choose General. In Settings, mark **T**yping Replaces Selection. Select OK or press Enter.

5. Position your cursor at the end of the address line, Los Angeles, CA 91073. Drag the cursor up to the beginning of the first line, Trey Research Company. Press the Del key.

    Word's MEMO template comes with text you'll have to replace for your own template. The reason you select the type this way is to preserve the paragraph return that identifies the type. Dragging from the top down may cause you to delete the formatting for the header.

6. You can type your own information, or type the following, pressing Enter as indicated:

    Humble Opinions Corporation (Enter)

    P.O. Box 174 (Enter)

    Oak Hill, WV 25901 (Enter)

    (304) 255-5555

7. Select the graphic (in Word's template) by clicking inside of it or by placing the cursor in front of the graphic, hold Shift, and press the right arrow key once. Delete it.

    You cannot import a graphic into this template; the option is not available on the Insert menu. If however, you have another Windows application with a graphic in it, you can copy the graphic to the clipboard and paste it into this template.

8. Select Humble Opinions Corporation. On the Ribbon, make the text 18-point Helv, bold.

9. Select the address lines and the phone number. Make the text 10-point Helv.

CHAPTER 10

Producing a Memo

10. Select the banner lines (To:, From:, Date:, and Subject:). Make the text 12 points. Delete the month, day, and year on the original template in the Date: line.

    Word's MEMO.DOT template uses 8- and 10-point type. For a memo, 12-point is better. If you prefer, you could leave it at 10.

11. With the banner lines still selected, select Forma**t**, **T**abs. In the Tabs dialog box, select Clear **A**ll. In the **T**ab Position box, type **.75**". Because the tab is **L**eft aligned, just click **S**et. Select OK or press Enter.

12. Position the cursor on the last paragraph return, under the Subject: line. Select Forma**t**, **S**tyle(s) and choose **D**efine, **C**haracter. Make the text 12 points.

13. Select OK twice.

13. Select OK and Apply or press Enter and Alt+A.

14. Select File, Save **A**s. The path and MEMO.DOT should appear in the File **N**ame box. Select OK or press Enter.

15. Select File, **C**lose.

Practicing with the Template

Now that you've saved the template, you can use it for all your memos. In this section, you can practice using the template. As the prompts appear on-screen, you fill them in, and then Word fills in the memo for you. Figure 10.2 shows the finished MEMO1.DOC.

To use the MEMO template in a document, perform these steps:

1. Select File, **N**ew.

2. Choose New **D**ocument, **U**se Template: memo. Select OK or press Enter.

   The Summary Info box appears (see fig. 10.3).

3. In **T**itle, type **Seminars** and press Tab. Don't press Enter; it closes the dialog box.

237

Humble Opinions Corporation

P. O. Box 174
Oak Hill, WV 25901
(304) 255-5555

To: David

From: Susan Plumley
        President

Date: January 21, 1992

Subject: Word Processing Seminar

As mentioned in the staff meeting, our company is offering seminars during the week of February 14 for all employees. The word processing seminar is one I think will interest you. It takes place at the Wyatt Hotel, February 16, from 8:00 a.m. to 4:00 p.m. Please let me know by Friday if you will attend. Thank you.

FIG. 10.2. *The memo produced by using the revised memo template.*

CHAPTER 10

Producing a Memo

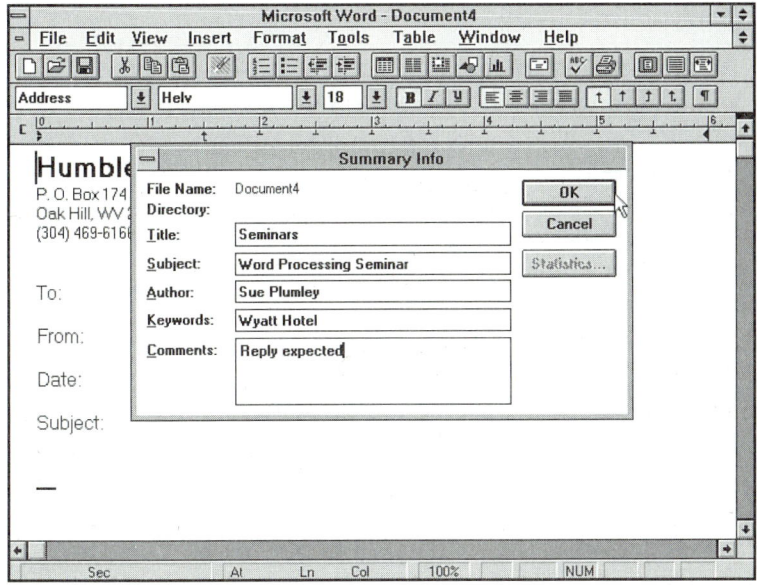

FIG. 10.3.
The Summary Info box for Word's memo document. This Figure is a Word Version 2.0 screen.

4. In **Subject**, type **Word Processing Seminar** and press Tab twice.

5. The **Author**'s name should be filled in from your licensing information. If not, type your name.

6. In **Keywords**, type **Wyatt Hotel** and press Tab.

7. In the **Comments** box, delete the instructions and type **Reply expected**. Select OK or press Enter.

   The Summary Info box is used to identify, search, and read documents. By using **F**ile, **F**ind, you can search through Subjects, Titles, Author's Names, Keywords, or Comments to find any memo you saved with a Summary Info box.

8. The next dialog box prompts you for the names of the recipients of the memo. Type **David** and Select OK or press Enter.

9. Next, a dialog box asks for the title of the author. Type **President** and Select OK or press Enter.

10. Word fills in the information and tells you it is ready to begin the memo. Select OK or press Enter.

239

PART II

Creating Business Documents

11. The cursor is in position. Type the following memo text:

    As mentioned in the staff meeting, our company is offering seminars during the week of February 14 for all employees. The word processing seminar is one I think will interest you. It takes place at the Wyatt Hotel, February 16, from 8:00 a.m. to 4:00 p.m. Please let me know by Friday if you will attend. Thank you.

12. Place the cursor after `Date:` and type **January 21, 1992**.

13. Select **F**ile, Save **A**s. Type **memo1**. Select OK or press Enter.

14. Select **F**ile, **P**rint. Select OK or press Enter.

This design is for people who are not familiar with Word or who are nervous around computers. An employee can follow these instructions for opening and saving the memo document, and Word does the rest.

Creating a Memo with a Numbered List

The next design is for longer memos. Very formal and business-oriented, this memo design includes numbered lists. The layout is similar to the last design, but you create your own template. You can add your own macros and fields if you like, but they are really not necessary.

First, create a template. Then, add the text. Figure 10.4 shows the completed memo2 document. To create the template, take these steps:

1. Select **F**ile, **O**pen. Change the extension in the File **N**ame box to *.DOT. Select OK or press Enter. Make sure that you're in the C:\WINWORD directory.

2. Open the NORMAL.DOT file. Select OK or press Enter.

3. Select Forma**t**, **D**ocument. The Document dialog box appears.

3. Select Forma**t**, Page Set**u**p. The Page Setup dialog box appears.

4. Set all margins to **1"**. Select OK or press Enter.

Humble Opinions
P. O. Box 174
Oak Hill, WV 25901
(304) 255-5555

DATE: January 21, 1992

TO: Michael Donner

FROM: Ellen Wickline

SUBJECT: Recent Regulations

Thanks for your recent inquiry. Our office is happy to supply you with the information you requested. The following regulations are those just passed by the Board. Enclosed are five copies for your office staff. Please do not hesitate to call if I can be of further service.

1. When working after hours, employees will sign in, noting date, time of arrival and time of departure. Time of departure must be initialed.

2. After hours, no employee shall enter the building with anyone who is not employed by this company.

3. Employees who leave and return must sign in and out and initial the times of departure and arrival.

4. Parking Building A closes at 9:00 p.m. Any cars in the parking building at this time will not be available until 7:30 a.m. the following business morning. Employees wishing to stay later than 9:00 p.m. must park in Parking Building C, which closes at 11:00 p.m.

Enclosures

FIG. 10.4.   A memo design with a numbered list.

PART II

Creating Business Documents

5. You may want to use your company name and address, or you can type the following memo text, pressing Enter and Tab as indicated:

   Humble Opinions (Enter)

   P.O. Box 174 (Enter)

   Oak Hill, WV 25901 (Enter)

   (304) 255-5555 (Enter, Enter, Enter)

   DATE:(Tab)(Enter, Enter)

   TO:(Tab)(Enter, Enter)

   FROM:(Tab)(Enter, Enter)

   SUBJECT:(Tab)(Enter, Enter)

6. Select `Humble Opinions`. On the Ribbon, make the text 14-point, bold.

7. With the text still selected, select For**m**at, **P**aragraph. In the **B**order box, choose Above. In the **P**attern box, choose Thick. Select OK or press Enter.

7. With the text still selected, select For**m**at, **B**order. In the Bo**r**der box, click the margin above. In the **L**ine box, choose the 2.25 rule. Select OK or press Enter.

8. Place cursor in the next line. Select For**m**at, **S**tyle(s). Press Del and type **Body**. Select **D**efine, **C**haracter. Make the text 12 points.

9. Select OK twice or press Enter twice.

9. Select OK and Apply or press Enter and Alt+1A.

10. Select all the text from the address down. In the Style box, choose Body.

11. Select the text from `DATE` to `SUBJECT`, including the Tab after Subject. Select For**m**at, **T**abs. In the **T**ab Position box, type **1"**. The Tab should be **L**eft aligned; select **S**et and OK or press Enter.

12. Select File, Save **A**s. You should be in the C:\WINWORD directory. In the File **N**ame box, type **memo2**. Select OK or press Enter. Select File, **C**lose.

CHAPTER 10

Producing a Memo

Using the Template

The template is now ready to use in any memo you want. This section shows you how to use the template as a document base and how to create a numbered list. You should outdent the numbered list or use a hanging indent. This procedure is simple in either version of Word. Word Version 2.0 offers a button on the Toolbar that automatically creates a numbered list with hanging indent. However, in this section, you create your own numbered list.

You also may want to practice creating a Summary Info box for this design. If so, do that before you select OK in the File, New box.

1. Select **F**ile, **N**ew. Choose New **D**ocument, **U**se Template: memo2. Select OK or press Enter.

2. Place the cursor behind the Tab after DATE:. Type the following, pressing Enter, Tab, and the down arrow as indicated:

   January 21, 1992 (down arrow to TO:)

   Michael Donner (down arrow)

   Ellen Wickline (down arrow)

   Recent Regulations (down arrow)

   Thanks for your recent inquiry. Our office is happy to supply you with the information you requested. The following regulations are those just passed by the Board. Enclosed are five copies for your office staff. Please do not hesitate to call if I can be of further service. (Enter, Enter)

   1.(Tab)**When working after hours, employees will sign in, noting date, time of arrival to match fig. 10.4 and time of departure. Time of departure must be initialed.** (Enter, Enter)

   2.(Tab)**After hours, no employee shall enter the building with anyone who is not employed by this company.** (Enter, Enter)

   3.(Tab)**Employees who leave and return must sign in and out and initial the times of departure and arrival.** (Enter, Enter)

PART II

Creating Business Documents

4.(Tab)**Parking Building A closes at 9:00 p.m. Any cars in the parking building at this time will not be available until 7:30 a.m. the following business morning. Employees wishing to stay later than 9:00 p.m. must park in Parking Building C, which closes at 11:00 p.m.** (Enter, Enter)

Enclosures

3. Select numbers 1 through 4 and their text. Select Forma**t**, **P**aragraph. In the Indents box, For From Le**f**t, type **1**". For From **R**ight, type **1**". For **F**irst Line, type **-.25**". Select OK or press Enter.

3. Select the numbers 1 through 4 and their text. Select Forma**t**, **P**aragraph. In the Indentation box, for From **L**eft, type **1**". For From **R**ight, type **1**". For **F**irst Line, type **-.25**". Select OK or press Enter.

4. Select **F**ile, Save **A**s. In the File **N**ame box, type **memo2**.

5. Select **F**ile, **P**rint.

Creating an Innovative Memo

Memos are not limited in design. A document with less text affords an opportunity to play with the white space. Wide margins on two sides, or four, creates an exciting expanse. Tamed by rules or boxes, white space can be quite eye-catching.

The memo design presented in this section makes use of Word's table feature to divide the space and create rules and boxes. The spacing in the table allows plenty of room to write or type. The wide margins, along with the centered text and table, make this memo inviting to read.

The company name is in large capitals. The name spans the width of the box, as does the address (see fig. 10.5). To create this template for later use, follow these steps:

1. Select **F**ile, **N**ew. Choose New **T**emplate, **U**se Template: Normal. Select OK or press Enter.

HUMBLE OPINIONS

P. O. BOX 174   OAK HILL, WV 25901   (304) 255-5555

TO:

FROM:

DATE:

SUBJECT:

REPLY:

FIG. 10.5.   *This memo shows an exciting way to use white space in a memo.*

PART II

Creating Business Documents

2. Select Forma**t**, **D**ocument. In the Margins box, set **T**op to **1.25**", **B**ottom to **1**", and **L**eft and **R**ight to **1.75**". Select OK or press Enter.

2. Select Forma**t**, Page Set**u**p. In the Margins box, set **T**op to **1.25**", **B**ottom to **1**", and **L**eft and **R**ight to **1.75**". Select OK or press Enter.

3. Type the following, inserting spaces and pressing Enter as indicated:

   HUMBLE OPINIONS (Enter)

   P.O. BOX 174 (four spaces) **OAK HILL, WV 25901** (four spaces) **(304) 255-5555** (Enter, Enter, Enter, Enter, Enter)

   TO: (Enter)

   FROM: (Enter)

   DATE: (Enter)

   SUBJECT: (Enter)

   REPLY:

4. Select `HUMBLE OPINIONS`. On the Ribbon, make the text 36 points, bold, center-aligned.

5. Select the address line. On the Ribbon, make the text 14 points, center-aligned. Place a bullet between the P.O. Box and the city, and another between the ZIP code and phone number.

To insert the bullet, use the Macro key you created in Chapter 5 (Ctrl+8).

To insert the bullet, select **I**nsert, **S**ymbol.

6. Select the text from `TO:` to `REPLY:`.

7. Select **I**nsert, **T**able. In the Number of **C**olumns, type **1**; in the Number of **R**ows, type **5**.

8. Choose the **F**ormat command button. In the **W**idth of Column, type **5**". The S**p**ace Between Cols should be **0**, and In**d**ent Rows should be **0**. In the Minimum Row **H**eight, delete `Auto` and type **.5**.

9. In Borders, for **O**utline, choose Thick; for **I**nside, choose Single. In the Align Rows box, choose **C**enter. Select OK or press Enter.

CHAPTER 10

Producing a Memo

10. Select SUBJECT: through REPLY:. Select Forma**t**, **T**able. In the Minimum Row **H**eight, type **2.15**". Select OK or press Enter.

   Figure 10.6 shows the Version 1.1 Format Table dialog box displaying the selections you should make.

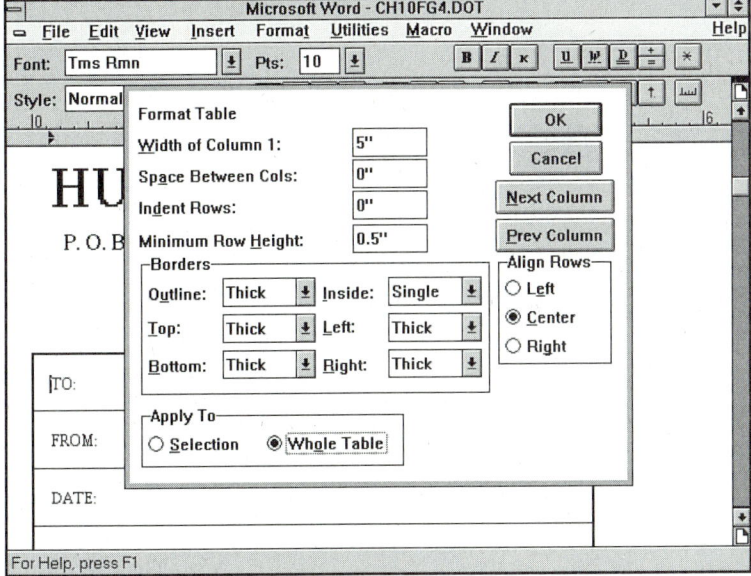

FIG. 10.6.
The Version 1.1 Format Table dialog box.

7. Select **T**able, **I**nsert Table. The table is selected. Select **T**able, Column **W**idth. In Width of Col, make sure that it says **5**". In **S**pace between Cols, type **0**. Select OK or press Enter.

8. Select the type from TO: to the end of DATE:. Select **T**able, Row **H**eight. In Height of Rows 1-3, choose At Least, for **A**t:, type **3li**. In Alignment, choose **C**enter. Select OK or press Enter.

9. Select SUBJECT: through REPLY:. Select **T**able, Row **H**eight. In Height of Rows 4-5, choose At Least, for **A**t:, type **2.15**". In Alignment, select **C**enter. Select OK or press Enter.

10. Select the entire table. Select Forma**t**, **B**order. In Preset, choose **G**rid. In the **L**ine box, choose the 1.25 rule. Word automatically applies a .75 rule to the inside lines of the table. Select OK or press Enter.

11. Select the text from TO: to REPLY:. Select Forma**t**, **P**aragraph. In the Spacing box, for **B**efore, type **1li**. In the Indents box, for From **L**eft:, type **.15**. Select OK or press Enter.

247

12. Position the cursor after TO: . Insert a Tab by pressing Ctrl+Tab. Repeat after FROM, DATE, SUBJECT, and REPLY.

13. Select the text in the table, from TO: to REPLY:. Select Forma**t**, **T**abs. In the **T**ab Position box, type **1.1**". Choose **S**et and OK.

14. Select File, Save **A**s and type **memo3**.

15. Select File, **P**rint.

Looking at Design

The basic memo contains a name, address, phone number, and banner lines. Using these fundamental items leaves room for many different variations in design. This section presents three ideas, but the possibilities are infinite.

Figure 10.7 is a landscape-oriented memo layout. A vertical bar borders the company name and the banner lines, but it also can border the text.

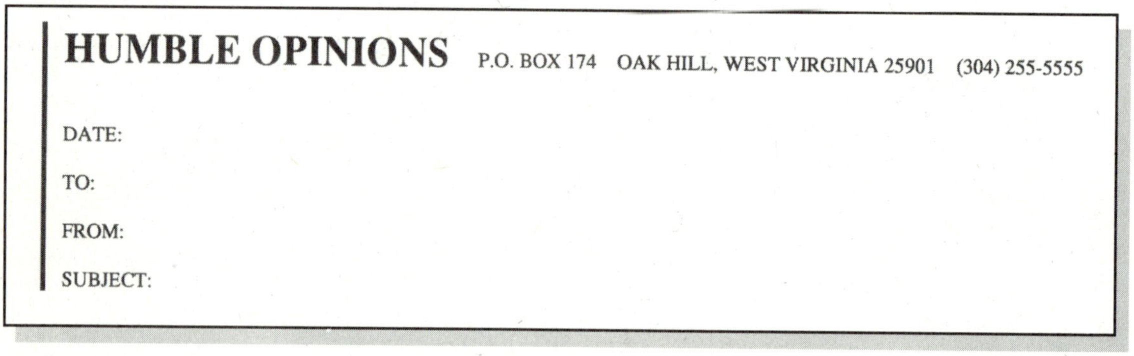

HUMBLE OPINIONS   P.O. BOX 174   OAK HILL, WEST VIRGINIA 25901   (304) 255-5555

DATE:

TO:

FROM:

SUBJECT:

FIG. 10.7. You can also use landscape orientation for a memo.

Landscape orientation is suitable for many types of messages. For example, a table of figures fits well on the page, or a spreadsheet, or a column of names or figures, or lists on tabs. You can divide the space into two or three columns by using Word's Section feature. Anything wide fits well in Landscape orientation.

Figure 10.8 shows another memo design. The boxes accent the wide left margin created by the logo. They keep the memo area confined, making it look neat and clean.

HUMBLE OPINIONS
P. O. BOX 174
OAK HILL, WV 25901
(304) 255-5555

DATE:

TO:

FROM:

SUBJECT:

REPLY:

FIG. 10.8. A memo with additional area for a reply.

PART II

Creating Business Documents

The horizontal rule along the top mirrors the margins. The rule also confines the head so that it isn't lost in all the space. The boxes divide the information. It's clear to the receiver where the answer goes, and the answer is apparent to the sender.

Figure 10.9 shows a memo created so that it will print "two up." *Two up* is a printing term, which means that two copies are printed on each sheet of paper. Printing half-page memo forms two to a page wastes less paper and is less expensive than using an entire sheet of paper for a short memo. If you have your memo forms professionally printed, it is less expensive to have them printed two up. The printer can cut them apart for you.

The design is a simple one. The head and address are right-aligned, and the banner lines are left-aligned. The rules define the margins. Notice that the margin between the two memos should be twice that of the bottom margin to allow for trimming.

Recapping

In this chapter, you learned about producing a variety of memos, from the conventional to the innovative. You learned that creating a memo template produces a basic stylesheet you can use over and over. Also, you learned how to incorporate design elements into something as simple as a memo.

In the next chapter, you learn how to produce a fax cover sheet.

humble opinions
P. O. Box 174
Oak Hill, WV 25901
(304) 255-5555

DATE:

TO:

FROM:

SUBJECT:

---

humble opinions
P. O. Box 174
Oak Hill, WV 25901
(304) 255-5555

DATE:

TO:

FROM:

SUBJECT:

FIG. 10.9. *You can arrange memos two up for printing or copying.*

DAILY EXPENSE REPORT

NAME: _____ DATE: _____

DIVISION: _____ VEHICLE: _____

DESTINATION: _____ CONTACT PERSON: _____

CO. ADDRESS: _____ PHONE NO.: _____

EXPENSE	DESCRIPTION	REIMBURSEMENT
HOTEL		
MEALS		
GAS/MILEAGE		
MISC.		

RESULTS OF TRIP/MEETING

SALES: _____

_____

CONTACTS: _____

_____

COMMENTS: _____

_____

_____

SIGNATURE: _____

Part III

Creating Business Forms

Includes

---

11. Producing a Fax Cover Sheet
12. Producing a Purchase Order
13. Producing a Travel or Expense Report
14. Producing an Order Form

11

Producing a Fax Cover Sheet

A fax, or facsimile transmission, is a transmission over phone lines. Businesses are increasingly sending faxes to customers, suppliers, employees, and other businesses. You can inform, confirm, and question with a fax. You can also order and purchase items, or even sell, by way of a fax. Mostly, however, a fax is for convenience. When you have information that must be sent quickly, such as copy or lists of customers, a fax will do the job.

A popular application is fax advertising. Companies create faxes that advertise their services or products and send them over the wires in the evening, when the rates are low. In the morning, when you check your fax machine, there may be ads galore.

A fax should have a cover sheet, identifying the material being sent, which usually contains the following information:

- The recipient
- The sender
- The sender's address and phone number
- The date of transmission
- The number of pages following the cover sheet
- Any additional message, such as special delivery instructions.

This information can be written or typed on a plain sheet of paper and sent as a cover sheet, but typewriter type or handwritten messages may not transmit well. An easy-to-read cover sheet is a must, especially for customers.

PART III

Creating Business Forms

Use a well-designed, easy-to-read fax cover sheet for all transmissions. Here are some guidelines for readability:

- Type should be no smaller than 10 points.
- Bold is fine for 12 points or larger, but is difficult to read in 10-point.
- Very large type, 14-point and above, faxes very well.
- Avoid condensed type, although expanded is fine.
- Leave at least 1-inch margins all around, because many fax machines cut off 1/4 inch to 1/2 inch of the margin.
- When using rules, use thicker ones—1.25 points and up. Thin rules may not show up on a faxed sheet.
- Don't use Scripts and Texts for a fax. Both are difficult to read before faxing, and impossible to read after going through a fax machine.
- Italic is very hard to read when faxed.

A good reason for using a well-designed cover sheet is fax paper. Most fax machines output to special fax paper, although some print to a laser printer for good, clean copies. Fax paper has a very hard, slick surface, and the print quality is often fuzzy or broken and hard to read. The transmission process itself may be a problem, as "noise" on the line may produce inferior output. Fax cover sheets, as well as any faxed material, must be clean and easy to read before transmission, as they often degrade after transmission.

Another good reason for an attractive fax cover sheet is the impression it makes on the recipient. When your company confirms sales or purchase orders, offers special bargains, or in any way deals with the customer through faxes, the impression made here may be the first—or the last.

The fax machine limits the size of your cover sheet. Most machines take 8 1/-2-inch-wide paper only; the length can be any size when fax paper comes on a roll, but is limited to 8 1/2 inches x 11 inches when the fax is printed on a laser printer. Faxes smaller than 8 1/2 inches x 11 inches are inconvenient to send or store. The designs in this chapter are all 8 1/2 inches x 11 inches.

Some of the cover sheets presented in this chapter are very formal and conventional, others are fresh and original. Additional attention-getting ideas that can be created with a draw or paint program are available at the end of this chapter .

CHAPTER 11

Producing a Fax Cover Sheet

The instructions in this chapter are for creating documents. You may, however, wish to save your designs as a template and then—when you're ready—use the template to create your own fax cover sheets. To create and save a new template, follow these steps:

> **NOTE**
>
> You may substitute your own information in these steps.

1. Choose **F**ile, and then **O**pen. Move to the `c:\winword` directory.

2. In the Open File **N**ame box, change the extension to `*.DOT` for template. Click OK or Enter.

2. In the List Files of **T**ype box, choose `Document Templates [*.dot]`. Click OK or Enter.

3. Choose the file `normal.dot`. Click OK or press Enter.

4. Make any desired changes in design such as margins, typeface and size.

5. Click **F**ile, then click Save **A**s. The path will be `c:\winword\`. Delete `NORMAL.DOT` and type the name for your template (perhaps FAXCOVER.DOT). Click OK to store your template on the hard drive, ready for later use.

Producing a Basic Fax Cover Sheet

Some companies use their letterhead as a cover sheet. This type of design works well, and provides a way of tying company information together. However, don't use the actual letterhead stock for the transmission, because paper with a linen or laid finish may not run through the fax machine very well, and because of the expense of the letterhead stock. For these reasons, copy your letterhead design onto a less expensive bond or sulphite paper. The customer doesn't see the quality of the paper, just the quality of the design.

PART III

Creating Business Forms

The first design created in this chapter is very common and uncomplicated, but serves the purpose. Important items on a cover sheet are the company name, phone number, and fax number, the names of the sender and receiver, and the number of pages (either to follow or including the cover sheet). An area is often provided for a comment or message. Figure 11.1 illustrates a basic fax cover sheet.

HUMBLE OPINIONS
(304) 255-5555
FAX (304) 251-1155

FACSIMILE TRANSMISSION FROM:

ATTENTION:

PAGES:

COMMENTS:

FIG. 11.1. *A basic fax cover sheet.*

CHAPTER 11

Producing a Fax Cover Sheet

The following steps are for creating a document; however, you can use your own information and save as a template.

1. Click **F**ile, then click **N**ew. In the **N**ew box, click **D**ocument. In the **U**se Template box, click Normal, and then click OK or press Enter.

2. Choose Forma**t**, and then **D**ocument. In the Margins box, change all to **1**".

2. Click Forma**t**, and then click Page Set**u**p. In **M**argins, change all to **1**".

3. Type the text for the fax cover sheet, pressing Tab and Enter where indicated:

   HUMBLE OPINIONS (Enter)

   (304) 255-5555 (Enter)

   FAX (304) 251-1155 (Enter, Enter, Enter)

       FACSIMILE TRANSMISSION FROM: (Tab) (Enter, Enter)

   ATTENTION: (Tab) (Enter, Enter)

   PAGES: (Tab) (Enter, Enter)

   COMMENTS: (Tab) (Enter, Enter)

4. Select HUMBLE OPINIONS. Change the type to 18 points, bold, center-aligned.

5. Select the two phone numbers. Change the type to center-aligned.

6. Select text from FACSIMILE... to COMMENTS. Choose Forma**t**, and then **T**abs. In the **T**ab Position box, type **3**". Choose **L**eft align, **S**et, and then click OK or press Enter.

7. Click **F**ile, and then click Save **A**s. Type **fax1**, and then click OK or press Enter.

8. To print the cover sheet, go to **F**ile, **P**rint, and then click OK or press Enter.

PART III

Creating Business Forms

Producing a Fax Cover with Rules

Graphics easily improve any design. Whether rules, boxes, or screens, graphics draw attention. The following design incorporates two horizontal rules in the heading. These rules extend to the margin, but the text indents on the left and right. This technique adds interest and variation to the cover sheet.

The tabs used in the address are left- and right-aligned. Combined with the rules, this creates a "boxed in" effect giving more significance to the heading. Figure 11.2 shows the finished cover sheet.

HUMBLE OPINIONS CORPORATION

P. O. BOX 174   (304) 255-5555
OAK HILL, WV 25901   FAX (304) 251-1155

DATE:

ATTENTION:

FROM:

PAGES (including cover):

COMMENTS:

FIG. 11.2.   *A fax cover sheet with the heading set off by graphic rules.*

CHAPTER 11

Producing a Fax Cover Sheet

To create the fax cover sheet shown in figure 11.2, follow these steps:

1. Choose **F**ile, and then **N**ew. In the **N**ew box, select **D**ocument. In the **U**se Template box, use Normal, and then click OK or press Enter.

2. Select Forma**t**, then **D**ocument. Set all margins to **1**", and click OK or press Enter.

2. Select Forma**t**, then Page Set**u**p. In **M**argins, set **T**op, **B**ottom, **L**eft and **R**ight to **1**", and then click OK or press Enter.

3. Type the text for the cover sheet, pressing Tab and Enter where indicated:

    HUMBLE OPINIONS CORPORATION (Enter)

    (Tab) **P. O. BOX 174** (Tab) **(304) 255-5555** (Enter)

    (Tab) **OAK HILL, WV 25901** (Tab) **FAX (304) 251-1155** (Enter, Enter, Enter)

    DATE: (Enter, Enter)

    ATTENTION: (Enter, Enter)

    FROM: (Enter, Enter)

    PAGES (including cover): (Enter)

    COMMENTS:

4. Select the text HUMBLE...., and change to 18 points, bold, and center-aligned.

5. With HUMBLE.... still selected, choose Forma**t**, then Charac**t**er. In the Character Spacing box, choose E**x**panded, **B**y:, and then type **1pt**. Click OK or press Enter.

6. With HUMBLE.... still selected, choose Forma**t**, then **P**aragraph. In the **B**order box, choose Above. In the **P**attern box, choose Thick.

7. In the Spacing box, choose **A**fter, type **.5li**, and then click OK or press Enter.

    or

5. With HUMBLE.... still selected, choose Forma**t**, then Charac**t**er. In the Spacing box, choose Expanded, **B**y: and then type **1pt**. Click OK or press Enter.

261

PART III

Creating Business Forms

6. With HUMBLE.... still selected, choose Forma**t**, then **B**order. In the Bo**r**der box, select the margin above. In the Line box, choose the 2.25 rule. Click OK or press Enter.

7. With HUMBLE.... still selected, choose Forma**t**, then **P**aragraph. In the Spacing box, select After, type **.5li**, and then click OK or press Enter.

8. Select the next two lines, from P. O. BOX... to the fax number (304)251-1155. Follow these steps:

    Choose Forma**t**, then **T**abs. In the **T**ab Position box, type **.5"**. Choose **L**eft align, **S**et, and then press the Del key.

    In the **T**ab Position box, type **6"**, choose **R**ight align, and then **S**et. Click OK or press Enter.

9. With P. O. BOX... still selected, choose Forma**t**, then **P**aragraph. In the Bo**r**der box, choose Below, In the Pattern box, choose Thick. Click OK or press Enter.

9. With P. O. BOX... still selected, choose Forma**t**, then **B**order. In the Bo**r**der box, select the margin below. In the Line box, choose the 2.25 rule. Click OK or press Enter.

10. Select the text from DATE... to PAGES, and change to bold. Repeat with COMMENTS:.

11. Select (including cover):, and change to 10-point type.

12. Click File, click Save **A**s, type **fax2**, and then click OK or press Enter.

13. To print the cover sheet, choose File, **P**rint, and then click OK or press Enter.

Producing a Cover Sheet with a Graphic Box

As mentioned earlier, graphics really contribute to a design. In the next cover sheet, shown in figure 11.3, a shadow box outlines the area set aside for the information. The box looks like a miniature page, surrounded by very wide left, right, and bottom margins. The heading within the box is similar to a letterhead, and adds to the overall effect.

CHAPTER 11

Producing a Fax Cover Sheet

FAX FROM:

HUMBLE OPINIONS
P. O. BOX 174 • OAK HILL, WV 25901
FAX (304) 551-1155
(304) 255-5555

DATE:

ATTENTION:

FROM:

MESSAGE:

FIG. 11.3. A "mini-page" fax cover sheet.

To create the fax cover sheet shown in figure 11.3, follow these steps:

1. Choose **F**ile, then **N**ew. In the New box choose **D**ocument. In the **U**se Template box, choose Normal, and then click OK or press Enter.

PART III

Creating Business Forms

2. Select Forma**t**, then **P**aragraph. In the B**o**rder box, choose Box. In the Patt**e**rn box, choose Shadow.

3. While still in the **P**aragraph dialog box, move to the Indents box, and set the **L**eft and **R**ight indents to **1.2**". Click OK or press Enter.

2. Select Forma**t**, then Bo**r**der. In the Preset box, choose S**h**adow. In **F**rom Text, choose 10pt. Move to the Line box, choose the 2.25 rule, and then click OK or press Enter.

3. Choose Forma**t**, then **P**aragraph. In the Indentation box, set the **L**eft and **R**ight margins at **1.2**", and then click OK or press Enter.

4. Type the following text for the cover sheet, pressing **E**nter where indicated:

   (Enter) **FAX FROM:** (Enter)

   HUMBLE OPINIONS (Enter)

   P. O. BOX 174 (space bar six times), **OAK HILL, WV 25901** (Enter)

   FAX (304) 551-1155 (Enter)

   (304) 255-5555 (Enter, Enter, Enter, Enter, Enter)

   DATE: (Enter, Enter)

   ATTENTION: (Enter, Enter)

   FROM: (Enter, Enter)

   MESSAGE:

5. Select the text FAX FROM, and change to bold.

6. Select the text HUMBLE OPINIONS, and change to center-aligned, 18 points, bold.

7. Select the next three lines, the address, fax number and phone number. Center align each line and set the type to 10 points.

8. Position the cursor between ...BOX 174 and OAK HILL..., and follow these steps:

   Insert a bullet by using the Macro key you created in Chapter 5 (Ctrl+8).

CHAPTER 11

Producing a Fax Cover Sheet

Select the text from DATE to MESSAGE:.

Select For**mat**, then **P**aragraph. In the Indents box, set First Li**n**e by typing **.15**". Click OK or press Enter.

Repeat to also indent the first line FAX FROM: by **.15** inch.

Version 1.1 of Word doesn't allow any other way to indent the text inside a box, unless you set tabs or use spaces. When you don't indent, the text is too close to the rule.

8. Position the cursor between ...BOX 174 and OAK HILL.... Insert a bullet by selecting **I**nsert, **S**ymbol, and double-clicking the bullet or by pressing the down arrows to select the bullet. Press Enter.

9. Select **F**ile, Save **A**s, type **fax3**, and then click OK or press Enter.

10. To print the cover sheet, choose **F**ile, **P**rint, and then click OK or press Enter.

Creating an Innovative Fax Cover Sheet

You can create many layouts with rules and boxes. You can vary the width of the rules, or the height and width of the boxes, or even their placement on the page. You can add screens or shadows.

The next cover sheet, shown in figure 11.4, is one method of changing the look of the page with graphic boxes. Separated by empty paragraph returns, each box has specific contents. The compartments of text create an interesting division of white space, as well. This design balances asymmetrically to the left, but could balance to the center instead.

To create the cover sheet shown in figure 11.4, follow these steps:

1. Select **F**ile, then **N**ew. In the New box, choose **D**ocument. In the **U**se Template box, choose Normal, and then click OK or press Enter.

2. Select For**mat**, then **D**ocument. Change the **L**eft margin to **1**", and then click OK or press Enter.

265

PART III

Creating Business Forms

HUMBLE OPINIONS
P. O. BOX 174
OAK HILL, WV 25901

FAX (304) 251-1155
(304) 255-5555

DATE:

ATTENTION:

FROM:

MESSAGE:

FIG. 11.4. *Compartments of text, balanced asymmetrically.*

CHAPTER 11

Producing a Fax Cover Sheet

2. Select Format, then Page Setup. Change the Left margin to 1", and then click OK or press Enter.

3. Type the following text for the cover sheet, inserting Enter where indicated:

   HUMBLE OPINIONS (Enter)

   P. O. BOX 174 (Enter)

   OAK HILL, WV 25901 (Enter, Enter)

   FAX (304) 251-1155 (Enter)

   (304) 255-5555 (Enter, Enter, Enter, Enter, Enter)

   DATE: (Enter, Enter)

   ATTENTION: (Enter, Enter)

   FROM: (Enter, Enter, Enter, Enter, Enter)

   MESSAGE: (Enter 10 times)

4. Select the text HUMBLE OPINIONS, and change to 18 points, bold.

5. Select the text from P. O. BOX... to the phone number, and change to Helv, 10 points.

6. Select the text from HUMBLE... to the end of the phone number.

7. To create the box, follow these steps:

   Choose Format, then Paragraph.

   In the Border box, choose the Box.

   In the Pattern box, choose Thick.

   In the Indents box, set First Line by typing **.15"**. Click OK or press Enter to create the box.

7. Choose Format, then Border. In the Preset box, choose Box. Set From Text by typing **5pt**. In the Line box, choose the 1.25 rule. Click OK to create the box.

8. Select the text beginning at the paragraph return above DATE to the paragraph return below FROM:. Repeat step 7.

9. Select the text from the paragraph return above MESSAGE: to the last return on the page. Repeat step 7.

PART III

Creating Business Forms

10. Select the entire page. Choose Forma**t**, and then **P**aragraph.

11. In the Indents box, set From R**i**ght by typing **3"**. Click OK or press Enter.

11. In the Indentation box, Set From **R**ight, by typing **3"**, and then click OK or press Enter.

12. Choose File, Save **A**s, type **fax4**, and then click OK or press Enter.

13. To print the cover sheet, choose **F**ile, click **P**rint, and then click OK or press Enter.

Looking at Design

You have many possibilities when working with a fax cover sheet. As long as you follow the guidelines for readability, you have no limits to your creativity. A cover sheet is an opportunity to have fun with different fonts and font sizes. Bookman, Century Schoolbook, Palatino, Avant Garde, all look good. With a paint or draw program, try using a display type, such as outlined, shadowed, rotated, or reversed. The previous designs did not incorporate logos, although you could easily add one. The logo can be text or graphic. The following designs for a cover sheet offer some ideas and variations for an attention-grabbing fax.

Figure 11.5 illustrates a cover sheet you can create with either version of Word. The table feature produced the boxed banner lines, using one column and five rows. This design uses a thick border on the outside. The even one-inch top, left, and right margins contrast with the wide bottom margin. This design is asymmetrical in balance.

The company name is very large, and helps to balance the wide graphic box above. The phone number and fax number are 18 points and separated with a bullet. You have plenty of room to write and this cover sheet is attractive, too.

Figure 11.6 is the letterhead glossary you saved in Chapter 5. Glossaries inserted in various company documents help tie those documents together, creating unity and consistency in material published by that company. A customer recognizes the letterhead on the fax and feels immediately familiar with it.

268

CHAPTER 11

Producing a Fax Cover Sheet

| Date: |
| Attention: |
| From: |
| Pages: |
| Message: |

HUMBLE OPINIONS
(304) 255-5555 • FAX (304) 251-1155

FIG. 11.5. *Fax cover sheet created with Word's table feature.*

The large caps/small caps repeat from the letterhead to the banner lines. Type is 10-point Helv in both the address and banner, also creating consistency.

PART III

Creating Business Forms

FIG. 11.6. *Cover sheet with Letterhead glossary from Chapter 5.*

Figure 11.7 illustrates another heading example. The logo was created in Version 2.0 by adding a frame, then typing and formatting the HH inside. You can reproduce all but the box in Version 1.1 by offsetting the H's with superscript and subscript. This design makes an attractive cover sheet or letterhead.

Humble Opinions is 18 points; the address and phone numbers are small (10 points) but readable. A 2.25-point rule divides the heading from the banner lines.

Figure 11.8 is a cover sheet you can do in either version of Word. The shadow box has a thick, 2.25-point, rule and extends to the margins. The arrow was imported from CorelDRAW! and the word

CHAPTER 11

Producing a Fax Cover Sheet

FIG. 11.7. *A fax cover sheet design with logo and horizontal rule.*

FAX is 125-point Palatino. Your printer governs your font type and size. Very large words like these really attract attention.

Figure 11.9 features a variation of the display type. Fax, in lower case letters, is vertically placed beside a thick, 4-point rule. The vertical rule meets a short horizontal rule at the top of the page. Version 1.1 can do this design except for the very thick rule and the corner. The type is 125 points; again your printer capabilities will control the font size and type.

Figure 11.10 is simple and basic, but with a twist. A 125-point exclamation mark not only attracts attention, but also makes the recipient look to see who sent the fax.

FIG. 11.8. *Very large FAX as a point of emphasis.*

FIG. 11.9. *An unusual fax cover design solution.*

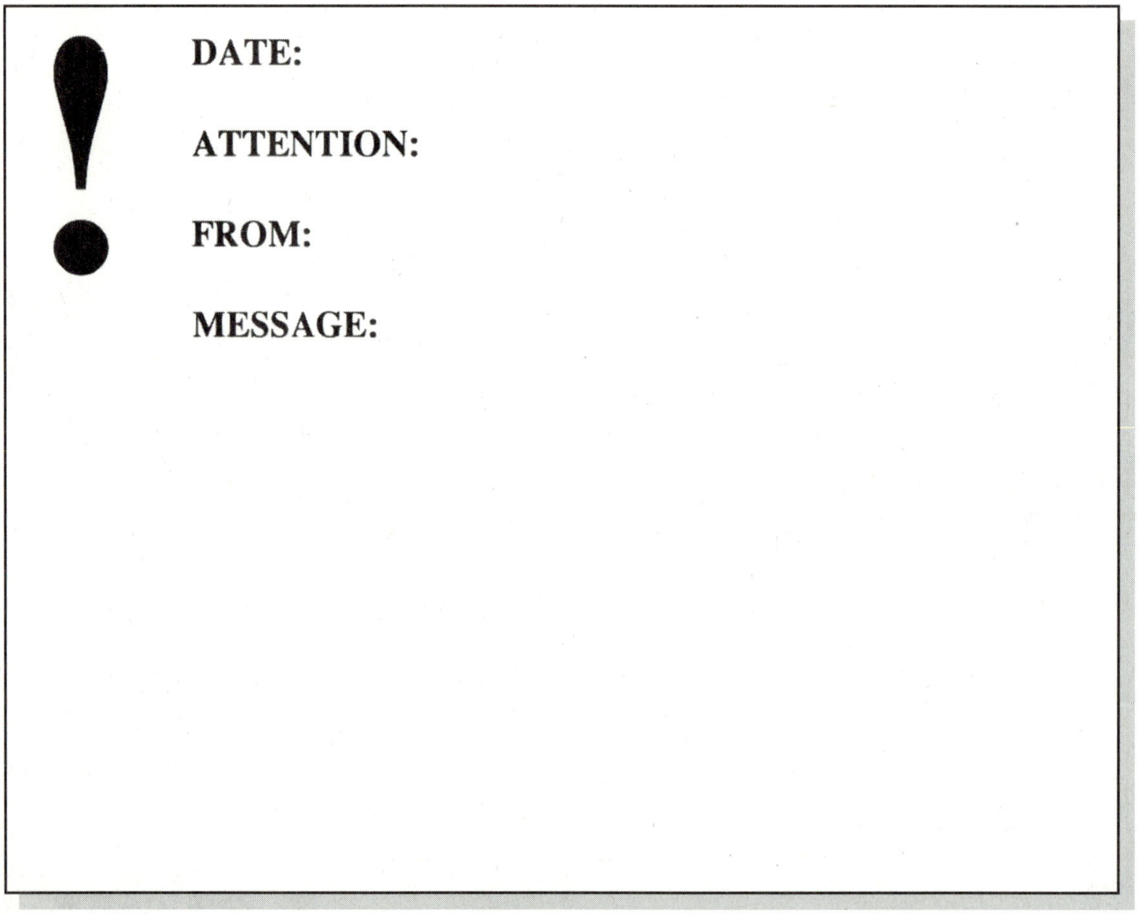

PART III

Creating Business Forms

DATE:

ATTENTION:

FROM:

MESSAGE:

FIG. 11.10. *A simple, basic, but eye-catching cover sheet.*

When a draw or paint program is available, consider a type variation for the word *fax*, or even your company logo. Use reversed type, apply a graduated screen, or conform the type to an envelope. These are just a few examples of the alterations you can do to type. Read the Reference program with your draw program, and experiment! Figure 11.11 shows examples of reversed type, screened type, and type shaped to an envelope, all created in CorelDRAW!.

Finally, figure 11.12 shows another design effect created in a draw program (CorelDRAW!): rotating type to any angle for an exciting change. Many programs allow you to rotate 90, 180, and 360 degrees, in 45-degree increments. In this example, the rotation, in addition to the play on words, may tempt the receiver to read further.

FIG. 11.11. The word **fax**, altered in a draw program, attracts attention on a cover sheet.

FIG. 11.12. *FACTS cover sheet, rotated in CorelDRAW!*

CHAPTER 11

Producing a Fax Cover Sheet

Recapping

In this chapter, you learned about the diverse uses of faxes and how to design and produce equally diverse fax cover sheets.

In Chapter 12, you learn how to produce a purchase order.

Producing a Purchase Order

I*n the business world, paperwork takes an inordinate amount of time, effort, and labor. Every day, business people are inundated with paperwork on purchases, sales, invoices, expenses, refunds, and so forth. Using standard forms helps reduce both the labor and the number of reports involved in completing paperwork.*

Forms summarize and organize the information that passes from department to department within a company, and from companies to customers. Standard forms provide a valuable time-saving feature by including the company's name, address, and phone number. In addition, forms ask for information related to their specific purpose. Also, forms can contain vertical and horizontal rules, boxes, or just a few lines to help establish order.

When you finish creating the forms in this and the following two chapters, you'll be able to produce forms of any type in Word. Word offers two distinct ways to create forms: by table, or by column. The table feature is by far the easiest method. The column feature may suit some designs as well. Both forms are discussed later on in this chapter.

Each design in this chapter is saved in document format. You may wish to enter your own company's name and address, and save the design as a template for later use. The procedure for opening and saving your own template was described in Chapter 11.

In addition to form design and creation, this chapter includes basic instructions and tips for writing macros and using fields to fill out a form, and then applying these techniques to one of the

PART III

Creating Business Forms

forms you created. After practicing these techniques, you can use macros and fields in any document you create in Word.

You can, of course, create forms on Word and then print the forms on your printer. Most forms, however, require at least two copies and sometimes four or more. When using printer-produced forms, and you need duplicates of the completed form, you must either fill them out individually or use carbon paper as you're filling them out. Consider doing the layout and master on Word and having them copied or printed at a print shop on carbonless paper. A form with carbonless paper copies (explained further in Chapter 4) consists of coated, color-coded sheets of paper that work like inserted carbon paper, but are much less expensive and less messy. Many copy shops can copy onto carbonless paper, then pad and even number your forms at a reasonable price.

Consecutive numbering is used on many forms and is essential on invoices and purchase orders. You can number forms yourself in your computer, but you must pay careful attention to the sequence. Print and copy shops can number them as well. When your print shop numbers your forms, follow these two guidelines in layout:

> Leave at least one inch (horizontally) for the number, usually in the upper right-hand area of the form.

> Ask your print shop how they handle the words or symbols for number (Number, No. or #), as most numbering machines automatically add *Number* or its symbol. However, you can add Number to your form, and then cover the word with white tape when not needed. Covering with white tape is a paste-up technique used to hide mistakes or unwanted text.

Finally, when using a typewriter to fill out forms, be careful of the spacing on the form. Typewriter type measures by line—single, one-half, double, triple, and so on. Setting your form by line spacing helps to ensure proper typewriter spacing. Normally, a form is set on at least one-half-line spacing, often double-line spacing, but never single-line spacing. Single-line spacing is too hard to fill in, and too hard to read after it's filled in.

CHAPTER 12

Producing a Purchase Order

Forms designed for typewriter use are measured from the top of the page to the first line that the typewriter fills in. The first line, and every line after, should begin on a 1/4 inch mark. When the first line does not begin on a 1/4 inch mark, adjust the line spacing within the heading or address. Before mass producing your form, first check for correct spacing by using your typewriter to type into the form. The first form you create in this chapter is on exact one-half-line spacing for use with a typewriter.

Producing a Purchase Order for Use With a Typewriter

The first design, shown in figure 12.1, is a basic purchase order. The order provides a heading, an area for information such as date, number, and purchased from, and uses a table for the purchase list. Although the information on a purchase order varies depending on the type of business, this form shows you how to produce a basic typewriter form.

The ruled lines for Date, Purchased From, and so forth are created with leader tabs. Leader tabs are an excellent way to do ruled lines because the ends are always even. Ruled lines are simple, they look good, and they're easy to make.

This particular sample, created on Version 2.0, uses 9-point type for the table heads. Although 8-point type works for forms, 9-point is much better. Version 1.1 allows 8- or 10-point type only, so the directions below reflect those limitations.

To create the form shown in figure 12.1, follow these steps:

1. Choose **F**ile, then **N**ew. In the New box, select **D**ocument. In the **U**se Template box, choose Normal, and then click OK or press Enter.

2. Choose Forma**t**, then **D**ocument. Change all Margins to **.5"**, and then click OK or press Enter.

2. Choose Forma**t**, then Page Se**t**up. In **M**argins, change all to **.5"**, and then click OK or press Enter.

3. Type the following text, or enter your own company's name, pressing Tab and Enter where indicated:

HUMBLE OPINIONS CORPORATION

P. O. Box 174
Oak Hill, WV 25901

FAX (304) 251-1155
(304) 255-5555

PURCHASE ORDER

Date: ______________________

Purchased From: ______________________

Attn.: ______________________

Address: ______________________

____

PO Number: ______________________

Purchased By: ______________________

Dept.: ______________________

Approved By: ______________________

QTY.	NUMBER	DESCRIPTION	UNIT PRICE	TOTAL

____
AUTHORIZED BY:

FIG. 12.1. Basic purchase order form using Word's table feature.

CHAPTER 12

Producing a Purchase Order

    HUMBLE OPINIONS CORPORATION (Enter)

    (Tab) **P. O. Box 174** (Tab) **FAX (304) 251-1155** (Enter)

    (Tab) **Oak Hill, WV 25901** (Tab) **(304) 255-5555** (Enter, Enter)

    PURCHASE ORDER (Enter, Enter, Enter)

    Date: (Tab, Tab) **PO Number:** (Tab) (Enter)

    Purchased From: (Tab, Tab) **Purchased By:** (Tab) (Enter)

    Attn.: (Tab, Tab) **Dept.:** (Tab) (Enter)

    Address: (Tab, Tab) **Approved By:** (Tab) (Enter) (Tab) (Enter four times)

4. Select the first line of text, HUMBLE...., and change to 24 points, bold, center-aligned.

5. Select the next two lines, from P. O. Box... to and including the second phone number (304)255-5555. Change the type to 12-point, Helv.

6. With this text still selected, follow these steps:

    Choose Forma**t**, then **T**abs. In the **T**ab Position box, type **.88"**, select **L**eft aligned, **S**et, and then press Del.

    In the **T**ab Position box, type **6.56"**, choose **R**ight aligned, **S**et, and then click OK or press Enter.

7. Select the text PURCHASE ORDER, and change to 12 points, bold, center-aligned.

8. Select the text from Date: to and including the tab below Address:, and change to 10-point, Helv.

9. With this text still selected, follow these procedures:

    Choose Forma**t**, then **T**abs. In the **T**ab Position box, type **3.5**, then choose **R**ight aligned. In the Leader box, choose **4**, **S**et, and then press Del.

    In the **T**ab Position box, type **3.75**, and choose **L**eft aligned, In the Leader box, choose None, **S**et, and press Del.

    In the **T**ab position box, type **7.5**, and choose **R**ight aligned. In the Leader box, choose **4**, **S**et, and then click OK or press Enter.

PART III

Creating Business Forms

10. Turn on Non-Printing Codes. Position the cursor on the next to the last paragraph return you typed.

11. Choose **I**nsert, then **T**able. For Number of **C**olumns, type **5**; For Number of **R**ows, type **24**. Select the gray command button labeled **F**ormat.

12. Select **N**ext Column. In the **W**idth of Column 1 box, type **.75"**. Choose **N**ext Column, and set Column 2 width for **1"**, select **N**ext Column, and set Column 3 width for **3.45"**, choose **N**ext Column, and set Column 4 width for **1.25"**, choose **N**ext Column, and set Column 5 width for **1.25"**. Click OK or press Enter.

13. Select the entire table, and follow these steps:

    Choose **F**ormat, then **T**able.

    In the Border box, for **O**utline choose Thick, and for **I**nside choose Single.

    Move to Minimum Row **H**eight, delete its contents, and type **1.5li**. Click OK or press Enter.

    If the gridlines don't appear on-screen, go to **V**iew, then **P**references, and turn on Table Gridlines. Click OK or press Enter.

11. Select Table, then Insert Table. For Number of **C**olumns, type **5**. For Number of **R**ows, type **24**. Click OK or press Enter.

    If the gridlines don't appear on-screen, go to **T**able, then **G**ridlines. A checkmark appears beside **G**ridlines in the menu to indicate that they are turned on.

12. Select the first column. Select Table, then Column **W**idth. For **W**idth of Column 1, type **.75"**. Select **N**ext Column, and set Column 2 width for **1"**, select **N**ext Column, and set Column 3 width for **3.45"**, select **N**ext Column, and set Column 4 width for **1.25"**, select **N**ext Column, and set Column 5 width for **1.25"**. Click OK or press Enter.

13. Select the entire table, and follow these procedures:

    Select **F**ormat, then **B**order. In the Preset box, choose Grid.

    In the Line box, choose the 1.25 rule, and then click OK or press Enter.

CHAPTER 12

Producing a Purchase Order

Select T**a**ble, then Row **H**eight. For **H**eight of Rows, choose At Least.

In the **A**t: box, type **1.5li**, and then click OK or press Enter.

14. Position the cursor in the left margin, beside the first row. When the cursor changes to a white arrow, double-click to select the first row of the table. Or with the keyboard, position the insertion point in the first cell. Press the F8 key (Extend Selection), then move to the last cell you want to select with the arrow keys. Choose Forma**t**, and then **T**able.

15. In the Border box, select **O**utline, and then choose Thick. For Minimum Row **H**eight, type **.35"**, and then click OK or press Enter.

14. Select the first row of the table. Choose Forma**t**, then **B**order. In the Bo**r**der box, click the bottom margin or use the down arrow key to highlight the bottom margin. In the **L**ine box, choose the 1.25 rule, and then click OK or press Enter.

15. Select the entire table. Select T**a**ble, then Row **H**eight. For Height of Rows, choose At Least. In the **A**t: box, type **1.5li**, and then click OK or press Enter.

16. Position the cursor in the first cell (first column, first row), Type the following text, pressing Tab where indicated:

    QTY., (Tab), **NUMBER**, (Tab), **DESCRIPTION**, (Tab), **UNIT PRICE**, (Tab), **TOTAL**.

17. Select the row you just typed, and change the type to 8-point, bold, Helv, center-aligned.

17. Select the row you just typed, and change the type to 9-point, bold, Helv, center-aligned.

18. Position the cursor on the last paragraph return at the bottom of the page.

    Press Enter and then press Shift-underline to make a signature line 2.5 inches to 3 inches long. Press Enter.

    Press Tab, and type **AUTHORIZED BY:**

19. Select and right align the underline. Use the Ribbon.

20. Select AUTHORIZED BY:, and change the type to Helv, 8-point. Use the Ruler and set the tab to 3".

285

PART III

Creating Business Forms

21. Select **F**ile, then Save **A**s. Type **po1**, and then click OK or press Enter.

22. Select **F**ile, **P**rint, and then click OK to print the form.

Both versions of Word offer an easy method of changing the widths of columns or cells. First select the column and then use the symbols on the ruler to adjust the boundaries of the table. In Version 1.1, click the Ruler icon, or activate the ruler by pressing Ctrl+Shift+F10, on the Ruler, to change the symbols. In Version 2.0, click the left-hand margin of the ruler to change symbols, or press Ctrl+Shift+F10 to activate the ruler. Symbols for tables appear as a T.

With Version 2.0, you can use a shortcut to insert a table at the cursor position. Choose the Table icon and drag the cursor to select the number of columns and rows (this option is available only to mouse users). Also in Version 2.0, you can add small boxes to a form for checking an answer, as in Yes and No questions. To create these boxes, go to Microsoft Draw.

Producing a Purchase Order for Reproduction

As mentioned in the introduction to this chapter, you may want to print or copy your purchase order forms onto carbonless paper. The next design, shown in figure 12.2, adapts to that purpose. The layout is in landscape orientation with two-up. Two-up refers to the way in which the form will print or copy—two forms per page. Running two forms on one sheet of paper, then trimming them down, is quick, easy, and inexpensive.

The trim size of this form is 5 1/2 inches x 8 1/2 inches. The inside space between the two columns, or *gutter*, is 1 inch, so that each form has a 1/2-inch margin all around. The word *gutter* has several meanings. In Word, gutter is listed with **M**argins, but gutter in the Margin dialog box is not for the space between columns, but rather for the binding margin of a page (see Chapter 4 for more details). For the space between columns, Word uses Spacing (Version 1.1) or Space between (Version 2.0), in the Columns dialog box.

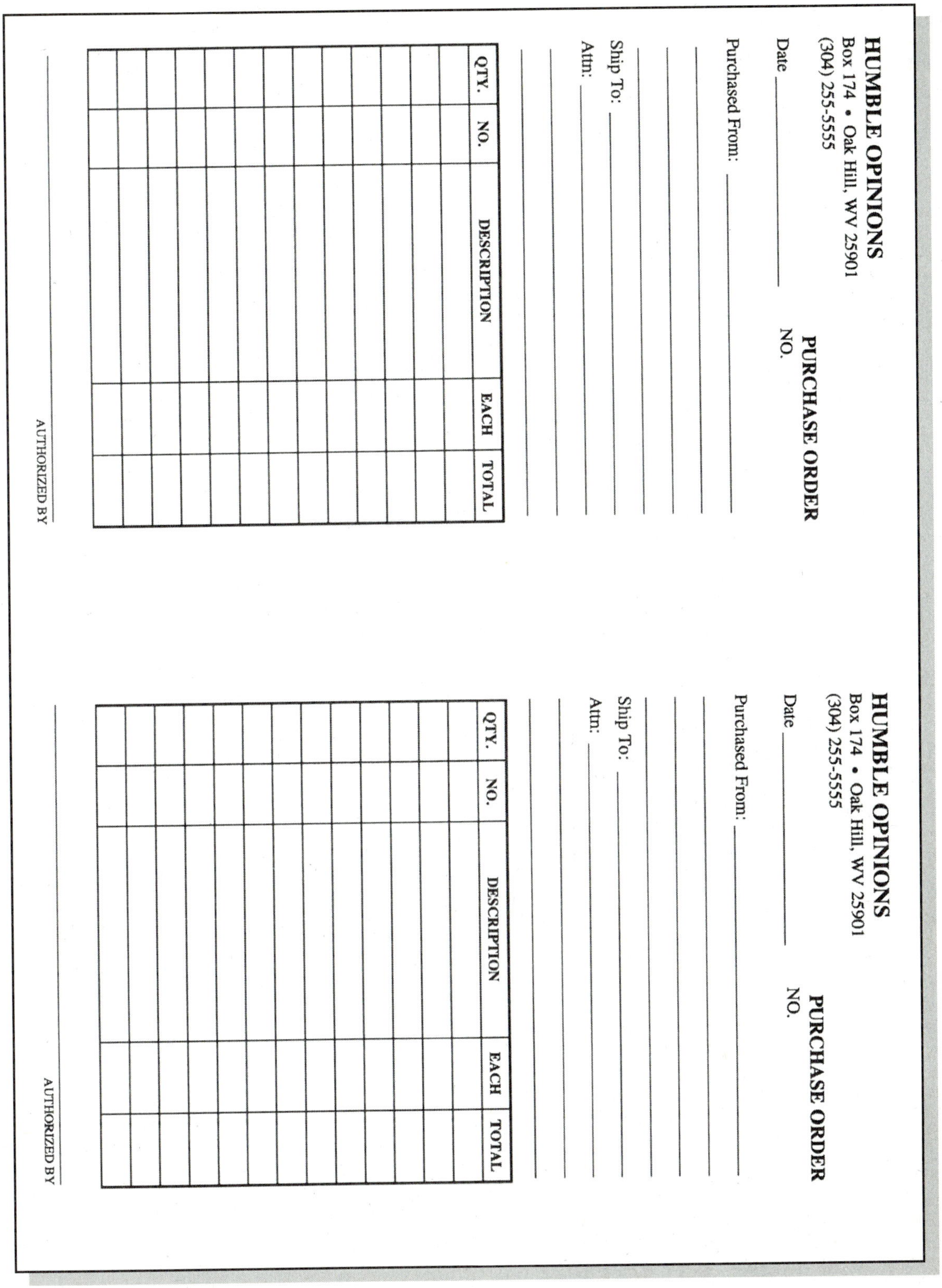

FIG. 12.2. *Purchase orders, set two up.*

PART III

Creating Business Forms

This purchase order is smaller than the others in this chapter, but may be sufficient when purchases are limited. Run these forms on your printer, or have them copied or offset-printed. Any quick print shop or commercial print shop can cut them in half for you, for a low price.

The lines for Purchased From, Ship To, and so on, are created with a right-aligned leader tab, like the previous design. The resulting lines are all even on the right, giving the form a neat appearance. Other details that make the form clean, sharp, and professional-looking are the slightly indented table (0.1 inch) to even the table with the rest of the form, and the two points of space added above the table heads to center them between the horizontal rules. Attention to intricate details like these separate the typesetters from the amateurs.

To create the form shown in figure 12.2, follow these steps:

1. Select **File**, then **New**. In the New box, choose **Document**. In the Use Template box, choose Normal, and then click OK or press Enter.

2. Choose **File**, **Printer Setup**, and then, in the dialog box, select **Setup**. Change the Orientation to **Landscape**, and click OK or press Enter. Word displays the message `Change current doc size...` Answer **Yes**.

3. Choose Format, then **Document**. Set all Margins to **.5"**, and then click OK or press Enter.

2. Choose Format, then Page Set**u**p. In the **S**ize and Orientation dialog box, change to **L**andscape.

3. In the **M**argins box, change all margins to **.5"**, and click OK or press Enter.

4. Choose Forma**t**, then **S**ection. For **N**umber of Columns, type **2**. For **S**pacing, type **1"**. For S**e**ction Start, choose No Break, and then click OK or press Enter.

4. Choose Forma**t**, then **C**olumns. For **N**umber of Columns, type **2**. For **S**pace Between, type **1"**. **A**pply to Whole Document, and then click OK

5. Type the text for the form, pressing Tab and Enter where indicated:

CHAPTER 12

Producing a Purchase Order

HUMBLE OPINIONS (Enter)

Box 174 (space bar four times) **Oak Hill, WV 25901** (Enter)

(304) 255-5555 (Enter)

(Tab) **PURCHASE ORDER** (Enter)

Date _____ (Tab) **NO.** (Enter, Enter)

Purchased From: (space bar) (Tab) (Enter)

(Tab) (Enter)

(Tab) (Enter)

(Tab) (Enter)

Ship To: (space bar) (Tab) (Enter)

Attn.: (space bar) (Tab) (Enter)

(Tab) (Enter)

(Tab) (Enter, Enter, Enter)

6. Select the text HUMBLE OPINIONS, and change the type to 14-point, bold. Use the Ribbon.

7. Position the cursor between ...Box 174 and Oak Hill..., and insert a bullet. Use the macro key created in Chapter 5 (Ctrl+8)

7. Position the cursor, choose **I**nsert, **S**ymbol, and then double-click the bullet or use the down and right arrow keys to select the bullet, and press Enter.

8. Select the text PURCHASE ORDER, and set a left-aligned tab at 2.5". Use the ruler.

9. Select the text Date and NO. Choose Forma**t**, click **T**abs. In the **T**ab Position box, type **2.44"**, set for **L**eft aligned, click **S**et, and then click OK or press Enter.

10. Select the text from Purchased From... to Attn: plus the following two paragraph returns (address lines). Choose Format, click **T**abs. In the **T**ab Position box, type **4"**, and set for **R**ight aligned. In the Leader box, choose number **4**, click **S**et, and then click OK or press Enter.

11. With the text still selected, Choose Forma**t**, then **P**aragraph. In Spacing, **L**ine type **1.5li**. Click OK or press Enter.

PART III

Creating Business Forms

11. With type still selected, choose Forma**t**, then **P**aragraph. For Line Spacing, type **1.5li**, and then click OK or press Enter.

12. Position the cursor on the next to the last paragraph return on the page. Choose **I**nsert, then **T**able. For the Number of **C**olumns, type **5**; for the Number of **R**ows, type **13**.

13. While still in this dialog box, choose the **F**ormat command button. Select **N**ext Column to begin setting the column widths. In **W**idth of Column 1 box, type **.5"**, and choose **N**ext Column. For the Width of Column 2, type **.5"**, and choose **N**ext Column. Repeat this procedure, setting Column 3 at **1.85"**, Column 4 at **.6"**, and Column 5 at **.6"**. Click OK or press Enter.

12. Choose T**a**ble, and then Insert Table. For the Number of **C**olumns, type **5**. For the Number of **R**ows, type **13**.

13. Select the first column. Select T**a**ble, and then Column **W**idth. In the Width of Column 1 box, type **.5"**, and choose **N**ext Column. For the Width of Column 2, type **.5"**, and choose **N**ext Column. Repeat this procedure, setting Column 3 at **1.85"**, Column 4 at **.6"**, and Column 5 at **.6"**. Click OK or press Enter.

14. Select the entire table. When the gridlines are not showing, go to **V**iew, choose P**r**eferences, and turn on Table **G**ridlines. Choose **F**ormat, then **T**able. For In**d**ent Rows, type **.1"**. For Minimum Row **H**eight, type **1.5li**.

15. While still in the dialog box, move to the Borders box. For **O**utline, choose Thick; for **I**nside, choose Single, and then click OK or press Enter.

14. Select the entire table. When the gridlines are not showing, choose T**a**ble and **G**ridlines. Choose T**a**ble, then Row Height. In the Indent from Left box, type **.1"**.

15. While in the same dialog box, move to **H**eight of Rows, and choose At Least. In the **A**t: box, type **1.5li**, and click OK or press Enter. With the entire table still selected, go to Forma**t**, and then **B**order. In the Preset box, choose **G**rid. In the Line box, choose the 1.25 rule, and then click OK or press Enter.

16. Position the cursor in the first cell—first column, first row—of the table. Type the following text, pressing Tab where indicated:

CHAPTER 12

Producing a Purchase Order

QTY., (Tab), **NO.**, (Tab), **DESCRIPTION**, (Tab), **EACH**, (Tab), **TOTAL**.

17. Select the row of type, and change to 8-point, bold, center-aligned. Use the Ribbon.

17. Select the row of type, and change to 9-point, bold, center-aligned. Use the Ribbon.

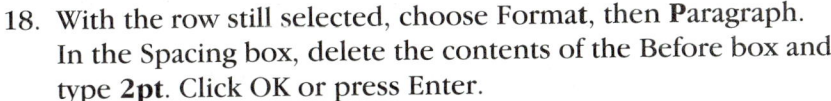

18. With the row still selected, choose Forma**t**, then **P**aragraph. In the Spacing box, delete the contents of the Before box and type **2pt**. Click OK or press Enter.

    This step lowers, and centers, the head vertically in the table. Word allows you to set spacing by lines (single, one-and-one-half, double, and so on). You may also set spacings by points for smaller increments.

19. Position the cursor on the last paragraph return in the column.

    Press Enter, Press Tab, and press Enter.

    Press Tab, type **AUTHORIZED BY**, and press Enter.

20. Select the line with only the tab. Choose Forma**t**, then **T**abs. Type **4"**, and set for **R**ight aligned. In the Leader choose number 4, **S**et, and then click OK or press Enter.

21. Select the text AUTHORIZED BY:, and change to 8 points. Set the tab on the Ruler, as right aligned at 4".

22. Position the cursor at the end of AUTHORIZED BY:. Choose **I**nsert, then **B**reak. Choose **C**olumn Break, and then click OK or press Enter.

23. Select the entire first column, from HUMBLE... to AUTHORIZED BY:. Choose **E**dit, then **C**opy (or press Ctrl+Insert). Position the cursor at the paragraph return in the second column. Choose **E**dit, then **P**aste (or Shift+Insert) to copy the form into the second column.

24. Select File, Save **A**s, type **po2**, and then click OK or press Enter.

25. Select File, **P**rint, and then click OK to print the two-up form.

291

PART III

Creating Business Forms

> **NOTE**
>
> Change the orientation of the page before beginning the next document. To change the orientation, select **F**ile, go to **P**rinter Setup, and then **S**etup. For Orientation, choose **P**ortrait, and then click OK or press Enter.

Producing a Purchase Order for Use with Fields

The purchase order shown in figure 12.3 incorporates two tables within one form. The first table merely separates the information with lines inside a box, to create an ordered look for the information. This design also enables you to apply fields and macros to the information table, described later in this chapter.

The second table of this form is similar to ones you produced earlier, except for the two-line heads, and the area for sub total, tax and total.

This design also demonstrates two methods of producing a table. One method converts text to table form, and the other method begins with a table, then adds the text.

To create the form shown in figure 12.3, follow these steps:

1. Choose **F**ile, **N**ew, and in the New box, click **D**ocument. In the Use Template box, choose Normal, and then click OK or press Enter.

2. Choose Forma**t**, **D**ocument, set all margins to **.5"**, and click OK or press Enter.

2. Choose Forma**t**, then Page Set**u**p. For **M**argins, set all to **.5"**, and click OK or press Enter.

HUMBLE OPINIONS

P. O. BOX 174
OAK HILL, WV 25901
(304) 255-5555

PURCHASE ORDER

DATE:	PO NUMBER:
PURCHASED FROM:	
SHIP ATTENTION TO:	
BILL ATTENTION TO:	
CONFIRMING ORDER REQUESTED BY:	SHIP BY:
TERMS:	
COMMENTS:	

QTY	ITEM NUMBER	DESCRIPTION	UNIT PRICE	TOTAL PRICE
			SUB TOTAL	
			STATE TAX	
			TOTAL	

AUTHORIZED BY: ______________________________

FIG. 12.3. *A purchase order created with two tables.*

PART III

Creating Business Forms

3. Type the text for the form, pressing Tab and Enter where indicated:

   HUMBLE OPINIONS (Enter)

   P. O. BOX 174 (Enter)

   OAK HILL, WV 25901 (Enter)

   (304) 255-5555 (Enter, Enter, Enter, Enter)

   PURCHASE ORDER (Enter, Enter)

   DATE: (Tab) **PO NUMBER:** (Enter)

   PURCHASED FROM: (Enter, Enter, Enter, Enter)

   SHIP ATTENTION TO: (Enter)

   BILL ATTENTION TO: (Enter)

   CONFIRMING ORDER REQUESTED BY: (Tab) **SHIP BY:** (Enter)

   TERMS: (Enter)

   COMMENTS: (Enter, Enter, Enter)

4. Select the text HUMBLE OPINIONS, and change to 24-point bold, center-aligned. Use the Ribbon.

5. Select the next three lines, the address to phone number, and change to 12-point, Helv, center-aligned. Use the Ribbon.

6. Select the text PURCHASE ORDER, and change to Helv, 14-point, bold, center-aligned. Use the Ribbon.

7. Position the cursor in front of DATE:. Select the next nine lines, to the end of COMMENTS:.

8. Use the Ribbon to change the type to Helv, 10-point, bold.

9. With this text still selected, Choose For**m**at, then click **T**abs. In the **T**ab Position box, type **4"**. Set for **L**eft aligned, choose **S**et, and then click OK or press Enter.

10. With the text still selected, choose For**m**at, then **P**aragraph. In the Spacing box, for Line, type **1.5li**, and then click OK or press Enter.

11. With the text still selected, choose **I**nsert, then **T**able. For the Number of **C**olumns, type **1**. The value for the Number of **R**ows is automatically entered.

CHAPTER 12

Producing a Purchase Order

12. While still in the Table dialog box, choose the **Format** button. For **W**idth of Columns, type **7.40"**.

13. In the same dialog box, move to the Borders box. For **O**utline, choose Thick; for **I**nside, choose Single, and then click OK or press Enter.

    When the table gridlines are off, choose **V**iew, then **P**references to turn them on.

10. With the text still selected, choose Forma**t**, then **P**aragraph. For Line Spacing, choose At Least, and in the **A**t: box, type **1.5li**. Click OK or press Enter.

11. With the text still selected, choose **T**able, then Insert Table. For the Number of **C**olumns, type **1**, and then click OK or press Enter.

12. Select Ta**b**le, then Row Height. For **H**eight of Rows, choose At Least, and in the **A**t: box, type **1.5li**. Choose OK or press Enter. Select **T**able, then Column Width. For **W**idth of Column, type **7.40"**, and then click OK or press Enter.

13. Select the entire table. Choose Forma**t**, then **B**order. In the Preset box, choose **G**rid. For **L**ine, choose the 1.25 rule, and then click OK or press Enter. If the tabs on the first and seventh lines don't appear, then position the cursor and press Ctrl+Tab.

14. Position the cursor on the next to the last paragraph return.

15. Choose Insert, then **T**able. For Number of **C**olumns, type **5**. For Number of **R**ows, type **19**.

16. While in the same dialog box, choose the **F**ormat button. Choose **N**ext Column to begin with Column 1. For **W**idth of Column 1, type **.70"**. Select **N**ext Column, and for the Width of Column 2, type **1"**. Repeat this procedure, setting Column 3 to **3.5"**, Column 4 to **1.10"**, and Column 5 to **1.15"**. Click OK or press Enter.

17. Select the entire table. Choose Forma**t**, then T**a**ble. For Minimum Row Height, type **1.5li**. In the Border box, for O**u**tline choose Thick; for **I**nside, choose Single. Click OK or press Enter.

15. Choose T**a**ble, then **I**nsert Table. In Number of **C**olumns, type **5**; in Number of **R**ows, type 19. Select the first column of the table.

295

PART III

Creating Business Forms

16. Choose Table, then Column Width. For Width of Column 1, type **.70"**. Select Next Column, and for the width of Column 2, type **1"**, choose Next Column. Repeat this procedure, setting Column 3 to **3.5"**, Column 4 to **1.10"**, and Column 5 to **1.15"**. Click OK or press Enter.

17. Select the entire table. Choose Format, then Border. In the Preset box, choose Grid. In the Line box, choose the 1.25 rule. Click OK or press Enter. Now choose Table, then Row Height. For Height of Rows, choose At Least. In the At: box, type **1.5li**, and then click OK or press Enter.

18. Position the cursor in the first cell—first row, first column—of the second table. Type the following, pressing Tab and Enter where indicated:

    QTY. (Tab) **ITEM** (Enter) **NUMBER**

    (Tab) **DESCRIPTION** (Tab) **UNIT** (Enter) **PRICE**

    (Tab) **TOTAL** (Enter) **PRICE**

19. Select these two lines of type, and using the Ribbon, change to Helv, 8-point, bold, center-aligned.

20. With the text still selected, choose Format, then Table. In the Border box, for Outline, choose Thick, and then click OK or press Enter.

19. Select these two lines of text, and using the Ribbon, change to Helv, 9-point, bold, center-aligned.

20. With the text still selected, choose Format, then Border. In the Border box, click in the bottom margin. In the Line box, choose the 1.25 rule, and click OK or press Enter.

21. Position the cursor in the bottom right-hand corner of the table, three lines up in the Unit Price column.

    Type **SUB TOTAL**, and reposition cursor on the next line.

    Type **STATE TAX**, and reposition cursor on the next line.

    Type **TOTAL**.

22. Select these three lines of type, and using the Ribbon, change to Helv, 10-point, bold, center-aligned.

23. Select the last three cells of the table, in the TOTAL PRICE column and to the right of the three lines of type.

CHAPTER 12

Producing a Purchase Order

24. Click Format, then click Table. In the Borders box, for Outline, click to choose Thick, and then click OK or press Enter.

24. Select Format, then Border. In the Border box, click the top margin, hold the Shift key and click the left margin. In the Line box, choose the 1.25 rule. and click OK or press Enter.

25. Position the cursor on the last paragraph return. Press Enter, and type

    AUTHORIZED BY: _____

    The signature line should be 2.5 inches to 3 inches long.

26. Select this last line of type, and change to Helv, 8-point.

26. Select this last line of type, and change to Helv, 9-point.

27. Choose File, Save As, type **po3**, and then click OK to save the form.

28. Choose File, Print, and then click OK to print the form.

Other options are available in tables. Figure 12.4 shows the shading option in Word Version 2.0. In this example, the first table of information is shaded, but you could shade only the TOTAL PRICE column or ITEM NUMBER column, and so forth. Shading directs attention to a particular area of the page and is often useful in forms. To add shading by using Version 2.0, follow these steps:

1. Select the block to be shaded.

2. Click Format, then click Border.

3. Click the gray command button labeled Shading. In Pattern, choose the percentage shading desired. Never use more than 20 percent shading with type in the block to be shaded. With too much shading, you can't read the type.

4. Click OK and then click OK again.

You may add shading when using Word Version 1.1, but not with the computer. A print shop can do the shading in its camera department. Remember to use no more than 20 percent shading with type in the box.

297

HUMBLE OPINIONS

P. O. BOX 174
OAK HILL, WV 25901
(304) 255-5555

PURCHASE ORDER

DATE:	PO NUMBER:
PURCHASED FROM:	
SHIP ATTENTION TO:	
BILL ATTENTION TO:	
CONFIRMING ORDER REQUESTED BY:	SHIP BY:
TERMS:	
COMMENTS:	

QTY	ITEM NUMBER	DESCRIPTION	UNIT PRICE	TOTAL PRICE
			SUB TOTAL	
			STATE TAX	
			TOTAL	

AUTHORIZED BY: ______________________________

FIG. 12.4. Purchase Order of figure 12.3 with shading added.

Adding Field Codes and a Macro to a Form

With some pre-planning, you may fill in your form on the computer, without using a typewriter or hand-written entries. Word allows you to type directly into a form like PO3.DOC, shown in figure 12.3. However, when you use a right-aligned leader tab to create lines for information, such as PO1.DOC and PO2.DOC, the lines disappear and the type starts on the right. When you plan to fill in this kind of form on the computer, leave these lines out altogether or use a table.

After you create a form by using tables, it's easy to fill. Just save the form as a template, then start new documents based on this template.

Two Word features that help you enter information into forms are Field Codes and Macros. As demonstrated in Chapter 10, Word prompts you for specific information and then inserts the information into the proper area for you. This feature is especially helpful to people who are not experienced with computers but must use them to fill out forms.

Brief Summary of Field Codes

Field Codes make some tasks in Word easier and more efficient. Field Codes direct Word to insert specific information into your document. Some of these items include dates, page numbers, text, pictures, indexes, tables of contents, and tables. Word supplies many choices of field types, and enables you to write your own instructions.

Each Field Code must contain at least three items—the Field Characters, the Field Types, and the instructions. You can add more items to clarify instructions, such as switches, arguments, nesting, and so on. Your Reference Manual covers each in detail.

The first item in a Field Code is the Field Characters, which are inserted with the Insert Field key. They are the braces that surround the instructions and Field Type. These braces {} look like those on your keyboard. You cannot, however, use the braces on the keyboard; you must use special characters for Fields.

PART III

Creating Business Forms

To insert the Field Characters, use the Insert Field key, Ctrl+F9, which inserts both the beginning and end characters, or braces. You then add the Field Type and instructions inside them.

The second item, the

Field Type, defines the action. A few Field Types are XE (Index Entry), Formulas, Glossary, Footnotes, and Fillin. Fillin and Date are the Field Types used in the example later in this section. In Word's menu, after clicking **I**nsert and then Fiel**d**, you choose the field you wish to use. Word then inserts the field codes at the cursor location, including Field Characters and Field Type. All you need do is write the instructions.

The third item is a set of instructions. These are directions to perform specific tasks. Instructions include telling the user to type something (fillin), formatting type, calculating equations, or even inserting information from another application. You must type a space between the Field Type and the instructions, or they will not work.

Many Field Types work with forms. As mentioned earlier, Fillin and Date are two used in the example later in this section. *Ask*, *Autonum*, *Seq*, and *Merge* are other fields you may wish to read more about in your Reference Manual.

Here are a few tips and shortcuts in using Field Codes in Word. For more detailed explanations, consult your Reference Manual. The on-line Help feature in both versions of Word is of great benefit for understanding Fields.

- To view the Field Codes after you enter them, you must turn them on by choosing **V**iew menu, then Field **C**odes. Similarly, to view the results of the Codes in a document, you must turn them off by choosing **V**iew, and then Field **C**odes.

- You cannot delete a single field character; deleting one deletes both. To edit a field, position the cursor in the field, then press Shift+F9 to display the codes. Edit the type or instructions, and press F9 to update and test the results.

- To format the contents or results of a field, select and format as usual. When you must jump to fields, for updating or formatting, use the Next Field key, F11 or Alt+F1. For the Previous Field key, use either Shift+F11 or Alt+Shift+F1. These Jump to Field keys don't work on XE (Index Entry), TC (Table of Contents) or RD (Reference Document) Field Codes. Consult your Manual for more information. Chapter 21 also creates and uses these Field Types.

CHAPTER 12

Producing a Purchase Order

Brief Summary of Macros

A macro is a sequence of commands. These commands can be typewritten text, formatting text, setting of options, or any command you or Word create to perform specific functions. Word comes with many macros ready for use, and allows you to create many, many more. In Chapter 5, you created a macro for inserting a bullet by using Version 1.1 instructions.

Word makes macros easy. All you do is Record the Macro. In Version 1.1, choose **M**acro and then turn on Re**c**ord. Or, in Version 2.0, turn on **R**ecord with the To**o**ls menu. After the macro begins to record, you just perform the tasks you want the macro to include. Choose **M**acro, Stop Re**c**ording, and **S**ave when you're finished.

The macro you use in the next set of instructions is *AutoNew*. AutoNew automatically performs the recorded tasks whenever you open a new document. In this example, you apply the macro only to the one template. You can, however, apply any macro globally when you wish the macro to activate upon beginning any new document.

Two other valuable macros you may want to use with forms, or any other document, are *AutoExec* and *AutoOpen*. For example, with a computer dedicated to doing only purchase orders, or invoices, an AutoExec macro loads the form template every time Word is started on that computer. Turning on the computer automatically loads the form and you're ready to begin. A switch is available for starting Word when you don't want the template to automatically load.

Creating Fields and a Macro for Your Form

In Chapter 10, you used Word's pre-written fields and macros. In this section, you create fields and a macro to automatically insert information into the form shown in figure 12.3 (PO3.DOC). After you complete this section, you'll be on your way to creating fields and macros for your other Word documents.

PART III

Creating Business Forms

These instructions are for two different fields. You can repeat the steps described here to fill in the entire first table. You can add your own fields and macros, as well. These instructions get you started.

Figure 12.5 shows the finished Fields in PO3.DOT with **V**iew, Field **C**odes on. This screen is the Version 2.0 screen, at 87 percent Zoom. Version 2.0 lets you customize the percentage of the Zoom screen so you can view any amount of the screen you want.

FIG. 12.5.
Purchase order template with Field Codes on.

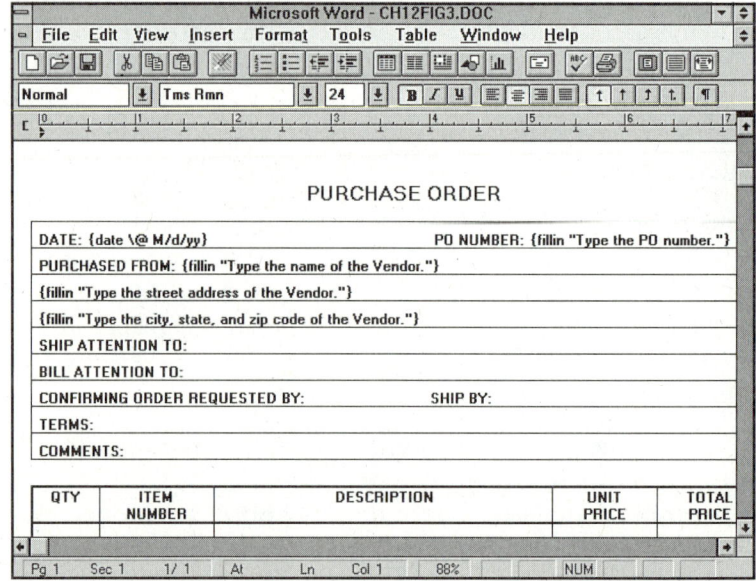

To create the template shown in figure 12.5, follow these steps:

1. Choose **F**ile, **O**pen, and open the document PO3.DOC.

2. Choose **F**ile, then Save **A**s. In the dialog box, choose the **O**ptions button. In **F**ile Format, choose Document Template. You may rename the file, but remember to change the extension to DOT. Click OK or press Enter.

2. Choose **F**ile, then Save **A**s. In Save File As **T**ype, choose Document Template [*.DOT]. You may rename the file, but remember to change the extension to DOT. Click OK or press Enter.

3. Turn on Field Codes by choosing View, then Field Codes.

302

CHAPTER 12

Producing a Purchase Order

4. Position the cursor after the word DATE:, and type: **space**. Click **I**nsert, then choose Fiel**d**. In the Insert Field type box, choose Date. In the Instructions box, choose M/d/yy, and then click OK or press Enter.

5. Position the cursor to the right of PO NUMBER:.

   Press the space bar, press Ctrl+F9, and type **fillin "Type the PO number."**

> **NOTE**
>
> Depending on your purchase order numbering system, you may be able to create a field for automatic numbering by using the SEQ field, but two problems make this difficult. One, if you use \r as a switch to refer to the number—so the next number increases with each PO completed—then all purchase orders have to be in the same document, which is not feasible with thousands of purchase orders. Second, for Word to recognize the numbering sequence, the instructions in the field must be rewritten when your number moves up another digit. For instance, from 999 to 1000, or from 9999 to 10,000. Again, this is not really practical. When you want to try writing a field for automatic numbering, call the Microsoft Word technical assistance folks. They are extremely competent and very helpful.

6. Position the cursor to the right of PURCHASED FROM:. Press the space bar, press Ctrl+F9, and type **fillin "Type the name of the Vendor."**

   Position the cursor in the next line (address line). Press the space bar, press Ctrl+F9, and type **fillin "Type the street address of the Vendor."**

   Position the cursor in the next line (city line). Press the space bar, press Ctrl+F9, and type **fillin "Type the city, state and zip code of the Vendor."**

7. Place the cursor at the beginning of the form. Choose **M**acro, then **R**ecord.

8. In Record Macro Name, type **autonew**. Choose **T**emplate, and click OK or press Enter.

303

PART III

Creating Business Forms

7. Place the cursor at the beginning of the form. Choose T**o**ols, then **R**ecord Macro.

8. In Record Macro **N**ame, type **autonew**. In Store Macro, choose **T**emplate, and click OK or press Enter.

9. Press F11 to select the first field, and then press F9 to update the field and display the dialog box. Click OK or press Enter.

10. Repeat this procedure with all the fields.

11. Place the cursor to the right of SHIP ATTENTION TO:. Press the space bar.

    By stopping the macro with the cursor positioned here, the cursor will position in the same spot when the macro runs in a new document.

12. Choose **M**acro, then Stop Re**c**order.

12. Choose T**o**ols, then Stop **R**ecorder.

13. Choose **F**ile, then **S**ave. Turn off Field Codes by choosing **V**iew, then Field **C**odes.

14. Choose **F**ile, then **C**lose.

You can now begin a new document and use this template. When Word starts the new doc, you're prompted with the questions just created. Take a moment to start a new document based on this template, so you can see the results of your macro and fields.

Looking at Design

You can produce simple or complicated forms in Word. A purchase order may need much more information than the samples included in this chapter. On the other hand, your purchase order may need less. Figure 12.6 shows a simple purchase order you can produce with the table feature or with tabs. When you use the table feature, you may turn on only a few lines. When using tabs to create this design, you apply the borders above and below.

This design works well when you have a lot of information that does not fit into a very strict form.

You can also produce a purchase order, or any form, with the use of columns instead of tables. Although tables are easier to control, columns may work in some situations. Figure 12.7 shows a purchase order created with columns in a landscape orientation.

HUMBLE OPINIONS
P. O. BOX 174 • OAK HILL, WV 25901
(304) 255-5555

PURCHASE ORDER

P O NUMBER

DATE

QTY	ITEM #	DESCRIPTION	PRICE	TOTAL

SUB TOTAL

SALES TAX

TOTAL

FIG. 12.6. *A purchase order with few lines dividing information.*

PART III

Creating Business Forms

FIG. 12.7. *A purchase order created with columns.*

The logo was drawn in CorelDRAW! and inserted as a picture. The margins are wide on the right and bottom for an interesting effect. The columns are all the same width, which may work for certain entries, and the lines between the columns were turned on in the column dialog box.

Recapping

This chapter showed you how to create purchase orders for use with a typewriter, for reproduction, and for use with fields and macros.

In Chapter 13, you learn how to produce an expense or travel report.

Producing a Travel or Expense Report

13

Business people who conduct work-related travel record their trips in a travel report, or log. Most companies compensate mileage for personal auto use, or require accounting for mileage when using the company car. A travel log is the most efficient method of tracking mileage.

Other expenses reimbursed as part of a business trip include authorized expenses for meals, hotels, and client entertainment. Forms are the perfect way to record these business expenses, as they organize the information, and keep all entries consistent for easy classification.

Because these are in-house forms, the company's name, logo, address, and phone are not necessary.

In this chapter, you create four forms: two variations of a travel log and two variations of an expense report. Besides organizing the information in different ways, you also learn more about tables. By varying borders, splitting tables, and merging cells in a table, you expand the form's application.

Producing a Travel Log

A travel log documents dates and mileage. Many companies require the time and mileage at departure, and upon arrival. The weekly Travel Log, shown in figure 13.1, divides those requirements into two columns, *OUT* and *IN*. The bold lines between entries make reading and identifying sections per trip easier. Varying the rule for just one cell or an entire row is easy with Word's table feature.

PART III

Creating Business Forms

Because travel logs are usually filled in by hand, rows, in most cases, are double-spaced to make these handwritten entries easier.

To create the Travel Log shown in figure 13.1, follow these steps:

1. Choose **F**ile, then **N**ew. In the New box, choose **D**ocument. In the **T**emplate box, choose Normal, and then click OK or press Enter.

2. Choose Forma**t**, **D**ocument, and set all margins to .5". Click OK or press Enter.

2. Choose Forma**t**, Page Set**u**p, and in **M**argins, set all to .5". Click OK or press Enter.

3. Choose Forma**t**, then **S**tyle(s). Choose **D**efine, click **C**haracter and then choose 10-point Helv.

Click OK or press Enter.

Click Apply or press Enter.

4. Type the following text, pressing Tab and Enter where indicated:

   TRAVEL LOG (Enter, Enter)

   NAME (Tab, Tab) **WEEK OF** (Tab) (Enter)

   STARTING MILEAGE (Tab, Tab) **ENDING MILEAGE** (Tab) (Enter, Enter, Enter, Enter)

5. Select TRAVEL LOG. Use the Ribbon to change the type to 18-point, bold, center-aligned.

6. Select the type from NAME up to and including the Tab after ENDING MILEAGE. Follow these steps:

   Choose Forma**t**, then **T**abs. In the **T**ab Position box, type **3.75"**, and choose **R**ight align. In the Leader box, choose 4, and choose **S**et.

   Press Del to delete the contents of the **T**ab Position box.

   In the **T**ab position box, type **4"**, choose **L**eft aligned, click **S**et, and press Del.

   In the **T**ab position box, type **7.45"**, and choose **R**ight align. In the Leader box, choose 4, choose **S**et, and then click OK or press Enter.

TRAVEL LOG

NAME _____ WEEK OF _____

STARTING MILEAGE _____ ENDING MILEAGE _____

OUT		IN	
DATE/TIME		DATE/TIME	
MILEAGE		MILEAGE	
DATE/TIME		DATE/TIME	
MILEAGE		MILEAGE	
DATE/TIME		DATE/TIME	
MILEAGE		MILEAGE	
DATE/TIME		DATE/TIME	
MILEAGE		MILEAGE	
DATE/TIME		DATE/TIME	
MILEAGE		MILEAGE	
DATE/TIME		DATE/TIME	
MILEAGE		MILEAGE	
DATE/TIME		DATE/TIME	
MILEAGE		MILEAGE	
DATE/TIME		DATE/TIME	
MILEAGE		MILEAGE	
DATE/TIME		DATE/TIME	
MILEAGE		MILEAGE	
DATE/TIME		DATE/TIME	
MILEAGE		MILEAGE	

SIGNATURE _____ TOTAL MILES _____

FIG. 13.1. *A weekly travel log to record dates and mileage.*

PART III

Creating Business Forms

7. Position the cursor on the next to the last paragraph return. Choose **Insert**, then **Table**.

8. For Number of **Columns**, type **4**. For Number of **Rows**, type **21**. Choose the **Format** button.

9. Select **Next** Column. In the **Width** of Column 1 box, type **1**". Select **Next** Column and set Column 2 for 2.75". Choose **Next** Column and set Column 3 for 1". Choose **Next** Column and set Column 4 for 2.75".

10. While still in this dialog box, move to Minimum Row **Height**, and type **2li**.

11. While still in this dialog box, move to the Borders box. For Outline choose Thick. For Inside choose Single, and then click OK or press Enter.

   When the gridlines are not showing, choose **View**, **Preferences**, turn on Table **Gridlines**, and then click OK or press Enter.

12. Select the first two cells in the first row of the table. Choose **Edit**, **Table**, and then **Merge Cells**. Repeat with the next two cells in the first row.

7. Position the cursor on the next to the last paragraph return. Choose **Table**, then **Insert Table**.

8. For Number of **Columns**, type **4**. For Number of **Rows**, type **21**, and click OK or press Enter.

   When the gridlines are not showing, choose **Table** and **Gridlines**.

9. Select the entire table. Choose **Table**, and then Row **Height**. Move to **Height** of Rows and choose At Least. In the **At:** box, type **2li**, and click OK or press Enter.

10. While in the Table dialog box, click Forma**t**, and then **B**order. In the Preset box, choose Grid. In the Line box, choose the 2.25 rule, and then click OK or press Enter.

   When the Gridlines don't appear on your screen, choose **T**able, then click **G**ridlines.

11. Select the first column of the table. Select **T**able, and then Column **W**idth. For **W**idth of Column 1, type **1**", and choose

CHAPTER 13

Producing a Travel or Expense Report

Next Column. Repeat this procedure, setting Column 2 at **2.75"**, Column 3 at **1"**, and Column 4 at **2.75"**. Click OK or press Enter.

12. Select the first two cells of the first row. Choose T**a**ble, then **M**erge Cells. Repeat with the next two cells of the first row.

13. Position the cursor in the first cell, and type the following text and press Tab and Enter where indicated:

    OUT (Tab) **IN** (Tab)

    DATE/TIME (Tab, Tab) **DATE/TIME** (Tab, Tab)

    MILEAGE (Tab, Tab) **MILEAGE** (Tab, Tab)

14. Select the last two lines, from the first DATE... up to and including the Tab following the last MILEAGE. Press Ctrl+C to copy. Position the cursor on the fourth row, and press Shift+Insert to paste. Reposition the cursor on the sixth row, and press Shift+Insert. Repeat this copy procedure to complete the table. Or, you can go to the **I**nsert menu, **P**aste.

15. Select the text OUT and IN. Use the Ribbon, and change the type to 14-point, bold, center-aligned.

16. With the text still selected, choose Forma**t**, and then **P**aragraph. In the Spacing box, choose **B**efore, type **3pt** and click OK or press Enter.

17. Select all DATE/TIME and MILEAGE text. Choose Forma**t**, and then **P**aragraph. In the Spacing box, click **B**efore, type **.5li**, and click OK or press Enter.

18. Select the entire first row of the table. Choose Forma**t**, and then T**a**ble. Move to the Borders box. For **B**ottom, choose Thick, and click OK or press Enter.

19. Select the entire third column of the table. Choose Forma**t**, and then T**a**ble. Move to the Borders box. For **L**eft, choose Thick, and click OK or press Enter.

20. Select the entire first MILEAGE row. Choose Forma**t**, then T**a**ble. Move to the Borders box. For **B**ottom, choose Thick, and click OK or press Enter. Repeat this procedure for each MILEAGE row throughout the table.

18. Select the entire first row of the table. Choose Forma**t**, then **B**order. Move to the Bo**r**der box, and click the bottom margin. In the **L**ine box, choose the 2.25 rule and click OK or press Enter.

19. Select the entire third column. Click Forma**t**, then click **B**order. In the Bo**r**der box, click the left margin. In the **L**ine box, choose the 2.25 rule and click OK or press Enter.

20. Select the entire first MILEAGE row. Choose Forma**t**, then **B**order. In the Bo**r**der box, click the bottom margin. In the **L**ine box, choose the 2.25 rule and click OK or press Enter. Repeat this procedure for each MILEAGE row throughout the table.

21. Position the cursor on the last paragraph return on the page.

    Press Enter, type **SIGNATURE**, press the space bar, and press Tab twice. Type **TOTAL MILES**, press the space bar, and press Tab.

22. Select the line of type, and follow these procedures:

    Choose Forma**t**, **T**ab, and then choose Clear **A**ll.

    In the **T**ab Position box, type **3.75"**, then choose **R**ight aligned. In the **L**eader box, choose 4, and **S**et.

    Press Del to delete the contents of the **T**ab Position box.

    In the **T**ab Position box, type **4"**, choose **L**eft aligned, **S**et, and press Del.

    In the **T**ab Position box, type **7.45"**, and choose **R**ight aligned. In the **L**eader box, choose 4, **S**et, and then click OK or press Enter.

23. To save this form, choose **F**ile, Save **A**s, type **travel1**, and click OK or press Enter.

24. To print this form, choose **F**ile, **P**rint, and click OK or press Enter.

Producing a Travel Report

This design for a Travel Report, shown in figure 13.2, includes the same items as the Travel Log design, with the addition of an area

CHAPTER 13

Producing a Travel or Expense Report

for the travel destination. The page is organized differently, and appears in landscape orientation. Because requirements for travel logs differ, one of these two forms should suit your purpose with perhaps only minor alterations.

TRAVEL REPORT

NAME: _____   POSITION: _____
WEEK OF: _____   BEGINNING MILEAGE: _____
TOTAL MILES: _____   ENDING MILEAGE: _____

DATE	TIME OUT	MILEAGE OUT	DESTINATION	TIME IN	MILEAGE IN	TOTAL

FIG. 13.2.   *Travel report in landscape orientation.*

To create the Travel Report shown in figure 13.2, follow these steps:

1. Select **F**ile, then **N**ew. In the New box, choose **D**ocument. In the **T**emplate box, choose Normal, and then click OK or press Enter.

PART III

Creating Business Forms

2. Select File, then **P**rinter Setup. Select the **S**etup button, and change the Orientation to Landscape. Choose OK, and click OK again or press Enter twice.

3. Choose Forma**t**, then **D**ocument. Set the **L**eft and **R**ight margins to **.5**", the **T**op margin at **.7**" and the **B**ottom margin at **.3**". Click OK or press Enter.

2. Choose Forma**t**, then Page Set**u**p. Move to **S**ize and Orientation, and change the Orientation to **L**andscape.

3. While still in the Page Setup dialog box, move to **M**argins and set the **L**eft and **R**ight margins to **.5**", the **T**op margin at **.7**" and the **B**ottom margin at **.3**". Click OK or press Enter.

4. Type the following text, pressing Tab, space bar, and Enter where indicated:

   TRAVEL REPORT (Enter)

   NAME: (space bar) (Tab, Tab) **POSITION:** (space bar) (Tab) (Enter)

   WEEK OF: (space bar) (Tab, Tab) **BEGINNING MILEAGE:** (space bar) (Tab) (Enter)

   TOTAL MILES: (space bar) (Tab, Tab) **ENDING MILEAGE:** (space bar) (Tab) (Enter, Enter)

5. Select TRAVEL REPORT. Use the Ribbon, and change the type to Helv, 18-point, bold, center-aligned.

6. Select the type from NAME: up to and including the Tab after ENDING MILEAGE. Use the Ribbon, and change the type to Helv.

7. With the text still selected, choose Forma**t**, then **P**aragraph. In the Spacing box, change the line spacing to Double, and click OK or press Enter.

8. With the text still selected, follow these steps:

   Choose Forma**t**, then **T**ab. In the **T**ab Position box, type **4.75**", and choose **R**ight aligned. In the Leader box, choose 4, and click **S**et.

   Press Del to clear the **T**ab Position box.

   In the **T**ab Position box, type **5**", choose **L**eft aligned, **S**et, and press Del.

CHAPTER 13

Producing a Travel or Expense Report

In the **T**ab Position box, type **10"**, and choose **R**ight aligned. In the Leader box, choose 4, **S**et, and then click OK or press Enter.

9. Position the cursor on the last paragraph return. Choose **I**nsert, then **T**able to display the Table dialog box.

10. For Number of **C**olumns, type **7**. For Number of **R**ows, type **15**. Choose the **F**ormat button.

11. Select **N**ext Column. In the **W**idth of Column 1 box, type **1"**. Choose **N**ext Column and set Column 2 for **1"**. Repeat this procedure, setting Column 3 for **1.5"**, Column 4 for **3"**, Column 5 for **1"**, Column 6 for **1.5"**, and Column 7 for **1"**.

12. While still in the Table dialog box, move to the Minimum Row **H**eight box, and type **2li**.

13. While still in the Table dialog box, move to the Borders box. For **O**utline, choose Thick. For **I**nside, choose Single, and click OK or press Enter.

14. When the gridlines are not showing, select **V**iew, P**r**eferences, turn on Table **G**ridlines, and then click OK or press Enter. Select the entire first row. Choose Forma**t**, then **T**able. In the Borders box, choose **B**ottom, choose Thick, and click OK or press Enter.

9. Position the cursor on the last paragraph return. Choose T**a**ble, then **I**nsert Table.

10. For Number of **C**olumns, type **7**. For Number of **R**ows, type **15**, and click OK or press Enter.

11. Select the first column, choose T**a**ble, then Column **W**idth. In the **W**idth of Column 1 box, type **1"**, then choose **N**ext Column. Repeat this procedure, setting Column 2 at **1"**, Column 3 at **1.5"**, Column 4 at **3"**, Column 5 at **1"**, Column 6 at **1.5"**, and Column 7 at **1"**.

12. Select the entire table. Choose T**a**ble, then Row **H**eight. For **H**eight of Row, choose At Least. In the **A**t: box, type **2li**, and click OK or press Enter.

13. With the table still selected, choose Forma**t**, then **B**order. In the Preset box, choose **G**rid. In the **L**ine box, choose the 1.25 rule, and click OK or press Enter.

315

PART III

Creating Business Forms

> When the Gridlines don't appear on your screen, choose Table, then select Gridlines.

14. Select the entire first row. Choose Forma**t**, then **B**orders. In the Bo**r**der box, click the bottom margin. In the **L**ine box, choose the 1.25 rule, and click OK or press Enter.

15. Position the cursor in the first column of the last row. Press Enter to create extra space in the last row for totals.

16. Position the cursor in the first cell of the first row:

    Type **DATE**, press Tab, type **TIME OUT**, press Tab, type **MILEAGE OU T**, press Tab, type **DESTINATION**, press Tab, type **TIME IN** , press Tab, type **MILEAGE IN** , press Tab, and type **TOTAL**.

17. Select this line of type, and use the Ribbon to change the type to Helv, bold, center-aligned.

18. With the text still selected, click For**ma**t, then choose **Pa**ragraph. In the Spacing box, choose **B**efore, type **3pt**, and click OK or press Enter.

19. To save the form, select File, Save **A**s, type **travel2**, and click OK or press Enter.

20. To print the form, click **F**ile, **P**rint, and then click OK or press Enter.

Before beginning the next document, reset the page orientation to portrait. Choose **F**ile, then **P**rinter Setup. Choose the **S**etup button, and change the Orientation to **P**ortrait. Click OK, and click OK again or press Enter twice.

Producing a Daily Expense Report

An expense report is usually required to provide documentation for expenditures. Sometimes prepared daily, an expense report includes hotel, meals, gas or mileage, or other expenses incurred while on company business. The Travel Log provides documentation for mileage claimed on the expense report. In addition, details of a sales call, such as contact person, address, phone

Producing a Travel or Expense Report

number, and the results of the trip, are required by some companies before they reimburse. The design shown in figure 13.3 provides space for these entries.

This form employs the right leader tab for some information, and a four-section table for other information. Although most forms use Helvetica as the typeface, this form uses Times Roman for which the small type is still readable. Remember from Chapter 3, that Times Roman is a smaller typeface than Helvetica. So, even though you're using 10-point type for both faces, Times Roman looks slightly smaller.

To create the form shown in figure 13.3, follow these steps:

1. Select **File**, then **New**. In the New box, choose **Document**. In the **Template** box, choose Normal, and then click OK or press Enter.

2. Click Forma**t**, click **Document**, and set all margins to **.5"**. Click OK or press Enter.

2. Choose Forma**t**, then Page Set**u**p. In **Margins**, set all to **.5"**, and click OK or press Enter.

3. Type the following text, pressing Tab, space bar, and Enter where indicated:

   DAILY EXPENSE REPORT (Enter, Enter)

   NAME: (space bar) (Tab, Tab) **DATE:** (space bar) (Tab) (Enter)

   DIVISION: (space bar) (Tab, Tab) **VEHICLE:** (space bar) (Tab) (Enter, Enter)

   DESTINATION: (space bar) (Tab, Tab) **CONTACT PERSON:** (space bar) (Tab) (Enter)

   CO. ADDRESS: (space bar) (Tab, Tab) **PHONE NO.:** (space bar) (Tab) (Enter, Enter, Enter)

4. Select DAILY EXPENSE REPORT. Use the Ribbon and change the type to 18-point, bold, center-aligned.

5. Select the type from NAME: up to and including the Tab following PHONE NO.: Click Forma**t**, then click **Paragraph**. In the Spacing box, click **Before**, and type **1li**. Click OK or press Enter.

DAILY EXPENSE REPORT

NAME: _____ DATE: _____

DIVISION: _____ VEHICLE: _____

DESTINATION: _____ CONTACT PERSON: _____

CO. ADDRESS: _____ PHONE NO.: _____

EXPENSE	DESCRIPTION	REIMBURSEMENT
HOTEL		
MEALS		
GAS/MILEAGE		
MISC.		

RESULTS OF TRIP/MEETING

SALES: _____
_____

CONTACTS: _____
_____

COMMENTS: _____
_____
_____

SIGNATURE: _____

FIG. 13.3. *An expense report with split tables and merged cells.*

CHAPTER 13

Producing a Travel or Expense Report

6. With the text still selected, follow these steps:

   Click For**mat**, then click **Tabs**. In the **T**ab Position box, type **3.5"**, and click to choose **R**ight aligned. In the Leader box, choose 4, and click **S**et.

   Press Del to delete the contents of the **T**ab Position box.

   In the **T**ab Position box, type **3.75"**, click **L**eft aligned, click **S**et, and press Del.

   In the **T**ab Position box, type **7.4"**, and click **R**ight aligned. In the Leader box, choose 4, click **S**et, and then click OK or press Enter.

7. Position the cursor on the next to last paragraph return. Choose Insert, then **T**able. For Number of **C**olumns, type **3**. For Number of **R**ows, type **9**. Choose the gray **F**ormat button.

8. Choose **N**ext Column. In the **W**idth of Column 1 box, type **1.2"**. Choose **N**ext Column and set Column 2 for **4.2"**. Repeat this procedure, setting Column 3 for **1.85"**.

9. While in the Table dialog box, move to Indent Rows, and type **.1"**. Move to Minimum Row Height, and type **2li**.

10. While still in the Table dialog box, move to the Borders box. For **O**utline choose Thick. For **I**nside choose Single, and click OK or press Enter.

    When the gridlines are not showing, choose **V**iew, **P**references, turn on Table **G**ridlines, and then click OK or press Enter.

7. Position the cursor on the next to last paragraph return. Choose **T**able, then choose **I**nsert Table. For Number of **C**olumns, type **3**. For Number of **R**ows, type **9**. Click OK or press Enter.

8. Select the entire table. Choose **T**able, then Row **H**eight. In **H**eight of Row, choose At Least. In the **A**t: box, type **2li**. Move to Indent From Left, type **.1"**, and click OK or press Enter.

9. With the table still selected, choose For**mat**, then **B**order. In Preset, choose Grid. In the **L**ine box, choose the 1.25 rule, and click OK or press Enter.

319

PART III

Creating Business Forms

10. Select the first column. Choose Table, then Column Width. In the Width of Column 1 box, type **1.2"**, then choose Next Column. Repeat this procedure, setting Column 2 at **4.2"**, and Column 3 at **1.85"**. Click OK or press Enter.

    When the Gridlines don't appear on your screen, choose Table, then Gridlines.

11. Position the cursor in the first row, first cell.

    Type **EXPENSE**, press Tab, type **DESCRIPTION**, press Tab, type **REIMBURSEMENT**, press Tab, and type **HOTEL**.

    Reposition the cursor to cell A-4, and type: **MEALS**. Reposition the cursor to cell A-6, and type **GAS/MILEAGE**. Reposition the cursor to cell A-8, and type **MISC**.

12. Select all lines just typed. Use the Ribbon, and choose bold and center align. Click Format, then click Paragraph. In the Spacing box, click Before and type **4pt**. Click OK or press Enter.

13. Select the first row of the table. Choose Format, then Table. Move to Borders, choose Bottom and Thick. Click OK or press Enter.

14. Position the cursor in row four—the row starting with MEALS. Press Ctrl+Shift+Enter to split the table. Repeat this procedure in row six—GAS/MILEAGE—and row eight— MISC.

15. Select row three. Choose Format, then Table. Move to Borders, choose for Bottom and Thick. Click OK or press Enter.

16. Select rows four and five. Choose Format, then Table. Move to Borders, choose Bottom and Thick. Choose Top, choose Thick, and click OK or press Enter. Repeat this procedure for rows six and seven.

17. Select rows eight and nine. Choose Format, then Table. Move to Borders, choose Top, Thick, and click OK or press Enter.

18. Select the first two cells, A-3 and B-3, in row three. Choose Edit, Table, then Merge Cells. Repeat this merge procedure with cells A-2 and B-2 of the MEALS table, the GAS/MILEAGE table, and the *MISC.* table.

320

CHAPTER 13

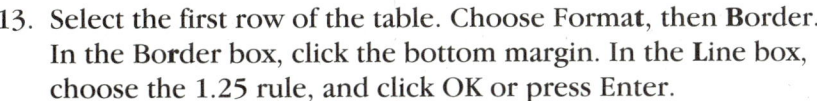

Producing a Travel or Expense Report

13. Select the first row of the table. Choose Forma**t**, then **B**order. In the Bo**r**der box, click the bottom margin. In the **L**ine box, choose the 1.25 rule, and click OK or press Enter.

14. Position the cursor in the MEALS cell. Choose **T**able, then **S**plit Table. Repeat the split at GAS/MILEAGE and MISC.

15. Select row three. Choose Forma**t**, then **B**order. In the Bo**r**der box, click the bottom margin. In the **L**ine box, choose the 1.25 rule, and click OK or press Enter.

16. Select rows four and five. Choose Forma**t**, then **B**order. In the Bo**r**der box, click the top margin, then hold the Shift key and click the bottom margin. In the **L**ine box, choose the 1.25 rule, and click OK or press Enter. Repeat with the GAS/MILEAGE table. For the keyboard, use the down arrow to select the top margin, press Enter, go back to the dialog box and select bottom margin.

17. Select rows eight and nine. Choose Forma**t**, then **B**order. In the Bo**r**der box, click the top margin. In the **L**ine box, choose the 1.25 rule, and click OK or press Enter.

18. Select the first two cells, A-3 and B-3, in row three. Choose **T**able, then **M**erge Cells. Repeat this merge procedure with cells A-2 and B-2 of the MEALS table, the GAS/MILEAGE table, and the MISC. table.

19. Position the cursor on the last paragraph return. Type the following, pressing Tab, space bar, and Enter where indicated:

    (Enter) **RESULTS OF TRIP/MEETING** (Enter)

    SALES: (space bar) (Tab) (Enter)

    (Tab) (Enter)

    CONTACTS: (space bar) (Enter)

    (Tab) (Enter)

    COMMENTS: (space bar) (Enter)

    (Tab) (Enter)

    (Tab) (Enter, Enter, Enter)

    (Tab) **SIGNATURE:** (space bar) (Tab)

20. Select RESULTS. . . . Use the Ribbon, and change the type to bold.

21. Select the type from SALES to the second line after COMMENTS, including the tab.

22. Choose Forma**t**, then **T**abs. In the **T**ab Position box, type **7.4"**, and choose **R**ight align. In the Leader box, choose **4**, **S**et, and click OK or press Enter.

23. With the text still selected, choose Forma**t**, then **P**aragraph. In the Spacing box, choose **B**efore and type **.5li**. Click OK or press Enter.

24. Select the text from SIGNATURE up to and including the Tab, and follow these steps:

    Choose Forma**t**, then **T**abs. In the **T**ab Position box, type **3.5"**, choose **L**eft aligned, click **S**et.

    Press Del to clear the **T**ab Position box.

    In the **T**ab Position box, type **7.4"**, and choose **R**ight aligned. In the Leader box, choose **4**, **S**et, and click OK or press Enter.

25. To save the form, choose **F**ile, Save **A**s, type **expense1**, and click OK or press Enter.

26. To print the form, choose **F**ile, **P**rint, and click OK or press Enter.

Producing a Small Expense/Reimbursement Form

Often, a small expense form is preferable to a large form. For employees who travel or incur expenses infrequently, the next form is perfect.

The small expense/reimbursement report, shown in figure 13.4, uses a simple table to itemize the date, description, location, and expense totals. The typeface in this table is a small, 7-point Times Roman (8-point in Version 1.1), and the head is only 12-point type. The type is small because of the small size of the form.

The final size of this expense report is 4 1/4 inches x 5 1/2 inches, and appears four-up on the page for printing and copying. Final sheets may be assembled in pads to keep them together.

EXPENSE/REIMBURSEMENT

NAME: ______________________________

DATE: ______________________________

NATURE OF TRIP: ______________________

DATE	DESCRIPTION	LOCATION	TOTAL

TOTAL REIMBURSEMENT: ______________________

SIGNATURE: ______________________________

EXPENSE/REIMBURSEMENT

NAME: ______________________________

DATE: ______________________________

NATURE OF TRIP: ______________________

DATE	DESCRIPTION	LOCATION	TOTAL

TOTAL REIMBURSEMENT: ______________________

SIGNATURE: ______________________________

EXPENSE/REIMBURSEMENT

NAME: ______________________________

DATE: ______________________________

NATURE OF TRIP: ______________________

DATE	DESCRIPTION	LOCATION	TOTAL

TOTAL REIMBURSEMENT: ______________________

SIGNATURE: ______________________________

EXPENSE/REIMBURSEMENT

NAME: ______________________________

DATE: ______________________________

NATURE OF TRIP: ______________________

DATE	DESCRIPTION	LOCATION	TOTAL

TOTAL REIMBURSEMENT: ______________________

SIGNATURE: ______________________________

FIG. 13.4. *Small Expense/Reimbursement set up four on a page.*

PART III

Creating Business Forms

To create the form shown in figure 13.4, follow these steps:

1. Choose **F**ile, then **N**ew. In the New box, choose **D**ocument. In the **T**emplate box, choose Normal, and then click OK or press Enter.

2. Choose Forma**t**, **D**ocument, and set the **T**op, **L**eft, and **R**ight margins to **.5**". Set the **B**ottom margin to **.3**", and click OK or press Enter.

3. Choose Forma**t**, then **S**ection. In the Columns box, choose **N**umber and type **2**. For **S**pacing, type **1**". For **S**ection Start, choose No Break, and click OK or press Enter.

2. Choose Forma**t**, then Page Set**u**p. In **M**argins, set the **T**op, **L**eft, and **R**ight margins to **.5**", and set the **B**ottom margin to **.3**". Click OK or press Enter.

3. Choose Forma**t**, then **C**olumn. For **N**umber of Columns type **2**. For **S**pace Between, type **1**".

4. Type the following, pressing Tab, space bar, and Enter where indicated:

   EXPENSE/REIMBURSEMENT (Enter, Enter, Enter)

   NAME: (space bar) (Tab) (Enter)

   DATE: (space bar) (Tab) (Enter)

   NATURE OF TRIP: (space bar) (Tab) (Enter, Enter)

5. Select EXPENSE.... Use the Ribbon, and change the type to 12-point, bold, center-aligned.

6. Select the type from NAME to ...OF TRIP, including the Tab. Choose Forma**t**, then **P**aragraph. In the Spacing box, choose **B**efore, type **.5li**, and click OK or press Enter.

7. With the text still selected, choose Forma**t**, then **T**abs. In the **T**ab Position box, type **3.2**", and **R**ight aligned. In the Leader box, choose **4**, **S**et, and click OK or press Enter.

8. Position the cursor on the next to the last paragraph return. Choose **I**nsert, then **T**able. For Number of **C**olumns, type **4**. For Number of **R**ows, type **10**. Choose the gray **F**ormat button.

CHAPTER 13

Producing a Travel or Expense Report

9. Select **N**ext Column. In the **W**idth of Column 1 box, type **.5**". Choose **N**ext Column and set Column 2 for **1.2**". Repeat this procedure, setting Column 3 for **.8**", and Column 4 for **.7**". Click OK or press Enter.

10. While in the Table dialog box, move to **I**ndent Rows and type **.1**". For Minimum Row **H**eight, type **1.5li**.

11. Move to Borders, and for **O**utline, choose Single. For **I**nside, choose Single, and click OK or press Enter.

    When the gridlines are not showing, choose **V**iew, **P**references, turn on Table **G**ridlines, and then click OK or press Enter.

8. Position the cursor on the next to the last paragraph return. Choose T**a**ble, then Insert Table. For Number of **C**olumns, type **4**. For Number of **R**ows, type **10**, and click OK or press Enter.

9. Select the entire table. Choose T**a**ble, then Row **H**eight. For **H**eight of Rows, choose At Least. In the **At**: box, type **1.5li**. For **I**ndent from Left, type **.1**", and click OK or press Enter.

10. With the table still selected, choose Forma**t**, then **B**order. In the Preset box, choose **G**rid. In the **L**ine box, choose the .75 rule, and click OK or press Enter.

    When the Gridlines don't appear on your screen, choose T**a**ble, then **G**ridlines.

11. Select the first column. Choose T**a**ble, then Column **W**idth. In the **W**idth of Column 1 box, type **.5**", then choose **N**ext Column. Repeat this procedure, setting Column 2 at **1.2**", Column 3 at **.8**", and Column 4 at **.7**". Click OK or press Enter.

12. Position the cursor in the first cell of the first row.

    Type **DATE**, press Tab, type **DESCRIPTION**, press Tab, type **LOCATION**, press Tab, and type **TOTAL**.

13. Select this line of type. Use the Ribbon, and change the type to 7-point, bold, center-aligned for Version 2.0. Change the type to 8-point, bold, center-aligned for Version 1.1.

PART III

Creating Business Forms

14. With the text still selected, choose Format, then choose **Paragraph**. In the Spacing box, choose **Before**, and type **3pt**. Click OK or press Enter.

15. Position the cursor on the last paragraph return. Type the following, pressing Tab space bar, and Enter where indicated:

    (Enter) **TOTAL REIMBURSEMENT:** (space bar) (Tab) (Enter)

    SIGNATURE: (space bar) (Tab) (Enter, six times)

16. Select the last two lines of type, from TOTAL... up to and including the Tab after SIGNATURE. Use the Ribbon and change the type to 7-point for Version 2.0. Change the type to 8-point for Version 1.1.

17. With this text still selected, choose Format, then **T**abs. In the **T**ab Position box, type **3.2"**, and choose **R**ight aligned. In the Leader box, choose **4**, **S**et, and click OK or press Enter.

18. With this text still selected, choose Format, then **P**aragraph. In the Spacing box, choose **B**efore and type **.5li**. Click OK or press Enter.

19. Move to the top of the form. Select the text from EXPENSE/ REIMBURSEMENT to the end of the SIGNATURE: line. Choose **E**dit and **C**opy, or press Ctrl+Insert.

20. Position the cursor on the last paragraph return in the column. Choose **E**dit and **P**aste, or press Shift+Insert.

21. Move to the top of the column and select the entire column. Choose **E**dit and **C**opy, or press Ctrl+Insert. Position the cursor at the very end of the column. Choose Insert, **B**reak, and choose Column Break.

22. The cursor should now be at the beginning of the second column. Choose **E**dit and **P**aste, or press Shift+Insert.

> **NOTE**
>
> If by chance, the second column jumps to the next page, position your cursor at the top of that column and press Backspace. The copied column will then position on the first page.

CHAPTER 13

Producing a Travel or Expense Report

23. To save the form, choose **File**, **Save As**, type **expense2**, and click OK or press Enter.

24. To print the form, choose **File**, **Print**, and click OK or press Enter.

Recapping

In this chapter, you learned how to produce different travel logs, travel reports, and small expense and reimbursement forms.

In the next chapter, you learn how to produce an order form.

14

Producing an Order Form

As many kinds of order forms exist as things to order. Some order forms list products, and others let you list the products. Many include specific areas for stock numbers, sizes, descriptions and prices. Most provide places for credit card information, shipping and handling charges, and tax. All ask for the name and address of the customer. Many order forms have special sections. Some include areas for purchase order numbers, bid numbers, terms of payment, or a place for gift orders.

Order forms come in sizes ranging from 5 inches x 3 1/2 inches to 11 inches x 17 inches. They may be cards, fliers, booklets, inserts, or part of another document. They may be mailed, handed out, or picked up. This chapter contains several kinds and sizes of order forms that best fit a laser printer.

The organization of information on an order form depends on the needs of the company. To expedite orders, you need to design the form in a way that supports the staff who fill the orders. A secondary consideration is the appeal of the form to the customer, although the catalog or sales sheet is more important for this purpose. In all cases, the form must be easy to read and fill out.

Most order forms contain a logo or some artwork. When you use Version 2.0 of Word, you can produce many logo options with Microsoft WordArt and Microsoft Draw. Logos are eye-catching; however, use logos only for a few words or one line of type. Some options are shown in the examples at the end of this chapter.

PART III

Creating Business Forms

The forms created in this chapter use Helvetica and Times Roman. Helvetica is generally considered to be the easiest type to read, especially when very small; however, Times Roman also works well. If you're using a great deal of small type, use Helvetica. Otherwise, type choice is a personal preference.

The following designs use tabs or tables to organize the information. The new table features introduced in this chapter provide you with more versatility for all your documents. The techniques you're learning in these business-form chapters can be used to produce any form.

Producing a Basic Order Form

The first order form design, shown in figure 14.1, is simple but functional. The company information includes a fax number, a toll-free phone number, and an address. The top half of the page is devoted to the customer's address, phone number, and payment criteria. The second half of the page is an order blank divided into five columns, but columns for size, color, page number, and so on, may be added easily. Right tabs and leaders are used to place totals and taxes under the total column.

To create the form shown in figure 14.1, follow these steps:

1. Choose **F**ile, then **N**ew. In the New box, choose **D**ocument. In the **T**emplate box, choose Normal, and then click OK or press Enter.

2. Choose Forma**t**, **D**ocument, and set all margins to **.5**". Click OK or press Enter.

2. Choose Forma**t**, then Page Set**u**p. In **M**argins, set all to **.5**", and click OK or press Enter.

3. Enter the following text, pressing Tab, space bar, and Enter where indicated:

   STARLIGHT PRODUCTIONS (Enter)

   P. O. BOX 174 (space bar six times) **OAK HILL, WEST VIRGINIA 25901** (Tab) **ORDER FORM** (Enter)

330

STARLIGHT PRODUCTIONS

P. O. BOX 174 • OAK HILL, WEST VIRGINIA 25901
(304) 215-5555   FAX (304) 215-1155

ORDER FORM
1-800-251-1155

ORDERED FROM: **SHIP TO:**

NAME _____   NAME _____
ADDRESS _____   ADDRESS _____
CITY _____   CITY _____
STATE (ZIP) _____   STATE(ZIP) _____
TELEPHONE _____   TELEPHONE _____

PAYMENT BY   _____ CHECK OR MONEY ORDER $ _____ AMOUNT ENCLOSED
             _____ CREDIT CARD: ____ VISA ____ MASTERCARD ____ AMEXP ____ DISCOVER
             CARD NUMBER _____ EXPIRES _____
             SIGNATURE _____

QTY.	ITEM NUMBER	DESCRIPTION	PRICE EACH	TOTAL

Subtotal _____
WV Res. Add 6% Tax _____
Shipping Add $3.95 _____
TOTAL _____

FIG. 14.1.   Basic order form using right leader tabs and a table.

PART III

Creating Business Forms

> **(304) 215-5555** (Tab) **FAX (304) 215-1155** (Tab) **1-800-251-1155** (Enter four times)
>
> **ORDERED FROM:** (Tab) **SHIP TO:** (Enter, Enter)
>
> **NAME** (space bar) (Tab, Tab) **NAME** (space bar) (Tab) (Enter)
>
> **ADDRESS** (space bar) (Tab, Tab) **ADDRESS** (space bar) (Tab) (Enter)
>
> **CITY** (space bar) (Tab, Tab) **CITY** (space bar) (Tab) (Enter)
>
> **STATE (ZIP)** (space bar) (Tab, Tab) **STATE (ZIP)** (space bar) (Tab) (Enter)
>
> **TELEPHONE** (space bar) (Tab, Tab) **TELEPHONE** (space bar) (Tab) (Enter, Enter)
>
> **PAYMENT BY** (Tab) _____ **CHECK OR MONEY ORDER** (Tab) $_____ **AMOUNT ENCLOSED** (Enter)
>
> (Tab) _____ **CREDIT CARD:** (space bar three times) ___**VISA** (space bar three times) ___ **MASTERCARD** (space bar three times) ___ **AM EXP** (space bar three times) ___ **DISCOVER** (Enter)
>
> (Tab) **CARD NUMBER** (space bar) (Tab, Tab) **EXPIRES** (space bar) (Tab) (Enter)
>
> (Tab) **SIGNATURE** (space bar) (Tab) (Enter five times).

4. Select STARLIGHT PRODUCTIONS, and use the Ribbon to change the type to 24-point, bold. With this text still selected, choose **Format**, then **Paragraph**. In the Spacing box, choose **After**, type **.5li**, and click OK or press Enter.

5. Select the two lines from P. O. BOX... to 1-800-251-1155. Use the Ribbon and change the type to Helv. With this text still selected, follow these steps:

   Click **Format**, then click **Tabs**.

   In the **Tab** Position box, type **1.95"**, click **Right** aligned, and press **Set**.

   Press Del to delete the contents of the **Tab** Position box.

   In the **Tab** Position box, type **6.56"**, click **Right** align, press **Set**, and click OK or press Enter.

CHAPTER 14

Producing an Order Form

6. Select the words ORDER FORM, and use the Ribbon to change the type to 14-point, bold. Select the phone number 1-800-251-1155, and use the ribbon to change the type to bold.

7. Position the cursor between ...BOX 174 and OAK HILL.... Insert a bullet.

   Use the Macro key you created in chapter 5 (Ctrl+8)

   Choose **I**nsert, **S**ymbol, then double-click to choose the bullet symbol. For the keyboard, use the down and right arrows to select bullet, then press Enter.

8. Select the line of type from ORDERED FROM to SHIP TO:, and use the Ribbon to change the type to Helv, bold. Choose Forma**t**, then **T**abs. In the **T**ab Position box, type 4", choose **L**eft aligned, and **S**et; alternately, set the tab on the Ruler as a 4", **L**eft aligned tab. Click OK or press Enter.

9. Select the text from NAME... up to and including the tab after TELEPHONE. Use the Ribbon to change the type to Helv. Choose Forma**t**, then **P**aragraph. In the Spacing box, choose **B**efore, type **.5li**, and type OK.

10. With this text still selected, follow these procedures:

    Choose Forma**t**, then **T**abs. In the **T**ab Position box, type **3.75"**, and choose **R**ight aligned. In the Leader box, choose 4, and **S**et.

    Press Del to delete the contents of the **T**ab Position box.

    In the **T**ab Position box, type 4", choose **L**eft aligned, **S**et, and press Del.

    In the **T**ab Position box, type **7.4"**, and choose **R**ight aligned. In the Leader box, choose 4, **S**et, and then click OK or press Enter.

11. Select the type from PAYMENT BY up to and including the tab after SIGNATURE. Use the Ribbon to change the type to Helv. Choose Forma**t**, then **P**aragraph. In the Spacing box, choose **B**efore, type **.5li**, and click OK or press Enter.

12. Select the two lines of text from PAYMENT... to ___ DISCOVER. Use the Ruler to set tabs or follow these procedures:

    Choose Forma**t**, then **T**abs. In the **T**ab Position box, type **1.13"**, choose **L**eft aligned, and **S**et.

333

Press Del to delete the contents of the **T**ab Position box.

In the **T**ab Position box, type **4.5"**, choose **L**eft aligned, **S**et, and click OK or press Enter.

13. Select the line starting with CARD NUMBER, and follow these procedures:

    Choose Forma**t**, then **T**abs. In the **T**ab Position box, type **1.25"**, choose **L**eft aligned, and **S**et.

    Press Del to delete the contents of the **T**ab Position box.

    In the **T**ab Position box, type **5.1"**, and choose **R**ight aligned. In the leader box, choose 4, **S**et, and press Del.

    In the **T**ab Position box, type **5.3"**, choose **L**eft aligned, **S**et, and then press Del.

    In the **T**ab Position box, type **7.4"**, and choose **R**ight aligned. In the leader box, choose 4, **S**et, and click OK or press Enter.

14. Select the SIGNATURE line, and follow these procedures:

    Click Forma**t**, then choose **T**abs. In the **T**ab Position box, type **1.25"**, choose **L**eft aligned, and **S**et.

    Press Del to delete the contents of the **T**ab Position box.

    In the **T**ab Position box, type **7.4"**, and choose **R**ight aligned. In the leader box, choose 4, **S**et, and click OK or press Enter.

15. Position the cursor on the next to the last paragraph return. Choose Insert, then **T**able. For Number of **C**olumns, type **5**. For Number of **R**ows, type **14**. Choose the gray **F**ormat button.

16. Select **N**ext Column. In the **W**idth of Column 1 box, type **.7"**. Choose **N**ext Column and set Column 2 for **1.5"**. Repeat this procedure, setting Column 3 for **3"**, Column 4 for **1.1"**, and Column 5 for **1.1"**.

17. While in the Table dialog box, move to Minimum Row **H**eight, type **1.5li**.

18. While still in the Table dialog box, move to Borders. For O**u**tline, choose Thick. For **I**nside, choose Single, and click OK or press Enter.

    If the gridlines don't appear, choose View, P**r**eferences, and then Table **G**ridlines.

CHAPTER 14

Producing an Order Form

19. Select the first row of the table. Choose Forma**t**, then **T**able. In Borders, choose **B**ottom, Thick, and click OK or press Enter.

15. Position the cursor on the next to the last paragraph return. Choose T**a**ble, then Insert Table. For Number of **C**olumns, type **5**. For Number of **R**ows, type **14**, and click OK or press Enter.

    If gridlines don't show, choose T**a**ble, then **G**ridlines.

16. Select the entire table. Choose T**a**ble, then Row **H**eight. For **H**eight of Row, choose At Least. In the **A**t: box, type **1.5li**, and click OK or press Enter.

17. With the table still selected, choose Forma**t**, then **B**order. In the Preset box, choose **G**rid. In the **L**ine box, choose the 1.25 rule, and click OK or press Enter.

18. Select the first column, choose T**a**ble, then Column **W**idth. In the **W**idth of Column 1 box, type **.7"**, then Next Column. Repeat this procedure, setting Column 2 at **1.5"**, Column 3 at **3"**, Column 4 at **1.1"**, and Column 5 at **1.1"**.

19. Select the first row of the table. Choose Forma**t**, then **B**orders. In the Bo**r**der box, click the bottom margin. In the **L**ine box, choose the 1.25 rule, and click OK or press Enter.

20. Position the cursor in the first row, first cell.

    Type **QTY.**, press Tab, type **ITEM NUMBER**, press Tab, type **DESCRIPTION**, press Tab, type **PRICE EACH**, press Tab, and type **TOTAL**.

21. Select the first row of the table, and use the Ribbon to change the type to Helv, bold, center-aligned.

22. With this row still selected, choose Forma**t**, then **P**aragraph. In the Spacing box, choose **B**efore, type **3pt**, and click OK or press Enter.

23. Position the cursor on the last paragraph return on the page. Type the following, pressing Tab, space bar, and Enter where indicated:

    (Enter)

    (Tab) **Subtotal** (space bar) (Tab) (Enter)

    (Tab) **WV Res. Add 6% Tax** (space bar) (Tab) (Enter)

335

(Tab) **Shipping Add $3.95** (space bar) (Tab) (Enter)

(Tab) **TOTAL** (space bar) (Tab)

24. Select the text from Subtotal up to and including the tab after TOTAL, and use the Ribbon to change the type to Helv. Follow these steps:

    Choose Forma**t**, then **T**abs. In the **T**ab Position box, type **6.2"**, choose **R**ight aligned, and **S**et.

    Press Del to delete the contents of the **T**ab Position box.

    In the **T**ab Position box, type **7.4"**, and choose **R**ight aligned. In the leader box, choose **4**, **S**et, and click OK or press Enter.

25. With this text still selected, choose Forma**t**, then **P**aragraph. In the Spacing box, choose **B**efore, type **.5li**, and click OK or press Enter.

26. Select the word TOTAL, and use the Ribbon to change the type to bold.

27. To save the form, choose **F**ile, and Save **A**s. Save the form as **order1**, and click OK or press Enter.

28. To print the form, choose **F**ile, **P**rint, and then click OK or press Enter.

Producing a Business-to-Business Order Form

When companies purchase products or services from other companies, the order form may change. For instance, the customer's billing and shipping addresses may be different. Also, a PO (Purchase Order) number, bid number, confirming date, and shipping date are usually included on the order form. Finally, most businesses add a request for a direct pay permit and state the terms of payment.

The order form shown in figure 14.2 adds the information in the preceding paragraph in an ordered, practical manner. Two tables divide the information; one table contains the business portion and the second table contains the product order information. An interesting change in this form appears at the bottom of the

CHAPTER 14

Producing an Order Form

second table, where some borders are turned off and the cells merged.

To create the order form shown in figure 14.2, follow these steps:

1. Choose **F**ile, then **N**ew. In the New box, choose **D**ocument. In the **T**emplate box, choose Normal, and then click OK or press Enter.

2. Choose Forma**t**, then **D**ocument. Set the **L**eft, **R**ight and **B**ottom margins to **.5**" and set the **T**op margin to **.7**". Click OK or press Enter.

2. Choose Forma**t**, then Page Set**u**p. In **M**argins, set the **L**eft, **R**ight and **B**ottom margins to **.5**" and set the **T**op margin to **.7**". Click OK or press Enter.

3. Enter the following text, pressing Tab, space bar, and enter where indicated:

   Starlight Productions (Enter)

   P. O. BOX 174 (space bar four times) **OAK HILL, WEST VIRGINIA 25901** (Enter)

   (304) 255-5555 (Enter four times)

   ORDER FORM (Enter three times)

   BILL TO: (Tab) **SHIP TO:** (Enter)

   (Tab three times) (Enter)

   (Tab three times) (Enter)

   (Tab three times) (Enter three times)

4. Select `Starlight Productions`, and use the Ribbon to change the type to 36-point, bold, italic, center-aligned.

5. Select the address and phone number, and use the Ribbon to change the type to Helv, 12-point, center-aligned.

6. Position the cursor and insert a bullet between `P. O. BOX 174` and `OAK HILL...25901`.

   Use the Macro key you created in Chapter 5 (Ctrl+8).

   Choose **I**nsert, **S**ymbol, and then double-click the bullet symbol.

337

Starlight Productions

P. O. BOX 174 • OAK HILL, WEST VIRGINIA 25901
(304) 255-5555

ORDER FORM

BILL TO:

SHIP TO:

PO NUMBER:	CONFIRM?	DATE:
CASH?	BID NO.:	SHIP VIA:
CHARGE?	C.O.D?	SHIP WHEN?

QTY	PRODUCT #	DESCRIPTION	PRICE EACH	TOTAL PRICE

If you are tax exempt or use a Direct Pay Permit, please enclose a copy.

TERMS: NET; DUE ON RECEIPT

SUBTOTAL	
STATE TAX	
TOTAL	

Thank You!

FIG. 14.2. *A new look with merged cells and turned off borders.*

CHAPTER 14

Producing an Order Form

7. Select ORDER FORM, and use the Ribbon to change the type to Helv, 12-point, bold, center-aligned.

8. Select BILL TO: and SHIP TO:, and use the Ribbon to change the type to bold. Use the Ruler to set the tab to 4", left aligned.

9. Select the next four lines, all tabs, and follow these steps:

    Choose Forma**t**, then **T**abs. In the **T**ab Position box, type **3.75"**, and choose **R**ight aligned. In the Leader box, choose 4, and **S**et.

    Press Del to delete the contents of the **T**ab Position box.

    In the **T**ab Position box, type **4"**, choose **L**eft aligned, **S**et, and press Del.

    In the **T**ab Position box, type **7.45"**, and choose **R**ight aligned. In the Leader box, choose 4, **S**et, and then click OK or press Enter.

10. With these lines still selected, choose Forma**t**, then **P**aragraph. In the Spacing box, choose **B**efore, type **.5li**, and click OK or press Enter.

11. Position the cursor on the next to the last paragraph return. Choose Insert, then **T**able. For Number of **C**olumns, type **3**; for Number of **R**ows type **3**. Choose the **F**ormat button.

12. For Minimum Row Height, type **1.5li**. The column widths will remain even.

13. In the same dialog box, move to Borders. For **O**utline, choose Thick. For **I**nside, choose Single, and click OK or press Enter.

    If the gridlines don't appear, choose View, P**r**eferences, and then Table **G**ridlines.

11. Position the cursor on the next to the last paragraph return. Click **T**able, then click **I**nsert Table. For Number of **C**olumns, type **3**; for Number of **R**ows type **3**. Click OK or press Enter.

    If gridlines don't appear, choose T**a**ble, then **G**ridlines.

12. Select the entire table. Choose T**a**ble, then Row **H**eight. In **H**eight of Row, choose At Least. In the **A**t: box, type **1.5li**, and then click OK or press Enter. The column widths will remain even.

PART III

Creating Business Forms

13. With the table still selected, choose For**m**at, then **B**order. In the Preset box, choose **G**rid. In the **L**ine box, choose the 1.25 rule, and click OK or press Enter.

14. Position the cursor in the first row, first cell. Type the following, pressing Tab where indicated:

    PO NUMBER: (Tab) **CONFIRM?** (Tab) **DATE:** (Tab)

    CASH? (Tab) **BID NO.:** (Tab) **SHIP VIA:** (Tab)

    CHARGE? (Tab) **C.O.D.?** (Tab) **SHIP WHEN?**

15. Select these three lines of type, and use the Ribbon to change the type to Helv, 8-point, bold.

16. With this text still selected, choose Forma**t**, then **P**aragraph. In the Spacing box, choose **B**efore, type **3pt**, and then click OK or press Enter.

17. Position the cursor on the last paragraph return on the page, and press Enter. Move the cursor up one line and choose **I**nsert, then **T**able. For Number of **C**olumns, type **5**; for Number of **R**ows, type **18**. Choose the **F**ormat button.

18. Select **N**ext Column. In the **W**idth of Column 1 box, type **.5"**. Choose **N**ext Column and set Column 2 for **1"**. Repeat this procedure, setting Column 3 for **3.5"**, Column 4 for **1.25"**, and Column 5 for **1.25"**.

19. In the same dialog box, move to Minimum Row **H**eight and type **1.5li**.

20. Move to the Borders box. For O**u**tline, select Thick. For **I**nside, select Single, and click OK or press Enter.

    If the gridlines don't appear, choose **V**iew, **P**references, and then click Table **G**ridlines.

21. Select the first row of the table. Choose Forma**t**, then **T**able. In the Borders box, choose **B**ottom, Thick, and then click OK or press Enter.

17. Position the cursor on the last paragraph return on the page, and press Enter. Move the cursor up one line, choose **T**able, then Insert Table. For Number of **C**olumns, type **5**; for Number of **R**ows, type **18**. Click OK or press Enter.

    If gridlines don't appear, choose **T**able, then **G**ridlines.

CHAPTER 14

Producing an Order Form

18. Select the entire table. Choose Table, then Row Height. For Height of Row, type **1.5li**, and click OK or press Enter.

19. With the table still selected, choose Format, then Border. In the Preset box, choose Grid. In the Line box, choose the 1.25 rule, and click OK or press Enter.

20. Select the first column of the table. Choose Table, then Column Width. In the Width of Column 1 box, type **.5"**, then choose Next Column. Repeat this procedure, setting Column 2 at **1"**, Column 3 at **3.5"**, Column 4 at **1.25"**, and Column 5 at **1.25"**. Click OK or press Enter.

21. Select the first row of the table. Choose Format, then Border. In the Border box, click the bottom margin. In the Line box, choose the 1.25 rule, and click OK or press Enter.

22. Position the cursor in the first row, first cell of the table.

    Type **QTY**, press Tab, type **PRODUCT #**, press Tab, type **DESCRIPTION**, press Tab, type **PRICE EACH** , press Tab, and type **TOTAL PRICE** .

23. Select this row of text, and use the Ribbon to change the type to Helv, 8-point, bold, center-aligned.

24. With the row still selected, click Format, then click Paragraph. In the Spacing box, choose Before, type **3pt**, and click OK or press Enter.

> **NOTE**
>
> The following instructions use letters and numbers to identify table cell locations. These cell identifiers are shown in figure 14.3 in a Version 1.1 screen.

25. Move to the bottom of this table and select the last three rows, cells A-16 through C-18. Choose Format, then Table. Move to Borders and choose None in all six boxes. Click OK or press Enter.

26. Select cells A-16, B-16 and C-16. Choose Edit, Table, then Merge Cells. Repeat for cells A-17 through C-17 and A-18 through C-18.

341

PART III

Creating Business Forms

FIG. 14.3.
Table cell identifiers for figure 14.2.

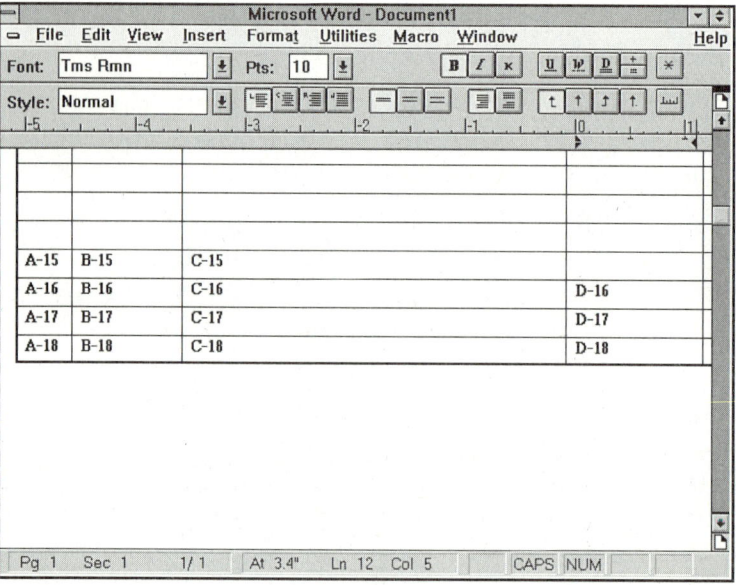

27. Select row 15. Click For**m**at, then choose **T**able. Move to Borders, choose **B**ottom, Thick, and click OK or press Enter.

28. Select cells D-16 through D-18. Choose For**m**at, then **T**able. Move to Borders, choose **L**eft, Thick, and click OK or press Enter.

25. Move to the bottom of this table, and select the last three rows, cells A-16 through C-18. Choose For**m**at, then **B**order. In the Preset box, choose **N**one, and click OK or press Enter.

26. Select cells A-16, B-16 and C-16. Choose T**a**ble, then **M**erge Cells. Repeat for cells A-17 through C-17 and A-18 through C-18.

27. Select row 15. Choose For**m**at, then **B**order. In the Bo**r**der box, click the bottom margin. In the **L**ine box, choose the 1.25 rule, and click OK or press Enter.

28. Select cells D-16 through D-18. Choose For**m**at, then **B**order. In the Bo**r**der box, click the left margin. In the **L**ine, choose the 1.25 rule, and click OK or press Enter.

29. Position the cursor in the first column of row 16, and type:

   If you are tax exempt or use a Direct Pay Permit, please enclose a copy.

CHAPTER 14

Producing an Order Form

Reposition the cursor in the first column of row 17, and type:

TERMS: NET; DUE ON RECEIPT

30. Select the text in row 17, TERMS...RECEIPT, and use the Ribbon to change the type to bold.

31. Position the cursor in cell D-16, and follow these steps:

    Type **SUBTOTAL**, and reposition the cursor in cell D-17.

    Type **STATE TAX**, and reposition the cursor in cell D-18.

    Type **TOTAL**.

32. Select these three lines of type, and use the Ribbon to change the type to Helv, 12-point, bold, right-aligned. Choose Forma**t**, then **P**aragraph. In the Spacing box, choose **B**efore, type **3pt**, and click OK or press Enter.

33. Select the cell with TOTAL and the cell to the right—cells D-18 and E-18. Choose Forma**t**, then **T**able. Move to Borders, **T**op, Thick, and click OK or press Enter.

33. Select the cell with TOTAL and the cell to the right—cells D-18 and E-18. Choose Forma**t**, then **B**order. In the Bo**r**der box, click the top margin. In the **L**ine box, choose the 1.25 rule. To screen this cell, move to the **S**hading box, choose Pattern, and then choose 10%. Click OK or press Enter.

34. Position the cursor on the last paragraph return, and type:

    Thank You!

35. Select this text, and use the Ribbon to change the type to Helv, 18-point, italic, center-aligned.

36. To save this form, choose **F**ile, and Save **A**s. Save the form as **order2**, and click OK or press Enter.

37. To print the form, choose **F**ile, **P**rint, and click OK or press Enter.

Producing an Order Form with Tabs

Many order forms provide a list of products that require customers to complete items such as quantity, size, and total price. You

343

PART III

Creating Business Forms

can create this type of order form by using a table, or tabs. The order form shown in figure 14.4 was created by using tabs. This short form is set two-up on a page for copying or printing.

Humble Opinions		ORDER FORM		
P. O. Box 174		ORDER TOLL FREE		
Oak Hill, WV 25901		1-800-551-1155		
(304) 251-5555				
NAME: _____				
ADDRESS: _____				
_____				
PHONE: _____				
QTY.	SIZE	DESCRIPTION	PRICE EA.	TOTAL
		T-SHIRT	$10.00	
		KID'S T-SHIRT	7.00	
		SWEATSHIRT	15.00	
		KID'S SWEAT	12.00	
		HAT #234	6.00	
		KID'S HAT #234	4.00	
		HAT #235	9.00	
		KID'S HAT #235	7.00	
		NEW CATALOG	1.00	
		RAIN POSTER	1.00	
		SUBTOTAL		
		WV Res. add 6% STATE TAX		
		TOTAL		
PLEASE ENCLOSE CHECK OR MONEY ORDER WITH ORDER.				
	SIZES:	SHIRTS	S, M, L, XL	
		KID'S SHIRTS	S, M, L	
		HATS	7, 8	
		KID'S HATS	5, 6	

FIG. 14.4. Order form created with tabs.

For some businesses, this type of order form is more customer-friendly. The description and price for each of the products listed is already completed for the customer.

An easy way to construct this form is with tabs. The horizontal rules are formatted through Paragraph in Version 1.1, or Border in Version 2.0. The form is then copied to the second column to create two identical forms.

To create the order form shown in figure 14.4, follow these steps.

1. Select **F**ile, then **N**ew. In the New box, choose **D**ocument. In the **T**emplate box, choose Normal, and then click OK or press Enter.

CHAPTER 14

Producing an Order Form

2. Choose **F**ile, then **P**rinter Setup. Choose **S**etup, change the orientation to **L**andscape, and click OK or press Enter.

3. Choose Forma**t**, then **D**ocument. Set all margins to **.5"**, and click OK or press Enter.

4. Choose Forma**t**, then **S**ection. In the Columns box, choose **N**umber and type **2**, then choose **S**pacing and type **1"**. For **S**ection Start, choose No Break, and click OK or press Enter.

2. Choose Forma**t**, then Page Set**u**p. For Size and Orientation, change the Orientation to **L**andscape.

3. For **M**argins, set all margins to **.5"**, and click OK or press Enter.

4. Choose Forma**t**, then **C**olumns. For **N**umber of Columns type **2**. For **S**pace Between, type **1"**, and click OK or press Enter.

5. Enter the following text, pressing Tab, space bar, and Enter where indicated:

   Humble Opinions (Enter)

   P. O. Box 174 (Tab) **ORDER FORM** (Enter)

   Oak Hill, WV 25901 (Tab) **ORDER TOLL FREE** (Enter)

   (304) 251-5555 (Tab) **1-800-551-1155** (Enter, Enter)

   NAME: (space bar) (Tab) (Enter)

   ADDRESS: (space bar) (Tab) (Enter)

   (Tab) (Enter)

   PHONE: (space bar) (Tab) (Enter three times)

6. Select this text, and use the Ribbon to change the type to Helv.

7. Select `Humble Opinions`, and use the Ribbon to change the type to 14-point, bold.

8. Select the next three lines, from `P. O. Box. 174` to `1-800-551-1155`. Choose Forma**t**, then **T**abs. In the **T**ab Position box, type **3.13"**, choose Center align, **S**et, and click OK or press Enter.

9. Select `ORDER FORM`, and use the Ribbon to change the type to 12-point, bold.

345

PART III

Creating Business Forms

10. Select the type from NAME: up to and including the tab after PHONE. Choose Forma**t**, then **P**aragraph. In the Spacing box, choose **B**efore, type **.5li**, and click OK or press Enter.

11. With this text still selected, choose Forma**t**, then **T**abs. In the **T**ab Position box, type **4.5"**, and choose **R**ight aligned. In the Leader box, choose 4, **S**et, and click OK or press Enter.

12. Position the cursor on the next to the last paragraph return.

    Press Tab, type **QTY.**, press Tab, type **SIZE**, press Tab, type **DESCRIPTION**, press Tab, type **PRICE EA.**, press Tab, and type **TOTAL**.

13. Select this line of text, and use the Ribbon to change the type to Helv, 8-point, bold.

14. With this text still selected, follow these procedures:

    Choose Forma**t**, **T**abs, and then Clear **A**ll. In the **T**ab Position box, type **.25"**, choose **C**enter aligned, and **S**et.

    Press Del to delete the contents of the **T**ab Position box.

    In the **T**ab Position box, type **.75"**, choose **C**enter aligned, **S**et, and press Del.

    In the **T**ab Position box, type **1.81"**, choose **C**enter aligned, **S**et, and press Del.

    In the **T**ab Position box, type **3.13"**, choose **C**enter aligned, **S**et, and press Del.

    In the **T**ab Position box, type **4"**, choose **C**enter aligned, **S**et, and click OK or press Enter.

15. With Word Version 1.1, you can't format a line above and below the same paragraph. To work around this limitation, follow these procedures:

    Select the paragraph return above the QTY. line.

    Choose Forma**t**, then **P**aragraph. For **Bo**rder, choose Below, for Pa**t**tern choose Single, and click OK or press Enter.

    Position the cursor on the paragraph return below the QTY. line.

    Choose Forma**t**, then **P**aragraph. For **Bo**rder, choose Above, for Pa**t**tern choose Single, and click OK or press Enter.

CHAPTER 14

Producing an Order Form

15. With the text still selected, choose Forma**t**, then **B**order. In the Border box, click in the top margin, then hold the Shift key and click in the bottom margin. In the Line box, choose the 1.25 rule, and click OK or press Enter.

16. To give the heading QTY. some space, position the cursor within that line. Choose Format, then **P**aragraph. In the Spacing box, choose **B**efore and type **3pt**, then choose **A**fter and type **3pt**. Click OK or press Enter.

17. Position the cursor on the last paragraph return. Type the following, pressing Tab and Enter where indicated:

    (Tab) **T-SHIRT** (Tab) **$10.00** (Enter)

    (Tab) **KID'S T-SHIRT** (Tab) **7.00** (Enter)

    (Tab) **SWEATSHIRT** (Tab) **15.00** (Enter)

    (Tab) **KID'S SWEAT** (Tab) **12.00** (Enter)

    (Tab) **HAT #234** (Tab) **4.00** (Enter)

    (Tab) **KID'S HAT #234** (Tab) **6.00** (Enter)

    (Tab) **HAT #235** (Tab) **9.00** (Enter)

    (Tab) **KID'S HAT #235** (Tab) **7.00** (Enter)

    (Tab) **NEW CATALOG** (Tab) **1.00** (Enter)

    (Tab) **RAIN POSTER** (Tab) **1.00** (Enter, Enter)

18. Select the text from the tab before T-SHIRT to the 1.00 after RAIN POSTER, and use the Ribbon to change the type to Helv.

19. With this text still selected, choose Forma**t**, then **P**aragraph. In the Spacing box, choose **B**efore, type **.5li**, and click OK or press Enter.

20. With this text still selected, follow these procedures:

    Choose Forma**t**, then **T**abs. In the **T**ab Position box, type **1.5"**, choose **L**eft aligned, and click **S**et.

    Press Del to delete the contents of the **T**ab Position box.

    In the **T**ab Position box, type **3.13"**, choose **D**ecimal aligned, **S**et, and click OK or press Enter.

21. Position the cursor in the last line, RAIN POSTER(tab)1.00.

347

PART III

Creating Business Forms

22. Choose For**mat**, then **P**aragraph. For **B**order choose Below, for Pa**tt**ern choose Thick, and click OK or press Enter.

22. Choose For**mat**, then **B**order. In the Bo**r**der box, click in the margin below. In the **L**ine box, choose the 1.25 rule, and click OK or press Enter.

23. Position the cursor on the last paragraph return. Type the following, pressing Tab and Enter where indicated:

    (Tab) **SUBTOTAL** (Enter)

    (Tab) **WV Res. add** (Enter)

    (Tab) **6% STATE TAX** (Enter)

    (Tab) **TOTAL** (Enter, Enter)

24. Select all four lines of text, and use the Ribbon to change the type to Helv, bold. Choose For**mat**, **T**abs, and then choose **C**lear All. In the **T**ab Position box, type **3.38"**, then choose **R**ight aligned, **S**et, and click OK or press Enter.

25. Select SUBTOTAL and WV Res. add. Choose For**mat**, then **P**aragraph. In the Spacing box, choose **B**efore, type **.5li**, and click OK or press Enter. Repeat this procedure for TOTAL.

26. Select WV Res. add, and use the Ribbon to change the type to 8-point.

27. Position the cursor in the TOTAL line of text. Choose For**mat**, then **P**aragraph. For **B**order choose Below. For Pa**tt**ern choose Thick, and click OK or press Enter.

27. Position the cursor in the TOTAL line of type. Choose For**mat**, then **B**order. In the Bo**r**der box, click in the margin below. In the **L**ine box, choose the 1.25 rule, and click OK or press Enter.

28. Position the cursor on the last paragraph return. Type the following, pressing Tab and Enter where indicated:

    PLEASE ENCLOSE CHECK OR MONEY ORDER WITH ORDER. (Enter, Enter)

    (Tab) **SIZES:** (Tab) **SHIRTS** (Tab) **S, M, L, XL** (Enter)

    (Tab, Tab) **KID'S SHIRTS** (Tab) **S, M, L** (Enter)

    (Tab, Tab) **HATS** (Tab) **7, 8** (Enter)

    (Tab, Tab) **KID'S HATS** (Tab) **5, 6**

CHAPTER 14

Producing an Order Form

29. Select PLEASE ENCLOSE...to...ORDER, and use the Ribbon to center-align the type.

30. Select the line of text from SIZES to ...XL, and follow these steps.

    Choose Format, Tabs, and then choose Clear All. In the Tab Position box, type **.75"**, choose Left aligned, and Set.

    Press Del to delete the contents of the Tab Position box.

    In the Tab Position box, type **1.5"**, choose Left aligned, Set, and press Del.

    In the Tab Position box, type **2.65"**, choose Left aligned, Set, and click OK or press Enter.

31. Move to the top of the column, and select all text to the bottom of the page. Choose Edit, then Copy, or press Ctrl+C.

32. Position the cursor at the bottom of the page, at the end of the line KID'S HATS(tab)5, 6. Choose Insert, then Break. Choose Column Break, and click OK or press Enter. The cursor should now appear at the top of Column 2.

33. Choose Edit, then Paste, or press Shift+Insert.

34. To save the form, choose File, then Save As. Save the form as **order3**, and click OK or press Enter.

35. To print the form, choose File, Print, and click OK or press Enter.

Looking at Design

As mentioned at the beginning of the chapter, there are many kinds of order forms. This section shows some examples of other types of forms. These forms were created in Version 2.0; however, with slight alterations, most of them can be done in Version 1.1.

Some order forms are created in card form, often appearing as inserts in a magazine or advertising letter. Figure 14.5 shows a simple order card for inclusion in an envelope. The head, KID'S DAY MAGAZINE, was created in Word Version 2.0 with Microsoft WordArt. The informational tabs are right leader tabs. The small check boxes for payment and subscriptions were done in Version 2.0's Microsoft Draw, then copied and pasted. Version 1.1 users

PART III

Creating Business Forms

may substitute lines for the check boxes. You may also produce logo type in Word by using expand, condense, change leading, and so forth, or import a TIFF from a draw program.

KID'S DAY MAGAZINE
2234 North Street, NW, Washington, DC 20202-2122

ORDER FORM

Name: _____ Age: _____

Address: _____

City: _____ State: _____ Zip: _____

☐ 12 MONTH SUBSCRIPTION - $14.00   ☐ 24 MONTH SUBSCRIPTION - $25.00
☐ THIS IS A HOLIDAY GIFT! (Gift card sent with your order)
☐ PAYMENT ENCLOSED   ☐ PLEASE BILL ME.

FIG. 14.5. *A postcard form, with boxes to check for information.*

Often, order cards have a mailing panel on the reverse side. When you produce an order form to be used as a postcard, remember the following postal regulations:

- The size must be no smaller than 3 1/2 inches x 5 inches.

- Include margins, at least 3/8 inch all around. When printing or copying the forms, set the cards two-up or three-up.

- The paper for a card that mails must be a cover stock. The post office requires at least a 7-point cover. Any weight of paper greater than 7-point is acceptable to the Postal Service. Index (110#), antique uncoated (65# or 80#), or even a coated cover (7- or 8-point) all work well.

For more information on Postal Regulations, refer to Chapter 7, "Producing Envelopes." For more information about paper, refer to Chapter 4, "Planning and Purchasing Printing."

The postcard design shown in figure 14.6 shows how to arrange the form to include a greater amount of information. Again, the head was created in Microsoft WordArt. The Postage and Handling information is set in a frame by using Version 2.0. The type is

CHAPTER 14

Producing an Order Form

much smaller, 7- and 8-point. The name, address, and so on, are on 1.5 line spacing, and the table is on single-line spacing. Version 1.1 users could paste-up the shipping and handling information, and use lines instead of check boxes.

GAN ANIN RECORDS AND TAPES
4714 N. ALVIS STREET, CHARLESTON, WEST VIRGINIA 25303

NAME: _____
ADDRESS: _____
CITY: _____
STATE & ZIP: _____
PHONE: _____

POSTAGE HANDLING
(Per Tape Or Record)
Up to 5 $2
5 to 10 $3
11 to 20 $4
Over 21   FREE

QTY	LABEL	NUMBER	TITLE/ARTIST	PRICE	TOTAL

☐ BILL ME ☐ PAYMENT ENCLOSED WV Residents add 6% sales tax.   TOTAL

FIG. 14.6. An order form card for use in an envelope.

Figure 14.7 shows another version of an order form using screens and merged cells for information. The shading was done in Version 2.0. When you use Version 1.1, a print shop can screen your forms before printing them. The shipping and handling charges appear in the table, with borders turned off and cells merged.

Word is an excellent program for complicated forms. With a little pre-planning, you can do any form. Figure 14.8 shows a form for gift orders being shipped to different addresses. The original table has 22 rows. However, with borders turned off and cells merged, the areas look quite different from a table full of rules. The shading adds importance to certain sections as well.

This form was produced in Version 2.0. This form can easily be created in Version 1.1, except for the shading and check boxes.

STARLIGHT PRODUCTIONS
P. O. BOX 174 • OAK HILL, WV 25901 ORDER TOLL FREE
(304) 215-5555   FAX (304) 215-1155   **1-800-251-1155**

ORDER FORM

ORDERED BY: **SHIP TO:** (If different from ORDERED BY)

Name: _____   Name: _____
Address: _____   Address: _____
_____   _____

QTY.	ITEM NO.	DESCRIPTION	SIZE	PRICE EACH	TOTAL

SHIPPING AND HANDLING CHARGES
Under $25.00 $3.95
$25.01 to $65.00 $5.25
$65.01 to $95.00 $6.95
Over $95.01   FREE

METHOD OF PAYMENT
Check or Money Order Preferred
Credit Card Only With Our Pre-approved Credit OK

Total Merchandise	
Add $3 For Catalog	
Subtotal	
WV Res. Add 6% Tax	
Shipping & Handling (see chart to left)	
TOTAL	

FIG. 14.7. *An order form with screening, merged cells, and some borders turned off.*

24 HOURS A DAY!! CALL TOLL FREE 1-800-251-1212

SOLD TO:
NAME: _____
ADDRESS: _____
_____
PHONE: _____

SHIP TO: (if different from SOLD TO)
NAME: _____
ADDRESS: _____
_____
PHONE: _____

Please make checks payable to:
Method of Payment:
☐ Check/MO
☐ Credit Card: _____
Acct. No. _____

STARLIGHT PRODUCTIONS
P. O. BOX 174 • OAK HILL, WEST VIRGINIA 25901

Signature: _____
Expires: _____

SHIP THIS ORDER TO THE ABOVE ADDRESS:

QTY	NUMBER	DESCRIPTION	PRICE EACH	TOTAL

FOR OFFICE USE ONLY			
ORDER NUMBER:		SUBTOTAL	
		SALES TAX	
		SHIPPING	
		TOTAL	

GIFT ORDER #1:

NAME: _____ SUBTOTAL
ADDRESS: _____ SALES TAX
CITY: _____ ST. ____ ZIP _____ SHIPPING
　　　　　　　　　　　　　　　　　　　　　　TOTAL #1

GIFT ORDER #2:

NAME: _____ SUBTOTAL
ADDRESS: _____ SALES TAX
CITY: _____ ST. ____ ZIP _____ SHIPPING
　　　　　　　　　　　　　　　　　　　　　　TOTAL #2

DELIVERY: ADD $7.00 FOR EACH ADDRESS　　　 DELIVERY
SHIPPING AND HANDLING: $10.50 PER ADDRESS　TOTAL

If you need more room, photocopy this form or attach an extra sheet of paper.
Express 2-day delivery for just $6.00 additional per address. Add to the Delivery column.

FIG. 14.8. *A complicated-looking form, easy to do in Word.*

PART III

Creating Business Forms

Recapping

This chapter discussed and showed you how to produce a variety of business order forms.

The next chapter shows you how to produce an advertisement.

HUMBLE OPINIONS
COMPUTER TRAINING CENTER

1127 E. Main Street
(304) 251-5151

Beckley, WV 25801
800-250-2369

INTRODUCTORY CLASSES

Basic Computers Learn about memory, DOS, files, directories, and popular software programs. Explore printers, modems, and hard and floppy drives. Discover new and innovative uses for the PC in your business!

Word Processing Learn basic editing, function keys, margin and tab settings, and editing codes. Use retrieve, save and print; use block operations for moving text, and spell checking.

Database Learn database concepts, create and edit a form, add and edit data, modify file structures, create reports and add and delete records. Also learn to sort data in variety of ways.

Spreadsheets Create, save, retrieve, and print a spreadsheet. Learn to use formulas, and copy rows and columns. Format ranges, change column widths, and use absolute cell addresses.

Desktop Publishing Become familiar with documents, mouse and keyboard functions, basic formatting of page such as typeface, type size and style; columns and margins; tabs and tables; frames, graphics, importing and exporting, bullets, and indents.

INTERMEDIATE CLASSES

Word Processing Learn about macros, tables, formatting columns, setting font types and sizes, and mail merge. Print envelopes, large and small paper sizes; learn the finer points of page make-up on the word processor.

Spreadsheets Become more efficient with spreadsheets by freezing titles, and using named ranges and windows. Perform logical evaluation, use cell protection, and control recalculation.

Desktop Publishing Learn to use desktop publishing to produce flyers, resumes, forms, newsletters, brochures, and any document you need for your business. Bring in your own word processing to format any document you want.

(304) 251-5151   CALL TODAY   800-250-2369

Part IV

Creating Sales Documents

Includes

---

15. Producing an Advertisement
16. Producing a Flier
17. Producing a Brochure

15

Producing an Advertisement

The purpose of an advertisement is to persuade someone to buy a product or service. Many ways exist to advertise, but the printed word probably is the most powerful of all advertising mediums.

Advertisements come in all kinds, shapes, and sizes. Newspaper and magazine ads, circulars, fliers, and brochures are just a few possibilities. Newspapers are a great way to advertise locally. Magazines widen the range of people who might read the ad. Circulars, fliers, and brochures allow you more room to describe a product or service and help you direct a more focused ad campaign. This chapter discusses ads, circulars, and direct mail. Chapters 16 and 17 cover fliers and brochures.

Examining Sources for Advertisements

Magazines are a good source for ads. Although seemingly expensive, the actual cost of advertising in magazines usually is not too high. Some nationally distributed magazines sell regional advertising, which means that this kind of ad appears only in your area. The cost of a regional ad is less when compared to the cost of a national ad. Magazine advertising can give your company a certain credibility. By focusing on a narrow group, you also can better target ads to the audience. Using color ads also is more effective in a magazine.

PART IV

Creating Sales Documents

All the ads in this chapter can work in magazines. Before designing your final piece, determine the prices the magazine charges and then decide about the size of ad you want to place.

Newspapers also are good sources for ads. You can advertise in many kinds of newspapers, such as national, metropolitan, and local. Most cities also have shopper-oriented, campus, business, or ethnic newspapers. Many newspapers have different frequencies of publication, ranging from twice a day to every other month. Before placing an ad, choose the newspapers with the publishing frequencies you need and that reach the proper audience. If you own a health food store, for example, advertise in campus and shopper-oriented newspapers. If, however, you sell business computers, place the ad in a business newspaper.

Planning and Designing Ads

Write the ad to match the intended audience. In a newspaper ad, keep the copy short and concise. Brief descriptions and a great deal of facts are important. You want to attract attention with the ad. Well-written copy and good ad design can draw a reader's attention. Before designing an ad, look through a newspaper to see what attracts you. Do you prefer ads with white space that create a light, airy feeling; do the ads with heavy borders and dark typefaces attract you? Make sure that you also look at competitors' ads. You want to design an ad to look completely different from ads run by the competition.

Consider the days on which you plan to run the ad. Most people read the paper cover-to-cover on Sundays. If the ad is male-oriented, consider Monday's paper, when the paper reports the weekend sports. A food-oriented ad may work best on Wednesday, when grocery stores advertise. If you design a *display ad*, try to place the ad near others in the same category. A display ad is one that is larger than a want ad, and one that can be placed anywhere in the newspaper. Don't be afraid of pitting your ad against your competitors. Giving the public a choice between your ad and the competition's—instead of just the competition's— is a good tactic.

CHAPTER 15

Producing an Advertisement

Using Type in Ads

In the design, use readable, clear type. Never use type smaller than the newspaper uses. If possible, use a typeface that differs from Times Roman (usually used in newspapers). Bookman, Palatino, Friz Quadrata—even Avant Garde—are great typefaces that attract attention by contrast. By the way, never let the newspaper design your ad because the result may look like everyone else's ad.

Using Art Work in Ads

Depending on the size of the ad, you might want to use art work or photos. Photos do attract attention, but use no more than three or four in one (half- or full-page) ad. Remember, too, that photographs in newspapers are not normally the best quality. Use photos in which the detail is not important. Art work, or display type is a great way to attract attention, but don't overdo it. If possible, design the art work yourself. Newspapers use clip art quite a bit, so it's not really unique. Display type is excellent. Find the emphasis point of the ad and use display type to stress it. For example, the words *sale*, *free*, *one day only*, and so on are good to use with large type. Limit the use of larger type to one word or phrase.

Although not art per se, coupons can nevertheless attract as much attention as art work. They also are beneficial to an ad. Offering a free sample, discount, or even a free brochure about the product, a coupon invites the reader to get involved. Be sure that you include the company's name, address, and phone number both in the coupon and elsewhere in the ad.

Using Color and Logos in Ads

If the ad is large, you may wish to add color. Full-color ads are not as noticeable as they once were. For a newspaper ad, you may be wasting money by purchasing color. Save the full-color work for a brochure or magazine. If you do use color, however, choose one that contrasts with other colors in the newspaper. You may not have a choice but if possible, try maroon, navy blue, or even forest green. These colors aren't usually used in newspapers or ads and therefore, your ad has a better chance of standing out.

PART IV

Creating Sales Documents

If your company has one, always include a logo. If workable, repeat the logo throughout the ad. Remember that consistency between company pieces gives the reader a sense of continuity and, therefore, a comfortable feeling about you.

Using Borders in Ads

Mention your offer in the headline and again in the subhead. You also can restate the offer in a coupon. Moreover, add a border of some kind to the ad. Word enables you to create several thicknesses of borders; you can draw a border or use a clip art border. Don't go overboard, however, and use a border that overwhelms the message. Never forget the all-powerful white space.

Placing the Ad

If possible, have the ad placed near the front of the paper, on the right hand page, above the fold. This part of the newspaper is the prime placement area for ads. This choice may not be an option but if you ask often enough, you might get the placement you want. Finally, consider using the same ad several times. Running the same ad is cheaper than creating a new one, and when people see the same ad every week for six months, they are more likely to consider buying from you. Also, repeat ads help to develop product and company recognition among readers.

Producing a Display Newspaper Ad

Several qualities make an ad stand out among the competition. Most newspaper ads are crowded, forcing more copy into a space than should reasonably fit. An ad that makes good use of white space stands out. An ad's main purpose is to get customers to visit your business, where you can show them the products or describe the details of the services you provide. Trying to crowd everything into one ad may drive customers away.

CHAPTER 15

Producing an Advertisement

The first design in this chapter uses a wealth of white space. As a basic design, the head states the offer and the discount, the body lists the items discounted, and the footer gives the name, address, and phone number of the business. Sale dates, unnecessary for an on-going sale, aren't listed.

A shadow border encloses the white space, helping to make the ad simple, straightforward, and attractive. The types used are Times Roman and Helvetica, although the 18-point Helvetica for the list of spices is an unusual choice. Figure 15.1 shows the first ad.

In contrast, figure 15.2 shows the same ad with a great deal more information included. You see entirely too much information in this ad. When you design the ad, consider not only the ad, but also how the ad looks on a page when surrounded by competing ads. This display ad measures 4 1/4 inches wide, or three columns in a daily newspaper. Before you design the ad, find out from the newspaper the cost of the different sizes of ad space.

To create the ad shown in figure 15.1, perform the following steps:

1. Go to **F**ile, **N**ew. Choose New **D**ocument and **U**se Template Normal. Select OK or press Enter.

2. Go to Forma**t**, **D**ocument. In **M**argins, set the **T**op and **B**ottom margins each to **2.5"**, the **L**eft to **2"**, and the **R**ight to **2.25"**. Select OK or press Enter.

3. Go to Forma**t**, **P**aragraph. In **B**order choose Box; in **P**attern choose Shadow.

In Word for Windows 2.0, the steps differ in the following ways:

1. Go to **F**ile, **N**ew. Choose New **D**ocument and **U**se Template Normal. Select OK or press Enter.

2. Go to Forma**t**, Page Set**u**p. In **M**argins, set the **T**op and **B**ottom margins each to **2.5"**, the **L**eft to **2"**, and the **R**ight to **2.25"**. OK.

3. Go to Forma**t**, **B**order. In the Preset box, choose S**h**adow; in **L**ine choose the 1.25 rule. OK.

4. Type the following text, pressing Tab and Enter where indicated:

   (Enter) **INDIAN SPICES** (Enter, Enter)

   1/3 - 1/2 OFF (Enter, Enter)

   (Tab) **Cumin** (Enter)

PART IV

Creating Sales Documents

(Tab) **Saffron** (Enter)

(Tab) **Tumeric** (Enter)

(Tab) **Coriander** (Enter)

(Tab) **Garam Masala** (Enter)

(Tab) **Black Mustard** (Enter)

(Tab) **Red Hot Chiles** (Enter three times)

We offer spices from around the world! (Enter)

OPEN DAILY 9 TO 5 (Enter)

Roghan Josh Spices (Enter)

2436 N. 24th Street (Enter)

871-9701 (Enter)

5. Select `INDIAN SPICES`. On the Ribbon, change the type to 32-point, bold, center-aligned.

6. Select `1/3 - 1/2 OFF`. On the Ribbon, change the type to Helv, 48 point, bold, and centered.

7. Select the 1 in 1/3. On the Ribbon, change the 1 to superscript (the plus button). Select the 3 in 1/3 and change to subscript (on the Ribbon, the equal button). Repeat with 1/2.

7. Select the 1 in 1/3. Go to **Format**, **Character**. In Super/subscript, choose Superscript. Press Enter. Select the 3 in 1/3, go to **Format**, **Character**. In Super/subscript, choose Subscript. Press Enter. Repeat with 1/2.

8. Select the text from `Cumin` to `Red Hot Chiles`. On the Ribbon, change the type to Helv, 18-point. On the Ruler, set the tab at 1 1/4", left-aligned.

9. Select `We offer....` On the Ribbon, change the type to 12-point, italic, center-aligned.

10. Select `OPEN DAILY...`, center-align.

11. Select `Roghan Josh Spices`. On the Ribbon, change the type to 18-point, bold, center-aligned.

12. Select the address and phone number. Change the type to 12-point, bold, center-aligned.

13. Go to **File**, Save **As**. Type **ad1**. OK.

14. Go to **File**, **P**rint.

CHAPTER 15

Producing an Advertisement

FIG. 15.1.
An attractive ad that employs a short list of facts and a profusion of white space.

> # INDIAN SPICES
> # 1/3 - 1/2 OFF
>
> Cumin
> Saffron
> Tumeric
> Coriander
> Garam Masala
> Black Mustard
> Red Hot Chiles
>
> We offer spices from around the world!
> OPEN DAILY 9 TO 5
> **Roghan Josh Spices**
> 2436 N. 24th Street
> 871-9701

Producing a One-Column Newspaper Ad

This ad also is a display ad, but it covers just one column. An ad doesn't need to be large to attract attention. The right-aligned type makes this ad unique. Most body type in a newspaper is fully

PART IV

Creating Sales Documents

justified; most ads use centered type. Many headlines are left-aligned, so right-aligned text stands out. Also incorporated in this ad is a simple stylized logo, designed in CorelDRAW!. The border is merely a rule on the top and bottom of the ad, allowing the white space to open even more. You also see that a single quotation mark added to Marie's name was created by pressing Alt+0146. Be sure that you use the keypad for the numbers. The quotation mark adds an air of sophistication and professionalism to the name and, therefore, to the ad.

FIG. 15.2.
Too much information in an ad rarely attracts readers.

GOURMET FOODS
INDIAN SPICES
1/3 - 1/2 OFF

(Spices On Sale Only - Everything Else Our Low Everyday Price)

CUMIN	BLACK MUSTARD	TUMERIC
CORIANDER	GARAM MASALA	SAFFRON
	RED HOT CHILES	

WE ALSO SELL:

BASUMATI	GHEE	YOGURT
PEPPERCORNS	GARLIC	BESAN
LAMB	GINGER ROOT	PARATHA
CARDAMON	ALMONDS	CLOVES
JALEBIS	ROSHGULLA	FIRNI

VISIT OUR GIFT SHOP:

COOK BOOKS	COCONUT MILK	KARHAIS
WOKS	DRESSES	SCARVES
COOKING UTENSILS		BOWLS

OPEN DAILY 9 TO 5
We offer spices from around the world!

Roghan Josh Spices
2436 N. 24th Street   871-9701

366

CHAPTER 15

Producing an Advertisement

As shown in figure 15.3, the ad consists of the name of the shop, a short list, the address, and a few other facts. The ad mentions the name of the shop twice. Repetition within even a small ad is a good practice.

FIG 15.3.
A one-column display ad using a customized logo.

To create the ad in figure 15.3, take the following steps:

1. Go to **F**ile, **N**ew. New **D**ocument, Use Template Normal. OK.

2. Go to Forma**t**, **D**ocument. In Margins, set the **T**op and Bottom margins to **2.5**". Set the **L**eft margin to **4**" and the right margin to **3.13**". OK.

PART IV

Creating Sales Documents

2. Go to Format, Page Setup. In Margins, set the Top and Bottom margins to **2.5**". Set the Left margin to **4**" and the Right margin to **3.13**". OK.

3. Type the following, pressing Enter where indicated:

   (Enter, Enter) **MARIE** (Alt+0146)**S** (Enter)

   CRAFT SHOP (Enter, Enter)

   POTTERY (Enter)

   WEAVINGS (Enter)

   JEWELRY (Enter)

   CANDLES (Enter)

   QUILTS (Enter, Enter)

   Handmade Gifts (Enter)

   Open Daily 10 to 5 (Enter, Enter)

   MARIE (Alt+0146)**S** (Enter)

   CRAFT SHOP (Enter)

   3041 Elks Circle (Enter)

   Huntington, WV (Enter)

   (304) 211-5505 (Enter)

4. Select all text. On the Ruler, right-align the text.

5. Place the cursor on the first paragraph return. Go to Format, Paragraph. In the Border box, choose Above. In Pattern choose Thick. OK.

6. Place the cursor on the last paragraph return. Go to Format, Paragraph. In the Border box, choose Below. In Pattern choose Thick. OK.

4. Select all of the type. On the Ribbon, right-align the text.

5. Place the cursor on the first paragraph return. Go to Format, Border. In the Border box, click in the top margin. On the keyboard, press the down arrow until the top margin is selected. In the Line box, choose the 1.25 rule. OK.

CHAPTER 15

Producing an Advertisement

Because you can choose thicker rules, you can go to a 2.25-point—or even a 4-point—rule for a nice effect in this ad. Both the top and bottom rules can be the same thickness, or you can make the bottom rule a bit heavier.

6. Position the cursor on the last paragraph return. Go to Forma**t**, **B**order. In the Bo**r**der box, click in the bottom margin. In the **L**ine box, choose the 1.25 rule. OK.

7. Select MARIE'S. On the Ribbon, change the type to 20-point, bold.

8. Select CRAFT SHOP. On the Ribbon, change to 14-point bold.

9. Select the type from POTTERY to QUILTS. On the Ribbon, change the type to Helv, 14-point.

10. Select Handmade Gifts and Open Daily 10 to 5. On the Ribbon, change the type to 12-point.

11. Select MARIE'S and CRAFT SHOP. Change the type to 12-point bold.

12. The address and phone number remain TmsRmn, 10-point.

13. If you have a logo or other art you can insert, do so above the first appearance of MARIE'S on-screen.

14. Go to **F**ile, Save **A**s. Type **ad2**. OK.

15. Go to **F**ile, **P**rint.

Producing a Five-Column Ad

A well-designed large ad demands attention. Some ads, such as used car ads, squeeze in so much information that unless you're dedicated to buying a car, you won't read them. A better way to design a used car ad, or any ad, is to use white space. The more white space an ad has, the more likely you are to read the ad. Larger ads also allow more room for information. Rather than listing facts, you have the room to describe, too.

The next display ad measures 7.13 inches wide, the width of five columns of want ad space. Of course, you can place any ad in a business section or other parts of the newspaper. As a contemporary subject, business oriented, refined, and reserved, however, this ad fits with the business news.

PART IV

Creating Sales Documents

The paragraph is full of facts that apply directly to the head. You also see that more line spacing exists within this paragraph for easier reading (see fig. 15.4).

To make the ad in figure 15.4, follow these steps:

1. Go to **F**ile, **N**ew. New **D**ocument, Use Template Normal. OK.

2. Go to Forma**t**, **D**ocument. In Margins, set the **T**op margin to **.5**", the **B**ottom margin to **.4**"; the **L**eft and **R**ight each to **.75**". OK.

3. Go to Forma**t**, **P**aragraph. In **B**order choose Box; in Pat**t**ern choose Double.

2. Go to Forma**t**, Page Se**t**up. In **M**argins, set the **T**op margin to **.5**", the **B**ottom margin to **.4**"; the **L**eft and **R**ight each to **.75**". OK.

3. Go to Forma**t**, **B**order. In the Preset box, choose **B**ox; in **L**ine choose one of the double rules. OK.

Again, you have the choice of various thicknesses of rules. The larger the ad, the thicker you can make the border. This ad looks fine with any double rule.

4. Type the following, pressing Tab and Enter where indicated:

COMPUTER TRAINING (Enter four times)

(Tab) **Training available in popular software programs:** (Enter)

(Tab) **WORD PROCESSING** (Enter)

(Tab) **DESKTOP PUBLISHING** (Enter)

(Tab) **SPREADSHEETS** (Enter)

(Tab) **DATABASES** (Enter)

(Tab) **ACCOUNTING PROGRAMS** (Enter)

(Tab) **DRAW AND PAINT PROGRAMS** (Enter three times)

(Tab) **Humble Opinions offers training in over 30 popular software programs.** (Enter)

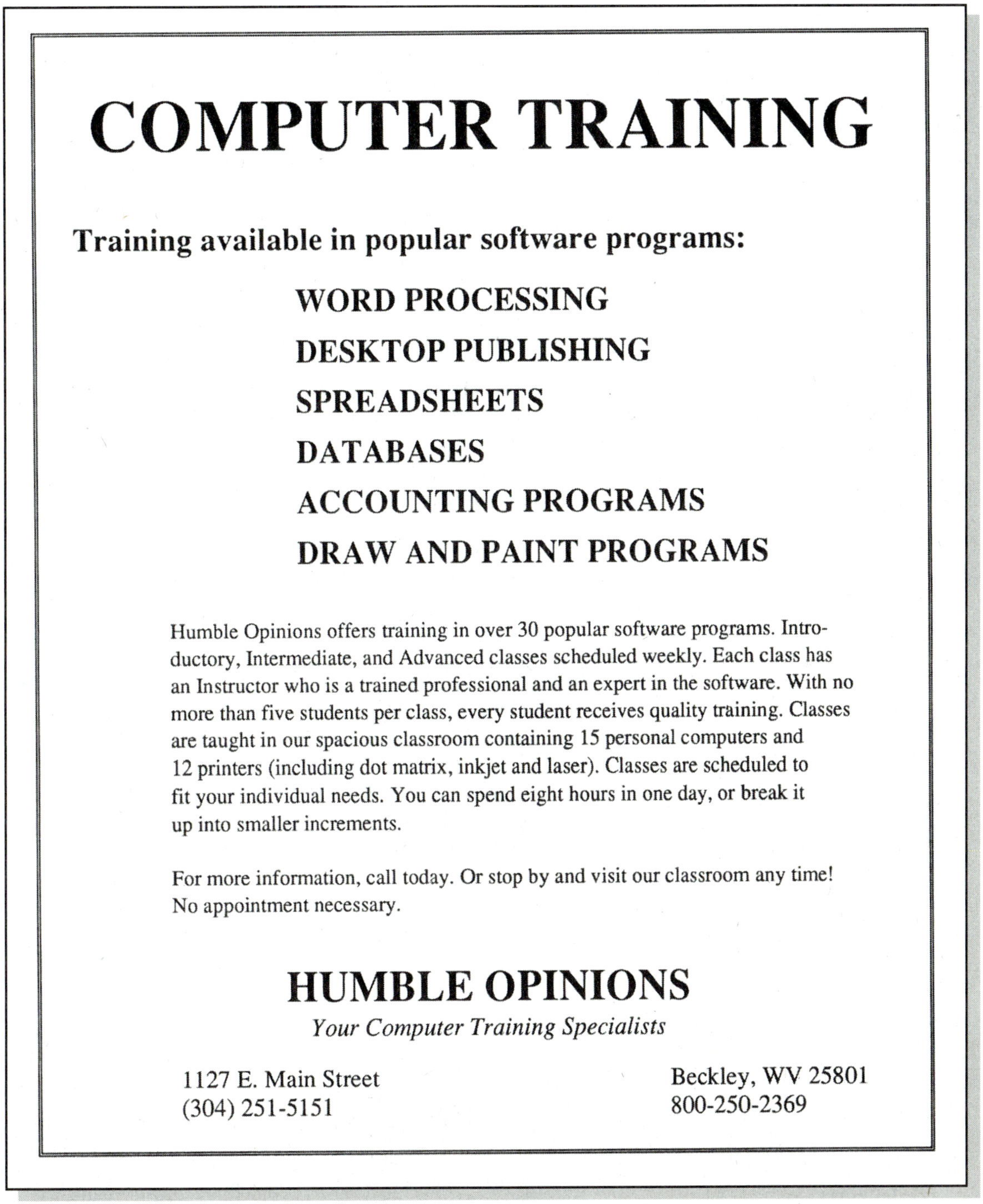

CHAPTER 15

Producing an Advertisement

COMPUTER TRAINING

Training available in popular software programs:

       WORD PROCESSING
       DESKTOP PUBLISHING
       SPREADSHEETS
       DATABASES
       ACCOUNTING PROGRAMS
       DRAW AND PAINT PROGRAMS

Humble Opinions offers training in over 30 popular software programs. Introductory, Intermediate, and Advanced classes scheduled weekly. Each class has an Instructor who is a trained professional and an expert in the software. With no more than five students per class, every student receives quality training. Classes are taught in our spacious classroom containing 15 personal computers and 12 printers (including dot matrix, inkjet and laser). Classes are scheduled to fit your individual needs. You can spend eight hours in one day, or break it up into smaller increments.

For more information, call today. Or stop by and visit our classroom any time! No appointment necessary.

HUMBLE OPINIONS
Your Computer Training Specialists

1127 E. Main Street   Beckley, WV 25801
(304) 251-5151   800-250-2369

FIG. 15.4. *A five-column newspaper ad.*

PART IV

Creating Sales Documents

(Tab) **Introductory, Intermediate, and Advanced classes scheduled weekly. Each class has an** (Enter)

(Tab) **Instructor who is a trained professional and an expert in the software. With no** (Enter)

(Tab) **more than five students per class, every student receives quality training. Classes** (Enter)

(Tab) **are taught in our spacious classroom containing 15 personal computers and** (Enter)

(Tab) **12 printers (including dot matrix, inkjet and laser). Classes are scheduled to** (Enter)

(Tab) **fit your individual needs. You can spend eight hours in one day, or break it** (Enter)

(Tab) **up into smaller increments.** (Enter, Enter)

(Tab) **For more information, call today. Or stop by and visit our classroom any time!** (Enter)

(Tab) **No appointment necessary.** (Enter three times)

HUMBLE OPINIONS (Enter)

Your Computer Training Specialists (Enter, Enter)

(Tab) **1127 E. Main Street** (Tab) **Beckley, WV 25801** (Enter)

(Tab) **(304) 251-5151** (Tab)**800-250-2369** (Enter)

5. Select COMPUTER TRAINING. On the Ribbon, change the type to 40-point, bold, center-aligned.

6. Select the line of type Training available.... On the Ribbon, set the type to 18-point, bold. On the Ruler, set the tab to .25", left-aligned.

7. Still selected, go to Format, Paragraph. In the Spacing box, After, type **.5li**. OK.

8. Select the list of programs, from WORD PROCESSING to DRAW AND PAINT PROGRAMS. On the Ribbon, change the type to 18-point, bold.

9. Still selected, go to Format, Paragraph. In the Spacing box, Before, type **.5li**. OK.

CHAPTER 15

Producing an Advertisement

10. With type still selected, go to the Ruler and set the tab at 2", left-aligned.

11. Select the type from `Humble Opinions...` to `No appointment necessary`. On the Ribbon, change the type to 12-point.

12. Still selected, go to For**m**at, **P**aragraph. In **Li**ne, type **.20**". OK. (The equivalent to size 12 type on 15-point spacing.)

12. Still selected, go to For**m**at, **P**aragraph. In **Li**ne Spacing choose At Least. In the **At**: box, type **.20**". OK. (The equivalent to size 12-point type on 15-point spacing.)

13. Still selected, on the Ruler set the tab to 1", left-aligned.

14. Select `HUMBLE OPINIONS`. On the Ribbon, change the type to 24-point, bold, center-aligned.

15. Select `Your Computer Training Specialists`. On the Ribbon, change the type to 14-point, italic, center-aligned.

16. Select the address and phone number. On the Ribbon, change the type to 14-point. On the Ruler, set the tabs to 1", left-aligned, and 5", left-aligned.

17. Go to **F**ile, Save **A**s. Type in **ad3**. OK.

18. Go to **F**ile, **P**rint.

Creating and Designing a Circular

This last ad can perform successfully as a newspaper ad, a newspaper insert, or a direct mail piece (circular). Almost any ad that you can expand or condense to a 5 1/2-inch x 8 1/2-inch sheet, an 8 1/2-inch x 11-inch sheet, or an 8 1/2-inch x 14-inch sheet, can be a circular.

Circulars are used mainly as a newspaper insert or for direct mail. As a newspaper insert, the circular can be printed either at the newspaper, or at a print shop. The best bet is to have the circular printed at a commercial or quick copy print shop. You have more control over the final piece, and the results look more professional.

PART IV

Creating Sales Documents

Because so many inserts are found in newspapers, make your insert unique. Design is important, but so is the paper and ink you choose. Select, for example, an ivory paper and maroon ink, or canary paper with forest green ink. The paper doesn't need to be expensive. Circulars are throwaway ads. A 50# or 60# offset works just fine. Actually, if you print only one side, a 20# bond paper might suffice. Ask for samples before you decide.

The ink also is of major importance. You usually don't see the colors mentioned in the preceding paragraph in newspaper ads. By choosing these colors, the piece attracts more attention. Be sure that you ask the newspaper about its circulation before printing so that you know how many circulars to print.

Using Direct Mail

The other use for a circular is direct mail. You can mail a circular by itself—folded, labeled, and stamped—or you can mail the circular in an envelope, with or without other related company pieces. A circular included with a bill is a great way to enhance its readership.

When direct mailing, you need a mailing list of customers with whom you previously did business. The existence of this list means that you know the recipients already have an interest in the product or service. Use care when buying a mailing list. Survey the list to see if it includes businesses or individuals or both. Check to see if the list covers a large geographical area around you. Remember that you want to target the advertising, and a mailing list is an essential point to consider when doing direct mail.

Looking at Design

The same design ideas for ads apply to circulars. Use large, eye-catching type. Coupons are a sensible addition. Borders, display type, art work, logos, and so on are all appropriate. Figure 15.5 is an example of a creation that you can use either as an ad or a circular. The larger size enables you to add more information. Here, adding a recipe is an excellent idea. The customer keeps the piece for the recipe and always has the store name, address, and phone number on hand.

ROGHAN JOSH GOURMET FOODS

Offering spices from around the world!

SPICE SALE 1/3 - 1/2 OFF

Cumin
Coriander
Tumeric
Red Hot Chilis

Black Mustard Seeds
Garam Masala
Saffron

MAY WE OFFER OUR MONTHLY RECIPE:
KELA KA RAYTA
(Yogurt with Banana and Coconut)

2 T. ghee
1 t. black mustard seeds
1/2 C. grated fresh coconut
1 C. unflavored yogurt

1 t. salt
1 medium banana (cut into 1/4" rounds)
1 t. fresh, chopped coriander
1/2 t. cumin

Heat ghee in small wok over moderate heat. Drop in mustard seeds. Fry 10 seconds. Drop in coconut. Stir for a few seconds, add coriander and cumin. Remove from heat. Stir in the yogurt, salt and chopped banana. Refrigerate for one hour before serving.

ROGHAN JOSH GOURMET FOODS
2436 N. 24th Street   871-9701
Open daily from 9:00 a.m. to 5:00 p.m.

VALUABLE COUPON

Bring this coupon with you for a FREE Jalebis, Roshgulla, or Shahitukra.
(Limit one per customer, not good with any other offer or coupon. Offer expires 12/11/92)

ROGHAN JOSH GOURMET FOODS
2436 N. 24th Street

FIG. 15.5. *A circular or newspaper ad design.*

PART IV

Creating Sales Documents

Including something like a recipe is a good idea because you give customers something, offering yourself as an authority on the subject, which builds the customer trust in you and your company. The next time customers have a question or need a particular item, they think of you first. A business can add any number of things to an advertisement. Computer software sales can offer keyboard shortcuts; a tax accountant can present a summary of new tax laws; a craft store can give instructions to create a specific craft item. Let the customer know you care.

Figure 15.5 also includes a coupon. As mentioned previously, coupons are great for getting customers to come to the store. Here, a coupon offers a small free Indian dessert. Who knows, if customers like the dessert, perhaps they may buy the ingredients to make it. Other ideas for coupon offers are a discount on a service or product or a free brochure describing your service. You also see the name, address, and phone number on both the coupon and the circular. After customers use the coupon, they still have all the information they need to contact you.

Creating Multipurpose Ads

Following are a few more ad ideas. Each ad uses something unique you may want to apply to your own ads. Figure 15.6 illustrates an ad with a border that makes the ad stand out among other ads in a newspaper. Furthermore, the heavy, black type draws attention. The list of desks, chairs, and other items is centered in the ad, which creates a pyramid effect in the line length and adds even more interest. When you use center-, left-, or right-aligned type, watch the ragged edges. Occasionally, these edges leave large gaps; at other times, you can create a design by rearranging the words. Finally, the 1/3 OFF is hard to miss, even at a glance.

Varying the edges of the border can make an ad unique, as in figure 15.7. The top border forces white space above the ad. Quite a bit of white space also was added within the ad. The type "What's in a Name?" is a display type from CorelDRAW!, but the rest of the ad is set in a simple sans serif type for contrast.

This ad is a good idea for a new business. Place the ad in the paper every day for two weeks before grand opening, and people

CHAPTER 15

Producing an Advertisement

will wonder what it's all about. Then, the day before grand opening, place a larger ad that explains the business, the products, services, and so on.

FIG. 15.6.
An ad with an unusual border that draws attention in a newspaper.

Figure 15.8 employs a landscape orientation to an ad. Because most ads are portrait, this design may entice the reader. The message is brief, yet effective.

Art work and logos are great for recognition. Figure 15.9 shows a logo design used in an ad. Original art work draws in the reader. The reversed type and stars of the logo also attract attention. The only border in this ad is part of the logo, which creates an interesting effect.

PART IV

Creating Sales Documents

FIG. 15.7. *An ad with unique border and wording to pique customer interest.*

ARE YOUR RETURNS TAXING YOU?
LUCRE INCOME TAX PREPARATION SERVICE   1-800-888-0090

FIG. 15.8. *A different orientation makes an ad unusual when placed near portrait-oriented ads.*

Display typefaces are great for any advertisement. If you have a draw or paint program, create heads for the ads. Figure 15.10 shows a display head created in CorelDRAW!. The graduated screen and the repeated word stand out in a crowd. Other effects you can use are outlined type, shadowed or screened type, rotated type, and reversed type.

Another idea for advertising is to use *jargon*, or buzz words, particular to your business. A computer business can use headlines such as "Is your memory shot? Try our new Office Organizer Software," or "HELP - we're the key." Figure 15.11 demonstrates another use of computer jargon. The simple computer screen was drawn in CorelDRAW! and adds appeal to the ad.

CHAPTER 15

Producing an Advertisement

FIG. 15.9.
The Starlight logo is stretched to fit as a headline for an ad.

FIG. 15.10.
Repetition of key words can attract attention, as does the use of display type.

379

PART IV

Creating Sales Documents

FIG. 15.11.
The use of jargon, aimed at a specific audience.

Recapping

In this chapter, you learned that the purpose of an advertisement is to persuade someone to buy a product or service. You also learned that print—newspaper and magazine ads, circulars, fliers, and brochures—is among the most powerful of all advertising mediums. Finally, you learned how to design a variety of ads for newspapers, magazines, and other print media.

In the next chapter, you learn how to produce a flier.

ROGHAN JOSH RESTAURANT

TAKE-OUT MENU
Call Anytime — 871-9701

APPETIZERS

Pakoras (6)	$3.95
Baingan Pakoras (6)	$4.50
Samosas (6)	$4.95
(Potato Filling or Lamb Filling)	
Chiura (6)	$3.95
Bhelpuris (6)	$4.95
Ekuri	$4.95

MAIN DISHES
FISH

Jhinga Kabab	$7.95
Jhinga Kari	$8.50
Tali Machli	$7.95
Machli aur Tamatar	$8.50

CHICKEN

Tandoori Murg	$8.95
Murg do Pyaza	$8.95
Tikka Murg	$8.95
Tithar	$8.95

LAMB

Kheema do Pyaza	$10.95
Badami Gosht	$10.95
Dhansak	$10.95
Kofta	$11.50
Husaini Kabab	$11.50
Raan	$10.95
Korma	$10.95

MAIN DISHES
PORK

Sorpotel	$10.95
Suvar Mas ka Vindalu	$10.95

BEEF

Kofta Kari	$11.95
Masaledar Raan	$11.95

VEGETABLES

Simla Mirch	$7.95
Aviyal	$7.95
Mattar Pannir	$7.95
Khumbi Bhaji	$7.95
Sag	$7.95

BREADS

Paratha (6)	$2.50
Alu Paratha (6)	$2.95
Chippatis (6)	$2.50
Puris (6)	$2.50

SALADS

Alu ka Rayta (serves 2)	$3.50
Pudine ka Rayta (serves 2)	$3.50
Rajma-Chana Salat (serves 6)	$5.50

DESSERTS

Jalebis (12)	$6.95
Roshgulla (12)	$6.95

ROGHAN JOSH RESTAURANT
OPEN DAILY FROM 11 A.M. TO 9 P.M.
2436 N. 24th Street
871-9701

FIG. 16.1. *A take-out menu in flier form; this layout also works well for price lists.*

PART IV

Creating Sales Documents

2. Go to **Format**, **D**ocument. Set all of the margins to .7".

2. Go to **Format**, Page Set**u**p. In **M**argins, set all to .7". Select OK.

3. Type the following listing, pressing Tab, space bar, and Enter where indicated:

ROGHAN JOSH RESTAURANT (Enter)

TAKE-OUT MENU (Enter)

Call Anytime (Alt+0151) (space bar) **871-9701** (Enter three times)

APPETIZERS (Enter)

Pakoras (6) (Tab) (space bar) **$3.95** (Enter)

Baingan Pakoras (6) (Tab) (space bar) **$4.50** (Enter)

Samosas (6) (Tab) (space bar) **$4.95** (Enter)

(Tab) **(Potato Filling or Lamb Filling)** (Enter)

Chiura (6) (Tab) (space bar) **$3.95** (Enter)

Bhelpuris (6) (Tab) (space bar) **$4.95** (Enter)

Ekuri (Tab) (space bar) **$4.95** (Enter)

MAIN DISHES (Enter)

FISH (Enter)

Jhinga Kabab (Tab) (space bar) **$7.95** (Enter)

Jhinga Kari (Tab) (space bar) **$8.50** (Enter)

Tali Machli (Tab) (space bar) **$7.95** (Enter)

Machli aur Tamatar (Tab) (space bar) **$8.50** (Enter)

CHICKEN (Enter)

Tandoori Murg (Tab) (Space bar) **$8.95** (Enter)

MURG DO PYAZA (Tab) (space bar) **$8.95** (Enter)

Tikka Murg (Tab) (space bar) **$8.95** (Enter)

Tithar (Tab)(space bar) **$8.95** (Enter)

LAMB (Enter)

Kheema do Pyaza (Tab) (space bar) **$10.95** (Enter)

CHAPTER 16

Producing a Flier

Badami Gosht (Tab) (space bar) **$10.95** (Enter)

Dhansak (Tab) (space bar) **$10.95** (Enter)

Kofta (Tab) (space bar) **$11.50** (Enter)

Husaini Kabab (Tab) (space bar) **$11.50** (Enter)

Raan (Tab) (space bar) **$10.95** (Enter)

Korma (Tab) (space bar) **$10.95** (Enter)

4. Before typing the next column, format the page. Select ROGHAN JOSH RESTAURANT. On the Ribbon, change the type to 30-point, bold, and centered.

5. With type still selected, go to For**mat**, **P**aragraph. In Spacing, After, type **.5li**.

6. In same dialog box, go to **B**order and choose Above. In Pa**t**tern, choose Thick and select OK.

5. With type still selected, go to For**mat**, **P**aragraph. In Spacing, After, type **.5li** and select OK.

6. With type still selected, go to For**mat**, **B**order. In Bo**r**der, click the top margin. On the keyboard, press the down arrow until the top margin is selected. In **L**ine, choose the 3-point rule and select OK.

7. Select TAKE-OUT MENU. On the Ribbon, change the type to 14-point, bold, and centered.

8. Select Call Anytime..., change the type to 12-point, bold, and centered.

9. Place the cursor on the next paragraph return symbol. Go to For**mat**, **P**aragraph. In **B**order, choose Below; in Pa**t**tern, choose Thick and select OK.

9. Place the cursor on the next paragraph return symbol. Go to For**mat**, **B**order. In the Bo**r**der box, click on the bottom margin or use the down arrow to select. In **L**ine, choose the 3-point rule and select OK.

10. Position the cursor on the next paragraph return next (just above APPETIZERS). Go to **I**nsert, **B**reak. In Section Break, choose Continuous and select OK.

11. Go to For**mat**, **S**ection. In Columns, **N**umber type **2**, **S**pacing should be .5". In Section Start, choose No Break and select OK.

PART IV

Creating Sales Documents

10. Place the cursor on the next paragraph return (just above APPETIZERS). Go to Forma**t**, **S**ection Layout. In **S**ection Start choose New Column and select OK. Go to Insert, **B**reak. In Section Break, choose Continuous and select OK.

11. Go to Format, **C**olumns. In **N**umber of Columns type **2**, **S**pace Between should be .5". Select OK.

12. Position the cursor at the end of the last line of type, Korma (Tab) (space bar) $10.95. Go to Insert, **B**reak. Choose Column Break and select OK.

13. Type the following, pressing Tab, space bar, and Enter where indicated:

    MAIN DISHES (Enter)

    PORK (Enter)

    Sorpotel (Tab) (space bar) **$10.95** (Enter)

    Suvar Mas ka Vindalu (Tab) (space bar) **$10.95** (Enter, Enter)

    BEEF (Enter)

    Kofta Kari (Tab) (space bar) **$11.95** (Enter)

    Masaledar Raan (Tab) (space bar) **$11.95** (Enter, Enter)

    VEGETABLES (Enter)

    Simla Mirch (Tab) (space bar) **$7.95** (Enter)

    Aviyal (Tab) (space bar) **$7.95** (Enter)

    Mattar Pannir (Tab) (space bar) **$7.95** (Enter)

    Khumbi Bhaji (Tab) (space bar) **$7.95** (Enter)

    Sag (Tab) (space bar) **$7.95** (Enter, Enter)

    BREADS (Enter)

    Paratha (6) (Tab) (space bar) **$2.50** (Enter)

    Alu Paratha (6) (Tab) (space bar) **$2.95** (Enter)

    Chippatis(6) (Tab) (space bar) **$2.50** (Enter)

    Puris (6) (Tab) (space bar) **$2.50** (Enter)

    SALADS (Enter)

    Alu ka Rayta (serves 2) (Tab) (space bar) **$3.50** (Enter)

CHAPTER 16

Producing a Flier

Pudine ka Rayta (serves 2) (Tab) (space bar) **$3.50** (Enter)

Rajma-Chana Salat (serves 6) (Tab) (space bar) **$5.50** (Enter)

DESSERTS (Enter)

Jalebis (12) (Tab) (space bar) **$6.95** (Enter)

Roshgulla (12) (Tab) (space bar) **$6.95**

14. Select APPETIZERS. On the Ribbon, change the type to 14-point, bold, and centered. Go to Forma**t**, **S**tyle(s). Type Major Head in the **S**tyle Name box and select OK. In Version 1.1, select OK again. In Version 2.0, select Apply. (Word Version 1.1 asks you to define the style based on the selection, respond with **Y**es.) Click on MAIN DISHES, in the Style box on the Ribbon, choose Major Head. Repeat with BREADS, SALADS, and DESSERTS.

15. Position the cursor in the line FISH. Go to Forma**t**, **S**tyle(s). In the **S**tyle Name box, type **H**ead. Click on **D**efine.

16. In Character, change the type to Helv, 12-point, and bold. Select OK.

    And OK again.

    Apply.

17. Click on CHICKEN. On the Ribbon, in the Style box, change it to Head. Repeat with LAMB, PORK, BEEF, and VEGETABLES.

18. Place the cursor in the line Pakoras (6).... Go to Forma**t**, **S**tyle(s). In the **S**tyle Name box, type **B**ody. Click on **D**efine.

19. In Character, change the type to Helv, 12 points. Select OK. In **T**abs, set the tab as **3.1"**, **R**ight aligned, Leader 2, **S**et. Select OK.

    And OK again.

    Apply.

20. Select the first section of food plus prices under APPETIZERS. On the Ribbon, in the Style box, choose Body. Repeat this step with each of the following sections of food and prices.

21. Select (Potato Filling or Lamb Filling) in the APPETIZERS section. Go to Forma**t**, **T**abs. Clear **A**ll. Set the tab to **.30**, **L**eft aligned, **S**et. Select OK.

387

PART IV

Creating Sales Documents

22. Position the cursor at the end of the last line, Roshgulla (12) (Tab) (space bar) $6.95. Go to Insert, **B**reak. In Section Break, choose Continuous and select OK.

23. Go to Format, **S**ection. In Columns, **N**umber, type **1**. In Section Start, choose New Column and select OK.

23. Go to Format, **C**olumns. In **N**umber of Columns, type **1** and select OK.

24. On the last paragraph return, type the following listing:

    ROGHAN JOSH RESTAURANT (Enter)

    OPEN DAILY FROM 11 A.M. TO 9 P.M. (Enter)

    2436 N. 24th Street (Enter)

    871-9701

25. Select ROGHAN JOSH.... Change the type to TmsRmn, 24-point, bold, and centered.

26. Go to Format, **P**aragraph. In B**o**rder, choose Above; in Pa**t**tern, choose Thick and select OK.

26. Go to Format, **B**order. In the Bo**r**der box, click in the top margin or use the down arrow to select. In **L**ine, choose the 3-point rule and select OK.

27. Select OPEN DAILY.... Change the type to TmsRmn, 12-point, and center.

28. Select the address, change the type to TmsRmn, 14-point, bold, and center.

29. Select the phone number. Change the type to TmsRmn, 18-point, bold, and center.

30. Still selected, go to Format, **P**aragraph. In B**o**rder, choose Below. In Pa**t**tern, choose Thick and select OK.

30. Still selected, go to Format, **B**order. In the Bo**r**der box, click in the bottom margin or use the down arrow to select. In **L**ine, choose the 3-point rule and select OK.

31. Go to File, Save **A**s. Type **flier1** and select OK.

32. Go to File, **P**rint.

CHAPTER 16

Producing a Flier

Producing a Coupon Flier

A flier that contains coupons is a valuable advertising tool. To use a coupon, a customer must visit the store. Once in the store, the chances are high that the customer will buy more than just the discounted item. Be sure that you add the name of the store on all coupons so that your store is the only place in which the customer tries to redeem the coupon. On the flier, outside the coupon border, also add the store name, address, and phone number. An expiration date on the coupons forces the customer to act quickly to receive the discount, which brings you business faster.

The next design includes 12 coupons set up in three columns. Again, section formatting applies. Notice also that the name of Roghan Josh appears in all the ads and fliers so far as all caps, TmsRmn, and 18- or 24-point bold. The typeface, type style, and sizes are similar in the rest of the flier and other ad pieces to create a sense of unity between this store's printed pieces (see fig. 16.2).

To create a flier similar to figure 16.2, follow these steps:

1. Go to **F**ile, **N**ew. New **D**ocument, **U**se Template Normal. Select OK.

2. Go to Forma**t**, **D**ocument. Set the **T**op and **B**ottom margins at **.75**". Set the **L**eft and **R**ight margins at **1.1**" and select OK.

2. Go to Forma**t**, Page Set**u**p. In **M**argins, set the **T**op and **B**ottom margins at **.75**". Set the **L**eft and **R**ight margins at **1.1**" and select OK.

3. Type:

   ROGHAN JOSH GOURMET FOODS (Enter)

   2436 N. 24th Street (Enter, Enter)

   VALUABLE COUPONS (Enter)

4. Select the first line. On the Ribbon, change the type to 24-point, bold, and center.

5. Select the address. On the Ribbon, change the type to 12-point and center.

6. Select VALUABLE COUPONS. Change the type to Helv, 18-point, bold, and center.

389

ROGHAN JOSH GOURMET FOODS
2436 N. 24th Street

VALUABLE COUPONS

| ASAFETIDA
1/2 oz. jar

$1.00 OFF
ROGHAN JOSH
Expires 3/29/92
Limit 1 Per Customer |

| JAGGERY
5 lb. bag

$2.00 OFF
ROGHAN JOSH
Expires 3/29/92
Limit 1 Per Customer |

| PHOA RICE
1 lb. bag

$1.00 OFF
ROGHAN JOSH
Expires 3/29/92
Limit 1 Per Customer |

| CARDAMOM
1/4 oz. jar

$.50 OFF
ROGHAN JOSH
Expires 3/29/92
Limit 1 Per Customer |

| FENUGREEK SEED
1/4 oz. jar

$.50 OFF
ROGHAN JOSH
Expires 3/29/92
Limit 1 Per Customer |

| ROSE WATER
1/4 oz. jar

$.50 OFF
ROGHAN JOSH
Expires 3/29/92
Limit 1 Per Customer |

| LOMBIA DAL
1 lb. bag

$1.20 OFF
ROGHAN JOSH
Expires 3/29/92
Limit 1 Per Customer |

| MUSTARD OIL
12 oz. bottle

$1.00 OFF
ROGHAN JOSH
Expires 3/29/92
Limit 1 Per Customer |

| TAMARIND
per pod

$.25 OFF
ROGHAN JOSH
Expires 3/29/92
Limit 1 Per Customer |

| RAJMA DAL
1 lb. bag

$1.00 OFF
ROGHAN JOSH
Expires 3/29/92
Limit 1 Per Customer |

| BASUMATI RICE
1 lb. bag

$1.00 OFF
ROGHAN JOSH
Expires 3/29/92
Limit 1 Per Customer |

| SAFFRON
1/4 oz. jar

$1.00 OFF
ROGHAN JOSH
Expires 3/29/92
Limit 1 Per Customer |

ROGHAN JOSH SPICES
We offer spices from around the world!

2436 N. 24th Street   871-9701

FIG. 16.2. *A coupon flier for Roghan Josh, set up in three columns.*

CHAPTER 16

Producing a Flier

7. Place the cursor on the last paragraph return. Go to **I**nsert, **B**reak. In Section Break, choose Con**t**inuous and select OK.

8. Go to Forma**t**, Section. In Columns, **N**umber, type **3**. Spacing is fine at .5". In **S**ection Start, choose New Column and select OK.

7. Position the cursor on the last paragraph return. Go to Forma**t**, **S**ection Layout. In **S**ection Start, choose New Column and select OK. Go to **I**nsert, **B**reak. In Section Break, choose Continuous and select OK.

8. Go to Forma**t**, **C**olumns. In **N**umber of Columns, type **3**. Space Between is OK at .5" and select OK.

9. Type **2xEnter**. Move the cursor up one line. Go to Forma**t**, **P**aragraph. In **B**order, choose Box. In Pa**t**tern, choose Double and select OK.

9. Type **2xEnter**. Move the cursor up one line to the first return. Go to Forma**t**, **B**order. In the Preset box, choose **B**ox. In **L**ine choose the .75 double rules and select OK.

10. On the Ribbon, center the paragraph return and type the following text:

    ASAFETIDA (Enter)

    1/2 oz. jar (Enter, Enter)

    $1.00 OFF (Enter)

    ROGHAN JOSH (Enter)

    Expires 3/29/92 (Enter)

    Limit 1 Per Customer

11. Select the first line, ASAFETIDA. Change the type to 12-point, bold.

12. Select $1.00 OFF. Change the type to 18-point, bold.

13. Select the next three lines, from ROGHAN... to Limit 1 Per Customer. Change the type to 8-point. Select ROGHAN... and bold.

14. Select the entire box plus the extra paragraph return after the box. Go to **E**dit, **C**opy. Position the cursor on the last return and go to **E**dit, **P**aste. Repeat this step two more times (so you have four boxes in the first column).

PART IV

Creating Sales Documents

15. Select all four boxes. Go to **Edit**, **Copy**. Position the cursor on the last paragraph return in the first column. Go to **Insert**, **Break** and choose **Column Break**. Select OK.

16. The cursor should be at the top of the second column. Go to **Edit**, **P**aste. Repeat the column break and paste the boxes in the third column.

17. The type in the boxes is already formatted. If you carefully delete one line at a time and type into it, the type remains formatted. Fill in each of the boxes with the following type by deleting a line and then typing the following text:

CARDAMOM

1/4 oz. jar

$.50 OFF

LOMBIA DAL

1 lb. bag

$1.20 OFF

RAJMA DAL

1 lb. bag

JAGGERY

5 lb. bag

$2.00 OFF

FENUGREEK SEED

1/4 oz. jar

$.50 OFF

MUSTARD OIL

12 oz. bottle

BASUMATI RICE

1 lb. bag

PHOA RICE

1 lb. bag

ROSE WATER

CHAPTER 16

Producing a Flier

1/4 oz. jar

$.50 OFF

TAMARIND

per pod

$.25 OFF

SAFFRON

1/4 oz. jar

18. Place the cursor on the last return in column 3. Go to **I**nsert, **B**reak. In Section Break, choose **C**ontinuous.

19. Go to Format, **S**ection. In Columns, **N**umber, type **1**. In **S**ection Start, choose No Break and select OK.

19. Go to Forma**t**, **C**olumns. In **N**umber of Columns, type **1** and select OK.

20. Type:

    ROGHAN JOSH SPICES (Enter)

    We offer spices from around the world! (Enter, Enter)

    2436 N. 24th Street(8 spaces)871-9701

21. Select ROGHAN.... On the Ribbon, change the type to 24-point, bold, and centered.

22. Select the next line, We offer.... Change the type to 14-point, italic, centered.

23. Select the address and phone number. Change the type to 14-point, centered.

24. Go to **F**ile, Save **A**s. Type **flier2** and select OK.

25. Go to **F**ile, **P**rint.

If you use Word 2.0, consider adding screened backgrounds to some or all of the coupon boxes. To perform this action to an entire box, select the box, go to Forma**t**, **B**order. Click on **S**hading. In the **P**attern box, choose the percentage of the screen. Figure 16.3 shows the above coupon flier with a 10 percent screen in some of the coupon boxes.

393

ROGHAN JOSH GOURMET FOODS
2436 N. 24th Street

VALUABLE COUPONS

ASAFETIDA	JAGGERY	PHOA RICE
1/2 oz. jar	5 lb. bag	1 lb. bag
$1.00 OFF	**$2.00 OFF**	**$1.00 OFF**
ROGHAN JOSH	ROGHAN JOSH	ROGHAN JOSH
Expires 3/29/92	Expires 3/29/92	Expires 3/29/92
Limit1 Per Customer	Limit1 Per Customer	Limit1 Per Customer

CARDAMOM	FENUGREEK SEED	ROSE WATER
1/4 oz. jar	1/4 oz. jar	1/4 oz. jar
$.50 OFF	**$.50 OFF**	**$.50 OFF**
ROGHAN JOSH	ROGHAN JOSH	ROGHAN JOSH
Expires 3/29/92	Expires 3/29/92	Expires 3/29/92
Limit1 Per Customer	Limit1 Per Customer	Limit1 Per Customer

LOMBIA DAL	MUSTARD OIL	TAMARIND
1 lb. bag	12 oz. bottle	per pod
$1.20 OFF	**$1.00 OFF**	**$.25 OFF**
ROGHAN JOSH	ROGHAN JOSH	ROGHAN JOSH
Expires 3/29/92	Expires 3/29/92	Expires 3/29/92
Limit1 Per Customer	Limit1 Per Customer	Limit1 Per Customer

RAJMA DAL	BASUMATI RICE	SAFFRON
1 lb. bag	1 lb. bag	1/4 oz. jar
$1.00 OFF	**$1.00 OFF**	**$1.00 OFF**
ROGHAN JOSH	ROGHAN JOSH	ROGHAN JOSH
Expires 3/29/92	Expires 3/29/92	Expires 3/29/92
Limit1 Per Customer	Limit1 Per Customer	Limit1 Per Customer

ROGHAN JOSH SPICES

We offer spices from around the world!

2436 N. 24th Street   871-9701

FIG. 16.3. In Word Version 2.0, add 10 percent screens to some or all of the coupon boxes.

Producing a Flier with Hanging Indents

If the flier has a list of subjects and descriptions or definitions, as shown in figure 16.4, then you may want to use a hanging indent. Here, the class names list to the left, and the descriptions indent to the right.

This design organizes the information so the customer can easily find the class name. Indenting the descriptions also allows a shorter line length so that the descriptions are easy to read. The graphic rules border the flier.

You also may note that the style of this flier is similar to the Humble Opinions' large ad in the previous chapter. Times Roman is the only typeface, type sizes are the same, and both designs present some information in paragraph form. These characteristics help create unity between the company pieces.

To create the flier in figure 16.4, perform these steps:

1. Go to **File**, **New**. Choose New **D**ocument, **U**se Template Normal. Select OK.

2. Go to Forma**t**, **D**ocument. Set all margins to .7" and select OK.

2. Go to Forma**t**, Page Set**u**p. Set all margins to .7" and select OK.

3. Type the following listing, pressing Tab and Enter where indicated:

   (Enter) **HUMBLE OPINIONS** (Enter)

   COMPUTER TRAINING CENTER (Enter, Enter)

   1127 E. Main Street (Tab) **Beckley, WV 25801** (Enter)

   (304) 251-5151 (Tab) **800-250-2369** (Enter three times)

   INTRODUCTORY CLASSES (Enter, Enter)

   Basic Computers (Tab) **Learn about memory, DOS, files, directories, and popular software programs. Explore printers, modems, and hard and floppy drives. Discover new and innovative uses for the PC in your business!** (Enter, Enter)

395

HUMBLE OPINIONS
COMPUTER TRAINING CENTER

1127 E. Main Street   Beckley, WV 25801
(304) 251-5151   800-250-2369

INTRODUCTORY CLASSES

Basic Computers   Learn about memory, DOS, files, directories, and popular software programs. Explore printers, modems, and hard and floppy drives. Discover new and innovative uses for the PC in your business!

Word Processing   Learn basic editing, function keys, margin and tab settings, and editing codes. Use retrieve, save and print; use block operations for moving text, and spell checking.

Database   Learn database concepts, create and edit a form, add and edit data, modify file structures, create reports and add and delete records. Also learn to sort data in variety of ways.

Spreadsheets   Create, save, retrieve, and print a spreadsheet. Learn to use formulas, and copy rows and columns. Format ranges, change column widths, and use absolute cell addresses.

Desktop Publishing   Become familiar with documents, mouse and keyboard functions, basic formatting of page such as typeface, type size and style; columns and margins; tabs and tables; frames, graphics, importing and exporting, bullets, and indents.

INTERMEDIATE CLASSES

Word Processing   Learn about macros, tables, formatting columns, setting font types and sizes, and mail merge. Print envelopes, large and small paper sizes; learn the finer points of page make-up on the word processor.

Spreadsheets   Become more efficient with spreadsheets by freezing titles, and using named ranges and windows. Perform logical evaluation, use cell protection, and control recalculation.

Desktop Publishing   Learn to use desktop publishing to produce flyers, resumes, forms, newsletters, brochures, and any document you need for your business. Bring in your own word processing to format any document you want.

(304) 251-5151   **CALL TODAY**   **800-250-2369**

FIG. 16.4. A flier of class descriptions, using a hanging indent.

CHAPTER 16

Producing a Flier

Word Processing (Tab) **Learn basic editing, function keys, margin and tab settings, editing codes. Use retrieve, save and print; use block operations for moving text, and spell-checking.** (Enter, Enter)

Database (Tab) **Learn database concepts, create and edit a form, add and edit data, modify file structures, create reports and add and delete records. Also learn to sort data in variety of ways.** (Enter, Enter)

Spreadsheets (Tab) **Create, save, retrieve, and print a spreadsheet. Learn to use formulas, and copy rows and columns. Format ranges, change column widths, and use absolute cell addresses.** (Enter, Enter)

Desktop Publishing (Tab) **Become familiar with documents, mouse and keyboard functions, basic formatting of pages such as typeface, type size and style; columns and margins; tabs and tables; frames, graphics, importing and exporting, bullets, and indents.** (Enter, Enter)

INTERMEDIATE CLASSES (Enter, Enter)

Word Processing (tab) **Learn about macros, tables, formatting columns, setting font types and sizes, and mail merge. Print envelopes, large and small paper sizes; learn the finer points of page make-up on the word processor.** (Enter, Enter)

Spreadsheets (tab) **Become more efficient with spreadsheets by freezing titles, using named ranges and windows. Perform logical evaluation, use cell protection and control recalculation.** (Enter, Enter)

Desktop Publishing (Tab) **Learn to use desktop publishing to produce fliers, resumes, forms, newsletters, brochures, and any document you need for your business. Bring in your own word processing to format any document you want.** (Enter, Enter)

(304) 251-5151 (8 spaces) **CALL TODAY**(8 spaces)**800-250-2369** (Enter)

4. Place the cursor on the first paragraph return. Go to Forma**t**, **P**aragraph. In the **B**order box, choose Above. In the Pa**t**tern box, choose Thick and select OK.

PART IV

Creating Sales Documents

4. Position the cursor on the first paragraph return. Go to Forma**t**, **B**order. In the Bo**r**der box, click in the top margin, or use the down arrow to select. In **L**ine, choose the 3-point rule and select OK.

5. Select `HUMBLE OPINIONS COMPUTER TRAINING CENTER`. On the Ribbon, change the type to 24-point, bold, centered.

6. Select the address and phone number lines. Change the type to 12-point. On the Ruler, set the tab as Right aligned at 7".

7. Select `INTRODUCTORY CLASSES`. Change the type to 14-point and bold.

8. Select all type from `Basic Computers...` to the end of the `Desktop Publishing...` paragraph. On the Ribbon, change the type to 12-point.

9. Still selected, go to Forma**t**, **P**aragraph. In the Indents box, From **L**eft type **1.75"**. In the First Li**n**e box, type **-1.75"** and select OK.

9. Still selected, go to Forma**t**, **P**aragraph. In the Indentation box, From **L**eft type **1.75"**. In the **F**irst Line box, type **-1.75"** and select OK.

10. Select and boldface `Basic Computers`. Repeat with the rest of the class names.

11. Select `INTERMEDIATE CLASSES`. On the Ribbon, change the type to 14-point and bold.

12. Select the last line of type, `(304) 251-5151.....` On the Ribbon, change the type to 18-point, bold, and centered.

13. Place the cursor on the last paragraph return. Go to Forma**t**, **P**aragraph. In the B**o**rder box, choose Below. In Pa**tt**ern, choose Thick and select OK.

13. Position the cursor on the last paragraph return. Go to Forma**t**, **B**order. In the Bo**r**der box, click in the bottom margin or press the down arrow until the bottom margin is selected. In **L**ine, choose the 3-point rule and select OK.

14. Go to **F**ile, Save **A**s. Type **flier3** and select OK.

15. Go to **F**ile, **P**rint.

CHAPTER 16

Producing a Flier

Looking at Design

You can also use any of the previous fliers as newspaper ads or circulars, just as you can use any of the circulars as fliers. Generally however, fliers contain more information. The flier can be two-sided if you have more information than fits on one side.

Figures 16.5 and 16.6 illustrate a two-sided flier. Space is not the reason for using both sides in this case. The front of the flier is designed to attract the attention of a specific audience, one that uses computers.

The use of the jargon word, HELP, on the front of the flier attracts attention as does the computer graphic. White space also adds to the effect.

Figure 16.6 shows the other side of the flier. A simple two-column schedule of classes, side two informs the reader of the class and the day and time the class is offered. Students who come to the training center may pick up and keep the schedule for later reference.

Fliers don't necessarily have to be in portrait orientation. Figure 16.7 illustrates a landscape orientation. Because the graphic's orientation is long, the flier's orientation mirrors it. The bullets attract attention to the contents of the book. The columns of artists' names fit well into landscape. Notice that the informational paragraph at the bottom is indented on both left and right to keep the correct line length for the type size. And the heavy rule along the bottom margin balances the graphic at the top.

Word Version 2.0's WordArt makes excellent display type for fliers. In figure 16.8, the type that runs up the side and across the top invites you to read it. The typeface is unusual and the rotation creates an exciting border. The rest of the type is Helvetica, to help emphasize the display type. Only necessary information is listed: date, place, subjects, hours. A form for more information enables interested parties to sign up, which gives the Trade Show additional names for later mailing lists.

FIG. 16.5. *The front of a flier, designed to attract the attention of a specific audience.*

HUMBLE OPINIONS
COMPUTER TRAINING CENTER

Schedule of Classes
May 1992

May 5
Intro to Word Processing 8-4
Intro to Spreadsheets 8-4

May 6
Intro to Office Mge 8-12
Intro to Database 8-4
Intro to Word Processing 8-4

May 7
Inter Word Processing 8-4
Inter Spreadsheet 8-4

May 8
Intro Desktop Publishing 8-4
Intro Acct. 8-4
Intro Word Processing 8-4

May 12
Inter Desktop Publishing 8-4
Inter Word Processing 8-4

May 13
Inter Database 8-4
Inter Acct. 8-4
Inter Spreadsheet 8-4

May 14
Adv Word Processing 8-4
Adv Spreadsheet 8-4
Adv Database 8-4

May 15
Adv Desktop Publishing 8-4
Adv Acct. 8-4

May 19
Intro to Word Processing 8-4
Intro to Spreadsheets 8-4

May 20
Intro to Office Mge 8-12
Intro to Database 8-4
Intro to Word Processing 8-4

May 21
Inter Word Processing 8-4
Inter Spreadsheet 8-4

May 22
Intro Desktop Publishing 8-4
Intro Acct. 8-4
Intro Word Processing 8-4

May 26
Inter Desktop Publishing 8-4
Inter Word Processing 8-4

May 27
Inter Database 8-4
Inter Acct. 8-4
Inter Spreadsheet 8-4

May 28
Adv Word Processing 8-4
Adv Spreadsheet 8-4
Adv Database 8-4

May 29
Adv Desktop Publishing 8-4
Adv Acct. 8-4

SATURDAY CLASSES

May 2
Intro to Word Processing 8-4
Intro to Spreadsheets 8-4

May 9
Intro to Office Mge 8-12
Intro to Database 8-4
Intro to Word Processing 8-4

May 16
Inter Word Processing 8-4
Inter Spreadsheet 8-4

May 23
Intro to Office Mge 8-12
Intro to Database 8-4

FIG. 16.6. *The other side of the flier.*

PART IV

Creating Sales Documents

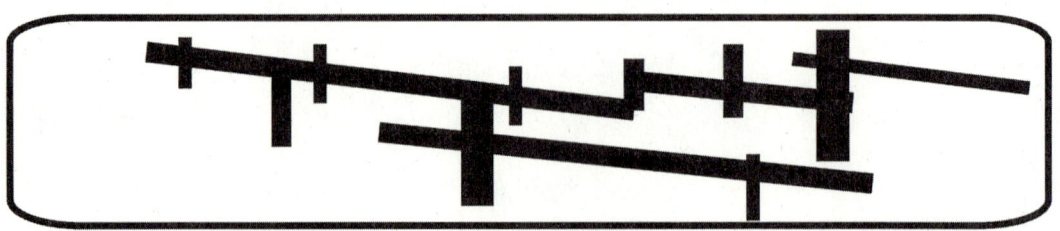

FIG. 16.7. *A landscape-oriented flier. White space creates an interesting space around the text.*

Design a flier to attract attention. Any layout that accomplishes this aim is appropriate. The flier in figure 16.9 looks like a newsletter. Because newsletters usually contain useful information, this flier is likely to be read. The masthead, designed in WordArt, attracts crafts people. A dateline and three columns make the flier look more like a newsletter. The right-aligned heads are consistent with Marie's ad in the newspaper, as are the listings of crafts in the first column. Leader tabs make the discounts easy to read, and the boxed type in the middle column helps to balance the masthead. Finally, the right column contains information useful to a potter, which also makes the flier a reference piece.

TRADE SHOW

APRIL 21 - 25, 1992
NEW HAVEN ARMORY

- **Personal Computers**
- **Output/Imaging Devices**
- **Monitors**
- **Compact Disk Drives**
- **Data Compression Utilities**
- **Networking**
- **Scanners**
- **Color**

SHOW HOURS:

APRIL 21	Noon to 6:00 p.m.
APRIL 22	10:00 a.m. to 6:00 p.m.
APRIL 23	10:00 a.m. to 6:00 p.m.
APRIL 24	10:00 a.m. to 6:00 p.m.
APRIL 25	10:00 a.m. to Noon

DTP 92 Trade Show
Three North 72, Suite 230
New Haven, NJ 23901

Please send me free brochure and registration forms. Please send your seminar brochure.

Name _____

Company _____

Address _____

City _____ State _____ Zip _____

DESKTOP PUBLISHING

FIG. 16.8. *A Trade Show flier with a fill-in form for more information.*

Decoupage Daily

MARIE'S CRAFT SHOP — MAY 1992 — ISSUE:5

MARIE'S CRAFT SHOP STOREWIDE SALE

MARIE'S CRAFT SHOP announces a pre-inventory **SALE**. Some items in the store discounted up to 75% off. Stop by Marie's Craft Shop today for craft bargains!!! Sale begins May 1 and ends May 14.

POTTERY
Georgia Clays	10% OFF
Pottery Tools	15% OFF
Glaze Components	10% OFF
Aprons	10% OFF

WEAVING
Looms	35% OFF
Fibers	25% OFF
Yarns	25% OFF
Shuttles	10% OFF

CANDLES
Wax	10% OFF
Hot plates	50% OFF
Wick	10% OFF
Coloring	10% OFF

TREMENDOUS SAVINGS!!

Many items in the store discounted up to 75% off. Some include:

POTTERY

Brens Pottery Wheels
Electric wheels: foot-controlled pedal, smooth speed control. Discounted **65%**!

Dister Pottery Wheels
Kick wheels built of sturdy steel frame. Flywheel evenly balanced. Discounted **75%**!

MAY 1 thru MAY 14 SALE

UP TO 75% OFF
MARIE'S CRAFT SHOP

TIPS ON POTTERY

1. Oxides and Talc

When working with a heavy mixture of talc clay, try adding various oxides for color before creating your pot. Chromium, cobalt, zinc, and red iron oxides are great. Take small amounts of the clay, one- or two-pound balls, and mix in anywhere from 1/4 oz. to 1 oz. of oxide.

Wedge until the oxide is thoroughly mixed. Then try blending two or even three of the oxided clays together to create a lovely hand-built or thrown pot.

2. Talc And Your Eyes

Remember that Talc is very hazardous to your eyes, and lungs. Be sure to wear goggles and a mask when working with the raw clay, or when trimming the bone dry pot. Dust particles can scratch your corneas, permeate your lungs, and damage mucous membranes.

FIG. 16.9. *An advertising flier that looks like a newsletter.*

CHAPTER 16

Producing a Flier

Recapping

This chapter taught you that a flier is a tool businesses use to advertise products, services, sales, or specials. You also learned that fliers are designed to inform customers and sell merchandise. Finally, you learned how to produce a variety of fliers.

In the next chapter, you learn how to produce a brochure.

17

Producing a Brochure

As one of the most effective forms of advertising, brochures explain and detail information about a company's products or services. When you design brochures, make sure that you concentrate on what the company can offer the customer. Brochures that describe only a company, its history, staff, qualities, and so on, hold little interest for customers who want to know what you can do for them.

Learning About Brochures

Brochures are soft-sell advertising. A well-designed brochure invites customers to read at their leisure, and to refer back through the material often. The cover design is attractive and draws the reader inside. Art work, graphics or photos help accomplish this task.

The material inside the brochure details products or services, or gives helpful facts to the customer. This information leads the eye in an organized, methodical way. Again, art, tables, and graphics reinforce the information. You can use spreadsheets, tables, and graphs in a brochure, but think about the stability of their content before making those kinds of additions.

Because brochures are reference pieces, don't include dated information. Brochures require general facts and enduring content. Try to add something in the brochure that makes the customer depend on it; something the customer may want to use later. For example, a paper company may add a list of paper

weights and types used for printing letterheads. Or a computer training business can list various keyboard shortcuts. Also, recipes, directions for complcting a task, a map, and important phone numbers, all are ways to make the brochure more useful to the customer.

Using Typesetting and White Space

Also remember that, as a reference piece, the typesetting of a brochure should be meticulous. Remember, customers may keep the brochure for reference and read it often. Therefore, the overall design must be attractive. In the following instructions, you find many typesetting details to assure that the brochure looks professional. One example is adding just three or four points of space above or below some lines of type or manually hyphenating some words that the automatic hyphenation misses. You find many more of these additions throughout this and the rest of the chapters in this book. You can of course, skip these details, but your resulting brochure might look amateurish and awkward.

Selecting the Paper and Ink

Brochures, as source pieces, usually look best when printed on heavy paper, such as 70# coated or uncoated offset. Smooth, linen, or enamel finishes also are good choices. Use white or pastel colored paper so that the customers' eyes don't tire easily.

Ink choices are many and varied. Using two, three, or even four colors of ink is both reasonable and recommended. The customer may keep an attractively printed brochure. Full color (four color process) is popular for brochures. If you have a good color photograph of your place of business, the staff, or of products, consider printing the front of the brochure in full color. Although more expensive than one-, two- or three-color printing, full-color printing certainly attracts attention and makes a lasting impression. When printing full color, remember that the side with the front panel can contain blue, black or magenta heads, rules, and so on, besides a full color photograph.

CHAPTER 17

Producing a Brochure

To save money, think about printing in full color on one side of the brochure only. The inside can be all in blue or black ink, for example. This method produces an attractive brochure, with emphasis on the front cover.

Determining the Size

Brochures come in all sizes. You might want a brochure that fits in a pocket, or on a rack, or in a binder. Traditionally, a brochure is 8 1/2 x 11 inches with two folds. Other common sizes are 5 1/2 inches x 8 1/2 inches with one fold and 8 1/2 inches x 14 inches with three folds. You can design your brochure any way you want to fit the information you have. You may want an 8 1/2-inch x 11-inch sheet printed on two sides (no folds), or an 11-inch x 17-inch sheet folded to 8 1/2 inches x 11 inches, or, 15 inches x 17 inches, folded to include a pocket along the inside bottom. The pocket is perfect for placing updated information, such as price lists, new products, and so on.

This chapter shows you how to produce one innovative and two traditional brochures. One design in this chapter should work for you and your company.

Notice that these brochures continue the ad campaign for three businesses—Humble Opinions, Roghan Josh, and Marie's Craft Shop—used in previous chapters for advertisements and fliers. This chapter finishes these ad campaigns by producing a brochure for each. Note the consistencies created between the ads and brochures. Logos, type faces and sizes, alignment, similar writing styles, and so on, add to the unity of the company pieces. Subtle changes are made for emphasis in art work, photos, or an unusual fold. Use these ideas as a guide when creating printed brochures.

Producing a Basic Brochure

The first design measures 8 1/2 inches x 11 inches, with one fold to make the final size 5 1/2 inches x 8 1/2 inches. When you design a brochure, plan each panel before you begin. Decide what goes on the cover, the inside, and the back. Then, working in Word, produce the brochure in a different order. Start typing and formatting the back panel first because this part of the brochure begins

PART IV

Creating Sales Documents

in the left column (see fig. 17.1). Then type and format the front panel (cover), and finally the inside.

ROGHAN JOSH GOURMET FOOD

Roghan Josh stocks the area's largest selection of gourmet foods. Our aisles represent the food of 12 countries. Spices, rice, beans and lentils, meats, canned and fresh vegetables, breads, and desserts are all represented here. Although our largest inventory is Indian food, we also stock spices and staples from:

India	Nepal	Thailand
China	Korea	Malaysia
Pakistan	Laos	Vietnam
Turkey	Borneo	Sumatra

ROGHAN JOSH SPICES

Within our spacious Gourmet store, you will find a special section dedicated to the Spices of various countries. Taking in more than half the Gourmet shop, Roghan Josh Spices stocks the finest, freshest herbs and spices found anywhere. We specialize in Indian spices, with a stockpile of more than 200. If you cannot find it here, we will order it for you and we will pay the shipping and handling charges.

ROGHAN JOSH RESTAURANT

Roghan Josh Restaurant, open from 11:00 a.m. to 9:00 p.m. daily, specializes in the food of India and Pakistan. Delicious meals prepared fresh daily at reasonable prices. Our menu includes appetizers, meat and vegetarian dishes, salads, breads, and desserts, all to delight your taste buds. Reservations are recommended; call ahead with a specified time of arrival. We have an entertainment lounge for those of you who would like a drink before dinner. Live Indian music is featured in the lounge nightly from 7:00 p.m. to 9:00 p.m.

ROGHAN JOSH
GOURMET FOODS
SPICES
RESTAURANT

2436 N. 24th Street
Washington, DC

871-9701

OPEN DAILY FROM 11:00 A.M. TO 9:00 P.M.

FIG. 17.1. *The front (right) and back (left) cover of a brochure.*

The front cover announces the name of the business, the address, phone number, and hours. Art work added to the front cover breaks up the space and, when printed, may add color.

The back panel describes each part of the store. When planning copy for the back panel, remember that customers usually look first at the front, and then the back of the brochure. If they're interested, they open the brochure.

When the brochure is open, make sure that you've included practical and effective information. Here, Roghan Josh lists definitions of spices, tips and basic ingredients to Indian cooking

CHAPTER 17

Producing a Brochure

(see fig. 17.2). Throughout the brochure, add helpful tips for the customer. Throughout this brochure, for example, Roghan Josh reminds the customer that the gourmet store stocks all these ingredients.

TIPS ON INDIAN COOKING

Avoid substituting spices within a recipe; the entire flavor of the dish could change. Your meal will be the best when you use exactly the spices called for in the recipe. Also, use whole spices whenever possible. Whole spices, such as peppercorns, mustard seeds, cumin, and coriander, retain their fresh, delicious flavor longer than those that are crushed. If you must use ground spices, use the same amount you would if using whole, then adjust the flavoring when the cooking is done.

Hot chili peppers are essential to most Indian foods. Whether just enough is added for flavor, or a lot is added for extremely hot food, always use the reddest chili available. Red does not signify hot as much as it means freshness. When preparing the peppers for your dish, wear rubber gloves. Rinse the peppers well in cold water. While holding the chili under the running water, remove the stem and seeds (you may leave the seeds for a hotter dish). Now slice or chop the pepper to add to the dish.

BASIC INGREDIENTS FOR INDIAN COOKING

GHEE

Ghee is an Indian butter that is boiled, then simmered, then strained to produce a perfectly clear, rich oil. Ghee is used for cooking and flavoring Indian food. Its taste is similar to the flavor of nuts. Roghan Josh stocks Ghee in 1-lb. and 5-lb. tubs.

GARAM MASALA

Masala is a spice blend; each masala is suited to particular dishes. Garam masala is the most widely used of the masala mixtures, and is available at our store. Various whole spices like cloves, cardamom, coriander, cumin, peppercorns and cinnamon are baked and then ground with a mortar and pestle to produce the finest mixture for your recipes.

Other masalas available at Roghan Josh include coriander masala, cardamom masala and a special masala blend for yogurt salads and rayta.

A SPICE GUIDE

ASAFETIDA is a garlic-flavored gum resin used mainly with vegetable dishes. The taste is definitely an acquired one, as it is very strong and often bitter.

CARDAMOM is a dried fruit in the ginger family. We carry both the pod and seed of cardamom. The flavor is somewhat lemony and makes an excellent addition to duck and chicken dishes.

CORIANDER is an herb related to the parsley family. Its seed and leaves are used in beef, lamb and vegetable dishes. Coriander is especially good for adding to rayta.

CUMIN is a basic ingredient of all Indian cooking. A member of the parsley family, its seed is extraordinarily aromatic.

MUSTARD SEEDS (black) are a member of the mustard family with far less strong flavor than the yellow mustard seed. Use mustard seeds in everything, but mostly rayta.

SAFFRON are dried stigmas of a flower in the crocus family. Mainly used for coloring, it has a mildly bitter flavor. Use to flavor and color chicken dishes, rice and vegetables.

JAGGERY is a raw, crude sugar. Use jaggery primarily in dessert dishes and chutneys.

TAMARIND is the pulp of a tropical tree. Its taste is sweet and biting. Use tamarind for fish, green vegetables and lamb.

TUMERIC is a member of the ginger family with a very pungent flavor. It's used to color food to a deep yellow-gold. Use tumeric in cauliflower and potato dishes.

THE ABOVE SPICES AND MORE AVAILABLE AT ROGHAN JOSH SPICES!

FIG. 17.2. *The inside of the brochure, brimming with valuable information for the customer.*

The type found in this brochure is similar to the type found in Josh's former ads and fliers. Bold, all cap heads in Times Roman create unity with other pieces. The art work, which prints in color, adds emphasis to the brochure. Justified type and indented first lines allows for more information. Also, notice the sufficient white space that makes reading the brochure easy on the eyes.

To produce the brochure shown in figures 17.1 and 17.2, follow these steps:

PART IV

Creating Sales Documents

1. Go to **F**ile, **N**ew. Choose New **D**ocument and **U**se Template, Normal. Then select OK.

2. Go to **F**ile, P**r**inter Setup. Click **S**etup. In Orientation, choose Landscape. Select OK two times.

3. Go to Forma**t**, **D**ocument. In Margins, type **.5"** for all. Select OK.

4. Go to Forma**t**, **S**ection. In Columns, **N**umber type **2**. In **S**pacing, type **1"**. **S**ection Start should be New Page. Select OK.

2. Go to Forma**t**, Page Set**u**p. In **S**ize and Orientation, choose Landscape.

3. Still in the dialog box, **M**argins. Type **.5"** for all. Select OK.

4. Go to Forma**t**, **C**olumns. In **N**umber of Columns type **2**. In **S**pace Between, type **1"** and select OK.

5. Go to Forma**t**, **St**yles. In the **S**tyle Name box, type **Body**. Click on **D**efine. Choose Character, change the point size to 12. Select OK.

6. Still in St**y**les dialog box, choose **P**aragraph. In Alignment, choose **J**ustified. In Indents, First Li**n**e, type **.25"**. Select OK twice.

5. Go to Forma**t**, St**y**le. In the **S**tyle Name box, type **Body**. Click on **D**efine. In Change Formatting, choose **C**haracter, change the point size to 12. Select OK.

6. Still in the Style dialog box, choose **P**aragraph. In Alignment, choose Justified. In Indentation, First Line, type **.25"**. Select OK and Apply.

7. Position the cursor in the top left-hand corner of column 1 (you may want to turn on non-printing characters from the Ribbon so you can see your column guides). On the Ribbon, in the Style box, choose Body.

8. Type the following text, pressing Tab and Enter where indicated:

ROGHAN JOSH GOURMET FOOD (Enter, Enter)

(Type the back cover paragraph as shown in fig. 17.1, or type your own data, then Enter, Enter.)

CHAPTER 17

Producing a Brochure

(Tab) **India** (Tab) **Nepal** (Tab) **Thailand** (Enter)

(Tab) **China** (Tab) **Korea** (Tab) **Malaysia** (Enter)

(Tab) **Pakistan** (Tab) **Laos** (Tab) **Vietnam** (Enter)

(Tab) **Turkey** (Tab) **Borneo** (Tab) **Sumatra** (Enter, three times)

ROGHAN JOSH SPICES (Enter, Enter)

(Type the back cover paragraph as shown in fig. 17.1, or type your own data, then Enter, Enter.)

ROGHAN JOSH RESTAURANT (Enter, Enter)

(Type the back cover paragraph as shown in fig. 17.1, or type your own data, then Enter, Enter.)

9. Select ROGHAN JOSH GOURMET FOOD. On the Ribbon, change the type to 18-point, bold, and centered. Repeat with ROGHAN JOSH SPICES and ROGHAN JOSH RESTAURANT.

10. Select the type from (Tab) India... to ...(Tab) Sumatra. On the Ruler, set the tabs as left aligned. The first at .63", the second at 2", the third tab at 3.25".

11. Position the cursor in the first tabbed line, India (Tab).... Go to Forma**t**, **P**aragraph. In Spacing, **B**efore, type **.5li** and select OK.

12. Select the entire column of type. Go to **U**tilities, **H**yphenate. Be sure to turn off **C**onfirm and select OK.

12. Select the entire column of type. Go to **T**ools, **H**yphenation. Be sure to turn off **C**onfirm and select OK.

13. Position the cursor at the bottom of this first column. Go to Insert, **B**reak. Choose **C**olumn Break. Select OK.

14. Type the following text, pressing Enter where indicated:

    ROGHAN JOSH (Enter)
    GOURMET FOODS (Enter)

    SPICES (Enter)

    RESTAURANT (Enter, five times)

    2436 N. 24th Street (Enter)

    Washington, DC (Enter, Enter)

413

PART IV

Creating Sales Documents

> **871-9701** (Enter, three times)
>
> **OPEN DAILY FROM 11:00 A.M. TO 9:00 P.M.** (Enter)

15. Select `ROGHAN JOSH`. On the Ribbon, change the type to 40-point, bold, and centered.

16. Select the next three lines of type, from `GOURMET FOODS` to, and including, `RESTAURANT`. Change the type to 24-point, bold, and centered.

17. If you want, you can insert a graphic on the third paragraph return down from `RESTAURANT`. You can always borrow Word's MONIQUE.TIF. To insert this file, go to Insert, Picture. In c:\winword\library choose MONIQUE.TIF and select OK.

18. Select the two address lines. On the Ribbon, change the type to 18-point, bold, and centered.

19. Select and change the phone number to 24-point, bold, and centered.

20. Select `OPEN DAILY....` Center-align this text.

21. Place the cursor on the last paragraph return. Go to Insert, **B**reak. Choose **C**olumn Break. Select OK. The cursor should be in the first column, page 2. Be sure that the Style in the Style box is Body.

22. Type the following text:

> **TIPS ON INDIAN COOKING** (Enter, Enter)
>
> *(Type the inside, left column paragraphs as shown in fig. 17.2, or type your own data, then Enter after the first paragraph and Enter, Enter after the second.)*
>
> **BASIC INGREDIENTS FOR INDIAN COOKING** (Enter)
>
> **GHEE** (Enter)
>
> *(Type the paragraph as shown in fig. 17.2, or type your own data, then Enter, Enter.)*
>
> **GARAM MASALA**(Enter)
>
> *(Type the paragraphs as shown in fig. 17.2, or type your own data, using Enter after the first and second paragraphs.)*

CHAPTER 17

Producing a Brochure

23. Format this column before continuing. Select TIPS ON INDIAN COOKING. Change the type to 18-point, bold, and center on the Ribbon.

24. Select BASIC INGREDIENTS.... On the Ribbon, change the type to 14-point, bold, and centered.

25. Select GHEE. On the Ribbon, change the type to bold. Go to Forma**t**, **P**aragraph. In Indents, First Li**n**e, delete the contents and type **0**. Select OK. Repeat with GARAM MASALA.

25. Select GHEE. On the Ribbon, bold it. Go to Forma**t**, **P**aragraph. In Indentation, **F**irst Line, delete the contents and type **0**. Select OK. Repeat with GARAM MASALA.

26. Select all the text in the column. Go to **U**tilities, **H**yphenate. Turn off **C**onfirm and select OK.

26. Select all the text in the column. Go to T**o**ols, **H**yphenation. Turn off **C**onfirm and select OK.

27. Position the cursor on the last paragraph return in the column. Go to Insert, **B**reak. Choose Column Break. Select OK.

28. Type the following text:

    (Make the lead-in word 12-point, all caps and bold, then type in the remainder of the data as shown in figure 17.2, remembering to press Enter, Enter at the end of each block of data. Or you can type in your own data.)

    A SPICE GUIDE (Enter)

    ASAFETIDA

    CARDAMOM

    CORIANDER

    CUMIN

    MUSTARD SEEDS

    SAFFRON

    JAGGERY

    TAMARIND

    TUMERIC

    THE ABOVE SPICES AND MORE AVAILABLE AT (Enter)

    ROGHAN JOSH SPICES!

PART IV

Creating Sales Documents

29. Select A SPICE GUIDE. On the Ribbon, change the type to 14-point, bold, and centered.

30. Select the entire column. Go to Utilities, **H**yphenate. Select OK.

30. Select the entire column. Go to **T**ools, **H**yphenation. Select OK.

31. Select the type from THE ABOVE SPICES... to ROGHAN JOSH SPICES!. On the Ribbon, change the type to bold and centered.

32. Go to **F**ile, Save **A**s. Type **broc1** and select OK.

33. Go to **F**ile, **P**rint.

Producing a Traditional Brochure

A traditional brochure uses landscape orientation, 11 inches x 8-1/2 inches and folds twice. The following design is popular, and the size, shape, and fold are traditional, yet the right-aligned heads make this brochure design unique. The style of the heads, the logo, and the single quotation marks make this brochure consistent with Marie's other advertising pieces.

The graphic rules along the top of each column tie together the front and back of the brochure. The justified type helps define the gutter space, and the large heads allow the reader to easily find specific areas of interest.

In the brochure, Marie offers information about the craft store, art gallery, and sculpture garden. The cover, or third column, on the front lists all three attractions and the hours, address, and phone number of the business. Included on the front cover are Marie's unusual logo (same as in the ad) and a spot for a four-color photograph of the sculpture gardens.

The first column explains the shop, gallery, and garden in greater detail. The people who saw the ads and fliers may not have known about the rest of the store. This brochure is designed to entice customers with this information, which covers more than just craft supplies.

CHAPTER 17

Producing a Brochure

Marie also adds a useful table of clay body recipes in the second column. Potters will be thrilled to find this table. Note also that all the ingredients in these recipes are available at Marie's shop.

Figure 17.3 illustrates the outside of the brochure.

FIG. 17.3. *The first side of Marie's brochure; the right column is the front cover.*

The inside of the brochure (see fig. 17.4) describes, in detail, the many art works and crafts available in the Gallery. Notice that Marie's Craft Shop is mentioned several times in the copy.

To create a brochure as shown in figures 17.3 and 17.4, take these steps:

1. Go to **File**, **New**. New **D**ocument, **U**se Template, Normal. Select OK.

417

PART IV

Creating Sales Documents

POTTERY

Beautiful earthenware, stoneware and porcelain pottery are in stock at Marie's Craft Shop. Many are functional, many are art works. No lead glazes are used in any of the pottery we stock. All are completely safe for eating and drinking. Over 50 potters represented.

JEWELRY

Pewter, silver, gold and polished stones adorn the lovely selections at Marie's Craft Shop. Earrings, necklaces, bracelets, pins and more created by local artists. Recently acquired inlaid onyx earrings fill out our selection of fine jewelry.

LEATHERWORK

Belts, wallets, and purses hand-made of buckskin, calfskin or suede, are available. Exquisite tanned hides, sewn and laced with narrow strips of leather, create a fine craft only available at Marie's Craft Shop.

DECOUPAGE

Wood, glass and ceramic pieces ornately hand-painted and lacquered with the most attractive prints and photographs. Many include gold leaf; many imported from China and Belgium.

CANDLES

Handsome molded, dipped, and layered candles in a variety of shapes and colors. All prepared with the finest mixture of paraffin, tallow and beeswax for a slow, even burning candle.

BASKETS

Baskets of all kinds including coiled, plaited, twined and wicker for sale at Marie's Craft Shop. Made from materials such as white ash, fiber rush, sea grass, raffia and even corn husks, our baskets make lovely gifts for you and a friend.

WEAVING

Brilliant colors and textures liven any room in these extraordinary wall hangings. Created from all natural fibers including wool, silk, linen and cotton. From checks and plaids to inlays and leno, our weavings are breathtaking!

BATIK

Imported Indian designs in both batik and tie-dye made from silk, cotton and linen in dazzling colors. Many of our batiks were created with all natural dyes, such as onion skins, tumeric and logwood.

STAINED GLASS

Decorative mosaics of colored glass created by combining stained glass and Gothic lead. Whether you need a sun-catcher or a full entrance window, Marie's Craft Shop has it all. In addition, we also carry terrariums and lamp shades.

QUILTS

Quilts made of corduroy, silk, velvet and cotton adorn the walls of Marie's Craft Shop. A multitude of patterns, including the Windmill, Dutchman's Puzzle, Grandmother's Choice, Dresden Plate and more available.

MOSAICS

Fragments of stone, glass, and ceramic tile form beautiful, colorful designs, most wall mosaics are small enough for framing. In addition, we have mosaic trivets, tables, and counter tops.

LAPIDARY

Lapped, faceted, cabochon and tumbled gems ready for you to use in your own art works. Some available stones are Amber, Emerald, Garnets, Ruby, Lapis Lazuli, Malachite, Opal, Tiger's-eye, Topaz and Turquoise.

FIG. 17.4. *The inside of Marie's brochure.*

2. Go to **F**ile, **P**rinter Setup. Click **S**etup. In Orientation, choose **L**andscape. Select OK twice.

3. Go to Forma**t**, **D**ocument. In Margins, type **.5"** for all and select OK.

4. Go to Forma**t**, **S**ection. In Columns, **N**umber type **3**. In **S**pacing, type **.35"**. **S**ection Start should be New Page. Select OK.

2. Go to Forma**t**, Page Set**u**p. In **S**ize and Orientation, choose **L**andscape.

3. Still in the dialog box, choose **M**argins. Type **.5"** for all and select OK.

4. Go to Forma**t**, **C**olumns. In **N**umber of Columns type **3**. In Space Between, type **.35"** and select OK.

CHAPTER 17

Producing a Brochure

5. Go to Forma**t**, St**y**les. In the **S**tyle Name box, type **Body**. Click on **D**efine. Choose **C**haracter, change the point size to 12. Select OK.

6. Still in the St**y**les dialog box, choose **P**aragraph. In Alignment, choose **J**ustified. In Indents, First Li**n**e, type **.25"**. Select OK twice.

5. Go to Forma**t**, Style. In the **S**tyle Name box, type **Body**. Click on **D**efine. In Change Formatting, choose **C**haracter, change the point size to 12. Select OK.

6. Still in St**y**le dialog box, choose **P**aragraph. In Al**i**gnment, choose Justified. In Indentation, **F**irst Line, type **.25"**. Select OK and Apply.

7. Place the cursor in the top left-hand corner of column 1 (you may want to turn on non-printing characters from the Ribbon so you can see your column guides). On the Ribbon, in the Style box, choose Body.

8. Type **2xEnter**. Move the cursor up one line to the top paragraph return.

9. Go to Forma**t**, **P**aragraph. In B**o**rders, choose Above. In Pa**t**tern, choose Thick and select OK. With the cursor still in position, press Ctrl+Insert to copy the rule.

9. Go to Forma**t**, Bo**r**der. In the Bo**r**der box, click the top margin or use the down arrow to select. In **L**ine, choose the 2.25 rule and select OK. With the cursor still in position, press Ctrl+Insert to copy the rule.

10. With the down arrow, move the cursor down one line, check to make sure that the Style still is Body, and type the following text:

    ABOUT MARIE(Alt+0146)**S** (Enter)

    CRAFT SHOP (Enter, Enter)

    (Type the back cover paragraphs as shown in fig. 17.3, or type your own data, pressing Enter after each paragraph.)

11. Format this column before continuing. Select ABOUT MARIE'S CRAFT SHOP. On the Ribbon, change the type to 18-point, bold, and right-aligned.

12. Select all the type in the first column. Go to **U**tilities, **H**yphenate. Turn off **C**onfirm and select OK.

419

PART IV

Creating Sales Documents

12. Select all of the type in the first column. Go to **T**ools, **Hy**phenation. Turn off **C**onfirm and select OK.

13. Go to the last paragraph return in the column. Go to **I**nsert, **B**reak, choose **C**olumn Break. Select OK.

14. Type **2xEnter**. Position the cursor on the first paragraph return in the column. Press Shift+Insert. This action pastes the rule at the top of the column. With the down arrow, move the cursor down one line and type the following text:

    COMMON RECIPES (Enter)

    FOR CLAY BODIES (Enter, Enter)

    (Type the paragraph as shown in fig. 17.3, or type your own data, pressing Enter, Enter after the paragraph.)

15. Select the first two lines of type, `COMMON RECIPES....` Change the type to 18-point, bold, and right-aligned.

16. Select and hyphenate the next paragraph. You need to position an optional hyphen in Stoneware because this word isn't in Word's hyphenation dictionary. Position the cursor between `Stone` and `ware`. Press Ctrl+hyphen.

    You can easily check for loose lines in any text and position these *optional* (often referred to as discretionary) hyphens. When using justified text, you must hyphenate, either with Word's help or on your own. If, in one line, you place an optional hyphen that isn't used, too much type might exist to fit on this line; try placing another optional hyphen elsewhere in the word. Always use Ctrl+hyphen instead of just a hyphen because if you edit type, the hyphen might move and therefore appear in the middle of a line.

17. Place the cursor on the last paragraph return. Go to Forma**t**, **P**aragraph. Remove the first line indent by changing the indent to **0** and selecting OK.

18. Go to **I**nsert, **T**able. In Number of **C**olumns, type **2**. In number of **R**ows, type **8**. Click on **F**ormat.

19. Click on **N**ext Column. In **W**idth of Column 1, type **2"**. Click Next Column, type **1.15"**.

20. Still in the dialog box, in Minimum Row Height, type **1.5li** and select OK.

CHAPTER 17

Producing a Brochure

18. Go to Table, Insert Table. In Number of Columns, type **2**. In number of Rows, type **8**.

19. Select the first column. Go to Table, Column Width. In Width of Column 1, type **2"**. Click Next Column, type **1.15"** and select OK.

20. Select the entire table. Go to Table, Row Height. In Minimum Row Height, type **1.5li** and select OK.

21. Position the cursor in the first cell, first row. If the grid lines don't show, turn them on.

    Go to View, Preferences. Click on Table Gridlines. Select OK.

    Go to Table, click Gridlines.

22. With the cursor in place, go to the Ribbon and click on left align. Type the following, pressing Tab and Shift+Enter where indicated:

    EARTHENWARE BODIES (Tab) **FORMULAS**

23. Select this line of type. On the Ribbon, change the type to 8-point, left-aligned. Position the cursor at the end of FORMULAS. Type the following text listing:

    (Tab) **Fires to a reddish color, matures between cones 08 and 1.** (Tab)

    60 red clay (Shift+Enter)

    22 red fire clay (Shift+Enter)

    8 ball clay (Shift+Enter)

    10 grog (Tab)

    Fires white, matures between cones 08 and 1. (Tab)

    50 fire clay (Shift+Enter)

    25 ball clay (Shift+Enter)

    7 flint (Shift+Enter)

    9 soda feldspar (Shift+Enter)

    8 talc (Tab)

    STONEWARE BODY (Tab) **FORMULAS** (Tab)

    Fires brown (when oxidized) matures between cones 6 and 9. (Tab)

PART IV

Creating Sales Documents

>   **42 fire clay** (Shift+Enter)
>
>   **26 stoneware clay** (Shift+Enter)
>
>   **25 red clay** (Shift+Enter)
>
>   **7 soda feldspar** (Tab)
>
>   **Fires orange-brown (reduction) matures at cone 9.** (Tab)
>
>   **30 stoneware clay** (Shift+Enter)
>
>   **40 fire clay** (Shift+Enter)
>
>   **8 red clay** (Shift+Enter)
>
>   **12 flint** (Shift+Enter)
>
>   **10 grog** (Tab)
>   **PORCELAIN BODY** (Tab) **FORMULAS** (Tab)
>
>   **Fires white (oxidized) or blue (reduced) matures at cone 10.** (Tab)
>
>   **50 kaolin** (Shift+Enter)
>
>   **24 potash feldspar** (Shift+Enter)
>
>   **24 flint** (Shift+Enter)
>
>   **2 bentonite**

24. Select EARTHENWARE BODIES (Tab) FORMULAS and change to bold. Repeat with STONEWARE... and PORCELAIN....

25. Select all the type in the table. Go to Format, Paragraph. In Spacing, Before, type **3pt** and select OK.

26. Still selected, go to Format, Table. In Borders, for Outline, choose Single. For Inside, choose Single. For Left and Right choose None. Select OK. Select column 2. Go to Format, Table. In Borders, Left, choose None. Select OK.

26. Still selected, go to Format, Border. In the Border box, click the top margin. Hold the Shift key, click the middle (horizontal) guideline, and click the bottom margin. In Line, choose the .75 rule and select OK.

27. Select the last line of the second column, 10 grog. Go to Format, Paragraph. In Spacing, type **2pt** and select OK. Repeat with each bottom line throughout the table, 8 talc, 7 soda feldspar, 10 grog, and 2 bentonite.

CHAPTER 17

Producing a Brochure

28. Position the cursor on the last paragraph return in the column. Go to **Insert**, **Break**, choose **Column Break**. Select OK.

29. At the top of the third column, type **Enter**. Move the cursor up to the first paragraph return. To paste the rule, press Shift+Insert. With the down arrow, move the cursor to the last return.

30. Type the following text:

    (Enter)

    MARIE(Alt+0146)**S** (Enter)

    CRAFT SHOP (Enter)

    ART GALLERY (Enter)

    SCULPTURE GARDEN (Enter, Enter)

    OPEN DAILY (Enter)

    10:00 A.M. TO 5:00 P.M. (Enter, Enter)

    3041 ELKS CIRCLE (Enter)

    HUNTINGTON, WV (Enter)

    (304) 211-5505

31. Select all the type in this column. On the Ribbon, change the alignment to right.

32. If you have a graphic, insert (and right-align) the picture above `MARIE'S`.

33. Select `MARIE'S`. Change the type to 40-point and bold.

34. Select the next three lines, from `CRAFT SHOP` to and including `...GARDEN`. Change the type to 18-point and bold.

35. Press enough enters to bring the line of type `OPEN DAILY` to 5.85" in the Status Bar.

36. Select the two address lines and phone number. Change the type to 14-point and bold.

37. Position cursor on the last return. Go to **Insert**, **Break**. Column Break. Select OK.

38. At the top of the second page, first column, repeat step 29.

39. Type the following text:

423

PART IV

Creating Sales Documents

(Make the lead-in word 18-point, all caps, bold, flush right, then type in the remainder of the data as shown in figure 17.4, remembering to press Enter, Enter at the end of each block of data. Or type in your own data.)

POTTERY

JEWELRY

LEATHERWORK

DECOUPAGE

40. Select the first column of type. Go to **U**tilities, **H**yphenate.

40. Select the first column of type. Go to **T**ools, **H**yphenation.

    You can create a style for heads by choosing Forma**t**, **S**tyle(s) and then defining the heads. Then click within the type and make all changes in the Style box on the Ribbon.

41. Place the cursor on the last paragraph return in the column. Go to **I**nsert, **B**reak, Column Break. Select OK.

42. At the top of the second column, type **2xEnter**. Position the cursor on the first paragraph return. Press Shift+Insert to paste the rule. Move the cursor down one line and type the following text (18-point, all caps, bold, flush right):

CANDLES

BASKETS

WEAVING

BATIK

43. Select the second column of type. Go to **U**tilities, **H**yphenate.

43. Select the second column of type. Go to **T**ools, **H**yphenation.

44. Select CANDLES. Change the type to 18-point, bold, right-aligned. Repeat with BASKETS, WEAVING, and BATIK.

45. Position the cursor on the last paragraph return in the column. Go to Insert, **B**reak, Column Break. Select OK.

46. At the top of the third column, type **2xEnter**. Place the cursor on the first paragraph return. Press Shift+Insert to paste the rule. Move the cursor down one line and type the following text (18-point, all caps, bold, flush right):

CHAPTER 17

Producing a Brochure

STAINED GLASS

QUILTS

MOSAICS

LAPIDARY

47. Select the third column of type. Go to **U**tilities, **H**yphenate. You may have to insert optional hyphens in `Windmill` and `Malachite`; you can perform this change by positioning the cursor and pressing Ctrl+hyphen.

47. Select the third column of type. Go to **T**ools, **H**yphenation. You may have to insert optional hyphens in `Windmill` and `Malachite`; you can perform this change by positioning the cursor and pressing Ctrl+hyphen.

48. Select `STAINED GLASS`. Change the type to 18-point, bold, and right-aligned. Repeat with `QUILTS`, `MOSAICS`, and `LAPIDARY`.

49. Go to **F**ile, Save **A**s. Type **broc2** and select OK.

50. Go to **F**ile, **P**rint.

Producing an Innovative Brochure

Brochures can be any size or shape. The following design employs an 8 1/2-inch x 14-inch page size with an unusual fold. If your printer doesn't allow you to print 8 1/2-inch x 14-inch, try a similar layout with 8 1/2 inches x 11 inches.

This brochure is *portrait oriented*. Rather than columns, a stair-stepped fold leads you to an information sheet on the inside. Run the brochure through the printer head-to-toe, as opposed to head-to-head, for the final product. Head-to-toe is a printer's term that means the head, or top, of the first side lines up with the toe, or bottom, of the second side.

The instructions also direct you to position type by using the inch measurements on the Status Bar. The second section of the Bar, `At...` shows the position of the cursor in inches, relative to the page. By paying close attention to these measurements, the type on the brochure falls between the folds for proper placement.

425

PART IV

Creating Sales Documents

Figure 17.5 illustrates the final folded front of the brochure. Humble Opinions is in very large type. The *steps* announce classes available and the phone numbers of the company. At first glance, the customer recognizes that this brochure is about software training in word processing, desktop publishing, and so on.

HUMBLE OPINIONS COMPUTER TRAINING

WORD PROCESSING		DESKTOP PUBLISHING
SPREADSHEET		DATABASE
(304) 251-5151	CALL TODAY	800-250-2369

FIG. 17.5. *The innovative brochure; the folded size is 8 1/2 inches x 4 5/8 inches.*

After opening the first fold of the brochure, the customer reads information about the company. This section contains a brief explanation of the equipment, instructors, classes, and method of training. Figure 17.6 shows the first stepped fold of the brochure. The phone numbers in the last *step* remind the customer to call today.

Figure 17.7 illustrates the unfolded first page of the brochure. At the top, you see a mailing panel with the return address and a place for mailing labels, followed by the front panel and the brief history of the company.

The inside of the brochure opens to a description of introductory, intermediate, and advanced classes (see fig. 17.8). Although not laid out in columns, the text is easy to read and follow. At the top of the brochure's inside, you see the name, address, and phone

CHAPTER 17

Producing a Brochure

numbers of the company. At the bottom of the brochure, you see the same *step* of phone numbers.

ABOUT HUMBLE OPINIONS

Humble Opinions offers training in more than 30 popular software programs; please call for a list of brand names. Introductory, Intermediate, and Advanced classes are scheduled weekly. No matter what level you are, we have a class to suit your needs. In business for more than 10 years, and serving the business community in the tri-state area, Humble Opinions is here to serve you!

Each class instructor is a professional. Two months of intensive training at our headquarters in West Virginia gives these instructors knowledge and experience with their particular software program. Each instructor trains in only two programs, and is therefore an expert in the software. With no more than five students per class, every student receives quality training. We feel it's important for the student to spend time with the instructors in a hands-on situation.

Classes are taught in our spacious classroom containing 15 personal computers and 12 printers. The personal computers are of various capacities and memories. The printers represented include dot matrix, inkjet and laser, so you work with a printer you are used to. Classes are scheduled to fit your individual needs. You can spend eight hours in one day, or break it up into smaller increments, as long as your return visit schedules with the same class.

SPREADSHEET   **DATABASE**

(304) 251-5151   **CALL TODAY**   **800-250-2369**

FIG. 17.6. The first section of the brochure when opened by the customer.

Figure 17.9 illustrates the flip side of the final, folded brochure. The mailing panel contains the return address and a place for labels and postage information. When mailing this kind of brochure, you should seal the steps. You can staple or add a small adhesive dot on each step.

HUMBLE OPINIONS
COMPUTER TRAINING
1127 E. Main Street
Beckley, WV 25801

HUMBLE OPINIONS COMPUTER TRAINING

WORD PROCESSING   **DESKTOP PUBLISHING**

ABOUT HUMBLE OPINIONS

Humble Opinions offers training in more than 30 popular software programs; please call for a list of brand names. Introductory, Intermediate, and Advanced classes are scheduled weekly. No matter what level you are, we have a class to suit your needs. In business for more than 10 years, and serving the business community in the tri-state area, Humble Opinions is here to serve you!

Each class instructor is a professional. Two months of intensive training at our headquarters in West Virginia gives these instructors knowledge and experience with their particular software program. Each instructor trains in only two programs, and is therefore an expert in the software. With no more than five students per class, every student receives quality training. We feel it's important for the student to spend time with the instructors in a hands-on situation.

Classes are taught in our spacious classroom containing 15 personal computers and 12 printers. The personal computers are of various capacities and memories. The printers represented include dot matrix, inkjet and laser, so you work with a printer you are used to. Classes are scheduled to fit your individual needs. You can spend eight hours in one day, or break it up into smaller increments, as long as your return visit schedules with the same class.

SPREADSHEET   **DATABASE**

FIG. 17.7. *The front page of the brochure, with mailing panel, front panel and first inside panel.*

HUMBLE OPINIONS COMPUTER TRAINING

1127 E. Main Street Beckley, WV 25801
(304) 251-5151 800-250-2369

Your Computer Training Specialists

INTRODUCTORY

BASIC COMPUTERS
If you're not familiar with computers but would like to know more, then this class is for you. Learn about operating systems such as DOS, and Windows. Discover the connections between directories, sub-directories, and files. Explore various printers and popular software programs.

WORD PROCESSING
We teach classes in more than 30 popular word processing programs. Learn basic editing, function keys, and margin and tab settings. Learn to use retrieve, and save and print. Use block operations.

DATABASE
Organize your mailing list, customer files, invoices, and any data you deal with daily. Learn basic concepts, create and edit a form, add and edit data, create reports, and add or delete records.

SPREADSHEETS
Regulate your accounting system with a spreadsheet program. Learn to create, save, retrieve, and print. Use formulas, copy rows and columns, format ranges, and use absolute cell addresses.

DESKTOP PUBLISHING
Produce professional-looking documents. Learn basic page formatting such as changing typeface, size and style, columns and margins, tabs and tables, frames, and graphics.

INTERMEDIATE

WORD PROCESSING
Learn about macros, tables, formatting columns, and mail merge. Print envelopes and odd page sizes. Learn the finer points of page make-up on your word processor.

SPREADSHEETS
Become more efficient with spreadsheets by freezing titles, and using named ranges and windows. Perform logical evaluation, use cell protection, and control recalculation.

DESKTOP PUBLISHING
Learn to use desktop publishing to produce fliers, resumes, forms, newsletters and long documents such as catalogs, books, and business reports. Bring your own word processing to format the documents you need for your business.

ADVANCED CLASSES

Advanced classes offered in any of the preceeding categories. Prerequisites are the Introductory and Intermediate classes. Advanced training covers tips and tricks of the programs, ways to improve speed and output, compatibility with other programs, and so on.

Advanced classes presented in Word Processing, Databases, Spreadsheets, and Desktop Publishing. For a complete list of software packages, call or stop by today!

FIG. 17.8. *The inside of the brochure with full class descriptions, address, and phone numbers of the company.*

PART IV

Creating Sales Documents

FIG. 17.9.
The mailing panel of the brochure.

> **HUMBLE OPINIONS
> COMPUTER TRAINING**
> 1127 E. Main Street
> Beckley, WV 25801

To create this innovative brochure, take the following steps:

1. Go to **F**ile, **N**ew. Choose New **D**ocument, **U**se Template Normal. Select OK.

2. Go to **F**ile, **P**rinter Setup, click **S**etup. In Paper Size, choose Legal 8-1/2 x 14 in. In Orientation, choose **P**ortrait. Select OK two times.

3. Go to Forma**t**, **D**ocument. In Margins, set the **T**op to .7", the **B**ottom to .3", and the **L**eft and **R**ight to .9". Select OK.

2. Go to Forma**t**, Page Set**u**p. In **S**ize and Orientation, change Paper Size to Legal (8-1/2 x 14 in); be sure it is **P**ortrait Orientation.

3. Still in the dialog box, choose **M**argins, set the **T**op to .7", the **B**ottom to .3", and the **L**eft and **R**ight to .9". Select OK.

4. Type the following text:

   HUMBLE OPINIONS (Enter)

   COMPUTER TRAINING (Enter)

   1127 E. Main Street (Enter)

   Beckley, WV 25801 (Enter)

5. Select the first two lines of type, HUMBLE OPINIONS COMPUTER TRAINING. On the Ribbon, change the type to 14-point and bold. The address lines remain 10 point and light-face.

6. Using the measurement on the Status Bar, type enough paragraph returns to position the cursor at 4.8" on the page. Type:

   HUMBLE OPINIONS (Enter)

   COMPUTER TRAINING (Enter)

7. Select these two lines of type. On the Ribbon, change to 44-point (or as close to this size as the printer allows), bold, and center aligned.

CHAPTER 17

Producing a Brochure

8. Still selected, go to Forma**t**, **C**haracter. In Character Spacing choose **C**ondensed. In the box, **By:** type **1.75pt** and select OK.

8. Still selected, go to Forma**t**, **C**haracter. In Spacin**g** choose Condensed. In the box, **By:** type **1.75pt** and select OK.

9. While watching the Status Bar, type enough paragraph returns to place the cursor on the page at 7.1". Type the following line:

   WORD PROCESSING (Tab) **DESKTOP PUBLISHING** (Enter)

10. Select and change this line of type to Helv, 18-point, bold. On the Ruler, set a right tab at 6.63".

11. Position the cursor at 8" (on the Status Bar). Type the following text:

    ABOUT HUMBLE OPINIONS (Enter, Enter)

    (Type the paragraphs as shown in the figure, or type your own data, pressing Enter, Enter after each paragraph except the last.)

12. Select the first line, `ABOUT HUMBLE OPINIONS`. Change the type to Helv, 18-point, bold, and center-aligned.

13. Select the next three paragraphs of type, from `Humble Opinions offers training...` to `...as long as your return visit schedules with the same class.` Change this type to 12-point. The text remains TmsRmn and left aligned.

14. With type still selected, go to Forma**t**, **P**aragraph. In the Indents box, From Le**f**t, type **.4"**, From **R**ight type **.4"**. In the Spacing box, **L**ine, type **15pt** and select OK.

14. With type still selected, go to Forma**t**, **P**aragraph. In the Indentation box, From **L**eft type **.4"**. From **R**ight type **.4"**. In Line Spacing, choose At Least. In the **At:** box, type **15pt** and select OK.

15. Place the cursor at 13.3" on the Status Bar and then type the following text:

    SPREADSHEET (Tab) **DATABASE** (Enter, Enter)

    You type the paragraph returns after typing this line to make sure that the next page is formatted with the same line spacing and indents as the body type on the current page.

431

PART IV

Creating Sales Documents

16. Select SPREADSHEET (Tab) DATABASE. Change the type to Helv, 18-point, and bold. On the Ruler, set the tab to right aligned at 6.63".

17. At the top of page two, type the following text:

    HUMBLE OPINIONS COMPUTER TRAINING (Enter)

    1127 E. Main Street (Tab) **Beckley, WV 25801** (Enter)

    (304) 251-5151 (Tab) **800-250-2369** (Enter)

    Your Computer Training Specialists (Enter, Enter)

    INTRODUCTORY (Enter, Enter)

    BASIC COMPUTERS (Enter)

    (Type the paragraphs as shown in the figure, or type your own data, pressing Enter, Enter after each paragraph except the last.)

    WORD PROCESSING (Enter)

    DATABASE (Enter)

    SPREADSHEETS (Enter)

    DESKTOP PUBLISHING (Enter)

    INTERMEDIATE (Enter, Enter)

    WORD PROCESSING (Enter)

    SPREADSHEETS (Enter)

    DESKTOP PUBLISHING (Enter)

    ADVANCED CLASSES (Enter, Enter)

    (304)251-5151 (Tab) **CALL TODAY** (Tab) **800-250-2369**

18. Select HUMBLE.... On the Ribbon, change the type to 24-point, bold, and center-aligned.

19. Still selected, go to Forma**t**, **P**aragraph. In Spacing, **A**fter, type **.5li** and select OK.

20. Still selected, go to Forma**t**, **C**haracter. In Spacing, choose **C**ondensed. In **B**y:, type **.75pt**. Select OK.

19. Still selected, go to Forma**t**, **P**aragraph. In Spacing, Af**t**er, type **.5li** and select OK.

432

CHAPTER 17

Producing a Brochure

20. Still selected, go to Forma**t**, **C**haracter. In Spacin**g**, choose Condensed. In B**y**:, type **.75pt**. Select OK.

21. Select the address and phone number. Change the type to 12 points. On the Ruler, set a right tab at 6.63".

22. Select `Your Computer....` Change the type to 14-point, italic, and center-aligned.

23. Select `INTRODUCTORY`. Change the type to Helv, 18-point, bold. The word should remain left aligned. Still selected, go to Forma**t**, **P**aragraph. In Indents, From Le**f**t. Change to **0** and select OK. Repeat this step with `INTERMEDIATE` and `ADVANCED CLASSES`.

23. Select `INTRODUCTORY`. Change the type to Helv, 18-point, and bold. The word should remain left aligned. Still selected, go to Forma**t**, **P**aragraph. In Indentation, From **L**eft. Change to **0** and select OK. Repeat this step with `INTERMEDIATE` and `ADVANCED CLASSES`.

24. Select each class title, `BASIC COMPUTERS`, `WORD PROCESSING`, and so on and select bold.

25. Select the last line of type, the phone numbers. Check the Status Bar to see if the line is positioned at about 13.3". Change the type to Helv, 18-point, bold. On the Ruler, set the first tab as centered at 3.38"; set the second tab as right at 6.63".

26. Go to **F**ile, Save **A**s. Type **broc3** and select OK.

27. Before printing, set the printer to legal size and manual feed if you don't have an 8 1/2-inch x 14-inch paper tray. Go to **F**ile, **P**rint. In Pages, choose From. Type **1**. In the **T**o box, type **1** and select OK.

> **NOTE**
>
> Depending on the printer and setup, Word may give you a message that concerns page size or margin sizes. If so, respond with **Y**es, to continue printing. Check the copy to ensure that all type prints and that the result looks similar to the figures in this chapter. If not, adjust the margins and reprint.

433

PART IV

Creating Sales Documents

27. Go to **File**, **Print** Setup. Click **Setup**. In Paper Size, choose Legal 8 1/2 x 14 in. Select OK and OK again. Before printing, set your printer to legal size, and manual feed if you don't have an 8 1/2 x 14-inch paper tray. Go to **File**, **Print**. In Range, choose **Pages**. In **From** type **1**. In **To**, type **1** and select OK.

> **NOTE**
>
> Depending on the printer and setup, Word may give you a message concerning page size or margin sizes. If so, respond with **Yes**, to continue printing. Check the copy to ensure that all type prints and that the result looks similar to the figures in this chapter. If not, adjust the margins and reprint.

28. Turn over and insert the printed sheet back in the printer, toe first. Go to **File**, **Print**, OK.

    Remember that you're supposed to change the printer and print(er) setup back to 8 1/2 inches x 11 inches after you finish this project.

29. To fold the brochure, with the inside page facing you (the descriptions of individual classes), bring the top toward you. Position the bottom edge of the page to align just above the phone numbers. The result should look like figure 17.6.

30. For the second fold, bring the top toward you and position it as shown in figure 17.5.

31. If you turn the final, folded piece over, your mailing address should show in the upper left corner.

Looking at Design

A brochure also can measure 8 1/2 inches x 11 inches in finished size. This kind of brochure inserts easily in a binder or folder for storage. Figure 17.10 shows the front cover of a brochure design that measures 8 1/2 inches x 11 inches. The thick border rules in combination with the large company name attract attention. Also listed on the brochure cover are the types of music described inside, the address, and phone number.

CHAPTER 17

Producing a Brochure

The rest of the brochure describes each kind of music, as shown by figure 17.11. The second page lists the company name, address, and phone number, as do the remaining pages of the brochure (not shown here). Each following page contains two boxes of type that describe the different kinds of music stocked by Gan Anin.

All type is Helv, 12-point. The graphic boxes help contain the left-aligned type and make an interesting layout to the page because each box varies slightly in height. The wide margins, both within and outside the graphic boxes, make the page easy and enjoyable to read.

Recapping

In this chapter, you learned that brochures are among the most effective forms of advertising in the marketplace today. You also learned that a well-designed brochure invites customers to read at their leisure, and to refer back through the material often. Finally, you learned how to create your own brochures.

In the next chapter, you learn how to produce a basic newsletter.

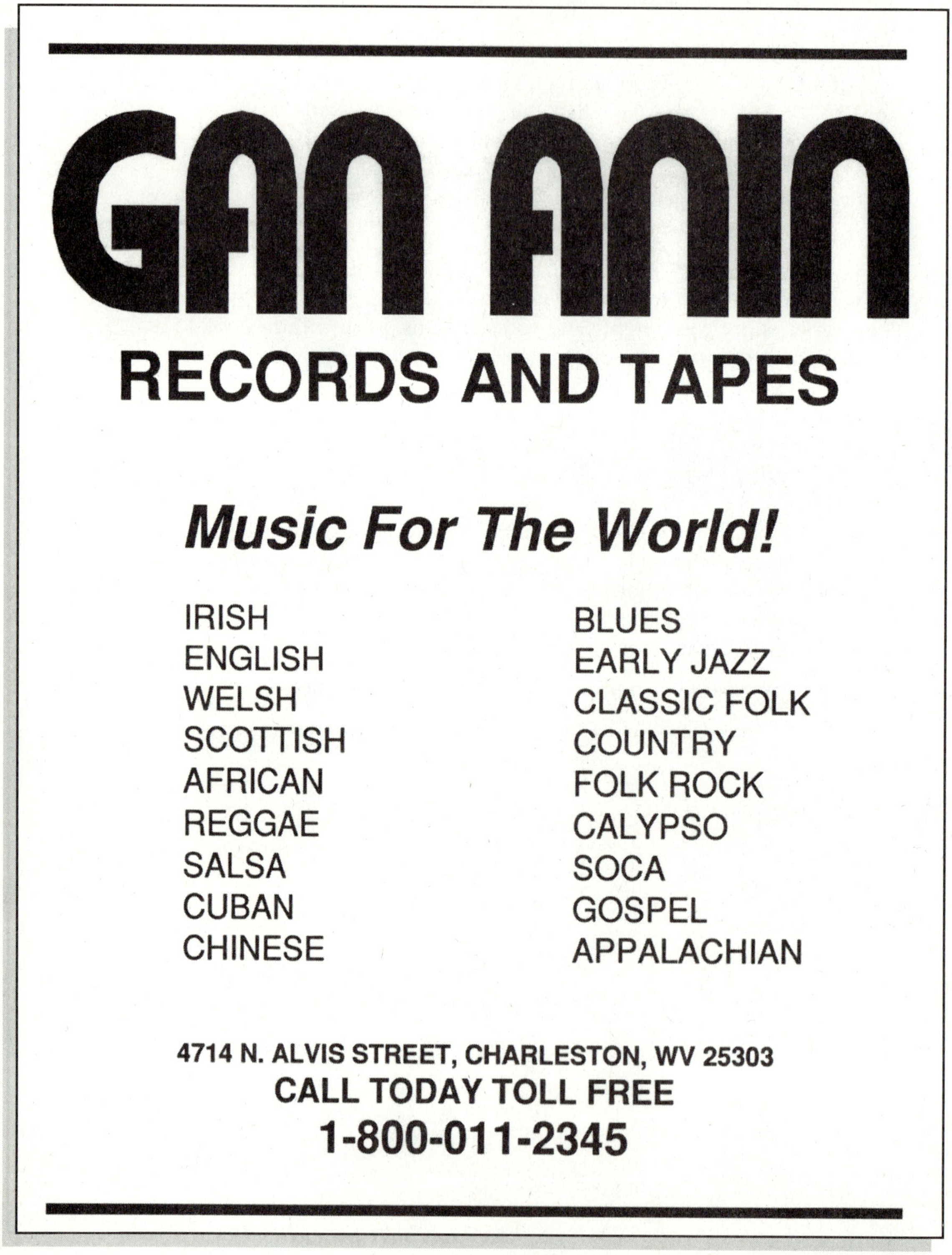

GAN ANIN

RECORDS AND TAPES

Music For The World!

IRISH	BLUES
ENGLISH	EARLY JAZZ
WELSH	CLASSIC FOLK
SCOTTISH	COUNTRY
AFRICAN	FOLK ROCK
REGGAE	CALYPSO
SALSA	SOCA
CUBAN	GOSPEL
CHINESE	APPALACHIAN

4714 N. ALVIS STREET, CHARLESTON, WV 25303
CALL TODAY TOLL FREE
1-800-011-2345

FIG. 17.10. *The cover of a different brochure layout.*

GAN ANIN RECORDS AND TAPES

4714 N. ALVIS STREET, CHARLESTON, WEST VIRGINIA 25303

CELTIC MUSIC

Offering the world's largest selection of Celtic music, GAN ANIN stocks more than 8,000 titles. Our largest inventory is Irish music, both from the Republic of Ireland and Northern Ireland. Fiddle, banjo, bouzouki, tin whistle, accordion (button and piano), mandolin, and bodhran instrumentals, both in compilations and individual artists.

Including the dance music and songs of Ireland, our collection of Irish music totals 3,000 titles. The biggest names in Irish music today, and in years past, stocked in our warehouses.

In addition, Scottish, Welsh, and English song and instrumental music round out our collection for your enjoyment. Send the reply card today for a free catalog.

WHOLE EARTH MUSIC

We stock a selection of 1,000 titles of world music including Greek, African, Chinese, and Mexican. Our African alternatives include African Pop, Funk, Pop Fusion, Zairean, and Ethiopian Pop. Our newest Chinese selections are blends of traditional and classical styles. Flute, keyboard, and percussion combine for expert arrangements and dynamic motion.

New to this publication are Cuban, Salsa, Reggae, Pakistani, Columbian, and Soca titles. Our new catalog describes them all. We also offer each selection on cassettes and CDs. Call or send the postage-paid reply card for our catalog today!

CALL TODAY TOLL FREE
1-800-011-2345

FIG. 17.11. *Page two of the brochure.*

TAITHNEAMH

MAY 1992

COUNTY KERRY

KILLARNEY

Welcome to the fourth issue of Taithneamh. This month we visit County Kerry in the West of Ireland. If you plan a trip to Ireland soon, you will not want to miss this lovely area. In the heart of Kerry is Killarney town. With its hustle and bustle of merchants, business and tourist centers, Killarney is a town you will never forget.

Through the center of town is Main Street, the business and market center. Connecting to Main are High and New Streets, two very popular day and night tourist spots. High Street is lined with rows of lights overhead; souvenir shops and cafes line the sides of the narrow, always populated street. The pubs on High are well known for the dance music in the late evenings. The fiddle, banjo and whistle ring out in merriment and revelry.

An offshoot of High Street is New. New Street has many guesthouses and it is home for the Post Office of Killarney. The guest houses welcome visitors with open doors, the smell of tea and scones, and of course, a nice, warm peat fire! What more could you want on a cold and rainy day. And the gardens, the wonderful, colorful gardens! New Street is the pride of the women's club in town, and so it should be! They plant every spring with new bulbs and seeds, making the street a virtual festival of dyestuff.

LEARNING IRISH

Taithneamh	Enjoyment, pleasure
Le fada an la	For many a day
Bail o Dhia ort	God bless you
A lainm	Beautiful, lovely

RING OF KERRY

During the day, if you base yourself in Killarney, there are a myriad of sights and attractions in the area. The Slieve Miskish Mountains, Ring of Kerry, and the Dingle Peninsula are jaunts that take no more than a day. Scenic beauty of the lakes, the heather and good roads make County Kerry a wonderful place to visit. The Ring of Kerry is a trip you must not miss!

Stretching 110 miles, the Ring of Kerry offers excitement at every turn. It is a mountainous road circling the Slieve Mish Mountains, through the Dingle Peninsula, and running parallel to the ocean during most of its length. Beginning in Killarney, the first leg of the Ring tenders a distant view of Macgillycuddy's Reeks, a glorious mountain range in the southwest of Ireland. Travelling further, you come to Killorglin, the scene of the famous Puck Fair. If, by chance, you visit in mid-August, do not miss the Puck Fair. Music, song, feasting and brotherhood envelop the city for three lively, fun-filled days.

As you travel further on the Ring, you come across Caragh Lake, one of Kerry's finest fishing spots. You may wish to take a boat trip to the Blasket Islands, or Skellig Rock. Skellig Michael is a massive rock, jutting 700 feet high out of the Atlantic; what a sight to behold! Or perhaps you will take a side trip to Puffin Island, Kerry's own bird sanctuary where over 10,000 puffins gather each year for breeding.

Whether you travel south or west on the Ring, to the Islands or the Burrin, you will never forget the beauty and solitude of the landscape, and the love of life from the people. It is a memory to cherish your whole life through.

Part V

Creating Newsletters

Includes

18. Producing a Basic Newsletter
19. Producing a Complex Newsletter

Producing a Basic Newsletter

18

A *newsletter informs, announces, reminds, advises, instructs, advertises, educates, entertains, and communicates. Newsletters can address management, employees, customers, or prospective customers. Because newsletters are so flexible, you can design them to fit any purpose.*

If you want better relations between management and laborers, for example, you can produce a newsletter that each issue details a different job in your plant. You also can focus on one employee each month, alternating between workers and managers.

Another purpose for a newsletter may be to advertise products and services to the customer. An article that shows how the new equipment you just bought speeds up service and guarantees quality and an article about a specific product and the product's applications are only two possibilities.

Newsletters must contain information that the audience can apply. Target the material to a specific group of people by including articles slanted toward the group. Selling your purpose, product, or service is a basic goal. You can add human interest stories that pertain to the audience and the subject. This focus keeps the reader's interest high. You don't have to use long stories; actually, short articles work better in newsletters.

Determining the Size

Newsletters come in almost any size and shape. The common size is 8 1/2 inches x 11 inches. Whether folded from 11 inches x 17 inches to form four-page newsletters, or from 11 inches x 25 1/2

PART V

Creating Newsletters

inches to form six-page ones, most newsletters are portrait oriented. The finished size also can go as small as 5 1/2 inches x 8 1/2 inches for mailing. Of course, you can experiment and change the size and shape of the newsletter, but keep in mind the kinds of paper and the run sizes available at a print or copy shop.

Working with Paper Stocks

Make sure that the paper you choose for a newsletter is heavy enough to prevent type and graphics from showing through. Paper of 60# or 70# are good choices. Smooth, vellum, enamel, and linen finishes all are appropriate, and each finish creates a different look and feel to the piece. Consider also method of distribution and the paper's effect on the reader. Newsletters that you mail should not be too heavy.

Learning the Basics

Many components of a newsletter are discussed in this and in the following chapter. Nameplate, dateline, mailing information, masthead, table of contents, header/footer and page numbers all are elements you might want to include. Points of emphasis—such as bullets, jumplines, call outs, art work, graphic rules, boxes, and screens—also are prospects. Depending on the size, design, and audience of the newsletter, you may add any or all of these elements.

This chapter concentrates on a basic newsletter, which uses attractive and professional, yet easy to create, designs. Some elements covered in the following instructions are nameplates, datelines, headers, two and three columns, graphic rules, and boxes.

Developing Consistency

Consistency between issues is a significant factor to consider in newsletter design. After you choose a writing style, stick with it, and adhere to the original design elements in each issue. If you start with three columns, Times Roman body text, Helvetica heads, rules between columns, and 3/4-inch margins, then make each issue of the newsletter correspond to these choices.

CHAPTER 18

Producing a Basic Newsletter

You can accomplish this consistency by using glossaries, style sheets, and templates. Word enables you to set up a basic template, with an attached style sheet for all documents. The instructions in this chapter cover new documents because the documents include stories and articles. If you like a design, however, after you complete the instructions, delete the stories and save the document as a template for later use. Each issue that you base on this template is consistent with the preceding issue.

A glossary is another way to ensure consistency, not only between issues of a newsletter but also between company pieces. The glossary you created in Chapter 5 can be inserted as a masthead in this newsletter. The first set of instructions include creating a glossary, which you're going to insert into a newsletter design.

Remember that, to save time and energy, you type the text only once, which you then copy each time you begin a new design. You spend more time designing the newsletter than you spend typing the text.

Creating a Nameplate

A nameplate is an identifier for the newsletter. Located on the front page and beginning at the top, the nameplate distinguishes your newsletter from all other newsletters. A nameplate consists of the name of the newsletter, the company's name, a catchy phrase, and an abbreviation, usually in a distinct typeface or type style. The type can be stretched, display, on an arc, slanted, vertical, or horizontal. You also can add a logo or art work, which adds to the newsletter's uniqueness. The nameplate can be in a box, bordered with rules, or screened. You also can use three or more colors. The possibilities are endless.

Word Version 1.1 limits you somewhat with nameplate possibilities. You can expand, condense, strikethru, subscript, and superscript type. You also can box and border the type. Figure 18.1 illustrates three ideas for nameplate designs, created in Version 1.1 by using type with no art or logo. You can import a TIFF graphic file to add to the type design.

Word Version 2.0 permits more options for type and graphic rules, boxes, and screens. Version 2.0 measures type in smaller increments, a point at a time. This feature is conducive to making

PART V

Creating Newsletters

the type fit from margin to margin. Version 2.0 also has WordArt, a display type program within Word. WordArt enables you to rotate, stretch, and place type on a curve, along with several other options. Many nameplates shown in this chapter were designed in WordArt, Word Version 2.0.

FIG. 18.1.   *Nameplate designs created in Word Version 1.1.*

Version 2.0 also easily adds various percentages of screens (shading) and several thickness choices for rules. Figure 18.2 shows three type designs from Version 2.0, without logos and without the use of WordArt. Notice that the second design is a different type style, Chancery. If you can choose from many typefaces, use a typeface completely different from the body text and heads for the nameplate.

444

CHAPTER 18

Producing a Basic Newsletter

FIG. 18.2. *Version 2.0 nameplate designs without the use of WordArt.*

In the first exercise of this chapter, you create a glossary for use in the newsletter. A glossary is stored text and or graphics imported to a document and can be used over and over again. A glossary, once created, can be used in subsequent newsletter designs. Two different glossaries are shown here, figure 18.3 illustrates a

PART V

Creating Newsletters

nameplate created in Word Version 1.1, and figure 18.4 exhibits a glossary created with WordArt in Version 2.0. Both nameplates have borders, display type, and a dateline. The directions to create both nameplates are detailed in the following series of steps.

FIG. 18.3. *Nameplate glossary created in Version 1.1 of Word.*

FIG. 18.4. *Nameplate glossary created in Version 2.0 of Word with the help of WordArt.*

The dateline identifies one or many facts about the newsletter. The date—whether month, year, season, or quarter—is almost always included. You also can add a volume number and issue number. The volume number refers to the number of years in publication, and the issue number refers to which edition of the present year. For example, Vol. 4, No. 5 means fourth year, fifth edition this year. Other information, such as subsequent titles, authors, editors, and so on also may go into the dateline.

To create the nameplate similar to those you've seen here, follow these steps:

CHAPTER 18

Producing a Basic Newsletter

1. Go to **F**ile, **N**ew. Choose New **D**ocument and **U**se Template Normal. Select OK or press enter.

2. Go to Forma**t**, **D**ocument. Change all margins to **.5"** and select OK or press enter.

2. Go to Format, Page Set**u**p. In **M**argins, change all to **.5"** and select OK or press enter.

3. Type **2xEnter**. Position the cursor on the first paragraph return.

4. Type the following line:

   (Enter) **TAITHNEAMH** (Enter)

5. Select the first paragraph return, TAITHNEAMH, and one paragraph return after. Go to Forma**t**, **P**aragraph. In **B**order, choose Box. In Patt**e**rn, choose Thick and Select OK or press enter.

6. Select the first T in TAITHNEAMH. On the Ribbon, change the type to Helv, 48-point (or as large as your printer allows), bold, and center-aligned. Repeat with the last H.

7. Select the inner letters, AITHNEAM. On the Ribbon, change the type to 40-point, bold.

4. Go to **I**nsert, **O**bject. Double click on MS WordArt or use the down arrow to select and press Enter. Type **TAITHNEAMH**.

5. Change the **F**ont to Wenatchee; the **S**ize to Best Fit; the **S**tyle to Plain; the F**i**ll should be Black; **A**lign Center. Click **A**pply, then select OK or press enter.

6. Click within the frame to turn on the *handles* of the graphic box. To crop, press the Shift key and drag the top and bottom handles of the box closer to the type (leave about 1/4-inch of space between the text and the box border). Or, select the graphic by positioning the cursor in front of the box. Hold Shift and press the right arrow. Size the graphic by going to Forma**t**, **P**icture. Repeat with the bottom of the frame. Position the cursor on the handle in the right bottom corner of the frame. Stretch the frame to the 7.5" mark on the ruler.

7. Go to Forma**t**, **B**order. In Bo**r**der, click the top margin, hold the Shift key and click the bottom margin or use the down arrow to select each margin. In **L**ine, choose the 3-point rule and select OK or press enter.

447

PART V

Creating Newsletters

8. Position the cursor on the last paragraph return. Type **2xEnter**.

9. Position the cursor on the first paragraph return after the nameplate's bottom border.

10. Go to Forma**t**, **P**aragraph. In **B**orders, choose Below. In Pat**t**ern, choose Single. Select OK or press enter. Move the cursor down two lines with the down arrow key. Go to Forma**t**, **P**aragraph. In B**o**rders, choose Above. In Pa**t**tern, choose Single. Select OK or press enter. Move the cursor up one line with the arrow key.

9. Move the cursor up one line.

10. Go to Forma**t**, **B**order. In Bo**r**der, click in the top margin, hold the Shift key, click in the bottom margin. On the keyboard, press the down arrow to select each margin. In the From Text box, type **4pt**. In **L**ine, choose the .75 rule and select OK or press enter.

11. Type the following line of text:

    MAY 1992 (Tab) **TRAVEL IRELAND** (Tab) **VOL. 1, NO. 4**

12. Select this line of type, go to the Ribbon. Change the type to Helv, 10-point.

    Still selected, go to Forma**t**, **P**aragraph. In the Spacing box, **B**efore, type **3pt**. In After, type **3pt** and select OK or press enter.

13. On the ruler, set the first tab as center aligned at 3.75"; set the second tab as right aligned at 7.5".

    You may have to adjust the right margin marker on the ruler to set the tab; once set, move the right margin marker back to its original position.

14. Select the entire nameplate and dateline. Go to **E**dit, **G**lossary. In the Glossary **N**ame box, type **newsletter**. Click on **D**efine.

15. You also can save this document as a template for later use. To do that, go to **F**ile, Save **A**s. Choose **O**ptions, in File Format choose Document template. Type the name and select OK or press enter.

448

CHAPTER 18

Producing a Basic Newsletter

15. You also can save this document as a template for later use. To do that, go to **F**ile, Save **A**s. In Save File as **T**ype: choose Document Template (*.DOT). Type the name and select OK or press enter.

Producing a Type Solution Newsletter

A basic newsletter may have no rules, screens, or boxes. Depending on the business, the information contained in a newsletter, and on the impression you want to make, you might prefer a text-only solution, similar to the first newsletter design example.

The two-column layout is common, as is the two-page layout. Printed on both front and back, the nameplate repeats in a smaller version on the back. For this reason, no matter which way you turn the newsletter, you see the newsletter's name. The nameplate is simple, yet recognizable.

The typeface used is Times Roman throughout the entire piece. Justified type defines the columns and interparagraph spacing adds white space. Figure 18.5 shows the front of the newsletter.

For consistency, the back page of the newsletter repeats the design of the front (see fig. 18.6). A mailing panel added at the bottom includes the return address and room for mailing labels, handwritten addresses, postage stamps, and so on. The piece can be easily folded twice and slipped into the mail.

As in some of the previous exercises, you type the information for the following newsletter designs only once. After typing, you save an extra copy of the text to use for the next design. Again, you may want to save this document as a template for subsequent use when you finish the layout.

To create the newsletter design shown in figure 18.5, take these steps:

1. Go to **F**ile, **N**ew. New **D**ocument, **U**se Template Normal. Select OK or press enter.

2. Go to Forma**t**, **D**ocument. Set all Margins to **.5**". Select OK or press enter.

449

TAITHNEAMH

MAY 1992

COUNTY KERRY

KILLARNEY

Welcome to the fourth issue of Taithneamh. This month we visit County Kerry in the West of Ireland. If you plan a trip to Ireland soon, you will not want to miss this lovely area. In the heart of Kerry is Killarney town. With its hustle and bustle of merchants, business and tourist centers, Killarney is a town you will never forget.

Through the center of town is Main Street, the business and market center. Connecting to Main are High and New Streets, two very popular day and night tourist spots. High Street is lined with rows of lights overhead; souvenir shops and cafes line the sides of the narrow, always populated street. The pubs on High are well known for the dance music in the late evenings. The fiddle, banjo and whistle ring out in merriment and revelry.

An offshoot of High Street is New. New Street has many guesthouses and it is home for the Post Office of Killarney. The guest houses welcome visitors with open doors, the smell of tea and scones, and of course, a nice, warm peat fire! What more could you want on a cold and rainy day. And the gardens, the wonderful, colorful gardens! New Street is the pride of the women's club in town, and so it should be! They plant every spring with new bulbs and seeds, making the street a virtual festival of dyestuff.

LEARNING IRISH

Taithneamh	Enjoyment, pleasure
Le fada an la	For many a day
Bail o Dhia ort	God bless you
A lainm	Beautiful, lovely

RING OF KERRY

During the day, if you base yourself in Killarney, there are a myriad of sights and attractions in the area. The Slieve Miskish Mountains, Ring of Kerry, and the Dingle Peninsula are jaunts that take no more than a day. Scenic beauty of the lakes, the heather and good roads make County Kerry a wonderful place to visit. The Ring of Kerry is a trip you must not miss!

Stretching 110 miles, the Ring of Kerry offers excitement at every turn. It is a mountainous road circling the Slieve Mish Mountains, through the Dingle Peninsula, and running parallel to the ocean during most of its length. Beginning in Killarney, the first leg of the Ring tenders a distant view of Macgillycuddy's Reeks, a glorious mountain range in the southwest of Ireland. Travelling further, you come to Killorglin, the scene of the famous Puck Fair. If, by chance, you visit in mid-August, do not miss the Puck Fair. Music, song, feasting and brotherhood envelop the city for three lively, fun-filled days.

As you travel further on the Ring, you come across Caragh Lake, one of Kerry's finest fishing spots. You may wish to take a boat trip to the Blasket Islands, or Skellig Rock. Skellig Michael is a massive rock, jutting 700 feet high out of the Atlantic; what a sight to behold! Or perhaps you will take a side trip to Puffin Island, Kerry's own bird sanctuary where over 10,000 puffins gather each year for breeding.

Whether you travel south or west on the Ring, to the Islands or the Burrin, you will never forget the beauty and solitude of the landscape, and the love of life from the people. It is a memory to cherish your whole life through.

FIG. 18.5. *The front page of a text-only newsletter.*

CHAPTER 18

Producing a Basic Newsletter

TAITHNEAMH

MUCKROSS ESTATE

Also located near Killarney, County Kerry, is a tremendous National Park called Muckross Estate. Over 10,000 acres of mountains, lakes and green, green flora preserved by the Republic for your enjoyment. Cars are not allowed on the estate; there are, however, alternatives. You may rent or bring your own bicycle. Or take a jaunting car. Jaunting cars line the entrance to the park (as well as line the streets of Killarney), ready to transport you to this scene of serenity and beauty. The horse-drawn carriages are driven by gents who spin tales and weave stories of old Ireland, Killarney, Muckross and the fairies.

Your first stop on the Estate is Muckross Abbey. A Francisian Abbey built in the 15th century, it is one of the best kept and restored Abbeys in all of Kerry. Your next stop is Muckross House. A monumental 19th century home donated, along with the land, to the people of Ireland by its former owners. The house is filled with intricately hand-carved furniture, home-made crafts, tapestries, and original art works. The basement contains a stable, and fully stocked print shop, pub, blacksmith shop, kitchen and weavers shop; all have presenters working as you tour, answer any and all questions.

THE LAKES

Contained with the National Park are three very famous, and pulchritudinous, lakes. The first you come to by jaunting car is the Lower Lake, also called Lough Leane. The second, or Middle Lake, is also called Muckross Lake. The third is simply the Upper Lake. In addition, don't miss Torc Mountain and its stupendous waterfall. Water from the Devil's Punch Bowl rushes over Torc's 60' waterfall, gushing and glorious, it is a sight you will not want to miss.

THE PEOPLE

Of course, as we have said before, the people of Ireland are its main tourist attraction. Their warm, friendly smiles await your visit. Their music greets you; their song welcomes you. Men resting along the side of the road from working in the peat bogs. Their worn, shiny suits a symbol of days gone by. The women, with their rosy red cheeks, shopping for fresh bread and potatoes; chatting with their frineds. The children, smiling and lighthearted, running and playing along the roadside. These are the people of Ireland; they welcome you to their country, their county, their homes, their hearts.

TAITHNEAMH
TRAVEL IRELAND
23 Killoglen Road
Killorglin, County Kerry
Ireland

FIG. 18.6. *The back page of the newsletter.*

2. Go to **Format**, Page Se**tu**p. In **M**argins, set all to **.5"**. Select OK or press enter.

PART V

Creating Newsletters

3. Type the following text:

   TAITHNEAMH (Enter, Enter)

   MAY 1992 (Enter, Enter)

   COUNTY KERRY (Enter, Enter)

   KILLARNEY (Enter, Enter)

   (Type the paragraphs as shown in fig. 18.5, or type your own data, pressing Enter after each paragraph.)

   (Enter, Enter) **LEARNING IRISH** (Enter)

   (Tab) **Taithneamh** (Tab) **Enjoyment, pleasure** (Enter)

   (Tab) **Le fada an la** (Tab) **For many a day** (Enter)

   (Tab) **Bail o Dhia ort** (Tab) **God bless you** (Enter)

   (tab) **A lainm** (Tab) **Beautiful, lovely** (Enter)

   RING OF KERRY (Enter, Enter)

   MUCKROSS ESTATE (Enter, Enter)

   THE LAKES (Enter, Enter)

   THE PEOPLE (Enter, Enter)

4. Go to File, Save **A**s. Type **newsbase**. Select OK or press enter. Go to File, Save **A**s **Newslet1**. Select OK or press enter.

5. Add a space between each letter of Taithneamh, and select this word. On the Ribbon, change to 48-point, bold, and centered.

6. With TAITHMEAMH still selected, go to Forma**t**, **C**haracter. In Character Spacing, choose **E**xpanded. In the **B**y: box, type **3pt** and select OK or press enter.

6. With TAITHMEAMH still selected, go to Forma**t**, **C**haracter. In Spacing, choose Expanded. In **B**y: type **3pt** and Select OK or press enter.

7. Select MAY 1992. Change the type to 14-point, italic, and centered.

8. With MAY 1992 still selected, go to Format, **P**aragraph. In Spacing, **B**efore type **.5li**. Select OK or press enter.

9. Select COUNTY KERRY. Change the type to 24-point, bold, and center-aligned.

CHAPTER 18

Producing a Basic Newsletter

10. With COUNTY KERRY still selected, go to Forma**t**, **P**aragraph. In Spacing, **A**fter, type **.5li**. Select OK or press enter.

10. With COUNTY KERRY still selected, go to Forma**t**, **P**aragraph. In Spacing, **A**fter, type **.5li**. Select OK or press enter.

11. Position the cursor to the left of KILLARNEY. Go to **I**nsert, **B**reak. In Section Break, choose Con**t**inuous. Select OK or press enter.

12. Go to Forma**t**, **S**ection. In Columns, **N**umber type **2**. **S**pacing should be .5". Select OK or press enter.

13. Select all text from the first paragraph, `Welcome to the fourth issue...` to the last paragraph on the second page, `...Their county, their homes, their hearts`. Go to Forma**t**, **P**aragraph. In Alignment, choose **J**ustified. In Spacing, Af**t**er, type **1li** and select OK or press enter.

14. Still selected, go to **U**tilities, **H**yphenate. Select OK or press enter.

12. Go to Forma**t**, **C**olumns. In **N**umber of Columns type **2**. **S**pace Between should be .5". In **A**pply To choose This Point Forward and select OK or press enter.

13. Select all text from the first paragraph, `Welcome to the fourth issue...` to the last paragraph on the second page, `...Their county, their homes, their hearts`. Go to Forma**t**, **P**aragraph. In Alignment, choose Justified. In Spacing, Af**t**er, type **1li** and select OK or press enter.

14. With the first paragraph still selected, go to **T**ools, **H**yphenation. Select OK or press enter.

15. Select KILLARNEY. On the Ribbon, change the type to 18-point, bold, and centered. Repeat this step with RING OF KERRY, MUCKROSS ESTATE, THE LAKES, and THE PEOPLE.

16. Select LEARNING IRISH. Change the type to 14-point, bold, and centered.

17. Select the text from LEARNING IRISH to `...Beautiful, lovely`. Set the tabs, either on the Ruler, or in Format, **T**abs, to left aligned .25" and 1.75".

18. With the preceding text still selected, go to Format, **P**aragraph. In Spacing, **A**fter, type **2pt**. Select OK or press enter.

PART V

Creating Newsletters

18. With the preceding text still selected, go to Forma**t**, **P**aragraph. In Spacing, Af**t**er, type **2pt**. Select OK or press enter.

19. Position the cursor at the bottom of the first column. Go to **I**nsert, **B**reak, choose Column Break. Select OK or press enter. Adjust the two column heads if necessary, with paragraph returns, so they're even.

20. Position the cursor at the bottom of page one, column two. Go to **I**nsert, **B**reak. In Section Break, choose **N**ext Page. Select OK or press enter.

21. At the top of the second page, go to Forma**t**, **S**ection. In Columns, **N**umber type **1**. In **S**ection Start choose No Break. Select OK or press enter.

21. At the top of the second page, go to Forma**t**, **C**olumns. In **N**umber of Columns, type **1**. In **A**pply To choose This Point Forward and select OK or press enter.

22. Type **TAITHNEAMH**, adding a space between each letter, type **3xEnter**, and select the word. On the Ribbon, change the type to 40-point, bold, and centered.

23. With TAITHMEAMH still selected, go to Forma**t**, **C**haracter. In Spacing choose **E**xpanded. In By:, type **3pt** and select OK or press enter.

23. With TAITHMEAMH still selected, go to Forma**t**, **C**haracter. In Spacing choose **E**xpanded. In **B**y: type **3pt** and select OK or press enter.

24. Position the cursor immediately to the left of MUCKROSS ES-TATE. Go to **I**nsert, **B**reak. In Section Break, choose Continuous and select OK or press enter.

25. Go to Forma**t**, **S**ection. In Columns, **N**umber type **2**. In Section Start, be sure it says No Break. **S**pacing should be .5". Select OK or press enter.

25. Go to Forma**t**, **C**olumn. In **N**umber of Columns, type **2**. In **A**pply To, choose This Point Forward. **S**pace Between should be .5". Select OK or press enter.

26. Position the cursor at the end of the second paragraph under MUCKROSS ESTATE, ending with ...answer any and all questions. Go to **I**nsert, **B**reak. Choose **C**olumn Break and select OK or press enter.

CHAPTER 18

Producing a Basic Newsletter

27. If necessary, adjust the two column heads, with paragraph returns to make sure that these heads are even.

28. Position the cursor at the end of the second column, `...their county, their homes, their hearts`. Go to **I**nsert, **B**reak. In Section Break, choose **C**ontinuous and select OK or press enter.

29. Go to Forma**t**, **S**ection. In Columns, **N**umber type **1**. In **S**ection Start, choose No Break and select OK or press enter.

29. Go to Forma**t**, **C**olumns. In **N**umber of Columns type **1**. In **A**pply To choose This Point Forward and select OK or press enter.

30. Type the following lines of text:

    (Enter, Enter)

    TAITHNEAMH (Enter)

    TRAVEL IRELAND (Enter)

    23 Killoglen Road (Enter)

    Killorglin, County Kerry (Enter)

    Ireland

31. Select the first two lines, `TAITHNEAMH` and `TRAVEL IRELAND`. On the ribbon, change the type to 14-point, bold.

32. Go to **F**ile, **S**ave.

33. Go to **F**ile, **P**rint. Select OK or press enter.

Producing a Type and Graphic Newsletter

This design combines type and graphic elements to create a two-page, four-page, or eight-page newsletter. Well-organized and easy to read, the layout adapts well to any length of piece. Graphic rules border the nameplate, dateline and header, and the headlines make the newsletter appear organized and the topics easy to find.

PART V

Creating Newsletters

The nameplate is the one you created at the beginning of the chapter and saved as a glossary. The sample shown here uses the Version 2.0 design, although either nameplate works well.

Due to the heavy nameplate in this example (see fig. 18.7), the main subject of the newsletter, County Kerry, centers under the dateline and is surrounded by a wealth of white space. The left alignment of the type and headlines, plus the interparagraph spacing, also add white space.

The body type used is Times but the headlines are Helvetica, which adds a bit of variety. The rule above the heads makes them easy to find and breaks up the space because no art, other than the nameplate, is used. Look at the jumpline at the end of the third column: jumplines lead the reader into another part of the newsletter.

Page two begins with a header that identifies the page number, topic, and date (see fig. 18.8). Headers, or footers, contain all information you deem necessary, although page numbers are customarily included. Notice that here, the page number is to the left. Remember, left-hand pages number on the left; right-hand on the right. Center-page numbering is fine in a footer but not in a header. Header type is smaller than the body type, and often is in bold or italic. The rule adds a division between the header and the articles.

A continued story from page one includes the name of the story and another jumpline. Always give the reader reference points. The headline type for the continued story is smaller, as well.

The style of page two is similar to that of page one—for consistency. If the newsletter were to run four, eight, or more pages, the style would still remain consistent with these two pages. Of course, emphasis points and variation are encouraged. Boxed or screened stories, art work, or photos are excellent additions.

To create the newsletter in figures 18.7 and 18.8, take the following steps:

1. Go to **F**ile, **O**pen. Open NEWBASE.DOC. Go to **F**ile, Save **A**s **newslet2**. Position the cursor at the beginning of the document. Type one **Enter**. Move the cursor up one line.

2. Go to Forma**t**, **D**ocument. Be sure all Margins are **.5"**. Select OK or press enter.

456

COUNTY KERRY

KILLARNEY

Welcome to the fourth issue of Taithneamh. This month we visit County Kerry in the West of Ireland. If you plan a trip to Ireland soon, you will not want to miss this lovely area. In the heart of Kerry is Killarney town. With its hustle and bustle of merchants, business and tourist centers, Killarney is a town you will never forget.

Through the center of town is Main Street, the business and market center. Connecting to Main are High and New Streets, two very popular day and night tourist spots. High Street is lined with rows of lights overhead; souvenir shops and cafes line the sides of the narrow, always populated street. The pubs on High are well known for the dance music in the late evenings. The fiddle, banjo and whistle ring out in merriment and revelry.

An offshoot of High Street is New. New Street has many guesthouses and it is home for the Post Office of Killarney. The guest houses welcome visitors with open doors, the smell of tea and scones, and of course, a nice, warm peat fire! What more could you want on a cold and rainy day. And the gardens, the wonderful, colorful gardens! New Street is the pride of the women's club in town, and so it should be! They plant every spring with new bulbs and seeds, making the street a virtual festival of dyestuff.

RING OF KERRY

During the day, if you base yourself in Killarney, there are a myriad of sights and attractions in the area. The Slieve Miskish Mountains, Ring of Kerry, and the Dingle Peninsula are jaunts that take no more than a day. Scenic beauty of the lakes, the heather and good roads make County Kerry a wonderful place to visit. The Ring of Kerry is a trip you must not miss!

Stretching 110 miles, the Ring of Kerry offers excitement at every turn. It is a mountainous road circling the Slieve Mish Mountains, through the Dingle Peninsula, and running parallel to the ocean during most of its length. Beginning in Killarney, the first leg of the Ring tenders a distant view of Macgillycuddy's Reeks, a glorious mountain range in the southwest of Ireland. Travelling further, you come to Killorglin, the scene of the famous Puck Fair. If, by chance, you visit in mid-August, do not miss the Puck Fair. Music, song, feasting and brotherhood envelop the city for three lively, fun-filled days.

As you travel further on the Ring, you come across Caragh Lake, one of Kerry's finest fishing spots. You may wish to take a boat trip to the Blasket Islands, or Skellig Rock. Skellig Michael is a massive rock, jutting 700 feet high out of the Atlantic; what a sight to behold! Or perhaps you will take a side trip to Puffin Island, Kerry's own bird sanctuary where over 10,000 puffins gather each year for breeding.

Whether you travel south or west on the Ring, to the Islands or the Burrin, you will never forget the beauty and solitude

(continued on page 2)

FIG. 18.7. Page one of a type and graphic solution for a newsletter.

2　　　　　　　　　　　　TRAVEL IRELAND　　　　　　　　　　　　MAY 1992

RING OF KERRY

(continued from page 1)
of the landscape, and the love of life from the people. It is a memory to cherish your whole life through.

MUCKROSS ESTATE

Also located near Killarney, County Kerry, is a tremendous National Park called Muckross Estate. Over 10,000 acres of mountains, lakes and green, green flora preserved by the Republic for your enjoyment. Cars are not allowed on the estate; there are, however, alternatives. You may rent or bring your own bicycle. Or take a jaunting car. Jaunting cars line the entrance to the park (as well as line the streets of Killarney), ready to transport you to this scene of serenity and beauty. The horse-drawn carriages are driven by gents who spin tales and weave stories of old Ireland, Killarney, Muckross and the fairies.

Your first stop on the Estate is Muckross Abbey. A Francisian Abbey built in the 15th century, it is one of the best kept and restored Abbeys in all of Kerry. Your next stop is Muckross House. A monumental 19th century home donated, along with the land, to the people of Ireland by its former owners. The house is filled with intricately hand-carved furniture, home-made crafts, tapestries, and original art works. The basement contains a stable, and fully stocked print shop, pub, blacksmith shop, kitchen and weavers shop; all have presenters working as you tour, answer any and all questions.

THE LAKES

Contained with the National Park are three very famous, and pulchritudinous, lakes. The first you come to by jaunting car is the Lower Lake, also called Lough Leane. The second, or Middle Lake, is also called Muckross Lake. The third is simply the Upper Lake. In addition, don't miss Torc Mountain and its stupendous waterfall. Water from the Devil's Punch Bowl rushes over Torc's 60' waterfall, gushing and glorious, it is a sight you will not want to miss.

THE PEOPLE

Of course, as we have said before, the people of Ireland are its main tourist attraction. Their warm, friendly smiles await your visit. Their music greets you; their song welcomes you. Men resting along the side of the road from working in the peat bogs. Their worn, shiny suits a symbol of days gone by. The women, with their rosy red cheeks, shopping for fresh bread and potatoes; chatting with their frineds. The children, smiling and lighthearted, running and playing along the roadside. These are the people of Ireland; they welcome you to their country, their county, their homes, their hearts.

LEARNING IRISH

Taithneamh	Enjoyment, pleasure
Le fada an la	For many a day
Bail o Dhia ort	God bless you
A lainm	Beautiful, lovely

THE FAIRIES

The children in Ireland have their own special fairies, the Pooka, sometimes affectionately called "Pookie". The Pooka is a mischievous fairy, but not mean or bad-natured. Each Pooka claims a child as his own and stays with that child from birth to age 13 or so.

The Pooka plays tricks on the child, hiding things like socks, or homework; breaking mum's valuable glassware and allowing the child to take the blame; mussing hair, or even the child's room.

The Pooka is a beloved fairy in Ireland. Children blame many everyday occurrences on their fairy, and who in the world would dare argue?

AND...

When one prominent man in Killarney was asked if he believed in fairies, he said, "Fairies, ahhh no, I don't believe in them! But ya know," he said as he still pondered the question, "Every night I leave a bowl of milk on me back porch, just in case."

FIG. 18.8. *Page two of the newsletter, consistent in style and layout.*

CHAPTER 18

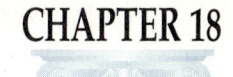

Producing a Basic Newsletter

2. Go to Forma**t**, Page Set**u**p. In **M**argins, be sure all margins are **.5**". Select OK or press enter.

3. Go to **E**dit, Gl**o**ssary. In the list of files, choose newsletter. **I**nsert.

4. Delete the first two lines of type from the original document, TAITHNEAMH and MAY 1992.

5. Select COUNTY KERRY. On the Ribbon, change the type to 24-point, bold, and center.

6. Position the cursor in front of KILLARNEY. Go to **I**nsert, **B**reak. In Section Break, choose Continuous and select OK or press enter.

7. Go to Forma**t**, **S**ection. In Columns, **N**umber type **3**. Spacing should be .5". In **S**ection Start, choose No Break and select OK or press enter.

7. Go to Forma**t**, **C**olumns. In **N**umber of Columns, type **3**. **S**pace Between should be .5". In **A**pply To, choose This Point Forward and select OK or press enter.

8. Select KILLARNEY. Go to Forma**t**, St**y**le(s). In the **S**tyle Name box, type **head**. Choose **D**efine.

9. Click on **C**haracter, change the type to Helv, 18-point, bold, and select OK or press enter.

10. Still in the dialog box, click on **P**aragraph. In Spacing, **A**fter, type **.5li**.

11. In the **P**aragraph box, in **B**order, choose Above. In Pat**t**ern, choose Thick. Select OK twice or press Enter twice.

10. Still in the dialog box, click on **P**aragraph. In Spacing, Aft**e**r, type **.5li**.

11. In dialog box, click on **B**order. In the Bo**r**der box, click in the top margin or use the down arrow to select. In **F**rom Text, choose 3pt. In the **L**ine box, choose the 1.25 rule. Select OK or press enter and Apply.

12. Position the cursor in the first paragraph of body text, Wel- come to the fourth issue.... Go to Forma**t**, St**y**le(s). In the **S**tyle Name box, type **body**. Click on **C**haracter. Change the point size to 12. Select OK or press enter.

PART V

Creating Newsletters

13. Still in the Style(s) dialog box, click on **P**aragraph. In Spacing, **Aft**er, type **1li**. Select OK twice or press Enter twice.

13. Still in the Style(s) dialog box, click on **P**aragraph. In Spacing, **Aft**er, type **1li**. Select OK or press enter and Apply.

14. Select all the text from the first paragraph, `Welcome to the fourth issue...` " to the end of the document. In the Ribbon, Style box, choose body. Go through the columns of type and insert optional hyphens (Ctrl+hyphen) in extremely short lines.

15. Select `RING OF KERRY` and, in the Style box, change the setting to head. Repeat with the heads `MUCKROSS ESTATE`, `THE LAKES`, and `THE PEOPLE` on page two.

16. Select the text from `LEARNING IRISH` to `A lainm(tab)-Beautiful, lovely`. Press Shift+Delete (Ctrl+X in version 2.0) to cut. Go to page two. Position the cursor at the end of the document and press Shift+Insert (Ctrl+V in version 2.0) to paste. Go back to page one; delete all extra paragraph returns left over from LEARNING IRISH.

17. On page one, the columns should form evenly without inserting breaks. Check to be sure that the tops and bottoms of the three columns are even. If the columns are uneven, adjust them.

18. Position the cursor at column three in the last paragraph, at the end of the line `...forget the beauty and solitude` and type the following line:

    (Enter, Enter) **(continued on page 2)**

19. Select `(continued on page 2)`. Change this text to italic.

20. With the preceding text still selected, go to Forma**t**, **P**aragraph. In Spacing, **A**fter, change to **0** and select OK or press enter.

20. With the preceding text still selected, go to Forma**t**, **P**aragraph. In Spacing, **Af**ter, change to **0** and select OK or press enter.

21. Position the cursor at the end of the line of type, `(continued...)`. Go to **I**nsert, **B**reak. In Section Break, choose **N**ext Page and select OK or press enter.

CHAPTER 18

Producing a Basic Newsletter

22. At the top of page two, go to Forma**t**, **S**ection. In Columns, **N**umber, type **1**. In **S**ection Start, No Break and select OK or press enter.

22. At the top of page two, go to Forma**t**, **C**olumns. In **N**umber of Columns, type **1**. In **A**pply To, choose This Point Forward and select OK or press enter.

23. Type **3xEnter**. With the up-arrow key, move the cursor to the first paragraph return. Type the following line:

    2 (Tab) **TRAVEL IRELAND** (Tab) **MAY 1992**

24. Select this line of type and change to 10-point, bold.

25. With the preceding text still selected, go to Forma**t**, **P**aragraph. In Spacing, **A**fter, change to **0**.

26. Still in the dialog box, in **Bo**rder choose Below. In Pa**tt**ern, choose Single and select OK or press enter.

25. Still selected, go to Forma**t**, **P**aragraph. In Spacing, Aft**e**r, change to **0**. Select OK or press enter.

26. With the preceding text still selected, go to Forma**t**, **B**order. In the Bo**r**der box, click in the bottom margin or use the down arrow to select. In **L**ine, choose the .75 rule. Select OK or press enter.

27. With the text still selected, go to the ruler and set the tabs. The first tab is centered at 3.75"; the second tab is right aligned at 7.5". You may need to adjust the right-hand margin marker to set the tab, then replace the marker.

    If you were to add pages 3 and 4 to this newsletter, you can simply copy and then insert this header at the top of page 3. You switch page 3's page number and the date so that the 3 is on the right. Page 4, or the last page of a newsletter, doesn't normally have a header, footer, or page number.

28. Position the cursor one paragraph return above MUCKROSS ESTATE. Go to **I**nsert, **B**reak. In Section Break, choose Con**t**inuous and select OK or press enter.

29. Go to Format, **S**ection. In Columns, **N**umber type **3**. In **S**ection Start choose No Break and select OK or press enter.

29. Go to Format, **C**olumns. In **N**umber of Columns, type **3**. In **A**pply To, choose This Point Forward and select OK or press enter.

PART V

Creating Newsletters

30. Type the following text:

    RING OF KERRY (Enter)

    (continued from page 1)

31. Select `RING OF KERRY`. Change the type to Helv, 14-point, bold.

32. Select `(continued...)`. Change the type to italic.

33. In the third column, check `LEARNING IRISH` to be sure that paragraph returns precede and follow and that two returns exist after `...Beautiful, lovely`. If not, add these returns now.

34. Select the type from the paragraph return above `LEARNING...` to and including one paragraph return after `...Beautiful, lovely`.

35. Go to Forma**t**, **P**aragraph. In Spacing, **A**fter, change to **0**.

36. Still in the dialog box, in **B**order choose Box. In Patt**e**rn, choose Single and select OK or press enter.

35. Go to Forma**t**, **P**aragraph. In Spacing, Aft**e**r, change to **0**.

36. Go to Forma**t**, **B**order. In the Preset box, choose **B**ox. In Line, choose the 1.25 rule and select OK or press enter.

37. Select and change the line of text, `LEARNING IRISH`, to 14-point, bold, and centered.

38. Select and change the type from `Taithneamh...` to `...Beautiful, lovely` to 10-point. On the Ruler, set the tabs as left aligned at .06" and 1". Be sure that the tops of the columns are even. If uneven, adjust the tops of the columns.

39. Position the cursor on the last paragraph return in the column and type the following text:

    THE FAIRIES (Enter)

    (Type the paragraphs as shown in figure 18.8, or type your own data, pressing Enter between each paragraph.)

    AND...(Enter)

40. Select `THE FAIRIES`. On the ribbon, in the Style box, change the type to head.

41. Select AND.... Change this text to Helv, 14-point, and bold.

42. Go to **File**, **S**ave.

43. Go to **File**, **P**rint.

Producing an Innovative Newsletter

You have many ways in which to lay out a newsletter. The customary format is portrait oriented, 8 1/2 inches x 11 inches, two or three columns. Retaining the basic format, you can vary columns and sections to create an innovative style.

In the following design example, each head represents a one-column section, whereas the body text is laid out in two columns. The style conforms to this format whether the newsletter contains four, eight, or more pages. Art or photos also fit naturally into the format.

Figure 18.9 shows page one of the newsletter. The simple nameplate and dateline are set off by a heavy rule along the top and a thinner rule along the bottom. The left-hand alignment allows for white space and mirrors the left-hand alignment of the headlines and body text. The rule above the headlines, and also the white space to the right of each head, divides the page. The rules, the headlines, and the white space impart a horizontal arrangement to the page, as opposed to the vertical you worked with in the preceding design.

Page two of the newsletter follows the same pattern. At the end of the page you see a short confirmation form that takes the full width of the page (see fig. 18.10). Usually, this newsletter would be four pages; you, however, design only three. Page three follows the same design and style as pages one and two.

For emphasis, the last page of the newsletter contains a calendar (see fig. 18.11). Created by using a table, the calendar is more interesting and easier to understand than a list of dates. Again, a return address placed at the bottom of the page affords a place for effortless labeling and mailing.

TAITHNEAMH

MAY 1992

COUNTY KERRY
KILLARNEY

Welcome to the fourth issue of Taithneamh. This month we visit County Kerry in the West of Ireland. If you plan a trip to Ireland soon, you will not want to miss this lovely area. In the heart of Kerry is Killarney town. With its hustle and bustle of merchants, business and tourist centers, Killarney is a town you will never forget.

Through the center of town is Main Street, the business and market center. Connecting to Main are High and New Streets, two very popular day and night tourist spots. High Street is lined with rows of lights overhead; souvenir shops and cafes line the sides of the narrow, always populated street. The pubs on High are well known for the dance music in the late evenings. The fiddle, banjo and whistle ring out in merriment and revelry.

An offshoot of High Street is New. New Street has many guesthouses and it is home for the Post Office of Killarney. The guest houses welcome visitors with open doors, the smell of tea and scones, and of course, a nice, warm peat fire! What more could you want on a cold and rainy day. And the gardens, the wonderful, colorful gardens! New Street is the pride of the women's club in town, and so it should be! They plant every spring with new bulbs and seeds, making the street a virtual festival of dyestuff.

LEARNING IRISH

Taithneamh	Enjoyment, pleasure
Le fada an la	For many a day
Bail o Dhia ort	God bless you
A lainm	Beautiful, lovely

RING OF KERRY

During the day, if you base yourself in Killarney, there are a myriad of sights and attractions in the area. The Slieve Miskish Mountains, Ring of Kerry, and the Dingle Peninsula are jaunts that take no more than a day. Scenic beauty of the lakes, the heather and good roads make County Kerry a wonderful place to visit. The Ring of Kerry is a trip you must not miss!

Stretching 110 miles, the Ring of Kerry offers excitement at every turn. It is a mountainous road circling the Slieve Mish Mountains, through the Dingle Peninsula, and running parallel to the ocean during most of its length. Beginning in Killarney, the first leg of the Ring tenders a distant view of Macgillycuddy's Reeks, a glorious mountain range in the southwest of Ireland. Travelling further, you come to Killorglin, the scene of the famous Puck Fair. If, by chance, you visit in mid-August, do not miss the Puck Fair. Music, song, feasting and brotherhood envelop the city for three lively, fun-filled days.

As you travel further on the Ring, you come across Caragh Lake, one of Kerry's finest fishing spots. You may wish to take a boat trip to the Blasket Islands, or Skellig Rock. Skellig Michael is a massive rock, jutting 700 feet high out of the Atlantic; what a sight to behold! Or perhaps you will take a side trip to Puffin Island, Kerry's own bird sanctuary where over 10,000 puffins gather each year for breeding.

Whether you travel south or west on the Ring, to the Islands or the Burrin, you will never forget the beauty and solitude of the landscape, and the love of life from the people. It is a memory to cherish your whole life through.

FIG. 18.9. Page one of an innovative newsletter.

MUCKROSS ESTATE

Also located near Killarney, County Kerry, is a tremendous National Park called Muckross Estate. Over 10,000 acres of mountains, lakes and green, green flora preserved by the Republic for your enjoyment. Cars are not allowed on the estate; there are, however, alternatives. You may rent or bring your own bicycle. Or take a jaunting car. Jaunting cars line the entrance to the park (as well as line the streets of Killarney), ready to transport you to this scene of serenity and beauty. The horse-drawn carriages are driven by gents who spin tales and weave stories of old Ireland, Killarney, Muckross and the fairies.

Your first stop on the Estate is Muckross Abbey. A Francisian Abbey built in the 15th century, it is one of the best kept and restored Abbeys in all of Kerry. Your next stop is Muckross House. A monumental 19th century home donated, along with the land, to the people of Ireland by its former owners. The house is filled with intricately hand-carved furniture, home-made crafts, tapestries, and original art works. The basement contains a stable, and fully stocked print shop, pub, blacksmith shop, kitchen and weavers shop; all have presenters working as you tour, answer any and all questions.

THE LAKES

Contained with the National Park are three very famous, and pulchritudinous, lakes. The first you come to by jaunting car is the Lower Lake, also called Lough Leane. The second, or Middle Lake, is also called Muckross Lake. The third is simply the Upper Lake. In addition, don't miss Torc Mountain and its stupendous waterfall. Water from the Devil's Punch Bowl rushes over Torc's 60' waterfall, gushing and glorious, it is a sight you will not want to miss.

THE PEOPLE

Of course, as we have said before, the people of Ireland are its main tourist attraction. Their warm, friendly smiles await your visit. Their music greets you; their song welcomes you. Men resting along the side of the road from working in the peat bogs. Their worn, shiny suits a symbol of days gone by. The women, with their rosy red cheeks, shopping for fresh bread and potatoes; chatting with their frineds. The children, smiling and lighthearted, running and playing along the roadside. These are the people of Ireland; they welcome you to their country, their county, their homes, their hearts.

♣ RESERVATION CONFIRMATION ♣

Your trip is scheduled to leave June 1, 1992. You must send this confirmation prior to May 16 with your first payment of $642. Be sure you have your passport in order.

Name: _____

Address: _____

Phone: _____

FIG. 18.10. *Page two of the newsletter, consistent in design and layout.*

PART V

Creating Newsletters

JUNE 1992

SUNDAY	MONDAY	TUESDAY	WEDNESDAY	THURSDAY	FRIDAY	SATURDAY
	1 Trip leaves New York for Shannon Airport	2	3 Tea on New St. 10 - 11 a.m. Kiloran Guest House	4	5 Open House Lahinch Guest House - 9 - 5 Refreshments	6
7	8	9 Boat Trip to Blaskets 9 a.m.	10	11 Muckross House Tour 9 to 11 a.m.	12	13
14	15	16	17 Jaunting Car Muckross Est. leaves - 2 p.m.	18	19 Free Lecture Gardens of Muckross 2 p.m.	20
21	22 Muckross Abbey Tour 11 a.m.	23	24	25 Weaving Workshop at Muckross 3 p.m.	26	27
28	29	30 Alpine Garden Tour 4 p.m.				

TRAVEL IRELAND
TAITHNEAMH
23 Killoglen Road
Killorglin
County Kerry, Ireland

FIG. 18.11. *The last page of the newsletter adds interest and emphasis with a calendar.*

To create the newsletter shown in figures 18.9 to 18.11, perform the following steps:

1. Go to **F**ile, **O**pen. Open NEWBASE.DOC. Save **As Newslet3** and select OK or press enter.

466

CHAPTER 18

Producing a Basic Newsletter

2. Go to Forma**t**, **D**ocument. Be sure all Margins are **.5**". Select OK or press enter.

2. Go to Forma**t**, Page Set**u**p. In **M**argins, be sure that all margins are **.5**". Select OK or press enter.

3. Select TAITHNEAMH and change the type to 48-point, bold.

4. With TAITHNEAMH still selected, go to Forma**t**, **P**aragraph. In Spacing, **A**fter, type **.5li**.

5. Still in the dialog box, **B**order, choose Above. In Patt**e**rn, choose Thick and select OK or press enter.

4. With TAITHNEAMH still selected, go to Forma**t**, **P**aragraph. In Spacing, Aft**e**r, type **.5li** and select OK or press enter.

5. With the text still selected, go to Forma**t**, **B**order. In the Bo**r**der box, click the top margin or use the down arrow to select. In **L**ine choose the 2.25 rule and select OK or press enter.

6. Select MAY 1992 and change the type to 14-point, bold.

7. Select COUNTY KERRY. Go to Forma**t**, Styles. In the **S**tyle Name box, type **head**. Choose **D**efine.

8. Click on **C**haracter, change the type to 18-point, bold. Select OK or press enter.

9. Still in the St**y**les dialog box, click on **P**aragraph. In **B**order choose Above. In **P**att**e**rn, choose Single. Select OK twice or press Enter twice.

7. Select COUNTY KERRY. Go to Forma**t**, Style. In the **S**tyle Name box, type **head**. Choose **D**efine.

8. Click on **C**haracter, change the type to 18-point, bold. Select OK or press enter.

9. Still in the St**y**le dialog box, click on **B**order. In the Bo**r**der box click in the margin above. In the **L**ine box, choose the 1.25 rule. Select OK or press enter and then Apply.

10. At the end of COUNTY KERRY, press delete twice. This step should bring KILLARNEY on the same line. Now press Shift+Enter to force KILLARNEY to the next line without a rule above it.

467

PART V

Creating Newsletters

11. Position the cursor in front of `Welcome to the fourth is-sue...` Go to **I**nsert, **B**reak. In Section Break, choose Continuous and select OK or press enter.

12. Go to Format, **S**ection. In Columns, **N**umber, type **2**. In Section Start, choose No Break and select OK or press enter.

12. Go to Format, **C**olumns. In **N**umber of Columns, type **2**. In A**p**ply To, choose This Point Forward and select OK or press enter.

13. With the cursor positioned within the first paragraph, go to Forma**t**, Styles. In the **S**tyle Name box, type **body**. Choose **D**efine.

14. Click on **C**haracter, change the type to 12-point and select OK or press enter.

15. Still in St**y**les dialog box, click on **P**aragraph. In Spacing, Aft**e**r, type **1li**. Select OK twice or press Enter twice.

13. With the cursor positioned within the first paragraph, go to Forma**t**, Style. In the **S**tyle Name box, type **body**. Choose **D**efine.

14. Choose **C**haracter, change the type to 12-point, and select OK or press enter.

15. Still in the Style dialog box, click on **P**aragraph. In Spacing, Af**t**er, type **1li**. Select OK or press Enter and then Apply.

16. Position the cursor at the end of the second paragraph, ending with the line `...ring out in merriment and revelry`. Go to Insert, **B**reak. Choose Column Break and select OK or press enter.

17. Position the cursor in front of `LEARNING IRISH`. Press Backspace twice to delete two paragraph returns.

18. Select the type from `LEARNING IRISH` to `...Beautiful, lovely`. Go to Forma**t**, **P**aragraph. In Spacing, **A**fter, delete the contents and type **0**.

18. Select the text from `LEARNING IRISH` to `...Beautiful, lovely`. Go to Forma**t**, **P**aragraph. In Spacing, Af**t**er, delete the contents and type **0**.

19. Still selected, on the Ruler set the tabs as left aligned at .25" and 2".

CHAPTER 18

Producing a Basic Newsletter

20. Select and bold the line, LEARNING IRISH.

21. Place the cursor at the end of the line ...Beautiful, lovely. Go to **I**nsert, **B**reak. In Section Break, choose **C**ontinuous and select OK or press enter.

22. Go to Forma**t**, **S**ection. In Columns, **N**umber, type **1**. In Se**c**tion Start, choose No Break. Select OK or press enter.

22. Go to Forma**t**, **C**olumns. In **N**umber of Columns, type **1**. In **A**pply To, choose This Point On and select OK or press enter.

23. Select RING OF KERRY. On the Ribbon, in the Style box, choose head.

24. Continue to format the page by following the previous steps for inserting breaks and formatting columns. At the end of the page, second column, position the cursor. Go to **I**nsert, **B**reak. In Section Break, choose **N**ext Page and select OK or press enter.

25. Continue to format the page by following the previous steps for inserting breaks and formatting columns.

26. At the beginning of the last section, after THE PEOPLE, type the following text:

    RESERVATION CONFIRMATION (Enter)

    Your trip is scheduled to leave June 1, 1992. You must send this confirmation prior to May 16 with your first payment of $642. Be sure you have your passport in order. (Enter)

    Name: (Tab) (Enter)

    Address: (Tab) (Enter)

    Phone: (Tab) (Enter)

27. Select RESERVATION CONFIRMATION. Change the type to bold, centered. You have no Symbol font in Word for the shamrock; however, if you have the Zaph Dingbat font, position the cursor and type **Alt+136**. Select the character and change its Font to Dingbat. Copy the character to the other side of CONFIRMATION. If you don't have the Dingbat font, you can create a shamrock in a draw or paint program and import as a TIFF file.

PART V

Creating Newsletters

27. Select RESERVATION CONFIRMATION. Change the type to bold, centered. Position the cursor in front of the R. Go to **I**nsert, **S**ymbol. Double click the shamrock or select it with arrows and press Enter. Copy the shamrock to the other side of CONFIRMATION.

28. Select the three lines of type from Name... to and including Phone.... Go to Forma**t**, **T**abs. In the **T**ab Position box, type **7"**. Right align, and choose Leader 4, **S**et. Select OK or press enter.

29. Position the cursor at the end of the page. Go to Insert, **B**reak. In Section Break, choose **N**ext Page and select OK or press enter.

30. At the top of page three, type the following line:

    JUNE 1992 (Enter, three times)

31. Select JUNE 1992, change to 24-point, bold, and centered. Position the cursor on the next to the last paragraph return.

32. Go to **I**nsert, **T**able. In Number of **C**olumns, type **7**. In Number of **R**ows, type **6**. Click on Format.

33. In Minimum Row Height, type **6li**.

34. Still in dialog box, Borders. For **O**utline, choose Thick. For **I**nside, choose Single and select OK or press enter.

35. Select the first row of the column. Go to Forma**t**, **T**able. In Minimum Row **H**eight, type **2li**.

36. Still in dialog box, in Borders, **B**ottom, choose Thick and select OK or press enter.

32. Go to Table, **I**nsert **T**able. In Number of **C**olumns type **7**; in Number of **R**ows, type **6** and select OK or press enter.

33. Select the first row. Go to T**a**ble, Row Height. In Height of Row 1 choose At Least. In **A**t:, type **2li** and select OK or press enter.

34. With first row still selected, go to Forma**t**, **B**order. In the Bo**r**der box, click the bottom margin. In **L**ine, choose the 1.25 rule and select OK or press enter.

35. Select the entire table. Go to T**a**ble, Row **H**eight. In Height of Rows 2-6 choose At Least. In **A**t:, type **6li** and select OK or press enter.

CHAPTER 18

Producing a Basic Newsletter

36. With table still selected, go to Forma**t**, **B**order. In Preset, choose **G**rid. In **L**ine, choose the 1.25 rule. Select OK or press enter.

37. Position the cursor in the first cell. Type the following text:

    SUNDAY (Tab) **MONDAY** (Tab) **TUESDAY** (Tab) **WEDNES-DAY** (Tab) **THURSDAY** (Tab) **FRIDAY** (tab) **SATURDAY** (Tab, Tab)

    1 (Tab) **2** (Tab) **3** (Tab) **4** (Tab) **5** (Tab) **6** (Tab)

    7 (Tab) **8** (Tab) **9** (Tab) **10** (Tab)

38. Continue typing the numbers of the calendar to **30**. Select the first row of text, SUNDAY.... On the Ribbon, change the type to 10-point, bold, and centered.

39. With the first row selected, go to Forma**t**, **P**aragraph. In Spacing, **B**efore, type **3pt** and select OK or press enter.

40. Select the numbers in the calendar. Change the type to 18-point.

41. To type entries in the calendar, position the cursor beside the number, press Shift+Enter. With the cursor in position, change the type size to 10-point and type the following text:

    Trip leaves (Shift+Enter)

    New York for (Shift+Enter)

    Shannon (Shift+Enter)

    Airport

42. If you want to practice typing into cells of the other dates, refer to figure 18.11 for examples.

43. Position the cursor on the last paragraph return on the page and type the following text:

    (Enter)

    TRAVEL IRELAND (Enter)

    TAITHNEAMH (Enter)

    23 Killoglen Road (Enter)

    Killorglin (Enter)

    County Kerry, Ireland

471

44. Select TRAVEL IRELAND. Change the type to 18-point, bold.
45. Select TAITHNEAMH. Change the type to 14-point bold.
46. Go to **F**ile, **S**ave.
47. Go to **F**ile, **P**rint.

Looking at Design

The design of a newsletter communicates to the reader. A newsletter with crowded text, a great number of graphics, and little white space says, "Don't Read Me!" If you must cut some copy, leave out a few graphics or add extra pages, but make these changes for the sake of the design. All of the following three examples of newsletter designs incorporate white space for comfortable reading.

Figure 18.12 illustrates an interesting layout. The arc of the letters in the nameplate creates exciting shapes of white space around the word. The margins are wide, as are the gutters. Intercolumn rules compliment the left-aligned body text. For variety, typefaces include both Times and Helvetica.

Figure 18.13 demonstrates a different columnar layout. The nameplate is vertical and in a narrow column. The next column (of text) is a bit wider; whereas the third column is even wider. This layout creates a distinct impression.

Finally, logos, graphics, art work, and photos are excellent additions to newsletters. Plan space in advance so that you don't crowd text or graphics. Art makes the nameplate even more recognizable to the reader, and graphics throughout make the newsletter more interesting to read.

Figure 18.14 illustrates a nameplate with art added. Keep the same nameplate in each issue. The map in the lower right corner helps balance the nameplate and illustrates the places named in the article. The logo is hand drawn and pasted up. The map was drawn in CorelDRAW!

COUNTY KERRY

KILLARNEY

Welcome to the fourth issue of Taithneamh. This month we visit County Kerry in the West of Ireland. If you plan a trip to Ireland soon, you will not want to miss this lovely area. In the heart of Kerry is Killarney town. With its hustle and bustle of merchants, business and tourist centers, Killarney is a town you will never forget.

Through the center of town is Main Street, the business and market center. Connecting to Main are High and New Streets, two very popular day and night tourist spots. High Street is lined with rows of lights overhead; souvenir shops and cafes line the sides of the narrow, always populated street. The pubs on High are well known for the dance music in the late evenings. The fiddle, and whistle ring out in merriment and revelry.

RING OF KERRY

During the day, if you base yourself in Killarney, there are a myriad of sights and attractions in the area. The Slieve Miskish Mountains, Ring of Kerry, and the Dingle Peninsula are jaunts that take no more than a day. Scenic beauty of the lakes, the heather and good roads make County Kerry a wonderful place to visit. The Ring of Kerry is a trip you must not miss!

Stretching 110 miles, the Ring of Kerry offers excitement at every turn. It is a mountainous road circling the Slieve Mish Mountains, through the Dingle Peninsula, and running parallel to the ocean during most of its length. Beginning in Killarney, the first leg of the Ring tenders a distant view of Macgillycuddy's Reeks, a glorious mountain range in the beautiful southwest of Ireland.

PUCK FAIR

Travelling further, you come to Killorglin, the scene of the famous Puck Fair. If, by chance, you visit in mid-August, do not miss the Puck Fair. Music, song, feasting and brotherhood envelop the city for three lively, fun-filled days.

As you travel further on the Ring, you come across Caragh Lake, one of Kerry's finest fishing spots. You may wish to take a boat trip to the Blasket Islands, or Skellig Rock. Skellig Michael is a massive rock, jutting 700 feet high out of the Atlantic; what a wonderful sight to behold!

Whether you travel south or west on the Ring, to the Islands or the Burrin, you will never forget the beauty and solitude of the landscape, and the love of life from the people. It is a memory to cherish your whole life through.

FIG. 18.12. Page one of a newsletter design; the shape of white space in the nameplate is notable.

TAITHNEAMH

COUNTY KERRY
KILLARNEY

Welcome to the fourth issue of Taithneamh. This month we visit County Kerry in the West of Ireland. If you plan a trip to Ireland soon, you will not want to miss this lovely area. In the heart of Kerry is Killarney town. With its hustle and bustle of merchants, business and tourist centers, Killarney is a town you will never forget.

Through the center of town is Main Street, the business and market center. Connecting to Main Street are High and New Streets, two very popular day and night tourist spots. High Street is lined with rows of lights overhead; souvenir shops and cafes line the sides of the narrow, always very populated street. The pubs on High are well known for the dance music in the late evenings. The fiddle, banjo and whistle ring out in merriment and revelry.

During the day, if you base yourself in Killarney, there are a myriad of sights and attractions in the area. The Slieve Miskish Mountains, Ring of Kerry, and the Dingle Peninsula are jaunts that take no more than a day. Scenic beauty of the lakes, the heather and good roads make County Kerry a wonderful place to visit. The Ring of Kerry is a trip you must not miss!

Stretching 110 miles, the Ring of Kerry offers excitement at every turn. It is a mountainous road circling the Slieve Mish Mountains, through the Dingle Peninsula, and running parallel to the ocean during most of its length. Beginning in Killarney, the first leg of the Ring tenders a distant view of Macgillycuddy's Reeks, a glorious mountain range in the southwest of Ireland. Travelling further, you come to Killorglin, the scene of the famous Puck Fair. If, by chance, you visit in mid-August, do not miss the Puck Fair. Music, song, feasting and brotherhood envelop the city for three lively, fun-filled days.

As you travel further on the Ring, you come across Caragh Lake, one of Kerry's finest fishing spots. You may wish to take a boat trip to the Blasket Islands, or Skellig Rock. Skellig Michael is a massive rock, jutting 700 feet high out of the Atlantic; what a sight to behold! Or perhaps you will take a side trip to Puffin Island, Kerry's own bird sanctuary where over 10,000 puffins gather each year for breeding.

Whether you travel south or west on the Ring, to the Islands or the Burrin, you will never forget the beauty and solitude of the landscape, and the love of life from the people. It is a memory to cherish your whole life through.

Also located near Killarney, County Kerry, is a tremendous National Park called Muckross Estate. Over 10,000 acres of mountains, lakes and green, green flora preserved by the Republic for your enjoyment. Cars are not allowed on the estate; there are, however, alternatives. You may rent or bring your own bicycle.

FIG. 18.13. *Page one of a newsletter; the three columns are different widths.*

# TAITHNEAMH

KILLARNEY COUNTY KERRY

Welcome to the fourth issue of Taithneamh. This month we visit County Kerry in the West of Ireland. If you plan a trip to Ireland soon, you will not want to miss this lovely area. In the heart of Kerry is Killarney town. With its hustle and bustle of merchants, business and tourist centers, Killarney is a town you will never forget.

Through the center of town is Main Street, the business and market center. Connecting to Main Street are High and New Streets, two very popular day and night tourist spots. High Street is lined with rows of lights overhead; souvenir shops and cafes line the sides of the narrow, always very populated street. The pubs on High are well known for the dance music in the late evenings. The fiddle, banjo and whistle ring out in merriment and revelry.

During the day, if you base yourself in Killarney, there are a myriad of sights and attractions in the area. The Slieve Miskish Mountains, Ring of Kerry, and the Dingle Peninsula are jaunts that take no more than a day. Scenic beauty of the lakes, the heather in bloom and good roads make County Kerry a wonderful place to visit. The Ring of Kerry is a trip you must not miss!

Stretching 110 miles, the Ring of Kerry offers excitement at every turn. It is a mountainous road circling the Slieve Mish Mountains, through the Dingle Peninsula, and running parallel to the ocean during most of its length. Beginning in Killarney, the first leg of the Ring tenders a distant view of Macgillycuddy's Reeks, a glorious mountain range in the southwest of Ireland. Travelling further, you come to Killorglin, the scene of the famous Puck Fair. If, by chance, you visit in mid-August, do not miss the Puck Fair. Music, song, feasting and brotherhood envelop the city for three lively, fun days.

As you travel further on the Ring, you come across Caragh Lake, one of Kerry's finest fishing spots. You may wish to take a boat trip to the Blasket Islands, or Skellig Rock. Skellig Michael is a massive rock, jutting 700 feet high out of the Atlantic; what a sight to behold! Or perhaps you will take a side trip to Puffin Island, Kerry's own bird sanctuary where over 10,000 puffins gather each year for breeding.

Whether you travel south or west on the Ring, to the Islands or the Burrin, you will never forget the beauty and solitude of the landscape, and the love of life from the people. It is a memory to cherish your whole life through.

Also located near Killarney, County Kerry, is a tremendous National Park called Muckross Estate. Over 10,000 acres of mountains, lakes and green, green flora preserved by the Republic for your enjoyment. Cars are not allowed on the estate; there are, however, alternatives. You may rent or bring your own bicycle.

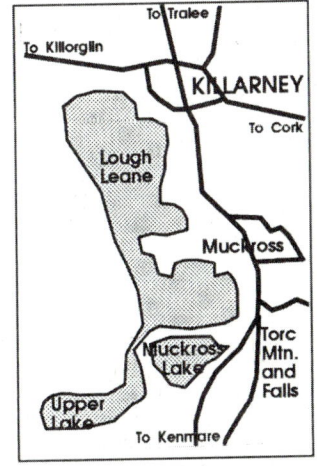

FIG. 18.14.   Example of a newsletter with graphics on the first page.

PART V
Creating Newsletters

Recapping

As you learned at the beginning of this chapter newsletters fulfill a variety of important functions. Newsletters inform, announce, remind, advise, instruct, advertise, educate, entertain, and communicate. You also learned that because newsletters are so flexible, you can design them to fit any purpose. Finally, you learned how to produce several sample newsletters.

In Chapter 19, things toughen up a bit when you learn how to produce a complex newsletter.

Producing a Complex Newsletter

19

In the last chapter, you created some nice looking documents by using the basic techniques of newsletter design. In this chapter, you learn more about technique and style in newsletter design. With the many newsletters produced and distributed in today's business world, yours should stand out in the crowd.

In this chapter, you design three distinctly different newsletter layouts. Because you now understand how to apply consistency and emphasis to a document, the directions for the following designs guide you through only the first two pages of each newsletter. After you see how the layout works, you can easily complete these designs for practice, or use them in your own documents.

You may want to save one of the following newsletters as a template for your own. By saving a design as a style sheet and template, and then removing all but the boilerplate text, you have a layout ready to use any time you wish. Consider again the possibility of using a glossary (see Chapter 5) as your nameplate; you can always save a glossary within your template.

Some new techniques for newsletter design introduced in this chapter are the masthead, headers, large first characters (drop caps or raised caps), tables of contents, callouts and varied column widths. The third design uses the table feature to create a wide column and a narrow column on each page for an interesting effect. This chapter also shows some techniques for using graphics such as photographs, art work, charts, tables, or anything that draws and keeps the attention of the reader. A few additional designs are included at the end of the chapter to give you more ideas.

Version 2.0 of Word provides many options for varying your newsletter design. Microsoft WordArt, Microsoft Draw and Microsoft Graph may be used for illustrations and nameplates. Also available are thicker rules, frames, and screens. Experiment with these features within your newsletters to dress up the final product.

Creating an Innovative Newsletter

Page one of the first newsletter design is shown in figure 19.1. This design is different than the typical newsletter. The nameplate, for example, is right-aligned and bordered on top with three rules of varying length. The rules, which guide the eye to the nameplate, help create interesting white space on the left. The heads are right-aligned, repeating the layout of the nameplate. Notice, too, that the heads are not bold. The unusual lightness of the heads and the use of white space create an openness and buoyant appearance to the newsletter.

In contrast, the first letter in the first paragraph of the story is large and bold. These large, bold letters (here, a raised cap) balance the right-aligned heads, and pull your attention to the text. The body text is justified with no indents to prevent detracting from other design points. Line spacing and interparagraph spacing add to the readability of the body text. Finally, a short table of contents at the bottom of the first page directs the reader's attention to the inside of the newsletter.

The second page of the newsletter, shown in figure 19.2, continues the style established on the first page by using repeated lines at the top, right-aligned heads and raised cap first characters.

As a point of emphasis, the area for `Our Spring Specials`, shown in figure 19.2, is one column with a centered head. The rules above and below tie this section to the header, as well as balance the page. The footer is just a left-hand page number. Page numbers on a right page would be on the right side.

MOUNTAIN SORREL

A Quarterly Newsletter of Herbal Curatives and Preventatives

The Healing Power of Lavender

Everyone knows of the delicious fragrance of lavender, especially English lavender, but few know of its medicinal qualities. Any of the three species of lavender make wonderful potions. A terrific calmative, lavender has the power to soothe headaches and nervous tension. Simply steep lavender flowers in hot water for 15 to 20 minutes, and sip a cupful of the tea two or three times during the day.

A stronger tea of lavender is good as a gargle for sore throats; it also relieves stomach aches and colic. We stock dried English and French lavenders in bunches and one pound bags, at a reasonable price. We also sell lavender oil extract for use as a medicinal oil.

Rosemary, More Than a Cooking Herb

Both the leaves and flowers of rosemary have been used to alleviate depression and insomnia. A simple rosemary tea, with a bit of ginger added, also comforts a nervous or upset stomach. Rosemary oil is widely known for its antibacterial properties, as well. Lastly, if you have dark hair, try a strong rosemary tea for a rinse after washing. It not only makes your hair shiny and soft, but it clears up your dandruff, too.

We stock a full supply of rosemary leaves, flowers, oil and our special home-made rosemary shampoo and rinses. Our supplies are limited, and believe us, they go fast! All natural, no preservatives, so order yours today, don't dare delay!

Catnip, Not Just For Cats

A member of the mint family, catnip contains many properties other mints do. As a pleasant tasting tea, catnip is an antispasmodic and a calmative. Treat stomach ailments, colic and intestinal complaints. Catnip calms nervousness and anxiety. Having a sleepless night? Try some catnip tea. If you have a cat, though, watch out, he'll try to drink your tea, too!

We stock catnip in one-half and one pound cans, as well as seeds to start your own plants in your garden.

It's Not Just a Weed, Joe-Pye Weed

Often seen growing along the railroad tracks or roadsides, in fields and meadows, Joe-Pye Weed is also known as Queen of the Meadow. The root is traditionally used to ease lower back pain and rheumatism. Leaves are sometimes used to break a fever by bringing on intense sweating. Use the root or leaves in teas and tinctures; but do be careful, too much, too often, can be toxic.

We keep Joe-Pye Weed roots in four and eight ounce containers.

INSIDE:

Salves	Page 3
Poultices	Page 2
Mushrooms	Page 4
Wild Edible Plants	Page 2

FIG. 19.1. *A newsletter projecting a light, open feeling.*

Mullein, Every Part Beneficial

The flowers, leaves and roots of this plant are all valuable medicines. Perfect as an antispasmodic, emollient and sedative, mullein is also an astringent. Prepare an infusion of one half cup mullein leaves and flowers to two pints water for most complaints; be sure to strain well. Mullein oil is very useful as a sedative. Simply place a few drops in your tea and sweet dreams. The root is very strong, leaves and flowers less so. Remember to never use the seed of mullein, except to plant. The seeds are very noxious.

We stock all parts of the mullein plant, roots, leaves, flowers, and oil.

Poultices Natural Healing

Poultices are used to treat the outer body. Skin ailments, muscle pain, cuts, burns, even colds and flu. Many herbs can make a natural poultice. The ever popular Mustard Plaster has been used for centuries to treat weakness and fatigue. Burdock is great for gout; cayenne is perfect for a cold or the flu. Of course, you're familiar with the properties of the Aloe plant for burns, but did you know borage, comfrey and plantain are excellent treatments as well? Plantain, by the way, is the best thing for a bee sting, especially when you're caught out in the garden, or the woods. Just chew the leaf for a moment or two and place it on the sting. It draws out the poison and reduces swelling.

Wild Edible Plants

If you like to gather your own plants and roots for cooking, we suggest the following for some of the most exciting dishes ever! Cookbooks of all kinds are available at our store to give you hints and tips on cooking your favorite wild, edible plants.

Fresh young flower buds of the cattail are great when boiled and served with lots of butter. The thick yellow pollen is just like flour when mixed 1/2 and 1/2 with white or wheat flour and used for baking. Peel the young stems to eat raw or cooked like vegetables. Fall roots, boiled like potatoes, taste great, too!

Arrowhead tubers bake, boil, cream or scallop just like potatoes. They are also good boiled then sliced up in salads.

Burdock, found in any meadow, is tasty when simmered and served with butter. Be sure to use two waters to simmer them in and each cooking should be for at least 20 minutes. Burdock leaves, when boiled in two waters, taste like greens. Add a little vinegar and bacon bits before serving. Use the inside of the flower stalks like a vegetable, too. Just boil, again in two waters, and serve with butter. The flower stalk piths, of the burdock plant, boiled with an equal amount of sugar, and a little orange juice make a delicious candy.

For recipes for these and many, many more edible wild plants, see our large selection of cookbooks.

Our Spring Specials

Silver Bark Brand:	**Tinctures:**	**Equipment:**
Chamomile Wash	Spearmint	Drying Racks
Peppermint After-Shave	Lemon Balm	Suribachis
Mugwort Bath Mixture	Cherry Bark	Beeswax
Sage Shampoo	White Pine	Pint Jars
Fennel and Mint Toothpaste	Thyme	Dehydrators

2

FIG. 19.2. Page two of the newsletter.

CHAPTER 19

Producing a Complex Newsletter

Creating Page One

Begin creating this newsletter by setting the margins and page format. To do so, follow these steps:

1. Choose **F**ile, then **N**ew. In the New box, choose **D**ocument. In the **T**emplate box, choose Normal, and then select OK or press Enter.

2. Select Forma**t**, then **D**ocument. Set the **T**op, **L**eft and **R**ight margins to **.75"**, and the **B**ottom margin to **.5"**. Select OK or press Enter.

2. Select Forma**t**, then Page Set**u**p. In Margins, change the **T**op, **L**eft and **R**ight margins to **.75"**; change the **B**ottom margin to **.5"**. Select OK or press Enter.

Newsletter Text

As in previous chapters, you type the information for the newsletters once only, and then copy the text for each subsequent design.

MOUNTAIN SORREL (Enter)

A Quarterly Newsletter of Herbal Curatives (Enter)

and Preventatives (Enter twice)

The Healing Power (Shift+Enter)

of Lavender (Enter)

(Type the paragraphs as they appear in figure 19.1, or type your own data, pressing Enter between each paragraph).

Rosemary, More Than (Shift+Enter)

a Cooking Herb (Enter)

Catnip, Not Just For Cats (Enter)

It's Not Just a Weed (Shift+Enter)

Joe-Pye Weed (Enter)

Mullein, Every Part Beneficial (Enter)

Poultices Natural Healing (Enter)

Wild Edible Plants (Enter)

Our Spring Specials (Enter)

Silver Bark Brand: (Tab) **Tinctures:** (Tab) **Equipment:** (Enter)

Chamomile Wash (Tab) **Spearmint** (Tab) **Drying Racks** (Enter)

Peppermint After-Shave (Tab) **Lemon Balm** (Tab) **Suribachis** (Enter)

Mugwort Bath Mixture (Tab) **Cherry Bark** (Tab) **Beeswax** (Enter)

Sage Shampoo (Tab) **White Pines** (Tab) **Pint Jars** (Enter)

Fennel and Mint Toothpaste (Tab) **Thyme** (Tab) **Dehydrators** (Enter)

Save this file twice, once for the newsletter design of figure 19.1 and once as a textbase for the other newsletter designs in this chapter. Select **F**ile, Save **A**s, save this document as **newbase**, and choose OK. Select **F**ile, Save **A**s and again save this document as **news1**, and choose OK.

Creating the Nameplate

To create the nameplate shown on page one, follow these steps:

1. Select the text MOUNTAIN SORREL. To create the 6-point spaces with rules above it, first use the Ribbon and change this type, temporarily, to 6-point.

2. With this text still selected, click Forma**t**, then click **P**aragraph. In the Spacing box, choose Line and type **.5li**. Move to **B**order and choose Above. Move to Pa**t**tern, choose Thick and select OK or press Enter.

2. With this text still selected, choose Forma**t**, then **P**aragraph. In the Spacing box, for Line Spacing, type **.5li**, and select OK or press Enter. Choose Forma**t**, and then **B**order. In the Border box, choose the margin above or use the down arrow to select. In the **L**ine box, choose the 2.25 rule, and select OK or press Enter.

3. Position the cursor in front of MOUNTAIN SORREL, and press Enter twice.

CHAPTER 19

Producing a Complex Newsletter

4. Position the cursor on the second line. Use the Ruler and indent this line .25 inches on the left. Position the cursor on the third line, and use the Ruler to indent this line .5 inches on the left.

5. Select MOUNTAIN SORREL, and use the Ribbon to change the type to Helv, 48-point, bold, right-aligned.

6. With this text still selected, choose Forma**t**, then **C**haracter. In the Character Spacing box, choose **C**ondensed. In the **B**y: box, type **1pt**, and select OK or press Enter.

6. With this text still selected, choose Forma**t**, then **C**haracter. In the **S**pacing box, choose Condensed. In the **B**y: box, type **1pt**, and select OK or press Enter.

7. Select the two lines of text from A Quarterly... to ...and Preventatives, and use the Ribbon to change the type to 10-point, bold, right-aligned.

8. Position the cursor in *and Preventatives*. Choose Forma**t**, then **P**aragraph. For B**o**rders, choose Below. For Pa**t**tern, choose Thick and select OK or press Enter.

8. Position the cursor in and Preventatives. Choose Forma**t**, then **B**orders. In the Bo**r**der box, choose the bottom margin or use the down arrow to select. In the **L**ine box, choose the 2.25 rule and select OK or press Enter.

9. Use the Ruler and set the left indent for 3.75 inches.

Column One

To create column one of this page, and format the heads and paragraphs for the newsletter, follow these steps:

1. Position the cursor in front of the first head, The Healing Power. Choose **I**nsert, then **B**reak. In the Section Break box, choose Continuous, and then Select OK or press Enter.

2. Choose Forma**t**, then **S**ection. In the Columns box, choose **N**umber and type **2**. Leave the value for **S**pacing at **.5**". In the **S**ection Start box, choose No Break and select OK or press Enter.

2. Choose Forma**t**, then **C**olumn. For **N**umber of Columns, type **2**. Leave **S**pace Between at **.5**". In the **A**pply To box, choose This Point Forward and select OK or press Enter.

PART V

Creating Newsletters

3. Select The Healing Power of Lavender, and use the Ribbon to change the type to 18-point, right-aligned.

4. With this text still selected, choose Forma**t**, then **P**aragraph. In the Spacing box, choose **A**fter, type **.5li**, and select OK or press Enter.

5. With this text still selected, choose Forma**t**, then Styles. In the Style Name box, type **Right Head** and select OK or press Enter. When asked whether you want to define the style based on the selection, answer **Y**es.

4. With the text still selected, choose Forma**t**, then **P**aragraph. In the Spacing box, choose Aft**e**r, type **.5li**, and select OK or press Enter.

5. With the text still selected, choose Forma**t**, then Styles. In the Style Name box, type **Right Head** and select OK or press Enter.

6. Select the first paragraph of body text, `Everyone knows of the delicious...` Choose Format, then Styles. In the St**y**le Name box, type **body text**, and click **D**efine.

7. Choose **C**haracter, in the Character dialog box, move to Font, choose 12 point, and select OK or press Enter.

8. In the Styles dialog box, choose **P**aragraph. In the Alignment box, choose **J**ustified. In the Spacing box, choose **A**fter, type **1li** and select OK or press Enter.

8. In the Style dialog box, choose **P**aragraph. In the Alignment box, choose Justified. In the Spacing box, choose Aft**e**r, type **1li** and select OK or press Enter.

9. Choose all body text on both pages of the document. Use the Ribbon, in the Style box, to change the selected type to body text, then hyphenate it.

10. Choose each head, `Rosemary, More Than...,Catnip, Not Just..., It's Not Just a Weed..., Mullein..., Poultices...,` and `Wild Edible....` On the Ribbon, in the Style box, change each head to a right head.

11. Select the letter `E` in `Everyone knows ...` in the paragraph following the head, `The Healing Power of Lavender`, and use the Ribbon to change the letter to 18-point, bold. Repeat this procedure for the first letter in each paragraph following a head.

CHAPTER 19

Producing a Complex Newsletter

12. At the end of the first column of the first page, position the cursor at the end of the line of type `...don't dare delay!`. Choose **I**nsert, **B**reak, choose **C**olumn Break and select OK or press Enter.

Column Two

To complete column two of the first page of this newsletter, follow these steps:

1. Check to ensure the two column heads are even. Position the cursor at the end of the second column, after the line `We keep Joe-Pye Weed roots in four and eight ounce containers.`

    (Enter, Enter) **INSIDE** (Enter)

    Salves (Tab) (space bar) **Page 3** (Enter)

    Poultices (Tab) (space bar) **Page 2** (Enter)

    Mushrooms (Tab) (space bar) **Page 4** (Enter)

    Wild Edible Plants (Tab) (space bar) **Page 2** (Enter)

2. Position the cursor on the paragraph return above `INSIDE`. Click Forma**t**, then click **P**aragraph. For **B**orders, choose Above. For Pat**t**ern, choose Thick and select OK or press Enter.

2. Position the cursor on the paragraph return above `INSIDE`. Select Forma**t**, then **B**order. In the B**o**rder box, select the top margin. In the **L**ine box, choose the 2.25 rule and select OK or press Enter.

3. Select `INSIDE` and use the Ribbon to change the type to Helv, bold, center-aligned.

4. With this text still selected, click Forma**t**, then choose **P**aragraph. In the Spacing box, choose **A**fter, type **4pt**, and select OK or press Enter.

4. With this text still selected, choose Forma**t**, then **P**aragraph. In the Spacing box, choose Af**t**er, type **4pt** and select OK or press Enter.

5. Select the next five lines of type from `Salves` to the paragraph return following `Wild Edible Plants`. Choose Forma**t**, then

485

PART V

Creating Newsletters

Paragraph. In the Spacing box, choose **A**fter and type **0**, then choose **B**efore and type **3pt**. Select OK or press Enter.

5. Select the next five lines of type, from `Salves` to the paragraph return below `Wild Edible Plants`. Choose Forma**t**, then **P**aragraph. In the Spacing box, choose Af**t**er and type **0**, then choose **B**efore and type **3pt**. Select OK or press Enter.

6. With this text still selected, choose Forma**t**, then **T**abs. In the **T**ab Position box, type **3"**, and choose **R**ight-aligned. In the Leader box, choose 2, **S**et, and select OK or press Enter.

7. With this text still selected, use the Ruler and set the indent to .25 inches.

8. Position the cursor on the last paragraph return. Choose Forma**t**, then **P**aragraph. For B**o**rder, choose Below. For Pa**t**tern, choose Thick and select OK or press Enter.

8. Position the cursor on the last paragraph return. Choose Forma**t**, then **B**order. In the Bo**r**der box, click the bottom margin or use the down arrow to select. In the **L**ine box, choose the 2.25 rule and select OK or press Enter.

9. Choose Insert, then **B**reak. In the Section Break box, choose Con**t**inuous and select OK or press Enter.

Creating Page Two

To complete page two of this newsletter, follow these steps:

1. At the top of the second page, position the cursor in front of `Mullein...` Be sure that there is an empty paragraph return above the head, `Mullein...` Choose Insert, then **B**reak. In the Section Break box, choose Continuous and select OK or press Enter. Position the cursor on the first paragraph return on the page.

2. Choose Forma**t**, then **S**ection. In the Columns box, choose **N**umber, type **1** and select OK or press Enter.

2. Choose Format, then **C**olumns. For **N**umber of Columns, type **1** and select OK or press Enter.

3. With the cursor in position (still in the first paragraph return on the page), type **dddd**. Select *dddd* and use the Ribbon to change the type to 6-point.

CHAPTER 19

Producing a Complex Newsletter

4. With this text still selected, choose Forma**t**, then **P**aragraph. In the Spacing box, choose Line, type **.5li** and select OK or press Enter. Press Enter twice, and then delete the text `dddd`.

   Creating a small space such as this in Word is difficult unless something is first typed onto the line. Using this procedure, you create a smaller space between lines than Word usually permits.

5. Select the three blank lines just created. Choose Forma**t**, then **P**aragraph. For **B**order, choose Above. For **P**attern, choose Thick and select OK or press Enter. Use the Ruler to set the left indent of the second line to .25" and the left indent of the third line to .5".

5. Select the three blank lines just created. Click Forma**t**, then click **B**order. In the Bo**r**der box, click the top margin. In the **L**ine box, choose the 2.25 rule and select OK or press Enter. Use the Ruler to set the left indent of the second line to .25 inches and the left indent of the third line to .5 inches.

6. Position the cursor at the end of the story, `Poultices...`, after the line `It draws out the poison and reduces swelling`. Choose Insert, **B**reak, choose **C**olumn Break and select OK or press Enter.

Finishing Page Two

To create the second column of page two, format the head, body, and large first character as in previous steps. To change section formatting for `Our Spring Specials`, follow these steps:

1. Position the cursor at the end of the second column, `...large selection of cookbooks`. Click Insert, then click **B**reak. In the Section Break box, choose Co**n**tinuous and select OK or press Enter.

2. Click Forma**t**, then click **S**ection. In the Columns box, choose **N**umber, type **1** and select OK or press Enter.

2. Select Forma**t**, then **C**olumns. For **N**umber of Columns, type **1** and select OK or press Enter.

3. Select `Our Spring Specials`, and temporarily change the type to 6 point. Position the cursor in front of the word `Our...` and press Enter. Move the cursor up one line.

4. Choose Forma**t**, then **P**aragraph. For **Bo**rder, choose Above. For **P**att**e**rn, choose Thick and select OK or press Enter.

4. Select Forma**t**, then **B**order. In the Bo**r**der box, choose the top margin. In the Line box, choose the 2.25 rule and select OK or press Enter.

5. Select Our Spring Specials and use the Ribbon to change the type to 18-point, center-aligned.

6. Select the text from Silver Bark Brand: to Dehydrators. Use the Ruler to set the tabs at 3 inches and 5.25 inches, left-aligned. Also on the Ruler, indent the beginning of these lines to .25 inches.

7. Position the cursor on the last paragraph return. Type **2**, select the type and change it to 6-point. Position the cursor in front of the 2 and press Enter.

8. Select the **2** and use the Ribbon to change it to 12 point. Add a border, thick for version 1.1 or a 2.25 rule for version 2.0, above it.

Save and Print

To save this newsletter, click **F**ile, and click **S**ave.

To print this newsletter, click **F**ile, click **P**rint, and select OK or press Enter.

Creating a Newsletter with a Page Border

The next design, shown in figures 19.3 and 19.4, applies graphic boxes and lines to the page. The box surrounds all type and the graphic rules further divide the information on the page. The graphic box, once created, repeats on every page of the newsletter. The box, in addition to the left-aligned heads and body text, creates interesting white space.

The first column of each page of this design uses a few sentences describing the essence of the stories, set in large italic type. The purpose of this short and easy-to-read text is to catch the interest of the reader. This text is not a callout; however, this first column

CHAPTER 19

Producing a Complex Newsletter

is a perfect spot for a callout. Just find an interesting statement within the text—something that will draw your reader—and place it in a format such as this. The first column is divided from the rest of the text with a vertical rule.

Notice the layouts of both page one, a right-hand page, and page two, a left-hand page, are exactly the same. That is, the first column of page one is not mirrored as the third column on the facing page, but appears as the first column on both pages. In this case, keeping the large text column on the left side of the page works best because the left-aligned text leads the eye into the middle column. Furthermore, the information in the first column is really designed to lead the reader into the middle and right-hand columns.

This design does not use jumplines. When your story continues in a logical manner, you don't need a jumpline. When, however, your story "jumps" two or three pages ahead, use jumplines to guide the reader. Similarly, you don't always need page numbers or a header or footer. Short newsletters, two or four pages in length, almost never use a header or footer. When your newsletter is eight pages or more, at least number the pages. When you use jumplines, or refer to a story or illustration within the document, page numbers are necessary.

To create this newsletter, complete the following steps:

1. Choose **F**ile, then **O**pen. Open the document *newbase*. Choose **F**ile, then Save **A**s and save this file as **news2**. Select OK or press Enter.

2. The margins were set in the original document at .75 inches; however, Choose Forma**t**, **D**ocument, place a minus sign in front of the **T**op margin, and select OK or press Enter.

3. Select **E**dit, then **H**eader/Footer. Choose Header and select OK or press Enter.

4. Click Forma**t**, then click **P**aragraph. For **B**order, choose box. For Patt**e**rn, choose Thick.

5. While still in the **P**aragraph dialog box, move to the Spacing box, choose Line, type **60li**, and select OK or press Enter.

2. The margins were set in the original document at .75 inches; however, Choose Forma**t**, Page Set**u**p, place a minus sign in front of the **T**op margin, and select OK or press Enter.

489

MOUNTAIN SORREL

A Quarterly Newsletter of Herbal Curatives and Preventatives

The North American Indians used many herbs and plants to promote health and vitality, to heal the afflicted, to strengthen the weak . . . Using common weeds, plants from the meadows, forests, and river's edge, the Indians created magnificent curative concoctions. Now, you can learn the Indian's secrets . . . the power of natural healing.

THE HEALING POWER OF LAVENDER

Everyone knows of the delicious fragrance of lavender, especially English lavender, but few know of its medicinal qualities. Any of the three species of lavender make wonderful potions. A terrific calmative, lavender has the power to soothe headaches and nervous tension. Simply steep lavender flowers in hot water for 15 to 20 minutes, and sip a cupful of the tea two or three times during the day.

A stronger tea of lavender is good as a gargle for sore throats; it also relieves stomach aches and colic. We stock dried English and French lavenders in bunches and one pound bags, at a reasonable price. We also sell lavender oil extract for use as a medicinal oil.

ROSEMARY, MORE THAN A COOKING HERB

Both the leaves and flowers of rosemary have been used to alleviate depression and insomnia. A simple rosemary tea, with a bit of ginger added, also comforts a nervous or upset stomach. Rosemary oil is widely known for its antibacterial properties, as well. Lastly, if you have dark hair, try a strong rosemary tea for a rinse after washing. It not only makes your hair shiny and soft, but it clears up your dandruff, too.

We stock a full supply of rosemary leaves, flowers, oil and our special home-made rosemary shampoo and rinses.

CATNIP, NOT JUST FOR CATS

A member of the mint family, catnip contains many properties other mints do. As a pleasant tasting tea, catnip is an antispasmodic and a calmative. Treat stomach ailments, colic and intestinal complaints. Catnip calms nervousness and anxiety. Having a sleepless night? Try some catnip tea. If you have a cat, though, watch out, he'll try to drink your tea, too!

We stock catnip in one-half and one pound cans, as well as seeds to start your own plants in your garden.

FIG. 19.3. A newsletter with a graphic box around the page.

Joe-Pye Weed was named after a New England Indian, Joe Pye, who used it to treat typhus. North American Indians also used Queen of the Meadow as a diuretic, to treat kidney and bladder stones. The flowers, which bloom from August to September, range from white to deep purple in color. Use both the flowers and the rootstock of this magnificent herb as a tonic, diuretic, and as an astringent.

IT'S NOT JUST A WEED, JOE-PYE WEED

Often seen growing along the railroad tracks or roadsides, in fields and meadows, Joe-Pye Weed is also known as Queen of the Meadow. The root is traditionally used to ease lower back pain and rheumatism. Leaves are sometimes used to break a fever by bringing on intense sweating. Use the root or leaves in teas and tinctures; but do be careful, too much, too often, can be toxic.

We keep Joe-Pye Weed roots in four and eight ounce containers.

MULLEIN, EVERY PART BENEFICIAL

The flowers, leaves and roots of this plant are all valuable medicines. Perfect as an antispasmodic, emollient and sedative, mullein is also an astringent. Prepare an infusion of one half cup mullein leaves and flowers to two pints water for most complaints; be sure to strain well. Mullein oil is very useful as a sedative. Simply place a few drops in your tea and sweet dreams. The root is very strong, leaves and flowers less so. Remember to never use the seed of mullein, except to plant. The seeds are very noxious.

We stock all parts of the mullein plant, roots, leaves, flowers, and oil.

POULTICES, NATURAL HEALING

Poultices are used to treat the outer body. Skin ailments, muscle pain, cuts, burns, even colds and flu. Many herbs can make a natural poultice. The ever popular Mustard Plaster has been used for centuries to treat weakness and fatigue. Burdock is great for gout; cayenne is perfect for a cold or the flu. Of course, you're familiar with the properties of the Aloe plant for burns, but did you know borage, comfrey and plantain are excellent treatments as well? Plantain, by the way, is the best thing for a bee sting, especially when you're caught out in the garden, or the woods. Just chew the leaf for a moment or two and place it on the sting. It draws out the poison and reduces swelling.

WILD EDIBLE PLANTS

If you like to gather your own plants and roots for cooking, we suggest the following for some of the most exciting dishes ever! Cookbooks of all kinds are available at our store to give you hints and tips on cooking

FIG. 19.4. Page two of the newsletter.

PART V

Creating Newsletters

3. Choose **V**iew, then **H**eader/Footer. Choose Header and select OK or press Enter.

4. Select Forma**t**, then **B**order. In the Preset box, choose **B**ox. In the **L**ine box, choose the 3-point rule and select OK or press Enter.

5. Choose Forma**t**, then **P**aragraph. In the Spacing box, move to **L**ine Spacing and choose Exactly. In the **A**t: box, type **60li** and select OK or press Enter. If you're in Normal view, **C**lose the Header pane.

6. Select MOUNTAIN SORREL and use the Ribbon to change the type to 40-point, bold, center-aligned.

7. Select only the M in MOUNTAIN and use the Ribbon to change this letter to 56-point, Subscript (the equal sign). Repeat with the S in SORREL.

7. Select only the M in MOUNTAIN and use the Ribbon to change this letter to 56-point. Click Forma**t**, then choose Character. For Super/Subscript, choose Subscript and select OK or press Enter. Repeat with the S in SORREL.

8. Select A Quarterly Newsletter... and use the Ribbon to change the type to Helvetica, 10-point, centered.

9. With this text still selected, choose Forma**t**, then **P**aragraph. For **B**order, choose Below. For **P**attern, choose Single and select OK or press Enter.

9. With this text selected, choose Forma**t**, then **B**order. In the Bo**r**der box, click the bottom margin or press the down arrow to select. In the Line box, choose the 1.25 rule and select OK or press Enter.

10. Position the cursor in front of *The Healing Power...* Choose Insert, then **B**reak. In the Section Break box, choose Continuous and select OK or press Enter.

11. Choose Forma**t**, then **S**ection. In the Columns box, choose **N**umber, type **3** and select OK or press Enter.

11. Choose Forma**t**, then **C**olumns. For **N**umber of Columns, type **3** and select OK or press Enter.

12. With the cursor still positioned in front of The Healing Power..., choose Insert, then **B**reak. Choose Column Break and select OK or press Enter.

CHAPTER 19

Producing a Complex Newsletter

13. Reposition the cursor in the first column and type the following, pressing Enter and Shift+Enter where indicated:

    (Enter, Enter) **The North American** (Shift+Enter)

    Indians used many (Shift+Enter)

    herbs and plants to (Shift+Enter)

    promote health and (Shift+Enter)

    vitality, to heal (Shift+Enter)

    the afflicted, (Shift+Enter)

    to strengthen (Shift+Enter)

    the weak . . . (Shift+Enter. Leave a space between each of the continuation periods)

    Using common weeds, (Shift+Enter)

    plants from the (Shift+Enter)

    meadows, forests, (Shift+Enter)

    and river's edge, (Shift+Enter)

    the Indians created (Shift+Enter)

    magnificent curative (Shift+Enter)

    concoctions. (Shift+Enter)

    Now, you can (Shift+Enter)

    learn the Indian's (Shift+Enter)

    secrets . . . (Shift+Enter. Leave a space between each of the continuation periods)

    the power of (Shift+Enter)

    natural healing.

14. Select the entire column of text and use the Ribbon to change the type to 14-point, italic.

15. With this text still selected, choose Forma**t**, then **P**aragraph. In the Spacing box, choose Line and type **2li**. In the Indents box, choose From **L**eft, type **.2"** and select OK or press Enter.

15. With this text still selected, click Forma**t**, then choose **P**aragraph. For Line Spacing, choose Double. For Indentation, choose From **L**eft, type **.2"** and select OK or press Enter.

493

PART V

Creating Newsletters

16. Select `The Healing Power....` Press Shift+F3 twice to change the type to all caps. Repeat these steps for all heads on both pages.

17. Again, select `The Healing Power...` and use the Ribbon to change the type to 14 point, bold, left-aligned. Choose Forma**t**, then **S**tyles. In the **S**tyle **N**ame box, type **head** and select OK or press Enter.

    When Word 1.1 asks whether you want to define the head style based on the selection, answer **Y**es.

18. Select the first paragraph of body text, `Everyone knows ...` and change the type to 12-point, left-aligned. Click Forma**t**, then choose **P**aragraph. In the Spacing box, choose **B**efore, type **1li** and select OK or press Enter.

19. With this text still selected, choose Forma**t**, then **S**tyles. In the **S**tyle **N**ame box, type **body** and select OK or press Enter.

    When Word 1.1 asks whether you want to define the head style based on the selection. Answer **Y**es.

20. Select the remainder of the text in this document and use the Ribbon, in the Style box, to change the type to body. Manually hyphenate any extremely short lines by positioning the cursor and pressing Ctrl+hyphen.

21. Select each head and use the Ribbon, in the Style box, to change each head. Press Shift+Enter to manually break the lines of the heads as shown in figures 19.3 and 19.4. Check to ensure that the heads and the body text at the tops of the columns are even.

22. Select the middle column of text. Click Forma**t**, then click **P**aragraph. For **B**order, choose Bar. For Pat**t**ern, choose Single and select OK or press Enter.

    With Word 1.1, you can't adjust the space between the bar and the text without using tabs. Because of this, the Word 1.1 version looks different than the figures here, which were created in Version 2.0.

22. Select the middle column of text. Choose Forma**t**, then **B**order. In the B**o**rder box, click the left margin or press the down arrow to select. For **F**rom Text, type **10pt**. For Line, choose the 1.25 rule and select OK or press Enter.

CHAPTER 19

Producing a Complex Newsletter

23. At the end of the story `ROSEMARY...`, delete the last two sentences, from `Our supplies are limited...` to `...don't dare delay!`.

> **NOTE**
>
> Editing to make stories fit, or look better, during layout is quite common. Do this only if you're the author, or the author has given you permission to do so.

24. At the end of the story `CATNIP...`, position the cursor at the end of the last line, `...seeds to start your own plants in your garden.` Choose **Insert**, then **Break**. Choose **Column** and select OK or press Enter.

25. At the top of page two, position the cursor in front of `IT'S NOT JUST A WEED....` Choose **Insert**, then **Break**. Choose **Column Break** and select OK or press Enter.

26. Position the cursor in the first column and type the following, pressing Enter and Shift+Enter where indicated.

    (Enter, Enter) **Joe-Pye Weed** (Shift+Enter)

    was named after (Shift+Enter)

    a New England (Shift+Enter)

    Indian, Joe Pye, (Shift+Enter)

    who used it to (Shift+Enter)

    treat typhus. (Shift+Enter)

    North American (Shift+Enter)

    Indians also used (Shift+Enter)

    Queen of the Meadow (Shift+Enter)

    as a diuretic, to (Shift+Enter)

    treat kidney and (Shift+Enter)

    bladder stones. (Shift+Enter)

    The flowers, which (Shift+Enter)

PART V

Creating Newsletters

bloom from August (Shift+Enter)

to September, range (Shift+Enter)

from white to deep (Shift+Enter)

purple in color. (Shift+Enter)

Use both the (Shift+Enter)

flowers and the (Shift+Enter)

rootstock of this (Shift+Enter)

magnificent herb as a (Shift+Enter)

tonic, diuretic, and as (Shift+Enter)

an astringent.

27. Select this first column of text and use the Ribbon to change the type to 14-point, italic.

28. With this text still selected, choose Format, then Paragraph. In the Spacing box, choose Line and type **2li**. In the Indents box, choose From Left, type **.2"** and select OK or press Enter.

29. Select the middle column of text. Choose Format, then Paragraph. For Border, choose Bar. For Pattern, choose Single.

28. With this text still selected, choose Format, then Paragraph. For Line Spacing, choose Double. For Indentation, choose From Left, type **.2"** and select OK or press Enter.

29. Select the middle column of type. Choose Format, then Border. In the Border box, click the left margin or press the down arrow. For From Text, type **10pt**. For In Line, choose the 1.25 rule and select OK or press Enter.

30. Check to ensure the tops of the second and third columns are even.

31. To save the newsletter, choose File, then Save.

32. To print the newsletter, File, Print and select OK or press Enter.

CHAPTER 19

Producing a Complex Newsletter

Creating an Innovative Newsletter with Tables

The newsletter shown in figure 19.5 is unusual because the design incorporates two uneven columns of type. Using Word's table feature, you can vary the column widths for a more unique document.

The justified body text and centered heads create a clean, ordered look to the document. Graphic boxes and rules act to emphasize certain portions of the newsletter.

This design also has a header which includes page numbers, the title of the newsletter, and the date. The header could contain other information, depending on your newsletter and personal preferences. The layout of the header is designed to change with left and right pages.

A masthead identifies key people and provides facts about the newsletter. Mastheads are usually in smaller type, boxed, sometimes screened, and customarily placed on page two of the newsletter. This design, created in Version 2.0, screens the mastheads. Although you cannot screen in Version 1.1 of Word, the box may suffice; if not, have your print shop do the screen.

In this newsletter, tables are used to create the columns. When you use tables, you may either convert text to table or insert text into a table. These instructions apply the latter option for two reasons. First, your text is already typed in a format not readily converted into a table; second, inserting text into a table is easier, and this design gives you the experience of switching windows and documents in Word.

To begin creating this newsletter, set the margins by following these steps:

1. Select **F**ile, then **O**pen. Open the file NEWBASE.DOC to use with this document.

2. Choose **F**ile, then **N**ew. In the New box, choose **D**ocument. In the **T**emplate box, choose Normal, and then select OK or press Enter.

497

MOUNTAIN SORREL

A Quarterly Newsletter of Herbal Curatives and Preventatives

The Healing Power of Lavender

Everyone knows of the delicious fragrance of lavender, especially English lavender, but few know of its medicinal qualities. Any of the three species of lavender make wonderful potions. A terrific calmative, lavender has the power to soothe headaches and nervous tension. Simply steep lavender flowers in hot water for 15 to 20 minutes, and sip a cupful of the tea two or three times during the day.

A stronger tea of lavender is good as a gargle for sore throats; it also relieves stomach aches and colic. We stock dried English and French lavenders in bunches and one pound bags, at a reasonable price. We also sell lavender oil extract for use as a medicinal oil.

Rosemary, More Than a Cooking Herb

Both the leaves and flowers of rosemary have been used to alleviate depression and insomnia. A simple rosemary tea, with a bit of ginger added, also comforts a nervous or upset stomach. Rosemary oil is widely known for its antibacterial properties, as well. Lastly, if you have dark hair, try a strong rosemary tea for a rinse after washing. It not only makes your hair shiny and soft, but it clears up your dandruff, too.

We stock a full supply of rosemary leaves, flowers, oil and our special home-made rosemary shampoo and rinses.

Catnip, Not Just For Cats

A member of the mint family, catnip contains many properties other mints do. As a pleasant tasting tea, catnip is an antispasmodic and a calmative. Treat stomach ailments, colic and intestinal complaints. Catnip calms nervousness and anxiety. Having a sleepless night? Try some catnip tea. If you have a cat, though, watch out, he'll try to drink your tea, too!

We stock catnip in one-half and one pound cans, as well as seeds to start your own plants in your garden.

It's Not Just a Weed, Joe-Pye Weed

Often seen growing along the railroad tracks or roadsides, in fields and meadows, Joe-Pye Weed is also known as Queen of the Meadow. The root is traditionally used to ease lower back pain and rheumatism. Leaves are sometimes used to break a fever by bringing on intense sweating. Use the root or leaves in teas and tinctures; but do be careful, too much, too often, can be toxic.

We keep Joe-Pye Weed roots in four and eight ounce containers.

Mullein, Every Part Beneficial

The flowers, leaves and roots of this plant are all valuable medicines. Perfect as an antispasmodic, emollient and sedative, mullein is also an astringent. Prepare an infusion of one half cup mullein leaves and flowers to two pints water for most complaints; be sure to strain well. Mullein oil is very useful as a sedative. Simply place a few drops in your tea and sweet dreams. The root is very strong, leaves and flowers less so. Remember to never use the seed of mullein, except to plant. The seeds are very noxious.

We stock all parts of the mullein plant, roots, leaves, flowers, and oil.

CALL TOLL FREE 1-800-099-8903

FIG. 19.5. *A newsletter designed using Word's table feature.*

Poultices, Natural Healing

Poultices are used to treat the outer body. Skin ailments, muscle pain, cuts, burns, even colds and flu. Many herbs can make a natural poultice. The ever popular Mustard Plaster has been used for centuries to treat weakness and fatigue. Burdock is great for gout; cayenne is perfect for a cold or the flu. Of course, you're familiar with the properties of the Aloe plant for burns, but did you know borage, comfrey and plantain are excellent treatments as well? Plantain, by the way, is the best thing for a bee sting, especially when you're caught out in the garden, or the woods. Just chew the leaf for a moment or two and place it on the sting. It draws out the poison and reduces swelling.

MOUNTAIN SORREL
Published Quarterly
Volume 9, Issue No. 2

Editor .... S. H. Schwimmer
Circulation Editor .... J. J. Rubel
Advertising Editor .... D. M. Herr

MOUNTAIN SORREL is the official publication of Silver Bark's Herbal Remedies and Book Store. Subscriptions to customers are free with purchase of yearly catalog at $7.95.

Orders for any product in this newsletter are welcomed by mail, phone, or in person. We do not guarantee our products, recipes or any advice in this newsletter as a medication or cure. We take no responsibility for misuse of any product we sell.

Wild Edible Plants

If you like to gather your own plants and roots for cooking, we suggest the following for some of the most exciting dishes ever! Cookbooks of all kinds are available at our store to give you hints and tips on cooking your favorite wild, edible plants.

Fresh young flower buds of the **cattail** are great when boiled and served with lots of butter. The thick yellow pollen is just like flour when mixed 1/2 and 1/2 with white or wheat flour and used for baking. Peel the young stems to eat raw or cooked like vegetables. Fall roots, boiled like potatoes, taste great, too!

Arrowhead tubers bake, boil, cream or scallop just like potatoes. They are also good boiled then sliced up in salads.

Burdock, found in any meadow, is tasty when simmered and served with butter. Be sure to use two waters to simmer them in and each cooking should be for at least 20 minutes. Burdock leaves, when boiled in two waters, taste like greens. Add a little vinegar and bacon bits before serving. Use the inside of the flower stalks like a vegetable, too. Just boil, again in two waters, and serve with butter. The flower stalk piths, of the burdock plant, boiled with an equal amount of sugar, and a little orange juice make a delicious candy.

For recipes for these and many, many more edible wild plants, see our large selection of cookbooks.

We also forage plants weekly for the freshest leaves, flowers, and roots.

Salves For Your Skin

Salves made from olive oil, beeswax and concentrated amounts of roots, leaves and flowers are the best medicines for skin irritations. All natural and pure, no preservatives or chemicals, our salves are the best around! Listed here are only a few of the salves we stock.

Chickweed	skin rashes, soothe itching
Calendula	insect bites, rashes
Comfrey	bee stings, burns
Plantain	bee stings, itches
Green Elder	cuts, bruises
Sage	sore muscles
Beech	blisters, swelling
Aloe	any skin problem
Mint Mixture	soothing and cooling

FIG. 19.6. Page two of the newsletter.

SPRING 1992　　　　　　　MOUNTAIN SORREL　　　　　　　3

TERRY MILFORT-HALE HERBALIST VISITS OUR STORE

Terry Milfort-Hale, an expert herbalist who's studied in Wyoming, Texas, West Virginia, North Carolina, and many other states visits our store on Friday, June 12, 1992. From 2:00 p.m. to 4:00 p.m., Terry will lecture on herbs and plants found in our area of the state.

Terry, who lives in Houston, lectures around the country about edible wild plants and herbs. She's world-famous for her tinctures, salves, oils and other herbal concoctions. Terry and her husband, John, have traveled throughout the US; she in search of unusual herbs; he in search of music. While both Terry and John play music, John is the more entranced of the two. Perhaps we can convince him to favor us with a bagpipe tune during their visit.

We're honored to have both Terry and John at our store for one day only. Don't miss your chance to discuss your herb garden and adventures with Terry!!! We'll also be selling Terry's latest best seller, *John and Terry's Garden*, as well as her other three books, and some of her favorite concoctions.

NEW!!!

STRAINED MUSCLES
BRUISES
ALL NATURAL
ALL HEALING

ORDER TODAY!!
Just $12.95
8 oz. jar

BAY AND EUCALYPTUS MASSAGE OIL

Herbal Terms

Infusion

An infusion is much like a tea, however, you actually boil the plant first, then steep it. Use 1 oz. or so of the herb (flower or leaves) to a pint of water. Bring the water and plant to a boil, then remove from heat and steep for at least 10 minutes. You may add honey or sugar while hot. Then cool to lukewarm before drinking.

Decoction

Similar to an infusion, decoction is used with the roots of the plant. Since they are hard, you must boil them for at least 10 minutes, then steep for 10 minutes more. Use 1 cup root to 1 pint water.

Arthritis

Many plants are suited for the pains of arthritis. Try infusions or decoctions of horseradish, black elder, chickweed, comfrey, drop wart and shave grass.

Make an arthritis liniment of yerba santa and wintergreen. Or try a poultice of cayenne, lobelia, mullein and slippery elm bark. We have recipes for all of the above.

Our Spring Specials

Silver Bark Brand:
Chamomile Wash
Peppermint After-Shave
Mugwort Bath Mixture
Sage Shampoo
Fennel and Mint Toothpaste
Natural Insect Repellent

Tinctures:
Spearmint
Lemon Balm
Cherry Bark
White Pine
Thyme
Anise

Equipment:
Drying Racks
Suribachis
Beeswax
Pint Jars
Dehydrators
2 oz. jars

FIG. 19.7. Page three of the newsletter.

CHAPTER 19

Producing a Complex Newsletter

3. Click File, then Save As. Save the document as **news3**, and select OK or press Enter. You now have two document windows open, *newbase* and *news3*.

4. Choose Format, then Document. In the Margins box, set the Left and Right margins at **.5"**, the Top margin at **.4"**, and the Bottom margin at **.2"**. Select OK or press Enter.

4. Choose Format, then Page Setup. In Margins, set the Left and Right margins at **.5"**, the Top margin at **.4"**, and the Bottom at **.2"**. Select OK or press Enter.

Creating the Nameplate

The first task for this newsletter is creating the nameplate at the top of page one. To create the nameplate, do the following:

1. Choose the control button to the left of the Menu bar. Choose Next Window to display the document NEWBASE.DOC.

> **NOTE**
>
> The keyboard shortcut for Next Window is Ctrl+F6. Use either the menu or shortcut key when directed to switch windows.

2. Select MOUNTAIN SORREL, and A Quarterly Newsletter... Choose Edit, then Cut, or press Shift+Delete (Ctrl+X in Version 2.0). Switch windows to return to news3.

3. Position the cursor in the new document, and press Enter five times. Move the cursor to the second paragraph return, click Edit and click Paste, or press Shift+Insert (Ctrl+V in Version 2.0).

4. Select MOUNTAIN SORREL use the Ribbon and change the type to 48-point, bold, center-aligned.

5. With the MOUNTAIN SORREL shell selected, choose Format, then Character. In the Character Spacing box, choose Condensed. For By:, type **1pt** and select OK or press Enter.

501

5. With MOUNTAIN SORREL still selected, choose Forma**t**, then **C**haracter. In the **S**pacing box, choose Condensed. For **B**y:, type **1pt** and select OK or press Enter.

6. Select only the M and use the Ribbon to change the letter to 62-point, or as close as is possible with your printer. Repeat with the S.

7. Select the lines from the first paragraph return to the paragraph return after MOUNTAIN SORREL. Click Forma**t**, then click **P**aragraph. For **B**order, choose box. For **Pa**tt**e**rn, choose Shadow and select OK or press Enter.

Border thicknesses can't be varied in Version 1.1, so your box will not look as thick as the figure created in Version 2.0.

7. Select the lines from the first paragraph return to the paragraph return after MOUNTAIN SORREL. Choose Forma**t**, then **B**order. In the Preset box, choose **S**hadow. In the **L**ine box, choose the 3-point rule and choose OK.

8. Select A Quarterly... and use the Ribbon to change the type to 12-point, bold, italic, center-aligned.

9. With this text selected, click Forma**t**, then choose **P**aragraph. For **B**order, choose Below. For **Pa**tt**e**rn, choose Thick and select OK or press Enter.

9. With this text selected, click Forma**t**, then click **B**order. In Bo**r**der, click the bottom margin or press the down arrow. In **L**ine, choose the 1.25 rule and select OK or press Enter.

Inserting Text into Tables

The two-column text layout on page one is created by inserting text into a table, and then setting the style format for the headings and body text of the newsletter. To create the table, insert the text, and format the text styles, follow these steps:

1. Position the cursor on the second paragraph return after A Quarterly.... Choose **I**nsert, then **T**able. For Number of **C**olumns type **2**. For Number of **R**ows, type **1**. Select OK or press Enter.

2. Select the table, choose Forma**t**, then **T**able. In **S**pace Between Cols box, type **.3"** and select OK or press Enter.

CHAPTER 19

Producing a Complex Newsletter

2. Position the cursor on the second paragraph return after A Quarterly.... Choose Table, then Insert Table. For Number of Columns, type 2. For Number of Rows, type 1. Select OK or press Enter.

3. Select the table. Choose Table, then Column Width. For Space between Cols, type .3" and select OK or press Enter.

4. Select the first column. Choose Format, then Table. In the Width of Column 1 box, type 4.5". Choose Next Column and set Column 2 for 2.25". Select OK or press Enter.

4. With the table selected, use the Ruler and change the width of the first column to 4 1/2". Change the width of the second column to 2 1/4" by moving the marker to 7 1/2".

5. Switch windows and return to the original document. Select the text from The Healing Power... to the end of the Catnip story, ...to start your own plants in your garden. Choose Edit, then Cut, or press Shift+Delete (Ctrl+X in Version 2.0). Switch windows.

6. Position the cursor in the first column of the table. Choose Edit then Paste, or press Shift+Insert (Ctrl+V in Version 2.0).

7. Switch windows and select the text from It's Not Just a Weed... to the end of the Mullein story, We stock all parts of the mullein plant, roots, leaves, flowers, and oil. Choose Edit, then Cut, or Press Shift+Delete (Ctrl+X in Version 2.0). Switch windows.

8. Position the cursor in the second column of the table. Choose Edit, then Paste, or press Shift+Insert (Ctrl+V in Version 2.0).

9. Select The Healing Power of... in the first column and use the Ribbon to change the type to Helv, 18-point, bold, italic.

10. With this text still selected, Choose Format, then Paragraph. In the Spacing box, choose After, type .5li and select OK or press Enter.

10. With this text still selected, select Format, then Paragraph. In the Spacing box, choose After, type .5li and select OK or press Enter.

PART V

Creating Newsletters

11. With the text still selected, select Forma**t**, then Styles. In the Style Name box, type **head** and select OK or press Enter.

    When Word 1.1 asks whether you want to define the head style based on the selection, answer **Yes**.

12. Select the first paragraph of body text and use the Ribbon to change the type to 12-point, justified. Use the Ruler and indent the first line .25 inches.

13. With this text still selected, select Forma**t**, then Styles. In the Style Name box, type **body** and select OK or press Enter.

    When Word 1.1 asks whether you want to define the head style based on the selection, answer **Yes**.

14. Select all the remaining text in the table and use the Style box on the Ribbon to change to body text.

15. Individually select each of the heads in the two columns of text and use the Style box to change each head to the head style. Press Shift+Enter to break the lines of the heads so they appear as shown in figure 19.5.

16. At the end of the Rosemary story, delete the lines of text from Our supplies are limited... to ...don't dare delay!.

17. Select all text in the two columns. Choose Utilities, **H**yphenate and select OK or press Enter.

17. Select all text in the two columns. Choose T**o**ols, **H**yphenation and then Select OK or press Enter.

Creating a Text Box

A framed toll-free telephone number appears at the bottom of page one. To create this boxed phone number, follow these steps:

1. Position the cursor on the paragraph return after the table. Type the following:

   CALL TOLL FREE 1-800-099-8903

2. Select this line and use the Ribbon to change the type to 18-point, bold, centered.

3. With this text selected, click Forma**t**, then choose **P**aragraph. For **B**order, choose Box. For Pattern, choose Shadow and select OK or press Enter.

Producing a Complex Newsletter

3. With this text selected, choose Forma**t**, then **B**order. In the Preset box, choose **S**hadow. In the **L**ine box, choose the 1.25 rule and select OK or press Enter.

Creating the Headers

A header appears at the top of page two and subsequent pages. Even-numbered pages have an even header and odd-numbered have an odd header. To create this header, complete the following steps:

1. At the top of the second page, press Enter twice and then position the cursor on the top paragraph return.

2. Select **V**iew, then **D**raft. Select **V**iew, **E**dit, then **H**eader/Footer. Choose Different First **P**age and **D**ifferent Odd and Even Pages. In the Select Header/Footer to **E**dit box, choose Even header and choose **O**ptions.

3. In the Page Numbers box, choose **S**tart at, Auto. In the Distance From Edge box, choose **H**eader, type **.7"** and select OK or press Enter.

4. A header pane appears on your screen. Choose the first icon on the left, the page number icon. Position the cursor after the number. In the text area, press Tab, type **MOUNTAIN SORREL**, press Tab, and type **SPRING 1992**.

5. Select this line of type. Choose Forma**t**, **P**aragraph, and change the type to 10-point, bold. In the same dialog box, move to B**o**rder and choose Below. For Pa**t**tern, choose Single and select OK or press Enter. Use the Ruler to set the tabs at 3 3/4 inches and 7 1/2 inches.

6. Click to **C**lose the header pane. Choose **V**iew, then **P**age Layout to view the header.

    For page three, create an odd page header by switching the page number with the date. Choose **D**raft view, **V**iew, **E**dit, then Header/Footer. Choose Odd Header and select OK or press Enter. Type **SPRING 1992**, press Tab, type **MOUNTAIN SORREL**, press Tab, and click the icon for the page number. Choose **C**lose.

2. Choose **V**iew, then **N**ormal. Select **V**iew, then **H**eader/Footer. Choose Different First **P**age and **D**ifferent Odd and Even

505

PART V

Creating Newsletters

Pages. In the From Edge box type **.7"**. In the Header/Footer box, choose Even Header and select OK or press Enter.

3. A header pane appears on your screen. Click the first icon on the left, the page number icon. Position the cursor after the number. In the text area, press Tab, type **MOUNTAIN SORREL**, press Tab, and type **SPRING 1992**.

4. Choose Close. Select View and then Page Layout to view the header.

   For page three, create an odd page header by switching the page number with the date. To do this, repeat steps 2 through 6, with the following two exceptions. In the Header/Footer box, choose Odd Header. In the header pane, type **SPRING 1992**, press Tab, type **MOUNTAIN SORREL**, press Tab, and click the page number icon.

5. Select the header. Use the Ruler and change the tabs to 3 3/4" and 7 1/2". Use the Ribbon and change the type to 10-point, bold.

6. With the header still selected, choose Format, then Border. In the Border box, click the bottom margin or press the down arrow. In the Line box, choose the 1.25 rule and select OK or press Enter.

Creating Page Two

Page two of this newsletter has two tables. The top table contains text imported from the original document, and the bottom table has a text box in one column and a list in the other. All the text for the bottom table is typed into the table.

To complete the top table, follow these steps:

1. Position the cursor on the second paragraph return after the header. To insert the table, repeat steps 1 and 2 of the section, *Inserting Text into Tables*. Make the first column 2 1/4" wide and the second column 4 3/4" wide.

2. Switch windows, cut and paste text, and format the two columns until they look like figure 19.6. In the second column under the story `Wild Edible Plants`, bold the words `cattail`, `Arrowhead` and `Burdock`. Also, at the end of this story, to even the columns, type **We also forage plants weekly for the freshest leaves, flowers, and roots.**

CHAPTER 19

Producing a Complex Newsletter

To create the bottom table and complete the masthead, follow these steps:

1. Position the cursor on the paragraph return after the table. Repeat steps 1 and 2 to insert another table. Set the columns to match the table at the top of the page. Position the cursor in the first column and type the following text, pressing Tab, space bar, and Enter where indicated:

   (Enter) **MOUNTAIN SORREL** (Enter)

   Published Quarterly (Enter)

   Volume 9, Issue No. 2 (Enter, Enter)

   Editor (Tab) (space bar) **S. H. Schwimmer** (Enter)

   Circulation Editor (Tab) (space bar) **J. J. Rubel** (Enter)

   Advertising Editor (Tab) (space bar) **D. M. Herr** (Enter, Enter)

   MOUNTAIN SORREL is the official publication of Silver Bark's Herbal Remedies and Book Store. Subscriptions to customers are free with purchase of yearly catalog at $7.95. (Enter, Enter)

   Orders for any product in this newsletter are welcomed by mail, phone, or in person. We do not guarantee our products, recipes or any advice in this newsletter as a medication or cure. We take no responsibility for misuse of any product we sell.(Enter)

2. Select `MOUNTAIN SORREL` and change the text to 12-point, bold, centered.

3. Select `Published Quarterly` and `Volume 9, Issue No. 2` and change the type to 10-point, bold, centered.

4. Select the text from `Editor...` to `...D. M. Herr` and change the type to 10-point, bold. Choose Forma**t**, then **T**abs. In the Tab Position box, type **2.13"**, and choose **R**ight aligned. In the Leader box, choose 2, **S**et and select OK or press Enter.

5. Select `MOUNTAIN SORREL` and use the Ribbon to bold this type. Select the rest of the text in the column and use the Ribbon to change the type to 10-point, justified. Use the Ruler to indent the first line .25" and hyphenate.

PART V

Creating Newsletters

6. Select the entire column. Choose **Format**, then **Paragraph**. For B**o**rder, choose Box. For **P**attern, choose Single and select OK or press Enter.

6. Select the entire column. Choose **Format**, then **B**order. In the Preset box, choose Box. In the Line box, choose the 1.25 rule. For **F**rom Text, type **2pt**. Click **S**hading. For **P**attern, choose the 10% screen and click OK twice.

To complete the list at the bottom right of page two, do the following:

1. Position the cursor in the second column and enter the following text, pressing Tab and Enter where indicated:

    Salves For Your Skin (Enter)

    Salves made from olive oil, beeswax and concentrated amounts of roots, leaves and flowers are the best medicines for skin irritations. All natural and pure, no preservatives or chemicals, our salves are the best around! Listed here are only a few of the salves we stock. (Enter)

    (Tab) **Chickweed** (Tab) **skin rashes, soothe itching** (Enter)

    (Tab) **Calendula** (Tab) **insect bites, rashes** (Enter)

    (Tab) **Comfrey** (Tab) **bee stings, burns** (Enter)

    (Tab) **Plantain** (Tab) **bee stings, itches** (Enter)

    (Tab) **Green Elder** (Tab) **cuts, bruises** (Enter)

    (Tab) **Sage** (Tab) **sore muscles** (Enter)

    (Tab) **Beech** (Tab) **blisters, swelling** (Enter)

    (Tab) **Aloe** (Tab) **any skin problem** (Enter)

    (Tab) **Mint Mixture** (Tab) **soothing and cooling**

2. Use the Style box on the Ribbon to change the head and body. Select the text from `Chickweed` to `soothing and cooling` and use the Ruler to set the tabs at 1" and 2 1/2", left-aligned.

3. With this text still selected, select **Format**, then **P**aragraph. In the Spacing box, choose **B**efore, type **.5li** and select OK or press Enter.

CHAPTER 19

Producing a Complex Newsletter

Save and Print the Newsletter

To save the newsletter, choose **F**ile, then **S**ave.

To print the newsletter, choose **F**ile, **P**rint and select OK or press Enter.

> **NOTE**
>
> When closing the original document, don't save. By not saving, the original newbase document is available for another practice session.

Looking at Design

In the preceding newsletter layouts, you produced only two pages for each design because the style is similar throughout a newsletter. In the last design, you created headers for odd and even pages, which are shown in figures 19.5 and 19.6.

Note the page number for page three (fig. 19.7), a right hand page, appears at the right side of the page. In addition, the layout of page three mirrors the column layout of page two so a facing page view would be interesting and consistent.

Two tables make up this page, plus a graphic box. The advertisement in the first table, second column, is screened, providing balance to the publication box on the facing page. The graphic box is shaded to repeat the design elements from page one.

Figure 19.8 illustrates a possible fourth page for the same newsletter. Because this is the last page, no header appears. A chart on poisonous mushrooms and plants adds graphic interest. The text was set up in a two-column table, with space left for the graphic. A mailing panel completes the newsletter.

Another design alternative, shown in figure 19.9 involves boxed drop-cap letters. The first letter of the first paragraph of each story is set in a framed 24-point, drop-cap. This design was created in Version 2.0. The option is not available in Version 1.1. Notice the frames around each letter contain plant drawings, as does the nameplate.

PART V

Creating Newsletters

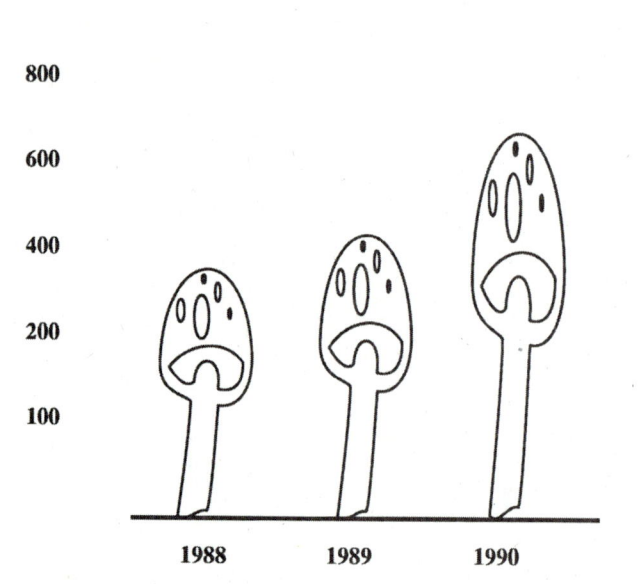

Danger, Poison

Each year hundreds of people in the United States die because they have ingested an herb, or plant that is toxic. When foraging, be sure you know what you are getting into! Some mushrooms, for example, can be deadly if eaten. Other plants such as tansy or foxglove are also harmful if prepared incorrectly or taken in too large a dose.

The chart to the right illustrates reported and proven deaths from the ingestion of poisonous plants over a three year period in the United States.

Always keep a field guide with you when foraging and refer to it often. Silver Bark's Herbal Remedies and Book Store has several field guides available to you at very low prices. See our full selection in our catalog. Your life could depend on it!

Silver Bark's Herbal Remedies and Book Store
13259 Main Street
Beckley, WV 25801

FIG. 19.8. Page four of the newsletter set up with tables.

To add a large graphic to your newsletter, you can choose among several options. You may use paragraph returns to separate text in a column and leave space for a paste-up. Alternatively you may import a graphic. With Version 2.0, you can draw and place a frame anywhere on the page. Figure 19.10 shows a two-column newsletter with a framed graphic. When inserting a frame such as this, make the columns wide enough for the text around the box to be easy to read. Left-aligned text is best because justified type would have either too many hyphens or too many wide spaces between words.

MOUNTAIN SORREL

A Quarterly Newsletter of Herbal Curatives and Preventatives

The Healing Power of Lavender

Everyone knows of the delicious fragrance of lavender, especially English lavender, but few know of its medicinal qualities. Any of the three species of lavender make wonderful potions. A terrific calmative, lavender has the power to soothe headaches and nervous tension. Simply steep lavender flowers in hot water for 15 to 20 minutes, and sip a cupful of the tea two or three times during the day.

A stronger tea of lavender is good as a gargle for sore throats; it also relieves stomach aches and colic. We stock dried English and French lavenders in bunches and one pound bags, at a reasonable price. We also sell lavender oil extract for use as a medicinal oil.

Rosemary, More Than a Cooking Herb

Both the leaves and flowers of rosemary have been used to alleviate depression and insomnia. A simple rosemary tea, with a bit of ginger added, also comforts a nervous or upset stomach. Rosemary oil is widely known for its antibacterial properties, as well. Lastly, if you have dark hair, try a strong rosemary tea for a rinse after washing. It not only makes your hair shiny and soft, but it clears up your dandruff, too. We stock a full supply of rosemary leaves, flowers, oil and our special home-made rosemary shampoo.

Catnip, Not Just For Cats

A member of the mint family, catnip contains many properties other mints do. As a pleasant tasting tea, catnip is an antispasmodic and a calmative. Treat stomach ailments, colic and intestinal complaints. Catnip calms nervousness and anxiety. Having a sleepless night? Try some catnip tea. If you have a cat, though, watch out, he'll try to drink your tea, too!

We stock catnip in one-half and one pound cans, as well as seeds to start your own plants in your garden.

It's Not Just a Weed, Joe-Pye Weed

Often seen growing along the railroad tracks or roadsides, in fields and meadows, Joe-Pye Weed is also known as Queen of the Meadow. The root is traditionally used to ease lower back pain and rheumatism. Leaves are sometimes used to break a fever by bringing on intense sweating. Use the root or leaves in teas and tinctures; but do be careful, too much, too often, can be toxic.

We not only keep Joe-Pye Weed roots in four and eight ounce containers. The flowers, and roots of this plant are all valuable medicines. It's perfect as an astringent, diuretic, and tonic. Prepare an infusion of one half cup Joe-Pye Weed flowers to two pints water for most complaints; be sure to strain well.

FIG. 19.9. *Newsletter with framed drop cap letters and art work.*

Mountain Sorrel

A QUARTERLY NEWSLETTER OF HERBAL CURATIVES AND PREVENTATIVES

The Healing Power of Lavender

Everyone knows of the delicious fragrance of lavender, especially English lavender, but few know of its medicinal qualities. Any of the three species of lavender make potions.

A terrific calmative, lavender has the power to soothe headaches and nervous tension. Simply steep lavender flowers in hot water for 15 to 20 minutes, and sip a cupful of the tea two or three times during the day.

A stronger tea of lavender is good as a gargle for sore throats; it also relieves stomach aches and colic. We stock dried English and French lavenders in bunches and one pound bags, at a reasonable price. We also sell lavender oil extract for use as a medicinal oil.

Rosemary, More Than a Cooking Herb

Both the leaves and flowers of rosemary have been used to alleviate depression and insomnia. A simple rosemary tea, with a bit of ginger added, also comforts a nervous or upset stomach. Rosemary oil is widely known for its antibacterial properties, as well. Lastly, if you have dark hair, try a strong rosemary tea for a rinse after washing. It not only makes your hair shiny and soft, but it clears up your dandruff, too.

We stock a full supply of rosemary leaves, flowers, oil and our special home-made rosemary shampoo and rinses.

Catnip, Not Just For Cats

A member of the mint family, catnip contains many properties other mints do. As a pleasant tasting tea, catnip is an antispasmodic and a calmative. Treat stomach ailments, colic and intestinal complaints.

Catnip calms nervousness and anxiety. Having a sleepless night? Try some catnip tea. If you have a cat, though, watch out, he'll try to drink your tea, too!

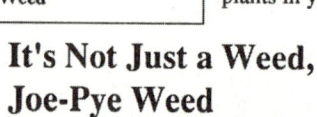
Joe-Pye Weed

We stock catnip in one-half and one pound cans, as well as seeds to start your own plants in your garden.

It's Not Just a Weed, Joe-Pye Weed

Often seen growing along the railroad tracks or roadsides, in fields and meadows, Joe-Pye Weed is also known as Queen of the Meadow. The root is traditionally used to ease lower back pain and rheumatism. Leaves are sometimes used to break a fever by bringing on intense sweating. Use the root or leaves in teas and tinctures; but do be careful, too much, too often, can be toxic.

We not only keep Joe-Pye Weed roots in four and eight ounce containers, but in 1 pound bags, as well. Our Joe-Pye is collected fresh each Saturday morning during the spring, and fall. From the moist forests and meadows within the area, only the most perfect roots and flowers are gathered. We then dry the herb by hanging it upside down in a cool, dark place, to guarantee you receive only the best.

FIG. 19.10. *A graphic with caption created in Version 2.0.*

CHAPTER 19

Producing a Complex Newsletter

Recapping

In this chapter, you learned new techniques for newsletter design, such as publication box, headers, large first characters (drop caps or raised caps), tables of contents, callouts, varied column widths, and table features to create a wide column and a narrow column on each page for an interesting effect. You also learned some techniques for using graphics such as photographs, art work, charts, and tables.

In the next chapter, you learn how to produce a business report.

TELEMARKETING

The telemarketing consisted of follow-up calls to seminars, demonstrations and mailings. Each call went strictly by a script; offered in the call was a key word the client could use for a discount when he signed up for class.

Out of the first 2,500 calls made, 75 people registered for classes. Total cost of the phone calls, including time and overhead, was $ .50 per call. Total cost per person per class is $100; therefore, total profit was $3,375.

SUMMARY OF DATA

Following is a spreadsheet of the above data so you can compare expenditures and profits as they applied to these three specific activities. Clearly, the direct mailing has demonstrated the highest return for the invested monies with 84.6% of total income from the three marketing methods. Telemarketing has an 8.8% share; the free seminars and demonstrations only 6.6%.

	DIRECT MAIL	SEMINARS	TELEMARKET
No. of Contacts	5,000	120	2,500
No. of Sales	490	42	75
Gross Income	$71,050.00	$6,090.00	$10,875.00
Cost of Marketing	$1,645.00	$300.00	$1,250.00
Cost of Class	$49,000.00	$4,200.00	$7,500.00
Gross Profit	$20,405.00	$1,590.00	$2,125.00
Market. Cost/Contact	$0.33	$2.50	$0.50
Total Cost/Sale	$103.36	$107.14	$116.67
Marketing Cost/Sale	$3.36	$7.14	$16.67
Profit/Sale	$41.64	$37.86	$28.33

The next section of this Marketing Summary details information about the Parallel Marketing plan. As we compare its great success to the results of the Direct Marketing plan, we believe you will see a need to continue the Plan for at least one year. With conservative changes in the basic approach, that is eliminating the free demonstrations and seminars, we believe the Marketing Plan will continue to succeed and benefit the company.

Part VI

Creating Long Documents

Includes

20. Producing a Business Report
21. Producing a Book

Producing a Business Report

20

Business reports inform and explain and usually focus on one specific project or one aspect of a project. Progress reports, annual reports, sales reports, inventory summaries, and marketing plans are only a few subjects for a business report. Almost all reports contain specific information regarding progress, profits, and expenditures. Finally, business reports incorporate figures, charts, spreadsheets, graphs, and text to explain these elements.

Planning the Design Elements

Some reports may include photographs. You also can add artwork or illustrations. Predominant, however, are spreadsheets or other figures to represent the budget, profit, or losses in easy-to-understand terms. If you use a spreadsheet program or graph maker, your figures easily import to Word. Microsoft Excel and Lotus 1-2-3 are two examples of spreadsheet program files you can import. Harvard Graphics for graphs and charts is another good program; Word 2.0 even contains a graph maker that you can use to create graphs. For specific information about saving and importing files to Word, refer to Appendix B. The instructions in this chapter refer to a spreadsheet and a graph and explain how to insert these elements into Word.

PART VI

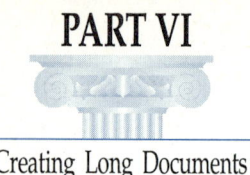

Creating Long Documents

Choosing the Layout

The layout of a business report usually is not complicated. One column or two printed on one side of an 8 1/2-inch x 11-inch page is a standard design. The report may include headers or footers (or both), logos, footnotes, cross-references, page numbers, a table of contents, index, and bibliography. The contents are up to you; you may want to include all components that make the report easy to read and understand. If a report is short, say eight to ten pages, you may decide not to use page numbers or a table of contents. If a report has many figures and refers to each figure often, perhaps an index or table of figures is appropriate.

By the way, proposals are similar to a business report in layout and design. Although proposals suggest a plan for the future, the subjects can be financial prospects, new business possibilities, marketing, and so on. You also may include graphs, charts, illustrations, and photographs. If you're planning a business proposal, apply the design and layout elements of this chapter to the proposal.

Determining the Size

Business reports and proposals usually print one side of a sheet of paper. Some reports, however, such as an annual report, are printed on both sides of 11-inch x 17-inch sheets, folded, and saddle-stitched to an 8 1/2-inch x 11-inch sheet. Most businesses invest a great deal of time, money, and effort in annual reports. Photographs, full color, perfect typesetting, and high-quality printing are common for annual reports. Proposals are often elaborate as well. Other business reports may be less refined. It all depends on the business, the report, and to whom the report is targeted.

Selecting the Paper and Binding

A good choice of paper for a business report is white or ivory, for comfortable reading. Customarily, the paper is 60# to 70#; the

CHAPTER 20

Producing a Business Report

finish smooth, vellum, linen, or enamel. The cover should match the paper in color and finish; use cover paper of 65# or 80# (65# runs through most laser printers with no problems; 80# usually will not run through a laser printer).

Reports usually are bound by stapling or by spiral binding. If you side-stitch the report, be sure that you leave the extra margin on the binding edge. If the report prints both sides, consider the design of the facing pages.

This chapter instructs you to format several pages of a traditional business report and shows you other innovative report designs. Contained in this chapter are cover pages, a table of contents, footers, logos, imported spreadsheets, graphs, and more.

Because you know about formatting procedures such as setting fonts, style sheets, tabs, tables, indents, and adding borders, the instructions in this and the following chapter are less detailed than previous chapters. However, keystrokes for new procedures are explained in detail.

Creating a Traditional Business Report

A traditional business report consists of a cover, text, tables, spreadsheets, graphs, or any combination of graphic elements. The design you'll work with contains all these elements and also is organized by using footers and a table of contents.

This particular report is a marketing summary. Included are text that explains the advertising techniques, the results of these techniques, and a spreadsheet and graph.

A binding margin on the left allows room for side stitching or spiral binding. As part of the design, the left margin can be made much larger than need be for a binding margin, which would make the line length comfortably readable.

The simple cover page consists of left-aligned heads and double rules that border both the top and bottom margins (see fig. 20.1). You can place a photograph in the center of the page for emphasis, or you can let the white space speak for itself. The style of the cover matches the design of the inside pages.

MARKETING SUMMARY FOR HUMBLE OPINIONS

BY PEAR ASSOCIATES, LTD.

JUNE 4, 1992

FIG. 20.1. *A traditional cover design for a business report.*

CHAPTER 20

Producing a Business Report

If the report contains more than eight or ten pages, a table of contents is important. Figure 20.2 shows the table of contents for the report. Word enables you to gather a table of contents by two methods. This design uses the TC fields. The TC field provides the text and page number for a table of contents. Notice that the footer repeats the double rule, and uses the traditional *ii* for the page number.

The first page of the body of the report repeats the cover design with double rules and left-aligned heads. The left-aligned type and interparagraph spacing make the text of a long report easier to read. Because all pages are right-hand pages, all the page numbers in the footer are on the right. In addition, beginning with this page, the page numbers change to numerals (see fig. 20.3).

Page four continues the design, incorporating a numbered list. Notice that the new head begins at the top of a page and leaves extra white space at the bottom of the previous page (see fig. 20.4).

Figure 20.5 shows page five, which contains two minor heads. These heads are bold and indented slightly to set them apart from major heads.

A table adds variation to the page (see fig. 20.6). Tables, charts, spreadsheets, graphs, and so on help the reader understand the text. You can use many illustrations in a business report for clarity, comprehension, and appeal.

Figure 20.7 shows a graph that represents the information in the text. You can import graphs from many programs into Word (see Appendix B).

Figure 20.8 includes a spreadsheet to summarize the data in the report. Two fields are available in Word that help you update information from other applications. If you use other Windows applications, such as Microsoft Excel, you can create Links to update your spreadsheet. Included is another field type that enables you to import, and then revise, files as the originals change. Most figures in a business report must be current, up to the minute. With Word, your report can be topical. Most spreadsheets also can be inserted as a file.

Notice that page two, the Table of Contents, is one of the last pages you produce. The entire text of the report must be in place before a table of contents can be compiled.

TABLE OF CONTENTS

Introduction 3
Customer List 4
Customer 4
Marketing Plan 5
Direct Marketing 5
Marketing Calendar 6
Direct Mailing 6
Demonstrations, Seminars 7
Telemarketing 8
Summary of Data 8

MARKETING PLAN

FIG. 20.2. *Table of Contents compiled by use of TC fields.*

MARKETING SUMMARY FOR HUMBLE OPINIONS
JUNE 4, 1992

Humble Opinions, a corporation dedicated to quality computer software training, initiated the Marketing Plan on June 4, 1991. Involved in this plan were many strategies for client expansion and increased financial gain. This summary analyzes the success of the Marketing Plan in terms of customer base increase and profit from services offered.

Current economic trends in our area greatly effect the figures of the past three months; however, earlier reports reveal that the basic premise of the Marketing Plan is working. Should future trends prove to follow the same path as the past three months, a new Marketing Plan will then be developed. We do suggest this plan be followed for an additional period of six months before any long-term decision is made.

Despite this recent decline in profits and sales, the Marketing Plan proved to be both beneficial and profitable to Humble Opinions in the first nine months of execution. The first three months, from June 1991 to August 1991, were considered the initiation period. Although contact with clients increased considerably, profits increased only slightly. During the second three months of the Marketing Plan, from September 1991 to November 1991, profits showed incredible growth. This is attributed to initial planning and advertising to build the customer base. The three-month period from December 1991 to February 1992 proved to support the objectives of the Plan through substantial client referrals and increased profits for the company.

We estimate the Marketing Plan, with minimum modifications, can and will benefit the company in countless ways over the next six months. Customer lists will continue to expand; profits will continue to rise at a reliable and constant rate.

FIG. 20.3. The design elements repeat in page three, and the footer number changes.

THE CUSTOMER LIST

Humble Opinions is a business based solely on the customer. Software instruction aimed specifically at people who buy and use personal computers in their business. The first requirement of the Marketing Plan was to accumulate a comprehensive list of clients who need software instruction. Many methods were implemented to accomplish this task.

As the list was compiled, pertinent information about each client was entered into a database for use in mailings, telemarketing and careful examination. Common data such as client name, address, and phone number as well as the company name, and key contact personnel and their phone numbers comprised the list. As time went on, we added specific information to each file, such as interest areas of the client, software products owned by their company, types of documents used by the company, and so on. In addition, comments were added to the files by the client about seminars, classes and demonstrations given by Humble Opinions that they attended. We then used these files as a basis for composing mailings and telemarketing scripts.

Following is a list of sources used for building the customer lists:

1. Customer records
2. Invoices from the last two years
3. Professional organizations' membership lists
4. Sign-up sheets from seminars, trade-shows, give-a-ways
5. Mailing lists purchased — specific to personal computer users
6. Salesman's cold calls

As part of the client listing process, we initiated a program to update customer files every six months. Executed by office staff members, telephone calls made regularly to the customer base serves to verify phone numbers, addresses, and key personnel. In addition, the telemarketing script includes questions directed to personal knowledge of new software instruction and training offered by the company.

MARKETING PLAN 4

FIG. 20.4. Page four of the report. When possible, start major heads at the top of the page.

THE MARKETING PLAN

Using the client list as a foundation, our people created advertising that addressed the specific needs and concerns of the customers. Each project was dedicated to individual software programs, and the particular features that applied to a targeted group of clients.

By approaching the Plan in this way, more attention was devoted to the details of the software training that applied to individual customers. Thus, each customer perceived himself as distinctive, unique.

We used two methods of marketing for this project, Direct Marketing and Parallel Marketing. More time and effort were aimed at Direct Marketing. Considerable advantages were realized from this effort. In addition, the Parallel Marketing concentrated on one specific program and proved to be extremely profitable.

DIRECT MARKETING

Among the Direct Marketing techniques utilized in the Plan were free demonstrations and seminars, direct mailing of fliers and letters, and telemarketing. Each approach was carefully researched and executed to enable us to measure results. Coupons for discounts identified clients who received the direct mailings. Different coupons distinguished seminar and demonstration attendants. Those customers accepting training through telemarketing efforts referred to a key word for a discount. Naturally, this summary is based solely on those clients whose proven response corresponds with each marketing technique. Any who did not reply with the coupon or key word could not feasibly be included in this report.

PARALLEL MARKETING

Parallel Marketing targeted customers of one computer store in the area. Customers of that store were given such advertising items as mouse pads, shortcut key cards, and fliers with class descriptions. All of these items displayed a special phone number that identified them with this particular marketing approach.

FIG. 20.5. *Modification of the indents set these topics apart from the rest of the text.*

Before analyzing the comprehensive outcome of the Marketing Plan, let us first look at the four stages divided into three-month periods. We first concentrate on Direct Marketing; the second half of the summary is devoted to Parallel Marketing. The following calendar of events illustrates the implementation of the Marketing Plan by use of Direct Marketing.

	1st period Jun. - Aug.	2nd period Sept. - Nov.	3rd period Dec. - Feb.	4th period Mar. - May
Direct Mail	2 mailings 10,000	1 mailing 7,500	2 mailings 10,000	1 mailing 7,500
Seminars	4 seminars 2 demos.	2 seminars 4 demos.	4 seminars 2 demos.	2 seminars 4 demos.
Telemarketing	2,500 calls	1,500 calls	1,500 calls	2,500 calls

To further demonstrate the expenses versus profits of the Marketing Plan, let us know examine a sampling of each Direct Marketing technique as shown on the calendar. Each of these examples directly quotes expenditures and revenues as they apply to Humble Opinions.

DIRECT MAILING

Our Direct Mailing campaign consisted of advertising letters and/or flyers dispatched to customers in the compiled database. The first mailing of 5,000 letters is typical in costs of subsequent ones, so following is an analysis of the expenses and proceeds from that mailing.

Primary costs include printing and postage. Humble Opinions personnel performed typesetting and composition of the letter. The printing company charged for paper and envelopes; camera, press, folding and inserting the letters; and printing and attaching the mailing labels. The total printing costs were $645. Postage was $1,000. A coupon attached to the letter identified it as the first mailing so response could be accurately measured.

Out of 5,000 letters mailed, 1,287 responded for more information. Out of those 1,287, 490 took classes at $145 each. The total cost of classes per person is $100, including the cost of printing and mailing, instructor, supplies, and overhead. At this rate, total profit resulting from this one mailing is $12,050.

MARKETING PLAN

FIG. 20.6. *Page six of the report contains a calendar of events in a table.*

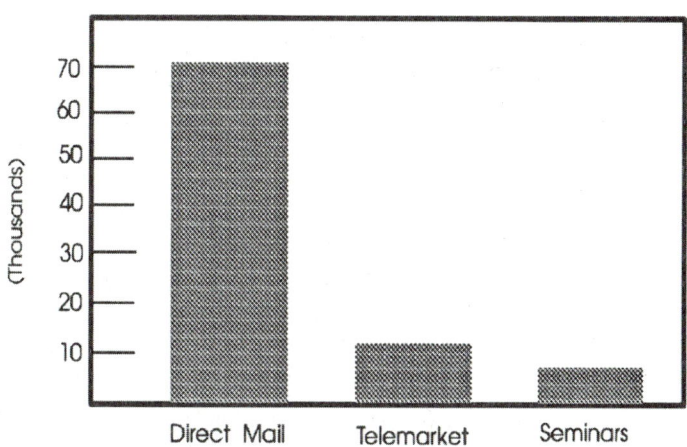

Figure 1 illustrates the prodigious difference in the three marketing techniques.

FREE DEMONSTRATIONS AND SEMINARS

Free seminars and demonstrations were advertised in the above mailings and by the use of fliers displayed in the company's office and classroom. Each seminar or demonstration concentrated on one particular software program and lasted about one hour. To add to the customer list, a sign-up list for a door prize was presented at each seminar. Refreshments served allowed the attendants to remain in the classroom for questions and discussion when the activity ended. A different coupon was utilized to measure response to the advertising.

Costs for each seminar or demonstration, including refreshments, door prize, lecturer, technicians, and overhead amounted to $300 per seminar. Attendance was 120 people at the first activity, 42 of which signed up for classes. At a cost of $100 per person per class, the total profit realized from the seminar was $1,890.

MARKETING PLAN 7

FIG. 20.7. *Add graphs to interpret results or illustrate text in a report.*

TELEMARKETING

The telemarketing consisted of follow-up calls to seminars, demonstrations and mailings. Each call went strictly by a script; offered in the call was a key word the client could use for a discount when he signed up for class.

Out of the first 2,500 calls made, 75 people registered for classes. Total cost of the phone calls, including time and overhead, was $ .50 per call. Total cost per person per class is $100; therefore, total profit was $3,375.

SUMMARY OF DATA

Following is a spreadsheet of the above data so you can compare expenditures and profits as they applied to these three specific activities. Clearly, the direct mailing has demonstrated the highest return for the invested monies with 84.6% of total income from the three marketing methods. Telemarketing has an 8.8% share; the free seminars and demonstrations only 6.6%.

	DIRECT MAIL	SEMINARS	TELEMARKET
No. of Contacts	5,000	120	2,500
No. of Sales	490	42	75
Gross Income	$71,050.00	$6,090.00	$10,875.00
Cost of Marketing	$1,645.00	$300.00	$1,250.00
Cost of Class	$49,000.00	$4,200.00	$7,500.00
Gross Profit	$20,405.00	$1,590.00	$2,125.00
Market. Cost/Contact	$0.33	$2.50	$0.50
Total Cost/Sale	$103.36	$107.14	$116.67
Marketing Cost/Sale	$3.36	$7.14	$16.67
Profit/Sale	$41.64	$37.86	$28.33

The next section of this Marketing Summary details information about the Parallel Marketing plan. As we compare its great success to the results of the Direct Marketing plan, we believe you will see a need to continue the Plan for at least one year. With conservative changes in the basic approach, that is eliminating the free demonstrations and seminars, we believe the Marketing Plan will continue to succeed and benefit the company.

MARKETING PLAN

FIG. 20.8. *A spreadsheet added to the report by linking.*

CHAPTER 20

Producing a Business Report

To create the report shown in figures 20.1 to 20.8, follow these steps:

1. Go to **F**ile, **N**ew, New **D**ocument, **U**se Template Normal. Select OK or press Enter.

2. Go to Forma**t**, **D**ocument. Set the **T**op, **B**ottom and **R**ight margins to **1"**, set the **L**eft margin to **2"**, and select OK or press Enter.

2. Go to Forma**t**, Page Set**u**p. In **M**argins, set the **T**op, **B**ottom and **R**ight margins to **1"**; the **L**eft margin to **2"**. Select OK or press Enter.

3. Type the following text, pressing Enter where indicated:

   (Enter, four times)

   MARKETING SUMMARY FOR HUMBLE OPINIONS (Enter, eight times)

   BY PEAR ASSOCIATES, LTD. (Enter, Enter)

   JUNE 4, 1992 (Enter, four times)

   MARKETING SUMMARY FOR HUMBLE OPINIONS (Enter)

   JUNE 4, 1992 (Enter, four times)

   (Here, and after each of the following headlines, type the paragraphs as shown in the figure, or enter your own data, pressing Enter after each paragraph.)

   THE CUSTOMER LIST (Enter)

   THE MARKETING PLAN (Enter)

       DIRECT MARKETING (Enter) (Indent your text)

       PARALLEL MARKETING (Enter)
   (After the line, `The following calendar of events...`, press Enter three times, then begin your table.)

   (Tab) **1st period** (Tab) **2nd period** (Tab) **3rd period** (Tab) **4th period** (Enter)

   (Tab) **Jun. - Aug.** (Tab) **Sept. - Nov.** (Tab) **Dec. - Feb.** (Tab) **Mar. - May** (Enter)

   Direct Mail (Tab) **2 mailings** (Tab) **1 mailing** (Tab) **2 mailings** (Tab) **1 mailing** (Enter)

   (Tab) **10,000** (Tab) **7,500** (Tab) **10,000** (Tab) **7,500** (Enter)

529

PART VI

Creating Long Documents

Seminars (Tab) **4 seminars** (Tab) **2 seminars** (Tab) **4 seminars** (Tab) **2 seminars** (Enter)

(Tab) **2 demos.** (Tab) **4 demos.** (Tab) **2 demos.** (Tab) **4 demos.** (Enter)

Telemarketing (Tab) **2,500 calls** (Tab) **1,500 calls** (Tab) **1,500 calls** (Tab) **2,500 calls** (Enter, Enter)

DIRECT MAILING (Enter)

FREE DEMONSTRATIONS AND SEMINARS (Enter)

TELEMARKETING (Enter)

SUMMARY OF DATA (Enter)

4. Select all of the type. On the Ribbon, change the type size to 12-point.

5. Go to the beginning of the document. Select MARKETING SUMMARY FOR HUMBLE OPINIONS. Change the type to 40-point, bold.

6. With the text shown in step 5 still selected, go to Forma**t**, **C**haracter. In Character Spacing, choose **C**ondensed. By: **1.25 pt**. Select OK or press Enter.

7. With type still selected, go to Forma**t**, **P**aragraph. In Spacing, Af**t**er, type **.5li** and select OK or press Enter.

8. Position the cursor in MARKETING. Go to Forma**t**, **P**aragraph. In **B**order, choose Above and in Pat**t**ern, choose Double. Select OK or press Enter.

6. With MARKETING still selected, go to Forma**t**, Character. In **S**pacing, choose Condensed. **B**y: **1.25 pt**, and select OK or press Enter.

7. With type still selected, go to Forma**t**, **P**aragraph. In Spacing, Af**t**er, type **.5li**. Select OK or press Enter.

8. Position the cursor in MARKETING. Go to Forma**t**, **B**order. In the Bo**r**der box, click the top margin. In **L**ine, choose a double rule. Select OK or press Enter.

Because the sample was created in Version 1.1, the double rule you see is the only choice. You have three choices available to you in Version 2.0. Be sure that you use the same thickness rules throughout the document.

CHAPTER 20

Producing a Business Report

9. Select BY PEAR ASSOCIATES, LTD. and JUNE 4, 1992. Change the type to Helv, 14-point, bold.

10. Position the cursor on the paragraph return after JUNE 4, 1992. Below this return, add a double rule. Press Enter.

11. With cursor in position, go to **Insert**, **Break**. Choose **P**age Break. Select OK or press Enter.

12. On page two, the double rule should be at the top of the page. Position the cursor on the paragraph return above MARKETING SUMMARY.... Go to **Insert**, **Break**. In Section Break, choose **N**ext Page and select OK or press Enter.

    The Section break is used here to divide the two types of page numbers. You compile the table of contents as the last step to formatting the document but add the footer now.

13. Go back to page 2. Go to **V**iew, **D**raft.

14. Go to **E**dit, **H**eader/Footer. Choose Footer; choose Different First **P**age; click **O**ptions. In Page Numbers, Format, choose i ii iii.... In Distance From Edge, **F**ooter, type **.7"** and select OK or press Enter.

15. In the Footer pane (Remember that you must be in **D**raft or **N**ormal view to see the footer pane), type the following line:

    MARKETING PLAN (Tab)

    Click the page number icon.

16. Select the line of type. On the Ribbon, change it to Helv, 10-point.

17. Still selected, go to Forma**t**, **P**aragraph. Place a Double rule Above the type. OK. **C**lose.

14. Go to **V**iew, **H**eader/Footer. Choose Footer; choose Different First **P**age; click Page **N**umbers. Choose i ii iii.... In From Edge, **F**ooter, type **.7"**. OK.

15. In the Footer pane, type the following line:

    MARKETING PLAN (Tab)

    Click the page number icon.

16. Select the line of type you added in step 15. On the Ribbon, change the type to Helv, 10-point.

531

PART VI

Creating Long Documents

17. With MARKETING PLAN still selected, go to Forma**t**, **B**order. In Bo**r**der, click the top margin or use the down arrow to select; in **L**ine, choose the double rule. Select OK or press Enter. **C**lose.

18. Go to **V**iew, **P**age to see the footer. You may need to adjust the right hand tab on the Ruler.

19. Move to page three. Position the cursor on the first paragraph return, go to Forma**t**, **P**aragraph and choose a double rule Above.

19. Move to page three. Position the cursor on the first paragraph return, go to Forma**t**, **B**order and choose a double rule.

20. Select MARKETING SUMMARY.... Change the type to Helv, 16-point.

21. With MARKETING SUMMARY.... still selected, go to Forma**t**, **C**haracter. Condense the type by **1.25 pt**. In Spacing, **A**fter, type **3pt**. Select OK or press Enter.

21. With MARKETING SUMMARY... still selected, go to Forma**t**, **C**haracter. Condense the type by **1.25 pt**. In Spacing, **A**fter, type **3pt**. OK.

22. Select JUNE 4, 1992. Go to the Ribbon and choose bold.

23. Select the first paragraph of body text. Go to Forma**t**, **S**tyle(s). In **S**tyle Name type **body**, click **D**efine. In **P**aragraph, Spacing, change **A**fter to **1.5li**.

23. Select the first paragraph of body text. Go to Forma**t**, **S**tyle(s). In **S**tyle Name type **body**, click **D**efine. In **P**aragraph, Spacing, change **A**fter to **1.5li**.

24. Move to page four. Select the text from the insertion point to and including the second paragraph under THE CUSTOMER LIST. On the Ribbon, in the Style box, choose Body.

25. To set the footers for the rest of the document, go to **V**iew, **D**raft. Follow steps 15 through 18 with two exceptions: don't choose Different First **P**age, and change the page numbers to 1 2 3....

26. Position the cursor at the end of the introduction (the paragraph preceding the THE CUSTOMER LIST head). Go to **I**nsert, **B**reak. Choose **P**age Break and select OK or press Enter.

27. At the top of page 4, place a double rule.

28. Select THE CUSTOMER LIST. Go to Forma**t**, **S**tyle(s). In **S**tyle Name, type **head** and click on **D**efine. Change the Charact**e**r to Helv, 14-point, bold, and select OK or press Enter. Select THE CUSTOMER LIST and on the Ribbon, in the Style box, change the setting to Head.

29. Select the type from Following is a list... to the end of number 6 on the list. On the Ruler, indent the type to .25" and set a left-hand tab at .5".

30. With the text in step 29 still selected, go to Forma**t**, **P**aragraph. In Spacing, Aft**e**r, type **.5li** and select OK or press Enter.

30. With the text in step 29 still selected, go to Forma**t**, **P**aragraph. In Spacing, Aft**e**r, type **.5li** and select OK or press Enter.

31. Select the next paragraph of type. In the Style box on the Ribbon, choose Body.

32. Position the cursor at the end of the paragraph, go to Insert, **B**reak. Choose **P**age Break and select OK or press Enter.

33. At the top of page 5, place a double rule above the first paragraph return. Select THE MARKETING PLAN. In the Style box on the Ribbon, change the type to head.

34. Select the rest of the text on the page. On the Ribbon, in the Style box, change the type to body.

35. Select the type from DIRECT MARKETING to the end of the paragraph under PARALLEL MARKETING. On the Ruler, indent the type .25" on the left and right.

36. Select DIRECT MARKETING. Bold it. Go to Forma**t**, **P**aragraph. In Spacing, Aft**e**r, type **.5li**. OK. Repeat with PARALLEL MARKETING.

36. Select and bold DIRECT MARKETING. Go to Forma**t**, **P**aragraph. In Spacing, Aft**e**r, type **.5li**. OK. Repeat with PARALLEL MARKETING.

37. Position the cursor at the end of the paragraph under PARALLEL MARKETING. Go to Insert, **B**reak. Choose **P**age Break and select OK or press Enter.

PART VI

Creating Long Documents

38. At the top of page 6, place a double rule on the first paragraph return. Select and format the body text and the head, `DIRECT MAILING`.

39. Select the type from (tab) `1st period...` to and including the `Telemarketing` line. Go to **I**nsert, **T**able and select OK or press Enter. On the Ruler, adjust column 1 to a width of 1.3".

40. Position the cursor on the paragraph return above the first line of the table. Go to Forma**t**, **P**aragraph. Place a Single rule Below. OK.

39. Select the type from (tab) `1st period...` to and including the `Telemarketing` line. Go to **T**able, **I**nsert Table. On the Ruler, adjust column 1 to a width of 1.3".

40. Position the cursor on the paragraph return above the first line of the table. Go to Forma**t**, **B**order. Place a 1.25 rule below the paragraph return and select OK or press Enter.

41. Select the first two lines of the table, from `1st period...` to `Mar. - May`. Change the type to 10-point, bold.

42. Select and bold `Direct Mail`. Repeat with `Seminars` and `Telemarketing`.

43. Position the cursor at the end of the text under `DIRECT MAILING`. Go to **I**nsert, **B**reak, choose **P**age Break. Select OK or press Enter.

44. At the top of page 7, insert the double rules, and format the head and body text.

45. If you plan to use a graph, bar, or pie chart, go to **I**nsert, **P**icture. Choose the graphic from the list of files and press Enter. Center the graphic. Position the cursor on the paragraph return under the graphic. Type a caption. Change the type to Helv, 8- or 9-point, centered.

46. Format the rest of the heads and body text for page 8.

47. If you have a table from another Windows application, such as Excel, open this application and the file you want to Link. The Word report document also should remain open.

48. In the original application, select the spreadsheet file. Copy the file. Switch to Word (Ctrl+Esc is a shortcut). Position the cursor.

CHAPTER 20

Producing a Business Report

49. Go to **E**dit, Paste **L**ink. Select the format in which you want to display the spreadsheet file.

50. Turn on **A**uto Update.

    The Windows application you use must support DDE, or Dynamic Data Exchange, for Linking with Word to work. Microsoft Excel Links with Word; check the reference manuals of other programs you use for more information.

47. If you have a table from another Windows application, such as Excel, open the application and the file you want to Link. Also, keep the Word report document open.

48. Select and then copy the spreadsheet file in the original application. Switch to Word (Ctrl+Esc is a shortcut). Position the cursor.

49. Go to **E**dit, Paste **S**pecial. Select the format in which you want to display your spreadsheet. (If you select "object," Word embeds instead of linking.)

50. Choose Paste **L**ink. If Paste Link is grayed, your application does not support linking; therefore, choose **P**aste.

    You can update linked spreadsheets either automatically or manually. Select one of these options in **E**dit, **L**inks.

    Format your spreadsheet as you normally format text.

51. To create a Table of Contents, go to page 3. Position the cursor in front of the H in Humble in the first sentence first paragraph. Go to **I**nsert, Fiel**d**. In Insert **F**ield Type, select TC. In Field **C**ode, after the TC (space), type **"Introduction."** OK. Be sure that you type the quote marks.

51. To create a Table of Contents, go to page 3. Position the cursor in front of the H in Humble in the first sentence first paragraph. Go to **I**nsert, Fiel**d**. In Insert **F**ield Type, select TC. In Field **C**ode, after the TC (space), type **"Introduction."** OK. Be sure that you type the quote marks.

52. Repeat the code inserting on page 4, first paragraph under The Customer List, Following is a list... (call it "Customer Sources"). Page 5, The Marketing Plan and Direct Marketing and Parallel Marketing. Page 6, Marketing Calendar and Direct Mailing. Page 7, Free Demonstrations and Seminars. Page 8, Telemarketing and Summary of Data.

535

PART VI

Creating Long Documents

The reason for placing all codes at the beginning of a paragraph, first line, is so that they are easy to find if you later need to change them. You also can turn on non-printing codes to see fields in the text.

53. Go to page 2, position cursor on the second paragraph return, and type the following two lines:

    (Enter, three times)

    TABLE OF CONTENTS (Enter, three times)

54. Go to **I**nsert, Table of **C**ontents. Use Table **E**ntry Fields. Select OK or press Enter. Word compiles the table of contents and inserts it at the cursor position.

55. Select TABLE OF CONTENTS. Change the type to Helv, 14-point bold.

56. Select the tabs, change the type to 12-point and on the Ruler, adjust the tab to 5.4".

57. With TABLE OF CONTENTS still selected, go to Forma**t**, **P**aragraph. In Spacing, **B**efore, type **.5li** and select OK or press Enter.

58. Go to **F**ile, **S**ave, **F**ile, **P**rint.

Looking at an Innovative Business Report

The formatting of business reports is a fairly straightforward process. You know how to perform the basic layout, such as formatting body text and heads, adding rules, converting text to tables, inserting breaks, and so on. The only difference with this report is the unusual page sizes. Figure 20.9 shows the finished report, with five levels at the bottom.

Each page, after the cover, contains a contents line of type and a rule above. You don't need page numbers or a table of contents for this report. The client chooses the subject he wants to read and opens right to the subject. This report in particular must be bound at the top. Side (top) stitch or spiral binding works well because the margin at the top is wide enough to accommodate the binding.

Marketing Summary for Humble Opinions

By Pear Associates, Ltd.
June 4, 1992

Introduction

Customer List

The Marketing Plan

The Marketing Plan — Direct

FIG. 20.9. *The front cover, and subsequent pages, die cut to form a table of contents.*

PART VI

Creating Long Documents

After the first five sheets, all page sizes remain 8 1/2-inches x 11-inches. To produce a small quantity—10 to 30 copies—of reports, you can print, cut, and assemble the job yourself. If you need a larger quantity, taking the work to a print shop or copy shop may be a better idea.

Figure 20.10 shows the basic style of the report, which uses justified type and a centered head. Look at the generous interparagraph spacing for easier reading. The rule along the top is Single, or 1.25, and the bottom rule is Thick, or 2.25. Because you have the choice of thicker rules in Version 2.0 of Word, you may try a 2.25-point rule at the top and a 6-point rule for the bottom heads.

Page one, or the cover, of the report cuts to 8 3/8 inches. Page two cuts to 9 inches. To position the word Introduction correctly, it must be at 8.6" on the Status bar ruler. When placing the bottom heads, you have to adjust paragraph returns with **B**efore and **A**fter (Aft**e**r) spacing in Forma**t**, **P**aragraph. Place the word as close to the measurement as possible, then choose one paragraph return, add three points of space and adjust from there.

Similar in style, page three contains the customer list. The numbered list of sources formats exactly like the one in the previous report (see fig. 20.11). This page cuts to 9 1/2 inches. The bottom head of Customer List is located at 9.2" on the Status bar ruler.

Although page four can contain graphics, charts, and so on, in this example, you see only text. The body is justified, and the subheads are boldfaced (see fig. 20.12). The head titled The Marketing Plan falls at 9.8" on the Status bar ruler. The page cuts at 10 1/8 inches.

Figure 20.13 shows page five, the longest page. The top head, the rules, and the table create an interesting variation to the other pages. The bottom head positions at 10.2" on the Status bar ruler, as do succeeding bottom heads.

Looking at Design

Varying the design and layout of a business report with illustrations, photos or graphics, rules, margins, and columns is possible. However, be conservative. A business report must be easy to read.

Figure 20.14 illustrates one way to create an interesting design.

Marketing Summary for Humble Opinions

June 4, 1992

Humble Opinions, a corporation dedicated to quality computer software training, initiated the Marketing Plan on June 4, 1991. Involved in this plan were many strategies for client expansion and increased financial gain. This summary analyzes the success of the Marketing Plan in terms of customer base increase and profit from services offered.

Current economic trends in our area greatly effect the figures of the past three months; however, earlier reports reveal the basic premise of the Marketing Plan is working. Should future trends prove to follow the same path as the past three months, a new Marketing Plan will then be developed. We do suggest this plan be followed for an additional period of six months before any long-term decision is made.

Despite this recent decline in profits and sales, the Marketing Plan demonstrated to be both beneficial and profitable to Humble Opinions in the first nine months of execution. The first three months, from June 1991 to August 1991, were considered the initiation period. Although contact with clients increased considerably, profits increased only slightly. During the second three months of the Marketing Plan, from September 1991 to November 1991, profits showed incredible growth. This is attributed to initial planning and advertising to build the customer base. The three month period from December 1991 to February 1992 proved to support the objectives of the Plan through substantial client referrals and increased profits for the company.

We estimate the Marketing Plan, with minimum modifications, can and will benefit the company in countless ways over the next six months. Customer lists will continue to expand; profits will continue to rise at a reliable and constant rate.

Introduction

FIG. 20.10. Page two of the innovative business report.

The Customer List

Humble Opinions is a business based solely on the customer. Software instruction aimed specifically at people who buy and use personal computers in their business. The first requirement of the Marketing Plan was to accumulate a comprehensive list of clients who need software instruction. Many methods were implemented to accomplish this task.

As the list was compiled, pertinent information about each client was entered into a data base for use in mailings, telemarketing and careful examination. Common data such as client's name, address, and phone number as well as the company's name, key contact personnel and their phone numbers comprised the list. As time went on, we added specific information to each file, such as interest areas of the client, software products owned by their company, types of documents used by the company, etc. In addition, comments were added to the files by the client about seminars, classes and demonstrations given by Humble Opinions that they attended. We then used these files as a basis for composing mailings and telemarketing scripts.

Following is a list of sources used for building the customer lists:

1. Customer records
2. Invoices from the last two years
3. Professional organizations membership lists
4. Sign-up sheets from seminars, trade-shows, give-a-ways
5. Mailing lists purchased — specific to personal computer users
6. Salesman's cold calls

As part of the client listing process, we initiated a program to update customer files every six months. Executed by office staff members, telephone calls made regularly to the customer base serves to verify phone numbers, addresses and key personnel. In addition, the telemarketing script includes questions directed to personal knowledge of new software instruction and training offered by the company.

Customer List

FIG. 20.11. Maintaining the layout and style, page three of the report.

The Marketing Plan

Using the client list as a foundation, our people created advertising that addressed the specific needs and concerns of the customers. Each project was dedicated to individual software programs, and the particular features that applied to a targeted group of clients.

By approaching the Plan in this way, more attention was devoted to the details of the software training that applied to individual customers. Thus, each customer perceived himself as distinctive, unique.

We used two methods of marketing for this project, Direct Marketing and Parallel Marketing. More time and effort were aimed at Direct Marketing. Considerable advantages were realized from this effort. In addition, the Parallel Marketing concentrated on one specific program and proved to be extremely profitable.

Direct Marketing

Among the Direct Marketing techniques utilized in the Plan were free demonstrations and seminars, direct mailing of flyers and letters, and telemarketing. Each approach was carefully researched and executed to enable us to measure results. Coupons for discounts identified clients who received the direct mailings. Different coupons distinguished seminar and demonstration attendants. Those customers accepting training through telemarketing efforts referred to a key word for a discount. Naturally, this summary is based solely on those clients whose proven response corresponds with each marketing technique. Any who did not reply with the coupon or key word could not feasibly be included in this report.

Parallel Marketing

Parallel Marketing targeted customers of one computer store in the area. Customers of that store were given such advertising items as mouse pads, shortcut key cards, and flyers with class descriptions. All of these items displayed a special phone number that identified them with this particular marketing approach.

Before analyzing the comprehensive outcome of the Marketing Plan, let us first look at the four stages divided into three month periods. We first concentrate on Direct Marketing; the second half of the summary devotes to Parallel Marketing. The following calendar of events illustrates the implementation of the Marketing Plan by use of Direct Marketing.

The Marketing Plan

FIG. 20.12. Page four of the report.

Calendar

	1st period Jun. - Aug.	2nd period Sept. - Nov.	3rd period Dec. - Feb.	4th period Mar. - May
Direct Mail	2 mailings 10,000	1 mailing 7500	2 mailings 10,000	1 mailing 7500
Seminars	4 seminars 2 demos.	2 seminars 4 demos.	4 seminars 2 demos.	2 seminars 4 demos.
Telemarketing	2500 calls	1500 calls	1500 calls	2500 calls

To further demonstrate the expenses versus profits of the Marketing Plan, let us know examine a sampling of each Direct Marketing technique as shown on the calendar. Each of these examples directly quotes expenditures and revenues as they apply to Humble Opinions.

Direct Mailing

Our Direct Mailing campaign consisted of advertising letters and/or flyers dispatched to customers in the compiled data base. The first mailing of 5000 letters is typical in costs of subsequent ones, so following is an analysis of the expenses and proceeds from that mailing.

Primary costs include printing and postage. Humble Opinions personnel performed typesetting and composition of the letter. The printing company charged for paper and envelopes; camera, press, folding and inserting the letters; and printing and attaching the mailing labels. The total printing costs totaled $645. Postage was $1000. A coupon attached to the letter identified it so response could be accurately measured.

Out of 5000 letters mailed, 1287 responded for more information. Out of those 1287, 490 took classes at $145 each. The total cost of classes per person is $100, including the cost of printing and mailing, instructor, supplies and overhead. At this rate, total profit resulting from this one mailing is $12,050.

Free Demonstrations and Seminars

Free seminars and demonstrations were advertised in the above mailings and by the use of flyers displayed in the company's office and classroom. Each seminar or demonstration concentrated on one particular software program and lasted about one hour. To add to the customer list, a sign-up list for a door prize was presented at each seminar. Refreshments served allowed the attendants to remain in the classroom for questions and discussion when the activity ended. A different coupon was utilized to measure response to the advertising.

The Marketing Plan — Direct

FIG. 20.13. *The fifth page of the report. Following pages would be the same length.*

CHAPTER 20

Producing a Business Report

Word Version 2.0 enables you to add frames and screens in a wide margin, such as you see in figure 20.14. The cover is simple but the screen adds a point of emphasis. If you use Version 1.1 of Word, consider a vertical bar, instead of the screen, to the left of the type.

All pages in the report repeat the design (see fig 20.15). The screen to the left and left-aligned heads follow through the entire document.

You can set a business report in two columns; however, avoid any more than that unless it's landscape orientation. Figure 20.16 shows a two-column report. The rules above and below the centered head distinguish this head from others. The footer in this design also is interesting. A horizontal rule leads the eye to the company logo on every page of the report. When typing in the header or footer pane, you also can insert an object, file, or picture.

Recapping

This chapter taught you that business reports inform and explain and usually focus on one specific project or one aspect of a project. You learned that almost all reports contain specific information regarding progress, profits, and expenditures. You learned that business reports can incorporate figures, charts, spreadsheets, graphs, and text to explain these elements. Finally, you learned how to produce your own business reports.

In Chapter 21, you learn how to produce a book.

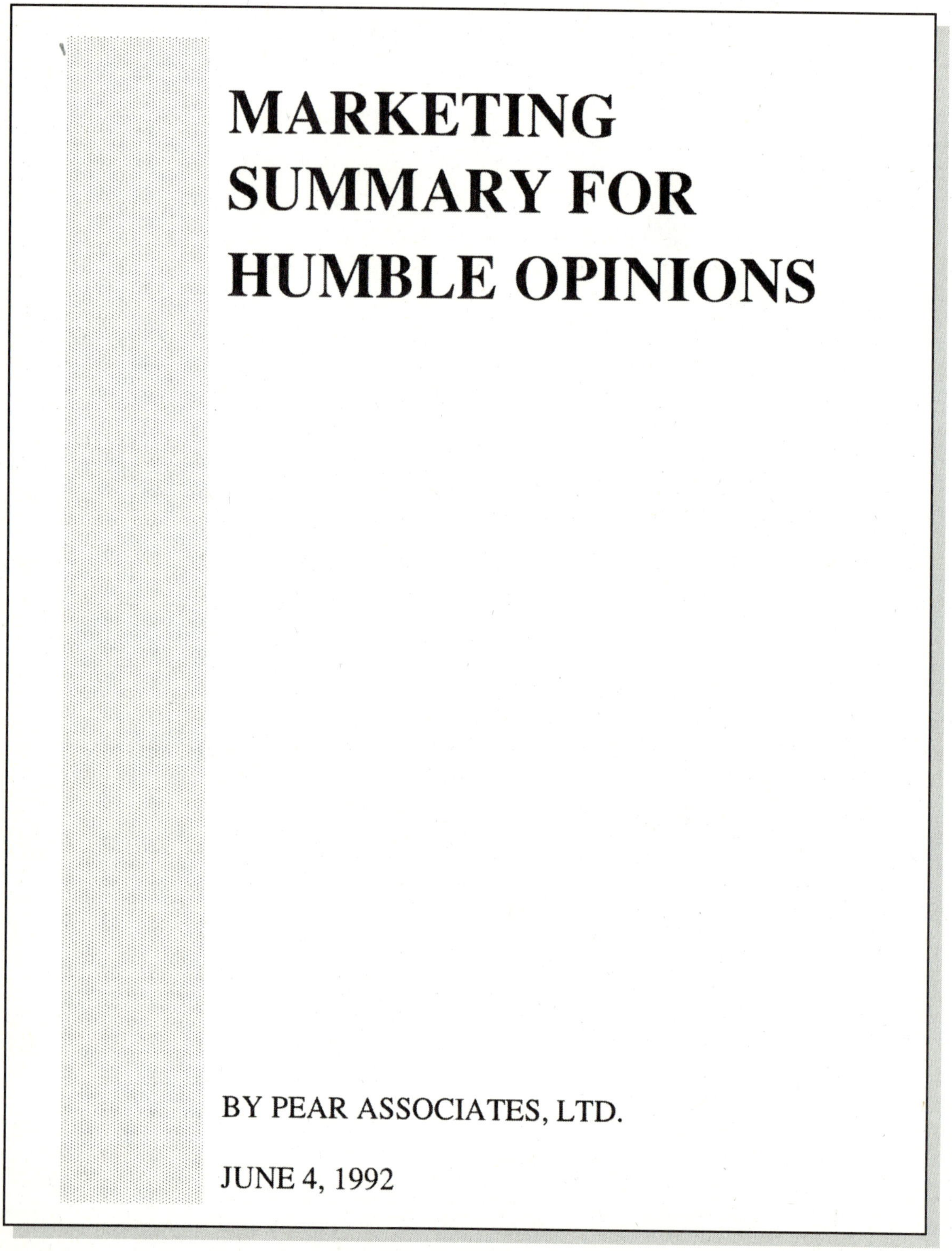

MARKETING SUMMARY FOR HUMBLE OPINIONS

BY PEAR ASSOCIATES, LTD.

JUNE 4, 1992

FIG. 20.14.   *A cover design that uses a screen in Word Version 2.0.*

MARKETING SUMMARY FOR HUMBLE OPINIONS
JUNE 4, 1992

Humble Opinions, a corporation dedicated to quality computer software training, initiated the Marketing Plan on June 4, 1991. Involved in this plan were many strategies for client expansion and increased financial gain. This summary analyzes the success of the Marketing Plan in terms of customer base increase and profit from services offered.

Current economic trends in our area greatly effect the figures of the past three months; however, earlier reports reveal the basic premise of the Marketing Plan is working. Should future trends prove to follow the same path as the past three months, a new Marketing Plan will then be developed. We do suggest this plan be followed for an additional period of six months before any long-term decision is made.

Despite this recent decline in profits and sales, the Marketing Plan demonstrated to be both beneficial and profitable to Humble Opinions in the first nine months of execution. The first three months, from June 1991 to August 1991, were considered the initiation period. Although contact with clients increased considerably, profits increased only slightly. During the second three months of the Marketing Plan, from September 1991 to November 1991, profits showed incredible growth. This is attributed to initial planning and advertising to build the customer base. The three month period from December 1991 to February 1992 proved to support the objectives of the Plan through substantial client referrals and increased profits for the company.

We estimate the Marketing Plan, with minimum modifications, can and will benefit the company in countless ways over the next six months. Customer lists will continue to expand; profits will continue to rise at a reliable and constant rate.

THE CUSTOMER LIST

Humble Opinions is a business based solely on the customer. Software instruction aimed specifically at people who buy and use personal computers in their business. The first requirement of the Marketing Plan was to accumulate a comprehensive list of clients who need software instruction. Many methods were implemented to accomplish this task.

As the list was compiled, pertinent information about each client was entered into a data base for use in mailings, telemarketing and careful examination. Common data such as client's name, address, and phone number as well as the company's name, key contact personnel and their phone numbers comprised the list. As time went on,

FIG. 20.15. *The next page of the report conforms to the basic design elements.*

MARKETING SUMMARY FOR HUMBLE OPINIONS

JUNE 4, 1992
BY PEAR ASSOCIATES, LTD.

Humble Opinions, a corporation dedicated to quality computer software training, initiated the Marketing Plan on June 4, 1991. Involved in this plan were many strategies for client expansion and increased financial gain. This summary analyzes the success of the Marketing Plan in terms of customer base increase and profit from services offered.

Current economic trends in our area greatly effect the figures of the past three months; however, earlier reports reveal the basic premise of the Marketing Plan is working. Should future trends prove to follow the same path as the past three months, a new Marketing Plan will then be developed. We do suggest this plan be followed for an additional period of six months before any long-term decision is made.

Despite this recent decline in profits and sales, the Marketing Plan demonstrated to be both beneficial and profitable to Humble Opinions in the first nine months of execution. The first three months, from June 1991 to August 1991, were considered the initiation period. Although contact with clients increased considerably, profits increased only slightly. During the second three months of the Marketing Plan, from September 1991 to November 1991, profits showed incredible growth. This is attributed to initial planning and advertising to build the customer base. The three month period from December 1991 to February 1992 proved to support the objectives of the Plan through substantial client referrals and increased profits for the company.

We estimate the Marketing Plan, with minimum modifications, can and will benefit the company in countless ways over the next six months. Customer lists will continue to expand; profits will continue to rise at a reliable and constant rate.

FIG. 20.16.   *A two-column layout for a business report.*

21

Producing a Book

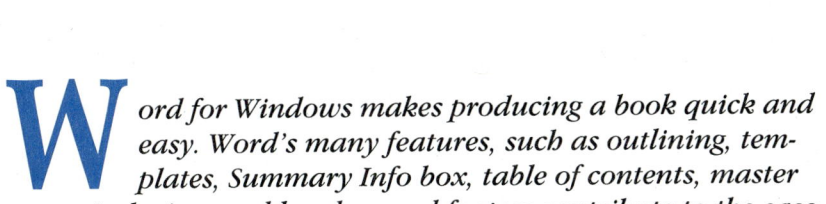

Word for Windows makes producing a book quick and easy. Word's many features, such as outlining, templates, Summary Info box, table of contents, master pages, indexing, and headers and footers contribute to the ease of formatting a book or other long document.

Planning Your Book

Before you do anything else, you must plan the book. First, consider the body of the book, such as the actual chapters, topics, and text. Word's Outline feature can help you with this process. You can list up to nine levels in an outline, and as you plan, you can add notes, thoughts, and key words under each heading. Then, when you're ready to begin the task of writing, you can use the outline as actual chapter titles, section headings, and so on. This chapter includes instructions for using the Outline feature of Word.

Setting Up Files and Directories

In addition to planning the text, plan how you might use all the files involved. If you use a hard disk, create a directory for the book; then create subdirectories for each chapter. You even can break each subdirectory into two separate directories, one for text and one for figures, illustrations, and graphics. If you plan to use floppy disks, use one disk for each chapter's text, and one for each chapter's illustrations.

If possible, working from the hard disk is preferable to working with floppies. Most computers work faster and more efficiently with long documents on the hard drive in procedures, such as gathering indexes and tables of contents. If you divide a book into chapter files on a hard disk, you can gather all these files together to create indexes or tables. If you keep the files on floppy disks, you need to transfer the files to the hard disk to accomplish this task. Floppy disks are excellent, however, for saving backups of all files.

Always back up every document, large or small. When you experience a power failure or a glitch in the program (and sooner or later, you will), you'll be glad you did. Furthermore, save your working files often.

An additional point: Word efficiently handles 20 to 40 pages in each file, and 20 pages is the optimum number. Split chapters that contain more than 40 pages into two or more documents.

Considering Front and End Material

Besides planning the body of the book, outline the front and end matter. Plan the length of the book, and include the front matter—the dedication, copyright, title pages, table of contents, list of illustrations, preface, foreword or introduction, and acknowledgments—in the plan. End matter includes appendix, glossary, index, notes, and bibliography. Naturally, many of these items are optional depending on the book and its needs. This chapter includes instructions on how to use the Word features to plan and form front and end matter effortlessly.

Front matter pages are usually numbered as lowercase Roman numerals. To accomplish this form of numbering, place these pages in a separate document and number them with headers or footers. As another option, you can format the first pages as a section, much as you did with the business report in the previous chapter, so that you can include these pages in the first chapter document.

CHAPTER 21

Producing a Book

Planning the Design Elements

Chapters always begin on a right page, even if the preceding page is blank. The first page of the chapter should not contain a header or footer. To also make the first page of the chapter stand out visually, add a wider top margin, or right-align the chapter number and head. You can use a large first character or drop cap for the first letter of the first paragraph of the chapter, which lets the reader know where a new chapter starts.

Remember that, when formatting, a book usually is made up of facing pages. Consistency in design and special attention to page numbers and also headers or footers (or both) is important. Furthermore, try to make all illustrations or graphics balance on the facing page.

Facing pages usually include running heads. A running head identifies the book title, author, chapter, or section, and the page number. Left and right pages also may differ; the left page header, for example, may include the chapter name and the page number, and the right page may contain the book title and page number.

Determining the Size

When planning the size of the pages of the book, consider several elements. If you print the book at a commercial print shop, match the page size in relation to the sheet size the printer stocks. You want to save money on paper, especially with this large of a job. Also, think about setting up the book in four-page signatures. For more information, see Chapters 2 and 4. If you plan to submit the book to a publisher, the publisher probably will specify the page size you use.

Three traditional page sizes for books are 5 1/2 inches x 8 1/4 inches, 6 1/8 inches x 9 1/4 inches, and 7 3/8 inches x 9 1/2 inches. Common sizes for printing at a commercial print shop are 8 1/2 inches x 11 inches, 5 1/2 inches x 8 1/2 inches and 6 inches x 8 inches. If possible, choose the paper type and finish when planning the size of the book.

PART VI

Creating Long Documents

Selecting the Paper

Book papers come in various finishes, weights and colors. Stick with 60# or 70# weight; 60 pound is optimum. Smooth or vellum finish is best for a book with a great deal of type; enamel finish is best for a book with photos. Usually, white paper is the only color used in a book; although ivory is a possibility.

Planning the Page Elements

The body of the book can be one or two columns. Two columns are used primarily in reference books, such as dictionaries and encyclopedias, although two columns also work in a landscape layout. Margins, traditionally, are even left and right, a slightly larger top, and even larger bottom. If the book is very thick, you may need to plan for a binding margin. White space in the margins is important for readability.

Also, consider the line length when planning the columns.

The type usually used is 10-point, although you may use 12-point if the text is aimed at an older group of people. A serif type font, such as Times Roman, Bookman, or even Trump, is easier to read. Also left-align or justify the body text. Be sure that you hyphenate all text you justify. *Rivers* of white space running through the paragraphs due to nonhyphenated justified type is distracting to the reader. Remember, the goal is to provide for comfortable reading.

Another matter important in book production is awkward page breaks. Avoid widows and orphans. A *widow* occurs when the last line of the paragraph ends on the top of a page and the rest of the paragraph is on the preceding page. An *orphan* is the first line of the paragraph at the bottom of the page, with the rest of the paragraph on the following page. Both versions of Word give you control over widows and orphans. In Version 2.0, go to T**o**ols, **O**ptions, in the Print category. In Version 1.1, go to Forma**t**, **P**aragraph.

Finally, be sure that you check all spelling within the documents. If you use Version 2.0, also check the grammar.

CHAPTER 21

Producing a Book

If you plan to produce a book, create a template and style sheet in Word *after* you choose the format. After it is created, use the template to begin each new chapter. This procedure saves time and ensures consistency. If you like one of the following book designs, after you complete the design, save it, then delete the text.

In the following exercises, you type the content of the book's first chapter only once. Then, as in previous chapters, you copy it for the second design. Because Word enables you to gather together all chapters for index and table of contents creation, you use the two chapters you design for this exercise as if the chapters were two chapters of your book.

After you format the sample chapters, you create a master document. In Word, a master document contains a built-in feature that pulls together each chapter in one file. You then can compile the index and table of contents from this file. You also can print the entire book from a master document.

Producing a Traditional Book Design

In this part of the chapter, you learn a traditional book design. The justified 10-point body type and interparagraph spacing used here enhance readability. The body also indents for a shorter line length (see fig. 21.1). The chapter number and title right-align for emphasis. Furthermore, extra space added above the chapter number and title create a visual division for the reader.

In figure 21.2, the major head hangs in the left margin so that the reader can easily see it. The left header includes the page number and the author's name (see fig. 21.2). The right header contains the page number and the book title as shown in figure 21.3. Both headers separate from the body with a rule.

Page four of the chapter completes the text. Additional white space commonly appears at the end of the last page of a chapter because the new chapter must start on a right-hand page (see fig. 21.4).

Chapter 1
Finding a Print Shop

What do you look for in a printer? What are your priorities? A quick turnaround? A superior print job? An inexpensive printing bill? Someone who treats you fairly and honestly? These are all attributes desired in a printer; but, unfortunately, you may not be able to find one who fills all of the above requirements.

Before you choose a printer, you should talk to and visit many printers. Ask questions, ask to tour their shop, meet the people with whom you will be working. If you are having a job typeset, meet the proofreader or head of that department. If you need artwork done, talk to the artist. If you need high-resolution output, talk to someone who has knowledge of the computer and desktop publishing programs. People who work in print shops are specialists in their fields. Rarely does one person know about all departments. Never depend on just one person in a print shop.

In addition, ask your friends and business associates who they use as a printer. Find out if they have had dealings with local shops, and what they think. If possible, find out who to talk to when you visit the shop, and who to stay away from. All print shops have at least one person who knows printing and is good at helping customers. A production manager, the head of composition, the person who schedules jobs, or perhaps a sales person could be your best contact at the shop. Similarly, most shops have employees you should avoid. One who knows more than anyone else, one who treats you like you're simple or tiresome, or one who doesn't care about you or your job. Take care of yourself when talking to your printer; if you don't like the way you're treated, either say so or find another printer.

FIG. 21.1. *The first page of the chapter minus a header or footer.*

2   S. Plumley

Printing Services

Of all the print shops available, try your local printers first. A local shop is convenient and keeps your money in your area. The convenience of touring the shop, placing your order in person, picking up your finished job, and registering complaints in person is far more beneficial to you than dealing with an out-of-state print shop. Sometimes, just looking them in the eye tells you everything you need to know.

The type of print shop you use depends on your job. Different shops cater to different types of printing. If you choose the right shop, your job looks better and the bill should be more to your liking. Following is a description of common print shops.

Commercial Printer

There are many types of print shops available. The commercial printer is most likely the one you will want to use. A commercial printer is one that will take on nearly any print job: books, forms, newsletters, letterheads, and so on; one who runs any number of ink colors from one color to four color process; one who has a typesetter, paste-up artist, camera department, presses, folders, and a bindery.

Although a commercial printer does the majority of work in-house, there may be some jobs he farms out to a trade shop. A trade shop specializes in one service: composition, or binding, four-color work, copy work.

Special Purpose Printer

A special purpose printer is one that specializes in specific print jobs: business cards or labels or business forms. A commercial printer might use them because they can do the work more efficiently and cheaper. But farmed out work may also be more expensive because the printer pays the trade shop and then charges you that price plus a mark-up (usually 25% of total). This is one reason you should get several quotes on your job before deciding upon one printer — you want the best price you can get (refer to Quotes on page 3).

Commercial print shops often farm out color separations. Small printers do not have the equipment or personnel to do their own separations. As color separation technology advances, less expensive equipment is becoming available. If your printer does separations in-house, always ask to see samples of his work. And always ask how much it will cost. Separations are very expensive.

FIG. 21.2.   Page two, a left-hand page that contains a left header.

Planning and Purchasing Printing 3

Quick Printer

A quick printer is one who does mostly photocopying by using a xerographic process that allows the copying of short-run quantities. The quality is usually low to medium; however some quick print shops do produce quality work. The standard page sizes for photo copying are 8-1/2" x 11" and 11" x 17". Quick print shops may also have a small press or two and do some offset printing. They may farm out work such as binding large jobs, typesetting, some camera work, and so on. A quick print shop is good to use for certain jobs: fliers, invitations, inserts, or jobs that don't require precision in width of margins, registration, and so forth.

The type of shop you choose depends upon your job. If you need high-quality printing within a reasonable amount of time, you may choose a commercial printer. If you need 500 fliers yesterday, then choose a quick print shop.

It is important to patronize several shops. Don't just get quote after quote. Actually take them some business once in a while. This way, when you are in need of something special or something fast, and one printer cannot do it — you have the option of taking it to another printer.

Estimates, Quotes

It's important to find out how much your job will cost before you have it printed. If you don't ask ahead of time, the printer could increase the price to whatever he wishes. Many print shop's are principled; many are not. There are two ways to find out the cost of your job, by an estimate or by a quote.

Estimates

Some printers will give estimates on the cost of your job. You would have to give complete details on your job, as you would with a quote, to get a reasonable estimate. Estimates, however, are not what the printer guarantees the price to be. An estimate is just that — an estimate. If the printer finds extra costs in running the job, he will raise the price accordingly. For this reason, it is important you get a quote instead of an estimate, if at all possible.

Quotes

It is important to get quotes on all of your jobs before you print them. A quote is the printer's stated price for the cost of your specific job. You should consider getting quotes from several printers because prices can vary greatly from shop to shop. Also, be sure your quote is in writing; keep your copy in case there is a question later. Most quotes are good for 30 days, so you'll have time to check out other printers. A quote should be honored by your printer as the price he will charge you — as long as you don't make any alterations after the piece is in process.

FIG. 21.3. *Page three contains a right header and continues the style of page two.*

A quote from the printer includes the cost of materials and labor for your job: composition, paste-up, camera, stripping, plate-making, paper, ink, press, and bindery. Not only that, but the quote also adds in a fee for overhead items such as electricity, cost of water, equipment, office help, and insurance for employees and building.

The more information you give printers, the better they will be able to quote your job. Describe your piece in a term the printer will recognize: newsletter, brochure, flier. This will give the printer an immediate basic understanding of your piece before the quote. If possible, include a mock-up of your job.

Make sure you provide all the information about your job to the person who quotes the job. If you omit details, expect the printer to alter the quote accordingly. Omitted details may also affect scheduling and delivery time. The printer has only the information you provide him when he quotes, plans and schedules your job.

FIG. 21.4. *The last page in the chapter, with plenty of white space.*

PART VI

Creating Long Documents

The final size of the book is 7 3/8 inches x 9 1/2 inches; look at the crop marks in figures 21.1 and 21.2. Because Word does not allow crop marks, you add them in paste-up. You can, however, adjust the margins of the page so that the text area is correct.

The following instructions include Word's Outline feature. Organizing chapter titles, major topics, and subtopics is much easier with an outline. Word also offers the option of compiling the table of contents from the headings selected in the outline (see fig. 21.5). This feature means that with a little preplanning, gathering the table of contents is made smooth and easy.

Once again, because you're now familiar with most page and type formatting, the instructions are detailed only when introducing new features.

To create the designs shown in figures 21.1 to 21.5, perform the following steps:

1. Go to **File**, **New**. Select New **Document**, **U**se Template Normal. Select OK or press Enter.

2. To create the em dashes in the text, as you type, press the following two-key combination:

    Alt+0150

    Alt+0151

FIG. 21.5.
The outline for chapter one of the book.

Chapter 1
Finding a Print Shop
Printing Services
Commercial Printer
Special Purpose Printer
Quick Printer
Estimates, Quotes
Estimates
Quotes

CHAPTER 21

Producing a Book

To enter the sample chapter, type the following text:

Chapter 1 (Shift+Enter)

Finding a Print Shop (Enter)

(Type in the paragraphs as shown in the figure, or enter your own data, pressing Enter after each paragraph.)

Printing Services (Enter)

Commercial Printer (Enter)

Special Purpose Printer (Enter)

Quick Printer (Enter)

Estimates, Quotes (Enter)

Estimates (Enter)

Quotes (Enter)

3. Go to File, Save **As chap2**. Go to File, Save **As chap1**. You format the CHAP1.DOC first.

4. Setting the margins must allow for not only the page trim size—7 3/8 inches x 9 1/2 inches—but also for the margins of the page. If you subtract the book's page size from the 8 1/2-inch x 11-inch sheet, you must take off 1.13 inches from a side and 1 inch from the top or bottom (these instructions divide the difference between the left and right, and the top and bottom). The actual margins of the book's page are .75 inches top, 1.25 inches bottom and .75 inches left and right. The following margins give you the correct final size.

    Go to Forma**t**, **D**ocument. Set the **T**op, **L**eft, and **R**ight margins at **1.3"**, set the **B**ottom margin at **1.5"** and select OK or press Enter.

    Go to Forma**t**, Page Se**t**up. Set the **T**op, **L**eft, and **R**ight margins at **1.3"**, set the **B**ottom margin at **1.5"** and select OK or press Enter.

5. To create the outline, go to **V**iew, **O**utline. Select `Chapter 1 Finding a Print Shop`. Go to the outline bar at the top of the text screen. Click the arrow for promotion of head (the arrow that points to the left). Or with the keyboard, press Alt+Shift and the left arrow key to promote a heading.

PART VI

Creating Long Documents

6. Select `Printing Services`. Click the promotes head arrow, then the demotes head arrow (the arrow that points to right) or press Alt+Shift and the right arrow key to demote the heading. Repeat this process with Estimates, Quotes.

   You also can select the heading in the Style box on the Ribbon; the chapter title is heading 1, Printing Services is heading 2, and so on.

7. Select, promote, and then demote `Commercial Printer`. Repeat the process with the following heads in the sample chapter: `Special Purpose Printer`, `Quick Printer`, `Estimates`, and `Quotes`.

8. To view only the headings of the chapter, click the number 3 button. If you prefer, you can print the outline of only the heads.

9. Go to **V**iew, **P**age.

9. Go to **V**iew, **P**age Layout.

10. Select `Chapter 1 Finding a Print Shop`. Go to Forma**t**, **S**tyle(s). Heading 1 appears in the **S**tyle Name box. Click **D**efine.

11. In **C**haracter, change to 24-point, **B**old, no **U**nderline. In **P**aragraph, change the spacing **B**efore, to **8.5li**. After to **4li**. Alignment to **R**ight. Select OK two times or press Enter twice.

11. In **C**haracter, change to 24-point, **B**old, no **U**nderline. In **P**aragraph, change the spacing **B**efore, to **8.5li**. After to **4li**. Alignment to Right. Select OK and Apply. Word asks if you want to change the properties of the style sheet. Select **Y**es.

12. Select the first paragraph of text. Go to Forma**t**, **S**tyle(s). Normal appears in the Style Name box. Click **D**efine.

13. In **P**aragraph, change the Alignment to **J**ustified. In Spacing, After type **1li**. In Indents, From Left, type **1.2"**. Select OK twice or press Enter twice.

13. In **P**aragraph, change the Alignment to **J**ustified. In Spacing, After type **1li**. In Indentations, From **L**eft, type **1.2"**. Select OK and Apply. **Y**es to Word's questioning of the style sheet.

558

CHAPTER 21

Producing a Book

14. To change heading 2, go to Format, Style(s). Change the Character to 14-point, bold. In Paragraph left align the head (no indents), add **1li** spacing after, and select OK or press Enter.

15. For heading 3, go to Format, Style(s). In Paragraph, left align with an indent from the left of 1.2", add **1li** spacing after, and select OK or press Enter.

16. Position the cursor in front of "Printing Services". Go to Insert, Break, choose Page Break and then select OK.

17. To add the header on page two, go to View, Draft.

18. Go to Edit, Header/Footer. Select Different First Page and Different Odd and Even Pages. Choose Options. In Distance From Edge, Header, type **.75"**.

19. In Select Header/Footer to Edit, select Even Header. In the header pane, choose the page number icon on the bar (Alt+Shift+P). Type **(tab) S. Plumley**.

20. Select the line of type. On the Ruler, adjust the indent to 0. Adjust the tab to right aligned at 5.88".

21. With the line of text still selected, on the Ribbon change the type to 8-point, italic. Go to Format, Paragraph. In Border, choose Below; in Pattern, choose Single and select OK or press Enter. Choose Close.

22. To set the Odd Header, go to View, Header/Footer. Select Odd Header.

23. In the header pane, type **Planning and Purchasing Printing(tab)**. Choose the page number icon (Alt+Shift+P). Format steps 20 and 21. Go to View, Page to see the results.

18. Go to View, Header/Footer. Select Different First Page and Different Odd and Even Pages. In From Edge, Header, type **.75"**.

19. In Header/Footer box, select Even Header. In the header pane, click the page number icon on the bar or press Alt+Shift+P. Type **(tab) S. Plumley**.

20. Select the line of type. On the Ruler, adjust the indent to 0. Adjust the right tab to right-aligned at 5.88".

559

PART VI

Creating Long Documents

21. With the line of text still selected, on the Ribbon change the type to 9-point, italic. Go to Format, **B**order. In the Bo**r**der box, click in the bottom margin or press the down arrow to select; in **L**ine choose the 1.25 rule and select OK or press Enter. **C**lose.

22. To set the Odd Header, go to **V**iew, **H**eader/Footer. Select Odd Header.

23. In the header pane type: **Planning and Purchasing Printing(tab)**. Click the page number icon or press Alt+Shift+P. Format following steps 20 and 21. Go to View, **P**age Layout to see the results.

24. Position the cursor in front of `Quick Printer`. Go to Insert, **B**reak. Choose **P**age Break and select OK or press Enter. Repeat the break in front of the second paragraph of text under `Quotes`, beginning with `A quote from the printer includes...`.

25. To create a cross-reference, go to page four. Position the cursor in the paragraph under `Quotes`. Go to Insert, Book**m**ark. In **B**ookmark Name, type **quoteref** and select OK or press Enter.

26. In the first paragraph under `Special Purpose Printer`, position the cursor after the `page(space)` in `(refer to Quotes on page )`. Go to Insert, Fiel**d**. On the keyboard, press P twice. In the Field **C**ode box, pageref appears.

27. In Instructions, select quoteref. Choose **A**dd and select OK or press Enter. Word inserts the page number at the position of the bookmark.

28. To create the index, you must mark entries throughout the text. Go to page two of the document.

29. Position the cursor in the first paragraph under `Commercial Printer`. Go to Insert, Index Entry. In the Index Entry box, type the following line:

    Printing Services:commercial printer

    Select OK or press Enter.

30. Repeat step 29 with each of the following:

    Same page, `Special Purpose Printer` **Printing**

CHAPTER 21

Producing a Book

> **Services:special purpose printer**
>
> Page 3, `Quick Printer` **Printing Services:quick printer**
>
> `Estimates` **Estimates**
>
> `Quotes` **Quotes**

31. Position the cursor at the end of the document. Go to **I**nsert, **B**reak. In Section Break, choose Continuous. Select OK and press **Enter**.

    The purpose of this section break is to guarantee that, when you include the document in the MASTER.DOC, the formatting remains constant.

32. Go to **F**ile, **S**ave. Choose **F**ile, **P**rint.

Producing Another Traditional-Styled Book

The following design employs headers that name the author and book title and footers that contain page numbers. This book design is a traditional layout; the size of the book is 6 3/4 inches x 8 3/4 inches. After completing the layout of this chapter, you combine this layout with the first design in a master document. You then compile an index and table of contents for the two chapters, which is standard practice for a book. To make the contents different from the first chapter, you change the heads. `Chapter 1, Finding a Printer`, for example, changes to `Chapter 2, Looking for a Printer`.

The first page of the chapter shows the page setup. The body text is not indented from the left, as was the case with the first design. The margins, however, offset on the left, then right, for a binding margin, as you may see from the crop marks. The justified type is indented, which creates a grayer page; the heads are left aligned. Figure 21.6 shows the first page of Chapter 2.

Page two of the chapter shows the left header with the author's name. The left footer is only a page number (see fig. 21.7). You renumber the pages in this chapter to continue from the last chapter, which is the usual practice in a book.

Chapter 2
Looking for a Printer

What do you look for in a printer? What are your priorities? A quick turn-a-round? A superior print job? An inexpensive printing bill? Someone who treats you fairly and honestly? These are all attributes desired in a printer, but unfortunately, you may not be able to find one who fills all of the above requirements.

Before you choose a printer, you should talk to and visit many shops. Ask questions, ask to tour their shop, meet the people with whom you will be working. If you are having a job typeset, meet the proofreader or head of that department. If you need artwork done, talk to the artist. If you need high resolution output, talk to someone who has knowledge of the computer and desktop publishing programs. Each person who works in a print shop is a specialist in his field. Rarely does one person know about all departments. Never depend on just one person in a print shop.

In addition, ask your friends and business associates who they use as a printer. Find out if they have had dealings with local shops, and what they think. If possible, find out who to talk to when you visit the shop, and who to stay away from. All print shops have at least one person who knows printing and is good at helping customers. A production manager, the head of composition, the person who schedules jobs, or perhaps a sales person could be your best contact at the shop. Similarly, most shops have employees you should avoid. One who knows more than anyone else, one who treats you like you're simple or tiresome, or one who doesn't care about you or your job. Take care of yourself when talking to your printer; if you don't like the way you're treated, either tell him so or find another printer.

FIG. 21.6. Page one of the design, without header, footer, or page number.

S. Plumley

What are the Types of Printers?

Of all the print shops available, try your local printers first. A local shop is convenient and keeps your money in your area. The convenience of touring the shop, placing your order in person, picking up your finished job, and registering complaints in person is far more beneficial to you than dealing with an out-of-state print shop. Sometimes, just looking them in the eye tells you everything you need to know.

The type of print shop you use depends on your job. Different shops cater to different types of printing. If you choose the right shop, your job looks better and the bill should be more to your liking, Following is a description of common print shops.

What is a Commercial Print Shop?

There are many types of print shops available. The commercial printer is most likely the one you will want to use. A commercial printer is one that will take on nearly any print job: books, forms, newsletters, letterheads, etc.; one who runs any number of ink colors from one color to four color process; one who has a typesetter, paste-up artist, cameral department, presses, folders, and a bindery.

Although a commercial printer does the majority of work in-house, there may be some jobs he farms out to a trade shop. A trade shop specializes in one service: composition, or binding, four-color work, copy work.

What is a Special Purpose Printer?

A special purpose printer is one that specializes in specific print jobs: business cards or labels or business forms. A commercial printer might use them because they can do the work more efficiently and cheaper. But farmed out work may also be more expensive because the printer pays the trade shop and then charges you that price plus a mark-up (usually 25% of total). This is one reason you should get several quotes on your job before deciding upon one printer — you want the best price you can get (refer to Quotes on page 8).

Commercial print shops often farm out color separations. Small printers do not have the equipment or personnel to do their own separations. As color separation technology advances, less expensive equipment is becoming available. If your printer does separations in-house, always ask to see samples of his work. And always ask how much it will cost. Separations are very expensive.

FIG. 21.7. *Page two of the chapter, page six of the book.*

PART VI

Creating Long Documents

Figure 21.8 shows the third page of the document. This right-hand page contains a right header, with the book title and a right footer.

The last page of the document is a left-hand page (see fig. 21.9).

To begin this design, follow the same pattern you used in the previous layout. Use an outline so that you can more easily collect the table of contents at the end. Mark index entries, and set headers and footers. If you were laying out a real book, you would use the template you created from the first chapter to begin this chapter.

To create the design as shown in figures 21.6 to 21.9, take these steps:

1. Go to **File**, **O**pen. Open the file CHAP2 and select OK or press Enter.

2. For the purpose of the table of contents, replace each head with the following lines:

    Chapter 2 (Shift+Enter)

    Looking for a Printer

    What are the Types of Printers?

    What is a Commercial Print Shop?

    What is a Special Purpose Printer?

    What is a Quick Print Shop?

    How Much Will it Cost?

    What is an Estimate?

    What is a Quote?

3. Go to **V**iew, **O**utline. Promote `Chapter 2...` to heading 1. Promote `What are the Types of Printers?` and `How Much Will it Cost?` to heading 2. Promote the other five heads to heading 3.

4. Go to Format, **D**ocument. Set both **T**op and **B**ottom margins to **2.15**"; set the Left and Right to **1.70**". In **G**utter, type **.5**". Click on **M**irror Margins for facing pages and select OK or press Enter.

CHAPTER 21

Producing a Book

4. Go to Forma**t**, Page Set**u**p. Set both **T**op and **B**ottom margins to **2.15**"; set the **L**eft and **R**ight to **1.70**". In **G**utter, type **.5**". Click on **F**acing Pages and select OK or press Enter. Note that the **L**eft and **R**ight now are Inside and Outside.

5. To format heading 1, select Chapter 2.... Go to Forma**t**, St**y**les. Click on **D**efine. In **C**haracter, change the type to 18-point, no **U**nderline, and select OK or press Enter. In **P**aragraph, change the Alignment to Left. In Spacing, change **B**efore to **2li** and After to **3li**. Select OK two times.

6. Select the first paragraph of body text. Go to Forma**t**, St**y**les. To format the Normal style, click on **D**efine. In **P**aragraph, Alignment, choose **J**ustified. In Indents, First Li**n**e type **.25**". Select OK twice or press Enter twice. Select the entire document and hyphenate.

7. Select Heading 2, What are the Types of Printers?. Go to Format, St**y**les. Change the **C**haracter to 14-point, bold. In **P**aragraph, change to no indent, left aligned. Change **A**fter to **.5li** and **B**efore to **1li**. Select OK twice or press Enter twice.

8. Select heading 3, What is a Commercial Print Shop?. Go to Format, St**y**les. In **P**aragraph, change to no indents, left aligned, **B**efore **1li**; After **.5li**. Select OK twice or press Enter twice.

5. To format heading 1, select Chapter 2.... Go to Forma**t**, Style. Click on **D**efine. In **C**haracter, change the type to 18-point, no **U**nderline, and select OK or press Enter. In **P**aragraph, change the Al**i**gnment to Left. In Spacing, change **B**efore to **2li** and After to **3li**. Select first OK and then Apply. When Word asks if you want to change the properties of the standard style, answer **Y**es.

6. Select the first paragraph of body text. Go to Forma**t**, Style. To format the Normal style, click on **D**efine. In **P**aragraph, Alignment, choose Justified. In Indentation, **F**irst Line type **.25**". Select OK, Apply, and **Y**es. Select the entire document and hyphenate.

7. Select Heading 2, What are the Types of Printers?. Go to Format, Style. Change the **C**haracter to 14-point, bold. In **P**aragraph, change to no indent, left-aligned. Change **A**fter to **.5li** and **B**efore to **1li**. Select OK, then Apply and Yes.

Planning and Purchasing Printing

What is a Quick Print Shop?

A quick printer is one who does mostly photocopying using a xerographic process that allows the copying of short run quantities. The quality is usually low to medium; however some quick print shops do produce quality work. The standard page sizes for photo copying are 8-1/2" x 11" and 11" x 17". Quick print shops may also have a small press or two and do some offset printing. They may farm out work such as binding large jobs, typesetting, some camera work, etc. A quick print shop is good to use for certain jobs: flyers, invitations, inserts, or jobs that don't require precision in width of margins, registration, etc.

The type of shop you choose depends upon your job. If you need high quality printing within a reasonable amount of time, you may choose a commercial printer. If you need 500 flyers yesterday, then choose a quick print shop.

It is important to patronize several shops. Don't just get quote after quote. Actually take them some business once in a while. This way, when you are in need of something special or something fast, and one printer cannot do it — you have the option of taking it to another printer.

How Much Will it Cost?

It's important to find out how much your job will cost before you have it printed. If you don't ask ahead of time, the printer could increase the price to whatever he wishes. Many print shop's are principled; many are not. There are two ways to find out the cost of your job, by an estimate or by a quote.

What is an Estimate?

Some printers will give estimates on the cost of your job. You would have to give complete details on your job, as you would with a quote, to get a reasonable estimate. Estimates, however, are not what the printer guarantees the price to be. An estimate is just that — an estimate. If the printer finds extra costs in running the job, he will raise the price accordingly. For this reason, it is important you get a quote instead of an estimate, if at all possible.

7

FIG. 21.8. Page seven of the book (page three of the chapter).

S. Plumley

What is a Quote?

It is important to get quotes on all of your jobs before you print them. A quote is the printer's stated price for the cost of your specific job. You should consider getting quotes from several printers because prices can vary greatly from shop to shop. Also, be sure your quote is in writing; keep your copy in case there is a question later. Most quotes are good for 30 days, so you'll have time to check out other printers. A quote should be honored by your printer as the price he will charge you — as long as you don't make any alterations after the piece is in process.

A quote from the printer includes the cost of materials and labor for your job: composition, paste-up, camera, stripping, plate-making, paper, ink, press, and bindery. Not only that, but the quote also adds in a fee for overhead items such as electricity, cost of water, equipment, office help, insurance for employees and building.

The more information you give your printer, the better he will be able to quote your job. Describe your piece in a term the printer will recognize: newsletter, brochure, flyer. This will give him an immediate basic understanding of your piece before he begins the quote. If possible, include a mock-up of your job.

Make sure you provide all the information about your job to the person who quotes the job. If you omit details, expect the printer to alter the quote accordingly. Omitted details may also affect scheduling and delivery time. The printer has only the information you provide him when he quotes, plans and schedules your job.

8

FIG. 21.9. *The final page of the chapter with the header and footer left-aligned.*

PART VI

Creating Long Documents

8. Select heading 3, `What is a Commercial Print Shop?`. Go to Format, Style. In Paragraph, change to no indents, left aligned, Before **1li**, After **.5li**. Select OK, then Apply and Yes.

9. Go to page one and position the cursor to the immediate left of `What are the Types of Printers?`. Go to Insert, Break. Choose Page Break and select OK or press Enter.

10. At the top of page two, go to View, Draft.

11. Go to Edit, Header/Footer. Select Different First Page and Different Odd and Even Pages.

12. In Select Header/Footer to Edit, select Even Header. In the header pane, type **S. Plumley**.

13. Select the line of type. On the Ruler, adjust the indent to 0.

14. With `S. Plumley` still selected, on the Ribbon change the type to Helv, 8-point, bold. Go to Format, Paragraph. In Border, choose Below; in Pattern, choose Double. In Spacing, Before, type **8li**. Select OK and choose Close.

15. To set the Odd Header, go to View, Header/Footer. Select Odd Header.

16. In the header pane type: **(tab)Planning and Purchasing Printing**. Set the tab as right aligned at 4.56" on the Ruler. Format following steps 13 and 14. Go to View, Page to see the results.

11. Go to View, Header/Footer. Select Different First Page and Different Odd and Even Pages.

12. In Header/Footer box, select Even Header. In the header pane, type **S. Plumley**.

13. Select the line of type. On the Ruler, adjust the indent to 0.

14. Still selected, on the Ribbon change the type to Helv, 9-point, bold. Go to Format, Border. In the Border box, click in the bottom margin or use the down arrow to select and, in Line, choose a double rule. Select OK or press Enter. Go to Format, Paragraph. In Spacing, Before, type **8li**. Close.

15. To set the Odd Header, go to View, Header/Footer. Select Odd Header.

CHAPTER 21

Producing a Book

16. In the header pane type: **(tab)Planning and Purchasing Printing**. Set the tab as right aligned at 4.56 inches on the Ruler. Format following steps 13 and 14. Go to **V**iew, **P**age Layout to see the results.

17. To set the even footer, go to **V**iew, **D**raft. Go to **E**dit, **H**eader/Footer. Select Even Footer. Choose **O**ptions. **S**tart at **5** and select OK or press Enter.

18. In the footer pane, click the page number icon or press Alt+Shift+P. Select the number and change to Helv, 8-point, bold. Go to Forma**t**, **P**aragraph. In Spacing, **A**fter, type **8li**. Select OK and choose **C**lose.

19. To set the odd footer, go to **V**iew, **H**eader/Footer. Select Odd Footer and then OK.

20. In the footer pane, type **tab** then click the page number icon or press Alt+Shift+P. Select and format as in step 18. Adjust the tab on the Ruler. **C**lose.

17. To set the even footer, go to **V**iew, **D**raft. Go to **V**iew, **H**eader/Footer. Select Even Footer. Click on Page **N**umbers. Start at **5**. Select OK or press Enter.

18. In the footer pane, click the page number icon or press Alt+Shift+P. Select the number and change it to Helv, 9-point, bold. Go to Forma**t**, **P**aragraph. In Spacing, Aft**e**r, type **8li**. Close.

19. To set the odd footer, go to **V**iew, **H**eader/Footer. Select Odd Footer and then select OK.

20. In the footer pane, type **tab**, then click the page number icon or press Alt+Shift+P. Select and format as shown in step 18. Adjust the tab on the Ruler and select **C**lose.

21. Insert a page break before `What is a Quick Print Shop?` and before `What is a Quote?`.

22. To create a cross reference, go to page 8. Position the cursor in the paragraph under `Quotes`. Go to **I**nsert, **B**ookmark. In **B**ookmark Name, type **quote2** and select OK or press Enter.

23. On page 6, in the first paragraph under `Special Purpose Printer`, position the cursor after the `page(space)` in `(refer to Quotes on page )`. Go to **I**nsert, Fiel**d**. On the keyboard, press P twice. In the Field **C**ode box, pageref appears.

569

24. In Instructions, select quote2. Choose **Add** and select OK or press Enter. Word inserts the page number on which the bookmark is located.

25. To create the index, you must mark entries throughout the text. Go to page 5.

26. Position the cursor in the second paragraph. Go to **Insert, Index Entry**. In the Index Entry box, type **Printers:key personnel**. Select OK or press Enter.

27. On page 6, under `What is a Commercial Print Shop?`, position the cursor in the first paragraph. Go to **Insert, Index Entry**. In the Index Entry box, type **Printing:in-house**. Continue to mark the index entries in:

    `What is a Special Purpose Printer?`, first paragraph, **Printing:farmed out**

    In same paragraph, **Mark-up**

    In the next paragraph, **Photographs:separations**

    On page 7, in the first paragraph, **Photocopying**

    Under `What is an Estimate?`, **Print Shop:cost:estimate**

    On page 8, under `What is a Quote?`, **Print Shop:cost:quote**

28. Position the cursor on the last paragraph return in the document. Go to **Insert, Break**. In Section Break, choose Continuous. Press **Enter**.

29. Go to **F**ile, **S**ave, **F**ile, **P**rint.

Creating a Master Document

Usually, you complete the entire book before creating a master document; but, using the two chapters you just finished, the following instructions demonstrate this procedure. A master document gathers the chapters into one file so that you can create a table of contents and an index. You also can print the chapter from a master document. To print from a master document, you must insert a section break at the end of each chapter, then press Enter to insure that all formatting remains the same. Word

CHAPTER 21

Producing a Book

changes the last paragraph return of all documents back to the original formatting. Formatting the index and table of contents in the style of the rest of the book also is important.

You can either format and print the table of contents and index within the master document, or you can copy each element and save to a document that contains other front and end matter.

1. To create the master document, go to **File**, **New**. Choose New Document, **U**se Template Normal (or the book template, if you created one). Select OK or press Enter.

2. Go to **V**iew, Field **C**odes. Click to turn on or press Alt+V,C.

3. Go to Insert, Fiel**d**. In Insert **F**ield Type, choose Include. In the Field **C**ode box, after `Include(space)`, type **CHAP1.DOC** and select OK or press Enter.

4. Press **E**nter. Go to Insert, Fiel**d**. In Insert **F**ield Type, choose Include. In the Field **C**ode box, after `Include(space)`, type **chap2.doc**, and select OK or press Enter.

5. Select the entire document, press the F9 key to update the fields.

6. Go to **F**ile, Save **As master** and select OK or press Enter. Go to **V**iew, turn off Field **C**odes. Word inserts the text of both documents. Don't close the document because you use it in the following set of instructions.

Creating an Index

The index is simple to create; you create it first so that the index is included in the table of contents. Using the same master document, you instruct Word to compile the index. You can use any format you want; refer to your reference manual for alternatives. Figure 21.10 shows the completed index for the two chapters.

To create an index, follow these steps:

1. Go to the end of the document. Position the cursor, go to Insert, **B**reak. Choose **P**age Break and select OK or press Enter.

2. Go to Insert, Index. Choose **N**ormal Index. In Heading Separator choose **B**lank Line. Select OK or press Enter. Word compiles and inserts the index.

571

PART VI

Creating Long Documents

FIG. 21.10.
One way to do an index in Word.

```
Index

Estimates, 3

Mark-up, 6

Photocopying, 7
Photographs
    separations, 6
Print Shop
    cost
        estimate, 7
        quote, 8
Printer
    key personnel, 5
Printing
    farmed out, 6
    in-house, 6
Printing Services
    commercial printer, 2
    quick printer, 3
    special purpose printer, 2

Quotes, 3
```

3. Type **Index** at the top; format as heading 2, and the page is completed. You may want to add headers and/or footers to the index pages.

4. Go to **F**ile, **S**ave, **P**rint. Don't close the document.

Creating a Table of Contents

Generating a table of contents is just as simple as the preceding steps. Using the master document, you insert a table of contents. Because you used heading paragraphs from the Normal style, Word easily gathers these headings to form the contents, a process which works much like forming an outline. Figure 21.11 shows the table of contents for the first two chapters.

Chapter 21
Producing a Book

FIG. 21.11.
A formatted table of contents for the book.

Table of Contents

```
Chapter 1
Finding a Print Shop ........................................................................... 1
        Printing Services ....................................................................... 2
                Commercial Printer ......................................................... 2
                Special Purpose Printer ................................................... 2
                Quick Printer .................................................................. 3
        Estimates, Quotes ..................................................................... 3
                Estimates ........................................................................ 3
                Quotes ............................................................................ 3
Chapter 2
Looking for a Printer .......................................................................... 5
        What are the Types of Printers? ................................................ 6
                What is a Commercial Print Shop? ................................. 6
                What is a Special Purpose Printer? ................................. 6
                What is a Quick Print Shop? ........................................... 7
        How Much Will it Cost? ............................................................ 7
                What is an Estimate? ...................................................... 7
                What is a Quote? ............................................................ 8
        Index .......................................................................................... 9
```

To create a table of contents, take these steps:

1. Go to the beginning of the master document (Ctrl+Home). Go to **I**nsert, **B**reak, choose **P**age Break, and then select OK. Go back to page one.

2. Go to Insert, Table of **C**ontents. Choose Use **H**eading Paragraphs, **A**ll. Select OK or press Enter.

3. By default, Word inserts the contents page. To format, go to the top of the page and type **3xEnter**. Position the cursor on the first paragraph return, type **Table of Contents**. Select and change this type to heading 2. You can adjust the indents at the beginning of each heading if you like. You should place a space between each tab and page number.

4. Go to **F**ile, **S**ave, **P**rint.

Looking at Design

When designing a book, restrain the urge to create layouts so innovative that they become difficult to read. Because books usually contain long blocks of text, the layout must be easy to read. Look at books in your library or in book stores to find layouts that inspire you. You may find the following two ideas for layouts interesting.

573

PART VI

Creating Long Documents

Figure 21.12 shows a larger page: 7 1/2 inches by 10 1/2 inches. Again, the type indents but this time the heads are in the margin beside the text. This layout makes finding each topic within a chapter easy. This design uses the standard justified text with interparagraph spacing.

Figure 21.13 shows the second page of the same design. The heads are in the margin, which makes finding the topic easy. This kind of design also can be used with callouts, rather than heads, in the margin.

Most books are portrait-oriented. Some books with photographs or illustrations, however, are landscape-oriented. Figure 21.14 shows a landscape orientation to the same printing book. The size of this book is 11 inches by 8 1/2 inches. The title of the chapter is left-aligned, with an inch of space above the title. Body text divides into two columns, first lines indent 1/4 inch and the text left-aligns.

Figure 21.15 shows the second page of the same book, with an area for an illustration or photograph. Using the modular form of layout, you can place an illustration that spans two columns (horizontally), or that fills one column (vertically) on the entire page, or you can place three or more smaller illustrations on the same page.

Because this book prints on one side of the paper only, all footers are on the right side. A binding margin also is added to the left of all pages.

CHAPTER 21

Producing a Book

Chapter 1
Finding a Print Shop

What do you look for in a printer? What are your priorities? A quick turn-a-round? A superior print job? An inexpensive printing bill? Someone who treats you fairly and honestly? These are all attributes desired in a printer, but unfortunately, you may not be able to find one who fills all of the above requirements.

Before you choose a printer, you should talk to and visit many shops. Ask questions, ask to tour their shop, meet the people with whom you will be working. If you are having a job typeset, meet the proofreader or head of that department. If you need artwork done, talk to the artist. If you need high resolution output, talk to someone who has knowledge of the computer and desktop publishing programs. Each person who works in a print shop is a specialist in his field. Rarely does one person know about all departments. Never depend on just one person in a print shop.

In addition, ask your friends and business associates who they use as a printer. Find out if they have had dealings with local shops, and what they think. If possible, find who to talk to when you visit the shop, and who to stay away from. All print shops have at least one person who knows printing and is good at helping customers. A production manager, the head of composition, the person who schedules jobs, or perhaps a sales person could be your best contact at the shop. Similarly, most shops have employees you should avoid. One who knows more than anyone else, one who treats you like you're simple or tiresome, or one who doesn't care about you or your job. Take care of yourself when talking to your printer; if you don't like the way you're treated, either tell him so or find another printer.

Services

Of all the print shops available, try your local printers first. A local shop is convenient and keeps your money in your area. The convenience of touring the shop, placing your order in person, picking up your finished job, and registering complaints in person is far more beneficial to you than dealing with an out-of-state print shop. Sometimes, just looking them in the eye tells you everything you need to know.

The type of print shop you use depends on your job. Different shops cater to different types of printing. If you choose the right shop, your job looks better and the bill should be more to your liking, Following is a description of common print shops.

FIG. 21.12. The first page of a chapter.

Chapter 1 Finding a Print Shop   2

Commercial

There are many types of print shops available. The commercial printer is most likely the one you will want to use. A commercial printer is one that will take on nearly any print job: books, forms, newsletters, letterheads, etc.; one who runs any number of ink colors from one color to four color process; one who has a typesetter, paste-up artist, cameral department, presses, folders, and a bindery.

Although a commercial printer does the majority of work in-house, there may be some jobs he farms out to a trade shop. A trade shop specializes in one service: composition, or binding, four-color work, copy work.

Special Purpose

A special purpose printer is one that specializes in specific print jobs: business cards or labels or business forms. A commercial printer might use them because they can do the work more efficiently and cheaper. But farmed out work may also be more expensive because the printer pays the trade shop and then charges you that price plus a mark-up (usually 25% of total). This is one reason you should get several quotes on your job before deciding upon one printer - you want the best price you can get (refer to Quotes on page 4).

Commercial print shops often farm out color separations. Small printers do not have the equipment or personnel to do their own separations. As color separation technology advances, less expensive equipment is becoming available. If your printer does separations in-house, always ask to see samples of his work. And always ask how much it will cost. Separations are very expensive.

Quick Printer

A quick printer is one who does mostly photocopying using a xerographic process that allows the copying of short run quantities. The quality is usually low to medium; however some quick print shops do produce quality work. The standard page sizes for photo copying are 8-1/2" x 11" and 11" x 17". Quick print shops may also have a small press or two and do some offset printing. They may farm out work such as binding large jobs, typesetting, some camera work, etc. A quick print shop is good to use for certain jobs: flyers, invitations, inserts, or jobs that don't require precision in width of margins, registration, etc.

The type of shop you choose depends upon your job. If you need high quality printing within a reasonable amount of time, you may choose a commercial printer. If you need 500 flyers yesterday, then choose a quick print shop.

It is important to patronize several shops. Don't just get quote after quote. Actually take them some business once in a while. This way, when you are in need of something special or something fast, and one printer cannot do it -- you have the option of taking it to another printer.

Cost

It's important to find out how much your job will cost before you have it printed. If you don't ask ahead of time, the printer could increase the price to whatever he wishes. Many print shop's are principled; many are not. There are two ways to find out the cost of your job, by an estimate or by a quote.

FIG. 21.13. *Page two of the same design.*

CHAPTER 1
FINDING A PRINT SHOP

What do you look for in a printer? What are your priorities? A quick turn-a-round? A superior print job? An inexpensive printing bill? Someone who treats you fairly and honestly? These are all attributes desired in a printer, but unfortunately, you may not be able to find one who fills all of the above requirements.

Before you choose a printer, you should talk to and visit many shops. Ask questions, ask to tour their shop, meet the people with whom you will be working. If you are having a job typeset, meet the proofreader or head of that department. If you need artwork done, talk to the artist. If you need high resolution output, talk to someone who has knowledge of the computer and desktop publishing programs. Each person who works in a print shop is a specialist in his field. Rarely does one person know about all departments. Never depend on just one person in a print shop.

In addition, ask your friends and business associates who they use as a printer. Find out if they have had dealings with local shops, and what they think. If possible, find out who to talk to when you visit the shop, and who to stay away from. All print shops have at least one person who knows printing and is good at helping customers. A production manager, the head of composition, the person who schedules jobs, or perhaps a sales person could be your best contact at the shop. Similarly, most shops have employees you should avoid. One who knows more than anyone else, one who treats you like you're simple or tiresome, or one who doesn't care about you or your job.

PRINTING SERVICES

Of all the print shops available, try your local printers first. A local shop is convenient and keeps your money in your area. The convenience of touring the shop, placing your order in person, picking up your finished job, and registering complaints in person is far more beneficial to you than dealing with an out-of-state print shop. Sometimes, just looking them in the eye tells you everything you need to know.

The type of print shop you use depends on your job. Different shops cater to different types of printing. If you choose the right shop, your job looks better and the bill should be more to your liking, Following is a description of common print shops.

FIG. 21.14. A landscape orientation with two columns.

PART VI

Creating Long Documents

COMMERCIAL PRINTER

There are many types of print shops available. The commercial printer is most likely the one you will want to use. A commercial printer is one that will take on nearly any print job: books, forms, newsletters, letterheads, etc.; one who runs any number of ink colors from one color to four color process; one who has a typesetter, paste-up artist, cameral department, presses, folders, and a bindery.

Although a commercial printer does the majority of work in-house, there may be some jobs he farms out to a trade shop. A trade shop specializes in one service: composition, or binding, four-color work, copy work.

SPECIAL PURPOSE PRINTER

A special purpose printer is one that specializes in specific print jobs: business cards or labels or business forms. A commercial printer might use them because they can do the work more efficiently and cheaper. But farmed out work may also be more expensive because the printer pays the trade shop and then charges you that price plus a mark-up (usually 25% of total). This is one reason you should get several quotes on your job before deciding upon one printer - you want the best price you can get.

Commercial print shops often farm out color separations. Small printers do not have the equipment or personnel to do their own separations. As color separation technology advances, less expensive equipment is becoming available. If your printer does separations in-house, always ask to see samples of his work. And always ask how much it will cost. Separations are very expensive.

QUICK PRINTER

A quick printer is one who does mostly photocopying using a xerographic process that allows the copying of short run quantities. The quality is usually low to medium; however some quick print shops do produce quality work. The standard page sizes for photo copying are 8-1/2" x 11" and 11" x 17". Quick print shops may also have a small press or two and do some offset printing. They may farm out work such as binding large jobs, typesetting, some camera work, etc. A quick print shop is good to use for certain jobs: flyers, invitations, inserts, or jobs that don't require precision in width of margins, registration, etc.

The type of shop you choose depends upon your job. If you need high quality printing within a reasonable amount of time, you may choose a commercial printer. If you need 500 flyers yesterday, then choose a quick print shop.

It is important to patronize several shops. Don't just get quote after quote. Actually take them some business once in a while. This way, when you are in need of something special or something fast, and one printer cannot do it -- you have the option of taking it to another printer.

It's important to find out how much your job will cost before you have it printed. If you don't ask ahead of time, the printer could increase the price to whatever he wishes. Many print shop's are principled; many are not. There are two ways to find out the cost of your job, by an estimate or by a quote.

FIG. 21.15. *Page two of the landscape orientation.*

CHAPTER 21

Producing a Book

Recapping

In this final chapter, you learned how quick and easy you can produce a book by using Word for Windows. You learned how Word's many features, such as outlining, templates, Summary Info box, table of contents, master pages, indexing, and headers and footers contribute to the ease of formatting a book or other long document.

You also learned how to plan the book by considering the body of the book, such as the actual chapters, topics, and text. You discovered how Word's Outline feature can help you with this process. You learned that you can list up to nine levels in an outline, and that as you plan, you can add notes, thoughts, and key words under each heading. Finally, you learned that you can use the outline as actual chapter titles, section headings, and so on.

Look Your Best with Word for Windows concludes with four appendixes that will add more depth to the expertise and proficiency you gained from this book.

Getting to Know Word

A

The document chapters in this book assume that you know Microsoft Word For Windows. If, however, you're not familiar with Word, this appendix gives a general survey of the screen, the mouse, and the keyboard features used in Word Versions 1.1 and 2.0. For more information about any feature or function, read the Reference Manual that comes with Microsoft Word.

Understanding Word Version 1.1

Word Version 1.1 is an excellent word processing program with many desktop publishing features. Word enables you to format characters, paragraphs and sections, create tables, perform macros, insert graphics and spreadsheets, and much more. The following descriptions of basic terminology are important to your understanding of the instructions in the document chapters of this book.

Figure A.1 shows the Word Version 1.1 screen. All parts of the Word screen are vital to your mastery of the program. The menu, shown at the top of the screen, is a necessity to working in Word. Many of the commands featured in the menu bar also are available on the Ribbon and Ruler. The scroll bars enable you to maneuver the page; the status bar identifies functions and locations.

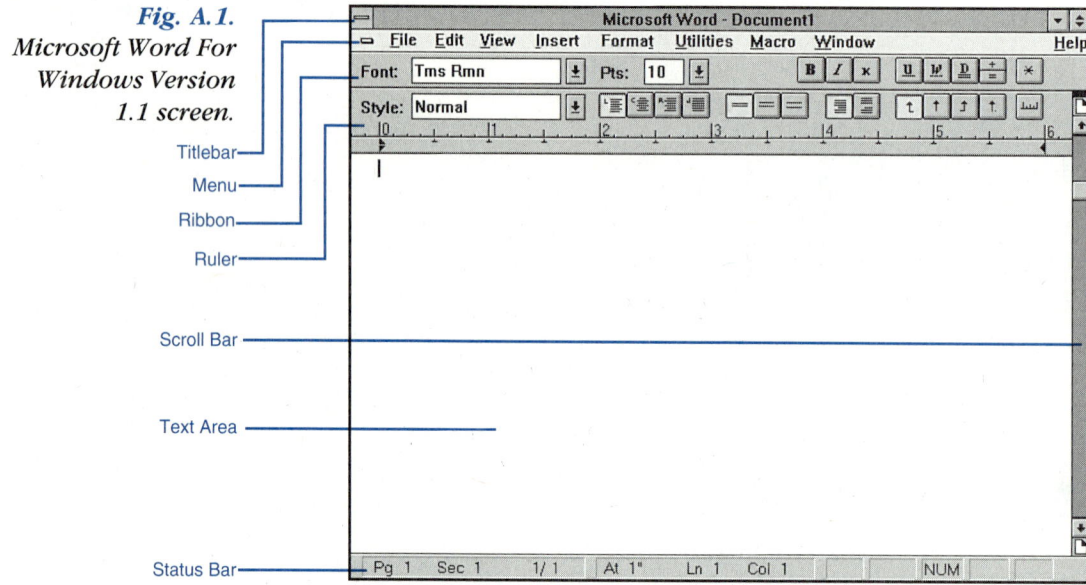

Fig. A.1. *Microsoft Word For Windows Version 1.1 screen.*

Working with the Titlebar

Along the top of the Word screen is the Titlebar. The Titlebar displays Microsoft Word and the name of the current document. Also located in the Titlebar is a control button (the rectangle to the left), which enables you to exit from Windows, reduce the program to an icon, or switch to another application. You use the two buttons at the far right of the Titlebar to minimize Word to an icon (the single triangle) and change and restore the size of the Word window (the double triangles).

Working with the Menu

Underneath the Titlebar is the menu. The menu performs functions essential to Word. When you click the mouse cursor (an arrow when used in the menus) on any command in this line, a drop-down menu appears. On the keyboard, access the command by pressing and holding down the Alt key while pressing the underlined letter of the command. In this book, those underlined letters are boldfaced. Figure A.2 shows the drop-down File menu.

APPENDIX A

Getting to Know Word

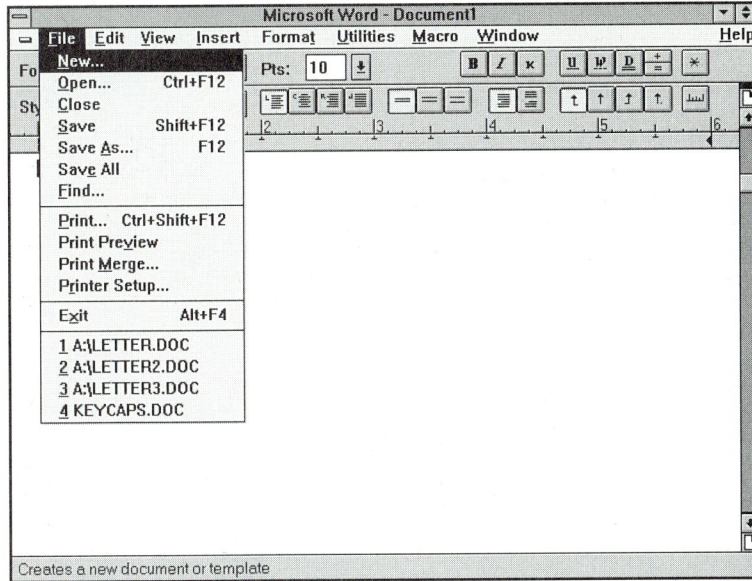

Fig. A.2.
The File menu in Word 1.1.

You choose one of the commands, and Word either performs a function or displays a dialog box. A dialog box appears when the command has three periods after it (**New...**, for example); otherwise a function is performed when the command is chosen.

When you choose a command that is followed by three periods, Word displays a dialog box. In the dialog box are choices relevant to the menu command.

In a dialog box, you may need to type something, choose from a list, or check a feature. Sometimes option buttons are available that enable you to access even more choices. Gray command buttons enable you to either accept the new choices with OK, or to select Cancel and close the box without changes. Figure A.3 shows a dialog box from the **Format** menu of Word Version 1.1.

Some commands on the drop-down menus appear gray at times, which indicates that the command is not available. On the **Edit** menu, for example, if no text is selected, you cannot select the **Cut**, **Copy**, or **Paste** commands.

Following is a brief summary of the options in each menu. For extensive details of each feature, read your Reference Manual.

Look Your Best with Word for Windows

Fig. A.3.
The Format Character dialog box showing default settings for a Normal template.

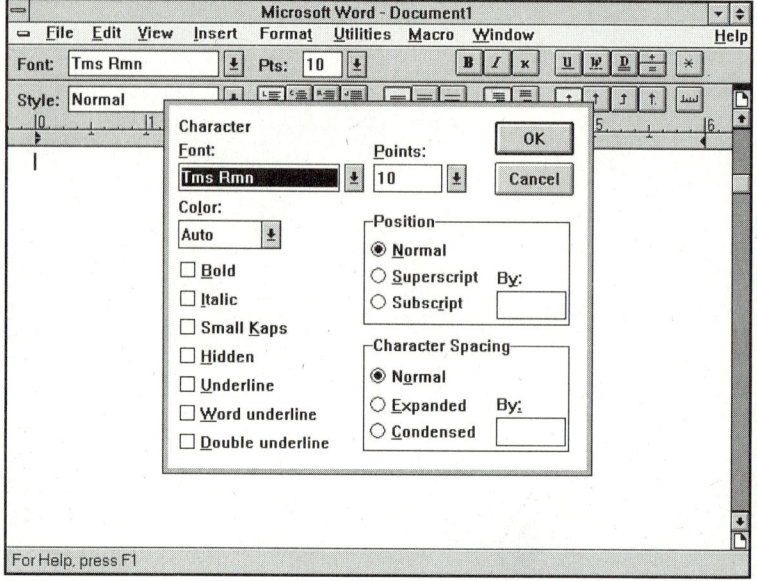

Option	Function
The Control Button	Enables you to Restore, Close a document, go to another document Window (Next Window) or Split a window.
The File Command	The File menu enables you to Open, Close, Save, and Save As a document. You also can begin a New document, Save All global template and macro changes, and Find files. From this menu, you can select Print, Print Preview, Print Merge, and Printer Setup. The four most recently opened documents are listed at the bottom of the menu for quick opening. You also can Exit from Word by using the File menu.
The Edit Command	The Edit menu lists commands for revising text and graphics. Cut, Copy, and Paste are functions that work with the clipboard.

APPENDIX A

Getting to Know Word

Option	Function
	The clipboard is an extra window that holds cut or copied text or graphics until you paste them to another location in your document. Only the most recently cut or copied text or graphic is stored in the clipboard; when you select Cu**t** or **C**opy again, the new text replaces the old text on the clipboard. The keyboard shortcut for Cu**t** is Shift+Del; for **C**opy, Ctrl+Ins; and for **P**aste, Shift+Ins.
	To access the clipboard window, click the Control button in the top left corner of your screen (on the Titlebar) or press Alt+Spacebar,U; then Alt+C and press Enter. From the menu that appears, select **R**un. If nothing is on the clipboard, you cannot open the window.
	The Edit menu also contains the **S**earch, R**e**place, **H**eader/Footer, Summary **I**nfo, Gl**o**ssary, **T**a**b**le, **U**ndo, and **R**epeat commands. You can use the **U**ndo command to reverse the action just taken. The **R**epeat command repeats the last command; however, **R**epeat doesn't work with all commands.
The **V**iew Command	Views of the page that are available are **O**utline (to create an outline), **D**raft (unformatted view for quick typing), and **P**age for looking at the formatted page. By using the View menu, you can turn on and off the Ri**b**bon, **R**uler, and **S**tatus bars by selecting the command.
	You also can show or hide **F**ootnotes, **A**nnotations, and Field **C**odes by using this menu. If you select P**r**eferences, you can turn on or off formatting codes, such as **T**abs, Spaces, **O**ptional Hyphens, Text **B**oundaries, and so forth. The View menu also enables you to display Short or Full **M**enus; you should use full menus when you are first learning Word.

continues

585

Look Your Best with Word for Windows

Option	Function
The **I**nsert Command	From the **I**nsert menu, you can select to insert various items into your document: **B**reak, Foot**n**ote, **F**ile, Bookma**r**k, Page N**u**mber, **T**able, **A**nnotation, **P**icture, Fie**l**d, Index **E**ntry, Table of Contents, and **I**ndex. All these items are inserted into your file at the cursor.
The Forma**t** Command	The Forma**t** menu enables you to select formatting for **C**haracters (size, typeface, style of the font), **P**aragraphs (spacing, borders, indents), **S**ections (columns, line numbering), and **D**ocuments (page size and margins). You also can apply **T**abs and **P**osition to certain parts of the text or graphics. You can **D**efine Styles in Word's templates or create your own **S**tyles. And, you can format Pict**u**res and **T**ables (with borders, rules, positioning).
The **U**tilities Command	Special features, such as **S**pelling, **T**hesaurus, and **H**yphenate, enable you to create better documents. Commands such as **R**enumber, Revision **M**arks, Compare **V**ersions, S**o**rt, **C**alculate, and Re**p**aginate Now help you organize your document. With the C**u**stomize command, you can select options such as Autosave, Unit of Measure, and Summary Info **P**rompt.
The **M**acro Command	From the **M**acro menu, you can select **R**ecord, **E**dit, and **R**un to set up macros. The Assign to **K**ey and Assign to **M**enu commands enable you to select options for applying the macros.
The **W**indow Command	The **W**indow menu lists the open windows. From this menu, you can choose to **A**rrange Windows and start a **N**ew Window.
The **H**elp Command	If you need help at any time while working in Word, you can choose the **H**elp command from the menu bar. When you choose any topic from the **H**elp menu, a small window appears. That Help window is another menu containing **F**ile, **E**dit, **B**rowse and Bookma**r**k, plus another **H**elp.

APPENDIX A

Getting to Know Word

Understanding the Ribbon

The Ribbon is the third line on the screen. The Ribbon enables you to quickly format characters, tabs, and paragraphs. To implement most of the options in the Ribbon, you first must select the text or position the cursor in the text, and then select the option. To access the Ribbon from the keyboard, use the Ctrl key with the icon letter.

Option	*Feature*
The Font Box	The Font box enables you to change the typeface of characters, words or paragraphs. The displayed font is the one currently in use. To activate the choices, click the arrow or press Ctrl+F and a box appears with the list of fonts. Click the font name to select it or press the down arrow key while pressing the Alt key. Then Press Enter. If you don't see the font you want in the box, use the scroll bar on the right of that box. By clicking the arrow at either the top or bottom of the scroll bar, you can view the entire list in the Font box. You exit from the Font box by clicking the mouse outside the box on the page or pressing the Esc key.
The Pts. Window	Pts. displays the size of the fonts used in the document in points. The size shown in the window is the current size. To change the size, click the arrow and a box appears or press Ctrl+P. Scroll to the size you want and click to select it or press Alt+down arrow key to scroll, and Enter to accept. You exit from the Pts. box by clicking the mouse outside the box on the page or pressing Esc.

continues

Look Your Best with Word for Windows

Option	Feature
The Attributes Buttons	The next buttons are *B* (bold), *I* (italic), *K* (small caps), *U* (continuous underlining), *W* (word underlining), and *D* (double underlining). Select the text to which you want to apply an attribute and click the appropriate buttons or press Ctrl+B, or Ctrl+I, and so on. To return the text to normal or turn off an attribute, select the text and click the button again or press the same combination keys again.
	You can subscript and superscript text by using the boxes with the = and the + signs, respectively. Again, from the keyboard, press Ctrl+(the plus sign) or =(the equal sign).
The Nonprinting Characters Icon	Selecting the asterisk reveals field codes, margin guides, tabs, returns, and any marks that don't print. This feature is handy if you have formatting you can't identify, such as a tab, or when you need to see a paragraph return so that you can select it.

Understanding the Ruler

The next line is the Ruler. You turn the Ruler on or off from the **View** menu by selecting **R**uler. The dark triangles on the left of the Ruler indicate indentations. The marks under the numbers on the Ruler signify tab stops. The default tab is every 1/2 inch; the default indentation is none.

APPENDIX A

Getting to Know Word

Option	Feature
The Style Box	Contained in the Ruler is a Style box that operates like the Font box. With styles, you can set a default font to use over and over in a template. The Normal style is body text. Word sets the typefaces, sizes, and alignment for these styles. Each template in Word has a different set of styles for the fonts used in that template. You can change Word's set styles by selecting Forma**t**, **D**efine Styles. You also can name and format your own styles by selecting Forma**t**, St**y**les. To access the Style box on the ruler, either click the down arrow with the mouse, or press Ctrl+S, select with Alt+down arrow, and press Enter.
The Paragraph Alignment Buttons	The next four buttons are for alignment. *L* is for left alignment; *C* is for center; *R* is for right, and *J* is for justified. To use any of these alignments, select the text or click in the line of text before selecting the alignment button. Click the button with the mouse, or press Ctrl+L, or Ctrl+C, and so on.
The Line and Paragraph Spacing Buttons	The next three buttons in the Ruler are for single-spacing (Ctrl+1), one-and-a-half-spacing (Ctrl+5), and double-spacing (Ctrl+2). After these boxes are two boxes that define spacing between paragraphs. The first box is for no extra space (Ctrl+E), and the second box is for a single line of space (Ctrl+O) between paragraphs selected.
The Tab Stop Buttons	The arrow buttons in the Ruler bar define tab stops. Use these buttons with the Ruler for placement of tabs. From left to right, these buttons are: left tab, centered tab, right tab, and decimal tab. (Ctrl+Shift+F10,1 for left; Ctrl+Shift+F10,2 for centered; Ctrl+Shift+F10,3 for right; Ctrl+Shift+F10,4 for decimal).

continues

Look Your Best with Word for Windows

Option	Feature
The Ruler Box	The Ruler box enables you to change Ruler views. Suppose, for example, that you format a table. By clicking the Ruler box or pressing Ctrl+Shift+F10, you can change the symbols from indenting for text, to indenting for the table. Click the Ruler box again to switch back or press Esc.

Understanding the Status Bar

Located at the bottom of the screen is the status bar. On the status bar you can see, from left to right, the following items:

- The page number
- The current section number
- The current page/total number of pages in the document
- The position of the insertion point from the top of the page
- The line number of the insertion point
- The character position of the insertion point (from the left margin)
- The macro record mode
- The extend mode
- The column select mode

Sometimes shown on the status bar are certain indicators: CAPS means Caps Lock is on, NUM means Num Lock is on, and OVR means overwrite or typeover is on.

Understanding the Scroll Bar

At the right side of the screen is a scroll bar. You use the scroll bar to move up and down the page. By clicking the arrow at the top or bottom of the scroll bar, you can move one line up or down the page. To move the insertion point with the keyboard, see the section on Using Direction Keys later in this chapter. By dragging

APPENDIX A

Getting to Know Word

the light gray square in the scroll bar, you can move up or down the page faster. If your document has more than one page, small page icons appear at the top and bottom of the scroll bar; use these icons to go to the next page (bottom icon) and the previous page (top icon). With the keyboard, use the GOTO key (F5).

Understanding the Text Area

The text area is the white part of the screen on which you type the text and format it. The blinking cursor shows where text will appear when you begin typing. You can use the mouse to click the place you want to edit, delete, or enter text, as well as to add a graphic.

Using the Mouse

Following is a list of terms that you need to know when using a mouse. You may want to practice these moves if you are not familiar with a mouse. Unless otherwise specified, all references to clicking are for the left mouse button.

Term	Meaning
Click	To quickly press and release the mouse button.
Double-click	To quickly press and release the button twice.
Drag	To press and hold down the mouse button while moving the pointer to another position. When the destination is reached, release the mouse button.
	When using the mouse, notice that the appearance of the cursor changes depending on where it is on your screen. In the text area, the mouse cursor is an I-beam; in the margin areas, scroll bar, status bar, menus, the Ribbon, and the Ruler, the mouse pointer is an arrow.
	When you click and drag using the right mouse button, you select columns of type, which is useful for selecting table columns if you need to cut or copy information.

Look Your Best with Word for Windows

Using the Keyboard

Word makes special use of several keyboard keys. Some of the following keys work alone; some work in conjunction with other keys.

Key	Function
Enter	Ends a paragraph; inserts blank lines; signifies OK in a dialog box.
Esc	Closes a dialog box, canceling any changes in that box.
Tab	Inserts a tab; moves through the choice boxes in a dialog box.
Delete	Deletes the character to the right of the cursor.
Backspace	Deletes the character to the left of the cursor.
Insert	Toggles between regular and typeover modes.

Microsoft Word For Windows Version 1.1 Shortcut Keys

Following is a list of the most commonly used shortcut keys. For a complete list, refer to your Reference Manual.

Using Function Keys

Word has programmed special functions into the function keys. The following keys sometimes are used alone, and sometimes in conjunction with other keys.

Key	Function
F1	Help
F2	Move
F3	Expand Glossary Name
F4	Repeat last editing or formatting action
F5	Go To
F6	Next pane

APPENDIX A

Getting to Know Word

Key	Function
F7	Spell Check selection
F8	Extend selection
F9	Update field
F10	Menu
F11	Next field
F12	File Save As
Shift+F2	Copy
Ctrl+F2	Grow font
Ctrl+Shift+F2	Shrink font
Shift+F3	Toggle case
Ctrl+F4	Close document window
Shift+F5	Go back to previous insertion point
Shift+F7	Thesaurus
Shift+F8	Shrink selection
Ctrl+F9	Insert field
Shift+F12	File Save
Ctrl+F12	File Open
Ctrl+Shift+F12	File Print

Using Direction Keys

These key combinations allow you to quickly move the insertion point within the screen and within the document; and to select text (highlight):

Key Combination	Function
Shift+left arrow	Highlights left one character
Shift+right arrow	Highlights right one character
Ctrl+left arrow	Moves left one word
Ctrl+right arrow	Moves right one word

continues

Look Your Best with Word for Windows

Key Combination	Function
Ctrl+Shift+left arrow	Highlights left one word
Ctrl+Shift+right arrow	Highlights right one word
Shift+Up	Highlights up one line
Shift+Down	Highlights down one line
Ctrl+Up	Moves up one paragraph
Ctrl+Down	Moves down one paragraph
Shift+Home	Highlights to beginning of line
Shift+End	Highlights to end of line
Ctrl+Home	Moves to beginning of document
Ctrl+End	Moves to end of document
Alt+Home	Moves to beginning of a row (table)
Alt+End	Moves to end of row (table)
PgUp	Moves up one window
PgDn	Moves down one window
Shift+PgUp	Highlights up one window
Shift+PgDn	Highlights down one window
Ctrl+PgUp	Moves to top of window
Ctrl+PgDn	Moves to bottom of window

Using Alphanumeric Keys

The following key combinations allow you to perform commands from the Ruler and Ribbon:

Key Combination	Function
Ctrl+B	Bold
Ctrl+C	Center paragraph
Ctrl+F	Assign font
Ctrl+G	Unindent hanging indent
Ctrl+I	Italic
Ctrl+J	Justified alignment

APPENDIX A

Getting to Know Word

Key Combination	Function
Ctrl+K	Small caps
Ctrl+L	Left alignment
Ctrl+R	Right alignment
Ctrl+T	Hanging indent
Ctrl+1	Single line spacing
Ctrl+2	Double line spacing
Ctrl+5	One-and-a-half line spacing
Ctrl+Shift+space bar	Insert non-breaking space
Ctrl+Backspace	Delete word to left
Alt+Backspace	Undo
Shift+Enter	Begin new line
Ctrl+Enter	Insert page break
Ctrl+Shift+Enter	Insert column break
Shift+Del	Cut to clipboard
Shift+Ins	Paste to clipboard
Ctrl+Ins	Copy to clipboard

Word Version 2.0

Microsoft Word For Windows Version 2.0 has many more features than Version 1.1. Version 2.0 supplies more features for the desktop publisher, with the addition of various border thicknesses, shading, grammar checking, bullets, outlining, and much more. Word Version 2.0 also offers more choices for converting text and graphics files. There also are more shortcuts using the Tool bar, and Version 2.0 has a revised Ruler and Ribbon.

Understanding the Screen

The menu in Version 2.0 has changed considerably from previous versions. Word 2.0 adds more detail in commands and dialog boxes. The Toolbar offers more shortcut commands, and the

Look Your Best with Word for Windows

Ribbon offers fewer. All parts of the screen are important to producing documents in Word. Figure A.4 shows the Word 2.0 screen.

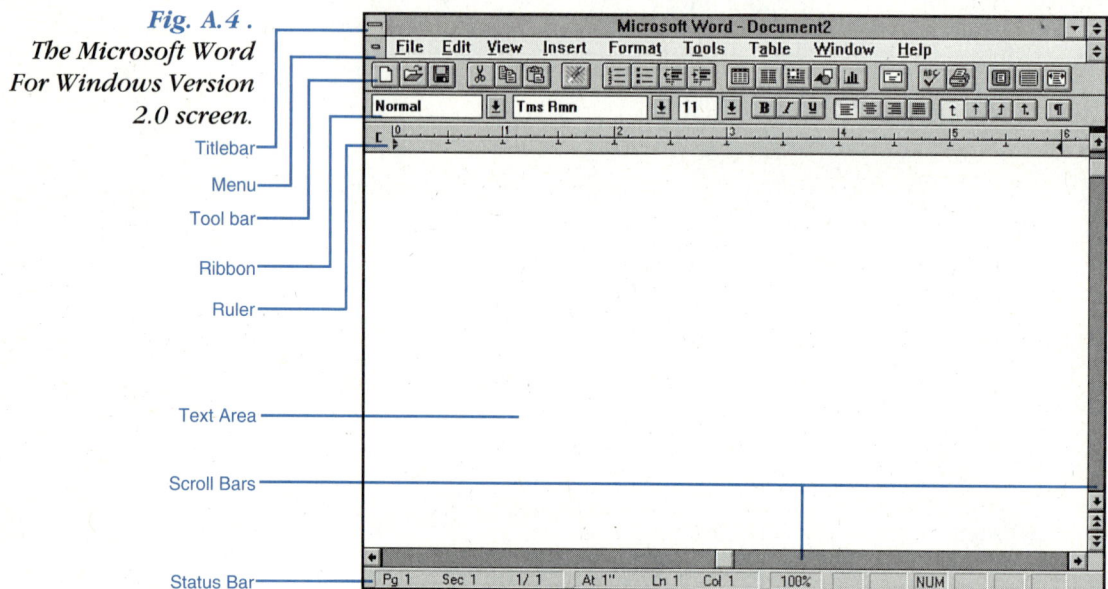

Fig. A.4.
The Microsoft Word For Windows Version 2.0 screen.

Understanding the Titlebar

Along the top of the Word screen is the Titlebar. In addition to `Microsoft Word`, the Titlebar displays the name of the current document. At the left of the Titlebar is the Control button (the rectangle), which enables you to **C**lose Windows, **R**estore, Mi**n**imize, Ma**x**imize, **M**ove, **S**ize, **S**witch to other applications, and R**u**n the clipboard. On the right of the Titlebar are two buttons with triangles. The button with one triangle reduces Word to an icon. The button with two triangles changes the size of the Word window.

APPENDIX A

Getting to Know Word

Understanding the Menu

Underneath the Titlebar is the menu. The menu performs functions essential to Word. When you select any command in this line, a drop-down menu appears. Figure A.5 shows the drop-down File menu.

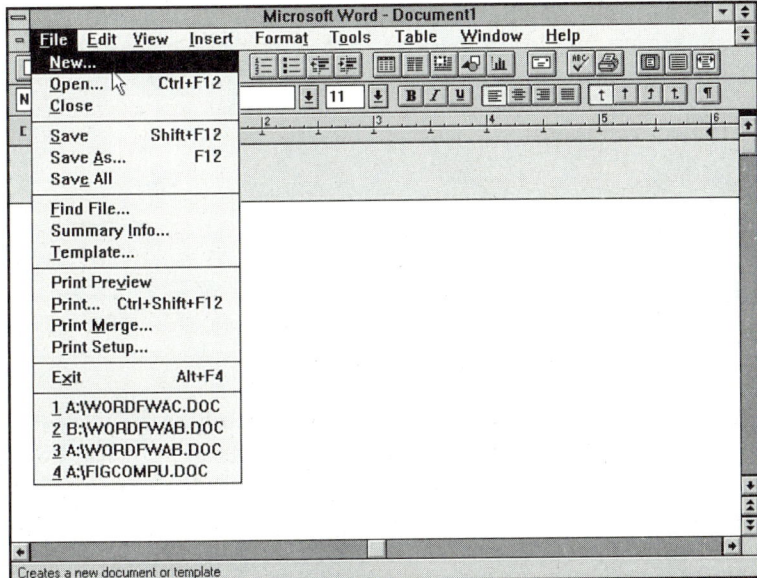

Fig. A.5.
The File menu in Word Version 2.0.

You click one of the commands or press and hold the Alt key in combination with the underlined letter, and Word either performs a function or displays a dialog box. A dialog box appears when the command has three periods after it (**New...**, for example); otherwise a function is performed.

When you choose a command that is followed by three periods, Word displays a dialog box. In the dialog box are choices relevant to the menu command.

In a dialog box, you may need to type something, choose from a list, or check a feature. Sometimes option buttons are available that enable you to access even more choices. Gray command buttons either enable you to accept the new choices with OK or Enter, or you can select Cancel (Esc) and close the box without changes. Figure A.6 shows a dialog box from the Format menu of Word Version 2.0.

597

Look Your Best with Word for Windows

***Fig. A.6.**
The Format Character dialog box showing default settings for a Normal template.*

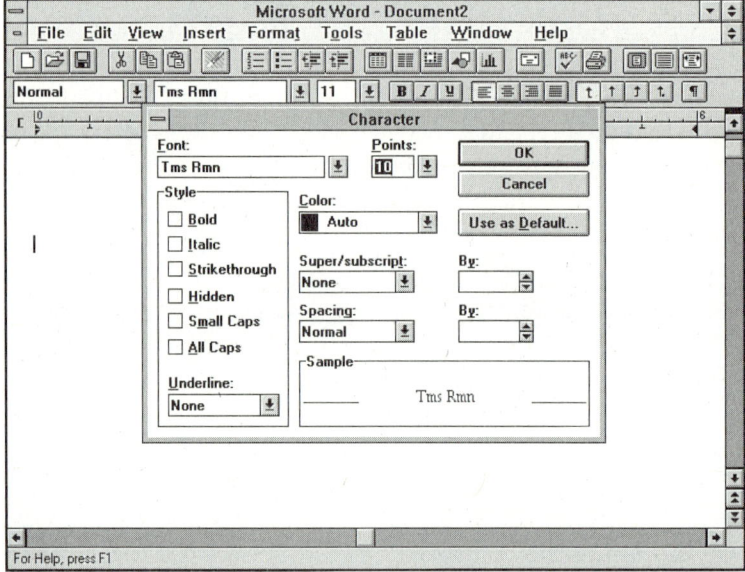

Some commands on the drop-down menus appear gray at times, which indicates that the command is not available. On the **Edit** menu, for example, if no text is selected, you cannot select the **Cu**t, **C**opy, or **P**aste commands.

Following is a brief summary of the options in each menu. For details of each feature, read your Reference Manual. To access the menu, either click on the file name with the mouse, or press and hold down the Alt key while pressing the underlined letter (in this book, the underlined letter is bold).

Option	Function
The Control Button	The Control button enables you to **R**estore, **M**ove, **S**ize, Maximize, **C**lose a document, switch to the **N**ext Window, or Spli**t** a window.
The **F**ile Command	The **F**ile menu enables you to begin a **N**ew document, **O**pen, **C**lose, **S**ave, or Save **A**s a document. You also can **F**ind File, create Summary **I**nfo, and attach a **T**emplate to a document. You can choose **P**rint, Print Preview, Print Merge, and P**r**int Setup. You also use the **F**ile menu to E**x**it from Word. At the bottom of the **F**ile menu are the last four documents you opened, so that you can open them quickly and easily.

APPENDIX A

Getting to Know Word

Option	Function
The **E**dit Command	Using the **E**dit menu, you can **C**ut, **C**opy, and **P**aste text, graphics, tables, and so forth. These are the most used functions of the **E**dit menu. Using the Cu**t**, **C**opy, or **P**aste functions involves using the clipboard.
	The clipboard is an extra window that holds the text or graphics you cut or copied, until you paste them to another location in your document. Only the most recently cut or copied item is stored in the clipboard. When you cut or copy something else, any previous material stored on the clipboard is erased. To run the clipboard, use the Control button in the titlebar. Click on the button or press Alt+spacebar+U, and press Enter. If nothing is on the clipboard, it will not open.
	You can use the **U**ndo command to reverse the action just taken. The **R**epeat command repeats the last command; however, **R**epeat doesn't work with all commands.
	The Paste **S**pecial command applies to data from other applications. Select **A**ll selects everything in the document. The **F**ind, R**e**place, and **G**o To commands help you revise text. The G**l**ossary, **L**inks, and **O**bject commands help to organize text and graphics.
The **V**iew Command	**V**iew offers different ways to view the page: **N**ormal (shows the page with soft and hard page divisions), **O**utline, **P**age Layout (the formatted page), and **D**raft View (displays without formatting).
	Using View, you can turn on or off the **T**oolbar, Ri**b**bon, and **R**uler. You can create **H**eaders/Footers, show **A**nnotations, **F**ootnotes, and Field **C**odes. Using the **Z**oom command, you can see the page in various magnifications.

continues

599

Look Your Best with Word for Windows

Option	*Function*
The Insert Command	You use the Insert menu to insert Breaks, Symbol, and Page Numbers for formatting; using this menu, you can add Footnotes, Bookmarks, Annotations, and the Date and Time. In addition, you can insert a Field, Index Entry, Index, and Table of Contents for organization, and a File, Frame, Picture, or Object.
The Format Command	Use the Format menu to choose specific Characters (typeface, size, and style), Paragraph (spacing and indents), Tabs (stop position, alignment, and leader characters), and Border (rules, boxes, and grids). Choose a Language, format Styles of text, change the Page Setup (margins, page size, and orientation), format Columns, the Section Layout and borders, and the placement and size of Frames and Pictures.
The Tools Command	The Tools menu helps you edit and revise your documents and customize Word. The Spelling, Grammar, Thesaurus, and Hyphenation commands enable you to write better documents. Bullets and Numbering customizes the Tool bar settings. The Create Envelope command automatically forms an envelope from your document. The Revision Marks, Compare Versions, Sorting, and Calculate commands help with organization. You can select the Record Macro and Macro commands. You can use Options to customize the Word program and commands.
The Table Command	Using the Table menu, you can Insert Table, Delete Columns, Merge Cells, and Convert Text to Table. In addition, the Table menu enables you to Select Row, Column, or Table, and change the Row Height and the Column Width. You can use the Split Table command and turn on and off Gridlines.

APPENDIX A

Getting to Know Word

Option	Function
The **W**indow Command	Using the Window menu, you can start a **N**ew Window, **A**rrange Windows, or switch to another Window if one is open.
The **H**elp Command	Word For Windows offers extensive on-line help. Included in the Help menu are the Help **I**ndex, **G**etting Started, **L**earning Word, and **A**bout Word commands. Each Help window has a menu including **F**ile, **E**dit, and **B**rowse commands. Included in the help files are underlined words. By selecting these words, you can read specific definitions.

Understanding the Toolbar

The Toolbar is a new addition to Word Version 2.0. With the Toolbar, you have many shortcuts available without going to the menus. Each button or icon has a picture on it to describe its use. To see a description of an icon or button's function, you can click and hold any button on the Toolbar. The Toolbar is only available to mouse users. For options within the Toolbar, access the menu with the keyboard. To release the button without performing the function, drag the cursor into the text area and release. You must first select text to perform some of the options on the Tool bar. Following is a brief outline of each button's function, beginning with the buttons on the left. For more detail, consult your Reference Manual.

Option	Function
The **F**ile Buttons	The first group of three buttons performs File commands. The first button creates a new document, the second opens an existing document, and the third saves the current document or active template.
The **E**dit Function Buttons	The next group of three buttons, **C**ut, **C**opy, and **P**aste, perform edit functions.

continues

601

Look Your Best with Word for Windows

Option	Function
The Undo Button	Select the Undo button to undo the most recent action. Some actions cannot be undone in the Edit menu.
The Format Buttons	The next buttons perform some indent actions. The first button formats a list with a 1/4-inch indent after the number. The second button does the same thing with bulleted lists. The third and fourth buttons move indents to either the next tab stop or the previous one.
The Insert Buttons	The first Insert button inserts a table; the second inserts columns. Either of these buttons enables you to specify the number of rows and columns in a table or number of columns. The third button inserts a frame; the fourth, a Microsoft Draw object; and the fifth, a Microsoft Graph object.
The Envelope Button	The Envelope button creates an envelope to print with the current document.
The Tools Buttons	With the Tools buttons, you can spell-check and print the current document.
The Page View Buttons	The first Page View button enables you to see the entire page (note that the margins are not accurate); the second page view button shows a 100 percent, or Normal, view; the third displays the full width of the sheet, margins included.

Understanding the Ribbon

The Ribbon offers more shortcuts for the menu commands. Sometimes, text must be selected to use the button. Use the Ribbon for formatting small amounts of text, adding attributes, and placing or adjusting tabs.

Option	Feature
The Style Box	To use the style box, choose any style from the current template. Click the arrow to the right of the Style box and a list appears from which you choose a style. Or with the keyboard, press Ctrl+S. Use the up and

APPENDIX A

Getting to Know Word

Option	Function
	down arrow keys to select, then press Enter. You can change the styles' definitions by using the Format, Style commands.
The Font Box	The font box lists the available fonts; the fonts with a printer icon beside them are the fonts available with your printer. Use the arrow to the right of the box to scroll the list, and click any typeface to select it. Or press Ctrl+F, select with the down or up arrows, then press Enter.
The Point Size Box	Choose the size of the fonts by clicking the arrow and scrolling. Or press Ctrl+P, type in the size, and press Enter. If you decide not to change the size, the font, or the style, click outside the box in the text area or press the Esc key.
The Attributes Buttons	The next three buttons enable you to apply attributes to characters, words or paragraphs. The B is for **Bold**, The I is for *Italic*, and the U is for continuous Underlining. If using the keyboard, press the Ctrl key with any of the letters on the icon.
The Alignment Buttons	Select a paragraph and click one of the next four buttons to apply alignment or press the Ctrl button in combination with the letter on the icon. The first button is for left alignment; the second is for center alignment. The third is for right alignment, and the last button is for justified alignment.
The Tab Stops Buttons	The tab buttons enable you to choose a tab type (left, center, right, or decimal) and apply it directly to the Ruler. With a mouse, click the type of tab you want, and then place it in position on the Ruler. To adjust or move the tab, click the symbol on the Ruler, and drag it to another location. With the keyboard, position the cursor and press Ctrl+Shift+F10 to activate the ruler. Use the left or right arrow key to move the

continues

Look Your Best with Word for Windows

Option	Function
	ruler cursor to the tab stop. To select the alignment, press 1 for left-aligned, 2 for center, 3 for right, and 4 for decimal.
The Display Non-printing Codes Button	The last button reveals codes, such as margin guidelines, paragraph return markers, tabs, and so forth. Click on the button or press Ctrl+Shift+8.

Understanding the Ruler

You can set the Ruler to three different scales: margin, indent, or table. Click the marker on the left side to change scales (you must have a table to use that scale). You position tabs, margins, or table borders on the Ruler. To activate the Ruler with the keyboard, press Ctrl+Shift+F10.

Understanding the Status Bar

Located at the bottom of the screen, the status bar shows you, from left to right, the following items:

The page number

The section number

Number of the page you are on/number of pages in the document

The position of the insertion point from the top of the page

The current line number

The current character position

The view mode

When Num Lock, Insert, or Caps Lock are on

APPENDIX A

Getting to Know Word

Understanding the Scroll Bars

With the scroll bars, you can move around on the page (text area) by clicking the arrows in the direction you want to go with the mouse. Each click takes you one line up or down, or 1/2 inch to the left or right. By clicking the light gray square on either scroll bar and dragging along the scroll bar, you can move across the page faster. If you have more than one page in your document, double-arrow buttons appear on the scroll bar in the bottom right corner that take you to the next or previous page quickly. To move within the page, the screen, or between pages with the keyboard, use the direction keys listed later in this chapter.

Understanding the Text Area

The text area is the white part of the screen on which you type and format text. The blinking cursor shows where text will appear when you begin typing. You can use the mouse to click the place in which you want to edit, delete, or type text, or add a graphic or use direction keys to quickly move around the text area.

Using the Mouse

When using the mouse, certain terms refer to specific movements of the mouse, the cursor, or the pointer. You may want to practice these moves if you are not familiar with a mouse. Unless otherwise indicated, all references to clicking apply to the left mouse button.

Term	*Definition*
Click	To press and release the mouse button quickly.
Double-click	To press and release the mouse button twice quickly.
Drag	To press and hold down the mouse button while moving the pointer to another position. When the destination is reached, you release the mouse button.
	When using the mouse, notice that the pointer changes depending on where it is on the screen. In the text area, the pointer is an I-beam, in the margin areas, scroll bar,

continues

Look Your Best with Word for Windows

Term	Definition
	status bar, menus, Ribbon, and Ruler, the mouse pointer is an arrow.
	When you click and drag using the right mouse button, you select a column. This feature is helpful when you are cutting or copying a column in a table or a column of tabbed items.

Using the Keyboard

Word makes special use of several keyboard keys. Some keys work alone; some work in conjunction with other keys.

Key	Function
Enter	Ends a paragraph; inserts blank lines; signifies OK in a dialog box
Esc	Closes a dialog box, canceling any changes in that box
Tab	Inserts a tab; moves through the choice boxes in a dialog box
Delete	Deletes the character to the right of the cursor
Backspace	Deletes the character to the left of the cursor
Insert	Toggles between regular and typeover modes

Microsoft Word For Windows Version 2.0 Shortcut Keys

Following is a list of the most commonly used shortcut keys. For a complete list, refer to your Reference Manual.

Using Function Keys

Word has programmed special functions into the function keys. These keys sometimes are used alone, sometimes in conjunction with other keys.

APPENDIX A

Getting to Know Word

Key	Function
F1	Help
F2	Move
F3	Glossary
F4	Repeat command
F5	Go To
F6	Next pane
F7	Spelling
F8	Extend selection
F9	Update field
F10	Menu
F11	Next field
F12	Save As
Shift+F2	Copy
Shift+F3	Toggle case
Shift+F7	Thesaurus
Shift+F8	Shrink selection
Shift+F12	Save
Ctrl+F2	Grow Font
Ctrl+F12	Open
Ctrl+Shift+F2	Shrink font
Ctrl+Shift+F10	Ruler mode
Ctrl+Shift+F12	Print
Alt+F2	Save As
Alt+F4	Quit Word
Alt+Shift+F2	Save

Look Your Best with Word for Windows

Using Direction Keys

To quickly move around the page or document, or to highlight (select) text with the keyboard, use the following keys:

Key	Function
Shift+left arrow	Highlights left one character
Shift+right arrow	Highlights right one character
Ctrl+left arrow	Moves left one word
Ctrl+right arrow	Moves right one word
Ctrl+Shift+left arrow	Highlights left one word
Ctrl+Shift+right arrow	Highlights right one word
Shift+Up	Highlights up one line
Shift+Down	Highlights down one line
Ctrl+Up	Moves up one paragraph
Ctrl+Down	Moves down one paragraph
Shift+Home	Highlights to beginning of line
Shift+End	Highlights to end of line
Ctrl+Home	Moves to beginning of document
Ctrl+End	Moves to end of document
Alt+Home	Moves to beginning of a row (table)
Alt+End	Moves to end of row (table)
PgUp	Moves up one window
PgDn	Moves down one window
Shift+PgUp	Highlights up one window
Shift+PgDn	Highlights down one window
Ctrl+PgUp	Moves to top of window
Ctrl+PgDn	Moves to bottom of window

APPENDIX A

Getting to Know Word

Using Alphanumeric Keys

Following are shortcut keys you can use to apply attributes listed on the Ribbon:

Key	*Function*
Ctrl+A	All caps
Ctrl+B	Bold
Ctrl+C	Copy
Ctrl+E	Center
Ctrl+G	Unindent hanging indent
Ctrl+I	Italic
Ctrl+J	Justify
Ctrl+K	Small caps
Ctrl+L	Left align
Ctrl+R	Right align
Ctrl+T	Hanging indent
Ctrl+V	Paste
Ctrl+X	Cut
Ctrl+1	Single line spacing
Ctrl+2	Double line spacing
Ctrl+5	One-and-a-half line spacing
Esc	Cancel
Shift+Enter	Begin new line
Ctrl+Enter	Insert page break

Using Other Programs with Word

B

With Word For Windows, you can import graphics and convert text files to Word. It is easy to convert other word processing programs to Word files and Word files to other programs. Importing graphics from draw and paint programs and scanned art also is effortless.

Before converting or importing, you must install the correct converter (for text) or filter (for graphics). Word cannot convert or import without it; you can, however, add filters and converters after initial installation. See your Reference Manual for more information.

Converting Text Files

You must convert text files instead of just opening them. Each word processing, spreadsheet, or database file has its own formatting codes. Usually, these codes are unrecognizable to other programs. Once converted, some formatting may not be exactly the same. You may notice different line endings, incorrect attribute conversion, or spaces inserted instead of tabs. However, most of the text and formatting will convert.

Word for Windows includes a users' guide called *Getting Right to Word*. This guide contains instructions and helpful hints for transferring your skills from various word processors to Word. If you're familiar with DisplayWrite, MultiMate, WANG, WordPerfect, or WordStar, this guide shows you how those word processors compare to Word in commands and functions.

Look Your Best with Word for Windows

Word Version 1.1

Converting files is easy in Version 1.1. When you open the document, Word prompts you for the file format. When you want to save a document in Word to another format, you simply tell Word which format you want.

Following is a list of applications you can convert to and from Word Version 1.1:

- Text Only (PC-8 with or without line breaks)
- DCA-RFT (DisplayWrite and DisplayWriter)
- RTF (Rich Text Format)
- Microsoft Windows Write
- Microsoft Word for DOS
- Microsoft Works word processing files
- Microsoft Excel BIFF
- Microsoft Multiplan and Multiplan BIFF
- MultiMate 3.3, 3.6, and Advantage II
- WordPerfect 4.1, 4.2, and 5.0
- WordStar 3.3, 3.4, and 4.0

Word Version 1.1 also converts to ASCII Text Only with or without line breaks. Word Version 1.1 can read ASCII, but will not convert from it.

To convert another format to Word format, follow these steps:

1. Select **File**, **Open**.
2. Word asks whether you want to convert the file. Answer **Yes**.

To convert a Word file to another application:

1. Select **File**, Save **As**.
2. Select **Options**. Choose **File** Format from the box and select OK or press Enter.

Remember, you must have the proper converter installed for each program you convert to or from.

Figure B.1 shows the **File**, Save **As** dialog box with the **Options** command selected.

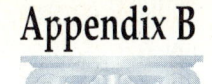

Appendix B

Using Other Programs with Word

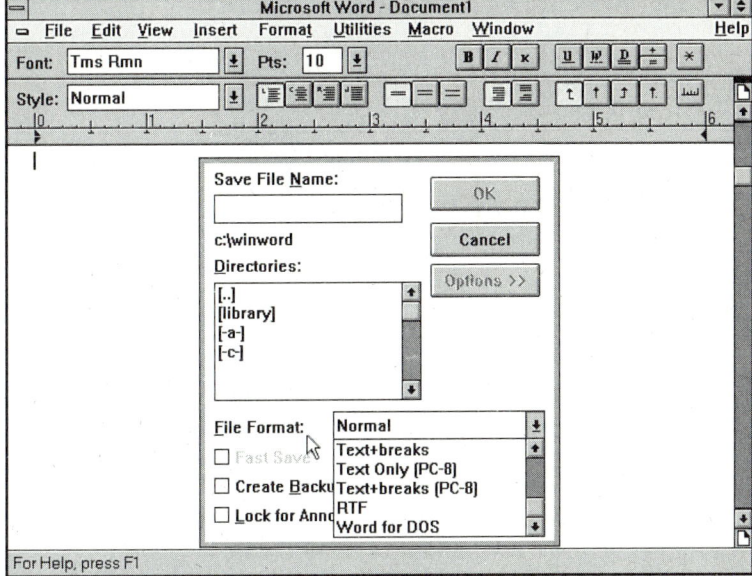

FIG. B.1.
The File, Save As dialog box with the Options command selected.

Word Version 2.0

With Version 2.0, you also can open documents from other applications directly into Word, including word processors, spreadsheets, and databases. Word enables you to save in other formats, as well. You must have the converters or filters installed to convert to or from certain programs.

Following is a list of applications you can convert to and from in Word Version 2.0:

- RTF-DCA (for DisplayWrite and IBM 5520)
- Text (Text Only, Text Only with line breaks, and Text with layout options)
- DOS Text (DOS Text Only, DOS Text Only with line breaks, and DOS Text with layout options)
- Rich Text Format (RTF)
- Word for Windows 1.*x* (Word for DOS 4.0, 5.0, and 5.5; Word for Macintosh 4.0 and 5.0)
- WordPerfect 4.1, 4.2, 5.0, and 5.1
- WordStar 3.3, 3.45, 4.0, 5.0, and 5.5

613

Look Your Best with Word for Windows

- Works for Windows and Works 2.0 for DOS
- Lotus 1-2-3 Versions 2.*x* and 3.0 (converts to Word only)
- Microsoft Excel BIFF 2.*x* and 3.0 (converts to Word only)
- Multiplan 3.0 and 4.2
- dBASE II, III, III PLUS, and IV

To open other file formats in Word, follow these steps:

1. Select **F**ile, **O**pen.
2. In the File **N**ame box, delete the DOC extension, type the extension of your file (**.TXT*, for example), and press Enter. Or, you can choose the proper format in the List Files of **T**ype box.
3. Select the file from the list of File **N**ames or type the file name in the File **N**ame box. Select OK or press Enter.
4. Word displays the Convert File dialog box. Make sure that the suggested format is correct. If it is not, choose the proper format. Select OK or press Enter.

To save a Word file in another format, follow these steps:

1. Select **F**ile, Save **A**s.
2. In the Save File **N**ame box, type the name of the file.
3. Choose **O**ptions, and in the **F**ile Format box, choose the format. Select OK or press Enter.

Figure B.2 shows the Version 2.0 **F**ile, Save **A**s dialog box.

Importing Graphics

Word makes importing graphics simple. Word can import graphics from many types of programs: draw, paint, scanners, and so forth. After you import a graphic, you can scale, crop, and add a border to it. Refer to your manual for details on scaling and cropping. Remember, you must have the proper filters installed to import graphics to Word.

Two basic types of graphic formats exist: bit-mapped and object. Bit-mapped graphics tend to be rough around the edges,

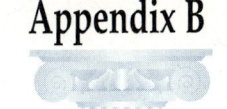

Appendix B

Using Other Programs with Word

especially when they are enlarged in Word (see fig. B.3). Object graphics are formed differently, thus the outline is smoother (see fig. B.4); object graphics reproduce well at any size.

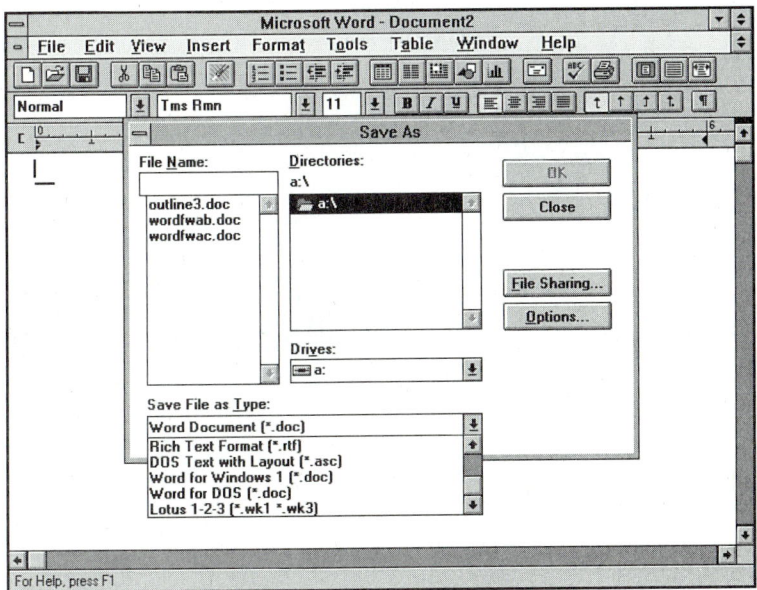

FIG. B.2.
The File, Save As dialog box in Version 2.0.

FIG. B.3.
Bit-mapped PC Paintbrush art.

615

Look Your Best with Word for Windows

FIG. B.4.
An object-oriented TIFF file from CorelDRAW!.

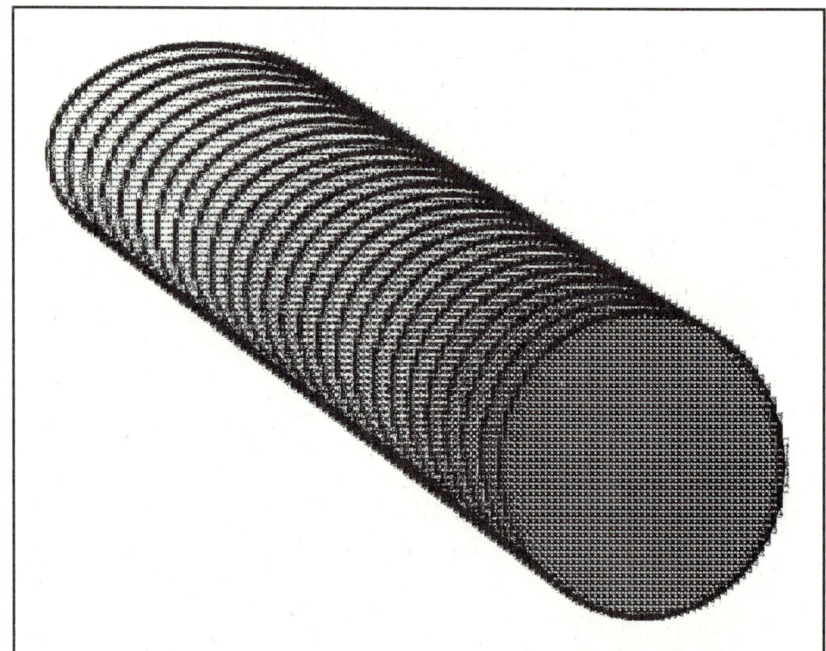

Bit-mapped graphics, also called paint graphics, images, and pixel-based graphics, are stored as patterns of 0's and 1's in the computer. The digital pattern has a one-to-one correspondence to the pattern of dots in the image. What this means to you is that the edges are noticeably ragged. If you can scan or draw images larger than you need them, and then reduce them in your document, the edges will appear less ragged.

PC Paintbrush files, available in Windows, can be imported or copied to the clipboard and pasted into Word.

Object graphics, or draw programs, are stored in the computer in a compact mathematical description. Graphics from programs, such as CorelDRAW!, AutoCAD, and Micrografx Designer, are compatible with Word. Some clip art programs, such as HP Graphics Gallery and Micrografx Designer, are object-oriented, and their files also can be imported into Word.

Word Version 1.1 can import TIFF files. Many programs, including HP Graphics Gallery, Micrografx Designer, CorelDRAW! and most scanners, enable you to store in the TIFF format.

With Word Version 2.0, you can import many different file formats. Many of the object file formats also are Windows applications, so you can copy and paste them with the clipboard, as well.

Appendix B

Using Other Programs with Word

Following is a brief summary of some of the formats and graphics programs you can use with Word Version 2.0:

- CGM (Computer Graphics Metafile) is object-oriented. The image is stored as geometric shapes. CGM is available in Harvard Graphics and Micrografx Designer.

- HPGL (Hewlett-Packard Graphics Language) is another object-oriented format. Originally developed for plotters (CAD), it also is available in CorelDRAW! and Micrografx Designer.

- EPS stands for Encapsulated PostScript Standard. You must have a PostScript printer to use it. EPS files are stored in various shades and patterns, but they take up huge amounts of disk space. Windows Metafile also is EPS and a space glutton.

- CorelDRAW! is a powerful art program for the PC. It runs on Windows, and can be saved in a variety of formats, TIFF included. Micrografx Designer can be exported to CGM, EPS, PCX, and TIFF.HP. Graphics Gallery can be saved in HPGL, PCX and TIFF.

Finally, a word about scanners. Scanners are great for line art (art without any gray), and you can save the files in a variety of formats, including TIFF. However, avoid scanning photos to print to a laser printer. A laser printer (300 dpi) cannot vary the dot size to produce the grays needed for a photograph. Scanned photos will, however, look fine if you output them to an image setter at 2,540 dpi or higher. If you don't have that option, have halftones shot at a print shop instead of scanning photographs.

Word Version 1.1.

Version 1.1 of Word enables you to import any graphic that is in TIFF format (Tagged Image File Format). Most draw and scanning programs enable you to save your files in this manner. TIFF is the only graphic format that you can import to Word Version 1.1. Figure B.5 shows a graphic imported in TIFF format.

To import a graphic with menu commands, complete these steps:

1. Position the cursor.
2. Select **I**nsert, **P**icture.

Look Your Best with Word for Windows

*FIG. B.5.
A scanned TIFF file
inserted with the
Picture command.*

3. Choose the correct **D**irectory, and then choose from the list of **F**iles. Or, type the name into the **P**icture File Name box.

4. Select OK or press Enter. Word inserts the picture at the cursor.

To import a graphic with the clipboard, follow these steps:

1. The application must be a Windows application and open. Copy the graphic in its original application.

2. Switch to or **O**pen Word. Position the cursor and select **P**aste.

Word Version 2.0.

Word Version 2.0 includes many more graphic formats for importing. After you import the graphic, you can scale, crop, add a border, and even position the graphic. Figure B.6 illustrates an imported, scaled, and cropped graphic that has a border added.

To import a graphic by using commands, follow these steps:

1. Position the cursor. Select **I**nsert, **P**icture.

2. In the File **N**ame box, select the graphic file. (Link by checking the box Link To File). Choose OK or press Enter.

Appendix B

Using Other Programs with Word

FIG. B.6.
A formatted graphic in Version 2.0, imported from CorelDRAW!.

If you Link (explained later in this appendix), you can update the graphic by first modifying the graphic in the original application. Then, in Word, follow these steps:

1. Choose **E**dit menu, **L**inks.

2. In the Links box, select the name of the graphic.

3. Choose the Update Now button. Links automatically updates your file.

To import a graphic with the clipboard, follow these steps:

1. With the graphic application open, select the graphic and copy it to the clipboard.

2. In Word, position the cursor.

3. From the **E**dit menu, choose **P**aste.

To import from Microsoft Draw, follow these steps:

1. In the Microsoft Draw window, select **F**ile, Import Picture.

2. You can edit most imported graphics in Microsoft Draw. You cannot, however, edit those with the format file extensions BMP, EPS, PCX, or TIF.

619

Following is a complete list of paint or draw programs that Version 2.0 accepts:

- Windows Metafile (*.WMF)
- Encapsulated PostScript (*.EPS)
- TIFF Tagged Image File Format (*.TIF)
- Computer Graphics Metafile (*.CGM)
- HP Graphic Language (*.HGL)
- DrawPerfect (*.WPG)
- Micrografx Designer 3.0/Draw Plus (*.DRW)
- PC Paintbrush (*.PCX)
- Windows Bitmaps (*.BMP)
- AutoCAD 2-D Format (*.DXF)
- AutoCAD Plotter Format (*.PLT)
- Lotus 1-2-3 Graphics (*.PIC)

Using Data Exchange

In addition to the methods of converting and importing, Word offers various forms of updating the information. Following is an introduction to the terms you should know. However, you should consult your Reference Manual for details.

Linking

Linking a file in Word allows you to share information between documents. By maintaining the original documents, any linked documents are automatically updated. For example, a budget worksheet produced in Microsoft Excel can be inserted into several reports in Word. If linked, any changes made in the original Excel documents are automatically updated in the reports in Word. This feature saves you time and provides consistency among your documents.

Appendix B

Using Other Programs with Word

Linking automatically updates any linked file in another application so that it updates in Word documents. The capability to update files, such as spreadsheets and databases, makes your reports timely and exact. You can link automatically, or link only when you specify. To link a file, you must select the Link box when you first choose Insert the Picture. Refer to the Manual for specific instruction for applications, updating, and editing links.

Embedding

Embedding means to copy information from one document to another with all the instructions used to create it originally. The advantage to embedding is that the information appears in Word in original formatting. If you need to edit the information, double-click it and Word opens the application for you. This feature makes editing and updating easy. Embedding is available only in Version 2.0.

Include

Include is a field type used to import all or a part of another file. Include automatically updates the file when you change the file in the original application. Lotus 1-2-3, MultiPlan, or TIFF file formats maintain their formatting.

DDE

DDE (Dynamic Data Exchange) is a way of transferring information (or files) between Windows applications. You can set DDE to update automatically or by prompt. It works in a manner similar to linking in Word.

DDE must be used with Windows applications that support it. Microsoft Excel, for example, supports DDE. Using linking with DDE means easier, faster updating of information.

C

Using Printers and Output

You should base your choice of a printer on the type and amount of work you do, and the quality of the printout you require. If you want draft-quality printouts, or you produce letters and other in-house documents, a dot matrix printer may suffice. If, however, you produce camera-ready masters, you need a laser printer.

Print quality is measured in terms of resolution of output. This appendix describes terms related to print quality, printer types, resolution output, and screen and printer fonts. At the end of this appendix are descriptions of printer setups for both versions of Word.

Understanding Resolution

Resolution describes the quality of the type and graphics output. Ragged, rough-edged type, much like that of dot matrix printers, is low resolution. Type that has smooth and refined edges, like that of a laser printer, is higher resolution.

Resolution is measured in dots per inch (dpi). The dpi describes how many dots, or pixels, make up a letter or graphic image. Most dot matrix 24-pin printers have about 70 to 75 dpi. Most laser printers have 300 dpi. Image setters (or image typesetters) have 1,265, 2,540, or even more dpi. Image setters are found almost exclusively in print shops and service bureaus because of their high price. For the average user, a 300-dpi laser printer is reasonably priced and the quality is very good. A laser printer can produce camera-ready masters.

Using Page Description Languages

Another factor to consider when purchasing a printer is the page description language it uses. Printer Command Language and PostScript are two common page description languages.

A laser printer with the Hewlett-Packard Printer Command Language or compatible (HPCL) can reproduce most of the formatting you do in Word. Adobe PostScript (PS) (or a PostScript-compatible language) is a more sophisticated language. The major difference between HPCL and PS languages is the way they form characters. PCL forms type by using bit-mapped images; PS forms type by using outlines.

Working with HP Printer Control Language

Bit-mapped text and images are made up of patterns of dots on a very fine rectangular grid. The arrangement of dots that make up each character is stored as an arrangement of digital bits in the laser printer. Bit-mapped images that output at 300 dpi are fairly good quality, but not the best.

A problem with the bit-mapped fonts is the amount of memory they take. Each typeface, type size, and style, is stored separately in memory, taking up quite a bit of space.

HPCL offers limited font choices and graphic capabilities. You should compare the limitations and advantages to your needs before choosing.

Working with PostScript Page Description Language

PostScript stores fonts as mathematical descriptions of the character outlines. The outline is formed, and then is filled in. For this reason, the edges are much smoother and more uniform than

APPENDIX C

Using Printers and Output

bit-mapped fonts. In addition, fonts formed by outline do not require much storage in memory. The PS language can make any size font from just one outline. With PS, you have more font choices, and you can use features such as type rotation, reversal, stretching, and filling with patterns.

Using Screen and Printer Fonts

Printer fonts are those that are included with the printer, either bit-mapped or outlined. You cannot print a document unless you have the proper printer fonts installed. Some printer fonts are resident, some are stored in the software program, others are downloaded. Resident fonts are those that come with the printer. Fonts stored in Word are Modern, Roman, and Script. Downloaded fonts include those from Adobe, or other companies, that you load to your printer before printing. When you turn your printer off, you lose these fonts until you download again.

Screen fonts are for the display, or monitor, only. You can print without screen fonts. Screen fonts are important for matching the appearance of the printed page with the actual output. If you don't see an accurate representation of the font on-screen, your formatting may not look right on the printed page.

Choosing a Printer

Be sure to choose the printer that is right for you and the job you do. Consider all the options—resolution, price, speed, and compatibility—before you buy a printer.

Dot Matrix Printers

A dot matrix printer is perfect for many situations. It is inexpensive and provides many capabilities. However, the output is grainy and rough, even on a 24-pin printer. It is not suitable for camera-ready material, or even for professional-looking correspondence (see fig. C.1).

FIG. C.1.
Sample output from a 24-pin dot matrix printer.

```
Dot Matrix
24 Pin Printer
```

Inkjet Printers

Inkjet printers are very popular. They're quiet, economical, and the print quality is better than dot matrix printers. Inkjet printers have wide carriages that can accommodate larger paper sizes. Their output is close to laser quality (see fig. C.2). Color Inkjet printers are now available at a relatively low cost. Inkjet printers are best suited for business correspondence, but not camera-ready material.

FIG. C.2.
Sample output from an Inkjet printer.

```
Inkjet
Printer
```

Basic Laser Printers

The basic laser printer is much more suitable for producing quality output. The higher resolution of 300 dpi to 600 dpi, produces type and graphics that are camera ready and of high quality (see fig. C.3). Usually employing the Printer Control Language, the basic laser printer offers many font choices for less money than a PostScript printer.

FIG. C.3.
Sample output from a laser printer with HP-PCL.

**HP-PCL
Laser Printer**

APPENDIX C

Using Printers and Output

PostScript Laser Printers

A PostScript laser printer is a high-quality printer. It offers many font choices and many type alternatives. The graphics are high quality, and many type and graphic options are offered (see fig. C.4). A PostScript laser printer offers a resolution of 300 dpi to 600 dpi. PostScript laser printers are more expensive than a basic laser printer and require more memory.

FIG. C.4.
Sample of PostScript laser printer output.

Image Setters

Image setters are very expensive, very high-resolution printers used in service bureaus and print shops. If you typeset a document in Word and plan to have it printed, consider using an image setter's high-resolution output. The type and images are sharp, clear, and very high quality (see fig. C.5).

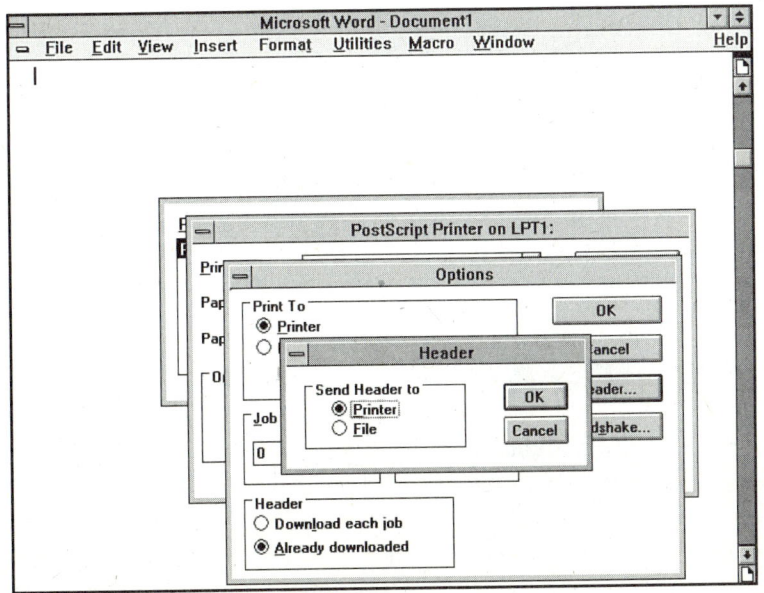

FIG. C.5.
Sample output from an image setter.

627

Usually reserved for large quantities (5,000 or 10,000 printed pieces or more) or material requiring very high quality, high-resolution output is sometimes available for all jobs. A print shop that deals with desktop publishing every day will often run text on an image setter for free, if the shop prints the job.

A service bureau is a specialty shop that only outputs type. Service bureaus specialize in high resolution, and usually charge a fairly reasonable (per page) fee for output.

If you take your job to a printer, or service bureau, for output, you should discuss several things with them before you commit to the job:

- Do they have a PC compatible system?
- Do they have Microsoft Word For Windows (Version 1.1 or 2.0)?
- What size disks do they use?
- Do they have the fonts you used in your document?

Understanding Printer Installation Terminology

Be sure, before you format documents in Word, that you have selected the correct printer in print setup. Word offers font choices depending on your printer; if you change printers after formatting a document, you may not have the right fonts.

You can choose the printer driver and the printer port, and you can configure your printer in either Windows (Control Panel) or in Word (Print Setup). For information and the steps for any of these procedures, consult your Windows Reference Manual.

Selecting Your Printer Driver

The printer driver file gives the program (Word) details about your printer features (descriptions and sizes of fonts, control sequences, and so forth). Windows lists common printer drivers in its setup. If your printer is not listed, check your printer manual

APPENDIX C

Using Printers and Output

for compatibility and emulation mode. If neither of these is an option with your printer, consult the Windows manual for further alternatives.

If your printer driver is not installed, you can choose the generic printer driver, but it will not print most page and type formatting.

Choosing a Printer Port

The printer port choices are serial, parallel, or file. Windows automatically sets common communications settings for serial printers. You might need to change some of the settings or choose another port. Again, it's best to consult your manual.

Configuring Your Printer

Configuring your printer consists of choosing the correct printer driver file, size and orientation of paper, paper source, amount of time out, cartridges, and so forth. These choices are all dependent on your printer. Some printers accommodate various paper sizes and various font cartridges.

If you use a PostScript printer, you need to download the PostScript header, located in the Print Setup box. When working with one program all day, for example Word, you should download the header at the beginning of the day. After it's downloaded, tell Word, in the Printer Setup box, that the header is downloaded. Your documents will output faster this way. If, however, you are using several different programs, say Word and CorelDRAW!, downloading the header with each job will give you the quickest output.

To change the download header option in Word, follow these steps:

1. Select **F**ile, **Pr**int Setup.
2. Click the **S**etup option button, and then the **O**ptions button.
3. Select the **H**eader button to download. You can click either **A**lready Downloaded or Down**l**oad for each job.

Look Your Best with Word for Windows

Setting Up Your Printer

The printer setup in Word is similar to the Windows printer setup. If you're familiar with the Windows setup, you'll have no problem with Word's.

To configure your printer in Word, follow these steps:

1. Select **F**ile, **Pr**inter Setup.

2. In the **P**rinter box, your printer should be listed. Click the gray command button, **S**etup. The dialog box that appears is about your printer.

3. In the **P**rinter: box, you can choose various printers that are installed in Windows (and therefore Word).

    Use the Paper **S**ource to choose feed.

    Paper Si**z**e has many options; however, your printer may not be able to print them all. You set the document orientation here.

    Use **C**opies to indicate how many copies you want printed. If you occasionally need extra copies, it's more convenient to set it in the **P**rint dialog box.

    Use Scali**n**g to reduce or enlarge a document by percentage. Many of these items may or may not be available depending on the printer you selected.

    The gray command buttons in this dialog box give you more choices for printer setup. Use the **O**ptions button to print to the **P**rinter or an En**c**apsulated PostScript File (EPS). You might print to an EPS, for example, if you take your file to a service bureau that doesn't have Word for Windows. The bureau can run an EPS file directly to a high-resolution PostScript image setter without the use of Word.

    Job Timeout enables you to set the amount of time that Word (or Windows) will try to print before it gives up. If you already have sent a job to the printer, the printer is busy. When you send the next job, Word will wait for the specified amount of time and try again. If the printer

APPENDIX C

Using Printers and Output

is not available, the program cancels printing. It's sometimes handy to set Timeout for 0 seconds; Windows will try to print all day.

The Header also is located in this dialog box (if you have a PostScript printer).

The Handshake is a device used for data transfer, between hardwares, or softwares. Refer to your Windows manual if you have a problem.

The **Ad**d Printer command button is a method of installing by inserting the disk with the printer driver. The Help command button displays Windows **H**elp on your specific printer. **A**bout tells you the printer driver that's installed in your Windows program.

Glossary of Desktop Publishing Terms

D

Alignment   Definition of text edge: flush right, flush left, justified, or centered.

Anchoring   Placement of boxes at a specific location: on the page or in a paragraph.

ascender   The portion of the lowercase letters b, d, f, h, k, l, and t that rises above the height of the letter x. The height of the ascender varies in different typefaces. See *descender*.

ASCII (American Standard Code for Information Interchange)   A standard computer character set devised in 1968 to enable efficient data communication and achieve compatibility among different computer devices.

The standard ASCII code consists of 96 displayed upper- and lowercase letters, plus 32 nondisplayed control characters. An individual character code is composed of seven bits plus one parity bit for error checking. The code enables the expression of English-language textual data but is inadequate for many foreign languages and technical applications. Because ASCII code includes no graphics characters, most modern computers use an extended character set containing needed characters.

ASCII file   A file that contains only characters drawn from the ASCII character set.

attribute   A character emphasis, such as boldface or italic, and other characteristics of character formatting, such as typeface and type size. See *formatting sequence*.

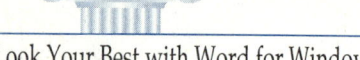

automatic font downloading   The transmission of disk-based, downloadable printer fonts to the printer, done by an application program as the fonts are needed to complete a printing job.

banner   A newsletter title.

baseline   The lowest point characters reach (excluding descenders). For example, the baseline of a line of text is the lowermost point of letters like a and x, excluding the lowest points of p and q. See *descender*.

bit-mapped font   A screen or printer font in which each character is composed of a pattern of dots. Bit-mapped fonts represent characters with a matrix of dots. To display or print bit-mapped fonts, the computer or printer must keep a full representation of each character in memory.

Because the computer's or printer's memory must contain a complete set of characters for each font you use, bit-mapped fonts consume enormous amounts of disk and memory space. Outline fonts, however, are constructed from mathematical formulas and can be scaled up or down without distortion. Outline fonts are considered technically superior. Printers that can print outline fonts, therefore, are more expensive.

bit-mapped graphic   A graphic image formed by a pattern of pixels (screen dots) and limited in resolution to the maximum screen resolution of the device being used. Bit-mapped graphics are produced by paint programs, such as PC Paintbrush, MacPaint, SuperPaint, GEM Paint, and some scanners.

bleed   A photograph, shaded box, bar, or other element that extends to the edge of the page. Laser-printed pages have a 0.3" margin and may not have bleeds.

blurb   A subtitle printed above or below a headline, usually set in a smaller type size than the headline.

body type   The font (normally 8- to 12-point) used to set paragraphs of text (distinguished from the typefaces used to set headings, subheadings, captions, and other typographical elements).

boldface   A character emphasis visibly darker and heavier in weight than normal type.

bowl   White space inside letters such as a, b, o, p, and q.

APPENDIX D

Glossary of Desktop Publishing Terms

brush style   A typeface design that simulates script drawn with a brush or broad-pointed pen.

byline   An author's name, often including the author's title.

callout   A quotation printed in large letters to spark interest in an adjoining article

caption   Descriptive phrase identifying a photograph, image, chart, or graph.

cartridge   A removable module that expands a printer's memory or font capabilities.

cartridge font   A printer font supplied in the form of a read-only memory (ROM) cartridge that plugs into a receptacle on Hewlett-Packard LaserJet printers and clones.

Hewlett-Packard LaserJet printers rely heavily on cartridge fonts that have some merits over their chief competition, downloadable fonts. Unlike downloadable fonts, the ROM-based cartridge font is immediately available to the printer and does not consume space in the printer's random-access memory (RAM), which can be used up quickly when printing documents loaded with graphics.

CGM (Computer Graphics Metafile)   An international graphics file format that stores object-oriented graphics in device-independent form so that you can exchange CGM files among users of different systems (and different programs).

Personal computer programs that can read and write to CGM file formats, including Harvard Graphics and Ventura Publisher.

character   Any letter, number, punctuation mark, or symbol that can be produced on-screen by pressing a key.

character set   The fixed set of keyboard codes that a particular computer system uses. See *ASCII (American Standard Code for Information Interchange)*.

characters per inch (cpi)   The number of characters that fit within a linear inch in a given font. Standard units drawn from typewriting are pica (10 cpi) and elite (12 cpi).

clip art   A collection of graphics images, stored on disk and available for use in a spreadsheet, page layout, or presentation graphics program.

clustering   A method of grouping small visual elements together on the page to create a single, larger illustration; for example, a series of small head-and-shoulder portrait photographs.

color separation   Separate color negatives (magenta, cyan, black, and yellow) created by a printer to produce four-color printed images.

compose sequence   A series of keystrokes that enables a user to enter a character not found on the computer's keyboard.

composite newsletter   A newsletter created with desktop publishing and traditional graphic design techniques; for example, when the newsletter is produced by desktop publishing methods except for photographic halftones, which are pasted into black squares.

condensed type   Type narrowed in width so that more characters will fit into a linear inch. In dot-matrix printers, condensed type usually is set to print 17 characters per inch (cpi). See *characters per inch (cpi)*.

constraining   A method used by many desktop publishing and drawing programs to maintain the original proportions of an image while reducing or enlarging its size.

continuous-tone photograph   A photographic print, which must be photographed through a halftone screen by the printer before it can be printed.

copyfitting   The common practice of designing the space for an article and then cutting or expanding the text to fit the allotted space.

counter   Concave space inside such letters as c, e, and s that opens onto the white space next to the letter.

Courier   A monospace typeface, commonly included as a built-in font in laser printers, that simulates the output of office typewriters.

crop marks   Marks on a page or photograph that tell the printer how to trim the page or position the photograph. Some desktop publishing programs can print crop marks on the page automatically.

cropping   Sizing a box to eliminate a portion of a photograph, image, chart, and so on.

APPENDIX D

Glossary of Desktop Publishing Terms

default font The font that the printer uses unless you instruct otherwise.

descender The portion of a lowercase letter that hangs below the baseline. Five letters of the alphabet have descenders: g, j, p, q, and y. See *ascender*.

desktop publishing (DTP) The use of a personal computer as an inexpensive production system for generating typeset-quality text and graphics. Desktop publishers often merge text and graphics on the same page and print pages on a high-resolution laser printer or typesetting machine.

dingbats Ornamental characters such as bullets, stars, and arrows used to decorate a page.

discretionary hyphen A hyphen that you insert manually and that the program uses to break a word at the end of a line; useful for telling the software where to hyphenate unusual words such as pneumococcus and Indianapolis.

display type A typeface, usually 14 points or larger and differing in style from the body type, that is used for headings and subheadings. See *body type*.

dot leader Pronounced "leeder"; a line of dots (periods) that leads the eye horizontally from one text element to another—for example, from a chapter title to a page number.

dot-matrix printer An impact printer that forms text and graphics images by pressing the ends of pins against a ribbon. Dot-matrix printers are fast, but the output they produce is generally poor quality because the character is not fully formed. These printers also can be extremely noisy. Some dot-matrix printers use 24 pins instead of 9, and the quality of their output is better.

dot pitch The size of the smallest dot that a monitor can display on-screen. Dot pitch determines a monitor's maximum resolution.

downloadable font A printer font that must be transferred from the computer's (or the printer's) hard disk drive to the printer's random-access memory before the font can be used.

drop cap A large initial capital letter used to guide the reader's eye to the beginning of body text.

drop out type White characters printed on a black background.

drop shadow A shadow placed behind an image, slightly offset horizontally and vertically, that creates the illusion that the topmost image has been lifted off the surface of the page.

elite A typeface that prints 12 characters per inch. See *pitch*.

ellipsis Three or four dots that represent omitted text.

em dash A long typographer's dash (—) used to separate phrases. The name indicates that the length of an em dash is the same as the width of the capital M in the current typeface.

em space A horizontal space equal to the width of a capital M in the current typeface.

en dash A typographer's hyphen, equal in width to a capital N in the current typeface.

en space Half an em space.

extended character set A character set that includes extra characters, such as foreign language accent marks, in addition to the standard 256-character IBM character set

eyebrow A word or phrase printed above an article heading that indicates a document department name; for example, "Lifestyles:" could be an eyebrow for an article titled "Boating on Snake River."

feathering Making very small changes in line spacing to line up the bottoms of adjacent columns of text.

flag A newsletter title.

flush left The alignment of text along the left margin, leaving a ragged right margin. Flush left alignment is easier to read than right-justified text.

flush right The alignment of text along the right margin, leaving a ragged left margin. Flush right alignment is seldom used, except for decorative effects or epigrams.

folio Printed next to a document title, the folio indicates issue date, volume, and issue number.

font One complete collection of letters, punctuation marks, numbers, and special characters with a consistent and identifiable typeface, weight (Roman or bold), posture (upright or italic), and font size.

APPENDIX D

Glossary of Desktop Publishing Terms

Technically, font still refers to one complete set of characters in a given typeface, weight, and size, such as Helvetica italic 12. The term, however, often is used to refer to typefaces or font families.

Two kinds of fonts exist: bit-mapped fonts and outline fonts. Each comes in two versions, screen fonts and printer fonts. See *bit-mapped font*, *font family*, *outline font*, *screen font*, *typeface*, *type size*, and *weight*.

font cartridge   Some printers accept plug-in font cartridges to add font variations to the printer's repertoire.

font editor   A software package that enables you to alter letters; generally used to create custom logos.

font family   A set of fonts in several sizes and weights that share the same typeface.

The following list describes a font family in the Helvetica typeface:

Helvetica Roman 10

Helvetica bold 10

Helvetica italic 10

Helvetica Roman 12

Helvetica bold 12

Helvetica italic 12

Helvetica bold italic 12

font metric   The width and height information for each character in a font. The font metric is stored in a width table.

footer   A short version of a document's title or other text positioned at the bottom of every page of the document. See *header*.

formatting   The process of changing the appearance of a page, by setting margins, choosing fonts, changing line spacing, alignment, column width, headers and footers, and other printed elements.

fountain effect   Smooth blending of print density from a dark to a light area.

frame   A box. Some desktop publishing and word processing programs use frames to hold various page elements, including body text, graphic images, charts, headers and footers, and so on.

frame-grabber   A combination of hardware and software that captures images from a video camera, still video camera, or videocassette.

full justification   The alignment of multiple lines of text along the left and the right margins. See *justification*.

graphics mode   In IBM and IBM-compatible computers, a mode of graphics display adapters in which the computer can display bit-mapped graphics.

graphics monitor   A computer monitor that can display both text and graphic images.

gray scale   A series of shades from white to black.

grayscale monitor   A monitor that can reproduce many shades of gray, typically 256 or more. Ordinary monitors can display only from 4 to 16 shades of gray.

greeking   Many word processing and desktop publishing programs display unreadably small text as solid lines or abstract symbols, called greeked text.

grid   The underlying design that establishes a consistent pattern for the position and style of columns, headings, fonts, line spacing, photos, and other document elements.

gutter   An additional margin added for two-sided printing to allow room for the binding. An extra margin is added to the left side of odd-numbered pages and to the right side of even-numbered pages. Also, the space between two columns of type.

halftone   A photo that has been copied through a printer's screen to create an image composed of dots or lines.

hanging indent   Paragraph formatting in which the first line extends into the left margin.

hard hyphen   A hyphen that prevents software from breaking a word; useful for preventing hyphenation of such words as "anti-inflammatory."

hard space   A space used to prevent two words from being separated by wordwrap at the end of a line; for example "Et Al."

header   Repeated text, such as a page number and a short version of a document's title, that appears at the top of each page in a document. See *footer*.

APPENDIX D

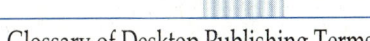

Glossary of Desktop Publishing Terms

Helvetica A sans serif typeface frequently used for display type applications and occasionally for body type. One of the most widely used fonts in the world, Helvetica is included as a built-in font with many laser printers. See *font family* for an example of Helvetica.

high-resolution output Typesetting; generally refers to printing quality of 1200 dots per inch or better.

hyphenation A program feature that automatically hyphenates words based on program rules (algorithmic hyphenation) or a list of hyphenated words (dictionary hyphenation).

image scanner Hardware that converts photos, drawings, or line images into computer-readable graphic files.

indentation The alignment of a paragraph to the right or left of the margins set for the entire document.

initial cap A large letter that indicates the beginning of body text. An initial cap can be dropped (inset) into the text, raised above the first line of text, or printed to the left of the body text.

jumpline Text placed at the bottom of a column of text to guide the reader to the page where the article continues—for example, "Continued on page 5" and "Continued from page 1."

justification The alignment of multiple lines of text along the left margin, the right margin, or both margins. The term justification often is used to refer to full justification, or the alignment of text along both margins.

kerning The reduction of space between certain pairs of characters in display type so that the characters print in an aesthetically pleasing manner.

label alignment In a spreadsheet program, the way labels are aligned in a cell (flush left, centered, flush right, or repeating across the cell).

landscape orientation The rotation of a page design to print text and/or graphics horizontally across the longer axis of the page. See *portrait orientation*.

laser printer A high-resolution printer that uses a version of the electrostatic reproduction technology of copying machines to fuse text and graphic images to the page.

Alternative technologies include light-emitting diode (LED) imaging printers that use a dense array of LEDs instead of a laser to generate the light that exposes the drum, and liquid crystal shutter (LCS) printers that use a lattice-like array of liquid crystal gateways to block or transmit light as necessary. See *resolution*.

layout In desktop publishing, the process of arranging text and graphics on a page.

leading The space between lines of type, measured from baseline to baseline. Synonymous with *line spacing*.

The term originated from letterpress-printing technology in which thin lead strips were inserted between lines of type to control the spacing between lines.

left justification The alignment of text along only the left margin. Synonymous with *ragged-right alignment*.

letter-quality printer An impact printer that simulates the fully formed text characters produced by a high-quality office typewriter.

ligature Combinations of letters printed in formal typography as a single letter: for example, ff and fl.

line spacing See *leading*.

Linotronic Brand name of the best-known PostScript-compatible typesetting machines. The Linotronic typesetters print at 1270 or 2540 dots per inch resolution.

live area The area of a page on which the printing hardware can print. Laser printers require a 0.3" margin around the live area on the page. Printing presses may require a nonprinting "gripper" area used to pull the sheet of paper through the press.

logo A business name, often designed for an artistic effect.

masthead An area that lists the staff, subscription information, ownership, and address of a newsletter or other publication, generally printed near the front of the issue.

mezzotint A photograph printed through a line or dot screen that adds an interesting texture or pattern to the image; for example, a pattern of fine concentric circles.

moire pattern A distracting pattern that may result when the printer makes a halftone screen of an already-halftoned photograph.

Glossary of Desktop Publishing Terms

monospace   A typeface such as Courier in which the width of all characters is the same, producing output that looks like typed characters. See *proportional spacing*.

nameplate   The title of a newspaper, newsletter, magazine, or other serial publication.

near-letter quality (NLQ)   A dot-matrix printing mode that prints typewriter-quality characters. As a result, printers using this mode print slower than other dot-matrix printers.

newspaper-style columns   Columns in which text "snakes" from the bottom of one column to the top of the next.

non-breaking space   A space that prevents the software from breaking two letters, words, or phrases at the end of a line—for example: US Mail, Pac Bell, and so on.

oblique   The italic form of a sans-serif typeface. See *sans serif*.

OCR (Optical Character Recognition)   A hardware and software system that can scan printed text into the computer for editing.

open, closed quote   True typographer's opening and closing quotation marks that curve toward the enclosed text

orientation   See *landscape orientation* and *portrait orientation*.

orphan   A formatting flaw in which the first line of a paragraph appears alone at the bottom of a page.

Most word processing and page-layout programs suppress widows and orphans; the better programs enable you to switch widow/orphan control on and off and to choose the number of lines for which the suppression feature is effective. See *widow*.

outline font   A printer or screen font in which a mathematical formula generates each character, producing a graceful and undistorted outline of the character, which the printer then fills in at its maximum resolution.

Because mathematical formulas produce the characters, you need only one font in the printer's memory to use any type size from 2 to 127 points. With bit-mapped fonts, you must download a complete set of characters for each font size into the printer's memory, and you cannot use a type size that you have not downloaded.

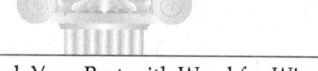

overstrike   The printing of a character not found in a printer's character set by printing one character, moving the print head back one space, and printing a second character on top of the first.

page layout program   An application program that assembles text and graphics from a variety of files with which you can determine the precise placement, sizing, scaling, and cropping of material in accordance with the page design represented on-screen.

page orientation   See *landscape orientation* and *portrait orientation*.

palette   An on-screen display containing the set of colors or patterns that can be used.

pica   A unit of measure equal to approximately 1/6 inch, or 12 points. In typewriting and letter-quality printing, a 12-point monospace font that prints at a pitch of 10 characters per inch (cpi).

Picas usually describe horizontal and vertical measurements on the page, with the exception of type sizes, which are expressed in points.

pitch   A horizontal measurement of the number of characters per linear inch in a monospace font, such as those used with typewriters, dot-matrix printers, and daisywheel printers.

By convention, pica pitch (not to be confused with the printer's measurement of approximately 1/6 inch) equals 10 characters per inch, and elite pitch equals 12 characters per inch. See *monospace*, *pica*, and *point*.

pixel   The smallest element (a picture element) that a device can display on-screen and out of which the displayed image is constructed. See *bit-mapped graphic*.

PMS (Pantone Matching System)   The universal standard for creating colors by mixing red, blue, black, white, and green.

point   The fundamental unit of measure in typography. 72 points equals an inch.

portrait orientation   The default printing orientation for a page of text, with the longest measurement oriented vertically. See *landscape orientation*.

APPENDIX D

Glossary of Desktop Publishing Terms

posterization High-contrast effect created by removing the gray mid-tones from a scanned image.

PostScript A sophisticated page description language for medium- to high-resolution printing devices.

PostScript, developed by Adobe Systems, Inc., is a programming language that describes how to print a page that blends text and graphics.

PostScript laser printer A laser printer that includes the processing circuitry needed to decode and interpret printing instructions phrased in PostScript—a page description language (PDL) widely used in desktop publishing.

pre-printing Printing color elements on a page before printing page elements in black in a second pass; an inexpensive way to print nameplates, logos, and other document elements in color.

presentation graphics Text charts, bar graphs, pie graphs, and other charts and graphs, which you enhance so that they are visually appealing and easily understood by your audience. See *presentation graphics program*.

presentation graphics program An application program designed to create and enhance charts and graphs so that they are visually appealing and easily understood by an audience.

A full-featured presentation graphics package such as Harvard Graphics includes facilities for making text charts, bar graphs, pie graphs, high/low/close graphs, and organization charts.

The package also provides facilities for adding titles, legends, and explanatory text anywhere in the chart or graph. A presentation graphics program includes a library of clip art so that you can enliven charts and graphs by adding a picture related to the subject matter (for example, an airplane for a chart of earnings in the aerospace industry). You can print output, direct output to a film recorder, or display output on-screen in a computer slide show.

printer font A font available for printing, unlike screen fonts available for displaying text on-screen.

process color A standard color that does not require custom ink mixing.

proof Preliminary draft, used to proofread and check layouts.

645

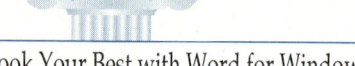

proportion scale   A graphic design tool used to size photos.

proportional spacing   The allocation of character widths proportional to the character shape so that a narrow character, such as i, receives less space than a wide character such as m. See *kerning* and *monospace*.

ragged-left alignment   The alignment of each line of text so that the right margin is even, but the left remains ragged. Synonymous with *flush right*.

raised cap   A large initial capital letter that extends above the first line of text. Raised and drop caps are used to guide the reader's eye to the beginning of body text.

registration mark   A printer's guide mark that ensures that color separations used in four-color printing will print in perfect alignment.

resident font   A font built into printer hardware—for example, most PostScript printers have 35 resident fonts

resolution   A measurement—usually expressed in linear dots per inch (dpi), horizontally and vertically—of the sharpness of an image generated by an output device such as a monitor or printer.

In monitors, resolution is expressed as the number of pixels displayed on-screen. For example, a CGA monitor displays fewer pixels than a VGA monitor, and, therefore, a CGA image appears more jagged than a VGA image.

Dot-matrix printers produce output with a lower resolution than laser printers.

reverse type   Type or graphic images printed in white on a dark background.

right justification   The alignment of text along the right margin and the left margin, producing a superficial resemblance to professionally printed text. The results may be poor, however, if the printer is incapable of proportional spacing; in such cases, right justification can be achieved only by inserting unsightly gaps of two or more spaces between words. For readability, most graphics artists advise computer users to leave the right margin ragged.

rotated type   In a graphics or desktop publishing program, text that has been rotated from its normal, horizontal position on the page. The best graphics programs, such as CorelDRAW!, enable the user to edit the type even after it has been rotated.

APPENDIX D

Glossary of Desktop Publishing Terms

rule line   Horizontal or vertical lines used to separate text and images. For example, horizontal rule lines often are used to separate a newsletter nameplate from the body text area.

sans serif   A typeface that lacks serifs, the fine cross strokes across the ends of the main strokes of a character.

Sans serif typefaces, such as Helvetica, are preferred for display type but are harder to read than serif typefaces, such as Times Roman, when used for body type. See *body type*, *display type*, *serif*, and *typeface*.

scalable font   See *outline font*.

scalloped columns   An informal design grid in which columns are allowed to end before they reach the bottom of the page.

screen   A shade of gray added to a box. Screens darker than 10% interfere with readability of black text; and screens lighter than about 60% may interfere with the readability of reversed (white) text.

screen font   A bit-mapped font designed to mimic the appearance of printer fonts when displayed on medium-resolution monitors.

script   A typeface that resembles handwriting.

separations   A negative used in four-color printing. Each layer contains one of the colors used to produce the four-color image.

serif   The fine cross strokes across the ends of the main strokes of a character.

Serif fonts are easier to read for body type, but most designers prefer to use sans serif typefaces for display type. (The body text in this book is serif text.) See *sans serif*.

service bureau   A business that provides phototypesetting of desktop published files.

shadow box   A box with a shadow that creates the illusion that the box is floating above the page.

sidebar   A short section of text accompanying a main article, usually set in a separate box.

sink   White space at the top of the pages of a document that remains the same on each page.

slide show   A predetermined list of on-screen presentation charts and graphs displayed one after the other.

Some programs can produce interesting effects, such as fading out one screen before displaying another and enabling you to choose your path through the charts available for display. See *presentation graphics*.

soft font   See *downloadable font*.

spot color   Color applied selectively to rules, boxes, headline text, and so on.

spread   Two facing pages.

standing head   A headline that introduces a regular feature, such as a department, in a newspaper, newsletter, or magazine.

stroke   The thickness of the letters of a font. Typeface stroke variations may include bold, narrow, and heavy.

subscript   A number or letter printed slightly below the typing line. See *superscript*.

superscript   A number or letter printed slightly above the typing line. See *subscript*.

text file   A file consisting of nothing but the standard ASCII characters (with no control characters or higher order characters).

template   A file containing the basic formatting commands for a certain type of document. For example, a newsletter template may contain the nameplate, column formatting codes, headers and footers, standard rule lines, and so on.

thumbnail   A small, hand-drawn or computer-generated sketch of one or more document pages. Some programs can print up to 16 thumbnails on an 8 1/2-by-11-inch page.

TIFF (Tagged Image File Format)   The file format used to store scanned images.

tombstone headlines   Two headlines that accidentally align horizontally in adjacent columns, creating unwelcome ambiguity for the reader.

trim size   The final size of a document page after the pages have been physically trimmed to equal size by the printer.

APPENDIX D

Glossary of Desktop Publishing Terms

type size   The size of a font, measured in points (approximately 1/72 inch) from the top of the tallest ascender to the bottom of the lowest descender. See *pitch*.

type style   The weight (such as Roman or bold) or posture (such as italic) of a font—distinguished from a font's typeface design and type size. See *attribute*.

typeface   The distinctive design of a set of type, distinguished from its weight and size.

Typefaces are grouped into two categories, serif and sans serif. Serif typefaces frequently are chosen for body type because they are more legible. Sans serif typefaces are preferred for display type. See *sans serif* and *serif*.

vertical justification   Aligning the bottoms of adjacent columns by selectively adding or subtracting small amounts of leading to text or by adding extra space between paragraphs, between text and headings, between photos and text, and so on.

weight   The overall lightness or darkness of a typeface design or the gradations of lightness to darkness within a font family.

A type style can be light or dark, and within a type style, you can see several gradations of weight (extra light, light, semilight, regular, medium, semibold, bold, extrabold, and ultrabold). See *typeface*.

widow   A formatting flaw in which the last line of a paragraph appears alone at the top of a new column or page.

Most word processing and page layout programs suppress widows and orphans; better programs enable you to switch widow/orphan control on and off and to choose the number of lines. See *orphan*.

word wrap   A feature of word processing programs (and other programs that include text-editing features) that wraps words down to the beginning of the next line if they go beyond the right margin.

WYSIWYG (What-You-See-Is-What-You-Get)   A design philosophy in which formatting commands directly affect the text displayed on-screen so that the screen shows the appearance of the printed text.

Index

A

About Word command, 601
accordion folds, 115
addresses, 131
advertisements
  borders, 362
  multipurpose, 376
  placing, 362
  planning, 360-362
  sources, 359-360
alignment, 633
  centered, 86
  flush left, 638
  flush right, 638
  fully justified, 87, 640
  label, 641
  left, 85-86, 642
  ragged-left, 646
  right, 86, 646
  vertical, 649
  see also, justification
alignment buttons, 589, 603
alley space, *see* gutter space
alphanumeric keys, 594-595, 609
anchoring, 633
Annotations command, 585-586, 599-600
Arrange Windows command, 586, 601
ascenders, 70, 633
ASCII files, 633

Assign to Key command, 132, 586
Assign to Menu command, 586
asymmetrical balance, 36
attributes, 78-79, 633
attributes buttons, 588, 603
Auto Update, 535
AutoExec macro, 301
automatic
  font downloading, 634
  hyphenation, 87
AutoNew macro, 234, 301
AutoOpen macro, 301

B

Backspace key, 592, 606
balance
  asymmetrical, 36
  modular, 37
  symmetrical, 35-36
balancing design elements, 35
banners, 634
barrel folds, 114
baselines, 71, 634
binding margins, 44
bit-mapped
  fonts, 634
  graphics, 614, 634
bleeds, 43, 103, 634
blurbs, 634
body
  text, 76, 91
  type, 634

boilerplate text, 51
boldface, 634
bond paper, 110
book paper, 110
Bookmark command, 560, 569, 586, 600
books, 62-63
  formats, 17
  planning, 547-548
Border command, 134, 140, 145-146, 158, 162, 165, 168, 184, 195-198, 201, 335, 340-343, 347-348, 363, 368-370, 385, 388, 391-393, 398, 419, 422, 447-448, 461-462, 467, 483-488, 492-496, 502, 505-508, 530-534, 560, 568, 600
Border dialog box, 122
borders, 53-54, 362
bowls, 634
boxes, 53-54
  dialog, *see* dialog boxes
  shadow, 53
  Summary Info, 243-244
Break command, 201, 349, 385-388, 391-393, 413-415, 420, 423-424, 454-455, 459-461, 468-470, 483-487, 492, 495, 531-534, 559-561, 568-573, 586, 600
brightness, 109
brochures, 57-59, 407-409
Browse command, 601

Look Your Best with Word for Windows

brush style, 635
bullets, 94, 132-133
bureaus, service, 647
business reports, 517-519
buttons
  alignment, 589, 603
  attributes, 588, 603
  control, 582, 596
  display nonprinting codes, 604
  Edit, 601
  Envelope, 602
  File, 601
  Format, 602
  Insert, 602
  option, 583
  Page View, 602
  spacing, 589
  tab, 603
  tab stop, 589
  Tools, 602
  Undo, 602
bylines, 635

C

Calculate command, 586, 600
callouts, 53, 93, 635
caps, initial, 641
captions, 90-91, 635
carbonless paper forms, 280
cartridge fonts, 635
cartridges, 635
cells
  locating, 341
  modifying, 286
centered text, 86
CGM (Computer Graphics Metafile), 617, 635
Character command, 81, 125, 132, 144-145, 183-185, 364, 431-432, 452-454, 483, 492, 501, 530-532, 586, 600
character sets, 635
characters, 635
  Field, 299
  nonprinting, 588
characters per inch (cpi), 635
charts, 21
checking spelling, 154
circulars, 373-376

clicking, 591, 605
clip art, 361, 635
clipboard, 585, 599
Close command, 584, 598
closed quotation marks, 643
clustering, 636
coated book paper, 110
coated cover paper, 111
Codes, Field, 299
color separation, 636
colors
  paper, 109
  process, 645
  spot, 648
Column command, 454-455, 483
Column Width command, 600
columns
  creating, 47-48
  modifying, 286
  newspaper-style, 643
  planning, 44-45
  scalloped, 647
Columns command, 201, 345, 386-388, 391-393, 412, 418, 453-454, 459-461, 468-469, 486-487, 492, 600
commands
  About Word, 601
  Annotations, 585-586, 599-600
  Arrange Windows, 586, 601
  Assign to Key, 132, 586
  Assign to Menu, 586
  Bookmark, 560, 569, 586, 600
  Border, 134, 140, 145-146, 158, 162, 165, 168, 184, 195-198, 201, 335, 340-343, 347-348, 363, 368-370, 385, 388, 391-393, 398, 419, 422, 447-448, 461-462, 467, 483-488, 492-496, 502, 505-508, 530-534, 560, 568, 600
  Break, 201, 349, 385-388, 391-393, 413-415, 420, 423-424, 454-455, 459-461, 468-470, 483-487, 492, 495, 531-534, 559-561, 568-573, 586, 600
  Browse, 601
  Calculate, 586, 600

Character, 81, 125, 132, 144-145, 183-185, 364, 431-432, 452-454, 483, 492, 501, 530-532, 586, 600
Close, 584, 598
Column Width, 600
Columns, 201, 345, 386-388, 391-393, 412, 418, 453-455, 459-461, 468-469, 483, 486-487, 492, 600
Compare Versions, 586, 600
Convert Text to Table, 600
Copy, 349, 391, 584, 599
Create Envelope, 600
Customize, 155, 586
Cut, 501-503, 584, 599
Date and Time, 600
Define Styles, 163, 194, 586, 589
Delete Columns, 600
Document, 124, 129, 135, 142, 152, 156, 163-165, 178-181, 191, 198, 330, 337, 345, 363, 367, 370, 384, 389, 395, 412, 418, 430, 447-449, 456, 467, 481, 490, 501, 529, 557, 564, 586
Draft, 505, 531-532, 568-569, 585, 599
Edit, 586, 601
Exit, 584
Field, 535, 560, 569-571, 586, 600
Field Codes, 571, 585, 599
File, 586, 600-601
Find, 584, 599
Find File, 598
Footnotes, 585-586, 599-600
Frame, 600
Getting Started, 601
Glossary, 148, 152, 448, 459, 585, 599
Go To, 599
Grammar, 600
Header/Footer, 165, 490-492, 505, 531, 559-560, 568-569, 585, 599
Help, 586
Help Index, 601
Hyphenate, 166, 413-416, 419, 424-425, 453, 504, 586

652

Index

Hyphenation, 166, 413-416, 420, 424-425, 453, 504, 600
Index, 571, 586, 600
Index Entry, 570, 586, 600
Insert Table, 600
Language, 600
Learning Word, 601
Links, 599, 619
Macro, 600
Maximize, 598
Merge Cells, 600
Move, 598
New, 124, 129, 135, 142, 152, 178-181, 191, 330, 337, 363, 367, 370, 382, 389, 395, 412, 417, 430, 447-449, 481, 497, 529, 556, 571, 584, 598
New Window, 586, 601
Next Window, 584, 598
Normal, 505, 599
Object, 447, 599-600
Open, 148, 195, 198, 456, 466, 490, 497, 564, 584, 598, 612-614
Options, 550, 600
Outline, 557, 564, 585, 599
Page, 124, 129, 135, 532, 558-559, 568, 585
Page Layout, 505, 506, 558-560, 569, 599
Page Number, 586, 600
Page Setup, 124, 129, 135, 142, 152, 156, 163-165, 178-181, 191, 199, 330, 337, 345, 363, 368-370, 384, 389, 395, 412, 418, 430, 447, 451, 459, 467, 481, 490, 501, 529, 557, 565, 600
Paragraph, 82, 126, 133-134, 140, 145-146, 158-159, 162, 165-168, 184-186, 195-198, 201, 332-336, 339-343, 346-348, 363, 368-373, 385, 388, 391, 397-398, 413-415, 419-422, 431-433, 447-448, 452-454, 460-462, 467-468, 471, 482-496, 502-505, 508, 530-538, 550, 559, 568-569, 586, 600
Paste, 349, 391-392, 501-503, 584, 599, 619
Paste Link, 535
Paste Special, 535, 599
Picture, 130, 146, 414, 447, 534, 586, 600, 617-618
Position, 586
Preferences, 334, 339-340, 421, 585
Print, 127, 134, 141, 147, 179, 186, 194, 198, 203, 336, 349, 364, 369, 373, 388, 393, 398, 416, 425, 433-434, 455, 472, 488, 496, 509, 536, 561, 570-573, 584, 598
Print Merge, 584, 598
Print Preview, 127, 134, 141, 147, 155, 162, 168, 179-181, 186, 194, 198, 203, 584, 598
Printer Setup, 179-181, 198, 345, 412, 418, 430, 584, 598, 629-630
Record, 132, 586
Record Macro, 600
Renumber, 586
Repaginate Now, 586
Repeat, 585, 599
Replace, 167, 585, 599
Restore, 584, 598
Revision Marks, 586, 600
Ribbon, 124, 129, 135, 585, 599
Row Height, 600
Ruler, 124, 129, 135, 585, 588, 599
Run, 586
Save, 148, 194, 198, 203, 455, 472, 488, 496, 509, 536, 561, 570-573, 584, 598
Save All, 132, 584
Save As, 127, 134, 141, 147, 155, 162, 168, 179-181, 184-186, 193-195, 336, 343, 349, 364, 369, 373, 388, 393, 398, 416, 425, 449, 452, 456, 490, 501, 557, 571, 584, 598, 612-614
Search, 585
Section, 47, 201, 345, 385, 388, 391-393, 412, 418, 453-455, 459-461, 468-469, 483, 486-487, 492, 586
Section Layout, 391, 600
Select All, 599
Select Column, 600
Select Row, 600
Select Table, 600
Size, 598
Sort, 586
Sorting, 600
Spelling, 154, 162, 166, 586, 600
Split, 584, 598
Split Table, 600
Status bar, 585
Stop Recorder, 132
Style(s), 197, 387, 412, 419, 424, 459, 467-468, 484, 494, 504, 533, 558, 565, 586, 589, 600, 603
Summary Info, 155, 162, 168, 585, 598
Symbol, 133, 159, 168, 183, 195, 333, 337, 470, 600
Table, 48, 159, 162, 334-335, 339-343, 420-422, 470, 502, 534, 585-586
Table of Contents, 536, 573, 586, 600
Tabs, 133, 144, 156, 161, 167, 186, 332-333, 336, 339, 345-349, 387, 453, 470, 486, 507, 586, 600
Template, 598
Thesaurus, 586, 600
Toolbar, 599
Undo, 585, 599
Zoom, 599
commercial print shops, 106-107
Compare Versions command, 586, 600
compose sequence, 636
composite newsletters, 636
Computer Graphics Metafile (CGM), 617, 635
condensed type, 145, 636
configuring printers, 629
constraining, 636
continuous-tone photographs, 636
control buttons, 582, 596
Convert Text to Table command, 600
converters, 611
converting text files, 611-614

Copy command, 349, 391, 584, 599
copy shops, 106
copyfitting, 636
CorelDRAW!, 274, 617
counters, 636
coupons, 361, 389
Courier fonts, 636
cover paper, 111
cover sheets, fax, 257-259
  designing, 268-274
  with graphic boxes, 262, 265-268
  with graphic rules, 260-262
cpi (characters per inch), 635
Create Envelope command, 600
creating
  bullets, 132-133
  columns, 47-48
  facing pages, 48-50
  headers, 505
  logos, 129-134
  macros, 132
  nameplates, 443, 446-449, 482-483
  rough drafts, 29-31
  tables of contents, 535
  vertical rules, 139-141
crop marks, 102, 636
cropping, 636
Customize command, 155, 586
Cut command, 501-503, 584, 599

D

dashes
  em, 556, 638
  en, 638
Date and Time command, 600
datelines, 86, 446
DDE (Dynamic Data Exchange), 535, 621
default fonts, 637
Define Styles command, 163, 194, 586, 589
Delete Columns command, 600
Delete key, 592, 606
descenders, 70, 637
design
  elements, 35
  flaws, 63, 96-97

designing
  envelopes, 177
  fax cover sheets, 268-274
  memos, 244-250
  purchase orders, 304-306
desktop publishing (DTP), 13, 637
dialog boxes, 583
  Border, 122
  Document, 135
  Spelling, 154
  Symbol, 133
  Table, 334
dingbats, 637
direct mail, 374
direction keys, 593-594, 608
discretionary hyphens, 82, 87, 420, 637
display heads, 89
display non-printing codes button, 604
display type, 76, 637
Document command, 124, 129, 135, 142, 152, 156, 163-165, 178-181, 191, 198, 330, 337, 345, 363, 367, 370, 384, 389, 395, 412, 418, 430, 447-449, 456, 467, 481, 490, 501, 529, 557, 564, 586
Document dialog box, 135
documents, master, 551, 570-571
dot leaders, 637
dot pitch, 637
dot-matrix printers, 625, 637
dots per inch (dpi), 105, 623
double-clicking, 591, 605
downloadable fonts, 637
dpi (dots per inch), 105, 623
Draft command, 505, 531-532, 568-569, 585, 599
drafts, rough, 29-31
dragging, 591, 605
drop caps, 93-94, 637
drop out type, 637
drop shadows, 638
DRW file format, 55
DTP (desktop publishing), 13, 637
Dynamic Data Exchange (DDE), 535, 621

E

Edit buttons, 601
Edit command, 586, 601
Edit menu
  Copy, 349, 391, 584, 599
  Cut, 501, 503, 584, 599
  Find, 599
  Glossary, 148, 152, 448, 459, 585, 599
  Go To, 599
  Header/Footer, 165, 490, 531, 559, 568-569, 585
  Links, 599, 619
  Object, 599
  Paste, 349, 391-392, 501-503, 584, 599, 619
  Paste Link, 535
  Paste Special, 535, 599
  Repeat, 585, 599
  Replace, 167, 585, 599
  Search, 585
  Select All, 599
  Summary Info, 155, 162, 168, 585
  Table, 341, 585
  Undo, 585, 599
editing
  graphics, 130-131
  text, 47
effects, fountain, 639
elite typeface, 638
ellipses, 638
em dashes, 556, 638
em spaces, 638
embedding, 621
emphasis techniques
  charts, 21
  color, 21
  graphic elements, 21
  typography, 21
  white space, 21
en dashes, 638
en spaces, 638
Encapsulated PostScript Standard (EPS), 617
Enter key, 592, 606
Envelope button, 602
envelopes
  boundaries, 175-176
  designing, 177
  planning, 174

Index

printing, 178-182
size, 175
EPS (Encapsulated PostScript Standard), 617
EPS file format, 55
Esc key, 592, 606
Exit command, 584
expense reports, 316, 319-322
expense/reimbursement forms, 322, 325-327
extended character sets, 638
eyebrows, 638

F

facing pages, 48-50
facsimile transmissions, *see* fax cover sheets
fastenings
 looseleaf, 116
 padding, 117
 saddle back, 117
 side stitch, 116
fax cover sheets, 257-259
 designing, 268-274
 guidelines, 256-257
 templates, 257
 with graphic boxes, 262-268
 with graphic rules, 260-262
feathering, 638
Field Characters, 299
Field Codes, 299
Field Codes command, 571, 585, 599
Field command, 535, 560, 569-571, 586, 600
Field Types, 300
fields, 301
File buttons, 601
File command, 586, 600-601
file formats
 ASCII, 633
 DRW, 55
 EPS, 55
 PCX, 55
 TIF, 55
 TIFF, 55, 127, 616
 WPG, 55
File menu, 191
 Close, 584, 598
 Exit, 584

Find, 584
Find File, 598
New, 124, 129, 135, 142, 152, 178-181, 191, 330, 337, 363, 367, 370, 382, 389, 395, 412, 417, 430, 447-449, 481, 497, 529, 556, 571, 584, 598
Open, 148, 195, 198, 456, 466, 490, 497, 564, 584, 598, 612-614
Print, 127, 134, 141, 147, 179, 186, 194, 198, 203, 336, 349, 364, 369, 373, 388, 393, 398, 416, 425, 433-434, 455, 472, 488, 496, 509, 536, 561, 570-573, 584, 598
Print Merge, 584, 598
Print Preview, 127, 134, 141, 147, 155, 162, 168, 179-181, 186, 194, 198, 203, 584, 598
Print Setup, 598, 629
Printer Setup, 179-181, 198, 345, 412, 418, 430, 584, 630
Save, 148, 194, 198, 203, 455, 472, 488, 496, 509, 536, 561, 570-573, 584, 598
Save All, 132, 584
Save As, 127, 134, 141, 147, 155, 162, 168, 179-181, 184-186, 193-195, 336, 343, 349, 364, 369, 373, 388, 393, 398, 416, 425, 449, 452, 456, 490, 501, 557, 571, 584, 598, 612-614
Summary Info, 598
Template, 598
files
 ASCII, 633
 linking, 620
 printer driver, 628
 text, 611-614
 TIFF, 55, 127, 616
filters, 611
Find command, 584, 599
Find File command, 598
finish, 108
finished size, 107
finishing techniques, 18
flags, 638
fliers, 56-57
 design, 399, 402
 formats, 17
 purpose, 381-382

flush left alignment, 638
flush right alignment, 638
folds
 accordion, 115
 barrel, 114
 French, 114
 parallel, 113
folios, 638
font boxes, 587, 603
fonts, 74, 638
 bit-mapped, 634
 cartridge, 635, 639
 Courier, 636
 default, 637
 downloadable, 637
 editors, 639
 families, 639
 Helvetica, 641
 metrics, 639
 monospaced, 80
 oblique, 643
 outline, 643
 printer, 625, 645
 resident, 646
 screen, 625, 647
 script, 647
 see also, typefaces
footer margins, 42
footers, 42-43, 60, 639
Footnotes command, 585-586, 599-600
Format buttons, 602
Format menu
 Border, 134, 140, 145-146, 158, 162, 165, 168, 184, 195-198, 201, 335, 340, 341-343, 347-348, 363, 368-370, 385, 388, 391-393, 398, 419, 422, 447-448, 461-462, 467, 483-488, 492-496, 502, 505-508, 530-532, 560, 568, 600
 Character, 81, 125, 132, 144-145, 183-185, 364, 431-432, 452-454, 483, 492, 501, 530-532, 586, 600
 Columns, 201, 345, 386-388, 391-393, 412, 418, 453-455, 459-461, 468-469, 483, 486-487, 492, 600
 Define Styles, 163, 194, 586, 589

655

Look Your Best with Word for Windows

Document, 124, 129, 135, 142, 152, 156, 163-165, 178-181, 191, 198, 330, 337, 345, 363, 367, 370, 384, 389, 395, 412, 418, 430, 447-449, 456, 467, 481, 490, 501, 529, 557, 564, 586
Frame, 600
Language, 600
Page Setup, 124, 129, 135, 142, 152, 156, 163-165, 178-181, 191, 199, 330, 337, 345, 363, 368-370, 384, 389, 395, 412, 418, 430, 447, 451, 459, 467, 481, 490, 501, 529, 557, 565, 600
Paragraph, 82, 126, 133-134, 140, 145-146, 158-159, 162, 165-168, 184-186, 195-198, 201, 332-336, 339-343, 346-348, 363, 368-373, 385, 388, 391, 397, 398, 413-415, 419-422, 431-433, 447-448, 452-454, 460-462, 467-468, 471, 482-496, 502-505, 508, 530-538, 550, 559, 568-569, 586, 600
Picture, 447, 586, 600
Position, 586
Section, 47, 201, 345, 388, 391-393, 412, 418, 453-455, 459-461, 468-469, 483, 486-487, 492, 586
Section Layout, 391, 600
Style(s), 197, 387, 412, 419, 424, 459, 467-468, 484, 494, 504, 533, 558, 565, 586, 589, 600, 603
Table, 159, 162, 335, 340-343, 422, 470, 502, 586
Tabs, 133, 144, 156, 161, 167, 186, 332-333, 336, 339, 345-349, 387, 453, 470, 486, 507, 586, 600
formats
  documents, 17
  file, *see* file formats
formatting, 639
  addresses, 131
  letterheads, 124-126, 138-139, 144
  printed progams, 228

forms, 61
  carbonless paper, 280
  small expense/reimbursement, 322, 325-327
fountain effect, 639
Frame command, 600
frame-grabbers, 640
frames, 639
French folds, 114
full justification, 82, 87, 640
function keys, 592, 606-607

G

Getting Started command, 601
glossaries, 148, 152, 445
Glossary command, 148, 152, 448, 459, 585, 599
glossary entries, 122
Go To command, 599
grabbers, 640
grain, 109
Grammar command, 600
graphics, 21, 50, 55
  bit-mapped, 634
  collecting, 17
  designing, 268-274
  editing, 130-131
  importing, 130, 614-620
  object, 615
  presentation, 645
  rules and boxes, 260-268
  sizing, 147
graphics mode, 640
graphics monitors, 640
gray scale, 640
gray space, 38
greeking, 640
gridlines, 334
grids, 30, 640
grippers, 40, 103
guidelines
  page layout, 256-257
  postal, 175-177
gutter space, 29, 47, 87, 286, 640

H

halftones, 103, 640
handles, 447
hanging indents, 88, 640
hard hyphens, 640
hard spaces, 640
head-to-toe, 425
header margins, 42
Header/Footer command, 165, 490-492, 505, 531, 559-560, 568-569, 585, 599
headers, 42, 43, 60, 505, 640
headings, 76
headlines, 86, 90, 648
Help command, 586
Help feature, 300
Help Index command, 601
Help menu
  About Word, 601
  Browse, 601
  Edit, 601
  File, 601
  Getting Started, 601
  Help Index, 601
  Learning Word, 601
Helvetica, 641
Hewlett-Packard Graphics Language (HPGL), 617
Hewlett-Packard Printer Command Language (HPCL), 624-625
high-resolution output, 641
horizontal layout mode, 31-33, 377, 641
horizontal rules, 51
horizontal-feed printers, 178-182
HPCL (Hewlett-Packard Printer Command Language), 624-625
HPGL (Hewlett-Packard Graphics Language), 617
Hyphenate command, 166, 413-416, 419, 424-425, 453, 504, 586
hyphenation, 641
Hyphenation command, 166, 413-416, 420, 424-425, 453, 504, 600
hyphens
  automatic, 87
  discretionary, 82, 87, 420, 637
  hard, 640

Index

I

image scanners, 641
image setters, 627
importing
　glossaries, 152
　graphics, 130, 614-620
indentation, 641
indents, 87
　hanging, 88, 640
　outdents, 88
Index command, 571, 586, 600
Index Entry command, 570, 586, 600
indexes, 571
initial caps, 641
ink, thermographed, 113
Inkjet printers, 626
inks, 408
Insert buttons, 602
Insert Field key, 300
Insert key, 592, 606
Insert menu
　Annotation, 586, 600
　Bookmark, 560, 569, 586, 600
　Border, 534
　Break, 201, 349, 385-388, 391-393, 413-415, 420, 423-424, 454-455, 459-461, 468-470, 483-487, 492, 495, 531-534, 559-561, 568-573, 586, 600
　Date and Time, 600
　Field, 535, 560, 569, 586, 600
　File, 586, 600
　Footnote, 586, 600
　Frame, 600
　Index, 571, 586, 600
　Index Entry, 570, 586, 600
　Object, 447, 600
　Page Number, 586, 600
　Picture, 130, 146, 414, 534, 586, 600, 617-618
　Section, 385
　Symbol, 133, 159, 168, 183, 195, 333, 337, 470, 600
　Table, 48, 334, 339-340, 420, 470, 502, 534, 586
　Table of Contents, 536, 573, 586, 600
Insert Table command, 600
inserting pictures, 201

J

jumplines, 92, 641
justification, 641
　see also, alignment
justified text, 82, 87

K

kerning, 81, 641
keyboard keys, 592, 606
keyboard shortcuts
　Alt-I,A (Insert Table), 48
　Alt-T,C (Character), 81, 125
　Alt-T,P (Paragraph), 82
　Alt-T,S (Section), 47
　Ctrl+- (hyphen), 82
　Ctrl+1 (single-space), 589
　Ctrl+2 (double-spacing), 589
　Ctrl+5 (One-and-a-half spacing), 589
　Ctrl+C (Copy), 349
　Ctrl+E (no extra space), 589
　Ctrl+F6 (Next Window), 501
　Ctrl+Ins (Copy), 585
　Ctrl+K (Small Kaps), 183
　Ctrl+O (extra line of space), 589
　Ctrl+V (Paste), 460, 501-503
　Ctrl+X, 501-503
　Ctrl+X (Cut), 460
　Shift+Del (Cut), 460, 501-503, 585
　Shift+Ins (Paste), 460, 585
　Shift+Insert, 501-503
keys
　Insert Field, 300
　keyboard, 592, 606

L

label alignment, 641
landscape (horizontal) mode, 31-33, 377, 641
Language command, 600
languages
　HPCL, 624-625
　page description, 624-625
　PostScript, 624-625, 645
laser printers, 626, 641
layout, 103, 642

layout modes
　landscape (horizontal), 31-33, 377, 641
　portrait (vertical), 31-32
leaders, 88
leading lines, 80-84, 144, 642
Learning Word command, 601
left justification, 85-86, 642
length, lines, 45-47
letter spacing, 80-81
letter-quality printers, 642
letterhead paper, 111
letterheads, 121
　formatting, 124-126, 138-139, 144
　printing, 127
　storing, 148
letters, kerning, 81
ligatures, 642
line spacing, 80-84, 144, 642
lines
　leading, 80-84, 144, 642
　length, 45-47
　rule, 647
linking files, 620
Links command, 599, 619
Linotronic typesetters, 642
lists
　bulleted, 94
　numbered, 95
live area, 642
locating cells, 341
logos, 59, 95, 129-134, 642
looseleaf fastening, 116

M

Macro command, 600
Macro menu
　Assign to Key, 132, 586
　Assign to Menu, 586
　Edit, 586
　Record, 132, 586
　Run, 586
　Stop Recorder, 132
macros, 51, 299
　AutoExec, 301
　AutoNew, 234, 301
　AutoOpen, 301
　creating, 132, 301
mailing documents, 104-105

657

margins, 39-44, 62, 103
 binding, 44
 bleeding, 43
 footer, 42
 header, 42
 setting, 152, 156
marks
 crop, 102, 636
 open quotation, 643
 registration, 646
master documents, 551, 570-571
mastheads, 60, 642
Maximize command, 598
memos, 233
 designing, 244-250
 templates, 234-237, 240-243
menus, 582-586
Merge Cells command, 600
mezzotint, 642
modes
 graphics, 640
 layout
  landscape (horizontal), 31-33, 377, 641
  portrait (vertical), 31-32
modifying
 graphics, 130-131
 text, 47
modular balance, 37
moire patterns, 642
monitors, 640
monospace, 643
monospaced fonts, 80
mouse, 591, 605
Move command, 598
multipurpose advertisements, 376

N

nameplates, 443, 446-449, 482-483, 643
near-letter quality (NLQ), 643
New command, 124, 129, 135, 142, 152, 178-181, 191, 330, 337, 363, 367, 370, 382, 389, 395, 412, 417, 430, 447-449, 481, 497, 529, 556, 571, 584, 598
New Window command, 586, 601

newsletters, 59-60
 basics, 441-443
 composite, 636
 formats, 17
 size, 441
newspaper-style columns, 643
Next Window command, 501, 584, 598
NLQ (near-letter quality), 643
non-breaking space, 643
nonprinting characters, 588
Normal command, 505, 599
normal type, 145
numbered lists, 95
numbering, 280, 303-304

O

Object command, 447, 599-600
object graphics, 615
oblique typeface, 643
OCR (Optical Character Recognition), 643
offset book paper, 110
opacity, 109
Open command, 148, 195, 198, 456, 466, 490, 497, 564, 584, 598, 612-614
open quotation marks, 643
opening templates, 182
Optical Character Recognition (OCR), 643
option buttons, 583
Options command, 550, 600
orientation, 643
 landscape, 228, 641
 page, 292
 portrait, 228, 644
orphans, 550, 643
outdents, 88
Outline command, 557, 564, 585, 599
outline fonts, 643
output, 105
overstriking, 644

P

pad fastening, 117
Page command, 124, 129, 135, 532, 558-559, 568, 585
page description languages, 624-625
page layout, 103
Page Layout command, 505, 506, 558, 560, 569, 599
page layout programs, 644
Page Number command, 586, 600
page orientation, 31-32, 292
Page Setup command, 124, 129, 135, 142, 152, 156, 163-165, 178-181, 191, 199, 330, 337, 345, 363, 368-370, 384, 389, 395, 412, 418, 430, 447, 451, 459, 467, 481, 490, 501, 529, 557, 565, 600
Page View buttons, 602
pages, facing, 48-50
palettes, 644
Pantone Matching System (PMS), 112, 644
paper
 bond, 110
 book, 110
 brightness, 109
 colors, 109
 cover, 111
 finish, 108
 grain, 109
 letterhead, 111
 opacity, 109
 scoring, 116
 size, 34-35, 108
 sulphite, 110
 types, 111-113
 weight, 108, 408
Paragraph command, 82, 126, 133-134, 140, 145-146, 158-159, 162, 165-168, 184-186, 195-198, 201, 332-336, 340, 343, 346-348, 363, 368-373, 385, 388, 391, 397-398, 413-415, 419-422, 431-433, 447-448, 452-454, 460-462, 467-468, 471, 482-488, 490-496, 502-505, 508, 530-538, 550, 559, 568-569, 586, 600

Index

paragraph spacing, 80, 84
parallel folds, 113
Paste command, 349, 391-392, 501-503, 584, 599, 619
Paste Link command, 535
Paste Special command, 535, 599
paste-up, 101
patterns, moire, 642
PCX file format, 55
permits, postal, 177
photographs, continuous-tone, 636
picas, 75, 644
Picture command, 130, 146, 414, 447, 534, 586, 600, 617-618
pictures, inserting, 201
Pictures command, 586
pitch, 644
pixels, 644
placing advertisements, 362
planning
   advertisements, 360-362
   books, 547-548
   columns, 44-45
   envelopes, 174
PMS (Pantone Matching System), 112, 644
PMTs, 103
point size box, 603
points, 75, 644
portrait (vertical) mode, 31-32, 644
ports, printer, 629
Position command, 586
postal
   permits, 177
   regulations and guidelines, 175-177
posterization, 645
PostScript (PS), 624-625
PostScript language, 645
PostScript laser printers, 627, 645
pre-printing, 645
Preferences command, 334, 339-340, 421, 585
presentation graphics, 645
presentation graphics program, 645
price quotations, 107-108

Print command, 127, 134, 141, 147, 179, 186, 194, 198, 203, 336, 349, 364, 369, 373, 388, 393, 398, 416, 425, 433-434, 455, 472, 488, 496, 509, 536, 561, 570-573, 584, 598
Print Merge command, 584, 598
Print Preview command, 127, 134, 141, 147, 155, 162, 168, 179-181, 186, 194, 198, 203, 584, 598
Print Setup command, 598, 629
print shops
   commercial, 106-107
   quick copy, 106
printer driver files, 628
printer fonts, 625, 645
printer ports, 629
Printer Setup command, 179-181, 198, 345, 412, 418, 430, 584, 630
printers
   configuring, 629
   dot-matrix, 625, 637
   horizontal-feed, 178-182
   image setters, 627
   Inkjet, 626
   laser, 626, 641
   letter-quality, 642
   PostScript laser, 627, 645
   setup, 630
   vertical-feed, 179
process colors, 645
programs
   common sizes, 207
   page layout, 644
   presentation graphics, 645
   printed, 207
      formatting, 228
      innovative design, 221-227
      sample design, 209, 212-214, 229-231
      symbols, 212
      tips on printing process, 220
      traditional format, 214, 215-220
   sample design, 211
proofs, 645
proportion scales, 646
proportional spacing, 646
PS (PostScript), 624-625

Pts. window, 587
purchase orders
   designing, 304-306
   numbering, 303-304
   producing, 281-291

Q

quick copy shops, 106
quotations, price, 107-108

R

ragged-left alignment, 646
raised caps, 646
Record command, 132, 586
Record Macro command, 600
registration marks, 646
regulations, postal, 175-177
Renumber command, 586
Repaginate Now command, 586
Repeat command, 585, 599
Replace command, 167, 585, 599
reports
   business, 517-519
   expense, 316, 319-322
resident fonts, 646
resolution, 623, 646
Restore command, 584, 598
resumes, 189-190
reversed type, 646
Revision Marks command, 586, 600
Ribbon, 587, 602
Ribbon command, 124, 129, 135, 585, 599
right justification, 646
right-aligned text, 86
Roman type family, 72
rotated type, 646
rough drafts, 29-31
Row Height command, 600
rule lines, 51-53, 139-141, 647
Ruler, 588, 604
Ruler box, 590
Ruler command, 124, 129, 135, 585, 588, 599
Run command, 586

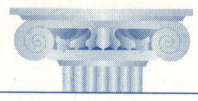

S

saddle back fastening, 117
sans serif typefaces, 73, 647
Save All command, 132, 584
Save As command, 127, 134, 141, 147, 155, 162, 168, 179-181, 184-186, 193-195, 336, 343, 349, 364, 369, 373, 388, 393, 398, 416, 425, 449, 452, 456, 490, 501, 557, 571, 584, 598, 612-614
Save command, 148, 194, 198, 203, 455, 472, 488, 496, 509, 536, 561, 570-573, 584, 598
scalloped columns, 647
scanners, 617
scoring paper, 116
screen fonts, 625, 647
screens, 55, 647
script fonts, 647
script type family, 73
scroll bars, 590, 605
Search command, 585
Section command, 47, 201, 345, 385, 388, 391-393, 412, 418, 453-455, 459, 461, 468-469, 483, 486-487, 492, 586
Section Layout command, 391, 600
Select All command, 599
Select Column command, 600
Select Row command, 600
Select Table command, 600
separations, 647
sequence, compose, 636
serif typefaces, 71, 647
service bureaus, 647
sets
 character, 635
 extended character, 638
setting margins, 152, 156
setting up printers, 630
shadow boxes, 53, 647
shelf life, 15
side stitch fastening, 116
sidebars, 647
sinks, 647
Size command, 598
sizes
 brochures, 409
 business reports, 518
 documents, 34-35
 envelopes, 175
 finished, 107
 newsletters, 441
 paper, 108
 trim, 107
sizing graphics, 147
sketches, thumbnail, 28, 648
slide shows, 648
small expense/reimbursement forms, 322, 325-327
snaking text, 47
Sort command, 586
Sorting command, 600
sources, advertisements, 359-360
spaces
 alley, see gutter space
 em, 638
 en, 638
 gray, 38
 gutter, 29, 47, 87, 286, 640
 hard, 640
 monospace, 643
 non-breaking, 643
 white, 38, 79
spacing
 letters, 80-81
 lines, 80-84
 paragraphs, 80, 84
 proportional, 646
 words, 80-82
spacing buttons, 589
spell checking, 154
Spelling command, 154, 162, 166, 586, 600
Spelling dialog box, 154
Split command, 584, 598
Split Table command, 600
spot colors, 648
spreads, 648
standing heads, 648
status bar, 590, 604
Status bar command, 585
Stop Recorder command, 132
storing letterheads, 148
stress, 71
strikethroughs, 186
stroke, 71, 648
styles, brush, 635
Style box, 589, 602
style sheets, 51, 96
Style(s) command, 197, 387, 412, 419, 424, 459, 467-468, 484, 494, 504, 533, 558, 565, 586, 589, 600, 603
subheads, 76, 86, 90
subscript, 184, 588, 648
sulphite paper, 110
Summary Info boxes, 155-156, 243-244
Summary Info command, 155, 162, 168, 585, 598
superscript, 184, 588, 648
Symbol command, 133, 159, 168, 183, 195, 333, 337, 470, 600
Symbol dialog box, 133
symbols, 212
symmetrical balance, 35-36

T

Tab key, 592, 606
tab stop buttons, 589, 603
Table command, 48, 159, 162, 334-335, 339-343, 420-422, 470, 502, 534, 585-586
Table dialog box, 334
Table menu
 Column Width, 600
 Convert Text to Table, 600
 Delete Columns, 600
 Insert Table, 600
 Merge Cells, 600
 Row Height, 600
 Select Column, 600
 Select Row, 600
 Select Table, 600
 Split Table, 600
Table of Contents command, 536, 573, 586, 600
tables, 292
Tables command, 586
tables of contents, 60, 535, 572
tabs, 88-89
Tabs command, 133, 144, 156, 161, 167, 186, 332-333, 336, 339, 345-349, 387, 453, 470, 486, 507, 586, 600
Tagged Image File Format (TIFF), 648
Template command, 598

Index

templates, 50, 62, 96, 648
  contents, 51
  fax cover sheets, 257
  memo, 234-237, 240-243
  opening, 182
text
  alignment, 85
  body, 76, 91
  boilerplate, 51
  centering, 86
  editing, 47
  fully justified, 82, 87
  Left-aligned, 85-86
  placing, 89-95
  right-aligned, 86
  snaking, 47
text area, 591, 605
text book paper, 110
text files, 611-614, 648
text type family, 74
thermographed ink, 113
Thesaurus command, 586, 600
thumbnail sketches, 28, 648
TIF file format, 55
TIFF (Tagged Image File Format), 648
TIFF file format, 55
TIFF files, 127, 616
Titlebar, 582, 596
tombstone headlines, 648
Toolbar, 601
Toolbar command, 599
Tools buttons, 602
Tools menu
  Calculate, 600
  Compare Versions, 600
  Create Envelope, 600
  Grammar, 600
  Hyphenation, 166, 413-416, 420, 424-425, 453, 504, 600
  Macro, 600
  Options, 550, 600
  Record Macro, 600
  Revision Marks, 600
  Sorting, 600
  Spelling, 154, 162, 166, 600
  Thesaurus, 600
transmissions, facsimile, *see* fax cover sheets
Travel Logs, 307, 310-312
Travel Reports, 312-316
trim size, 107, 648

type, 70
  body, 634
  condensed, 145, 636
  families
    Roman, 72
    sans serif, 73
    script, 73
    text, 74
  display, 76
  normal, 145
  reversed, 646
  rotated, 646
  size, 75-78, 649
  styles, 74, 649
typefaces, 70, 361, 649
  elite, 638
  oblique, 643
  sans serif, 647
  serif, 647
  see also, fonts
typesetters, 27, 642
typewriters, 28
typography, 21, 69

U

uncoated cover paper, 111
Undo button, 602
Undo command, 585, 599
Utilities menu
  Calculate, 586
  Compare Versions, 586
  Customize, 155, 586
  Hyphenate, 166, 413-416, 419, 424-425, 453, 504, 586
  Renumber, 586
  Repaginate Now, 586
  Revision Marks, 586
  Sort, 586
  Spelling, 154, 162, 166, 586
  Thesaurus, 586

V

vertical justification, 649
vertical layout mode, 31
vertical rules, 52, 139-141
vertical-feed printers, 179
View menu
  Annotations, 585, 599
  Draft, 505, 531-532, 568-569, 585, 599

Field, 571
Field Codes, 571, 585, 599
Footnotes, 585, 599
Header/Footer, 165, 492, 505, 531, 559-560, 568-569, 599
Normal, 505, 599
Outline, 557, 564, 585, 599
Page, 124, 129, 135, 532, 558-559, 568, 585
Page Layout, 505-506, 558-560, 569, 599
Preferences, 334, 339-340, 421, 585
Ribbon, 124, 129, 135, 585, 599
Ruler, 124, 129, 135, 585, 588, 599
Status bar, 585
Toolbar, 599
Zoom, 599
viewing gridlines, 334

W

weight, paper, 108, 649
What-You-See-Is-What-You-Get (WYSIWYG), 649
white space, 21, 38, 79, 369
widows, 550, 649
Window menu
  Arrange Windows, 586, 601
  New Window, 586, 601
word spacing, 80-82
word wrap, 649
WPG file format, 55
writing copy, 16
WYSIWYG (What-You-See-Is-What-You-Get), 649

X–Z

x-height, 70

Zoom command, 599

661

Computer Books from Que Mean PC Performance!

Spreadsheets

1-2-3 Beyond the Basics	$24.95
1-2-3 for DOS Release 2.3 Quick Reference	$ 9.95
1-2-3 for DOS Release 2.3 QuickStart	$19.95
1-2-3 for DOS Release 3.1+ Quick Reference	$ 9.95
1-2-3 for DOS Release 3.1+ QuickStart	$19.95
1-2-3 for Windows Quick Reference	$ 9.95
1-2-3 for Windows QuickStart	$19.95
1-2-3 Personal Money Manager	$29.95
1-2-3 Power Macros	$39.95
1-2-3 Release 2.2 QueCards	$19.95
Easy 1-2-3	$19.95
Easy Excel	$19.95
Easy Quattro Pro	$19.95
Excel 3 for Windows QuickStart	$19.95
Excel for Windows Quick Reference	$ 9.95
Look Your Best with 1-2-3	$24.95
Quattro Pro 3 QuickStart	$19.95
Quattro Pro Quick Reference	$ 9.95
Using 1-2-3 for DOS Release 2.3, Special Edition	$29.95
Using 1-2-3 for Windows	$29.95
Using 1-2-3 for DOS Release 3.1+, Special Edition	$29.95
Using Excel 4 for Windows, Special Edition	$29.95
Using Quattro Pro 4, Special Edition	$27.95
Using Quattro Pro for Windows	$24.95
Using SuperCalc5, 2nd Edition	$29.95

Databases

dBASE III Plus Handbook, 2nd Edition	$24.95
dBASE IV 1.1 Qiuck Reference	$ 9.95
dBASE IV 1.1 QuickStart	$19.95
Introduction to Databases	$19.95
Paradox 3.5 Quick Reference	$ 9.95
Paradox Quick Reference, 2nd Edition	$ 9.95
Using AlphaFOUR	$24.95
Using Clipper, 3rd Edition	$29.95
Using DataEase	$24.95
Using dBASE IV	$29.95
Using FoxPro 2	$29.95
Using ORACLE	$29.95
Using Paradox 3.5, Special Edition	$29.95
Using Paradox for Windows	$26.95
Using Paradox, Special Edition	$29.95
Using PC-File	$24.95
Using R:BASE	$29.95

Business Applications

CheckFree Quick Reference	$ 9.95
Easy Quicken	$19.95
Microsoft Works Quick Reference	$ 9.95
Norton Utilities 6 Quick Reference	$ 9.95
PC Tools 7 Quick Reference	$ 9.95
Q&A 4 Database Techniques	$29.95
Q&A 4 Quick Reference	$ 9.95
Q&A 4 QuickStart	$19.95
Q&A 4 Que Cards	$19.95
Que's Computer User's Dictionary, 2nd Edition	$10.95
Que's Using Enable	$29.95
Quicken 5 Quick Reference	$ 9.95
SmartWare Tips, Tricks, and Traps, 2nd Edition	$26.95
Using DacEasy, 2nd Edition	$24.95
Using Microsoft Money	$19.95
Using Microsoft Works: IBM Version	$22.95
Using Microsoft Works for Windows, Special Edition	$24.95
Using MoneyCounts	$19.95
Using Pacioli 2000	$19.95
Using Norton Utilities 6	$24.95
Using PC Tools Deluxe 7	$24.95
Using PFS: First Choice	$22.95
Using PFS: WindowWorks	$24.95
Using Q&A 4	$27.95
Using Quicken 5	$19.95
Using Quicken for Windows	$19.95
Using Smart	$29.95
Using TimeLine	$24.95
Using TurboTax: 1992 Edition	$19.95

CAD

AutoCAD Quick Reference, 2nd Edition	$ 8.95
Using AutoCAD, 3rd Edition	$29.95

Word Processing

Easy WordPerfect	$19.95
Easy WordPerfect for Windows	$19.95
Look Your Best with WordPerfect 5.1	$24.95
Look Your Best with WordPerfect for Windows	$24.95
Microsoft Word Quick Reference	$ 9.95
Using Ami Pro	$24.95
Using LetterPerfect	$22.95
Using Microsoft Word 5.5: IBM Version, 2nd Edition	$24.95
Using MultiMate	$24.95
Using PC-Write	$22.95
Using Professional Write	$22.95
Using Professional Write Plus for Windows	$24.95
Using Word for Windows 2, Special Edition	$27.95
Using WordPerfect 5	$27.95
Using WordPerfect 5.1, Special Edition	$27.95
Using WordPerfect for Windows, Special Edition	$29.95
Using WordStar 7	$19.95
Using WordStar, 3rd Edition	$27.95
WordPerfect 5.1 Power Macros	$39.95
WordPerfect 5.1 QueCards	$19.95
WordPerfect 5.1 Quick Reference	$ 9.95
WordPerfect 5.1 QuickStart	$19.95
WordPerfect 5.1 Tips, Tricks, and Traps	$24.95
WordPerfect for Windows Power Pack	$39.95
WordPerfect for Windows Quick Reference	$ 9.95
WordPerfect for Windows Quick Start	$19.95
WordPerfect Power Pack	$39.95
WordPerfect Quick Reference	$ 9.95

Hardware/Systems

Batch File and Macros Quick Reference	$ 9.95
Computerizing Your Small Business	$19.95
DR DOS 6 Quick Reference	$ 9.95
Easy DOS	$19.95
Easy Windows	$19.95
Fastback Quick Reference	$ 8.95
Hard Disk Quick Reference	$ 8.95
Hard Disk Quick Reference, 1992 Edition	$ 9.95
Introduction to Hard Disk Management	$24.95
Introduction to Networking	$24.95
Introduction to PC Communications	$24.95
Introduction to Personal Computers, 2nd Edition	$19.95
Introduction to UNIX	$24.95
Laplink Quick Reference	$ 9.95
MS-DOS 5 Que Cards	$19.95
MS-DOS 5 Quick Reference	$ 9.95
MS-DOS 5 QuickStart	$19.95
MS-DOS Quick Reference	$ 8.95
MS-DOS QuickStart, 2nd Edition	$19.95
Networking Personal Computers, 3rd Edition	$24.95
Que's Computer Buyer's Guide, 1992 Edition	$14.95
Que's Guide to CompuServe	$12.95
Que's Guide to DataRecovery	$29.95
Que's Guide to XTree	$12.95
Que's MS-DOS User's Guide, Special Edition	$29.95
Que's PS/1 Book	$22.95
TurboCharging MS-DOS	$24.95
Upgrading and Repairing PCs	$29.95
Upgrading and Repairing PCs, 2nd Edition	$29.95
Upgrading to MS-DOS 5	$14.95
Using GeoWorks Pro	$24.95
Using Microsoft Windows 3, 2nd Edition	$24.95
Using MS-DOS 5	$24.95
Using Novell NetWare, 2nd Edition	$29.95
Using OS/2 2.0	$24.95
Using PC DOS, 3rd Edition	$27.95
Using Prodigy	$19.95
Using UNIX	$29.95
Using Windows 3.1	$26.95
Using Your Hard Disk	$29.95
Windows 3 Quick Reference	$ 8.95
Windows 3 QuickStart	$19.95
Windows 3.1 Quick Reference	$ 9.95
Windows 3.1 QuickStart	$19.95

Desktop Publishing/Graphics

CorelDRAW! Quick Reference	$ 8.95
Harvard Graphics 3 Quick Reference	$ 9.95
Harvard Graphics Quick Reference	$ 9.95
Que's Using Ventura Publisher	$29.95
Using DrawPerfect	$24.95
Using Freelance Plus	$24.95
Using Harvard Graphics 3	$29.95
Using Harvard Graphics for Windows	$24.95
Using Harvard Graphics, 2nd Edition	$24.95
Using Microsoft Publisher	$22.95
Using PageMaker 4 for Windows	$29.95
Using PFS: First Publisher, 2nd Edition	$24.95
Using PowerPoint	$24.95
Using Publish It!	$24.95

Macintosh/Apple II

Easy Macintosh	$19.95
HyperCard 2 QuickStart	$19.95
PageMaker 4 for the Mac Quick Reference	$ 9.95
The Big Mac Book, 2nd Edition	$29.95
The Little Mac Book	$12.95
QuarkXPress 3.1 Quick Reference	$ 9.95
Que's Big Mac Book, 3rd Edition	$29.95
Que's Little Mac Book, 2nd Edition	$12.95
Que's Mac Classic Book	$24.95
Que's Macintosh Multimedia Handbook	$24.95
System 7 Quick Reference	$ 9.95
Using 1-2-3 for the Mac	$24.95
Using AppleWorks, 3rd Edition	$24.95
Using Excel 3 for the Macintosh	$24.95
Using FileMaker Pro	$24.95
Using MacDraw Pro	$24.95
Using MacroMind Director	$29.95
Using MacWrite Pro	$24.95
Using Microsoft Word 5 for the Mac	$27.95
Using Microsoft Works: Macintosh Version, 2nd Edition	$24.95
Using Microsoft Works for the Mac	$24.95
Using PageMaker 4 for the Macintosh	$24.95
Using Quicken 3 for the Mac	$19.95
Using the Macintosh with System 7	$24.95
Using Word for the Mac, Special Edition	$24.95
Using WordPerfect 2 for the Mac	$24.95
Word for the Mac Quick Reference	$ 9.95

Programming/Technical

Borland C++ 3 By Example	$21.95
Borland C++ Programmer's Reference	$29.95
C By Example	$21.95
C Programmer's Toolkit, 2nd Edition	$39.95
Clipper Programmer's Reference	$29.95
DOS Programmer's Reference, 3rd Edition	$29.95
FoxPro Programmer's Reference	$29.95
Network Programming in C	$49.95
Paradox Programmer's Reference	$29.95
Programming in Windows 3.1	$39.95
QBasic By Example	$21.95
Turbo Pascal 6 By Example	$21.95
Turbo Pascal 6 Programmer's Reference	$29.95
UNIX Programmer's Reference	$29.95
UNIX Shell Commands Quick Reference	$ 8.95
Using Assembly Language, 2nd Edition	$29.95
Using Assembly Language, 3rd Edition	$29.95
Using BASIC	$24.95
Using Borland C++	$29.95
Using Borland C++ 3, 2nd Edition	$29.95
Using C	$29.95
Using Microsoft C	$29.95
Using QBasic	$24.95
Using QuickBASIC 4	$24.95
Using QuickC for Windows	$29.95
Using Turbo Pascal 6, 2nd Edition	$29.95
Using Turbo Pascal for Windows	$29.95
Using Visual Basic	$29.95
Visual Basic by Example	$21.95
Visual Basic Programmer's Reference	$29.95
Windows 3.1 Programmer's Reference	$39.95

**For More Information,
Call Toll Free!
1-800-428-5331**

*All prices and titles subject to change without notice.
Non-U.S. prices may be higher. Printed in the U.S.A.*

Word Processing Is Easy When You're Using Que!

Using Word for Windows 2, Special Edition
Ron Person & Karen Rose

Complete coverage of program basics and advanced desktop publishing hints. Includes Quick Start lessons and a tear-out Menu Map.

Version 2
$27.95 USA
0-88022-832-6, 900 pp., 7³/₈ x 9¹/₄

Using LetterPerfect
Robert Beck

A comprehensive guide to this all-new condensed version of WordPerfect! Includes reference for error messages and formatting codes.

Version 1
$22.95 USA
0-88022-667-6, 620 pp., 7³/₈ x 9¹/₄

Using Professional Write
Katherine Murray

Quick Start tutorials introduce word processing basics and help readers progress to advanced skills. Packed with easy-to-follow examples!

Through Version 2.1
$22.95 USA
0-88022-490-8, 343 pp., 7³/₈ x 9¹/₄

More Word Processing Titles from Que

Microsoft Word Quick Reference
Que Development Group
Through Version 5.5
$9.95 USA
0-88022-720-6, 160 pp., 4³/₄ x 8

Using Ami Pro
James Meade
Version 2.0
$24.95
0-88022-738-9, 600 pp., 7³/₈ x 9¹/₄

Using Microsoft Word 5.5: IBM Version, 2nd Edition
Bryan Pfaffenberger
Through Version 5.5
$24.95
0-88022-642-0, 702 pp., 7³/₈ x 9¹/₄

Using PC-Write
Trudi Reisner
Through Version 3.03
$22.95 USA
0-88022-654-4, 400 pp., 7³/₄ x 9¹/₄

Using Professional Write Plus for Windows
George Beinhorn
Version 1
$24.95
0-88022-754-0, 500 pp., 7³/₈ x 9¹/₄

To Order, Call (800) 428-5331 OR (317) 573-2500

Personal computing is easy when you're using Que!

Using 1-2-3 for DOS Release 2.3, Special Edition
$29.95 USA
0-88022-727-8, 584 pp., 7³/₈ x 9¹/₄

Using 1-2-3 for DOS Release 3.1+, Special Edition
$29.95 USA
0-88022-843-1, 584 pp., 7³/₈ x 9¹/₄

Using 1-2-3 for Windows
$29.95 USA
0-88022-724-9, 584 pp., 7³/₈ x 9¹/₄

Using 1-2-3/G
$29.95 USA
0-88022-549-7, 584 pp., 7³/₈ x 9¹/₄

Using AlphaFOUR
$24.95 USA
0-88022-890-3, 500 pp., 7³/₈ x 9¹/₄

Using AmiPro
$24.95 USA
0-88022-738-9, 584 pp., 7³/₈ x 9¹/₄

Using Assembly Language, 3rd Edition
$29.95 USA
0-88022-884-9, 900 pp., 7³/₈ x 9¹/₄

Using BASIC
$24.95 USA
0-88022-537-8, 584 pp., 7³/₈ x 9¹/₄

Using Borland C++, 2nd Edition
$29.95 USA
0-88022-901-2, 1,300 pp., 7³/₈ x 9¹/₄

Using C
$29.95 USA
0-88022-571-8, 950 pp., 7³/₈ x 9¹/₄

Using Clipper, 3rd Edition
$29.95 USA
0-88022-885-7, 750 pp., 7³/₈ x 9¹/₄

Using DacEasy, 2nd Edition
$24.95 USA
0-88022-510-6, 584 pp., 7³/₈ x 9¹/₄

Using DataEase
$24.95 USA
0-88022-465-7, 584 pp., 7³/₈ x 9¹/₄

Using dBASE IV
$24.95 USA
0-88022-551-3, 584 pp., 7³/₈ x 9¹/₄

Using Excel 3 for Windows, Special Edition
$24.95 USA
0-88022-685-4, 584 pp., 7³/₈ x 9¹/₄

Using FoxPro 2
$24.95 USA
0-88022-703-6, 584 pp., 7³/₈ x 9¹/₄

Using Freelance Plus
$24.95 USA
0-88022-528-9, 584 pp., 7³/₈ x 9¹/₄

Using GeoWorks Ensemble
$24.95 USA
0-88022-748-6, 584 pp., 7³/₈ x 9¹/₄

Using Harvard Graphics 3
$24.95 USA
0-88022-735-4, 584 pp., 7³/₈ x 9¹/₄

Using Harvard Graphics for Windows
$24.95 USA
0-88022-755-9, 700 pp., 7³/₈ x 9¹/₄

Using LetterPoerfect
$24.95 USA
0-88022-667-6, 584 pp., 7³/₈ x 9¹/₄

Using Microsoft C
$24.95 USA
0-88022-809-1, 584 pp., 7³/₈ x 9¹/₄

Using Microsoft Money
$19.95 USA
0-88022-914-4, 400 pp., 7³/₈ x 9¹/₄

Using Microsoft Publisher
$22.95 USA
0-88022-915-2, 450 pp., 7³/₈ x 9¹/₄

Using Microsoft Windows 3, 2nd Edition
$24.95 USA
0-88022-509-2, 584 pp., 7³/₈ x 9¹/₄

Using Microsoft Word 5.5: IBM Version, 2nd Edition
$24.95 USA
0-88022-642-0, 584 pp., 7³/₈ x 9¹/₄

Using Microsoft Works for Windows, Special Edition
$24.95 USA
0-88022-757-5, 584 pp., 7³/₈ x 9¹/₄

Using Microsoft Works: IBM Version
$24.95 USA
0-88022-467-3, 584 pp., 7³/₈ x 9¹/₄

Using MoneyCounts
$24.95 USA
0-88022-696-X, 584 pp., 7³/₈ x 9¹/₄

Using MS-DOS 5
$24.95 USA
0-88022-668-4, 584 pp., 7³/₈ x 9¹/₄

Using Norton Utilities 6
$24.95 USA
0-88022-861-X, 584 pp., 7³/₈ x 9¹/₄

Using Novell NetWare, 2nd Edition
$24.95 USA
0-88022-756-7, 584 pp., 7³/₈ x 9¹/₄

Using ORACLE
$24.95 USA
0-88022-506-8, 584 pp., 7³/₈ x 9¹/₄

Using OS/2 2.0
$24.95 USA
0-88022-863-6, 584 pp., 7³/₈ x 9¹/₄

Using Pacioli 2000
$24.95 USA
0-88022-780-X, 584 pp., 7³/₈ x 9¹/₄

Using PageMaker 4 for Windows
$24.95 USA
0-88022-607-2, 584 pp., 7³/₈ x 9¹/₄

Using Paradox 4, Special Edition
$29.95 USA
0-88022-822-9, 900 pp., 7³/₈ x 9¹/₄

Using Paradox for Windows, Special Edition
$29.95 USA
0-88022-823-7, 750 pp., 7³/₈ x 9¹/₄

Using PC DOS, 3rd Edition
$24.95 USA
0-88022-409-3, 584 pp., 7³/₈ x 9¹/₄

Using PC Tools 7
$24.95 USA
0-88022-733-8, 584 pp., 7³/₈ x 9¹/₄

Using PC-File
$24.95 USA
0-88022-695-1, 584 pp., 7³/₈ x 9¹/₄

Using PC-Write
$24.95 USA
0-88022-654-4, 584 pp., 7³/₈ x 9¹/₄

Using PFS: First Choice
$24.95 USA
0-88022-454-1, 584 pp., 7³/₈ x 9¹/₄

Using PFS: First Publisher, 2nd Edition
$24.95 USA
0-88022-591-2, 584 pp., 7³/₈ x 9¹/₄

Using PFS: WindowWorks
$24.95 USA
0-88022-751-6, 584 pp., 7³/₈ x 9¹/₄

Using PowerPoint
$24.95 USA
0-88022-698-6, 584 pp., 7³/₈ x 9¹/₄

Using Prodigy
$24.95 USA
0-88022-658-7, 584 pp., 7³/₈ x 9¹/₄

Using Professional Write
$24.95 USA
0-88022-490-8, 584 pp., 7³/₈ x 9¹/₄

Using Professional Write Plus for Windows
$24.95 USA
0-88022-754-0, 584 pp., 7³/₈ x 9¹/₄

Using Publish It!
$24.95 USA
0-88022-660-9, 584 pp., 7³/₈ x 9¹/₄

Using Q&A 4
$24.95 USA
0-88022-643-9, 584 pp., 7³/₈ x 9¹/₄

Using QBasic
$24.95 USA
0-88022-713-3, 584 pp., 7³/₈ x 9¹/₄

Using Quattro Pro 3, Special Edition
$24.95 USA
0-88022-721-4, 584 pp., 7³/₈ x 9¹/₄

Using Quattro Pro for Windows, Special Edition
$27.95 USA
0-88022-889-X, 900 pp., 7³/₈ x 9¹/₄

Using Quick BASIC 4
$24.95 USA
0-88022-378-2, 713 pp., 7³/₈ x 9¹/₄

Using QuickC for Windows
$29.95 USA
0-88022-810-5, 584 pp., 7³/₈ x 9¹/₄

Using Quicken 5
$19.95 USA
0-88022-888-1, 550 pp., 7³/₈ x 9¹/₄

Using Quicken for Windows
$19.95 USA
0-88022-907-1, 550 pp., 7³/₈ x 9¹/₄

Using R:BASE
$24.95 USA
0-88022-603-X, 584 pp., 7³/₈ x 9¹/₄

Using Smart
$24.95 USA
0-88022-229-8, 584 pp., 7³/₈ x 9¹/₄

Using SuperCalc5, 2nd Edition
$24.95 USA
0-88022-404-5, 584 pp., 7³/₈ x 9¹/₄

Using TimeLine
$24.95 USA
0-88022-602-1, 584 pp., 7³/₈ x 9¹/₄

Using Turbo Pascal 6, 2nd Edition
$29.95 USA
0-88022-700-1, 800 pp., 7³/₈ x 9¹/₄

Using Turbo Pascal for Windows
$29.95 USA
0-88022-806-7, 584 pp., 7³/₈ x 9¹/₄

Using Turbo Tax: 1992 Edition Tax Advice & Planning
$24.95 USA
0-88022-839-3, 584 pp., 7³/₈ x 9¹/₄

Using UNIX
$29.95 USA
0-88022-519-X, 584 pp., 7³/₈ x 9¹/₄

Using Visual Basic
$29.95 USA
0-88022-763-X, 584 pp., 7³/₈ x 9¹/₄

Using Windows 3.1
$27.95 USA
0-88022-731-1, 584 pp., 7³/₈ x 9¹/₄

Using Word for Windows 2, Special Edition
$27.95 USA
0-88022-832-6, 584 pp., 7³/₈ x 9¹/₄

Using WordPerfect 5
$27.95 USA
0-88022-351-0, 584 pp., 7³/₈ x 9¹/₄

Using WordPerfect 5.1, Special Edition
$27.95 USA
0-88022-554-8, 584 pp., 7³/₈ x 9¹/₄

Using WordStar 7
$19.95 USA
0-88022-909-8, 550 pp., 7³/₈ x 9¹/₄

Using Your Hard Disk
$29.95 USA
0-88022-583-1, 584 pp., 7³/₈ x 9¹/₄

Find It Fast with Que's Quick References!

Que's Quick References are the compact, easy-to-use guides to essential application information. Written for all users, Quick References include vital command information under easy-to-find alphabetical listings. Quick References are a must for anyone who needs command information fast!

  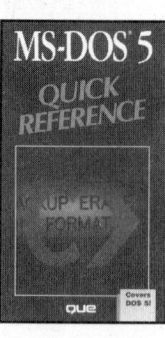

1-2-3 for DOS Release 2.3 Quick Reference
Release 2.3
$9.95 USA
0-88022-725-7, 160 pp., 4¾ x 8

1-2-3 for DOS Release 3.1+ Quick Reference
Releases 3, 3.1, & 3.1+
$9.95 USA
0-88022-845-8, 160 pp., 4¾ x 8

1-2-3 for Windows Quick Reference
1-2-3 for Windows
$9.95 USA
0-88022-783-4, 160 pp., 4¾ x 8

AutoCAD Quick Reference, 2nd Edition
Releases 10 & 11
$8.95 USA
0-88022-622-6, 160 pp., 4¾ x 8

Batch File and Macros Quick Reference
Through DOS 5
$9.95 USA
0-88022-699-4, 160 pp., 4¾ x 8

CorelDRAW! Quick Reference
Through Version 2
$8.95 USA
0-88022-597-1, 160 pp., 4¾ x 8

dBASE IV 1.1 Quick Reference
Through Version 1.1
$9.95 USA
0-88022-905-5, 160 pp., 4¾ x 8

DR DOS 6 Quick Reference
Version 6
$9.95 USA
0-88022-827-X, 160 pp., 4¾ x 8

Excel for Windows Quick Reference
Excel 3 for Windows
$9.95 USA
0-88022-722-2, 160 pp., 4¾ x 8

Fastback Quick Reference
Version 2.1
$8.95 USA
0-88022-650-1, 160 pp., 4¾ x 8

Hard Disk Quick Reference, 1992 Edition
Major hard disks & MS-DOS 5
$9.95 USA
0-88022-826-1, 160 pp., 4¾ x 8

Harvard Graphics 3 Quick Reference
Version 3
$9.95 USA
0-88022-887-3, 160 pp., 4¾ x 8

Harvard Graphics Quick Reference
Version 2.3
$8.95 USA
0-88022-538-6, 160 pp., 4¾ x 8

Laplink III Quick Reference
Laplink III
$9.95 USA
0-88022-702-8, 160 pp., 4¾ x 8

Microsoft Word Quick Reference
Through Version 5.5
$9.95 USA
0-88022-720-6, 160 pp., 4¾ x 8

Microsoft Works Quick Reference
Through IBM Version 2.0
$9.95 USA
0-88022-694-3, 160 pp., 4¾ x 8

Paradox 3.5 Quick Reference
Version 3.5
$9.95 USA
0-88022-824-5, 160 pp., 4¾ x 8

MS-DOS Quick Reference
Through Version 3.3
$8.95 USA
0-88022-369-3, 160 pp., 4¾ x 8

Norton Utilites 6 Quick Reference
Version 6
$9.95 USA
0-88022-858-X, 160 pp., 4¾ x 8

PC Tools 7 Quick Reference
Through Version 7
$9.95 USA
0-88022-829-6, 160 pp., 4¾ x 8

Q&A 4 Quick Reference
Versions 2, 3, & 4
$9.95 USA
0-88022-828-8, 160 pp., 4¾ x 8

Quattro Pro Quick Reference
Through Version 3
$8.95 USA
0-88022-692-7, 160 pp., 4¾ x 8

Quicken 5 Quick Reference
Versions 4 & 5.0
$9.95 USA
0-88022-900-4, 160 pp., 4¾ x 8

Windows 3 Quick Reference
Version 3
$8.95 USA
0-88022-631-5, 160 pp., 4¾ x 8

Windows 3.1 Quick Reference
Through Version 3.1
$9.95 USA
0-88022-740-0, 160 pp., 4¾ x 8

WordPerfect 5.1 Quick Reference
WordPerfect 5.1
$9.95 USA
0-88022-576-9, 160 pp., 4¾ x 8

WordPerfect Quick Reference
WordPerfect 5
$8.95 USA
0-88022-370-7, 160 pp., 4¾ x 8

WordPerfect for Windows Quick Reference
WordPerfect 5.1 for Windows
$9.95 USA
0-88022-785-0, 160 pp., 4¾ x 8

To Order, Call: (800) 428-5331
OR (317) 573-2500